The Future of Newspapers

The future of newspapers is hotly contested. Pessimistic pundits predict their imminent demise while others envisage a new era of participatory journalism online, with yet others advocating increased investment "in quality journalism" rather than free gifts and DVDs, as the necessary cure for the current parlous state of newspapers.

Globally, newspapers confront highly variable prospects reflecting their location in different market sectors, countries and journalism cultures. But despite this diversity, they face similar challenges in responding to the increased competition from expansive radio and 24 hour television news channels; the emergence of free "Metro" papers; the delivery of news services on billboards, pod casts and mobile telephony; the development of online editions, as well as the burgeoning of blogs, citizen journalists and User Generated Content. Newspapers' revenue streams are also under attack as advertising increasingly migrates online.

This authoritative collection of research based essays by distinguished scholars and journalists from around the globe, brings together a judicious mix of academic expertise and professional journalistic experience to analyse and report on the future of newspapers.

This book was published as special issues of *Journalism Practice* and *Journalism Studies*.

Bob Franklin is Professor of Journalism Studies in the School of Journalism, Media and Cultural Studies at Cardiff University; Editor of *Journalism Studies* and *Journalism Practice* and author of *Pulling Newspapers Apart; Analysing Print Journalism* (2008) Routledge, *Local Journalism and Local Media: Making the Local News* (2006) Routledge and many more.

The Future of Newspapers

Edited by Bob Franklin

Routledge
Taylor & Francis Group

LONDON AND NEW YORK

First published 2009 by Routledge
2 Park Square, Milton Park, Abingdon, Oxon, OX14 4RN

Simultaneously published in the USA and Canada
by Routledge
270 Madison Avenue, New York, NY 10016

Routledge is an imprint of the Taylor & Francis Group, an informa business

© 2009 Edited by Bob Franklin

Reprinted 2009, 2010

Typeset in Helvetica by Value Chain, India
Printed and bound in Great Britain by the MPG Books Group

British Library Cataloguing in Publication Data
A catalogue record for this book is available from the British Library

ISBN10: 0-415-47379-9
ISBN13: 978-0-415-47379-8

Contents

NOTES ON CONTRIBUTORS

Jose A. García Avilés is an Assistant Professor of Communication Theory at the University Miguel Hernandez de Elche, Spain. He has published several books on broadcast journalism, including *El periodismo en la televisión digital* [Digital Television Journalism] and *Broadcast Journalism in the Age of Digital Convergence*. He is currently researching newsroom convergence in Spanish and European media.

Piet Bakker studied Political Science at the University of Amsterdam. He worked as a journalist for newspapers, magazines and radio stations and was a teacher at the School for Journalism in Utrecht. From 1985 onwards, he worked at the Department of Communications at the University of Amsterdam/Amsterdam School of Communications Research (ASCoR) as an associate professor. From September 2007, he is also professor of Cross Media Content at the Research Centre for Communication and Journalism at the Hogeschool, Utrecht. He has published books and articles on reading habits, media history, local journalism, Internet, Dutch media, international news, investigative journalism, the music industry and free newspapers.

Els De Bens retired in 2005 as a professor in the Department of Communication Sciences at Ghent University, Belgium. She continues to be involved in several research projects mainly funded by the Interdisciplinary Institute for Broadband Technology (IBBT). She is the chair of the Flemish Media Council and of the taskforce Media and Science of the Flemish Board for Science Policy. She is also a member of several evaluation committees for research projects abroad (Switzerland, United Kingdom, Germany and Portugal). She is co-editor of the *European Journal of Communication* and author of 80 publications. Her research interests lie in media economics, ICT and media polity. She was active as a guest professor in universities in the United States (Berkeley), Russia (Moscow), Germany (Nurnberg and Dortmund) and South Afrika (Stellenbosch). She is a member of several international academic networks on European research projects for the European Science Foundation (e.g. The Euromedia Research Group).

Katrien Berte studied Communication Sciences at Ghent University, Belgium. After graduating in 2001, she worked for a commercial market research agency. She joined the research Group for Media and ICT in the Department of Communication Sciences at Ghent University and the Interdisciplinary Institute for Broadband Technology (IBBT) in 2005. Her research interests and publications lie in the field of quantitative survey analysis, new media and advertising. She is currently working on a PhD thesis on advertising in a digital media environment based on the IBBT research project ADME (http://projects.ibbt.be/adme).

Colette Brin is Associate Professor at the Département d'information et de communication, Université Laval, in Quebec City. A former journalist with experience in radio, TV and print media, Dr Brin's research focuses on the sociology of journalism and media institutions, particularly in regard to recent and ongoing changes in professional and industry practices. Her published work includes several articles and book chapters as well as *Nature et transformation du journalisme* (2004), which she co-edited with Jean Charron and Jean de Bonville. Her current projects include studies of economic journalism, the influence of convergence on news content; media credibility, and a history of television news in Quebec.

Miguel Carvajal has a PhD in Journalism and he is lecturer of journalism writing at the University Miguel Hernandez de Elche, Spain. Previously he was lecturer assistant at University of Navarra, was also assistant to the Head of school. He was funded by the Spanish Government to carry out his doctoral dissertation on media management from 2001 to 2004. He was a visiting researcher at the University of Westminster. He has published several monographs and papers on media concentration and media management in Spain. He is currently researching media convergence and strategic management of media companies.

Yuen-Ying Chan is Director of the Journalism and Media Studies Centre at the University of Hong Kong.

Jaci Cole is a graduate student at Louisiana State University's Manship School of Mass Communication. She is co-editor, with J. M. Hamilton, of the recently published *Journalism of the Highest Realm: the memoir of Edward Price Bell*.

Martin Conboy is Reader in Journalism Studies at the University of Sheffield. He is particularly interested in the confluence of language, national identity and cultural debate within both contemporary and historical journalism. His publications include *The Press and Popular Culture* (2002), *Journalism: a critical history* (2004), *Tabloid Britain: Constructing a community through language* (2006) and *The Language of the News* (2007). He is also the co-editor of a series of books entitled Journalism Studies: Key Texts.

David Domingo is Assistant Professor at the Communication Department of Universitat Rovira i Virgili, Tarragona, Catalonia. He has been Visiting Assistant Professor in the School of Journalism and Mass Communication at the University of Iowa, USA and is co-editor (with Chris Paterson) of *Making Online News: the ethnography of new media production* (Peter Lang, 2008). His research focuses on the development of online journalists' working routines and values, and their adoption of convergence and audience participation.

Geneviève Drolet is a Masters student at the Département d'information et de communication, Université Laval, in Quebec City. A former radio journalist, her thesis project is a case study of *Le Soleil*, a local broadsheet, which recently converted to compact format. She is particularly interested in the recent evolution and future of local and regional news in Quebec, the practice and discourse of working journalists, as well as the ecology of small media markets.

Bob Franklin is Professor of Journalism Studies in the Cardiff School of Journalism, Media and Cultural Studies. He is the Editor of *Journalism Studies* and *Journalism Practice* and co-editor of a new series of books to be published by Sage, entitled Journalism Studies: Key Texts. His publications include *Pulling Newspapers Apart: Analysing print journalism* (2008), *Local Journalism and Local Media: Making the local news* (2006), *Television Policy: The MacTaggart Lectures* (2005), *Key Concepts in Journalism Studies* (2005) and *Packaging Politics: Political communication in Britain's media democracy* (2004).

John Maxwell Hamilton is Dean and Hopkins P. Breazeale Professor of the Manship School. A long-time journalist, he has reported on foreign affairs for The Christian Science Monitor, ABC Radio, and many other news media. He is the author or co-author of five books.

John Hartley is Australian Research Council Federation Fellow and Research Director of the ARC Centre of Excellence for Creative Industries and Innovation at Queensland University of Technology in Australia. He was foundation dean of the Creative Industries Faculty (QUT) and previously founding head of the School of Journalism, Media and Cultural Studies at Cardiff University. He is the author of 18 books, translated into a dozen languages, including *Television Truths* (Blackwell, 2008), *Creative Industries* (Blackwell, 2005), *A Short History of Cultural Studies* (Sage, 2003), *The Indigenous Public Sphere* (with Alan McKee, Oxford, 2000), *Uses of Television* (Routledge, 1999) and *Popular Reality* (Arnold, 1996).

Laurence Hauttekeete is a senior researcher at the Department of Communication Sciences. She is a member of the research group "Media and ICT" (MICT) and her research focuses on new media trends, media economics and media policy.

Ari Heinonen is Senior Lecturer, Journalism, at the Department of Journalism and Mass Communication at the University of Tampere, Finland, and Docent of Journalism both at the University of Tampere and University of Jyväskylä. His research interests include journalism and new media, changing journalistic and professional and journalism ethics. He has directed and participated in several national and international research projects on the changing nature of journalism in the Age of the Net.

Alfred Hermida is an assistant professor at the School of Journalism at the University of British Columbia. He is an award-winning online news pioneer, having been a founding member of the BBC News website. During a total of 16 years at the BBC, he gained extensive professional experience in television, radio and online, covering regional, national and international news. His research interests include the impact of digital communications technology on journalism and new multiplatform models of journalism education. Professor Hermida is a frequent commentator on Internet trends, such as the rise of social media and the role of citizen content, and writes on developments in digital journalism at Reportr.net.

Tim Hoebeke is a researcher at the Department of Communication Sciences and a member of the Center for Journalism Studies. His research focuses on NIE-programmes and on the relationship between journalism and language studies.

Sofia Johansson is Lecturer in Media and Communication Studies at Södertörn University College, in Stockholm, Sweden. She is the author of *Reading Tabloids: Tabloid newspapers and their readers* (2007), and has published a number of articles on popular newspapers and their audiences. Sofia is a founding board member of the journal *Westminster Papers in Communication and Culture*, and her research interests cover the press, popular culture and media reception.

Andrew T. Kenyon is Director of the CMCL—Centre for Media and Communications Law, and Associate Professor in the University of Melbourne Law School. He researches in comparative media and communications law, especially defamation, free speech, copyright and digital media. He is editor of the *Media & Arts Law Review* and a participant in the Australian Research Council Cultural Research Network. Recent books include *Defamation: Comparative law and practice* (UCL Press, 2006), *New Dimensions in Privacy Law* (co-edited with Megan Richardson, Cambridge University Press, 2006) and the edited collection *TV Futures: Digital television policy in Australia* (Melbourne University Press, 2007).

Risto Kunelius is a professor at the Department of Journalism and Mass Communication, University of Tampere, Finland. He is currently working on projects focusing on professional journalism in the context of late modern public spheres.

Hagar Lahav, Head of the Journalism Program, School of Communication, Sapir Academic College, Tel Aviv, specializes in critical journalism study and in feminist media study.

Tim Marjoribanks is TR Ashworth Senior Lecturer in Sociology, in the School of Political Science, Criminology and Sociology at the University of Melbourne. His media-related research focuses on areas including the relationship between defamation law and news production, debates around objectivity, new technology and media, and media–sport relations. His work has been published in journals including *Media, Culture and Society*, *Journal of Sociology*, and *Australian Journalism Review*.

Catherine O'Connor is a Senior Lecturer in Journalism at Leeds Trinity and All Saints. Before joining the college in January 2007 she spent 15 years working in regional newspapers, including the *Halifax Courier*, the *Yorkshire Evening Post*, where she was deputy news editor, and the *Telegraph & Argus*, Bradford, where she spent seven years as deputy editor. She is still involved in industry training and her research interests include journalism–source relations and the future of local newspapers.

Deirdre O'Neill is an Associate Principal Lecturer in Journalism at Leeds Trinity and All Saints. Before joining Leeds Trinity she worked on magazines, was a college press officer and ran training for the newspaper industry. Her research interests are in the field of news selection, sources, access and influence.

John O'Sullivan lectures in journalism and related areas at the School of Communications, Dublin City University, and is a member of the Centre for Society Information and Media (SIM). A journalist for more than 20 years, he has worked in editing and reporting with newspapers, magazines and online ventures, with particular focus on ICT. Previous and current research activities and interests at national and international levels include journalism practice in online publishing, the migration of established media online, and news design and format in print and online. He currently is completing a PhD thesis, investigating the interaction of journalism and online media.

Henrik Örnebring is Axess Research Fellow in Comparative European Journalism at the Reuters Institute for the Study of Journalism, University of Oxford. He has previously published articles about journalism and journalism/media history in *Journalism Studies*, the *European Journal of Communication* and several edited collections.

Michael Palmer is professor of the history and geopolitics of international information and the media, University of Sorbonne Nouvelle-Paris 3, and director of the research centre CIM (Communication Information Media), University of Sorbonne Nouvelle-Paris 3. He is the author of 10 books including: *Dernières nouvelles d'Amérique* (éditions de l'Amandier, Paris, 2006), *Quels mots pour le dire? Correspondants de guerre, journalistes et historiens face aux conflits dans l'ex-Yougoslavie* (l'Harmattan, Paris, 2003), *Des petits journaux aux grandes agences: naissance du journalisme moderne* (Aubier, Paris, 1983; director), *International News Viewed from France* (CIM, Paris, 2007), and with Jeremy Tunstall, *Media Moguls* (Routledge, London, 1991) and *Liberating Communications Policy Making in France and Britain* (Basil Blackwell, Oxford and Cambridge, MA, 1990).

Steve Paulussen is senior researcher at the Department of Communication Sciences at Ghent University. His research interests lie in the fields of journalism studies, new media and the Internet. Since 2006, Paulussen has been involved in the multidisciplinary research project FLEET (FLEmish E-publishing Trends), which investigates the changing roles of publishers, journalists and users in the digital news environment. As a member of the research group for Media and ICT (MICT), he is also doing research for several projects of the Interdisciplinary Institute for Broadband Technology (IBBT).

Zhen-Mei Peng is a graduate student in the Cheung Kong School of Journalism and Communication at Shantou University, Guangdong, China.

Robert G. Picard, Hamrin professor of media economics and director of the Media Management and Transformation Centre at Jönköping International Business School, Jönköping University, Sweden, is author and editor of 20 books and numerous articles. He is editor of the *Journal of Media Business Studies* and was previously editor of the *Journal of Media Economics*. He has been a fellow at the Shorenstein Center at the John F. Kennedy School of Government at Harvard University, has consulted and carried out assignments for governments in North America and Europe and for international organisations including the European Commission, UNESCO, and the World Intellectual Property Organisation. He has been a consultant for leading media companies in North America, Europe, Asia, Africa, and Latin America.

Peter Preston is one of the United Kingdom's most distinguished journalists, columnists and Editors. He joined the *Guardian* in 1963 and edited the paper between 1975 and 1995. He continues to contribute regular columns to the *Guardian* and writes a media page for the *Observer's* Business and Media Supplement. He was a member of the Scott Trust from 1979 to 2003 and Chaired the International Press Institute and the Association of British Press Editors.

Thorsten Quandt is a Professor of Communication Studies at the Free University Berlin. He has worked previously as a lecturer and researcher at the LMU Munich, the Berlin University of the Arts, the University Trier, the University of Applied Sciences (FHW) in Vienna, the University of Applied Sciences (FH) Bremen and the Technical University Ilmenau. His research and teaching fields include journalism studies, online communication, media innovation research and communication theory. Currently, he is the Chair of the research network "Integrative Theories in Communication Studies" and the co-Chair of the Journalism Division in the German Communication Association (DGPuK). He has (co) published more than 50 scientific articles and several books, many of them on new forms of journalism on the Internet.

Karin Raeymaeckers is professor at the Department of Communication Studies and she is the director of the Center for Journalism Studies. She teaches and publishes on journalism studies, media structures and media policy, readership market trends, and political communication.

Zvi Reich is a lecturer at the Department of Communication Studies, Ben-Gurion University of the Negev. His research focuses on practices of news. His book, *Sourcing the News*, will soon be published by the Hampton Press. Dr Reich is a former senior editor at *Yedioth Ahronoth*, the most popular Israeli daily.

Aude Rouger is a PhD student at the University of Paris 3, Sorbonne nouvelle. Her thesis deals with the crisis of the French regional daily newspapers, their relation to territories and their treatment of local news. She is the president of Parcoursic, a French association of young researchers in media and communication studies (http://parcoursic.-free.fr). Her publications include: Camille Laville, Laurence Leveneur and Aude Rouger (forthcoming in 2008) *Construire son parcours de thèse. Manuel réflexif et pratique*,

Aude Rouger (2005) "Entre presse nationale parisienne et journaux locaux de province: la presse régionale en Ile-de-France", *Le Temps des Médias* 5, pp. 177-88.

Laura Ruusunoksa is a doctoral student at the Department of Journalism and Mass Communication, University of Tampere, Finland. Her PhD research is on Finnish journalists' professional understanding of public journalism.

Jane B. Singer is the Johnston Press Chair in Digital Journalism at the University of Central Lancashire. Her research explores digital journalism, including changing roles, perceptions, and practices. Before earning a PhD in journalism from the University of Missouri, she was the first news manager of Prodigy Interactive Services. She also worked as a newspaper reporter and editor. Jane serves on the editorial boards of *Journalism Practice* and *Journalism Studies*, and is president of Kappa Tau Alpha, the national US journalism honor society. She is on leave from the University of Iowa School of Journalism and Mass Communication, where she is an associate professor.

Nigel Starck a former journalist and broadcaster, is director of the University of South Australia's MA and BA awards in Communication. His book *Life After Death* (Melbourne University Press, 2006) offers a definitive account of newspaper obituary history and practice.

John Steel is a Lecturer in the Department of Journalism Studies at the University of Sheffield. His research interests include political thought and 19th-century newspapers, ideology and language in the media, press freedom and journalism education.

Neil Thurman is a senior lecturer in the Department of Journalism and Publishing at City University, London. His work on online journalism also appears in *Journalism: Theory, Practice & Criticism*, *New Media & Society*, and in Richard Keeble's *Print Journalism: A critical introduction*.

Marina Vujnovic is a PhD candidate at the School of Journalism and Mass Communication, University of Iowa. She is currently the Managing Editor of the *Journal of Communication Inquiry*. In 2006 she was named an Outstanding Graduate Teaching Assistant by the UI Council on Teaching, and in 2005 she won the John F. Murray Outstanding Doctoral Student in Research award. She is co-author of two scholarly articles and a co-author of several book chapters. Her research interests fall into the category of critical and cultural studies with an emphasis on the political economy of media and qualitative methodologies in communication. She is especially interested in globalization and media, gender and media history, international communication, Eastern European area studies and media, and public relations.

Herman Wasserman lectures in Journalism, Communication and Cultural Studies at Sheffield University, UK and is Associate Professor Extraordinary of Journalism, Stellenbosch University, South Africa. He is editor of the journal *Ecquid Novi: African Journalism Studies* and editorial board member of the *Journal of Global Mass*

Communication, the *Journal of African Media Studies* and the *Journal of Mass Media Ethics*. His research interests include African media, postcolonial theory and journalism and globalization.

Wendy M. Weinhold is a third-year PhD student in Mass Communication and Media Arts at Southern Illinois University Carbondale. She supplements her studies through work as the Daily Egyptian writing coach; as on-air talent for WSIU-FM, the Carbondale-based National Public Radio affiliate; and as a reporter for In Focus, a program that airs on WSIUTV, the Carbondale-based Public Broadcasting Service station. She has more than five years of professional experience as a print journalist. Her research uses political economy of media, ethnographies of journalists and audiences, and legal analysis to explore the myriad definitions of the American journalist.

Xiang Zhou is a professor at the Cheung Kong School of Journalism and Communication, Shantou University, Guangdong, China. Her research interests include the development of the Internet and social change, framing, and international communication. Her recent work has also appeared in *Journalism & Mass Communication Quarterly*, *Journal of Computer-mediated Communication*, and *International Communication Gazette*.

INTRODUCTION

Bob Franklin

Newspapers around the globe are in a state of flux, reflecting the influence of a number of technological, cultural, economic and political changes. These changes are sometimes dramatic, invariably rapid and prompt reconsideration of three fundamental questions. First, the availability of online editions means that commonsense understandings of newspapers as simply the printed "hard copy" edition no longer provide an adequate response to the question, "What is a newspaper?" Second, in an age of citizen journalism, when news is gathered, but less frequently reported and edited, by amateurs as well as professionals, the issue of "Who is a journalist?" is attracting considerable but often contested consideration. Finally, given the possible tensions between the global trend towards tabloid journalism and the traditional public service emphasis on newspapers as providers of informed argument and debate, as much as providers of entertainment, the question arises "What is the function of a newspaper?"

The Future of Newspapers Conference, hosted by the Cardiff School of Journalism, Media and Cultural Studies and sponsored by the publishers Routledge, Taylor & Francis, provided a forum for more than 170 scholars from 29 countries to analyse and discuss these questions and to debate recent developments in newspapers and their implications for journalism studies and journalism practice. The conference was the first in a series of planned biennial conferences intended to address key issues in journalism studies and, in keeping with the current emphasis on multimedia practice in newspaper journalism, the opening plenary delivered by distinguished journalist and ex *Guardian* Editor Peter Preston, was streamed live across the Web.

The response to the Conference's initial Call for Papers was unanticipated, but quite remarkable; the Future of Newspapers theme certainly seemed to strike a chord with journalism academics and practitioners. An extraordinarily large number of high-quality, wide-ranging and research-based papers were submitted by scholars from around the globe. More than 100 papers were received for review from which 60 were eventually selected, focusing on the five conference themes of: (1) new media and the changing newspaper environment; (2) newspapers as businesses; (3) local, regional and community newspapers; (4) global trends and developments; and (5) newspapers' changing contents, design and formats. A selection of these revised papers reflecting the various conference themes and incorporating conference discussions are published in this issue.

This strong response from the academic community suggests that the Future of Newspapers *is* a crucial topic within journalism studies and worthy of the sustained attention which such conferences allow. But the diverse experiences reported in the various papers below, suggest that a better title for the conference might have been the *Futures* of Newspapers, since newspapers confront distinctive and highly variable prospects reflecting their location in different regions of the world, market sectors and journalism cultures.

The Future of Newspapers; Contested Assessments

It is undeniably a pivotal moment in the history of newspapers understood literally as "news" printed on "paper", but also understood as news content on multiple media platforms which is now delivered by the Internet, pod casts and mobile telephony, more often than by newspaper delivery boys and girls.

There is, moreover, an evident Manichaeism in the different futures which unravel for newspapers in the scholarly literature. Some observers are pessimistic; and not without some justification. They cite the sustained decline in newspaper titles, the dramatic losses in circulations, the growing attractiveness of the Internet and television advertising channels for readers and advertisers and the emergence of free "Metro"-style newspapers, along with recent scandals involving journalists like Jayson Blair which undermine public trust in media credibility. But some pundits go on to make unrealistic extrapolations based on declining circulations to predict, with a curiously bizarre precision, the exact date on which the last newspaper reader will vanish. They seem to spoil a good case by overstating it.

Some pundits are more optimistic. They acknowledge that newspapers need to strike an urgent editorial and financial accommodation with the Web, but they believe that newspapers are adapting both their contents and formats in response to developments in media technology, pressures of market forces and readers' changing requirements for news. They believe this "editorial Darwinism" explains how newspapers have survived previous challenges to their business and editorial environment, often driven by technological innovation. From telegraph to television, newspapers' ability to adapt to changing circumstances has always provided them with a survival strategy and secured their future; this editorial Darwinism is central to understanding the history of newspapers.

Others express even more positive visions for the future of newspapers in which the availability and popularity of new media technologies—in living rooms no less than newsrooms—empower a growing army of citizen journalists, bloggers and readers wishing to post comments online, to construct a more pluralist and democratic debate about matters of public interest. In this new vision, the role of newspapers becomes more to hold the ring in a genuinely public debate than to dictate an agenda formulated in editorial offices and articulated by journalists. The model of journalism which previously witnessed journalists, columnists and leader writers handing down authoritative opinions in the manner of "tablets of stone", is retreating to make way for a new journalism which seeks to encourage readers to join journalists in a more open and interactive discussion.

Which vision for the future of newspapers will be vindicated by events is currently unclear, but the essays published here reflect the assessments of both pessimists and optimists although rarely in pure form. Amid the diversity, a number of central themes or concerns emerge.

Declining Newspaper Titles and Readers?

First, the precocious pessimism and unwarranted hyperbole of those who wish to proclaim the imminent demise of the newspaper, is clearly unsustainable. It articulates a curiously North American and Eurocentric view of the press which seems blinkered to the explosion of new titles and readerships in other parts of the world; the future of newspapers is more open and considerably more nuanced than some observers imagine. Globally, there is no cause for pessimism about the future of newspapers with the most recent data gathered by the World Association of Newspapers (2007) detailing unprecedented growth. Daily paid titles, for example, recorded an average 17 per cent growth from 9533 to a record-breaking 11,142 titles between 2002 and 2006, although rates varied markedly across Asia (33.1 per cent), Africa (16.7 per cent), South America (12.6 per cent), Europe (5.6 per cent) and Australia (1.4 per cent). The circulations of paid daily newspapers also increased by 8.7 per cent across the same five-year span to a record high of 510 million copies, while the distribution of free daily newspapers expanded three-fold from 13,795 million to 40,802 million. Again, regional variations are evident, but these data offer a sobering corrective to the pessimists' case; the global newspaper business is booming.

It is also important to highlight the distinctive fortunes and *futures* which newspapers confront in different sectors of the newspaper market. In the United Kingdom, for example, aggregate circulations of daily and Sunday titles across all sectors are in sharp decline from 38.4 million in 1965 to 32.6 million in 1985, plummeting to 22.7 million in 2007: 15.7 million copies lost in the paid newspaper market (41 per cent) with an accelerating rate of decline in reader numbers. But if the detail in this broad canvas is examined closely, a different picture emerges. The Sunday tabloid/mid-market tabloid newspapers illustrate the most striking decline (20.9 million copies in 1965, 15.1 million in 1985 but only 8.7 million in 2007), with weekday tabloids faring slightly better but still losing 28.9 per cent of their market since 1985 (12.5 million to 8.8 million), despite the circulation success of the highly popular mid-market *Daily Mail*. By contrast, across the same period (1965–2007) the "quality" dailies have enjoyed 27.5 per cent circulation growth from 2.03 million in 1965 to 2.6 million in 2007 and even in the Sunday market, quality newspaper readerships have declined only 8 per cent across the last four decades; the Sunday popular market has declined by 58 per cent across the same period.

Locally and regionally, the same story fails to make the headlines. Evening papers like the *Birmingham Evening Mail* have lost 54 per cent of their readership between 1995 and 2005 and morning papers fare little better; the *Yorkshire Post* has lost 36 per cent of circulation across the decade. But the 526 paid weekly and 637 free weekly papers have enjoyed relative stability, with some paid weekly titles showing a modicum of growth.

Those who advocate the pessimist's case, moreover, occasionally underestimate the impact of the emergence of online editions of newspapers, as well as the new "Metro"-style and other free papers which now enjoy substantial readerships and generate advertising revenues for the press industry, compensating in part for those lost by the paid daily and Sunday editions. In the United Kingdom, the 10 titles in the Associated Metro series alone, distribute 1.9 million copies daily with the *London Lite* and *LondonPaper* adding a further 750,000 copies daily to readers and revenues. Similarly, while the readership of the *Guardian* has declined across the last 20 years (487,000 in 1985 compared to 363,562 in 2007), the online *Guardian Unlimited* claims 16 million readers and 147 million page impressions every month.

Lifestyle Change Not Technology

A second common theme suggests that the impact of the Internet, as a factor explaining the decline of the traditional newspaper market, has perhaps been overstated or, expressed differently, other factors—such as the growth of free newspapers which generate revenues but also challenge and cannibalise the content, circulation and advertising revenues of existing paid titles in the same newspaper group—have perhaps been more influential although they have tended to be ignored.

Significantly, more sociological accounts identify longer-term changes in patterns of work and lifestyles as crucial in explaining the decline in titles and readers. In the United States and United Kingdom for example, the decline in newspaper titles and circulation in some press sectors predate the existence of the Web; and by a good while! Peter Preston nails the argument neatly in his plenary address. "The death of evening newspapers . . . in their hundreds across the United States" he asks, were they "victims of the Net?" His answer is worth citing at some length. "The London *Evening News* and the *Star*" he argues:

> were killed off long before the Net was invented. What disposed of them, and many more like them, was a combination of malignant factors. People didn't work set hours in offices and factories any longer, they worked at home or in industrial estates on the edge of town; they drove home rather than got a train: they found they couldn't get an evening paper delivered any longer because the traffic was too impenetrable: and the paper they could sometimes get—because it went to press at noon rather than 3.30— didn't have any of the facts that drove purchase . . . no late racing results or cricket scores, for instance. You could get that stuff on TV anyway, in the office canteen, in the betting shop, in the pub, off Ceefax or the radio (never mind the Net!). So the reason for buying a paper which often wasn't in the right place at the right time anyway, was hugely diminished.
>
> Simply, life changed but evening newspapers didn't, or couldn't. A whole slice of newspaper life died in the States and is withering here now as the evenings that remain are turned into single-edition late morning papers, updated on the Net in a further burst of suicide fever fuelled by short-term accountancy. Note the basic situation, though: the Net may be the deliverer of the *coup de grace* here, but it's not truly to blame for what's gone wrong over decades. Human living patterns, changing, moving on, have done that. Complain about the dying years of evening journalism and all you're doing is complaining about life.[1]

But there is an additional, more general, argument in this context of overstating or misattributing the impact of the Internet on the future of newspapers. This argument stresses the "resistance" of a range of actors such as journalists, to the incorporation of new technologies in the production of commodities whether newspapers, lollipops or motor cars. This argument suggests that technological innovation and capacity is a necessary but not always sufficient condition for change. The impetus which technological development provides may be slowed, resisted and knocked off course by a number of political, economic and cultural factors which mediate its impact. In the newspaper industry, the strength, character and direction of this resistance to change reflects a host of factors which may be workplace specific (journalists' attitudes to change, for example, along with the strength of trade union membership); title specific (a newspaper's market position, circulation strength, profitability); company or group specific (the relative willingness of different newspaper companies to commit resources to change), and finally resistance may be reader or consumer specific (readers' preferences for certain types of news, how it is presented and on which platform, as well as their willingness/ability to pay) (Williams and Franklin).[2]

But while it is important not to exaggerate the role of the Internet in triggering changes in the traditional newspaper industry, a third and perhaps obvious point of consensus stresses the significance of the Web's current impact on newspapers, as well as its influence on their likely future development.

The Internet, Newspapers and Journalism

Advertising. One significant feature of the Internet for newspapers is the potential threat it poses to their vital advertising revenues (Picard). But scholars typically stress both the potential opportunities, which online editions of newspapers offer for enhancing advertising revenues, as well as the threats posed by this potential predator of newspapers' advertising share (Berte and De Bens). Globally, Internet advertising revenues certainly increased in 2005; and by a striking 24 per cent. But such growth is from a relatively low baseline. In 2006 the Internet won a modest 5.7 per cent share of the $425 billion global advertising market, while newspapers secured 29.4 per cent of revenues, rising to 42.3 per cent when magazines are included. Newspaper advertising revenues, moreover, have risen by an average 15.6 per cent between 2002 and 2006, with regions such as Latin America (32.5 per cent), Asia, Pacific and India (20.8 per cent) and the United States and Canada (15.7 per cent) enjoying above-average increases. In some countries the growth in newspapers' advertising revenues has been unprecedented; 128 per cent across five years in China. Revenue projections for 2006–2010 average 17 per cent with some regional variations (World Association of Newspapers, 2007).

News contents and participatory journalism. A second impact of the Internet on newspapers has been the explosion in the availability of news online which has been accompanied by the promise of increased interactivity between readers and journalists (beyond that provided by the letters' page), the prospect for readers to contribute to news stories by posting comment and writing blogs, along with journalists' eager courtship of citizen journalists and user-generated content. Online editions of newspapers also have the potential to create new formats for writing and telling stories, along with radical changes in page design and layout as those pages are increasingly scrolled at the click of a mouse rather than turned between a moistened thumb and finger. Early enthusiasts of these changes identified a coming "revolution" in editorial contents and formats which promised nothing less than a "whole new journalism" (Quandt).

But the summary conclusion of much of the scholarly literature suggests that online news has failed to live up to these expectations. Thorsten Quandt's analysis of the editorial contents of 10 online news media in the United States, France, Britain, Germany and Russia suggests that "the revolution did not happen". The news sites in his study revealed some distinctive national features reflecting particular journalistic cultures and audience interests, but broadly they exhibited a lack of multimedia content (only seven of the 10 sites enhanced more than a fifth of their stories with multimedia content), an absence of options for direct contact and interaction with journalists (such as email or a single chat link to journalists in any of the 1600+ news items analysed), as well as missing bylines, references to authors or attributions to news sources (such as news agencies) which did little to contribute to transparency in the editorial process. Significantly, much of the editorial content was quite traditional and focused on the coverage of national political and economic events, human-interest stories, crime, sport and culture (Quandt).

Online news has also disappointed advocates by its failure to deliver on some aspects of its promise of a more participatory journalism. Reporting the findings of a study of readers' participation in online newspapers in nine countries (Belgium, Croatia, Finland, France, Germany, Spain, Slovenia, United Kingdom and the United States), David Domingo and his fellow researchers report a "general reluctance to open up most of the production process to the active involvement of citizens" so that "the core journalistic culture remains largely unchanged". Readers are offered only limited opportunities for engagement with the editorial process which are largely restricted to opportunities to "debate current events" while being firmly excluded from other aspects of news production (Domingo et al.). A similar study examined the user-generated content initiatives (UGCIs) of 12 UK newspaper websites. Findings revealed a "dramatic increase" in opportunities for contributions from readers, but concluded that while news sites seemed eager to "open their doors to the public", editors retain their "traditional gate-keeping role", reflecting concerns about "reputation, trust and legal liabilities". Consequently, the contributions of citizen journalists to these UK sites are monitored and moderated with only 12 of the 118 blogs identified in the sample, allowing readers to post directly without comment being vetted by journalists (Hermida and Thurman; see also Ornebring).

Journalism practice. The Internet has exercised a more discernible effect on daily journalism practice in local and national newsrooms. Virtually all print journalists are now required to work across multiple media platforms which involves not only delivering copy for print and online editions of their newspapers, but also shooting brief video clips, reading pieces to camera, as well as recording podcasts which can be downloaded from the newspaper's website. This commitment to multiplatform working has typically been viewed sceptically by journalists' trades unions who complain that newsrooms are already understaffed and that removing journalists from work on the print editions to produce video clips for use online, perhaps without adequate training or additional remuneration, is inefficient, deprives newsrooms of key workers and detracts from the core business of the company which is the print edition. Journalists claim the inevitable consequence here is a decline in the quality of the print product (Williams and Franklin).

The shift to an "online first" policy on news reporting, moreover, means that a newspaper's website might cannibalise and publish the paper's major news story of the day as much as three to four hours ahead of the print edition's evening publication, leaving the newspaper without a strong front-page story. Consequently, print journalists are no longer "breaking" the news so much as discussing existing news, thereby encouraging the further "featurisation" of news journalism (Williams and Franklin). Early publication of news online, moreover, poses considerable dilemmas for journalism practice. If a story posted on a newspaper website wins a good deal of readers' attention and attracts considerable comment as the news day unravels, for example, will editors be tempted to retreat from an earlier decision made at conference to lead with a different story in the print edition, and replace this original story with the popular Web item; in brief will (and should) the "popular" judgement of readers trump journalistic assessments of news value (Williams and Franklin, 2007).

Research also reveals that journalists attach great value to the Internet and the ways in which it facilitates many day-to-day news-gathering and reporting routines. A survey of 239 journalists in 40 news outlets in 11 European countries, which asked journalists to rank traditional and online methods of researching news stories, discovered that the three most popular methods included journalists' everyday use of Web search engines alongside more traditional methods such as face-to-face conversations and telephone conversations; likewise emails and Web news sites ranked equally with the use of archives and discussions with newsroom colleagues. Journalists also declared (overwhelmingly) that they would miss the Internet in the newsroom and that without the Web they would find it difficult to keep up to date with news, as they use the Web routinely to verify information and to find information on local and national government. The study also discovered that few journalists believed that bloggers and citizen journalists posed a significant threat to their ways of working or journalism in the round (O'Sullivan and Heinonen). The Internet is a formidable presence in newsrooms, is highly valued by the majority of journalists and is deeply embedded in their daily news-gathering and reporting practices.

Online journalism; business models.   Paradoxically, despite the significance of the Internet to journalists and the future of newspapers, there is no agreed and consensual industry-wide business model for how to turn a profit from online editions. But since newspapers are essentially economic organisations, the further development of online editions will prove problematic unless they can move to profitability. *Independent* Executive Editor Simon Kelner is highly sceptical claiming that "there is absolutely no model for a newspaper website to make money" (Thomas, 2006). Such intransigent claims ignore recent research (Dal Zotto; Bleyen and Van Hove), but the majority of online news sites are "a financial drain on the newspapers that support them" (Crosbie, 2004). The first financial review by the BBC Trust published in June 2008 highlighted that bbc.co.uk, the most elaborate and widely consulted news website in Europe, overspent by £36 million in 2007, overshooting its allocated budget of £74.2 million by 48 per cent (*MediaGuardian*, 2 June 2008, p. 8)

Newspaper companies have identified three sources of income from online news: subscription, advertising and *"ad hoc"* sales (Herbert and Thurman, 2007), although each identified element in the revenue stream is problematic and there are economic tensions between them. Consequently, companies' business plans typically deploy a judicious and inclusive balance of all three.

The problem with subscriptions to online editions, compared to paying the cover price for a newspaper, is that it is not clear why anyone should pay to buy news from the former when broadly the same news is available for free from many other newspaper websites. So charging is problematic except for worldwide quality brands which specialise in a particular news/information sector, such as the *Wall Street Journal online*. But if companies *are* successful in persuading readers to move online, they cannibalise their own print readership and reduce their revenue base. The consequences of this cannibalism are severe. Advertising represents newspapers' vital revenue source accounting for up to 80 per cent of paid papers' revenues and 100 per cent of free newspaper income. Web-based advertising revenues are growing (and rapidly) but from a low baseline and constitute a very modest proportion (5.7 per cent in 2006) of global revenues ($425 billion) while newspapers receive 29.4 per cent. Each convert to online editions is won at a substantial financial cost; such victories are pyrrhic. But companies cannot return to a subscription-based strategy since charging for site access reduces reader traffic and with it the vital advertising revenues. Companies compromise by selling what is popular with readers but unique to their brand. Consequently, in the United Kingdom, *The Times* charges for its crossword, the *Independent* for the features by its distinguished Middle East correspondent Robert Fisk (Herbert and Thurman, 2007, pp. 215–20). *Ad hoc* sales involve newspapers using their valued brand to associate themselves with a range of goods from travel, cars, property and dating. These goods and services provide the fastest growing revenue stream for the sites (20–30 per cent a year) but also attract further reader traffic and in turn, advertising income.

Newspapers' Changing Style and Contents

A final theme to emerge in the discussion of the future of newspapers centres on the changing shape (literally) of newspapers, the emphasis on newspaper relaunches and redesigns, as well as the constant "tweaking" and shifting of editorial content resulting in an enhanced editorial emphasis on news and features about lifestyle, fashion, leisure and travel as well as a tendency to focus on celebrity and human-interest stories. The reasons informing such shifts are broadly economic. Newspapers are obliged to operate in increasingly competitive and fragmented markets for readers and advertising revenues and it is this "hypercompetition" (Brin and Drolet), more than developments in media technology, which has motivated newspapers' constant changes to their design and contents to meet readers' shifting requirements for news and its presentation. Technological change has played more of an enabling or under labourer role in this context, with the latest printing presses offering the possibility of colour pictures on every page, the inclusion of illustrative graphics, an enhanced quality for photographic reproduction and crisper typefaces. Redesigns are a constant feature of editorial life; in June 2008, the London *Times*, produced its revamped 72-page newspaper, with colour on every page and Leading articles rather curiously tucked away on page 2 some 20 pages remote from the remainder of the Op-Ed pages. The changes to newspaper format, layout and design are striking and undeniable; the shifts in contents have proved more contentious.

Globally, there has been a move to tabloid formats and away from the old broadsheet newspapers; 28 newspapers moved to tabloid size in 2005 confirming a trend of 86 "converts" since 2001. In the United Kingdom, owners and editors have preferred to use the term compact to describe their new products in an effort to avoid the anticipated opprobrium associated with the term tabloid and to defuse any suggestions of "Dumbing down".

The move to compact editions was pioneered by *The Independent* in September 2003 and undoubtedly reflected the title's sustained loss of readers from 400,000 in 1990 to 220,000 a decade later. Research revealed that compact editions would be popular with young readers, women and commuters but, more significantly, with advertisers. Sales of the new-style *Independent* soared by 40,000 a day; *The Times* promptly launched its own compact edition. The *Guardian* editor was deeply concerned about the potential impact of the shift to tabloid on editorial contents and argued that the change in size would inevitably be reflected in content (Rusbridger 2005). He opted for the Berliner format, more common on mainland Europe and exemplified by *Le Monde* which, in terms of page size, sat somewhere between the tabloid and broadsheet.

Visually the most striking feature of the new compact editions is the increased use of photography for telling stories, especially on the front page above the fold. Given the shrinking page size, there are obviously fewer stories with fewer words on each page. The *Independent* exemplifies this design shift by adopting a "poster"-style front page featuring a single story, illustrated by a colourful graphic or photograph with virtually no text or even headline. The editor's preference for columnists and editorial comment above "straight" factual news coverage is reflected in his proud boast that the *Independent* is a "viewspaper" not a newspaper.

Similar trends in editorial style and contents are evident following the Quebec newspaper *Le Soleil*'s recent move to tabloid (Brin and Drolet). The paper, for example, offers a new column devoted to provincial politics but also features: an expanded Arts and Entertainments section; a gossip column about Hollywood celebrities; a column offering advice about child rearing written by a psychologist who hosts a popular reality television programme, and all this in a new chatty and friendly style of writing. News stories have disappeared from the front page which simply features a large photograph and accompanying headline. Local and regional newspapers illustrate similar editorial shifts. In her study of three French regional newspapers *Ouest-France* (Rennes), *Le Parisien* (Paris) and *Le Progrès* (Lyon), Aude Rougier identified a number of editorial changes designed to win readers including an emphasis on more "persona-lised" news, a focus on themes such as education, the environment, health and housing, along with an emphasis on readers' letters and a readers' forum.

But while this trend to move to tabloid newspapers is global, it is not always motivated by declining sales but occasionally by a mix of economic, political and cultural factors. Wasserman, for example, notes the remarkable popularity of the new South Africa tabloids like the *Daily Sun* which have "taken the market by storm" creating a "tabloid revolution". They are highly popular with readers achieving unprecedented readerships of 3.8 million. Their editorial content offers highly personalised and often sensationalised accounts of issues like poverty, HIV and crime, but significantly offers its black working-class readership a voice on these and other issues. For their part, the South African journalism establishment has been highly critical of the new tabloids alleging that they ignore professional commitments to objectivity and neutrality and bring journalism into disrepute because of their sensationalism and the partisanship of their coverage; a charge reminiscent of mainstream (and competitor) newspaper criticism of the innovatory editorial style and contents of the popular penny press in the United States in the 1830s.

Peter Preston and The Curse of Introversion

Having settled on the title "The Future of Newspapers" for the first Cardiff *Journalism Practice* and *Journalism Studies* biennial conference, Peter Preston seemed an obvious person to deliver the keynote plenary session, which heads up this collection of essays.

Peter is one of the UK's most distinguished, well-regarded and celebrated editors, journalists and columnists. He was educated at Loughborough Grammar School and St John's College Oxford where he discovered his love for printer's ink as Editor of the student newspaper *Cherwell*. He moved to the *Guardian* in 1963 and went on to become Editor of that paper for the 20 years between 1975 and 1995. He then began a "second career" as a prolific columnist contributing regular columns to the *Guardian*—typically addressing a wide range of domestic and international political and social concerns. On Sundays, he writes a media column for the *Observer*'s Business and Media supplement. The analysis of newspapers and their very disparate futures is a common theme on that page. In addition to this editorial work Peter has exercised considerable influence within the press industry more broadly. He was a member of the Scott Trust from 1979 to 2003, but was also Chair of the International Press Institute and the Association of British Press Editors.

The theme of his Plenary Address is The Curse of Introversion. I believe it offers an extraordinarily insightful and eloquent account of the problems and prospects for the future of newspapers.

NOTES

1. Peter Preston, The Curse of Introversion, the Plenary Address delivered to The Future of Newspapers Conference at the Cardiff School of Journalism, Media and Cultural Studies, Cardiff University, 13 September 2007 and printed in this issue.
2. A list of papers presented to The Future of Newspapers Conference is given in the Appendix.

REFERENCES

CROSBIE, VIN (2004) "What Newspapers and Their Websites Must Do To Survive", *Online Journalism Review*, 4 March, www.ojr.org/ojr/business/1078349998.php, accessed June 2008.

HERBERT, JACK and THURMAN, NEIL (2007) "Paid Content Strategies for News Websites: an empirical study of British newspapers' online business strategies", *Journalism Practice* 1, pp. 208–26.

RUSBRIDGER, ALAN (2005) "What Are Newspapers For?", the inaugural Hugo Young Lecture, University of Sheffield, 9 March.

THOMAS, LOU (2006) "'Website Must Come Second' Says Independent's Kelner", Press Gazette, 20 July, www.pressgazette.co.uk/article/200706/independent_website_second, accessed June 2008.

WILLIAMS, ANDREW and FRANKLIN, BOB (2007) *Turning Around the Tanker: implementing Trinity Mirror's online strategy*, Cardiff: Cardiff University.

WORLD ASSOCIATION OF NEWSPAPERS (2007) "*Newspaper Circulation Rises Worldwide*", www.wan~press.org/print.php3?id_article=14032, accessed June 2008.

Appendix: Papers presented to The Future of Newspapers Conference, Cardiff University, 13–14 September 2007

1. **Piet Bakker**, The Simultaneous Rise and Fall of Free and Paid Newspapers in Europe.
2. **Annika Bergström**, Audience Participation in Publishing.
3. **Katrien Berte, J. Gysels, and Els De Bens**, Newspapers Go for Advertising! Challenges and opportunities in a changing media environment.
4. **Valérie-Anne Bleyen and Leo Van Hove**, To Bundle or Not to Bundle? How Western European newspapers price their online content.
5. **Henrik Bødker**, Constructing Lives, Constructing Politics.
6. **Paul Bradshaw**, Wiki Journalism: Are wikis the new blogs?
7. **Marie Brandewinder**, Views on the Future of Newspapers and Present Stakes: How balance of forces and evaluation criteria evolve in the French press.
8. **Vincent Campbell, Rachel Gibson, Barrie Gunter, and Maria Touri**, News Blogs and the Future of Newspapers.
9. **Miguel Carvajal and Jose A. García Avilés**, From Newspapers to Multimedia Groups: Business growth strategies of the regional press in Spain.
10. **Christina Chan-Meeton**, Newspapers in Mauritius: Will their apparent vitality be sustained?
11. **Lenka Waschkova Cisarova**, The Future of Local and Regional Press in the Czech Republic: Does monopoly owner establish development trends?

Chapter 1 THE CURSE OF INTROVERSION

Peter Preston

Have newspapers a future? As a matter of fact, we at the *Guardian*[1] asked one huge multinational consultancy to tell us about that some nine years ago—and many hundreds of thousands of pounds later they declared Fleet Street dead for lack of advertising and circulation within five years. But it didn't quite happen. Indeed, it's absolutely not happened so far. In our trade, to be frank, prophets fall flat on their faces, nothing emerges on cue, and any honed, sharp, simplified notion is rapidly proved false. What we have to deal with instead is complexity, how one thing goes with another: a compote of theses. And if there's a theme that links them, then it's the situation of an industry—our media industry—that, on examination, behaves like no other industry I know.

It has difficulties. It witters about them constantly. It faces challenges.

Jeremy Paxman, with a descant from John Humphrys,[2] proclaims them mountainous, going on cataclysmic. It treats every change, every innovation, with suspicion and something akin to fear. It constantly announces the end of its world and evokes a golden age nobody but its own practitioners remember. It is, in short, the very model of a great business bringing itself to dust in a welter of navel gazing. It forgets to communicate with those who pay its bills. Day to day, it remains wrapped in its own pre-occupations. This is the curse of introversion.

Let's step back then and start with national newspapers, where most of the wittering starts: with perceived decline and fall. Thirty years ago—in June 1977—the *Daily Mirror* sold 3,879,000. This June that figure was 1,565,711. In June 1977, the *Daily Express* sold 2,312,152. Make that just 770,403. The *Telegraph* over 1.3 million 30 years back. Make that 892,000 now—hugely bolstered by cheap subscriptions, foreign sales and a word I barely remember from the seventies ... bulks. And so on and so dismally forth. Where have 1.5 million *News of the World* customers gone? And over three million former *People*-reading people? Why are national daily sales down to 11.6 million when those with not-so-long memories can recall 14 million? Why is our universe contracting year after year, as though inexorably?

Answer: it can't be anything we're doing wrong. So it must be outside forces. It must be the menace of the Internet, a digital screen come to sweep us all away. Arthur Sulzberger Junior openly talks of a New York without his beloved *Times*. "One day there were tablets and the next day there weren't".

Look around and see how everyone's suffering. Why, the regional press is posting lousy figures year after year now; 90,000 paid copies of the *Manchester Evening News*? I remember when they sold 350,000. I remember when the *Liverpool Echo* topped 400,000. I remember when London had three evening papers, competing with brutal ferocity, selling nearly 3 million copies between them. Just 200,000 actually bought a copy of the *Evening Standard* last June.

There was nothing else, either, that they could buy.

And are things better in the big country where trends begin? They are, if anything, lousier. Consider this, the 2007 assessment from Fitch Ratings, the financial analysts who report regularly on the US newspaper industry. Newspapers are doing "even worse" than

Fitch expected as 2007 began. And their outlook for the sector remains resolutely "negative".

Sure enough, Internet advertising continues to grow apace.

Sure enough, newspapers are opening and developing their own Internet news sites as though their futures depended on it—which may well be true. But, increasingly, the figures don't add up. Increasingly, the 25–30 per cent profitability ratios Wall Street expects are failing and flailing. Increasingly, the premium prices family newspaper owners expected when they sold their precious babies aren't being realised.

So there's the received wisdom. It applies to broadcasting, too. Look at the TV figures and another million US viewers have vanished. The network will soon be partworks. Listen to the soliloquies of Michael Grade,[3] never mind Jeremy Paxman, and you know that more channels—many, many more channels—really means more desperation in a world where power has shrunk and resources are very finite indeed. If the press is in trouble, you think, then TV, as we know it, is sinking. The old order is changing very fast. But our difficulty is understanding what the new order may turn out to be.

Thus I'm standing here on a familiar spot, expected to animadvert about the death of newspapers—and therefore about an industry that has been my life, and which some of you hope will be your life, too. Let the cries of woe ring out! Or, more rationally, not. Because there are other shows and other elections of indicative facts here. Because we're really talking about far more complex trends covered by a slurry of self-regarding pessimism.

The death of evening newspapers, for instance ... were they, in their hundreds across the United States, victims of the Net? Hardly: the London *Evening News* and the *Star* were killed off long before the Net was invented. What disposed of them, and many more like them, was a combination of malignant factors. People didn't work set hours in offices and factories any longer, they worked at home or in industrial estates on the edge of town; they drove home rather than got a train: they found they couldn't get an evening paper delivered any longer because the traffic was too impenetrable: and the paper they could sometimes get—because it went to press at noon rather than 3.30—didn't have any of the facts that drove purchase ... no late racing results or cricket scores, for instance. You could get that stuff on TV anyway, in the office canteen, in the betting shop, in the pub, off Ceefax or the radio (never mind the Net!). So the reason for buying a paper which often wasn't in the right place at the right time anyway was hugely diminished.

Simply, life changed but evening newspapers didn't, or couldn't. A whole slice of newspaper life died in the States and is withering here now as the evenings that remain are turned into single-edition late morning papers, updated on the Net in a further burst of suicide fever fuelled by short-term accountancy. Note the basic situation, though: the Net may be the deliverer of the *coup de grace* here, but it's not truly to blame for what's gone wrong over decades. Human living patterns, changing, moving on, have done that. Complain about the dying years of evening journalism and all you're doing is complaining about life.

The enemies of the evenings were inertia, fatalism and cost-cutting. You can take exactly those elements and apply them to other situations, too. I wrote recently in the *Observer* about American papers' propensity—from the *New York Times* down—to opt for a narrow 12-inch wide sheet, carving an inch and half or so (and usually a column) from what they offer the punter. Pay more for less? It's a potty pitch nobody outside the closed world of newspaper introspection would give house room to. It isn't even disguised by the kind of thorough-going redesign that the *Guardian* has implemented as it has turned Berliner. The Americans have just pared away to produce a curiously long, thin sheet with the standard number of tales still turning inside as before and the standard number of separate sections—Metro, Classified, Real Estate—falling out of a hopelessly confusing bundle behind. (I liked the arts and entertainment section in the *Denver Post* in that regard. It's called A and E.) Should we be surprised, if this rather hapless performance encourages cyclical decline? Of course not. It is almost designed to encourage it. And pause for a moment for greater thought, because already we have a pattern worth a post mortem.

Have evening newspapers, here and there, fought back with investment, zeal and ingenuity? Did the *Evening Standard*, for instance, counter too early deadline problems and too many traffic distribution problems, by setting up satellite plants in Croydon and Watford and taking the paper closer to readers it otherwise couldn't reach, with more intensive editionising of news for a city the size of Austria? No: it cut back on news and shelved editions. It didn't expand coverage, it contracted. Intrinsically, following received wisdom industry-wide, it gave up the ghost. And, on a much wider scale, that's also what American papers have done when adversity comes knocking. They have given up the ghost.

And there is a huge, linking theme, conditioning such behaviour—one that has nothing to do with the Net. For newspaper ownership—the way they're owned and run— is also a massive factor here, perhaps the greatest factor.

Look with a beady glint of history in your eye and you can see what's happened over the decades. Once—as I remember saying to David Dimbleby—there were family companies like his own, proud to own newspapers large and small. They made good money. They offered a community status and a pleasing life style. And then along came an entrepreneur—a Conrad Black, an Art Neuhaus, a Vere Rothermere, a Freddie Johnston— making an offer they couldn't refuse. Maybe the founding family itself had lost interest in newspaper life. Maybe there wasn't a son or a daughter who could take over the helm. Maybe the struggle to overcome union resistance and find enough cash to buy new presses was becoming onerous. But, certainly, the offer the big boys made seemed munificent. They were growing year by year. They were public companies with a share price soaring ever higher. They could turn in shareholder returns in that 25–30 per cent region—even 32 per cent at their market peak. They could afford to offer 15 or 16 times earnings for another juicy little property. If there was anything better than earning a local paper, it was selling it.

But see what happens when the music stops. The economy dips, as economies still do from time to time, and the price premium isn't right any longer. The *Chicago Tribune* goes to Zell and back. Knight Ridder is wrecked from the inside by the equity merchants on its board who want the old earnings ratios restored; but that time is past and the United States's second biggest chain is dismembered. In Britain, in the past few months, Northcliffe newspapers has come to market, then withdrawn for lack of interest; and Trinity Mirror's sell-off of holdings it deems peripheral has ended in something close to humiliation.

The world has changed, in short. The equity and corporate raiders have got a lot of tough new problems to chew on. The day of the big, ever-expanding chain, moving onwards and upwards on a tide of debt and expectation of profit levels that would make Tesco look puny, is over. But, crucially, we don't know what comes next—which is absolutely as big a question, and probably more of a threat, than the Net.

Ask yourself . . . why should anyone want to own a newspaper? There are two main reasons around (if I exclude the saintly Scott trustees of the *Guardian*, who get neither money nor glory from their stewardship). One reason is cash. A mass circulation paper bringing in millions of 40 or 50ps over a newsagent's counter every morning enjoys a cash-flow situation other industries can barely dream of. The profits, even in decline, can still seem pretty appetising. Richard Desmond didn't buy the *Express* and *Sunday Express* in some unlikely spasm of altruism. The chains we still have are built on good returns and better promises to the City. The opportunities for tax refinement across many countries are seemingly limitless. (Another Murdoch memorial lecture!)

And then—the other reason—there is influence. You can have both, of course. The aforementioned Mr Murdoch wants his cake and eats it. The Barclay brothers bought the *Telegraph*, I guess, as a nice little earner that the family could own and gain authority from long after the twins had passed to some great Channel island in the sky. It's good to be a media mogul, after all. It prevents other papers writing too much about your family indiscretions. It traditionally opens Downing Street's doors at tea time. It will throw in a peerage to anybody who asks hard enough. (The Conrad Black memorial lecture!)

But where do these ancestral motivations rank in today's pantheon? The money motive, as we've seen, has lost much of its allure. Big corporations are in trouble, often big trouble. Like EMAP, they're nightmare jigsaws with any bits up for sale if they'll get a good price. And the glory game isn't quite what it was either. The sons of the cavaliers—like the latest Viscount Rothermere—may not actually be very keen on the limelight; indeed, may shun it almost entirely. Their special share structures are under City pressure. It's a fight to hang on and to look for an heir who'll want to hang on, too. (A real Rupert Murdoch memorial lecture.)

Why not buy a chunk of Chelsea or Manchester City instead? And as for TV, where's the buzz in owning this or that battling cable channel, one of hundreds, in competition with the BBC, which has a licence to raise money, or an ITV which no longer has a licence to print money? It's neither a particularly glamorous nor a particularly lucrative game. All of which makes media ownership itself a massive and growing problem. Sam Zell's Chicago foray isn't a one-off phenomenon here. He's the new owner of last resort, unable or unwilling to invest the big capital the business needs, available only to wheel, deal and pick up any juicy pieces. The reasons why people, historically, have bought and run newspapers, are no longer valid. The reasons why successor regimes would step in are wholly obscure. If there are questions of faith, vision and resource to be answered, then we're all in trouble.

Pause for some quick stocktaking. We've perused an industry in a dither that doesn't seem able to adjust to change: change in its financial status, change in society's working patterns, change in ownership perception and resilience. Is the Internet to blame? It's part of the problem, to be sure. But that problem was burgeoning long before doom topped media agendas. America's top 20 papers were sliding steadily in sales—a point or more down every year—long before the Net crossed their horizon. Fleet Street has been puffing distress for just as long, if not longer: and, again, the net played no part in that to begin with. Instead, we have introversion to deal with. Introversion means that we adjust slowly to change, if we adjust at all. Introversion means we don't notice the world changing around us. Introversion means a fatal lack of communication in the communications business, a blinkered refusal to make connections or form fresh alliances. Introversion brings a kind of imbecility along with it.

Consider one, as yet untrumpeted, factor, doing quite as much current circulation damage as the Internet: the rise and rise of the freesheets.

It's only 12 years since some bright young Swedes decided that a free morning paper for Stockholm—maybe 20 minutes' worth of reading for young, moneyed commuters on their way into the office—could fill a niche that Sweden's staider, more traditional, paid-for papers couldn't reach; and only a few years less than that since Associated Newspapers decided that Scandinavian *Metros* would cause havoc in the British market if they didn't move fast and beat them to the punch. It's only just over a year since News International, which Associated did indeed beat to the morning market punch, launched the *LondonPaper* as a free, with Associated moving in to try to block that via *London Lite*.

The result? If you put in other frees like *CityAM*, then well over two million copies that don't cost a penny are out there to be picked up, or fended off, every weekday. Has that had an impact on paid-for circulation? Of course. London in particular is a sales disaster for many titles: pain for the *Guardian*, woe for the *Independent*, but real trouble, too, for the *Mail* and *Times* and *Sun*.

Consider, too, the logic of that. A relatively successful product that makes a profit—though, at £14 million or so in good economic times, the morning *Metro* is not exactly a gold-plated winner—actually depresses the profits and prospects of the house that publishes it. Worse, an unproven London free evening paper in a sector (the evening) which is dying on its feet all over the western world, enters and on every possible indicator loses money without any prospect of making it, especially while it faces a free competitor launched to defend a paid-for paper that, in turn, loses pots of money—somewhere on an oscillating scale between £10 and £20 million in recent years. That might just be understood if the evening market were provenly fertile: but it's not, really anywhere in Europe or America. And it might just be worth a punt if daily freesheets were financial certainties. But they're not: indeed, some of the Swedes' latest European ventures have failed and their overall profitability sets few pulses racing.

What kind of introversion, I wonder, commits newspaper managements to such visceral games? But what kind of introversion, in turn, also means that they and the journalists they employ don't include those extra two million printed copies in the story they tell about news printed on paper? Here's introversion within introversion.

If I write an article for the *Guardian* then, somehow or other, I regard the 80 pence the reader paid to have it on his breakfast table as some kind of personal validation. If you pay to read me, that counts. If *Guardian* syndication sells that article on to a freesheet, however, then it doesn't count at all, because it's free and therefore rather demeaning. But register even more confusion as you read that same piece on the *Guardian*'s very successful website. It's free there, too, but that counts hugely because . . . because we choose to count it. Free news on paper is beyond the pale. Free news on your Apple is greatly blessed. If we chose to add paid-for and free copies together in a newspaper universe, putting two million-plus copies on top of the 11.5 million nationals currently sold every day, then the decline that we complain about so morosely would turn out to be no overall decline at all, just a shifting of furniture. If we wanted a good story to tell, we could have it without the least strain.

But here, as in so many other instances, our future is our past. The war between *London Lite* and the *LondonPaper* is the past, a kind of printed Paschendale. The future—as

Rupert Murdoch, say, ploughs $5 billion into the *Wall Street Journal*, £750 million into new UK presses and endless millions into his Internet vision—is covered in mist.

Newspaper journalists, who work under great daily stress in closed offices, churning out edition after edition, are instinctively dependent on team-playing and routine. That's why, of necessity, they grow anxious when the world throws up new challenges. But I think they are also justified in asking those who lead, own and pay them what's happened to the vision thing? The press—and, to a large extent, conventional broadcasting—hasn't been engulfed by crisis. Rather, it has wandered into it, perpetually surprised by the predictable. And that, in turn, hampers any attempt to see the challenge everybody talks about, the challenge of the Net, with any reasonable clarity.

Where will we be in five/10/15 years? If you're a journalism student, perhaps in Cardiff, wondering whether the trade you're training for has any future—and I am of course asked this question—then the difficulty isn't just seeing what the Internet we have is doing to newspapers ... the impact, perhaps, of Craig's List. No: the difficulty is seeing how the Net itself, in ambition and technology, will have changed. And not all of that is negative.

Some supposedly unstoppable phenomena may have stopped growing. The number of bloggers, for instance, appears probably finite on some current research. Craig's List itself has a host of newer, younger rivals to contend with. Newspapers have already begun to fight back via a plethora of their own websites. The latest hand-held computers may prove a fantastic tool for delivering hard, terse news, but no use at all for longer analysis pieces. (Actually, we have no idea what those computers will do come 2022.)

In short, both sides of the equation are utterly uncertain.

It's not merely newspapers, dying or not, that we have to contend with: it's a rush of change that can whisk Facebook from zero to hero in a few weeks—or see the *Daily Mail* website zoom from nowhere to number 2 in a month. There's no slow build in this new business now. There's no established audience, no basic constituency, no settled achievement. You're as good as your last idea—and anybody can have good ideas.

There is, though, one job with tolerable certainty attached. Does news matter? Does it matter if you know what's going on in your world, your street, your town, your country? If it does, then you'll want someone to discover, collect, edit and distribute that news—and you will want it done with some professionalism. There's a deal too much blather about "trust" in journalism these days, I think, but facts that bear some relation to truth are better than facts confected or simply got wrong. There is a need for solid facts. Therefore, there is a continuing need for organisations that can dig out those facts. Therefore there will—on screen or in print—be a continuing need for journalism and journalists.

It doesn't matter much whether the facts that the news factory produces are put down on paper, or transmitted on the Net. Killing forests is only one ancient way of approaching a task that may be far better done digitally. Journalism itself—good, responsive journalism, meeting a need—is not threatened by the Net. Indeed, its opportunities and possibilities are much enhanced. It won't die, though more trees may live.

No, what we're talking about here isn't the end of everything we hold dear, but transition. How long before newsprint is gone, if it ever goes entirely? How long before screens, large and small, are everything? And I think, rather tediously for the Net's most vehement devotees perhaps, that the road may be far longer and rougher than they suppose.

I was looking, a few months ago, at the 2006 world press picture as painted pretty authoritatively by the World Association of Newspapers: global newspaper sales up 2.3 per cent last year (and 9.48 per cent in the past five years), ad revenues up 3.7 and 15.7 per cent over the same two spans. Now that, of course, is much bolstered by Asian tigerishness. China is up 15.5 per cent since 2002 and India 53.6 per cent. European paid-for daily titles sold 0.74 per cent more copies last year than the year before. Add in free dailies—and why not?—and that's a 10.2 per cent circulation rise year on year, or 12.2 per cent since 2002.

Whatever happened to supposedly inexorable connections—like the law that sees online grow and print sink as though they were yoked together in some suicide pact? Japan, where they sold 69.1 million copies a day in 2006, has computers on every desk. China—at 98.7 million copies a day—is also a supreme Internet growth area. It's much too facile to hail simple cause and effect.

Of course there are special circumstances everywhere you turn. Former Communist countries in eastern Europe got a shot of democratic adrenaline when they joined the union—more sales, more titles—and now see that slip back a bit as the thrill wears off. Immigration (influxes of people who don't read too easily or recognise many of the cultural icons) can be a bit of a dampener. But look at the larger developed countries hanging in or around G8 status. After Italy (up year on year, but a bit down over five years) there is France at -1.55 per cent (-5.7 per cent over five years) and Germany at -2.1 and -9.35 per cent. Spain—at -2.14 and -1.13 per cent—did rather better.

US dailies lost 1.9 per cent in 2006 and 5.18 per cent over five years—but those figures are warped by the collapse of what's left of the evening paper market there (down 19.62 per cent over five years). America's morning papers have merely seen 2.52 per cent of readers toddle away—and their ad revenue grew 5.69 per cent in 2006. For all the sound and gnashing fury, that is not nemesis.

So there, again, is the curse of introspection. We exaggerate our own demise. We paint an artificially gloomy picture. We plump—like our own headline writers—for one angle or another, rather than creating a rounded picture. We lay blame at the most convenient (for us) door.

Some of this blame-shifting is really simple bemusement or frustration.

If you're an editor in the van of pushing readership on the Internet, then it's galling to be sacked because your newsprint sales have dipped. If you're a Sunday editor (called Wheatcroft, say) then you won't want to be accounted a failure because all the journalists who should have been providing you with something special have been made to unload it days earlier by the editor of the daily paper who thinks he runs you "in chief". Where are the current rewards for future success, real or promised, if this supposed future, as at the *Telegraph*, means eight changed editors in the last four years?

See? Introspection comes naturally—and with it comes a kind of anxiety that carries its own seeds of destruction within it. If you don't know what "success" is, then you won't know how to achieve it. And if—more important for the moment, I think, than most things that happen on the editorial floor—the managers who run your place and the owners who choose them are similarly perplexed, then we have a lethal prescription: managements which can't recruit top talent, owners fighting a dour, doomed rearguard action or flipping and flopping back and forth.

What's the future? We don't know. Why can't we make it for ourselves? We can, because the news we gather and sell is a staff of continuing life. But do we, examining our navels again, have the faith to put that first? Do we concentrate on the main event—or are we stuck in the mud defending Caxton and what we learned as trainees 30 years ago?

You know by now how I'd answer all that. You also know that, to my fury, the next 20 years will be as challenging and invigorating as any in journalism's history. And I hope, 20 years on, that you'll come to agree.

Straightforwardly.

NOTES

1.   A left-of-centre, quality newspaper published in the United Kingdom.
2.   Two well-known BBC broadcasters celebrated for their adversarial interview style.
3.   Michael Grade is currently Chief Executive of ITV, the United Kingdom's major commercial broadcaster; previously he Chaired the Board of Governors at the BBC.

Chapter 2

THE FUTURE OF NEWSPAPERS
Historical perspectives

Martin Conboy and **John Steel**

Introduction

Historical understanding of any cultural form allows us to appreciate not only their distinctiveness but also their relationship to other forms and their "constructedness" (Poster, 2002). By viewing them as constructed within such a network of influences, we might be better able to consider the prospects they have in the future. Many of the political, economic and cultural functions of newspapers today have survived from previous technological regimes and it is these functions which surely need to be secured if they are to survive through a period of radical technological reorganisation. This paper opens by summarising the ways in which newspapers have always, hitherto, combined economic, technological and cultural imperatives that have sought to represent systems of shared beliefs through the emergence of differentiation. The paper then focuses on news and debates about "information society", suggesting that the radical and rapid technological transformation witnessed towards the end of the 20th century and gathering pace at the start of the 21st century, should be seen as a continuation of socio-economic trends that go back as far back as the 17th century. Finally, the paper considers debates central to the political imperative of newspapers and reflects on how the current trends of what we term "hyper-differentiation" might impact on political formations of the future.

Newspapers and the Emergence of "Differentiation"

It may seem obvious but it is worth stressing from the start that newspapers have always produced readers, not news, as their primary goal; creating a selection of news tailored for a particular readership to create profit and/or exert influence on that readership. Bearing this in mind will help focus our discussion on what future newspapers will continue to do, if they wish to survive, in changing technological circumstances. We can trace the emergence of newspapers in Britain to the regular production of the proceedings of Parliament in the 1640s (Raymond, 1996; Sommerville, 1996). This was in itself, given the political tensions of the time, a partisan development despite the naming of periodicals as "True" or "Perfect" Diurnals. It was a continuation of the contestation of authority which had accompanied such publications as it constituted a challenge to previous hierarchies of information dissemination (Conboy, 2004). The first regular periodical newspapers may have restricted themselves to reports of the latest political developments but this in itself did more than merely communicate political events; it served to generate a community of information, a community of political preference for an informed middle-ranking citizenship. Of course, this deployment of technology for political purposes had a profitable advantage for the printers who took the attendant risks in producing such new products since they could make good money from the requirements of this new audience of readers.

The need for newspapers to develop a differentiated readership became more apparent with the division of publications along broadly Royalist and Parliamentary lines from 1643. Many of these were also entitled as being "true" or "perfect" accounts but this truth was being increasingly manufactured from a particular perspective. The Restoration of the monarchy in 1660 saw more control exerted on the publication of news and as a consequence the reporting of political debate in Parliament on a regular basis was to wait over a hundred years before it was once again to be permitted. For the rest of the century up until the lapsing of the Licensing Acts in 1695, newspapers concentrated on dealing with the commercial interests of their readers in their formal reports. From 1695, the technology of printing became permitted, once again by political shifts, to allow a cultural experimentation with the communicative form of the newspaper and this, once again, was to provide evidence of the imperative in this format to address and influence a carefully defined readership. Political restrictions still meant that the readerships were much more likely to be expressed in terms of their lifestyle, tastes and broadly emergent bourgeois identity. The quantity and range of journalistic experimentation produced a great variety of attempts to articulate more specific readerships from the first women's periodicals (Adburgham, 1972) to the first regular daily newspaper from 1702, the *Daily Courant*. One of the most celebrated and important experiments was conducted from 1709 by Addison and Steele in *The Tatler* and later *The Spectator*. *The Tatler* began by incorporating news but after its 83rd edition this was dropped. The paper produced criticisms of newspapers and newswriters which indicated a certain cultivated cynicism about the exigencies of producing a regular supply of topical information, particularly about foreign wars (*Tatler* 18, 1709 and *Tatler* 77, 1709). Addison and Steele preferred to concentrate on what had become the distinctive identity of their output which was the articulation of the tastes of the rising class, the bourgeoisie.

The Tatler has more of the tone of the coffee-house, even of the tavern. It appealed, and was designed to appeal, more to the fashionable world than *The Spectator*. The latter, as benefited the character of its silent and retiring "writer", Mr Spectator, was addressed more to the morning tea-table, to the reflective hours of the civil servants and merchants represented in its subscription lists (Ross, 1982, p. 37).

Newspapers through the 18th century tended to treat their audience as more or less a homogenous readership with similar interests in court and commerce. Differentiation and experimentation with readerships based on class, gender or special interest took place within other periodical publications. For instance, throughout the 18th century it was the writing of letters, anonymously or pseudonymously, to the newspapers which allowed political factions to express themselves in more guarded fashion and cluster around particular publications (Adburgham, 1972; Shattock and Wolff, 1982; Tusan, 2005; White, 1970). Added to this was the increasing tendency for single-issue sheets to address a readership via the radical views of the author, or the narrow range of authors around a particular political perspective. This tradition, which Chalaby (1998) identifies as a precursor to modern journalism, was enhanced by the work of men who he sees as "publicists", from Wilkes, Gayle and Paine to Cobbett, Carlile and Wooler.

The great era of consolidation for daily newspapers was the 19th century. This was accomplished to a large extent through a growing emphasis on the consistency of appeal to a particular audience. The key to the success of the newspapers was industrialisation. This enabled steam printing and distribution by train during the exponential growth of the economy at this time. Yet, the assertiveness of newspapers as articulators of the reflected glories of Empire throughout the period was less to do with technology and more to do with the continuing refinement of the address to a specific readership through the careful orchestration of different newspapers by distinctive editors. It is from the late 18th century onwards that this phenomenon emerges. Men like James Perry on the *Morning Chronicle* and Daniel Stuart with his *Morning Post* laid the foundations for the function of the editor. The word is first used in the context of a newspaper in 1802 and was refined throughout the century to the point where the editor became the driving identification of the newspaper's articulation of its audience. Barnes, Delane, Stead, O'Connor, Scott and Massingham all contributed to the consolidation of the newspaper as a voice consistently fashioned for a particular readership identified by its political persuasion and social identity.

The narrative conventions of newspapers have always been tentative in their claims to truth and reliability (Toolan, 1998). Sommerville (1996) has also commented on the ways in which the eruption of newspapers created a shift in understanding the world which for the first time foregrounded simplicity and brevity. What newspapers can perhaps be more reliably credited with are those longer narratives of ideological coherence and identity. The *Times* at its height of mid-Victorian influence became the textual identification of confident, aspiring professional classes and an upper bourgeoisie while the weekly popular papers created narratives which crafted a carefully marketed version of the aspirations, frustrations and tastes in entertainment of the working classes (Humphreys, 1990). This propensity for narrating a particular version of events, crafted for a specifically targeted audience in terms of class and political orientation, became amplified from the late Victorian period. Increased pressure on space because of advertisements, increased

flow and quantity of news through improved technologies of transport and communication, meant that the structure of newspapers was oriented away from reports and more to
the modern configuration of the "story", chopped and shaped to fit the template of the
newspaper's available space and directed by the ascendant figure of the sub-editor
Matheson (2000). The *Daily Mail* came to embody the aspiring lower-middle classes' views
of themselves in similar ways to the dominant newspapers of the 20th century which may
have distinct news agendas but they are always differentiated by an astute commercial
consideration of the cultural and political inclinations of their readerships. This can be best
appreciated when viewing the "audience design" (Bell, 1994) of newspapers. The
monopoly of newspapers on reliable accounts about the latest events in the world was
broken by the advent of radio. As the radio consolidated its influence on communities of
listeners who tuned in for the latest news, so the newspapers turned increasingly to
various forms of product and even medium differentiation in order to retain their
readerships. They achieved this by enhancing the textual performance of audience
especially in the popular market (Conboy, 2002; Smith, 1975) and promoting this above
the function of simply providing the news to an audience imagined, as with radio, as an
ideal homogenised group. Television news drove this search for audiences in print further
as experiments in form and content reached the elite press from the 1980s. All newspapers
subsequently had to redefine their place in the media ecology. These experiments saw the
rise of feminised content, especially in the *Daily Mail*, and developments in lifestyle and
consumer journalism in a daily elite newspaper, the *Guardian*, in the 1980s and were to
culminate in the shift of elite newspapers from broadsheet to compact format in the new
millennium. With the further development of media technologies, they have had to
continue this process of refinement, increasing their function as arbiters of taste, opinion
and identity to such an extent that their news function now seems almost entirely
obsolete (Preston, 2004).

Carey (1989) has argued that newspapers have always been more concerned with
rituals of identity formation rather than any positivist contribution to knowledge about the
world. He therefore sees news as a cultural form and one which was created by and for the
bourgeoisie in the 18th century and one which set the template for developments to
follow even as it broadened out its social and economic base—not information but drama,
conflict between rival forces not a world of fact impacting upon fact. He elaborates this
"ritual" view over the "transmission" model of communication.

> The ritual view of communication, though a minor thread in our national thought, is by
> far the older of these views—old enough in fact for dictionaries to list it under "archaic."
> In a ritual definition, communication is linked to terms such as "sharing", "participation,"
> "association," "fellowship," and "the possession of a common faith," . . . a ritual view of
> communication is directed not toward the extension of messages in space but toward
> the maintenance of society in time; not the act of importing information but the
> representation of shared beliefs. (Carey, 1989, pp. 20–1)

This perspective would seem to reinforce the impression which emerges from the
summary of newspapers' articulation of readerships across history above. Apart from
moments of radical intervention, the majority of newspapers have, in their appeal to
audience, been responding to the primary imperative in a capitalist era of production,
offering optimal engagements with the latest configurations of capitalist culture for

well-targeted sections of the national community. What we might be witnessing at the start of the 21st century is the continuation of ritual by other, technological, means.

What makes the Internet such an interesting phenomenon in the contemporary history of newspapers is that it is at one and the same time a rival and a medium for the continuation of the newspaper in a radically altered form. Various explorations offer us a glimpse of the activity which newspapers are engaged in to try to adapt their traditional appeal to readership for a new technological era. Sumpter (2000) considers the ways in which editorial evaluation of news values for the readership of specific newspapers has long been a matter of hierarchical hunches rather than anything based in scientific market research. Site-metrics based on readership of online newspapers threatens this sort of traditional assessment of what is suitable for particular readerships. Gasher (2007) considers the limitations of reach of even online newspapers as they remain rooted in a national "cartography" of readership which contrasts with much of the hyperbole surrounding the global reach of Internet news media. Niblock (2007) identifies the ways in which newspapers are reacting to the challenges of the Internet by further reinforcing older patterns of identification with readerships through more sophisticated "lifestyle identities" expressed in their pages. All newspapers are using aspects of the interactive facilities of the Internet to promote the impression of a greater accountability to a generalised readership. It may be that the development of the Internet is simply a technological reconfiguration of older aspects of audience identification. On the other hand, it may be worth considering such modification in line with McLuhan's "Four Laws of the Media". Levinson summarises McLuhan's interpretation of any innovation in media technology as follows:

> What does it enhance or amplify in the culture? What does it obsolesce or push out of prominence? What does it retrieve from the past, from the realm of the previously obsolesced? And—and here the tetrad projects into the future—what does the medium reverse or flip into when it reaches the limits of its potential. (2001, p. 16)

Our initial contribution to this debate involves asking a set of fundamental questions of this new technological shift in newspapers. Are the changes in relations between informers and informed (Deibert, 1997) allowing a blossoming of human agency or are they merely assisting in the redrafting of the future so that it conforms to the ideological predispositions of communication in a capitalist world, confirming the suspicions of Carey that:

> Such transformations involve not only technical change but the complex alteration of physical, symbolic, and media ecologies which together will determine the impact of the medium ... [and] attempts to domesticate the future, to bring it under rational, predictable control ... [are] ... less predictions of the future than attempts to legislate and control it, to make sure the future conformed to particular ideological predispositions. (1998, p. 28)

News and the "Information Society"

In order to assess whether the current shifts in newspaper practice and potential are simply reconfigurations of traditional articulations of readership, and indeed ones which promise much to benefit these readers, we will need to first consider the structural implications of the information society as it is currently framed, and its relationship to the production of news. The phrase "information society" can be broadly understood to denote the social, political, economic and cultural shifts in society that have come about primarily because of relatively recent innovations in information and communications technology. Thinking about how technology might impact on society began to emerge as early as the 1950s, but the most notable and systematic contribution to the debate about the impact of technology came with Daniel Bell's *The Coming of Post-Industrial Society* (1973) (Bell, 1999). Bell suggested that capitalist society had shifted from an industrial, to a knowledge-based economy.

> What is different now is that the new information age is founded not on a mechanical technology but on an intellectual technology and that the new conceptions of time and space transcend the boundaries of geography (is there any portion of the world that is now exempt from some searching voice or image?) and take place in "real time," making the phrase "virtual reality" seem like a truism rather than a trendy slogan. (Bell, 1999, p. liii)

What is particularly interesting about the idea of the "information society" is its advocates suggest that it is both descriptive as well as explanatory: it describes a society (essentially global) that is characterised by an abundance of information that is available to all those with a computer and Internet connection. It is also explanatory in that the phrase has come to be understood as providing a catch-all term that neatly sums up and encapsulates the impact that information, and technology, have had on our very existence. Information is both the currency (Lennon, 1999) and the commodity of the "globalised" world in which we live (Castells, 1996). Though information society perspectives vary to a large extent, a key theme amongst information society scholars is the claim that the quantitative increase in the amount of information available necessarily leads to a qualitative change in social formations (Webster, 2002). Change seems to be the watchword here and the proliferation of newspapers offering digital online content, seems to support, or at least reflects the perspective that news production and distribution has changed beyond all recognition. News as an "important category of information" (Hill, 1999, p. 178) seems now to be central to contemporary economic, cultural and social life, yet the "news" provided by newspapers has been redefined and rearticulated to take into account such change in society. Indeed one author has suggested "the survival of the newspapers as a mass medium has been achieved by adaptation to changed circumstances" (Feather, 1994, p. 64). Circumstances which presumably induce the majority of British newspapers to focus on celebrity gossip, political scandal and salacious content. Such an analysis, however, underplays the cultural power of newspapers in whatever form (digital or paper) to define and thereby (re)-create their readership.

Rather than signalling dramatic and revolutionary change, technology and technological innovation can be seen as part of the continuous development of capitalist production relations, in Webster's view this should be seen as part of the continuing process of "'informatisation' of life, a process which has been ongoing, arguably for several centuries ..." (Webster, 2002, p. 265). In emphasising continuity rather than change, Webster's analysis of the so-called information society does not see technological innovation as bringing forth a completely new form of society. Change certainly takes place, but as an element of the perpetual development of capitalist production relations. Webster takes issue with much of the technologically determinist literature prevalent in analyses of modern communications technology. Instead he aligns himself with Shiller's

(1996) analysis of technology which focuses on the economic dynamic within technological innovation; Giddens's (1990, 1991) focus on elite development and use of technology; and Habermas's (1962) critique of the reformulation of the public sphere. Though Webster does not dismiss post-modern approaches to the information society debate, he suggests that in emphasising change and "newness" what these approaches miss out are the continuities of media and information production that have their seeds in the 16th and 17th centuries. He is of course not suggesting that nothing has changed, rather that the pace of change has given a false impression of "newness". What we have is an intensification of information production and distribution which he terms "the informatisation of life".

If one looks to the historical record the idea of rapid change and development heralding a new era is nothing new (see Marvin, 1988). In relation to the press in the 19th century, there was an awareness of the capacity for new technology to deliver what might be described as an "enhanced conversation" with expanding audiences across time and space (Marvin, 1988, p. 194). The following extended quote from John Pendleton in his book *Newspaper Reporting in Olden times and To-day* (1890), enthusiastically embraces the "immediacy" of news production:

> Nearly every daily newspaper had sent out the instruction "Gladstone, first person, verbatim". Twelve, sixteen, even twenty reporters formed the corps of some newspapers; and the half-hour "turns" were suspended for three, five, or ten minute takes, the reporters deftly working hand over hand, section by section; so that when Mr. Gladstone resumed his seat at eight o'clock in the evening, having spoken since thirty five minutes past four o'clock in the afternoon, nearly the whole of his speech, sent either by telephone or messenger, was in the offices of the London morning papers, and so on the wires for the country. It was an anxious time in many a telegraph office and in many a sub-editors room, but the speech, which contained 24,700 words, was nearly all in type in Manchester, Leeds and Edinburgh before midnight—before the great statesman who delivered it had emptied his pomatum pot of voice restorative and gone home to bed. (Pendleton, 1890, pp. 103–4)

In a seemingly prophetic speech on the future of newspapers Robert Donald, the then Chairman of the Institute of Journalists in 1913, suggests that one day news could be delivered to a person's home in the same way as electricity or gas was currently delivered (cf. McEwen, 1982; Taylor, 1934). Such enthusiastic speculation about the possibilities of future media was not unusual in the late 19th century; nor was fevered speculation about the potential impact of such technology on the circumstances of the day (Marvin, 1988, p. 193). Even in the 1940s we see discussions of how the press of the future might look. For example, Harris predicts that if the popular press "deteriorated seriously" because of market pressures, a "public utility newspaper" not unlike the BBC could be a possibility (1943, pp. 132–3). This would only be necessary, however, if the monopolisation of the press continued and over-commercialisation became predominant. In discussing the impact of technology, Harris also suggests that air travel has offered new possibilities for the internationalisation of the press, either in terms of an Anglo-American or Anglo-European venture. He argues that the technicalities of such a venture are not the issue but there are issues about language, culture and profitability. The point being that technology may enable commercial ventures but does not drive them; if there is no market, the venture will fail and Harris is crucially aware of this.

Technology, Differentiation and Democracy

It has been suggested that the recent Internet "revolution" offers both opportunities and barriers to enhanced political participation and democracy. In terms of expanding the existing traditional political context, such technologies can be seen as providing opportunities for an increased sense of connectedness both to the political system and to those who inhabit this system on our behalf. Though the potentialities of this technology have yet to be realised in practice, there seems to be a willingness by the political elite to pay at least some lip service to the "interactivity" and "democratic" potentials of this new technology, though it is unclear whether their motives are purely instrumental or genuine. Similarly from the perspective of what might be termed "alternative" politics, the potential to break down existing barriers to communication and participation are being realised in newsgroups, discussion boards, websites and so on. The optimistic view is that technology has liberated us from the tyranny of control, where "closed" information pathways have now given way to open information flows (Castells, 1996; McNair, 2006). Indeed there have been many discussions focusing on how traditional political formations might make use of such technologies in order to enhance and augment existing political institutions (Coleman, 2001; Coleman and Ward, 2005; Rheingold, 1995; Ward and Vedel, 2006). Cyber optimists see this current era in our history as heralding new opportunities which will enable us all (should we choose to) to become active citizens. Information can be viewed as the core material that enables us to "make sense" of the world and thus aid our participation in it. "News" and its production and dissemination can be seen as one of the important strands of this information society and recent attention has been given to exploring how news production and delivery can take advantage of the "information revolution" that the information society has given rise to. News, though a commodity, is available to nearly everyone with a computer, PDA or mobile phone. Not only is news different from that dry stale content that we see on paper, that terribly old-fashioned media, it is up-to-date, personalised and just for me! Current trends in newspaper digitisation allow content to be tailored to the end-user that enables them to manage content in ways that best reflect their own personal choices. "News" then becomes the picture of the world that we have some power in creating. This power to filter out content and information that the consumer might deem irrelevant and uninteresting enables the end-user not only to have the ultimate power as a consumer—the power to define what it is they read; it also enables individuals to bracket off information and content that is outside their sphere of interest. In short, the consumer has ultimate power over content. This power is taken even one step further when one considers the increasing preponderance of user-generated content (UGC). Not only can users now discriminate against undesirable content, they can now create their own content that reflects their particular view of the world and speaks to the values that they might wish to promote. This has long been the aim of techno-centric movers and shakers such as Nicholas Negroponte and of course Bill Gates, who envisage a consumer society in which the consumer has power to change the frame of reference through which he or she engages with the world, or not, as the case may be.

Though many variations of optimism exist, there are also numerous critiques of Internet technology in the political sphere, for example a number of radical critiques emphasise how Internet technologies come to replicate existing technologies and thereby replicate existing structures of power. In short, the Internet has become a reflection of more traditional communications technologies which have been appropriated by the elite and reflect their corporate agenda (Ford and Gil, 2001; McChesney, 2000). Moreover, journalistic norms increasingly have more to do with "packaging and marketing information than with ensuring the integrity of the data conveyed" (Brown, 1997, p. 168; cf. also Franklin, 2004).

Sunstein (2001) and Winston (2005) suggest, however, that such hyper-differentiation may place tensions on public discourse and democratic politics. For example, Cass Sunstein suggests that in societies that are based on a deliberative model of democracy, such hyper-differentiation may hamper or even undermine such deliberative processes. He suggests that a deliberative democracy involves individuals being confronted with ideas and information that otherwise they might have chosen to avoid. The physical act of reading a newspaper, which is chaotic and unsystematic in character, leads to unexpected outcomes. For example, the reader's attention may randomly be caught by an interesting story about EU farming policy; they may come across an article written by someone whose views they have no time for, yet might still read that article to confirm their suspicions that the person is an idiot! By filtering out and personalising content readers are in effect denying themselves access to some greater deliberative context. Hyper-differentiation in effect cuts off opportunities to engage with issues that readers might have never considered engaging with in the first place. The worst-case scenario for Sunstein is that issues become even more sectarian and secular space for debate is closed off. Active, open deliberation, which is informed by a wide spectrum of opinion, is placed under severe pressure by closed, atomised sectarian perspectives. The model of a deliberative democracy is therefore ultimately replaced by a consumer democracy in which the tendency for fragmentation and atomisation has a real impact on political debate. The newspapers of the future will no doubt continue to have an important role in defining and shaping the audience, however, it would be lamentable if the construction of hyper-differentiated audiences undermines rather than enhances the deliberative component of democratic societies.

Conclusion

We can tentatively conclude that the evidence to date suggests that the impact of the Internet on contemporary newspaper practice and indeed on the potential future of newspapers is far from a simple switch of technological engagement with readerships. It is rather a switch which has within its institutional and political dynamic a great deal which destabilises traditional notions of citizenship and community. Hyper-differentiation may indeed place pressure on the deliberative ideal, yet ultimately it is the producers and the readers of newspapers who have the ultimate say and even responsibility for the future. Beyond the sort of technological determinism which disempowers both of these parties, we need to be able to restore confidence that it is human intervention in the processes of technology which will determine the quality of social readership available to us in the near future and therefore the quality of our media communication as a ritual of shared beliefs.

REFERENCES

ADBURGHAM, ALISON (1972) *Women in Print: writing women and women's magazines from the restoration to the accession of Victoria*, London: George Allan and Unwin.

BELL, ALLAN (1994) *Language in the News*, Oxford: Blackwell.

BELL, DANIEL (1999) *The Coming of the Post-Industrial Society: a venture in social forecasting*, New York: Basic Books (1st edition published in 1973, Harmondsworth: Penguin, Peregrine).

BROWN, DAVID (1997) *Cybertrends, Chaos, Power, and Accountability in the Information Age*, London: Viking.

CAREY, JAMES W. (1989) *Communication as Culture: essays on media and society*, Boston: Hyman Publishers.

CAREY, JAMES W. (1998) "The Internet and the End of the National Communication System: uncertain predictions for an uncertain future", *Journalism and Mass Communications Quarterly* 75(1), pp. 28–34.

CASTELLS, MANUEL (1996) *The Information Age: economy, society and culture*, Vol. 1: *The rise of the network society*, Oxford: Blackwell.

CHALABY, JEAN K. (1998) *The Invention of Journalism*, Basingstoke: Macmillan.

COLEMAN, STEPHEN (2001) *Elections in the Age of the Internet: lessons from the United States*, London: Hansard.

COLEMAN, STEPHEN and WARD, STEPHEN (Eds) (2005) *Spinning the Web: online campaigning in the 2005 General Election*, London: Hansard Society.

CONBOY, MARTIN (2002) *The Press and Popular Culture*, London: Sage.

CONBOY, MARTIN (2004) *Journalism: a critical history*, London: Sage.

DEIBERT, RONALD (1997) *Parchment, Printing, and Hypermedia: communication in world order transformation*, New York: Columbia University Press.

FEATHER, JOHN (1994) *The Information Society: a study of continuity and change*, London: Library Association.

FORD, TAMARA V. and GIL, GENÈVE (2001) "Radical Internet Use", in: John D. H. Downing (Ed.), *Radical Media*, London: Sage.

FRANKLIN, BOB (2004) *Packaging Politics: political communication in Britain's media democracy*, London: Arnold.

GASHER, MIKE (2007) "The View From Here: a news-flow study of on-line editions of Canada's national newspapers", *Journalism Studies* 8(2), pp. 299–319.

GIDDENS, ANTHONY (1990) *The Consequences of Modernity*, Cambridge: Polity.

GIDDENS, ANTHONY (1991) *Modernity and Self-identity: self and society in the late modern age*, Cambridge: Polity.

HABERMAS, JÜRGEN (1962) *The Structural Transformation of the Public Sphere: An Inquiry into a Category of Bourgeois Society*. Translated by Thomas Burger with the assistance of Frederick Lawrence, Cambridge: Polity, 1989.

HARRIS, WILSON (1943) *The Daily Press*, Cambridge: Cambridge University Press.

HILL, MICHAEL (1999) *The Impact of Information on Society: an evaluation of its nature, value and usage*, London: Bowker-Saur.

HUMPHREYS, A. (1990) "Popular Narrative and Political Discourse in *Reynold's Weekly Newspaper*", in: Laurel Brake, Aled Jones and Lionel Madden (Eds), *Investigating Victorian Journalism*, Basingstoke: Macmillan.

LENNON, DAVID (1999) "The Future of 'Free' Information in the Age of the Internet", *Aslib Proceedings* 51(9), pp. 285–9.

LEVINSON, PAUL (2001) *Digital McLuhan: a guide to the Information Millennium*, London and New York: Routledge.

MARVIN, CAROLYN (1988) *When Old Technologies Were New: thinking about electric communication in the late nineteenth century*, New York: Oxford University Press.

MATHESON, DONALD (2000) "The Birth of News Discourse: changes in news language in British newspapers, 1880–1930", *Media, Culture and Society* 22(5), pp. 557–73.

MCCHESNEY, ROBERT W. (2000) *Rich Media, Poor Democracy: communication politics in dubious times*, New York: The New Press.

MCEWEN, JOHN M. (1982) "The National Press During the First World War: ownership and circulation", *Journal of Contemporary History* 17, pp. 459–86.

MCNAIR, BRIAN (2006) *Cultural Chaos: journalism, news and power in a globalised world*, London: Routledge.

NIBLOCK, SARAH (2007) "From 'Knowing How' to 'Being Able': negotiating the meanings of reflective practice and reflexive research in journalism studies", *Journalism Practice* 1, pp. 20–32.

PENDLETON, JOHN (1890) *Newspaper Reporting in Olden times and To-day*, London: Elliot Stock.

POSTER, MARK (2002) "Culture and New Media: a historical view", in: L.A. Lievrouw and S. Livingstone (Eds), *Handbook of New Media: social shaping and social consequences of ICTs*, London: Sage.

PRESTON, PETER (2004) "Are Newspapers Burnt Out?", *Observer*, 21 November.

RAYMOND, JOAD (1996) *The Invention of the Newspaper: English newsbooks, 1641–1649*, Oxford: Oxford University Press.

RHEINGOLD, HOWARD (1995) *The Virtual Community: finding connection in a computerized world*, London: Minerva.

ROSS, ANGUS (Ed.) (1982) *Selections from the Tatler and the Spectator*, Harmondsworth: Penguin.

SHATTOCK, JOANNE and WOLFF, MICHAEL (1982) *The Victorian Periodical Press: samplings and soundings*, Leicester: Leicester University Press.

SHILLLER, HERBERT L. (1996) *Information Inequality: the deepening social crisis in America*, New York: Routledge.

SMITH, ANTHONY C. H. (with IMMIRZI, ELIZABETH and BLACKWELL, TREVOR) (1975) *Paper Voices: the popular press and social change, 1935–1965*, London: Chatto and Windus.

SOMMERVILLE, JOHN (1996) *The News Revolution*, Oxford: Oxford University Press.

SUMPTER, R. S. (2000) "Daily Newspaper Editors' Audience Construction Routines: a case study", *Critical Studies in Media Communication* 17(3), pp. 334–45.

SUNSTEIN, CASS (2001) *Republic.Com*, Princeton, NJ: Princeton University Press.

TAYLOR, HENRY A. (1934) *Robert Donald, Being the Authorized Biography of Sir Robert Donald, Journalist, Editor and Friend of Statesmen*, London: S. Paul.

TOOLAN, M. J. (1998) *Narrative: A Critical Linguistic Introduction*, London: Routledge.

TUSAN, MICHELLE (2005) *Women Making News: gender and the women's periodical press in Britain*, Champaign: University of Illinois Press.

WARD, STEPHEN and VEDEL, THIERRY (2006) "The Potential of the Internet Revisited", *Parliamentary Affairs* 59(2), pp. 210–25.

WEBSTER, FRANK (2002) *Theories of the Information Society*, London: Routledge.

WHITE, CYNTHIA L. (1970) *Women's Magazines 1693–1968*, London: Michael Joseph.

WINSTON, BRIAN (2005) *Messages, Free Expression, Media and the West from Gutenberg to Google*, London: Routledge.

Chapter 3

MAPPING PROFESSIONAL IMAGINATION
On the potential of professional culture in the newspapers of the future

Risto Kunelius and **Laura Ruusunoksa**

Introduction

Debates on the future of newspapers—and the future of professional journalism—often focus heavily on the external conditions in which journalism operates. In such a framework, journalism is seen to be facing a series of problems. Indeed, predicting the end of journalism has been a common figure of speech in this literature for at least the past 15 years (cf. Deuze, 2007; Hardt, 1996; Katz, 1992). On the other hand, some of the same conditions have been interpreted as a ray of hope illuminating a more democratic role for journalism (cf. McNair, 2006).

In these debates, there is a tendency to see the professional culture of journalists as a reflection of its institutional and organisational contexts. It is indeed impossible to comprehend the actions of individual journalists without a sense of the occupationally situated ideologies that motivate their decisions and routines. But when we are discussing the *future* of newspapers or journalism, an overtly structural framework entails a danger of reducing journalism to its conditions. This does not help us to understand or *appreciate the role of professionals and professional culture in defining the future of newspapers*, or more importantly the future of the democratically useful practices that newspaper journalism has cultivated (cf. Sparks, 2007).

Thus, understanding the role of professionals in the current changes requires considering several viewpoints. The first task is to see journalism and the development of newspapers contextually. Secondly, we need an anti-reductionist conceptual frame through which to scrutinise journalistic professional culture. Therefore we need an approach that acknowledges the limits of the journalists' professional horizon but also appreciates the dynamics between the professional culture and its context. For this purpose, this article coins the term *professional imagination* to refer to the collective potential of agency inherent in the professional culture of journalists.

Thirdly, any culturally valid prediction must draw on empirical evidence. We will discuss the role of professional culture in the future of journalism and newspapers with reference to interviews with a small but strategically important group of Finnish journalists. By interpreting the ways in which mid-level managing editors and news directors in Finnish newspapers view the changes in journalism we attempt to provide an insight into the ways in which dominant professional discourse modifies current contextual imperatives into professionally acceptable aims and ideals. This material enables us to consider some inner tensions of the professional culture.

Newspapers and Journalism in Finland

Journalism is contextual by nature. Thus, in order to understand the professional culture of Finnish newspaper journalism in the early 2000s, let us offer a concise account of its recent past and present from four perspectives: economic, technological, cultural and political.

Towards the end of the 1980s, Finnish newspapers had developed into financially prosperous, politically important but rather passive institutions of "public service". In commercial terms, the provincial newspapers especially were successful: many of them enjoyed a virtual monopoly in regional advertising and readership markets. They were tightly linked to everyday consumer advertising and local identities. Prosperous papers were often locally owned and newspaper publishing was viewed as a particular branch of industry. Technologically, newspapers had been eager to develop their printing facilities. Under the protection of a stable economy and home delivery tradition (with high household penetration levels) they had invested heavily in printing plants and the quality of the material print product. By the end of the 1980s, digitalisation was well under way *in* the journalistic production process but had few or no implications for delivery and printing. Culturally, the paradigmatic Finnish newspaper at that point considered itself a well-regarded cultural institution, part of the local identity. Politically, the main newspapers had largely assumed a party-politically neutral stance by the end of 1980s. The papers addressed their readers mainly as a-political national citizens and saw it as their main task to inform the public about the functioning of the consensus-oriented political and administrative apparatus of the welfare state. In this environment, journalists had become neutral professionals with a relatively co-operative relationship to official sources. The profession had a broad "public ethos" and a strong focus on the transmission of generally important public information. So, its particularities notwithstanding, until the 1990s, Finnish newspapers presented a fairly good case of what Hallin and Mancini have called the "democratic-corporatist" media model (Hallin and Mancini, 2004).[1] But the current trends now suggest that this position has been re-negotiated.

Economic Pressures

In recent decades, newspaper publishing has become a branch of a diversified and consumer-driven media industry, as evidenced by somewhat paradoxical development of declining circulations and growing profit expectations. Due to the previously advanta-geous position in their branch, newspapers have been rather good targets for rationalisation and raising of profit margins. According to profit logic, target audiences are addressed exclusively according to their needs and interests, which runs contrary to the inclusive tradition of "public" professionalism. Concentration of ownership, slowly but surely, has also taken place in Finland, separating the management of the papers from their local communities. Finally, a steady decline in the market share of print mass media and the rise of free sheets (*Metro* etc.), the magazine branch and the new media testify to the loss of the stable environment of the newspapers. The economic changes in the Finnish newspaper business have been somewhat slower than elsewhere, even though generally the economic tendencies are familiar from other Western contexts.

Technological Challenges

The new media environment and the rapid development of information and communication technologies have posed a challenge for Finnish newspapers. The challenge has remained in spite of the generally positive attitude towards technology. Only the beginning of the new millennium marked a turning point towards digital and interactive technologies. Pressures to develop newspapers into multimedia news organisations have become an everyday concern. As a result of this, journalists execute more phases in the work process than before (Heinonen, 1999; Luostarinen and Uskali, 2004). Of course, even if such an internal change in the newsroom is strongly motivated by economic profits, technological change also indicates other challenges for the professional culture. The explosion of "social media" and "peer production" (cf. Benkler, 2006) erodes the boundary of production and consumption, and thus the boundaries of profession-alism. At the same it is believed that technology can help mainstream media to overcome some of its weaknesses, such as lack of trust and transparency (cf. Gillmor, 2004). However, Finnish newspapers have been rather slow to introduce social media elements in their products. Certainly, at the time of our interviews (2005–6), these innovations were still far from prevailing.

Cultural Change

Newspapers used to be an integral part of a system of collective identities, national, political or local. This constellation has been contested by intensified individualism and secularisation, with a trend towards individualistic values gaining strength during 1980–90 in Finland. Increasing affluence and leisure have accentuated the process of moving towards consumer culture lifestyles, and the media have become an increasingly important provider of frames of reference by which people define themselves and their place in society. Consequently, the newspaper is now merely one player among others, and competition in this environment has increased the entertainment function of the newspapers. This trend partly overlaps with signs of tabloidisation—overall personalisa-tion, visualisation, polarisation and shortening of news stories (Herkman, 2005). Socio-cultural questions of age, gender and multiculturalism also impose new demands on newspaper journalism. In a nutshell: the central, national and serious role of newspaper journalism is in transition. (E.g. Nieminen et al., 2006.)

Political Transitions

Many scholars see the 1980s as a significant turning point for Finnish political culture. At that point, the first critical remarks about the Finnish welfare state system emerged and "competition" as a form of social organisation began to gain legitimacy (e.g. Alasuutari, 1996). This trend, combined with the merging of ideological differences among the main political parties and an era of administratively oriented coalition governments, has led to a decline in political activity and voting turnouts. These changes have been paralleled by the more "professional" routines of political journalism, which traditionally emphasise a more critical stance towards the state, politics and administrative expertise. On the other hand, there have been signs of emerging civic activism outside traditional political organs. Lifestyle and issue-based political activity has posed a clear challenge for political journalism. Moreover, the current governmental ideals themselves—such as subsidiarity and transparency—call for an improvement in the status of "ordinary people" in the public discussion. In a Finnish professional discussion these trends are sometimes reminiscent of ideas of public journalism (cf. Heikkilä and Kunelius, 2003; Ruusunoksa, 2006).

Journalistic Field and Professional Imagination

Recent scholarship has suggested a number of ways in which to define journalism or its professional culture (cf. Hanitzsch, 2007; Zelizer, 2005). Looking at professionalism *as culture* entails an insight into what things *mean to journalists* (culture is a system of meanings), and an understanding of how these *meanings and actions are related* (culture is a system of meaningful practices). Thus, the context is always communicated by language and practical interpretations within the culture, and journalism should not be reduced to effects of its "external" context.

A long tradition in journalism studies has focused on the culture of everyday newsroom work. These studies—beginning at least from Tuchman in 1972 and having a long following—have provided us with a detailed view of how the news work applies its own organisationally grounded distinctions to the social reality around it, thus making it possible for reporters to act (Gans, 1980; Tuchman, 1978, etc.). Here, however, we will relate our discussion to a recent adaptation of Pierre Bourdieu's "field theory" to the analysis of journalism (cf. Benson and Neveu, 2005; Schultz, 2007).

Field theory usefully reminds us of two interrelated aspects of culture: change and power. It emphasises that when we look at a culture as a *field* (cf. Bourdieu, 2005, p. 30), we also look at a structure in change. In a field, the value of certain *capitals* (skills, experience, credentials) may increase as the structure of the field changes. Changes in the structure of a field are affected by the "objective" conditions of the field (its relationship to other fields, or its context), but also partly by the actions of the people in the field. Thus, a journalistic field has a current structure, but it also carries with it—in the *habituses* of its actors—traces of its old structures. Therefore, a field of journalism is always potentially more than just the dominant cultural order we recognise at a given moment. This is also because in any field there is—in addition to the *rules* which reflect the dominant order of the field—always an element of *game*. A certain amount of unpredictability can be expected, and even individual virtuosity can play a significant role. Field theory thus helps us to shape one perspective in which not only the context and the dominant values can be highlighted, but also the more marginal values of the field can be taken into account.

In addition to change, field theory includes a dynamic notion of *power*: change in the journalistic field requires that dominant interpretations are able to gain a position of hegemony in the struggle to define what journalism can and what it should be. This helps us to think about the way in which the *inner order* of a professional field is shaped. Power and position in a field are based on "objective" and strategic structural relations, such as money, other resources or relations to other powerful agents. Thus, dominant forms of symbolic or other capital are supported by a relation to other fields. In journalism, for instance, the increasing submission of journalistic autonomy to the economic field (Bourdieu's claim, 2005) has increased the value of seeing journalism as a business—also *in* the field of professional debates. This can be seen as a clear change in the inner order of the field, offering new agents more power and decreasing the power of some older arguments.

Furthermore, the concept of a field highlights the symbolic struggle needed in order to legitimate changes *within* the professional field. In order to be professionally legitimated, new capitals in the field will have to be partly translated into the inherited language of the field. Thus, even if the journalistic field has become less autonomous, it is still characterised by the fact that its actors themselves consider it autonomous. Hence, changes in journalism reflect the transformations in its surroundings, but at the same time changes in journalism are affected by certain patterns of *inherited symbolic capital within* the field. This symbolic terrain carries with it traces of earlier power relations and role definitions, and therefore it is partly incompatible with the demands of the new structures.

Field theory, however, also has limitations that can be illustrated particularly well in the case of journalism. For although the theory helps us to see the potential of resistance and agency embedded (for instance) in the idea of the autonomy of the journalistic field, it easily prevents us from seeing how the potential of agency embedded in the value of "autonomy" is linked to a broader system of meanings. Thus while it is plausible to argue for the autonomy of journalism from financial interests (cf. Glasser and Gunther, 2005), it is not quite as simple to argue for autonomy from powerful sources, for instance (cf. Kunelius, 2006). Thus, the symbolic capital in a professional field is also always connected to discourses that cut across fields. Particularly in journalism, professionalism has always been strongly connected to the idea of serving the public and thus explicitly linked to broader discourses about democracy. Hence, its professional culture is connected to rhetorical sources of power that are situated "outside" the field itself.

In order to underline this dimension of journalism, we refer to our object of study as the *professional imagination* of journalists. By referring to imagination we draw on the work of Charles Taylor (2004, pp. 23–5). For Taylor *imaginaries* are a form of knowledge embedded not only in theories, but also in less elaborated but more ordinary forms like "images, stories and legends". Imaginaries are not merely "lay theories"; they play a powerful and active part in any culture, because they make "possible common practices and a widely shared sense of legitimacy". Hence social imaginaries are widely shared by the *ordinary* members of a society. Taylor's *modern* social imaginaries refer to developing forms of shared background "knowledge" and assumptions that form an important part of the imagined environment in which we act. By discussing these imaginaries (for instance the "objectified reality of economy", the "public sphere", the "sovereign people", etc.) Taylor reminds us of the broad symbolic landscape in which all modern "autonomous" fields are obliged to act. Consequently, we think that professional journalists play an active role in translating the conditions of their work into a language that works inside the professional field. In order to succeed in the field, the actors have to either align themselves with the dominant interpretations in the field or to struggle to make their own perspectives viable. In this struggle social imaginaries reaching beyond the local rules and limits of the field are important resources.[2]

A rich understanding of both the limits of innovation and the creative potential embodied in the professional imagination of journalists would demand multiple methods and data, as well as contextually grounded skill in interpretation. Here, we will have to settle for a somewhat more general and modest goal. We will try to grasp the professional imagination of journalists through a close reading of interviews with professional journalists. Our material consists of in-depth interviews (spring 2006) in which 16 managing news editors from 10 different Finnish newspapers talk about the challenges to journalism. We consider these interviewees to constitute a strategically chosen sample: they are all journalists who have distinguished themselves in the current newsroom culture. Thus, they represent the dominant discourse of current professional culture. At the same time, however, their position as managers requires them to be sensitive to the resistance against the dominant interpretation. Hence, their views on journalism also contain hints about the conflicts and diversity in the newsrooms.

Below, we will outline two layers of cultural professional imagination. The first layer consists of the discourses with which the dominant professional culture makes sense of the changes in its environment. We will look at how our interviewees define the necessities dictated by contextual changes of journalism and how these imperatives are interpreted journalistically. The second layer consists of (discourse about) changing newsroom practices. We will look at how some of the interpretations concerning challenges to journalism are translated into more practical changes in news work.

Discursive Environment: Dominant Readings of Challenges to Journalism

One way of scrutinising professional imagination is to observe how journalists view their relationship to the "world outside", i.e. how they make sense of the social changes affecting newspaper journalism in four domains: economy, technology, culture and politics. Naturally, this division is not the way the respondents explicitly categorise their concerns. However, sticking to the categories with which we made preliminary sense of the context is a way of emphasising the cultural approach: we need to both pinpoint changes and to see how the agents interpret them. While we cannot offer an exhaustive inventory of our interviews from all these sectors here, we present some of the main trends in all four contexts.

The Economic Frame

Managing editors describe economic pressures and challenges to newspaper journalism mainly in the frame of *competition*. In the respondents' discourse, competition is described as "intensified" or "hard". The ongoing struggle for the audience's time and attention is often compared to the secure and almost idyllic era of newspaper journalism in the past. This paradise is now lost; the newspaper "has to compete" both with other media outlets and other media genres.

The struggle is a hard but worthy one, mainly because newspaper journalism is here equated with quality, seriousness and reliability. Thus competition as a necessity in the new environment gains positive connotations inside the culture itself; it emphasises the demanding nature of journalism. It takes special commitment and skill to maintain the circulation and hold people's attention from day to day.

Another constantly recurring economic theme in the vocabulary of the news managers is *business thinking:* the necessity to keep an eye on the day-to-day success of the paper. Again, respondents draw a clear distinction between past and present: there used to be a time when newsrooms "stubbornly" did not care about the circulation figures and when marketing people were considered "outsiders". Today, there is a shared business vocabulary within the whole corporation. In the respondents' talk, business logic is quickly translated into its internal consequences: into "co-operation" between journalists and the business side, into "flexibility" of practices. Co-operation—both inside papers and between papers with joint ownership—is a positive interpretation of the business logic. It emphasises the collective nature of news work and leans on a frame of professional solidarity. News managers also point out that understanding the business logic is a proactive capacity and a source of power and competence:

> The thing is that media houses, newsrooms, will have to live in economic frames which get tighter all the time, and all this is developing into a content production industry. We should not go back to the kind of journalism education where everything is based on criticising journalistic practices. Instead, we need to be able to change these practices, and you have to understand what it is all about, and start thinking how journalism can be renewed from within in these financial frames.

On the whole, in the realm of economics, the view of professional culture is mostly adaptive and reactive. The power of economic challenges—and the way economy is imagined as "objectified reality" (in Taylor's terms)—is reflected in the ways in which these pressures are taken for granted and dealt with by making them into virtues of necessity: hard work, competitiveness and co-operation. To be sure, the managing editors are not blind to the dangers that these pressures exert on journalism: most of them would *not totally* agree that journalism is a business just like any other. Rather, there is a sense of struggle: business is journalism's second nature, and has to be dealt with with skill.

Technology as Adaptation and Solution

On a general level, the managing editors express a sense of confidence in their ability to meet the challenges of developing technology. This may be a reflection of both the general Finnish ideology of technological innovation and a reflection of the past culture of the newspaper corporations. However, when studied in more detail, certain concerns are also evident.

Just like economy, technological development is mostly a taken-for-granted, naturalised force. Consequently, there is a profoundly felt *need to adapt to its imperatives.* The news managers see technology as something "external" to journalism as such. This externality sometimes feeds pessimism: "we have to make changes", "now we have 86,000 deadlines a day", or that "we end up not being able to do anything well enough". There is also a sense of professional uncontrollability of the new media environment.

But again, just as in the case of economy, technological challenges are also useful tools for managing editors. The new imperatives serve as a kind of Trojan horse:

introducing new kinds of technologies can also mean introducing new kinds of *discipline* and new kinds of journalistic demands into the newsroom:

> [The new layout system] had a fundamental effect on journalism as well, we began to use clearly defined story formats, we have a leading story on each page. This had an impact on the work of the managing news editor, who now has to plan for a major leading story for each page.

Thus, talk about technology clearly exposes how newspapers are moving towards a more *format-driven* model of journalism (more below). This can, on the one hand, be seen as a reactive move to the increasing media competition and business pressures (disguised as technological and thus neutral), a move in which planning is equated with effectiveness. But on the other hand, technological imperatives reflect a drive towards journalism that makes clearer judgements of what is important and what is not, that is, towards a more active journalistic institution. Thus, in a sense, the interviewees depict a new kind of technically aided and affected professionalism, which includes a more interactive approach, more professional reflection and perhaps more independence from routine information sources.

In terms of technology, ideal journalism appears as *medium-neutral*. The skills of journalism are seen as universal, not something materialised in a particular cultural and technological setting, but rather as something that transcends them: the gadgets may change but journalism remains the same.

Cultural Trends

The cultural trends recognised by managing editors appear to be much more varied and less coherently articulated than economic and technological trends. As examples of the cultural trends, we focus on two themes: consumerism as a context for newspaper reading and perceived audience demand for greater sensations and entertainment.

The need to adapt to the *consumer orientation* of the readers is manifested in two ways. First, news editors emphasise the notion of service journalism, i.e. providing news stories and materials that are immediately and individually useful for readers. This means writing about consumer issues or framing issues as consumer choices. Second, the consumer orientation assumes that people regard the newspaper as just another consumer product. This, in turn, is connected to the need to emphasise "news packaging":

> We have to fight for their [audience's] time and attention. So we also need to pay attention to the way we serve things up, the layout and stuff like that become more important ... It used to be easier ... Now it has to be served up nicely on a plate. It is a bit like comparing a big mac to a gourmet portion.

While "packaging" is partly a submissive move to please the imagined audience (and again partly reflects the idea that journalism is essentially independent of its modes of delivery), it can also be seen as a sign of professional change and innovation. It directs newspapers away from "mass produced sausage journalism" into more dynamic forms with greater impact and more demand for interactivity.

Packaging and visualisation are also important elements in *experience-driven journalism*, another theme through which the perceived cultural trends are interpreted. According to this frame, detached facts of news narration are no longer enough, instead "every story has to be a sensation". One can sense a profound re-negotiation of a general professional attitude. The editors are clearly struggling to broaden the cultural repertoire of newspapers, and in this vein, entertainment values are seen as professionally welcome.

Regarding the dialectics of adaptation and innovation, cultural changes clearly differ from the economic and technological themes. Cultural trends are seen more as interpretations or beliefs whereas economic and technological changes are more often experienced concretely in the newsroom. It also seems that interpretations of the cultural changes have a more legitimate claim to call journalistic professionalism into question. Perhaps cultural trends are seen as emerging from the life-world of the readers, and since the audience enjoys a particularly important position in the symbolic order of journalism, these claims gain further strength.

The Changing Political Scene

Explicit talk about the role of journalism on the changing political scene is fairly weak in our material. In fact, managing editors seem to ignore many interesting issues, such as life politics, identity politics, or new social movements. However, they take up two broadly political themes: a belief in a trend of depolitisation and a need to detach journalism from bureaucratic power.

The trend of general *depolitisation* in society is mostly taken for granted. The managing editors firmly believe that the public no longer associates itself with politically collective identities. Depolitisation is seen as a welcomed part of the "natural history" of journalism from a political to an independent profession. Depolitisation does not necessarily mean a passive form of journalism, however. The newspaper as an institution can align itself with the prosperity and viability of the region. In this way, depolitisation is transformed into stronger localisation, and political representation is translated into local representation.

The need to emphasise *detachment from bureaucratic power* grows out of the legacy of welfare state journalism. News editors take great pride in their attempt to tackle the news from an everyday life perspective, instead of seeing the world through the eyes of system experts:

> Twenty years ago it [journalism] was worse in the sense that it was more bureaucratic, the general feeling of newspapers was that they were directed to a small circle. Now everyone writes for a larger audience and I think that is good, that we think more about the readers.

On the other hand, we can hear an echo of an older professional discourse which says that everyday life cannot possibly be as important as powerful institutions and keeping them under control. Furthermore, in an ever-more complicated world (where political and economic interests are more intertwined and more global) journalistic monitoring of socially important issues has become more lazy than it should be—or than it used to be. According to this view, there used to be more "passionate" journalism and "save-the-world-spirit" in the newsrooms. Thus, the price of accommodating to changes in political landscape has been that journalism has become less ambitious in terms of societal issues.

From Discursive to Practical: Consequences and Contradictions in the Newsroom

In addition to the *discursive* level of sense making, we can also think of the ways in which the culture reacts to its environment by modifying its everyday *practices*. By looking at how the managing editors talk about new practices we can get a glimpse of how the broad interpretations described above are translated into changing routines on the level of newsroom work. This turns our attention also to some internal contradictions arising when some of the contextual pressures described above are materialised as changing newsroom practices. In order to exemplify the inner dialectics and the practical level of professional imagination, we will discuss three themes: project enthusiasm, teamwork and template-driven planning.

The Culture of Projects

Being a mid-level managing news editor in a Finnish newspaper means that you have to deal with *continuous change* and constantly negotiate about the change process with the staff. The news editors have adapted to their role as organisational developers and project leaders. Indeed, they have often made their mark in the organisation by being in charge of various kinds of internal projects. Project-talk reflects the technological and economic trends: almost all the interviewees have taken part in more than one big newspaper redesign project. The never-ending—and therefore also tiresome—nature of the development work is underscored:

> In fact, we have come to the point where you have to make journalistic and strategic decisions and reforms on a daily basis. It is actually very hard to even get a picture of all of these things [projects] that you are part of, because it is so continuous . . .

It is, however, clear that the managers are proud of these projects. The reforms serve as career milestones. This project ethos suggests that mastering a major journalistic reform project is an important act of distinction in the professional field. The interviewees also believe that distinction has been earned: almost all their reforms have encountered contradictions and criticism in the newsroom, but slowly the staff has adapted to the situation and thus recognised the dominant views—and the managers' journalistic authority.

On a practical level, therefore, Finnish newspapers react to change pressures by constant organisational reform projects: layout development projects, structural changes in the newsroom, reorganisation of journalists' positions etc. Some other studies also suggest that a kind of "project fatigue" is apparent among Finnish newspaper reporters (e.g. Ruusunoksa, 2006). Indeed, our interviewees, too, hint that continuous reform projects sometimes blur the journalistic reasons behind them. In an ironic vein, one respondent put it like this: "Journalistic development will soon need a project on its own".

The Ideal and the Reality of Teamwork

The second theme that characterises the present organisational culture in the newspapers is *teamwork*. The teamwork ethos emerges from the economic-cultural domain: it is a special case inside the discourse of co-operation within the whole organisation:

> We have to think how we can do these things in a new way, and often it takes many people to tackle that: you have the reporter, the managing editor, some visual people. You have to accept that you are no longer the only person having a say on a story, already in the planning stage you have to negotiate with others.

Teamwork, however, is a somewhat ambivalent trend in the newsroom. What is considered a necessity by the managing editors is often experienced as a loss of authority by rank and file journalists. Indeed, in a survey of Finnish journalists in 1987, most journalists reported they had freedom to choose news items, plan their perspectives and decide on their story formats (Kehälinna and Melin, 1988). In contrast, journalists in a 2007 survey seem to *want* more guidance and instructions before they set out on a story assignment: 45 per cent say they would like to have "somewhat" or "considerably" more guidance and instructions in their assignments (Jyrkiäinen, 2008).

Here newsroom culture seems to be in a state of change; the new dominant mode of journalism emphasises teamwork but many journalists are still tuned into the idea of individual autonomy (cf. Nerone and Barnhurst, 2003). Other findings suggest that it is problematic to introduce teamwork ideals into newsrooms that were previously more autonomously organised. Some reporters refuse to co-operate, some choose to be marginalised and some are allowed by management to stay as they are (Seppi et al., 2007[3]).

Thus, even if teamwork is a dominant value in the field, it also creates tensions—both with the everyday reality of newsrooms and with some other new ideals. In terms of reality, many journalists feel that they are left outside the strategic teamwork processes and thus feel excluded from the most important discussions. In terms of other emerging ideals, the teamwork ethos seems to run counter to the trend of seeing journalists as public personalities rather than anonymous reporters.

Template Journalism and Planning

The managing editors interviewed all emphasise that newsroom work has come to be increasingly planned both in terms of form and contents. Planning emerges as an answer to a combination of economic and cultural pressures, such as effectiveness and visualisation. Form-oriented planning can be described as *template journalism* in which pages and their elements are defined and structured before the actual news content is decided. Every page has a distinct format that is only slightly modified from day to day. Ideally, all news stories are written to a pre-designed length. In a sense then, an abstract ideology of layout affects journalistic decisions more than before.

The idea of templates or story formats is of course not a new one. In fact, much of the professional values and skills have been materialised in such routines. As one of our news editors puts it, one of the most important qualities in a journalist is an ability to see the world in the form of stories:

> Two things are pretty crucial [in a reporter]. You get along with people ... because usually they have the information you need ... Another one is what I have begun to call journalistic imagination: that you see the world as stories and story ideas.

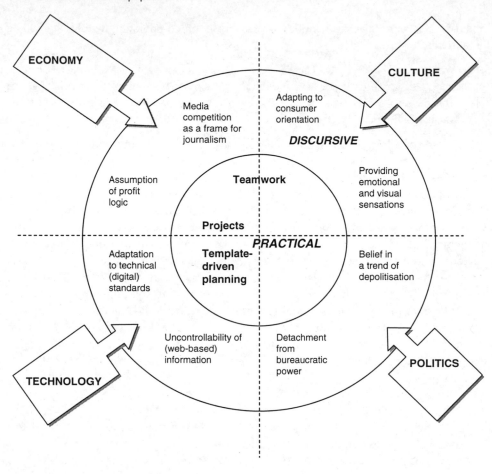

FIGURE 1
Summary: professional discourse and newsroom practice in the journalistic field

The interviewee neatly recognises the way in which professional imagination is partly embedded in a very practical mastery of the "grammar" of journalism. At the same time, however, the interviewee sees this skill mainly as an "intuitive" competence: some have the talent to see the world in journalistic terms, others do not. Thus, professional imagination is recognised, but it is seen as a functional skill that works for the demands of effectiveness and the logic of template journalism.

In addition to format-driven planning, there is a clear tendency to plan journalistic *content*. Almost 70 per cent of the journalists in the 2007 survey said that planning had increased or remained the same (Jyrkiäinen, 2007). In our interviews there is also a sense that planning needs to be centralised: "someone" has to control what is going to be in the paper the same day and know what is planned for the next day. This need to "look ahead" is crucial for the news managers not only because of effective story production. Newspapers are also more eager than before to position themselves as the leading discussion arenas, and this demands a certain amount of active work on the public agenda, instead of merely reacting to the initiatives of other institutions.

Just as in the case of the project ethos and teamwork ideals, talk about more centralised planning as an organisational virtue reveals tensions. Particularly when connected to the centralisation of editorial decisions, more intensive planning is problematic. In the 2007 survey "bad organisation" of work was a problem for 44 per cent, and the level of co-operation was "inadequate" for 43 per cent. Furthermore, 33 per cent thought that an "authoritarian" leadership style is an obvious problem, or that the workplace is too "hierarchical" (Jyrkiäinen, 2008). Also some managers themselves hint at alarming consequences of increased template planning. While such planning, they say, helps to guarantee "standard quality", it also weakens the element of surprise and innovation in the newspaper.

On the Potential of Professionalism

Our account of the mental landscape of newspaper professionalism in Finland is presented in condensed form in Figure 1. In our attempt to understand the state of professional imagination in Finnish newspapers, the *discursive* level acts as the matrix through which the contextual trends are interpreted and converted into *practical* consequences in newsrooms. Even this brief summary of our materials suggests three points for further reflection.

First, our account offers fairly convincing evidence of journalism that *mainly adapts to external pressures*. It seems clear that economic and technological trends are seen as the dominant driving forces of change; they set the agenda for re-negotiating journalism, its ideals and practices. Cultural changes are widely discussed, but the lessons learned from this terrain often coincide with the competition-adaptation logic provided by the techno-economic discourse. Interestingly, current changes in the political environment are not much discussed in the dominant interpretation. Aggressively put, then, interviews with successful managing editors reveal that understanding competition and adaptation are the most valued sources of symbolic capital in the journalistic field.

However, the interviews also testify to a professional culture that actively participates in designing some of the structures of its future action. Although project mentality, teamwork and template journalism may well be seen as mainly practical interpretations of techno-economic demands, they are also practical attempts to retain or save something from the earlier professional ideals: that journalists themselves develop their practice (project ethos), that newspaper is a collective (teamwork) and that it has a distinct language of its own (templates). Thus, even on the surface level of the dominant interpretation of change, we can—with the help of a healthy dose of optimism—argue that professional cultures should not be reduced to the effects of their immediate contextual changes.

Secondly, levels of power (managers versus reporters) and dimensions of time (old versus new ethos) produce creative fissures in the professional culture. These inner tensions and symbolic struggles are already apparent when news editors themselves articulate the dominant values. Thus, in the shadow of the techno-economic imperatives, there are moments of alternative thoughts that struggle to defend perhaps more demanding roles for journalists—or which at least recognise the need for a plurality of values inside the profession. For instance, newsroom leaders are indeed engaged in serious soul searching when they try to view the mastery of the business logic of journalism as a professional resource: they realise they have to learn the rules of the game but they have also become acutely aware of the limits that the business frame imposes on innovative professional discussion.

When one moves from the discursive level to the more practical one, the contradictions of the field seem to be revealed in a more contrasted way. The practical consequences of the dominant discourse (or values of the field) also provoke criticism of ethos of teamwork, project culture and template journalism. One form of counter-argument is that these new goals have not been genuinely achieved. In this criticism, the earlier values of journalism have been projected into new practices. Another form of resistance is the claim that even if the new forms are true, they are developing newspaper journalism in a questionable direction, leaving less room for the traditional virtues of journalism, such as professional autonomy and detachment. In this kind of criticism, earlier (or alternative) values are seen as distinct from the new practices. In both cases, the resources of criticism are to a large extent drawn from the earlier dominant order of professionalism. Broadly speaking, these counter-discourses are informed by the older Finnish ethos of "public service" journalism.

In the framework of field theory these tensions inside the journalistic field are crucial. If journalistic organisations fail to recognise the diversity of professional identities and the competences related to these identities, they severely restrict their reflexive potential. In a sense, then, the degree of "autonomy" of the field depends on the degree of its heterogeneity. The notion of professional imagination points to yet another question. In our interviews, there are only a few instances of professional imagination which would draw its inspiration from an alternative or utopian view of what journalism might be. The relative silence about the changing political scene is rather telling here. The only legitimate category "outside" the newsroom which still carries some power is the notion of the *public*. Despite (or parallel to) the attempts to redefine the public as customers, the public is also viewed in an interactive manner. Thus, in a sense, the audience is not positioned merely at the receiving end of information delivery. One can—with some interpretative leverage—suggest that this new interactive role of the public could transform from the "right to be informed" into the "right to communicate". Perhaps late modern newspaper journalists have to admit that journalism's legitimacy will be based more on relevance for and communication with the public than on an earlier claim to being autonomous. The crucial point is that professional journalism should learn to see the landscape of changing social imaginaries as a resource for re-energising the profession in a more articulated manner.

Thirdly, a note on research. While we think that our findings suggest that the professional culture in Finnish newspapers is mostly driven by the techno-economic calculus, we also think that the current conjuncture emphasises the importance of research in sustaining the diversity of this debate. For research it is of vital importance to be able to stay in a communicative relationship with the professional community of practitioners and to point out that the essential resources of developing journalism also include other aspects on top of money and new gadgets. We hope that the idea of professional imagination is a small constructive step in this direction. We offer it tentatively as a way of complementing the analytical grasp of field theory by pointing to the way in which symbolic capitals in professional fields refer outside their own field, to broader, shared imaginaries.

One particular final finding can support this idea. One of the recurring characteristics we found in our materials was the idea that despite all the contextual changes there is still something constant and stable in journalism. For journalists, there seems to be a core of journalism that is independent of form, technology or subject matter. The idea of professional imagination points to understanding this finding in two equally important ways. First, it may be that this belief in the untouchable core of journalism is one of the most tragic misunderstandings cherished by professionalism, for it prevents journalists from seeing the potential and limits of their professional practice. If you think technology is merely a "conduit" for journalism, you are ill equipped for the future; and if you think the core of the "old" journalism is something to be defended—and not re-imagined—you are not well equipped to identify the opportunities in the changing context of the profession. Secondly, however, professional imagination suggests that we must also remember that this idea of a core of journalism reflects a genuine mission and independent purpose for journalism: that which makes the profession worth defending and developing. Thus, while researchers must question this sacred belief, they should perhaps bear in mind that it represents an important motivational source for keeping journalism connected (or re-connecting it) to the broad political processes which the dominant professional imagination nowadays seems to have pushed rather far.

ACKNOWLEDGEMENTS

This study is part of a research project "Journalism: Public Profession and Late Modernity" funded by the Academy of Finland. Interviews were conducted by Pekko Ylönen and Tuomo Tamminen.

NOTES

1. On the history of Finnish journalism, see for instance Tommila (2001) and Salokangas (1999).
2. For another attempt to connect imaginaries to professional identities, see Heikkilä and Kunelius (2006).
3. Our claims about the rank and file journalists are based on our earlier empirical findings: interviews with some 60 Finnish journalists of all kinds of media at all ranks from 2004 to 2005 (Seppi et al., 2007).

REFERENCES

ALASUUTARI, PERTTI (1996) *Toinen tasavalta, Suomi 1946–1994 [The Second Republic, Finland 1946–1994]*, Tampere: Vastapaino.

BENKLER, YOCHAI (2006) *The Wealth of Networks: how social production transforms markets and freedom*, New Haven, CT: Yale University Press.

BENSON, RODNEY and NEVEU, ERIC (Eds) (2005) Bourdieu and the Journalistic Field, Cambridge: Polity Press.

BOURDIEU, PIERRE (2005) "The Political Field, the Social Science Field, and the Journalistic Field", in: Benson Rodney and Neveu Eric (Eds), *Bourdieu and the Journalistic Field, Cambridge: Polity Press*, pp. 29–47.

DEUZE, MARK (2007) *Media Work*, Cambridge: Polity Press.

GANS, HERBERT (1980) *Deciding What's News: a study of CBS Evening News, NBC Nightly News, Newsweek, and Time*, London: Constable.

GILLMOR, DAN (2004) *We the Media: grassroots journalism by the people, for the people*, Sebastopol, CA: O'Reilly.

GLASSER, THEODORE L and GUNTHER, MARK (2005) "The Legacy of Autonomy in American Journalism", in: Overholser Geneva and H. Jamieson Kathleen (Eds), *The Press: institutions of American democracy*, Oxford and New York: Oxford University Press, pp. 384–99.

HALLIN, DANIEL and MANCINI, PAOLO (2004) *Comparing Media Systems: three models of media and politics*, Cambridge: Cambridge University Press.

HANITZSCH, THOMAS (2007) "Deconstructing Journalism Culture: towards a universal theory", *Communication Theory* 17(4), pp. 367–85.

HARDT, HANNO (1996) "The End of Journalism: media and newsworkers in the United States", *Javnost/The Public* 3(3), pp. 21–41.

HEIKKILÄ, HEIKKI and KUNELIUS, RISTO (2003) "Ajatuksia lainaamassa. Miten kansalaisjournalismin ideat istuvat meille?" ["Borrowing Ideas. How do the ideas of public journalism fit into the Finnish context?"], in: Malmelin Nando (Ed.), *Välittämisen tiede*, Helsinki: University of Helsinki, Department of Communication, pp. 179–204.

HEIKKILÄ, H.EIKKI and KUNELIUS, R.ISTO (2006) "Journalists Imagining the European Public Sphere: professional discourses about the EU news practices in ten countries", *Javnost/The Public* 13(4), pp. 63–80.

HEINONEN, ARI (1999) *Journalism in the Age of the Net: changing society, changing profession*, Tampere: University of Tampere.

HERKMAN, JUHA (2005) *Kaupallisen television ja iltapäivälehtien avoliitto. Median markkinoituminen ja televisioituminen* [*Commercial Television and the Tabloid Press: an open marriage*], Tampere: Vastapaino.

JYRKIÄINEN, JYRKI (2008) *Journalistit muuttuvassa mediassa* [*Journalists in the changing media system*], Department of Journalism, Journalism Research Centre, Publications B 50/2008, Tampere: University of Tampere.

KATZ, ELIHU (1992) "End of Journalism: notes of watching the war", *Journal of Communication* 42(3), pp. 5–13.

KEHÄLINNA, HEIKKI and MELIN, HARRI (1988) *Tuntemattomat toimittajat. Tutkimus Suomen Sanomalehtimiesten Liiton jäsenistä* [*The Unknown Reporters. A study on the Members of the Finnish Union of Journalists*], Porvoo: Suomen Sanomalehtimiesten Liitto.

KUNELIUS, RISTO (2006) "Good Journalism", *Journalism Studies* 7(5), pp. 671–90.

MCNAIR, BRIAN (2006) *Cultural Chaos: journalism, news and power in a globalised world*, London: Routledge.

NERONE, JOHN and BARNHURST, KEVIN (2003) "US Newspaper Types, the Newsroom, and the Division of Labor 1750–2000", *Journalism Studies* 4(4), pp. 435–49.

NIEMINEN, HANNU, ASLAMA MINNA and PANTTI, MERVI (2005) *Media ja demokratia Suomessa. Kriittinen näkökulma* [*Media and Democracy in Finland: a critical view*], Oikeusministeriön julkaisu 11, Helsinki: Ministry of Justice.

LUOSTARINEN, HEIKKI and USKALI, TURO (2004) Suomalainen journalismi ja yhteiskunnan muutos 1980–2000 [Finnish Journalism and Social Change 1980–2000], Helsinki: Sitra, http://www.sitra.fi/Julkaisut/Heiskala.pdf.

RUUSUNOKSA, LAURA (2006) "Public Journalism and Professional Culture: local, regional and national public spheres as contexts of professionalism", *Javnost/The Public* 13(4), pp. 81–98.

SALOKANGAS, RAIMO (1999) "From Political to Regional and Local: the newspaper structure in Finland", *Nordicom Review* 20(1), pp. 77–105.

SCHULTZ, IDA (2007) "The Journalistic Gut Feeling", *Journalism Practice* 1(2), pp. 190–207.

SEPPI, SIRPA, NISSI, EMMI and KUNELIUS, RISTO (2007) "Report on Interviews with Journalists, 2004–2005", unpublished manuscript, University of Tampere.

SPARKS, COLIN (2007) "Extending and Defining the Propaganda Model", *Westminster Papers in Communication and Culture* 4(2), pp. 69–84.

TAYLOR, CHARLES (2004) *Modern Social Imaginaries*, New York: Planet Books.

TOMMILA, PÄIVIÖ (2001) "Sanomalehdistön historia" ["The History of Newspapers in Finland"], in: Nordenstreng Kaarle and Wiio Osmo A. (Eds), *Suomen mediamaisema [The Finnish Media Landscape]*, Helsinki: WSOY, pp. 45–61.

TUCHMAN, GAYE (1978) *Making News: a study in the construction of reality*, New York: Random House.

ZELIZER, BARBIE (2005) "Definitions of Journalism: the legacy of autonomy in American journalism", in: Overholser Geneva and Jamieson Kathleen H. (Eds), *The Press: institutions of American democracy*, Oxford and New York: Oxford University Press, pp. 66–80.

Chapter 4

"THE SUPREMACY OF IGNORANCE OVER INSTRUCTION AND OF NUMBERS OVER KNOWLEDGE"
Journalism, popular culture, and the English constitution

John Hartley

Popular Culture: Subject or Object?

> In this way a reading public which was increasingly working class in character was forced to organize itself. (E.P. Thompson, 1968, p. 799)

Popular culture, understood as modern, industrialised, urban "associated life" (Veblen, 1899) and media, is both "object" and "subject" of representation in journalism. As object, popular culture is the familiar consumer market, over which the press barons and their international corporate successors preside. Here, professionals and proprietors take it upon themselves not only to sell representations of the world in commodity form to "the people," but also to set themselves up as representatives of their readership (using that term to cover all forms of semiotic engagement), whose abilities to choose and act— e.g. to buy, vote, or riot—they arrogate to themselves as part of their power to influence economic and political decisions. But as subject, popular culture is the source and means of self-representation by various self-constituted versions of "the people." It is the place where individually and collectively, as persons or as classes, ordinary people get to speak for themselves. Clearly journalism takes a different form, depending on whether popular culture is understood as object ("they"), or subject ("we"), in the process of production (Sonwalkar, 2005).

Journalism studies is interested in journalism; cultural studies is interested in culture, as you would expect. Each field has properly concentrated on its own object of study, investigating with its own evolving set of methods and problems, to such an extent that the two specialisms now present to the observer as two different species. If they ever were varieties of the same discipline, it seems that at last they have speciated; intermarriage among their populations is impossible. In this divergent evolution, journalism studies has tended to take the view that popular culture is an object (of manipulation; behaviour), while cultural studies has tended to view popular culture as a subject (of emancipation; action). Journalism research tends to prioritise the perspective of the producer (the professional, the industry, the firm); cultural studies that of the consumer (identity, meaning, use).

It seems that fear of miscegenation among journalism educators means that neither cultural studies nor popular culture are welcome in J-school environments; i.e. in the context of the professional training of newsroom journalists. From that perspective, studying popular culture is seen either as siding with a depoliticised celebration of consumerism, or as giving way to theory-driven relativism (*Media International Australia, 1999*; Windschuttle, 1998). But such a view of popular culture and of cultural studies is mistaken, both historically and conceptually. Journalism studies would benefit from recognising more directly that the historical co-evolution of journalism and popular culture, the "subjective" tradition of self-representation, and the methodological purposes of cultural studies, are all important to a proper understanding of journalism's place in contemporary culture.

In short, the object of study has not speciated, so the means of study ought not to either. Journalism and popular culture are part of the same unified field. To adopt an "objective" or a "subjective" stance is not a matter of discipline but of politics (or interest at least). And while it might seem obvious that an "objective" stance is preferable for journalism, the history of how popular culture was turned into an object suggests that this is by no means a reliable conclusion. Rather, popular culture as subject is the source of popular self-representation, a practice that was decisive in the evolution of mass communication, and which is now resurgent. With the current emergence of digital online self-made media, the need for an integrated understanding of journalism and popular culture is once again urgent, and cultural studies can assist in reaching it. Journalism studies would therefore benefit from giving consideration to the "subjective" as well as to the "objective" traditions; for example to *YouTube* as well as to "newspapers of record," because they are part of the same system, and any research field that focuses on just one of them is the poorer for it.

Liberty and Libertinage

> We are forced to ask ourselves how inflammatory language and mythologizing can offer a legitimate exegesis on the politics of the day. (Antoine de Baecque, 1989, p. 168)

Popular culture is the true seed-bed of modern popular journalism. Although newspapers for the gentry and merchant classes had been around since the 17th century, it was only when they became popular that they took on contemporary shape, and only then that journalism achieved its potential of communicating with entire populations regardless of their local class or status. In turn, journalism played a strong role in developing popular culture as a modern, urban, mediated experience, as opposed to the prevailing notion of it at the time as craft-based folk art.

Popular journalism was born of the European Enlightenment, French Revolution, and British industrialisation and urbanisation during the period from the 1790s to the 1840s. In that half-century, motivated by a desire for political emancipation as well as an entrepreneurial bid for profit, radical journalists and publishers, from Tom Paine and William Cobbett to Richard Carlile and Henry Hetherington (see Spartacus, nd), perfected the means for secular, cross-demographic communication about public (and private) affairs to "ordinary" readers numbering in the hundreds of thousands and—by the time the ultra-radical Sunday newspaper *The News of the World* came on to the scene in 1843— in the millions. This was, as historian Robert K. Webb puts it, "a pioneering effort to solve the problem of getting ideas across from one man, or one class, to another" (1955, p. 35; and see Hartley, 1996, pp. 94–9). The "pauper press" succeeded in creating the popular "reading public"; an achievement won by people without the vote, often poor, in the teeth of government suppressions, and with no established business infrastructure or market.

"Getting ideas across" was not a merely cerebral business, however. Modern political journalism was founded as much in scandal, gossip and sensationalism as it was in reason and truth. As the *ancien régime* slid towards political modernisation via the French Revolution, salacious novels and pornographic pamphlets were the "real sources from which political journalism originated in France," according to the historian Robert Darnton (1982), 203). Sex and politics were coterminous; as the bedroom antics of *Thérèse philosophe* (Anonymous, 1748) and her many successors demonstrated by the simple narrative device of equating the achievement of orgasm with that of freedom. Sexual gossip, scandal and innuendo about the king, queen, courtiers and clerics were used to undermine deference towards royalty and aristocracy, while stories of sexual awakening and libertinage were grand metaphors for political self-realisation and philosophical freedom. The most celebrated writers of the Enlightenment—Diderot, Voltaire, Montesquieu, Mirabeau—wrote bawdy and pornographic works as well as political journalism and philosophy, without making a distinction between the personal (popular culture) and the political (journalism). On the contrary, the genre of publishing that gave birth to popular journalism in France, the *"livres philosophiques,"* lumped porn together with philosophy (Darnton and Roche, 1989, pp. 27–49). In short, and not only in France (see McCalman, 1992, 1993), the radical underground was not squeamish about where journalism stopped and other forms of writing and representation began. "Liberty" and "libertinage" shared the same philosophical history (Grayling, 2005, pp. 116–8).

Representation—Two Models for "Two Nations"

It was not easy to escape from politics in nineteenth-century Britain. It filled the newspapers; it was a principal means of mass entertainment. (Robert K. Webb, 1955, p. 83)

During the early 19th century, when industrialisation took hold, first of all in Britain, only three men in a hundred and no women had the vote. There was a sharp divide between the working class and the political class: they were, in Disraeli's famous phrase, "two nations" (Disraeli, 1845, p. 149). The propertied, educated and enfranchised class, both conservative and liberal (as famously satirised in *Iolanthe*), followed public affairs in papers such as *The Times* and *The Economist*. These were dedicated to politics (confidence or otherwise in the government of the day), public administration (e.g. campaigns for army reform, or against slavery or capital punishment), and the economy (e.g. promotion of or opposition to free trade). Meanwhile, the other nation, the unenfranchised popular majority, developed their own press, both radical-popular (e.g. the *Republican*, *Poor Man's Guardian*, *Northern Star*) and, increasingly in and after the 1840s, commercial-popular (e.g. *Lloyd's Weekly News*, *Reynold's News*). There was a telling mismatch between scale of readership and degree of political influence. With a circulation in the low thousands, *The Times* could topple governments; with sales in the hundreds of thousands, and multiple readers per copy (Webb, 1955, pp. 33–4), the pauper press was physically attacked *by* the government: their premises were raided, their property seized and their proprietors imprisoned.

Because of these asymmetric purposes and powers, the respectable and the radical press were expressions of different models of communication. *The Times* and *The Economist* developed journalism as professional expertise, to serve a readership with a stake in both economic and political questions. These papers connected the minority of emancipated citizens to each other, and for them a three-link supply chain of sender–text–receiver was appropriate, because the producer and consumer were co-subjects, equal in status if not in information. The pauper press, meanwhile, saw itself as part of the struggle against the current economic and political arrangements and, as the current phrase has it, sought to "speak truth to power" (Kennedy, 2000). Its mode was as much to accuse opponents as to address its own readers, because it spoke on behalf of—as the voice of—a class that had not attained citizenship (and therefore the idea of the informed citizen did not apply). The poorest sections of that class were not even counted in the census (Mayhew, 1849, preface). For activists, who agreed that "the ideas of the ruling class are in every epoch the ruling ideas," a two-term base/superstructure model was appropriate (Marx, 1845). The productive or labouring classes and the poor were on one side, confined by penury and policing to a rather direct relationship with the economic base; the titled, landed, and educated (middle) classes were on the other side, occupying the super-structural heights of politics and culture (while benefiting from basic economic power). Here already there appeared to be a chalk and cheese distinction between professional journalism (*The Times*) and popular culture (*Poor Man's Guardian*), even though journalistic skills were to be found on both sides of the fence.

This was the basis for a divergence between journalism that saw popular culture as object (to be feared and controlled) and journalism that saw popular culture as subject; "we the people." The early mass-circulation newspapers were produced by radicals among whom were also entrepreneurs, who had the "ability to harness commercialism for the purposes of political dissent and cultural populism," and who were proud to use the latest high-tech industrial inventions such as the steam-powered rotary press (Haywood, 2004, p. 164) in order to reach a mass reading public. They pioneered the "mass" media. However, as time unfolded the commitment to oppositional self-representation in these newspapers declined as their scale and profits increased. As the 19th century progressed, wages, leisure, literacy and the franchise were progressively increased and extended. The "radical-popular" (we) press began to give way to the "commercial-popular" (they) press. A good example is the *News of the World*, launched as an unstamped "ultra-radical" Sunday newspaper in 1843 (Maccoby, 2001, p. 420). Eventually it became the newspaper with the largest circulation in the world, when it was widely known as the "News of the Screws" because of its penchant for exposing sex scandals, in the honourable tradition of the *livres philosophiques* and in ample fulfilment of its own longstanding motto of "All Human Life is There." It was Rupert Murdoch's first Fleet Street acquisition in 1969. It remains the Sunday stablemate of News Corp's *Sun*. The *Sun*'s own career followed the same route in the 20th century. It began in 1911 as the *Daily Herald*, a strike-sheet published by printing unions as part of an industrial dispute. It was taken over by the Trades Union Congress and with the help of the publisher Odhams, it became the official mouthpiece of the union movement and the Labour Party. For a while in the 1930s it too was the biggest-selling newspaper in the world, but suffered in brutal circulation wars with the *Daily Express*. When the Mirror Group took over Odhams in the 1960s they revamped the *Herald*, changed its name to the *Sun*, and then sold it to Rupert Murdoch in 1969 (see National Museum of Photography, Film & Television, 2000). Both papers were transformed from radical-popular agents of workers' self-representation to commercial popular mechanisms for turning them into a market; from "subject" to "object."

Constitutional Journalism—A "Certain Charmed Spectacle"

It is nice to trace how the actions of a retired widow and an unemployed youth become of such importance. (Walter Bagehot, 1867)

By the turn of the 20th century the popular press had largely fallen to conservative press barons, who launched commercial picture-tabloids like the *Daily Mail* and *Daily Mirror*. Their proprietors addressed the labouring classes and their families not as radical activists but domestic consumers (and biddable voters). They boosted their circulation with stunts and prizes and pretty girls rather than firebrand politics (although the *Mirror* did a bit of both). During World War I they were fully incorporated into the purposes of the state, their proprietors becoming cabinet ministers. They ushered in the *Citizen Kane* era of press lords whose political clout was based on popular reach. They were exemplified by Lords Northcliffe, Rothermere, Beaverbrook, Kemsley, Camrose and Thomson on one side of the Atlantic, and on the other by William Randolph Hearst ("you furnish the pictures, I'll furnish the war!"; *Time*, 1942).

In the process, the self-representative communication model of the radical press was recast into the sender–receiver model that still characterises journalism research. The latter model connects journalism to popular culture only indirectly. Journalism is seen as a production system that conveys news to the public, while popular culture is a consumption system of commercially purveyed entertainment. But despite the asymmetry, each side needs the other: no readers, no news; no entertainment, no readers. However, compared with the earlier radical-popular press upon which commercial-popular journalism is built, in this model representation has shifted from the demand to the supply side.

What kind of representation did commercial-popular journalism proceed to supply? In 1867 Walter Bagehot, journalist, influential editor of *The Economist* for 17 years and author of the standard work on the English constitution, made a famous distinction between those component parts of the constitution that excite "the reverence of the population" and those "by which it, in fact, works and rules" (Bagehot, 1867). He called them the "dignified" and "efficient" parts, respectively. The monarchy and aristocracy

(House of Lords) were the dignified part; the Cabinet and the House of Commons were the efficient part.

Following the extension of the vote to unskilled male labourers in the 1867 Reform Act, Bagehot feared what he called "the supremacy of ignorance over instruction and of numbers over knowledge." Indeed, he wrote, "I am exceedingly afraid of the ignorant multitude of the new constituencies," in the industrialised metropolises. To counter their numerical supremacy Bagehot made a less well-remembered distinction between "deference" and "democracy." He preferred deference, where electors defer to wealth and rank, and thence to "the higher qualities of which these are the rough symbols and the common accompaniments," over democracy, which exalts the "vacant many" over the "inquiring few."

Bagehot felt, however, that the parliamentary system itself could be used "to prevent or to mitigate the rule of uneducated numbers," so long as deference was maintained. By deference he did not mean—or mean alone—the forelock-tugging deference of what Marx called "rural idiocy" towards the country squirearchy. Bagehot had something much more modern in mind:

> In fact, the mass of the English people yield a deference rather to something else than to their rulers. They defer to what we may call the theatrical show of society. A certain state passes before them; a certain pomp of great men; a certain spectacle of beautiful women; a wonderful scene of wealth and enjoyment is displayed, and they are coerced by it. Their imagination is bowed down; they feel they are not equal to the life which is revealed to them. Courts and aristocracies have the great quality which rules the multitude, though philosophers can see nothing in it—visibility. (Bagehot, 1867)

Bagehot is describing nothing less than the genesis of what is now more easily named as celebrity culture (Plunkett, 2003; see also Rojek, 2004; Turner, 2004). Rather than siding with those "philosophers" who would "deride this superstition," he makes celebrity journalism central to the constitutional arrangements of what was at the time the most powerful empire on earth. He argued that the "charmed spectacle" and human values of the royal and aristocratic families could succeed in preserving popular deference, under the cloak of which the mundane business of government could continue in few but expert hands:

> What impresses men is not mind, but the result of mind. And the greatest of these results is this wonderful spectacle of society, which is ever new, and yet ever the same; in which accidents pass and essence remains; in which one generation dies and another succeeds ... The apparent rulers of the English nation are like the most imposing personages of a splendid procession: it is by them the mob are influenced; it is they whom the spectators cheer. The real rulers are secreted in second-rate carriages; no one cares for them or asks about them, but they are obeyed implicitly and unconsciously by reason of the splendour of those who eclipsed and preceded them. (Bagehot, 1867, VIII)

This distinction between the dignified (deferential) and efficient (ruling) parts of the constitution is crucial to any consideration of the relationship between journalism and popular culture. It makes of the "charmed spectacle," and thus of the popular/media culture which is the stage for it, what may be called a ruse to rule. Journalism on both sides of this divide is part of the "constitutional" mechanism for social order: there is journalism for efficiency (*The Times*, *The Economist*), and journalism for deference (celebrity spectacle). The overall system requires both parts for the ordered continuation of good government in a polity governed by fear of a democratic majority which has no direct role to play in rule. Bagehot's schema makes clear what subsequent familiarity may well have blurred; that the spectacle of "wealth and enjoyment," the celebrity of "great men" and "beautiful women," and the "theatrical show of society," are all *an essential part of government* (Hartley, 2008a).

"A Universal Fact ... Rivets Mankind"

> A *family* on the throne is an interesting idea also. It brings down the pride of sovereignty to the level of petty life. (Walter Bagehot, 1867)

Popular culture is the domain of spectacle and celebrity. These are communicated to the "mob" of "spectators" via popular journalism. Therefore, in line with Bagehot's insight about the need for both rule and the spectacle of rule—and that these are distinct but equally necessary as the efficient and dignified parts of the constitution—journalism also has two essential "constitutional" components: one that follows the "real rulers secreted in second-rate carriages," and another that follows the "charmed spectacle" of high society.

> No feeling could seem more childish than the enthusiasm of the English at the marriage of the Prince of Wales ... But no feeling could be more like common human nature as it is, and as it is likely to be ... A princely marriage is the brilliant edition of a universal fact, and, as such, it rivets mankind. (Bagehot, 1867)

The 1867 Reform Act enfranchised over a million working men. Modern journalism (as part of Bagehot's constitution) is founded on the fear of this newly sovereign demos. How to "rivet" the popular mind to a constitution in which "real rule" might remain with those "secreted in second-rate carriages," so as to avoid succumbing to "the supremacy of ignorance over instruction and of numbers over knowledge"? The cultivation of deference via popular culture, using "universal facts" and "common human nature" to "rivet mankind" was, however, not straightforward but a hazardous venture, not least because a "princely marriage" may swiftly be followed by royal adultery and marital scandal—as has duly unfolded for not one but three princes of Wales since then (Edwards VII and VIII, Charles). Further, the people who really enjoyed that "great quality" of visibility seemed to be the respectable classes themselves, not to mention the courtiers whose job it was to attract the attention of the press. As Lord McGregor (then chair of Reuters Trust) noted:

> At the time of the wedding of the Prince of Wales [1863], sales of *The Times* increased to 108,000 copies compared with its average of around 60–65,000 during the 1860s. In 1864, the Prince and Princess visited Denmark accompanied by Lord Spencer who ... went on to complain that court officials with their *"adulation of reporters* show great want of dignity." (McGregor, 1995, my emphasis)

In short, it was not by any means a case of the posh papers providing rational information for rulers while popular culture laid on celebrity, spectacle, spin and bread and circuses for the masses. It was if anything the other way around. Circulation of *The Times* nearly doubled on Royal Wedding day. For the have-nots, on the other hand, the spectacle was not always so welcome—it served to inflame "the knockabout anti-monarchism of the popular press ... and ... the republican political rumblings in the 1860s and 1870s, some of which found a parliamentary voice opposing grants to the Queen's children on occasions such as royal marriages" (Thompson, 2001, p. 75).

Similarly, it should not be assumed that the respectable press was always pro-*government* (it was always pro-*rule*). Thomas Barnes in *The Times* joined with Richard Carlile in the *Republican* in denouncing the Peterloo Massacre of 1819. *The Times* thundered: "nearly a hundred of the King's unarmed subjects have been sabred by a body of cavalry in the streets of a town of which most of them were inhabitants, and in the presence of those Magistrates whose sworn duty it is to protect and preserve the life of the meanest Englishmen" (19 August 1819). *The Times* was in favour of the 1932 Reform Bill to extend the franchise, while the *Morning Chronicle* commissioned both Charles Dickens's "sketches by Boz" and Henry Mayhew's reports on the condition of the labouring poor in England and Wales (Mayhew, 1849). In other words, the top people's press was averse neither to spectacle and sensation nor to social reform. What really differentiated the two types of journalism discussed here was their *readership*: understood at the time as "two nations" and still now not fully integrated into one public, politically, journalistically or culturally.

Walter Bagehot was candid about the rationale for a constitution with a dignified part that was literally useless but vital in terms of "visibility," spectacle and narrative. It was straightforward fear of "numbers over knowledge." He was "exceedingly afraid" that popular sovereignty would overwhelm established arrangements. To counter the influence of the "ignorant multitude," however, Bagehot proposed not to educate the masses as to their "real rulers," (much less to rule themselves), but to put on a good show—"not mind, but the result of mind." In this endeavour he was aided and abetted by the "efficient" papers, the conservative press barons, and the sender–text–receiver model of communication, all of which were dedicated to riveting mankind; that is, trying to hold on to real rule, albeit from a second-rate carriage, and seeking to unite the two nations under one constitution. It is this model of communication that underlies commercial-popular journalism to this day, and this is also the model most widely taught to journalists.

Plus ça Change?

The logic of the history I have been outlining . . . is for the industry to keep flogging the dead horse of its weary old formats until they lose their audience entirely. At that point, the networks can claim to have proved there is no market for current affairs programs any more, and replace them with a game show. (Graeme Turner, 2005, p. 159)

Since its invention in the French and the Industrial Revolutions, the popular reading public has migrated from press to broadcasting and thence to online media, and the scale of the potential readership has expanded from a class or a nation to a globalised social network market (which can sometimes also be a public). But the pioneering effort of the radical press to solve the problem of "getting ideas across" demographic boundaries in conditions of economic change, political contestation and cultural division, was the crucial R&D for what later became a thoroughly commercialised media environment. The current period is experiencing a return to self-representation or demand-led rather than supply-led journalism, via user-generated content, citizen journalism and self-made or DIY media of various kinds, all of which can be used for journalism as well as for self-expression and entertainment, including plenty of bawdy stuff that retreads the fuzzy line between liberty and licentiousness. These activities too are proving to be an energetic and surprising locus of innovation, as ideas and social networks form in the sphere of self-representation (daydreaming and mischief as well as freedom and comfort), and some are subsequently adopted in that of economic enterprise and professionalised production, crossing from culture to economy—subjective to objective—in the process.

Perhaps the model of communication established in the early pauper press is due for a revival. Certainly there are straws in the wind: one that blew by as I was writing this was a newspaper story in *The Australian*, syndicated from *The Times*—both newspapers of record. It reports on the popularity of a *YouTube* video of a model (Amber Lee Ettinger), "prancing around New York in various stages of undress while lip-synching the words of a song declaring she had a crush on presidential candidate Barack Obama" (*The Australian*, 2007a). Among the lyrics quoted are these:

> Baby I cannot wait
> Till 2008,
> Baby you're the best candidate. . . .
> You're into border security,
> Let's break this border between you and me.
> Universal healthcare reform,
> Mmmm—it makes me warm. (Obama Girl, 2007)

Quite apart from the combination of humour, sexuality, and politics, what links this to self-representative journalism is its non-canonical provenance and its popular reach. It was published on the "broadcast yourself" platform, where it attracted over a million hits, thousands of comments, and the attention of "over 200 TV stations around the world" (Obama Girl, 2007). Although it appears to have been professionally made, it personifies the perspective of the citizen (whose part is performed by "Obama Girl"), while using the resources of popular culture, including comedy, music, dance and a pretty girl, to say something that is serious, at least to the extent that it addresses a notoriously non-voting demographic in the name of anti-Bush politics.

Fusing sex and politics (and rock and roll) in the name of liberty has remained a well-trodden route to fame (and sometimes fortune) from the *livres philosophiques* onwards. It has been continued in the present era via such figures as Felix Dennis (from *Oz* to *Maxim*) and Larry Flynt (*Hustler*). An endless succession of scandals, from royal mistresses to Monica Lewinsky, continually remind us that sex remains one of the most potent elements of political journalism. The staples of popular culture—scandal, celebrity, bedroom antics—are the very propellant of modern journalism and therefore of modern ideas (Hartley, 1996, pp. 114–20).

In a similar vein, during the Australian federal election campaign of 2007, the first *YouTube* election in that country, a 23-year-old law student at Sydney University named Hugh Atkin trumped the political professionals by uploading a self-made spoof called "Kevin Rudd—Chinese Propaganda Video" (Atkin, 2007). As Australian voters knew, this referred to Labor leader Kevin Rudd's fluency in Mandarin (he had previously served as a diplomat). It scored over 80,000 views and hundreds of comments, favourites, honours and responses. It was shown on *The 7.30 Report*, the ABC's flagship current affairs programme, and received copious coverage in the news media, most of which concurred with this assessment: 'The two main political parties, with their multi-million advertising budgets, are proving no match for the power and creativity of the guerilla videomakers of the internet" (*Sydney Morning Herald, 2007*). While its qualities as satire were admired, its politics were ambivalent, as noted by a comment on the site: 'This is pure, absolute, unadulterated genius. But I can't figure out if it's pro-Liberal or pro-Labor. Can I get some help here??? WHAT SHOULD I THINK??!?' (au.youtube.com/user/mpesce). This was posted by Mark Pesce, a prominent new-media entrepreneur and writer (see markpesce.com/). In the conversational mode of social networks, his rhetorical question was answered by Atkin, among a long string of others debating the issues. Another comment recommended viewers to look at an "even funnier" video by "Cyrius01" (Stefan Sojka; see www.cyrius.com.au/), called "Bennelong Time" (Bennelong is the name of Prime Minister John Howard's constituency; Cyrius01, 2007). It re-voiced a Led Zeppelin classic with apposite anti-Howard lyrics, ending with a call to vote for the Greens. This too went viral, attracted over 50,000 views and was featured on ABC TV. Sojka was interviewed on ABC Radio and in *The Australian*, where he said:

> For years and years you sit there looking at the television and screaming at it, trying to put your arguments across during all the political current affairs shows, and then I thought, well, there is a place where I can actually do it and say something and maybe be heard. (*The Australian*, 2007b)

The Australian commented: "It's unofficial, unauthorised and may yet have an influence on the voting intentions of generations X and Y." In terms of popular appeal, it seemed that these spoofs were upstaging not only the parties and advertising agencies, but also straight political journalism, which proved all too willing to limp along behind the YouTubers in search of the authentic voice of the populace.

Is this what has become of the tradition of popular self-representation; popular culture as subject? Certainly popular culture is the ground on which new experiments in journalism are propagating. Developments in online media are a definite challenge to expert, top-down, producer-led, supply side journalism, as is well recognised in industry and in the commentariat. The industrial-era model of one-way, one-to-many, read-only, mass communication that sees the populace as an object (of policy and campaigns) is now supplemented if not supplanted by two-way, peer-to-peer, read & write, networked communication where popular culture is once again the subject and agent of its own representation. The reading public is at last evolving into a writing public. Now, in principle, everyone can be a journalist; anyone can publish journalism (Hartley, 2008b). The tradition of self-representation has found a mechanism to cut out (or never cut in) the intermediary agency of the professional expert and the political activist alike. People can and do speak for themselves in an expectation of being heard, whether by a small group of peers or more widely. In short, the supply-chain model of journalism is again in conflict with the self-representation model, as was the case at the beginning of modern journalism in the period 1790–1830.

Both journalism and popular culture currently face the challenge of citizen consumers who produce as well as consume creative content across all domains including information, entertainment and deliberative debate. The popular extent of this challenge is contestable, but it does bring into focus serious questions about the future of the modern professional, expert, representative journalist, especially when so many of this group are employed on non-news journalism, while traditional political journalism is driven by ideological agendas (Fox) and formula-driven reporting (*Daily Mail*).

That challenge extends to the study of journalism too. The curriculum of J-schools and the range of topics in academic journals have tended to restrict what counts as journalism to the democratic process (politics—including war and other forms of social conflict), the career of policy (public administration and its maladministration) and the business cycle (economics and its downside). Much of what journalists actually do is missing from the record. You would not guess that they do astrology, beauty, captions, celebrity, competitions, crime, desire, domestic life, emotional experience, fashion, fear, fiction, gossip, human interest, jokes, liberation, lifestyle, media, medical procedures, oratory, pin-ups, puns, real estate, reviews, scandal, sex, shopping, sport, travel, TV-listings and a lot else besides; or that they are active agents in PR, marketing, spin, propaganda, impression management and the "economy of attention" (Lanham, 2006) just as much as in the democratic process or in constitutional journalism, whether dignified or efficient. Such aspects of journalistic practice go back to the 18th century. They are deeply embedded in popular culture even if they do not all originate there; but have had remarkably little impact on the *study* of journalism.

The familiar and widespread allergic response towards cultural studies (or any other theory) by professional journalism educators has had a negative effect on the academic advancement of the field (Zelizer, 2004), but at the same time journalism courses in universities are increasingly popular as skills-based information management and writing programmes, whose graduates may have no ambition to work in professional newsroom practice. Future research in the field might want to investigate the extension of journalistic capabilities into popular culture (and vice versa) via such training schemes, along with impact of anti-expert DIY formats from blogs to *YouTube*. Are journalism and popular culture finally dissolving into each other? Is it possible to imagine both numbers and knowledge, subject and object, radical and commercial, in the rule and representation of (what's left of) modernity?

REFERENCES

ANONYMOUS [Attributed to Marquis Boyer d'Argens] (1748) *Thérèse Philosophe, ou Mémoires pour servir à l'histoire du père Dirrag et de mademoiselle Éradice*, du.laurens.free.fr/auteurs/Boyer_Argens-Therese_philo.htm.

ATKIN, HUGH (2007) "Kevin Rudd—Chinese Propaganda Video", *YouTube*, au.youtube.com/watch?v =ptccZze7VxQ.

BAECQUE, ANTOINE DE (1989) "Pamphlets: libel and political mythology", in: R. Darnton and D. Roche (Eds), *Revolution in Print: the press in France 1775–1800*, Berkeley: University of California Press, pp. 165–76.

BAGEHOT, WALTER (1867) *The English Constitution*, www.gutenberg.org/etext/4351 (1872 rev. edn).

CYRIUS01 (2007) "John Howard 2007 Bennelong Time Since I Rock and Rolled", *YouTube*, au.youtube.com/watch?v =8_zulGddP6o.

DARNTON, ROBERT (1982) *The Literary Underground of the Old Regime*, Cambridge, MA: Harvard University Press.

DARNTON, ROBERT and ROCHE, DANIEL (Eds) (1989) *Revolution in Print: the press in France 1775–1800*, Berkeley: University of California Press.

DISRAELI, BENJAMIN (1845) *Sybil: or the two nations*, London: Henry Colburn (reissued 1980 by Penguin Books).

GRAYLING, A. C. (2005) *Descartes: the life of René Descartes and its place in his times*, London: The Free Press/Pocket Books.

HARTLEY, JOHN (1996) *Popular Reality: journalism, modernity, popular culture*, London: Arnold.

HARTLEY, JOHN (2008a) *Television Truths: forms of knowledge in popular culture*, Oxford: Blackwell.

HARTLEY, JOHN (2008b) "Journalism as a Human Right: the cultural approach to journalism", in: Martin Löffelholz and David Weaver (Eds), *Global Journalism Research: Theories, Methods, Findings, Future*, London: Routledge, pp. 40–50.

HAYWOOD, IAN (2004) *The Revolution in Popular Literature: print, politics and the people, 1790–1860*, Cambridge: Cambridge University Press.

KENNEDY CUOMO, KATHERINE (2000) *Speak Truth to Power: human rights defenders who are changing our world*, New York: Crown Publishers.

LANHAM, RICHARD A. (2006) *The Economics of Attention: style and substance in the age of information*, Chicago: Chicago University Press.

MACCOBY, SIMON (2001) *English Radicalism: 1832–1852*, London: Routledge.

MARX, KARL (1845) *The German Ideology*, www.marxists.org/archive/marx/works/1845/german-ideology/ch01b.htm.

MAYHEW, HENRY (1849) *London Labour and the London Poor*, etext.virginia.edu/toc/modeng/public/MayLond.html.

MCCALMAN, IAIN D. (1992) "Popular Irreligion in Early Victorian England: infidel preachers and radical theatricality in 1830s London", in: R. W. Davis and R. J. Helmstadter (Eds), *Religion and Irreligion in Victorian Society: essays in honor of R.K. Webb*, London: Routledge, pp. 51–67.

MCCALMAN, IAIN D. (1993) *Radical Underworld: prophets, revolutionaries and pornographers in London, 1795–1840*, Oxford: Clarendon Press.

MCGREGOR OF DURRIS, LORD OLIVER ROSS (1995) "Rights, Royals and Regulation: the British experience", Harold W. Andersen Lecture (World Press Freedom Committee), www.wpfc.org/AL1995.html.

MEDIA INTERNATIONAL AUSTRALIA (1999) "Media Wars", themed section of *Media International Australia incorporating Culture & Policy*, No. 90.

NATIONAL MUSEUM OF PHOTOGRAPHY, FILM & TELEVISION (2000) "The *Daily Herald*' Newspaper and Archive", Bradford: National Museum of Photography, Film & Television, nmpft.org.uk/insight/info/5.3.29.pdf.

OBAMA GIRL (2007) "I Got a Crush . . . on Obama", *YouTube*, www.youtube.com/watch?v = wKsoXHYICqU.

PLUNKETT, JOHN (2003) *Queen Victoria: first media monarch*, Oxford: Oxford University Press.

SONWALKAR, PRASUN (2005) "Banal Journalism: the centrality of the 'us–them' binary in news discourse", in: S. Allen (Ed.), *Journalism: critical issues*, Maidenhead: Open University Press, pp. 261–73.

ROJEK, CHRIS (2004) *Celebrity*, London: Reaktion Books.

SPARTACUS (nd) (by John Simkin) "Journalists", *Spartacus Educational* website, www.spartacus.schoolnet.co.uk/journalists.htm.

SYDNEY MORNING HERALD (2007) "YouTube Revolutionaries Upstage the Party Machine", 26 October, www.smh.com.au/news/federalelection2007news/rudd-faces-youtube-revolution/2007/10/25/1192941243230.html?s_cid = rss_news.

THE AUSTRALIAN (2007a) "'Obama Girl' Highlights Senator's YouTube Dilemma", 19 June, p. 9, www.theaustralian.news.com.au/story/0,20867,21929093-2703,00.html.

THE AUSTRALIAN (2007b) "Political Ads Mocked on YouTube", 25 October, www.theaustralian.news.com.au/story/0,25197,22643204-26077,00.html.

THOMPSON, DOROTHY (2001) "The English Republic", *The Republic*, Issue 2 (*The Common Good*), pp. 72–80, www.republicjournal.com/02/contents002.html.

THOMPSON, E.P. (1968) *"The Making of the English Working Class"*, Harmondsworth: Pelican Books.

TIME (1942) "Hearst's Third War", 23 March, www.time.com/time/magazine/article/0,9171, 802309-1,00.html.

TURNER, GRAEME (2004) *Understanding Celebrity*, London: Sage Publications.

TURNER, GRAEME (2005) *Ending the Affair: the decline of current affairs in Australia*, Sydney: UNSW Press.

VEBLEN, THORSTEIN (1899) *The Theory of the Leisure Class*, xroads.virginia.edu/~hyper/VEBLEN/ veblenhp.html.

WEBB, ROBERT K. (1955) *The British Working Class Reader 1790–1848*, London: George Allen & Unwin.

WINDSCHUTTLE, KEITH (1998) "Journalism Versus Cultural Studies", *Australian Studies in Journalism* 7, pp. 3–31.

ZELIZER, BARBIE (2004) "When Facts, Truth, and Reality Are God-terms: on journalism's uneasy place in cultural studies", *Communication and Critical/Cultural Studies* 1(1), pp. 100–19.

Chapter 5

NEWSPAPERS GO FOR ADVERTISING!
Challenges and opportunities in a changing media environment

Katrien Berte and **Els De Bens**

Introduction

In the traditional media mix, newspapers have always been very valuable advertising channels. The medium is suitable for promotional campaigns, e.g. couponing, retailer ads etc., informative campaigns which provide extensive product information and pure branding campaigns (De Bens, 2001, p. 152). Newspapers are a flexible medium which can reach large audiences although they can also be used to address local targets (Belsch and Belsch, 2003, p. 462; Kotler et al., 2004, p. 453). Printed ads are not as intrusive as television ads or Internet pop-ups. The reader remains in control of the content and decides what articles or advertisements he or she is interested in. Newspaper ads are also often more relevant to the reader than television ads (Ephron, 2005).

The advances in digital media have shaken up relations in the traditional advertising and media markets. These innovations entail an increase in the number of advertising channels as well as sweeping shifts in marketing budgets. Interactive advertising channels such as the Internet and mobile applications, are gaining in importance at the expense of the traditional media like newspapers and commercial television, both media which are very dependent on advertising revenue streams. Newspapers, for example, are considered to be financially healthy when 40–70 per cent of their income is derived from advertising revenues (De Bens, 2001, p. 88).

Newspaper advertising is mostly threatened by the Internet which makes the "core business" of newspapers, news, available for free on numerous websites. New competitors, pure play Internet companies like Google and Yahoo challenge newspapers by offering free news from all over the globe and thus attract large audiences and advertising revenues (World Association of Newspapers (WAN), 2007b, p. 10). Young readers are accustomed to the free "culture" of the Internet and therefore do not perceive free news as less reliable or less accurate (Bruninx, 2007). Classified advertising, one of the major sources of advertising income has moved to the Internet (WAN, 2006a, p. 9).

If newspapers cannot maintain their position on the advertising market, some major changes are inevitable. Firstly, the retail price of newspapers. While most consumers perceive advertisements as unpleasant, they often forget that commercial messages decrease the price of media (Berte, 2006). Raising the retail price of a newspaper can be a valid response to a drop in advertising investments although this is not the most sociably accepted solution.

Secondly, and much more likely to occur, are mergers between publishers or other types of media companies. Mergers enlarge the potential readers market, making the publishing company more attractive to advertisers (Gustafsson, 2004). Worldwide, mergers between traditional media companies, telecom operators and pure play Internet companies are a reality. They result from the economical logic of market expansion, although this type of merger can have enormous consequences for a small media market like Belgium. Fierce competition is inevitable when the investments of advertisers remain stable (Picard, 1988, p. 38). Diversity and pluralism of the press are seriously threatened by these evolutions (Van Der Wurff and Van Cuilenburg, 2001).

The aim of this paper is therefore to identify the challenges that newspapers face in this rapidly changing media environment with regard to the advertising market. Not only do we study the negative consequences of these developments, we also focus on the opportunities of these new technologies for newspaper advertising. The paper is not limited to advertising in the printed newspaper; considerable attention has been paid to advertising on the newspaper's website.

The examples used in this paper are mostly based on the current newspaper market in Belgium, although most trends can be generalized to the situation of advertising in print media in the developed countries.

Methods

This paper originates from a research project on "Advertising in a Digital Media Environment" (ADME). This project examines how traditional media can regain a strong position in the advertising market by responding adequately to technological advances and by developing new advertising models. The research project is funded by the Flemish Interdisciplinary Institute for Broadband Technology and, therefore, is mostly focused on the Belgian media market.

We began by collecting data on the advertising investments in the Belgian mass media. The CIM Media Data Base (MDB pige) was used. This database contains advertising expenditures in Belgian mass media collected by Mediaxim for Carat Belgium, a media specialist company. This instrument was developed to measure the level of clutter in media and is subdivided into economical sectors, products, brands and advertisers (CIM, 2006). It provides data on advertising expenditures in cinema, outdoor media, radio, television, newspapers and magazines (Carat, 2006, p. 16). Financial considerations prevented us from accessing the actual database. Carat Belgium, on the other hand, was a partner in a larger research project on interactive advertising and provided us with the necessary information.

In order to draw accurate conclusions from the trends in the CIM Media Data Base, we conducted several interviews with managers from different media companies. Although most of these managers work for a company that targets the Flemish consumer market, we focused our interviews on general trends which can be applied to both Belgian and European media markets. Several newspaper groups,[1] television networks[2] as well as an advertising agency[3] and a media specialist company[4] are included in this study.

In addition to the interviews, national and international literature was consulted to interpret the findings and identify general trends.

Results

Challenges for Newspaper Advertising in a Changing Media Environment

Digitalisation has led to the birth of a wide range of new media channels like the Internet, mobile media (e.g. mobile phones and PDAs), digital television etc. This evolution has a large impact for the newspaper market which is mainly threatened by the Internet, currently the fastest growing advertising channel worldwide (WAN, 2007e, p. 15). Both the readers' market and the advertising market were affected by this evolution. In the following paragraphs, we discuss the consequences for both markets.

The Internet has drastically changed the newspaper market due to the arrival of new competitors in an already crowded media space (WAN, 2007e, p. 9). Newspapers not only compete on their local market with other local media firms, now they are also threatened by international companies like Google, Yahoo, MSN etc. and, thus, are entering a global market place. These companies are all pure play Internet (dot.com) firms which are fully dependent on advertising revenue for their existence. Their main goal is to reach a large audience and attract major international advertisers. One of the strategies to achieve this goal is offering attractive content like news on their website. It mostly concerns different types of international news offered for free to the websites' visitors.

Other types of Internet competitors also cause some major distortions in the revenue stream of classified ads which is a major source of income for newspapers. According to the World Association of Newspapers (WAN, 2004b, p. 12), an average 26 per cent of all newspaper revenue is derived from classified advertising. Our research on the Belgian market, along with other studies and examples from other companies, show that there is a significant decrease in these revenue streams reflecting the arrival of the Internet (Aris and Bughin, 2005, p. 25; Berte and Gysels, 2007; WAN, 2005a, 2005b, 2005c, 2006a). Companies like Ebay, Stepstone, Monster and local variations of these sites attract classified ads that would otherwise be published by newspapers. Placing ads on this kind of website is free and accessible for both dealers as well as individuals while online databases with classified ads are easily searchable. It is difficult to assess the damage caused by these online classified sites since recent and accurate data are unavailable and vary according to the type of classified ad. Newspapers, for example, maintained a fairly strong position on the recruitment market while almost all private-sector ads have migrated to the Internet (Berte and Gysels, 2007).

The arrival of new media and news distribution channels also leads to the fragmentation of the audience (McQuail, 2005, p. 540). The consumer has access to a wide range of news channels and often consumes two or more media at the same time (EIAA, 2007; TNS Media Intellinger/Cmr, 2004) In general, we all consume more media than a few years ago but lately the time spent on new media has increased rapidly while time spent on newspapers and magazines has decreased (Glorieux et al., 2004; TNS Media Intellinger/Cmr, 2004). Other research shows that the Internet took 2 per cent of the time spent on reading newspapers when comparing 2006 to 2004 (EIAA, 2007). The declining reach of newspapers inevitably has consequences for the advertising market since both markets are inextricably bound up with each other. This evolution can lead to a negative circulation spiral. A newspaper which loses reach is not as attractive to advertisers as before, so it will also experience losses on the advertising market, therefore missing out on money to invest in the paper or forcing it to augment the retail price, which again has a negative effect on the readers market (De Bens, 2001, p. 51; Picard, 1988, p. 59).

In order to reach a significant amount of consumers, advertisers have to divide their budgets over a larger amount of channels so traditional media often lose part of their advertising income. Newspapers are competing with new media in order to maintain their position on the advertising market.

This fragmentation of the audience leads us to the paradox of the digital age. Despite the large number of communication channels available to most consumers making it easier to send a message to a group of consumers, it seems to be more difficult to capture the attention of the consumer to a specific message (Berte and Gysels, 2007, p. 19).

As a result of the augmented amount of advertising channels, the consumer is confronted with a large number of commercial messages on a daily basis. Several studies show that a consumer sees between 1500 and 4000 commercial messages on a daily basis (Yeshin, 2006, p. 156). A natural, human reaction to cope with this information overload is to be selective and avoid unnecessary information (Ingram, 2006). So there is not only an economical battle for advertising income, there is an enlarged competition to capture the attention of the consumer as well. Newspapers fight a battle for the attention of the consumer not only with other media channels but also within its own publications. Despite the low intrusive character of the advertisements (DoubleClick, 2005; WAN, 2007c, p. 18), ad avoidance also occurs in printed media. A study of Millward Brown shows that 45 per cent of all print advertisements are skipped by the readers (Ingram, 2006).

In general, consumers gain more and more control over the messages they are exposed to. New techniques like pop-up blockers and personal video recorders are tools to easily skip commercial messages. Before, the marketer decided which message he wanted to send to an audience, today, consumers decide for themselves which messages they want to see (Jaffe, 2005). Relevancy and the context of (commercial) information gain more importance.

Finally, there is a general trend for shifting advertising budgets from above-the-line media to below-the-line media or from mass media to targeted, interactive or direct media (WAN, 2006b, p. 7). Research from WAN (WAN, 2005a) shows that there is a large difference between the advertising spending in 1980 and 2000. In 1980, almost 70 per cent of all investments worldwide were spent on traditional media while this proportion dropped to

30 per cent in 2000 (WAN, 2005a). Despite their first and second place as advertising media worldwide, television and newspapers are affected by budget shifts towards Internet marketing, direct marketing, mobile marketing and other new types of marketing like guerrilla marketing and viral marketing. In addition to this, retailers are also trying to take a place in the media market. Research shows that three out of four decisions to buy a product are made inside a store (Temmerman et al., 2005), thus making them the ideal place to advertise products. Mainly producers of fast moving consumer goods invest more and more in point-of-sale advertising like couponing, billboarding, product trials and in-store television networks. Their products are more targeted to specific customer needs, so mass media like newspapers are not always suitable to promote these products. Jaffe comments

> Why would you even want to reach a mass audience at a time when there are truthfully very few remaining mass products? With more than 40.000 products up for grabs in your average supermarket, the only mass that is present these days is mass confusion, distraction and clutter. Even the once revered Coca Cola is not as mass as it thought it was ... With C2, Diet Coke, Diet Coke with lemon, Classic Coke, Cherry Coke and Vanilla Coke ... It is a much diversified product line against a segmented audience. (2005, p. 5)

Besides these trends, being the first mass medium on the advertising market, newspapers have a rather old-fashioned image, especially when compared to some of their competitors which are characterized by audiovisual properties and interactivity. Advertisers expect bad printing quality (Belsch and Belsch, 2003, p. 463) while consumers also think that TV and magazines have more attractive ads than newspapers (Newspaper Association of America, 2006).

Other problems for newspapers can be found in changing advertising legislations and social changes. More and more advertising bans menace the media advertisement market based on product type or ethical foundations. Not only tobacco but also alcohol (in many countries) and recently in the United Kingdom in children's programmes, advertising for products containing high fat, sugar and salt is banned thus significantly decreasing the amount of products which can be advertised in the mass media (De Bens and Raymaeckers, 2007).

Opportunities and Strategies for Newspaper Advertising in a Changing Media Environment

The first part of this results section revealed some major challenges for newspapers especially for the printed versions. New media also offer a lot of opportunities for newspapers to fortify their position on the advertising market and transform their existing newspaper brand to a multimedia brand. In this section of the paper, the opportunities of digital media for newspapers are discussed for both the printed and online newspapers.

Firstly, we need to start with the unique selling proposition (USP) of newspapers, their content and specifically, the interpretation and the contextualization of the news. Newspapers have always been and remain the main source of information for local news (WAN, 2007d, p. 13). USPs, contextualization of news and the local focus are transformed into new strategies to counter Internet sites offering free international news. In Belgium, national newspapers are expanding the amount of their local editions. *Het Laatste Nieuws*, a popular newspaper with the largest circulation on the market, has plans to expand its 19 regional editions to 25 editions while other popular newspapers also have plans to follow this strategy (Temmerman, 2007). The different sections in a newspaper offer the advertiser a wide range of possibilities for contextual advertising, a combination of the advantages of a wide range of editorial content combined with commercial messages, e.g. advertising for sports goods is only in the sports section. Contextual advertising can also be based on the content of the newspaper but also on the local context of the reader, his interests, his community or socio-demographic characteristics like age or origin etc. (WAN, 2007a, p. 38).

According to Kotler (quoted in WAN, 2007a, p. 38), the future of newspapers is a targeted approach. Concepts like audience aggregation, audience portfolio and the long tail promoting this kind of targeted products (Anderson, 2006; WAN, 2007a, p. 6) can also be applied to newspapers. A newspaper company should attract different small segments of audiences by publishing targeted products in order to reach a mass market. So it should focus on specific topics or target specific groups. In Belgium, *Het Nieuwsblad*, a popular newspaper, focuses mainly on sports and local news (Temmerman, 2007). The economical newspaper, *De Tijd/L'echo*, changed its positioning to a general quality newspaper in 2003 in order to reach a larger readers and advertisers market. In May 2006, it changed its focus back to an economical newspaper, with great success on the advertisers and readers market. Sales were up by 3.6 per cent (Temmerman, 2007).

Secondly, newspapers are also using new printing techniques which are beneficial in order to attract both readers and advertisers. Newspapers decided to boost sales by publishing on smaller formats. Since 1991, 97 newspapers worldwide have changed their formats. This trend originated from the success of the free newspaper and the attraction of young readers to the "compact" formats thus ensuring future readership (WAN, 2007a, p. 59). Advertisers also seem pleased with this new compact format although some had to adjust their ads to the new style.

After the change to the compact formats, Belgian newspapers started to charge for modules instead of media space calculated by millimeters per column. In order to break through the clutter, new print formats were available to advertisers. These formats differ from the traditional ads in squares or columns. It is currently possible to advertise within

FIGURE 1
The growing beer glass (advertiser =Duvel) in *La Dernière Heure*

an article or to highlight a product using new printing techniques. For example, Figure 1 shows a campaign for Duvel in *La Dernière Heure*, a Belgian newspaper.

Newspapers have always been suitable for couponing and retail ads and through all these new printing techniques, the more attractive compact formats and new standard advertising formats, newspapers have become excellent tools for branding campaigns (De Bens and Raymaeckers, 2007).

Sales houses like Scripta and Via Fred in Belgium also changed tariffs in order to make newspapers more attractive to smaller advertisers. The Newspaper Deals (NP), official discounts for advertisers who bought ads in all Belgian newspaper titles on a single day, were less successful since only large, national advertisers like Coca Cola were using them (De Bens et al., 2007).

Finally, the synergy between the printed newspaper and the Internet is the most powerful tool for publishers to retain/regain their position in the changing media market.

In order to gain some profit from the migration of classified advertising from print media to the Internet, newspapers started their own classified websites (WAN, 2005b). Using the link between the offline brand and the local character of these sites, sites like www.autozone.be, a site for selling cars, and www.spotter.be, a site for for private-sector ads, became popular local versions of sites like Ebay. Both sites are owned by traditional publishing groups, De Persgroep and Corelio.

Not only can websites of newspapers be used to counter the loss of income from classified ads, they can also be used to benefit from the trend of moving advertising budgets from above-the-line to below-the-line media. Using the many possibilities of the Internet for direct marketing, newspapers now have an interactive platform to offer advertisers a direct line of communication with the readers. Although most Belgian newspaper sites remain very close to the "newspaper" concept, some sites like

FIGURE 2

Website HLN.be, a multichannel strategy. Source: www.hln.be, page view of the showbizz channel, 1 August 2007

www.hln.be, the electronic version of *Het Laatste Nieuws*, has a totally different strategy (Figure 2). The site aims to be the largest portal site in Belgium and, therefore, directly competes with large portal sites like the local MSN or sites from Telecom operators like Skynet or Telenet. The strategy is not only to attract a large audience but also much segmented audiences through the different sections or channels of the site (Bruninx, 2006).

FIGURE 3

The launch of *The Simpsons Movie*—3 AD Model, *Het Laatste Nieuws* site. Source: www.hln.be, a view of the home page, 25 July 2007

Although classified advertising is possible in the different channels, the site also offers possibilities for branding online by using its 3 AD Model. This online format combines a leader board, a skyscraper and a large message unit, all containing messages from one advertiser (Figure 3). The banner on top (leader board) is mostly used for branding purposes; the skyscraper on the right is used for promotional goals while the message unit in the middle acts as repeated call to action (Bruninx, 2006).

Newspaper sites can also respond to new advertising techniques using digital technologies. Video advertising and search advertising, personalization, mobile video content and user-generated content are the latest trends in advertising (WAN, 2007c, p. 35).

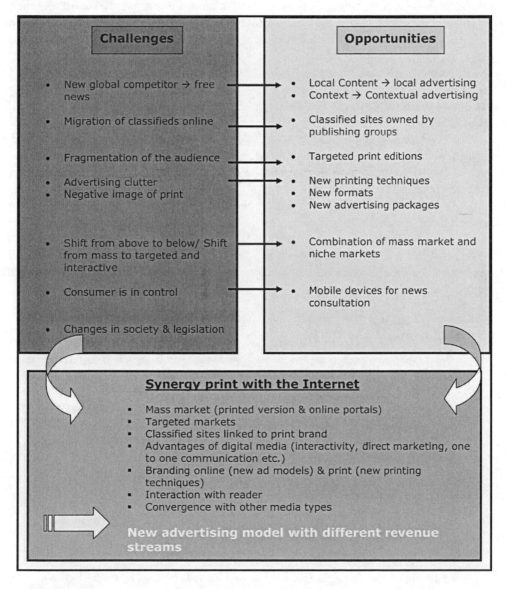

FIGURE 4
Challenges for newspaper advertising countered by the opportunities of new media

Convergences with other types of media like mobile devices can also bring some large revenue streams for newspapers. This personal media is a perfect way to give the consumer control over the news he wants to receive, e.g. news alerts of his favourite news topics. It is also a way to interact with readers and attract a new audience of young readers (WAN, 2004a).

Conclusion

The results of our research reveal the different challenges, opportunities and strategies for newspaper advertising in a changing media environment. Although digitalization and new advertising channels pose a serious threat for advertising revenues, it is our belief that newspapers will remain very important and effective advertising channels in the future, if they are willing to accept the challenges of new media and use them to their advantage.

Examples from the newspaper market (Belgian and other markets in the developed countries) show that they have bent the challenges into opportunities and show us that newspapers go for advertising! Publishing companies have used the opportunities of digital media to counter the threats and have transformed into multimedia companies. For almost every challenge identified in this study, a solution or opportunity has been found, e.g. the focus on local news is a response to the availability of free international news online. We have summarized the links between the challenges and the opportunities of new advertising channels in Figure 4.

Finally, it is our belief that the strength of newspapers in the digital media environment resides in the synergy between the printed medium and the online version which combines the advantages of both media platforms. This results in a different business model containing a large number of advertising channels and revenue streams. This complicated business model is clearly an issue which requires further exploration.

ACKNOWLEDGEMENTS

This article originated from the project 'Advertising in a Digital Media Environment (ADME)' supported by project grants from the Interdisciplinary Institute for Broadband Technology (IBBT). This project was conducted by a consortium of companies: Vmma, Vitaya, De Persgroep, Concentra Media, Corelio Media, Saatchi & Saatchi Belgium, Carat Belgium, Zappware, Belgacom Skynet and Telenet; in cooperation with the IBBT research groups: MICT (Ghent University), CUO (University of Leuven), ICRI (University of Leuven), IBCN (Ghent University) and WiCa (Ghent University).

NOTES

1.   Concentra Media, Corelio Media and De Persgroep.
2.   Vitaya and De Vlaamse Media Maatschappij (Vmma), both commercial television stations based in Flanders, the northern part of Belgium.
3.   Saatchi Belgium, the Belgian division of the International Saatchi & Saatchi Group.
4.   Carat Belgium, the Belgian division of Carat International, part of the Aegis Media Group.

REFERENCES

ANDERSON, CHRIS (2006) *The Long Tail: Waarom we in de toekomst minder verkopen van meer*, Amsterdam: Nieuw Amsterdam.

ARIS, ANNET and BUGHIN, JACQUES (2005) *Managing Media Companies: harnessing creative value*, Chichester: John Wiley & Sons.

BELSCH, G. E. and BELSCH, M. E. (2004) *Marketing Communicatie. Reclame en Promotie*, Academic Service: Den Haag.

BERTE, KATRIEN (2006) "The Evolution of the Advertising Investments in the Belgian Mass Media (2000–2005): trends and interpretations", paper presented to the 5th conference on Mass Media and Communication (ATINER), Athens, 21–22 May.

BERTE, KATRIEN and GYSELS, JAN (2007) "ADME WP 1.2. Problemen met reclame-inkomsten in de print media in een digitale omgeving. Update 1", unpublished research report, Department of Communication Sciences, MICT-IBBT, Ghent.

BRUNINX, SERGE (2006) *"HLN.be, binnenkort de grootste?"*, *Pub* 30(12), pp. 36–7.

BRUNINX, SERGE (2007) *"Terminus Noord? Krantenbonzen over CIM 2006"*, *Pub* 30(15), pp. 38–40.

CARAT (2006) *Media Key Facts 2006*, Brussels: Aegis Media Group Belgium.

CIM (2006) "Jaarverslag 2005", unpublished annual report, Brussels.

DE BENS, ELS (2001) *De Pers in België. Het verhaal van de Belgische dagbladpers gisteren, vandaag en morgen*, Tielt: Lannoo.

DE BENS, ELS and RAYMAECKERS, KARIN (2007) *De Pers in België. Het verhaal van de Belgische dagbladpers gisteren, vandaag en morgen*, 2nd edn, Tielt: Lannoo.

DE BENS, ELS, BERTE, KATRIEN and GYSELS, JAN (2007) "ADME 1.1. Analyse van de inkomstenstructuur van de dagblad en de audiovisuele sector. Update 1", unpublished research report, Department of Communication Sciences, MICT-IBBT, Ghent.

DOUBLECLICK (2005) "ROI Research", January, *Onderzoeksgroep TOR, Vakgroep Sociologie, Vrije Universiteit Brussel*, http://www.emarketer.com, accessed 12 July 2007.

EIAA (2007) *Mediascope. Media Consumption Study Europe 2006*, http://www.eiaa.net/Ftp/casestudiesppt/EIAA_2007_PRESENTATION_PAN-EUROPEAN,%20for%20website.pdf, accessed 26 July 2007.

EPHRON, ERWIN (2005) "The Softer Intrusion of Print", *Admap*, June, p. 40.

GLORIEUX, IGNACE, MINNEN, JOERI AND VANDEWEYER, JESSIE (2004) *Vlaanderen de klok rond. 2004. Enkele resultaten van het Vlaamse tijdsbestedingsonderzoek (TOR '04)*.

GUSTAFSSON, KARL ERIK (2004) "Stability and Change: success and failure of newspapers in Europe since the 1970's", in: Robert Picard (Ed.), *Strategic Responses to Media Market Changes*, Jonkoping: Jonkoping International Business School.

INGRAM, ANDREW (2006) "The Challenge of Ad Avoidance", *Admap*, May, pp. 30–2.

JAFFE, JOSEPH (2005) *Life After the 30-Second Spot*, Hoboken: John Wiley & Sons.

KOTLER, PHILIP, ROBBEN, HENRY and GEUENS, MAGGIE (2004) *Marketingmanagment: de essentie*, 2nd edn, Benelux: Pearson Education Benelux.

MCQUAIL, DENNIS (2005) *Mass Communication Theory*, 5th edn, London: Sage Publications.

NEWSPAPER ASSOCIATION OF AMERICA (2006) "Newspaper Reader Engagement", presentation, http://www.naa.org/research/newspaper-reader-engagement-06.pdf, accessed 26 July 2007.

PICARD, ROBERT (1988) "Pricing Behavior of Newspapers", in: Robert Picard, James Winter, Maxwell McCombs and Stephen Lacy (Eds), *Press Concentration and Monopoly: new perspectives on newspaper ownership and operation*, Norwood, NJ: Ablex Publishing Corporation, pp. 55–69.

TEMMERMAN, WOUTER (2007) "Kranten wikken en wegen hun content", *MediaMarketing* 13(119), pp. 52–4.

TEMMERMAN, WOUTER, LAURIJS, STEPHAN and BOUCHAR, FRÉDÉRIC (2005) "POS-marketing, voor het moment van de waarheid", *MediaMarketing* 11(102), p. 57.

TNS MEDIA INTELLINGER/CMR (2004) "The Outlook for Advertising", *Adwatch*.

VAN DER WURFF, RICHARD and VAN CUILENBURG, JAN (2001) "Impact of Moderate and Ruinous Competition on Diversity", *Journal of Media Economics* 14(4), pp. 213–29.

WAN (2004a) "The Mobile Opportunity", Shaping the Future of the Newspaper Strategy Report 3(1), http://www.futureofthe newspaper.com.

WAN (2004b) "New Classified Models", Shaping the Future of the Newspaper Strategy Report 3(2), http://www.futureofthe newspaper.com.

WAN (2005a) "Circulation Science", Shaping the Future of the Newspaper Strategy Report 4(2), http://www.futureofthe newspaper.com.

WAN (2005b) "Classified Models Revisited", Shaping the Future of the Newspaper Strategy Report 4(3), http://www.futureofthe newspaper.com.

WAN (2005c) "Media Landscapes: beyond advertising", Shaping the Future of the Newspaper Strategy Report 4(6), http://www.futureofthe newspaper.com.

WAN (2006a) "Digital Classifieds Survey", Shaping the Future of the Newspaper Strategy Report 5(3), http://www.futureofthe newspaper.com.

WAN (2006b) "Advertising Science", Shaping the Future of the Newspaper Strategy Report 5(5), http://www.futureofthe newspaper.com.

WAN (2007a) "New Print Products", Shaping the Future of the Newspaper Strategy Report 6(1), http://www.futureofthe newspaper.com.

WAN (2007b) "Benchmarking New Digital Revenues", Shaping the Future of the Newspaper Strategy Report 6(2), http://www.futureofthe newspaper.com.

WAN (2007c) "Advertising Best Practices", Shaping the Future of the Newspaper Strategy Report 6(3), http://www.futureofthe newspaper.com.

WAN (2007d) "The Power of the Local Focus", Shaping the Future of the Newspaper Strategy Report 6(4), http://www.futureofthe newspaper.com.

WAN (2007e) "World Digital Media Trends", Shaping the Future of the Newspaper Special Report, http://www.futureofthe newspaper.com.

YESHIN, TONY (2006) *Advertising*, London: Thomson.

Chapter 6

SHIFTS IN NEWSPAPER ADVERTISING EXPENDITURES AND THEIR IMPLICATIONS FOR THE FUTURE OF NEWSPAPERS

Robert G. Picard

Introduction

From a business model rather than journalistic standpoint, the primary function of the newspaper is an advertising delivery system. Advertising accounts for about two-thirds of the content and 75–85 percent of income for the average newspaper in the United States and similar situations are found in many European nations. The operations of contemporary newspapers are completely dependent upon the resources provided by this advertising base and changes to the income stream affect choices about employment, work processes, and costs throughout newspapers.

This study uses a US dataset because no comparable long-term European-wide dataset is available. Its findings, however, will be relevant to European publishers because the basic advertising trends are similar on the two continents and advertising buying choices and decision-making are based on comparable factors. In general, commercial trends in the newspaper industry tend to lag slightly behind in Europe—absent recession or other economic factors—so the commercial developments in the United States serve as a bellwether.

It is important, however, to understand a structural difference in the US newspaper industry. Newspaper industries worldwide differ in that they are primarily based on national, regional, or local structures. The US structure is local, that is, most circulation results from papers tied to local municipalities spread across the nation. By comparison, the United Kingdom has a national structure with most circulation accounted for by London-based papers and Germany has a regional structure with the largest circulation based in large regional papers operated from the largest metropolitan areas. These structural elements are significant because they influence where and how advertising is sold and the types of advertisers that use newspapers. Thus one must be aware of structural differences when interpreting newspaper trends.

The link between newspaper advertising and gross domestic product (GDP) has long been established (Jones, 1985; Picard, 2001; Shaver and Shaver, 2005; Swerdlow and Blessios, 1993) and advertising expenditures fluctuate with the economy because newspaper advertising is primarily retail advertising and classified advertising. Sales of those who purchase retail advertising (department stores, furniture stores, etc.) and classified (especially employment, automobile, and real estate advertising) are affected by economic changes and they adjust their advertising spending accordingly (Hooley and Lynch, 1985; Schmalensee, 1972). The relationship between advertising and GDP is found globally as well as in nations with well-developed economies. Chang and Chan-Olmsted (2005) found a positive relationship between the two indicators in 70 markets from 1991 to 2001, Picard (2001) found the relationship in six of nine major economies in North America, Europe, and Asia, and Shaver and Shaver (2005) found it to exist in six of eight nations studied in the 1990s.

We are all well aware that the newspaper industry is in the midst of a transformation. For most of the second half of the 20th century the newspaper industry was a stable, comfortable and highly profitable industry and it was incredibly profitable during the second half of the century because of the growth of the economy and heavy growth in advertising expenditures. In 2000, US newspapers were receiving two and a half times more advertising dollars in real terms than they received at mid-century (Picard, 2002). Profit margins averaged in the high teens and most large newspaper companies had profit margins exceeding 20 percent during the last decades of the century.

During the second half of the century, however, more and more media began to appear and audiences began facing multiple choices among their newspaper and television stations, radio stations, magazines, weekly and alternative newspapers, Internet and other types of content offerings. The availability of more media led many readers to choose other forms of media for their informational needs. This trend is seen in the fact that in 1950, 356 persons out of 1000 in the United States received a newspaper but only 198 did so in 2000. These changes also affected advertising rates, reducing the annual average increases for advertising rates as the end of the century approached.

The development of the Internet and its advertising abilities, particularly those as a substitute for newspaper classified advertising, added more pressures on newspapers and raised concern about if and when its effects would lead to the demise of newspapers (Picard, 2003; Price, 2006; World Association of Newspapers, 2002, 2005).

The environmental changes became especially significant in the early 21st century as advertisers began to reconsider the whole of their advertising spending patterns. Growing concerns over the effectiveness of all advertising expenditures came to a head with the economic downturn and recession in newspaper advertising from 2001 to 2003. When that recession ended, advertisers did not return to their previous pattern of spending across media.

Although trends in some categories of newspaper advertising are still relatively positive, the classified advertising category is declining and threatened because it is more effective on the Internet than in print. This is particularly problematic for newspapers because it has been the primary category of advertising sales growth for the past decade and a half.

Today, the newspaper industry is a mature industry with little growth potential and facing the potential for decline so managers are becoming increasingly vigorous in marketing and sales efforts as they try to maintain circulation to maintain their current income. The lack of growth in the industry is critical. Growth in sales and revenue are a basic indicator of the health of an industry and its firms. The problems of growth in the newspaper industry have created a "capital crisis" that is leading to strong pressures and ownership changes throughout the US newspaper industry (Picard, 2006). This is occurring because if firms are not able to grow over time, they stagnate, become less interesting to investors, lose resources for product development and reinvestment, and ultimately decline.

Thus trends and developments regarding advertising sales are the primary indicator of the future financing of the newspaper industry and the focus of this paper.

Methods and Results

Data on GDP were acquired from the national economic accounts data of the US Department of Commerce, Bureau of Economic Analysis (2007) and data on newspaper advertising were compiled from governmental statistical data maintained by the Department of Commerce and the Newspaper Association of America.

Share of Advertising

As the number of media choices rose and newspaper reading declined in the 20th century, advertisers began increasing advertising expenditures in other media. The result is that the newspaper share of total advertising expenditures has declined by about one-third since 1970 (Figure 1).

The primary beneficiaries of the changing expenditure patterns over time have been television and direct mail, with the Internet making significant gains in the past decade (Figure 2).

The clear shift in advertising expenditures away from newspapers over time has attracted the attention of many observers, but the trend must be considered with care. If newspapers' share of expenditures declined while total advertising expenditures were

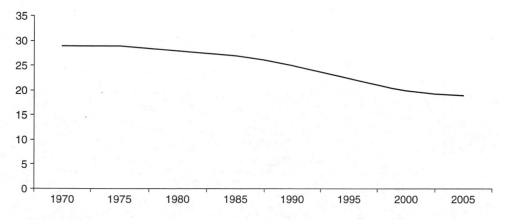

FIGURE 1
Newspaper share of total US advertising expenditures (%)

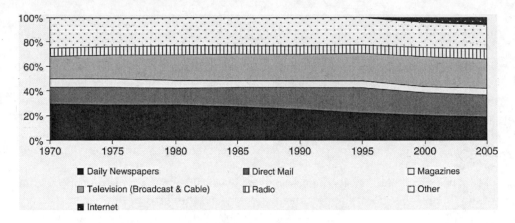

FIGURE 2
Division total US advertising expenditures among media (%)

stable or declining, the result would be less income for newspapers. However, if the share declined but total expenditures increased, newspapers would receive more income despite the declining share.

Advertising Expenditures

From 1950 to 2005 gross domestic product in the United States grew from $293.8 billion to $12,445.8 billion dollars, as a result of the remarkable economic growth that made the United States the world's leading economy in the second half of the 20th century (Figure 3). The growth was fueled by the creation of a unified single national market, by the development of finished goods, by investments in physical and human capital, by population growth, by the development of large firms and managerial capitalism, and by technological change (Chandler, 1977; Heilbronner and Singer, 1998; Lipsey et al., 2005). Other Western nations grew dramatically as well in the 20th century,

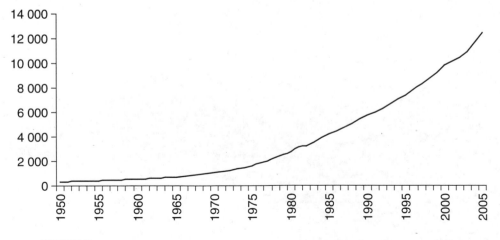

FIGURE 3
US GDP (billions, current dollars)

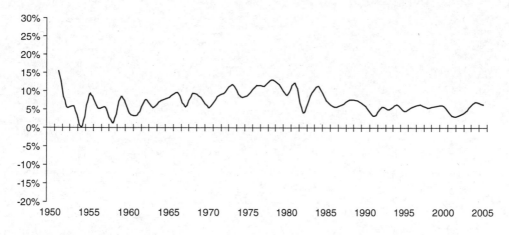

FIGURE 4
Change in GDP

but many Western European nations first had to recover from the devastating effects of damage from the Second World War and their individual market sizes were well below that of the United States.

The large prolonged scale of growth in GDP shown in Figure 3 was, of course, interrupted by upswings and downturns in the economy which appear if annual change in GDP is considered (Figure 4). Prolonged downturns that meet the definitions of recessions occurred approximately every 11 years with particularly significant recessions beginning in 1950, 1955, 1960 and 1980.

General Trends in Newspaper Advertising

During the 55-year period total US newspaper advertising grew from $2 billion to $47.4 billion (Figure 5). Its growth pattern was long and sustained until the recessions of 1990 and 2001.

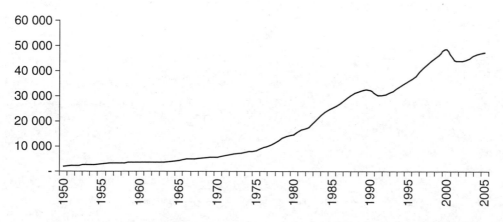

FIGURE 5
US newspaper advertising expenditures (millions, current dollars)

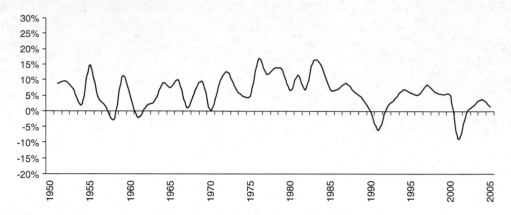

FIGURE 6
Annual change in US newspaper advertising expenditures (%)

As with GDP, the large overall growth was affected by upswings and downturns in the economy which are clear when annual change is considered (Figure 6). Particularly notable downward changes are seen in the 1955, 1960, 1990 and 2001 recessions.

Newspapers' advertising expenditures typically rose higher than GDP growth in good times and fell further than GDP declines during recessions and downturns in the economy across the 55-year period (Figure 7).

This pattern of similar growth and decline is clear until the 2001 recession when—for the first time in 50 years—growth in newspapers' advertising expenditures after a recession did not exceed growth in the GDP. Viewed over a shorter time period, the fact that advertising did not recover after the 2001 recession as it had in the past becomes very clear (Figure 8).

Trends in Categories of Newspaper Advertising

Newspaper advertisers are not all alike, of course, and are driven by somewhat different needs and motives. In the United States, they are grouped in three major

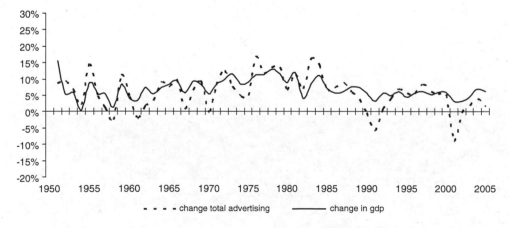

FIGURE 7
Change in GDP and change in newspaper advertising expenditures

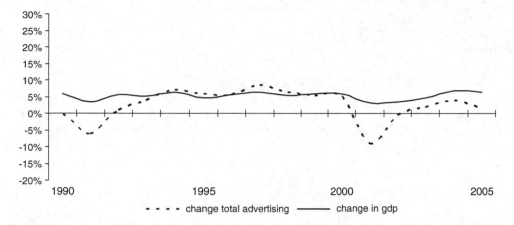

FIGURE 8
Change in GDP and change in newspaper advertising expenditures, 1990–2005

categories, retail, classified, and national, and data on expenditures for those categories are maintained. Retail advertising is display advertising from retailers in local markets; classified advertising includes local business advertisers such as those offering jobs, houses, and automobiles through ads in the classified section, as well as individual non-business advertisers selling household goods, animals, etc. National advertisers are large nationwide companies that purchase advertising simultaneously in newspapers across the country. In the United States, approximately 85 percent of advertising comes from local advertisers or from large national firms advertising in a local newspaper to support the shops and service firms they have in the local municipalities.

Retail advertising has grown regularly since mid-20th century (Figure 9), but major disruptions during the recessions in the early 1990s and first years of the 21st century are evident.

Changes in newspaper retail advertising expenditures have generally followed the trend for change in GDP (Figure 10), but began diverging and underperforming about 20 years ago.

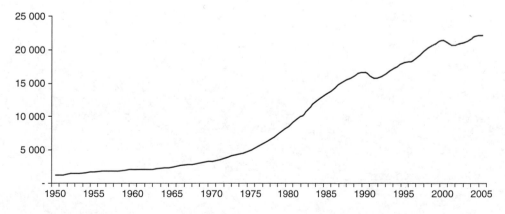

FIGURE 9
Newspaper retail advertising expenditures (millions, current dollars)

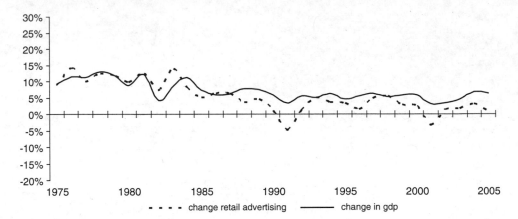

FIGURE 10
Change in GDP and change in newspaper retail advertising expenditures

Classified advertising expenditures grew overall in the second half of the 20th century (Figure 11), but were badly affected by the recession in the 1990s and the recession and growth of Internet advertising in the early years of the 21st century.

Classified advertising change follows the general trends of GDP (Figure 12) but with much more volatility rising and dropping at a greater pace than the general economy, primarily because of classified advertising for employment, automobile, and housing are more affected by economic changes than advertisers in the retail category.

National advertising expenditures have also shown regular growth but were significantly affected in the early 20th century (Figure 13).

The rate of change of national advertising compared to GDP shows it is particularly susceptible to downturns in the economy (Figure 14). However, it is less volatile than that for classified advertising (Figure 12) but more so than retail advertising (Figure 10).

When considered as a group, the changing contributions of the three major categories are evident (Figure 15). Retail advertising today accounts for about half the advertising income and its contribution to the total is increasing. Classified advertising

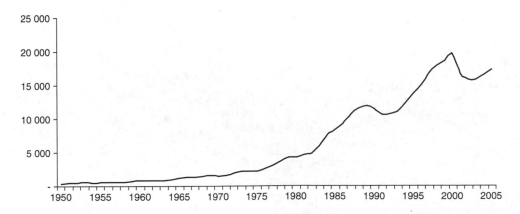

FIGURE 11
Newspaper classified advertising expenditures (millions, current dollars)

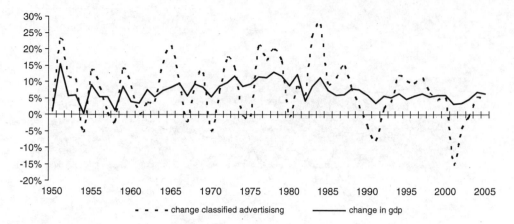

FIGURE 12

Change in GDP and change in newspaper classified advertising expenditures

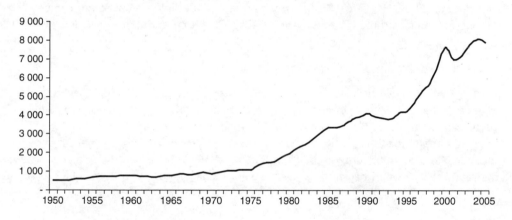

FIGURE 13

Newspaper national advertising expenditures (millions, current dollars)

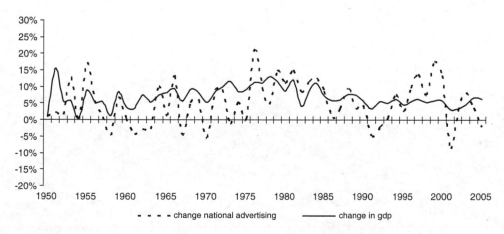

FIGURE 14

Change in GDP and change in newspaper national advertising expenditures

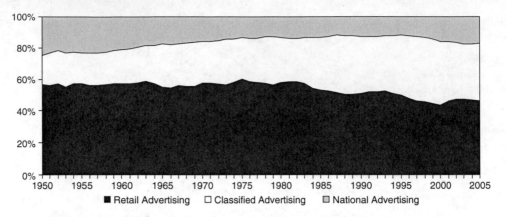

FIGURE 15
Contributions of advertising categories to overall advertising revenue

accounts for about 30 percent, but its contribution is declining after being a driver of growth for the past three decades. National advertising's contribution is also increasing.

Advertising Growth and Inflation

Growth of advertising over time is, of course, affected by inflation. Nevertheless, when adjusted to constant currency the real growth across the 55-year period is evident— particularly after the 1970s—and advertising is still growing (Figure 16).

Although growth is continuing, the strength of that growth has changed, as shown in Figure 17. Since 2000, growth of advertising has exceeded the inflation rate only once, indicating that inflation has eaten away the gains made in those years.

Summary of Trends

Although it is clear that the economy and newspaper advertising expenditures remain linked, the relationship is changing. Table 1 shows the correlation between newspaper advertising expenditures and GDP in different time frames. As the time period

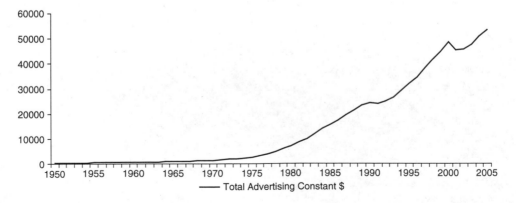

FIGURE 16
Newspaper advertising expenditures (millions, constant dollars), 2000 index

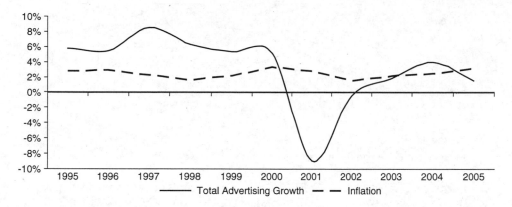

FIGURE 17
Change in newspaper advertising expenditures (constant currency) and inflation rate, 2000 index

is moved closer to the contemporary time, the relationship between expenditures and GDP diminishes, with an especially dramatic breakdown in the relationship between classified advertising and GDP (which also accounts for most of the less dramatic breakdown in total newspaper advertising expenditures and GDP).

Overall, the shifts in newspaper advertising trends can be summed up as:

1. The relationship between GDP and newspaper advertising is weakening somewhat, particularly for classifieds.
2. Growth of newspaper advertising overall is not now keeping pace with inflation.
3. There is greater volatility in rates of change with a few peaks upward and deepening downward thrusts.
4. Retail advertising trends remains relatively healthy.
5. Classified advertising trends are problematic, but are slightly better in the last couple of years because of joint sales with Internet classifieds. The heavy downward thrusts when GDP declines are particularly worrisome.
6. National advertising growth is relatively positive, but greater volatility exists than in the past.

Implications for the Future of Newspapers

The trends in advertising are not as bad as some in the industry have feared, nor are they good enough to ignore or feel great confidence in the future financing that advertising will provide newspapers.

TABLE 1
Correlations between newspaper advertising expenditures and GDP by years

	1950–2005	1985–2005	1995–2005
Newspaper advertising and GDP	0.982827	0.947443	0.78308
Retail advertising and GDP	0.971009	0.973506	0.927363
Classified advertising and GDP	0.975353	0.862909	0.298424
National advertising and GDP	0.991307	0.961623	0.931986

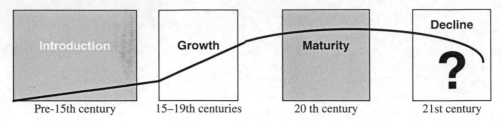

Introduction	Growth	Maturity	Decline
			?
Pre-15th century	15–19th centuries	20 th century	21st century

FIGURE 18
Industry life cycle and the newspaper industry

The trends indicate that basic retail display advertising will remain a pillar of newspapers' income for some years to come, but that one cannot expect it to grow significantly beyond rates of inflation in the future if current trends hold. National advertising expenditures are less stable, but can be expected to be maintained as well for some time. The classified advertising category is highly problematic and decline can be expected in the years to come, unless newspapers are able to stem the flow of classified advertising expenditures to the Internet.

Overall, the trends indicate the advertising expenditures will plateau and decline in the future, denying newspapers revenue growth that is critically needed for sustainability.

This pattern of newspaper history thus seems to be following a basic industry life cycle pattern (Figure 18), but by comparison to other industries it has had an unusually long life cycle.

Although the shifts in newspaper advertising are removing the unusually high profitability of the industry, they are not yet dooming it to demise or altering the basic structural element of the local newspaper markets in the United States. The changes, however, would seem to be moving the industry back to a period in which the newspaper industry was less financially interesting to investors who were primarily interested in profits and asset growth.

REFERENCES

CHANDLER, JR. and ALFRED, D. (1977) *The Visible Hand: the managerial revolution in American business*, Cambridge, MA: Harvard University Press.

CHANG, B.-H. and CHAN-OLMSTED, SYLVIA M. (2005) "Relative Constancy of Advertising Spending: a cross-national examination of advertising expenditures and their determinants", *Gazette* 67(4), pp. 339–57.

HEILBRONNER, ROBERT L. and SINGER, AARON (1998) *The Economic Transformation of America: 1600 to present*, Belmont, CA: Wadsworth.

HOOLEY, GRAHAM J. and LYNCH, JAMES E. (1985) "How UK Advertisers Set Budgets", *International Journal of Advertising* 4(3), pp. 223–31.

JONES, JOHN P. (1985) "Is Total Advertising Going Up or Down?", *International Journal of Advertising* 4(1), pp. 47–64.

LIPSEY, RICHARD G., CARLOW, KENNETH I. and BEKAR, CLIFFORD T. (2005) *Economic Transformations: general purpose technologies and long term economic growth*, New York: Oxford University Press.

PICARD, ROBERT G. (2001) "Effects of Recessions on Advertising Expenditures: an exploratory study of economic downturns in nine developed nations", *Journal of Media Economics* 14(1), pp. 1–14.

PICARD, ROBERT G. (2002) "US Newspaper Ad Revenue Shows Consistent Growth", *Newspaper Research Journal* 23(4), pp. 21–33.

PICARD, ROBERT G. (2003) "Cash Cows or Entrecôte: publishing companies and new technologies", *Trends in Communication* 11(2), pp. 127–36.

PICARD, ROBERT G. (2006) "Capital Crisis in the Profitable Newspaper Industry", *Nieman Reports* 60(4), pp. 10–12.

PRICE, CINDY L. (2006) *Rewriting the Future for Newspaper Investors*, Dallas, TX: International Newspaper Marketing Association.

SCHMALENSEE, RICHARD (1972) *The Economics of Advertising*, Amsterdam: North-Holland Publishing Company.

SHAVER, MARY ALICE, and SHAVER, DAN (2005) "Changes in the Levels of Advertising Expenditures During Recessionary Periods: a study of advertising performance in eight countries", paper presented to the Asian-American Academy of Advertising, Hong Kong, June.

SWERDLOW, ROBERT A. and BLESSIOS, V.I. (1993) "A Model for Predicting Advertising Expenditures: an inter-industry comparison", *International Journal of Advertising* 12(2), pp. 143–53.

US DEPARTMENT OF COMMERCE, BUREAU OF ECONOMIC ANALYSIS (2007) "Current Dollar and 'Real' Gross Domestic Product", http://www.bea.gov/national/ index.htm#gdp.

WORLD ASSOCIATION OF NEWSPAPERS (2002) "Internet Strategies for Newspapers Revisited", Shaping the Future of the Newspaper Strategy Report 1(3), http://www.futureofthe newspaper.com.

WORLD ASSOCIATION OF NEWSPAPERS (2005) "Classified Models Revisited", Shaping the Future of the Newspaper Strategy Report 4(3), http://www.futureofthe newspaper.com.

Chapter 7

(NO) NEWS ON THE WORLD WIDE WEB?
A comparative content analysis of online news in Europe and the United States

Thorsten Quandt

Introduction

From its early days, the Word Wide Web has been the object of both visionary expectations and fears alike. This is especially true for journalism. In the 1990s, hopes were high that technological developments would also change the face of journalism: researchers and the public expected a "revolution" (Stephens, 1998), the "age of the net" (Heinonen, 1999) or the "future of journalism" (Pavlik, 1999), following Quittner's visionary article on "a whole new journalism" (1995). Interaction between writers and audiences seemed to be possible, and the inclusion of multi-media content promised to open up new spheres of story telling.

With the dotcom-bust of the late 1990s and early 2000s, companies around the globe reduced their online staff and decreased investments considerably (Chyi and Sylvie, 2000). While this cooled down some of the wildest expectations, there are still hopes for a new—and more democratic—idea of journalism (Hartley, 2000), backed by the techno-logical possibilities of the Internet. Lately, journalism researchers focus on participatory forms of journalism, where the "people formerly know as the audience" (Rosen, 2006) actively contribute to the news content, resulting in a convergence between producers and consumers (also labeled "produsage"; Bruns, 2005).

While these concepts of a new journalism are helpful for thinking about our research objects in new and inspiring ways, actual research that backs up the underlying concepts is not always available. In the last few years, journalism researchers have primarily studied online journalists, their motives, opinions and work routines (Deuze, 2002; Quandt et al., 2006; Singer, 2003). The actual content of mainstream journalistic online media has been somewhat neglected: while numerous smaller studies focus on specific aspects of online news, there is just a limited number of studies that aim for a broader description of the formal and topical characteristics of the overall news content. In contrast to the above expectations, these empirical studies consistently indicate that mainstream media companies have been slow in embracing the Internet's new possibilities. With recent developments like blogs and wikis—and a growing competition from participatory journalism—these media companies now claim they will finally fulfill the visionary promises of a "whole new journalism", incorporating new forms of story telling and interactivity (Paulussen et al., 2007).

This comparative content analysis of 10 online news media in five countries (United States, France, United Kingdom, Germany and Russia) is a "reality check" to assess whether these claims are true. By analyzing approximately 1600 full-text articles, we investigate what kind of topics and regions/countries are reported in stories in online newspapers, whether there are advanced multi-media features and possibilities for interaction, how the source attributions and link structures work, and whether we find user-generated content. Furthermore, the large dataset allows us to identify national specifics as well as general trends that are true for online journalism in Europe and the United States.

Literature Review

The overall content of online news has been a somewhat weak point in journalism research in the past, as noted above. Nevertheless, there are a few content-oriented studies scattered amongst the numerous pieces on online journalism. In the late 1990s, Neuberger et al. (1998; see also Neuberger, 1999) analyzed the news of five online media and their print counterparts in Germany. They counted the amount of "shovel ware", interactive elements and links. According to this early study, between 5.6 and 37.2 percent of content in online media was taken from the parent medium. It was concluded that "edits are just minor, links to other offerings with similar topics are seldom, multi media and interactivity aren't happening here" (Neuberger, 1999, p. 262, translated by author). In an exploratory content analysis of 100 US online newspapers, Schultz also focused on the interactive options of online media. The researcher coded the presence of various forms of interactivity, i.e. e-mail, chats, polls and surveys as well as online forums; on this basis, an index score was calculated to describe the overall level of interactivity. The overall scores were underwhelming, and Schultz concluded that "media organizations do not necessarily exploit this opportunity (to increase interactivity) effectively" (Schultz, 1999). In a similar way, Tankard and Ban analyzed news sites that were selected on the basis of the newslink.org site for interactivity, multi-media content and hypertext links. According to them, the sites under analysis were not "living up their potential" (Tankard and Ban, 1998)—94 percent of articles did not even contain a single link.

Overall, these and other studies during the early phase of online journalism in the late 1990s (cf. Dibean and Garrison, 2001; Gubman and Greer, 1997; Massey and Levy, 1999; Peng et al., 1999) focused primarily on the formal and structural properties of the news content. They concurrently sketched a picture of online journalism lacking interactive, multi-media content, primarily relying on "shovel ware" taken from the print parents. An exception to the concentration on technological options is the trend study by Kamerer and Bressers (1998). In this study, the news content itself was also analyzed for the presence of national and local news. The authors found that the percentage of sites featuring national news was increasing, while local news was present in nearly all of the news sites under analysis.

After this first wave of studies, the output of research was shrinking considerably, due to the dotcom bust dampening the hopes and interest in online journalism. However, in recent years, a number of content analyses continued to follow the research route outlined above. Much in the same vein as the early studies, Rosenberry (2005) content analyzed 47 online newspaper sites exploring the inclusion of links and interactive options, and whether they serve the purpose to improve public communication. As web technology has evolved in the meantime, there are some new options considered in this study—like blogs and links to community sites—however, the findings resemble the early studies: "few newspapers are using the Internet's interactive technologies to improve the coverage of public affairs" (Rosenberry, 2005, p. 61). With similar ambitions, Oblak (2005) analyzed the front pages of 10 online papers (most of them located in Slovenia) and compared them with four print papers. She also differentiated between various forms of hypertextuality and interactivity, with mixed results: online-only news was more advanced both in its use of links and interactive options, while such options were very limited in the online offsprings of traditional (print) media.

The impression that online websites do not fully use the potential of the Web might be due to a lack of a comparative perspective, though: when looking at the development of multi-media and interactive elements of 83 online news publications in the United States between 1997 and 2003, Greer and Mensing found that "Web sites are increasingly more sophisticated in news presentation, ... multimedia and interactive elements" (2004, p. 98). So when comparing the status quo with earlier stages of development, some improvements are evident.

Comparisons over time are a helpful tool to get things into perspective. It has to be noted, though, that this is not the only way of contrasting data: most of the studies described here were conducted in a US context. While the United States is certainly the Internet pioneer in many ways, there are still some doubts that findings can be transferred directly. Poor (2007) therefore compared the content of four news portals in four different countries (United States, Spain, Japan and Germany) over one week, and specifically looked for overlaps or nation-specific content. To his surprise, the author found limited evidence of connecting patterns—"there was not large overlap between the sites for the sample week" (Poor, 2007, p. 21). He concluded that the sites, while being similar in their basic formal principle, are "different in terms of national culture, with its linguistic and historical factors" (2007, p. 21). With a much broader comparative approach, van der Wurff, Lauf and others organized a content analysis in 16 European countries (van der Wurff and Lauf, 2005). Much in the vein of the other studies mentioned above, they could identify a lack of advanced features in online news throughout Europe. They also found that the news was mostly dealing with domestic topics (especially national politics, economy and crime).

As a result of these comparative findings, one has to conclude that there is no "World Wide" journalism on the Web, but a system of clearly defined language or even national zones. This is supported by other studies as well: as Halavais (2000) could convincingly show in a link analysis of websites, the national boundaries and language zones still play an important role in defining strongly linked sub-clusters of websites that are only loosely connected to the rest of the World Wide Web. These findings contradict the notion of a homogeneous worldwide journalism on the Internet and the simple transfer of US studies. On the other hand, there are also authors who stress that there is a tendency towards a Western professional norm that influences journalism throughout the world (Hanitzsch, 2007), resulting in a "cosmopolite" (Reese, 2001, p. 178) journalism. This effect might be strengthened by the dominance of English as the *lingua franca* of the Internet (Dor, 2004), thus making the journalistic patterns of English-speaking websites the role model for all other countries. These contradictory positions demonstrate the problem with current knowledge about online journalism content: given the importance of news sites, read by millions worldwide on a daily basis, we need to know more about them and their actual content. Most studies so far have only looked at the formal attributes of the websites from a technology-oriented perspective, analyzing whether the full potential of the Web is exploited by the news sites. These findings convincingly describe a very slow adoption of new technological options in the past, but it remains to be seen whether this still holds true nowadays. The content itself has been largely invisible in past studies, and there are no signs of clear reporting patterns; there are hints at national differences, which leave some doubts about the transfer of findings from the mostly US-based studies to other countries around the globe. So obviously, pressing questions regarding the content of news sites remain.

Objectives and Methodology

In a first step of the study, and following the above discussion, we further clarified the research questions. The results of this process were three main research directions:

- First, we would like to know whether news websites actually use new forms of (multi-media) presentation and offer opportunities for interaction, as indicated by the early prophecies of a "whole new journalism".
- Second, we wonder whether websites worldwide are depending on content from the same types of news sources (i.e. news agencies, parent companies etc.) and whether they indicate if they are just using "shovel ware" (re-using content); and in which direction they will lead the user by the means of specific links.
- Last but not least, we would like to identify the main topics and actors of news on the World Wide Web, as well as their geographic extension. By doing so, we can clarify whether there is some kind of "world wide journalism", which covers the same (types of) topics, or whether the well-know (language) boundaries and national reporting patterns still exist.

These research directions led to the design of a study which differs from most other online content analyses in several ways: We had to work comparatively, analyzing data from websites that are based in different countries. Furthermore, we had to code the theme structure and the content, and not only formal aspects, as was the case in most early online content analyses.

We realized this study using some methodological innovations, which were only possible due to the advancement of computer technology: just recently, the growth of storage capacities and broadband connections allowed for making fully functional offline copies of websites with the help of a specialized software (in our case: Teleport Pro). Using such software in conjunction with a scheduler (which works much like a video recorder) and an arrangement of five download computers, we could download multiple websites synchronously.

For the country selection of our study, we chose a "most similar systems" approach, as described in more detail by Esser (2004) and others (Przeworski and Teune, 1970): the websites were chosen from the most important online media in the largest and most influential European countries (France, Germany, Russia,[1] United Kingdom) and the United States. The selection of the sites was based on (1) orientation towards professionalized "quality" journalism (as opposed to some heavily entertainment-oriented offerings, like Bild.T-Online.de in Germany), (2) market leadership (number of users), and (3) accessibility by the general public. Hence, the selected sites can be regarded as being the most relevant online news sites in their respective countries.[2] For our comparative study presented here, we analyzed the news sites of sueddeutsche.de, spiegel.de (Germany), news.bbc.co.uk, timesonline.co.uk (United Kingdom), le-monde.fr, lefigaro.fr (France), kommersant.ru, lenta.ru (Russia), newyorktimes.com, usatoday.com (United States) between 31 January and 13 February 2005 (see Table 1).[3] All websites were accessed and saved at 12:00 of the respective local time, as this snapshot reflects very much the main "news of the day" that are produced by the main editorial staff and accessed by most users (although peak usage and production shifts also vary between countries and sites). Since a website might contain more than 200 articles that are accessible within two links from the front page, we applied some selection rules based on the importance of the articles: basically, only the prominently placed articles with teasers on the front page (i.e. that did not consist of a link only) were coded, since we expect them to be read by most users.

The analysis of these articles is based on a standardized codebook with items focusing on formal categories as well as various content categories. The codebook has been prepared with comparability in mind, and the individual language versions were checked for equivalence of constructs and items with the help of native speakers that were able to identify problematic items. All websites have been coded by native speakers or people with long time first-hand experience within the respective countries, and they were trained and supervised by the same scientist. Furthermore, problematic codings were discussed using a project Web forum, allowing for a decentralized project management. As a result, inter-coder reliability was satisfying (at least >0.8 in most cases, with the exception of tendency ratings, which are not discussed in this paper). Overall, by planning and organizing the whole study "in house" with the help of native speakers, we could follow the guidelines for maximizing equivalence (for example described by Esser, 2004).

A first look at the websites in our sample already reveals some similarities: on a basic structural level, the news sites in the four countries look pretty similar (cf. Figure 1). The layouts follow two main principles: the "weblog" style (spiegel.de, sueddeutsche.de, lemonde.fr), which structures the news in a uni-directional way from top to bottom, mostly based on importance and age, with the sub-division of various sections) and the "newspaper style" (visible in the other pages; here, several columns are used, so the hierarchical ordering is not as strict).

Although the basic structures of international websites are fairly standardized, there are differences when it comes to the information depth and amount of text that is accessible from the front page. Our content analysis reveals that there are two groups of websites here: the German and Russian sites, as well as the *Times*, offer 11.6–18.0 articles (with at least a teaser text) off the front page, whereas the French and American sites, as well as the BBC, only give access to 6.4–9.4 articles on average. Some of these "low front page content" pages use many links instead: the French sites, for example, look very much

TABLE 1
The sample (left to right: German, English, French, US and Russian websites)

	sueddeutsche.de	spiegel.de	news.bbc.co.uk	Times-online.co.uk	Le-monde.fr	lefigaro.fr	Newyorktimes.com	Usatoday.com	kommersant.ru	lenta.ru	Overall
Abbreviation	SD.DE	SP.DE	BBC.UK	TIME.UK	MON.FR	FIG.FR	NY.US	US.US	KO.RU	LE.RU	
N (articles)	252	202	89	163	123	131	95	100	225	223	1603
Average N per issue	18.0	14.4	6.4	11.6	8.8	9.4	6.8	7.1	17.3*	15.9	11.6
Average words per article†	586.0	636.0	573.0	939.7	684.5	712.2	1233.0	660.9	636.5	221.5	644.8

*kommersant.ru was offline on 31 January; so the average N per issue has been calculated on the basis of 13 sample days here.
†ANOVA reveals that the differences are significant on a level <0.000, with df $=9$, $\bar{F}=57.847$.

FIGURE 1

Analyzed websites, basic structure (at the time of the study) (upper left to lower right: spiegel.de, sueddeutsche.de (Germany), news.bbc.co.uk, timesonline.co.uk (United Kingdom), lemonde.fr, lefigaro.fr (France), newyorktimes.com, usatoday.com (United States), kommersant.ru, lenta.ru (Russia) like commented link lists. One might speculate that there are some nation-specific differences when it comes to the information presentation on the websites, given the fairly low variance between sites of one country origin (with the exception of the British sites; however, the BBC's broadcast heritage obviously plays a significant role here).

However, the average number of articles does not tell us the whole story: the information depth is also depending on the average length of the articles. Here, the *New York Times* and the *Times* take the lead, followed by the French sites. They offer very long pieces, up to 1233 words on average for the *New York Times*. It is interesting to note that at the same time, these sites do not position many pieces on the front page—this seems to be a deliberate "reduction" that stresses the focus on news depth rather than on news variation. The Russian *Lenta* marks the opposite extreme: while there are many articles featured on their front site, most of them are very short pieces (221.5 words on average). It is notable, though, that the most websites in our sample offer many long articles, with up to 5372 words (for *New York Times*, reflecting the nature of stories in the print edition of this paper, with an above average length of articles). This contradicts some early predictions that online news pieces have to be short and concise. In contrast to this assumption, we found background articles and "documentation packages" that used the unlimited space on the Internet for an exhaustive coverage of the respective events.

Findings

In this section, we would like to answer the questions developed in the previous sections of this article. We will present the findings according to our research directions, starting with formal characteristics, followed by a discussion of the websites' relational qualities, and the analysis of the content and actors.

Formal Characteristics of the Sample

Early research on journalistic websites assumed that, freed from the constraints of papers and television, they will offer new ways of covering events (Neuberger et al., 1998). The basic idea behind this is the notion that limited space, the static layout of paper-based news, the pressures of a linear medium like TV and other limiting factors do confine the news production to a rather inflexible and limited coverage. So do the news sites finally use the Internet's potential, or do they still remain in the traditional boundaries of print journalism, as described in earlier studies?

When looking at the types of articles in our sample (cf. Table 2), we get a somewhat mixed impression: the German and British sites do experiment with various forms of reporting. Besides the standard news items, there are a fair number of background pieces, reports, comments and subjective forms of writing. The French, Russian and American sites, on the other hand, stick to neutral, informative, but standard news items. There is nearly no variation, with only a few background pieces and comments. So this points to a different understanding of writing for online news: while the German and British news people use the Internet's unlimited space for offering analysis and comments, their French, Russian and American colleagues obviously have an informative, less subjective journalism in mind; this echoes findings from journalism surveys in conventional journalism (see Weaver, 1998).

TABLE 2
Type of article (% of all coded items per medium*)

	SD.DE	SP.DE	BBC.UK	TIME.UK	MON.FR	FIG.FR	NY.US	US.US	KO.RU	LE.RU	Mean share
Standard news item	64.7	60.9	47.2	42.3	95.9	83.2	73.7	99.0	82.2	96.4	74.6
Interview	5.2	2.5	0.0	2.5	0.8	0.8	0.0	0.0	2.2	0.4	1.4
Background/analysis	7.1	15.3	21.3	15.3	3.3	16.0	1.1	0.0	3.1	2.7	8.5
Info/encyclopedia	0.4	0.0	2.2	0.0	0.0	0.0	0.0	0.0	3.6	0.0	0.6
Lead	0.0	0.5	3.4	3.7	0.0	0.0	2.1	0.0	0.0	0.0	1.0
Report	14.7	6.9	13.5	8.6	0.0	0.0	18.9	1.0	1.8	0.0	6.5
Comment/critique	6.3	8.9	1.1	17.8	0.0	0.0	3.2	0.0	7.1	0.4	4.5
Other subject forms	1.2	5.0	11.2	8.0	0.0	0.0	1.1	0.0	0.0	0.0	2.7
Others	0.4	0.0	0.0	1.8	0.0	0.0	0.0	0.0	0.0	0.0	0.2

*Nearly all group differences (and in the multiple codings: nearly all row differences) were significant at $p < 0.000$. This is true for all of the tables with distribution analyses, and a result of the high number of cases. However, we have to stress that due to the nature of the codings, most analyses showed a considerable number of empty cells, which is problematic even for non-parametric tests. Therefore, we feel that it is necessary to interpret the data carefully, and excluded an argumentation on the basis of the (somewhat misleading) statistical significance.

TABLE 3
Multi-media content (% of articles with respective content per medium)

	SD.DE	SP.DE	BBC.UK	TIME.UK	MON.FR	FIG.FR	NY.US	US.US	KO.RU	LE.RU	Mean share
Slide show	8.7	13.4	3.4	0.0	4.9	1.5	13.7	7.0	0.4	0.0	5.3
Video stream	0.4	2.0	23.6	0.0	0.8	0.0	6.3	11.0	0.0	0.0	4.4
Audio stream	0.8	0.0	4.5	0.0	0.0	0.0	0.0	1.0	0.0	0.0	0.6
Combinations	0.0	2.0	14.6	0.0	0.8	0.0	3.2	19.0	0.0	0.0	4.0
Other	0.0	2.0	0.0	0.0	6.5	0.0	2.1	2.0	0.0	0.0	1.3
No multi-media	90.1	80.7	53.9	100.0	87.0	98.5	74.7	60.0	99.6	100.0	84.5

The analysis of multi-media content reveals more differences between the websites—but these differences are only partially country specific (cf. Table 3). Actually, seven of the 10 websites do not enhance more than one-fifth of their articles with multi-media content, so there is some sort of cross-national consent that this is not a required part of online journalism. If websites offer multi-media content, they mostly use slide shows (which can be also used as a means of producing more clicks and boosting the stickiness of the site). There are some exceptions to the rule, the most obvious one being the BBC website, which offers many of the multi-media elements that were expected by the early visions of a "whole new journalism". This can be clearly attributed to the television/radio heritage of this site—obviously, the website tries to transport the parent medium's characteristics to the Internet and can rely on pre-produced material from the BBC's various radio and TV studios.

However, to a somewhat lesser extent, the *USA Today* and *New York Times* websites also offer video streaming and some video/audio combinations or animations. It is probably not a coincidence that these are US-based sites—as Internet development started in the United States, online journalism is most advanced there (as it had more time to develop, reaches a higher readership in general, and therefore is relying on a healthier economic basis—which is important when offering the more expensive ways of online coverage).

The pattern is not as clear when it comes to the options for interaction (cf. Table 4). Here, we do not find a standard set of options that unifies the international websites. The German and English websites as well as the *New York Times* offer specific e-mail addresses of the authors and feedback forms, as well as contact addresses. In some cases, they also offer linked forums and other options. The French *Le Monde* and the Russian *Kommersant* do offer discussion forums on a much more regular basis, with *Kommersant* linking nearly every article with a (user-driven) forum. They do not use other types of interaction, though. *USA Today* only offers e-mail addresses in some articles. Finally, *Figaro* and *Lenta* do not offer any options for interaction at all.

That said, while there are ways to contact the journalists offered by some websites, this does not guarantee that they are reached directly. As has been noted elsewhere (Quandt, 2005), e-mails are very often filtered by editorial assistants who pre-select and answer some user posts. Furthermore, more direct ways of contact and interaction are missing completely: we could not find one single chat link in more than 1600 coded articles—so basically, the user's interaction possibilities with the media still remain indirect and without "obligations" (to answer or even read the users' input) on the side of the journalists. Overall, we can conclude that there is no coherent way of organizing user contacts and interaction; however, the level of interaction options is underwhelming throughout the sample, especially when taking the early expectations for online journalism into account. The finding echoes other studies that also found just limited or no interaction options in current online journalism (see above), so this is no singular result, but a broadly supported description of the status quo in online journalism.

Sources and Links

Earlier research indicates that online journalism is highly dependent on external sources and parent media. The "copy & paste" principle seems to be acceptable for some online journalists (Quandt, 2005), so "shovel ware" is the core material for many of the

TABLE 4

Options for interaction (% of articles with respective content per medium); multiple codings were possible, therefore the columns can add up to more than 100 percent

	SD.DE	SP.DE	BBC.UK	TIME.UK	MON.FR	FIG.FR	NY.US	US.US	KO.RU	LE.RU	Mean share
E-mail	61.1	18.3	1.1	9.8	0.0	0.0	21.1	24.0	0.0	0.0	13.5
Feedback form	8.3	0.0	16.9	11.7	0.0	0.0	0.0	0.0	0.0	0.0	3.7
Contact address	1.2	0.0	3.4	2.5	0.0	6.1	2.1	0.0	0.0	0.0	1.5
Forum link	5.6	7.4	1.1	0.0	22.8	0.0	16.8	0.0	96.4	0.0	15.0
Chat link	0.0	0.0	0.0	0.0	0.0	0.0	0.0	0.0	0.0	0.0	0.0
Other options	0.4	3.0	3.4	0.0	0.0	0.0	1.1	0.0	0.0	0.0	0.8

smaller news sites. While we could not realize a full input–output analysis here, in order to check for the use of external source material, we coded explicit (author/source mentioned at the beginning or end of the text) or implicit (name mentioned in the text) author attributions in the articles (cf. Table 5). With the exception of two media (Spiegel and BBC), the news sites indicate an author or source in nearly every individual case. It might seem surprising that the two quality media Spiegel and BBC do not always mention the author in each case, however their sites imply that if not otherwise indicated, the article is written entirely by (unknown) members of their newsrooms.[4]

But what is more remarkable is that in approximately three-quarters of all cases, the news sites name a specific journalist as the (mostly sole) author. Other authors and sources are only indicated for some media. Most notably, the German sueddeutsche.de (43.7 percent of all cases), the French Le Monde (85.4 percent) and USA Today (80.0 percent) mention news agencies quite often, while the other media usually do not reveal that they used agency material. Other authors and sources are negligible: only the German media mention other media as the authors in a fair number of cases, which is due to the inclusion of cross-promoted magazine articles on these websites. These findings are astonishing, given journalism studies' knowledge about news production processes: it is highly unlikely that news media do not rely heavily on agency material; some studies actually found that up to 80 percent of material was coming from agencies (Baerns, 1991 [1985]). So Le Monde's source attribution is probably the most reliable, while other sites simply did not make their editorial practice transparent. We have to stress that these findings are very unfortunate—with the increased possibilities of searching and re-using information on the net, near-time production and high market pressure, we feel that there is a clear danger that copy & paste becomes the basic principle, whilst the user simply does not know where the material is actually coming from.

The information flow on the Internet does not only allow for copying information from other sources, though—it also offers the possibility of linking the articles to other websites, thus leading the user to new websites (cf. Table 6). All of the coded media made heavy use of links inside the website. Some also linked inside the articles—this was the case if they offered very long background pieces in several parts. A fair number of media also added hyperlinks to other websites where the user can find additional information concerning that topic (see "other links" in Table 6). Four media (the French and German sites) also used links for cross-promotion: linking to other (online) publications belonging to the same publisher. Actually, we also found links to partner websites, and even commercial sites. This might indicate a blurred line between editorial and commercial content; in most countries, there are explicit rules to clearly separate ads and news content in print or TV media—obviously, the separation is eroding in the online environment.

Topics, Actors, Regions

Last but not least, we turned to the contents of the articles and coded the respective content categories and the geographic extension of the content. A first look at these topic categories (cf. Table 7) reveals that there seem to be some nation-specific patterns in the coverage, as well as some overall tendencies. Generally speaking, the main emphasis of the coverage is on national politics and the economy, followed by human-interest stories, international politics, crimes, sport and culture. This distribution pattern is reflecting similar patterns that are known from content analyses of press and TV coverage (e.g. Heinderyckx,

TABLE 5

Source/author (% of articles with mention of respective author per medium)

	SD.DE	SP.DE	BBC.UK	TIME.UK	MON.FR	FIG.FR	NY.US	US.US	KO.RU	LE.RU	Mean share
Specific author	97.6	69.3	40.4	98.8	100.0	97.7	100.0	100.0	96.0	100.0	90.0
Editor/journalist											
Implicit	8.7	5.4	0.0	1.2	80.5	11.5	3.2	2.0	0.0	98.7	21.1
Explicit/byline	65.5	50.5	39.3	89.0	13.0	84.0	85.3	19.0	94.7	0.0	54.0
News agency											
Implicit	5.6	2.0	0.0	0.0	3.3	0.8	6.3	3.0	0.0	0.0	2.1
Explicit/byline	43.7	0.0	0.0	1.8	85.4	9.9	12.6	80.0	0.9	0.0	23.4
Other media											
Implicit	6.0	15.8	0.0	0.0	0.0	0.0	0.0	0.0	0.0	1.3	2.3
Explicit/byline	8.7	6.4	0.0	0.0	6.5	0.0	1.1	0.0	0.0	0.0	2.3
User											
Explicit/byline	0.4	0.5	0.0	0.0	0.0	0.0	0.0	0.0	0.0	0.0	0.1
Other sources											
Implicit	0.4	1.5	0.0	0.6	0.0	0.0	0.0	0.0	0.0	0.0	0.3
Explicit/byline	3.2	0.5	1.1	8.0	0.0	0.0	0.0	0.0	0.4	0.0	1.3

TABLE 6

Links (% of articles with respective link per medium); multiple codings were possible, therefore the columns can add up to more than 100 percent

	SD.DE	SP.DE	BBC.UK	TIME.UK	MON.FR	FIG.FR	NY.US	US.US	KO.RU	LE.RU	Mean share
Internal link inside article	42.9	11.4	1.1	31.3	0.0	0.0	57.9	1.0	0.0	0.0	14.6
Link inside website	52.8	64.4	89.9	63.8	84.6	61.8	86.3	66.0	69.3	96.0	73.5
Link to publications of same publisher	11.5	7.4	0.0	0.6	7.3	3.1	0.0	0.0	0.0	0.9	3.1
External link to partner	3.2	4.0	0.0	0.6	7.3	1.5	0.0	0.0	0.0	0.0	1.7
External link to e-commerce	2.8	5.4	1.1	0.0	0.0	0.0	15.8	4.0	0.0	0.0	2.9
Other links	3.2	14.9	83.1	12.3	4.1	0.8	29.5	12.0	0.0	87.0	24.7

TABLE 7
Topics (% of articles mentioning the respective topic category per medium)

	SD.DE	SP.DE	BBC.UK	TIME.UK	MON.FR	FIG.FR	NY.US	US.US	KO.RU	LE.RU	Mean share
Politics, national	13.9	22.8	36.0	25.8	47.2	39.7	42.1	36.0	37.8	27.8	32.9
Economy	27.0	19.8	5.6	16.0	3.3	9.9	12.6	9.0	17.3	14.8	13.5
Human interest	10.7	7.4	22.5	22.1	4.9	6.9	9.5	15.0	4.9	3.6	10.8
Politics, international	3.2	7.4	4.5	4.3	13.0	13.0	9.5	12.0	7.6	6.3	8.1
Crimes	3.6	5.0	5.6	1.8	6.5	6.9	9.5	10.0	11.1	18.4	7.8
Sport	12.7	9.4	2.2	9.8	4.9	0.0	3.2	2.0	8.0	5.8	5.8
Culture, art, media	9.5	10.9	3.4	2.5	2.4	8.4	3.2	0.0	9.3	6.7	5.6
Medicine, health	4.0	1.5	5.6	1.8	5.7	6.1	5.3	2.0	0.0	6.3	3.8
Research, technical	6.3	6.9	3.4	1.2	2.4	4.6	2.1	2.0	1.3	7.2	3.7
Disasters	2.4	2.0	2.2	2.5	4.9	1.5	1.1	7.0	1.3	1.8	2.7
Social affairs	4.8	1.5	6.7	11.0	0.0	0.0	1.1	0.0	0.4	0.0	2.6
Other	2.0	5.4	2.2	1.2	4.9	3.1	1.1	5.0	0.9	1.3	2.7

1993; see also Shoemaker and Cohen 2006). While it might not come as a surprise, it stresses that—in contrast to earlier expectations—online journalism is fairly conventional when it comes to topic categories.

That said, there are considerable differences between the individual websites, and they seem to be linked to national news habits as well. There are striking similarities between the websites inside a country, while they differ considerably from country to country. The German websites feature less national politics in relation to the other countries' sites; on the other hand, they offer more economy news, sports and culture. Overall, they offer a varied spectrum of news, with a less-pronounced focus than the sites in other countries. The British websites feature an average number of political news, but many more human-interest stories than the websites in other countries, and a considerable amount of "social affairs" news. The French websites primarily offer political news: Overall, 60 percent of Le Monde's articles and more than 50 percent of Figaro's news can be seen as political, with 13 percent of each site's articles being international politics. The US sites show a somewhat similar pattern, also with about 50 percent of political news content for each site. Furthermore, we find an above-average number of crime-related stories on both US sites. Last but not least, the Russian websites also hint at some national preferences: they cover mostly politics, economy, but also a lot of stories on crime as well as cultural news. Again, the pattern here is conventional in the sense that it clearly reflects the news interests of the audiences in the respective countries, and echoes the patterns found in other news media as well. For example, it is not surprising that crime stories play a more important role in the US and Russian media, as crimes are a more central problem to the public in these nations.

Beyond these basic content categories, the meaning of articles can be defined by other variables as well, one of the most important being geographical extension. This tells us about the perceived relevance of nations, and the resulting construction of power relations in the world. The importance of the United States as the remaining super power is obvious when looking at the geographic scope of the coverage (cf. Table 8): in the German and UK media, US-related news can be observed in a considerable number of cases, and the same is true for the Russian Lenta. Only the French websites largely ignore the United States in their news.

Besides this detail, we find some interesting patterns here: most obviously, the bulk of articles focus on the national context only. So while the World Wide Web could offer possibilities for covering much more, the news sites mostly stick to the expected news interests of their audiences, thus reproducing the well-known geographic bias in the news coverage. It is also obvious that the websites only refer to regions where the respective countries have a vital interest: so the websites of the EU members Germany, France and the UK also discuss topics of the EU, while the Russian sites turn towards the former Soviet states and their "old" allies from the former "Eastern Bloc", and US news is very much influenced by the news on Iran/Iraq, Afghanistan and the Middle East. Actually, the news from the Middle East clearly tops all other parts of the world (excluding the United States itself) in the US online news. Largely non-existent are other parts of the world: South America, Australia, the Far East and Africa only play a minor role in the coverage.

Overall, we find that the World Wide Web is not as "global" as we might believe, at least when it comes to news. The content is very much limited by the traditional, national context and the (expected) interests of the users. Even the US and UK sites, which are not "handicapped" by language barriers, focus very much on domestic news.

TABLE 8
Regions/countries (% of articles relating to that country/region per medium)

	SD.DE	SP.DE	BBC.UK	TIME.UK	MON.FR	FIG.FR	NY.US	US.US	KO.RU	LE.RU	Mean share
France	0.8	1.5	0.0	0.6	28.5	45.8	0.0	1.0	0.0	0.9	7.9
Germany	52.0	43.1	0.0	0.0	0.8	0.8	0.0	0.0	0.0	0.0	9.7
United Kingdom	2.8	1.0	58.4	59.5	0.8	1.5	1.1	2.0	0.9	4.0	13.2
Russia	0.0	0.0	0.0	0.0	0.0	0.0	0.0	0.0	58.2	35.4	9.4
United States	6.3	11.9	3.4	12.9	3.3	0.8	58.9	39.0	3.6	11.7	15.2
Italy	1.6	1.5	4.5	1.8	1.6	1.5	4.2	9.0	1.3	0.0	2.7
Other EU countries	5.6	4.0	2.2	5.5	4.1	1.5	0.0	2.0	4.0	3.6	3.3
Europe (rest)	6.0	4.5	2.2	2.5	7.3	12.2	0.0	4.4	4.4	4.0	4.4
Former Soviet States	0.0	0.5	1.1	1.2	2.4	0.8	1.1	1.0	9.8	5.8	2.4
Middle East*	0.8	2.0	6.7	3.7	10.6	6.1	24.2	30.0	1.3	10.8	9.6
Far East/Asia	1.6	1.5	0.0	0.6	5.7	0.8	4.2	6.0	2.7	7.6	3.1
Canada	0.0	0.5	0.0	0.6	0.0	0.0	0.0	0.0	0.0	0.0	0.1
North America	0.0	0.0	2.2	0.0	0.0	0.0	0.0	0.0	0.0	0.0	0.2
South America	0.0	0.5	0.0	1.2	0.8	0.0	0.0	1.0	0.0	0.4	0.4
Africa	0.4	0.0	1.1	0.6	4.1	0.8	0.0	0.0	0.4	1.3	0.9
Australia	0.8	0.5	0.0	0.0	0.0	0.0	0.0	1.0	0.4	0.9	0.4
Multinational/global	17.9	23.3	18.0	9.2	30.1	27.5	6.3	7.0	12.0	12.6	16.4
None	3.6	4.0	0.0	0.0	0.0	0.0	0.0	0.0	0.9	0.9	0.9

*Including Israel and Palestine (both were coded individually; however, to our surprise, the number of articles relating to Israel and Palestine was very low, actually 0 for most media, so that we decided to use the sum index for the data presentation). Numbers above 40% in dark grey; numbers above 10% in light grey.

Conclusions

The technological and social changes connected with the Internet are assumed to have a huge impact on democracy and journalism. As we have described above, a lot of journalism scholars expected online journalism to become the driving force behind a revolution in journalism. Looking at the sum of our findings described in the previous section, we have to conclude that the revolution did not happen. What unifies the websites analyzed here is a similar formal structure, the lack of multi-media content, the missing options of direct interaction with the journalists, a fairly standardized repertoire of article types, missing source/author attributions, a general trend towards the coverage of national political events, and the limited scope of the news (which is dominated by events of regional or national proximity). There are many national specifics, though, which can be attributed to differing journalistic cultures and audience interests in the respective countries.

Overall we can condense these findings to the following conclusion. Online journalism, as it is offered by the market leaders in the respective countries, is basically good old news journalism, which is similar to what we know from "offline" newspapers. Obviously, audiences and journalists alike are not thinking journalism across national boundaries but are still limited by their use and reporting habits. That said, this might be just natural, following the traditional news values, which reflect the relevance for the users. Furthermore, the websites do not make use of the World Wide Web's potential for new types of writing, producing, linking and interacting—but maybe that is also not an issue for the users. It is highly likely that they just want their usual news—fast and reliably.

However, our study also offered a comparative look at topical patterns and the geographical coverage, which make national specifics in international online journalism visible for the first time. It would be very interesting to see whether the same patterns apply to more unconventional ways of news production and distribution on the Web. Do weblog and community news have similar limitations? And do their users really care, if this will be the case? These are important questions for further research, as participatory forms are heavily discussed in journalism studies today. So maybe beyond the cautious online strategies of the media companies and the organized settings of online newsrooms, there is the place for experimentation and innovation that we could not find in the leading online news in the five countries analyzed here.

NOTES

1. Russia can be seen as a deviation from the "most similar systems" approach—its political, economic and social structure is different from the Western European countries. However, we felt that it might be helpful to contrast the findings of the largest EU countries with a large Eastern European country in order to see whether similarities are only due to the Western European context or more general trends in online journalism.
2. There are more top sites in most countries under analysis, and the choice of two is certainly a difficult one in many cases. For example, the inclusion of the BBC as the only site without a newspaper parent is somewhat inconsistent with the other sites. However, we still decided to include it here based on its importance as an online news source in the United Kingdom (and around the world).

3.   The two weeks analyzed here were chosen since they did not include any nation-specific specialities (like elections) or international topics that could influence the composition of the news portfolio worldwide (like the outbreak of a disease or a war).
4.   For a discussion of the meaning and development of bylines in journalism, see also Reich (2007).

REFERENCES

BAERNS, BARBARA (1991 [1985]) *Öffentlichkeitsarbeit oder Journalismus? Zum Einfluß im Medien-system*, 2nd edn, Köln: Verlag Wissenschaft und Politik.

BRUNS, AXEL (2005) *Gatewatching. Collaborative online news production*, New York: Peter Lang.

CHYI, HSIANG IRIS and SYLVIE, GEORGE (2000) "Online Newspapers in the U.S.: perceptions of markets, products, revenue and competition", *International Journal of Media Management* 2(2), pp. 69–77.

DEUZE, MARK (2002) "National News Cultures: a comparison of Dutch, German, British, Australian and U.S. journalists", *Journalism & Mass Communication Quarterly* 79(1), pp. 134–49.

DIBEAN, WENDY and GARRISON, BRUCE (2001) "How Six Online Newspapers Use Web Technologies", *Newspaper Research Journal* 22(2), pp. 79–93.

DOR, DANIEL (2004) "From Englishization to Imposed Multilingualism: globalization, the Internet, and the political economy of the linguistic code", *Public Culture* 16(1), pp. 97–118.

ESSER, FRANK (2004) "Journalismus vergleichen. Komparative Forschung und Theoriebildung", in: Martin Löffelholz (Ed.), *Theorien des Journalismus. Ein diskursives Handbuch*, 2nd rev. edn, Wiesbaden: Verlag für Sozialwissenschaften, pp. 151–79.

GREER, JENNIFER and MENSING, DONICA (2004) "The Evolution of Online Newspapers: a longitudinal content analysis, 1997–2003", *Newspaper Research Journal* 25(2), pp. 98–112.

GUBMAN, JON and GREER, JENNIFER (1997) "An Analysis of Online Sites Produced by U.S. Newspapers: are the critics right?", paper presented to the Annual AEJMC Conference, Chicago, July/August.

HALAVAIS, ALEXANDER (2000) "National Borders on the World Wide Web", *New Media & Society* 2, pp. 7–25.

HANITZSCH, THOMAS (2007) "Deconstructing Journalism Culture: towards a universal theory", *Communication Theory* 17(4), 367–85.

HARTLEY, JOHN (2000) "Communicative Democracy in a Redactional Society: the future of journalism studies", *Journalism* 1(1), pp. 39–48.

HEINDERYCKX, FRANÇOIS (1993) "Television News Programmes in Western Europe: a comparative study", *European Journal of Communication* 8(4), pp. 425–50.

HEINONEN, ARI (1999) *Journalism in the Age of the Net. Changing society, changing profession*, Tampere: University of Tampere.

KAMERER, DAVID and BRESSERS, BONNIE (1998) "Online Newspapers: a trend study of news content and technical features", paper presented to the Annual AEJMC Conference, Baltimore, MD, August.

MASSEY, BRIAN L. and LEVY, MARK R. (1999) "Interactivity, Online Journalism, and English-language Web Newspapers in Asia", *Journalism & Mass Communication Quarterly* 76(1), pp. 138–51.

NEUBERGER, CHRISTOPH (1999) "Regionale Plattform oder Schaufenster zur Welt? Fallstudien über das Online-Engagement von fünf Tageszeitungen", in: Christoph Neuberger and Jan

Tonnemacher (Eds), *Online—Die Zukunft der Zeitung*, Opladen: Westdeutscher Verlag, pp. 124–44.

NEUBERGER, CHRISTOPH, TONNEMACHER, JAN, BIEBL, MATTHIAS and DUCK, ANDRÉ (1998) "Online—the future of newspapers? Germany's dailies on the World Wide Web", *The Journal of Computer-mediated Communication* 4(1), http://jcmc.indiana.edu/vol4/issue1/neuberger.html, accessed August 2007.

OBLAK, TANJA (2005) "The Lack of Interactivity and Hypertextuality in Online Media International Communication", *Gazette* 67, pp. 87–106.

PAULUSSEN, STEVE, HEINONEN, ARI, DOMINGO, DAVID and QUANDT, THORSTEN (2007) "Doing It Together: citizen participation in the professional news making process", *Observatorio (OBS) Journal* 1(3), pp. 131–54, http://obs.obercom.pt/index.php/obs/article/view/148/107, accessed July 2008.

PAVLIK, JOHN V. (1999) "New Media and News: implications for the future of journalism", *New Media & Society* 1, pp. 54–9.

PENG, FOO YEUH, THAM, NAPHTALI IRENE and XIAOMING, HAO (1999) "Trends in Online Newspapers: a look at the U.S. Web", *Newspaper Research Journal* 20(2), pp. 52–63.

POOR, NATHANIEL D. (2007). "A Cross-national Study of Computer News Sites: global news, local sites", *The Information Society*, 23(2), http://www.indiana.edu/~tisj/23/index.html#2, accessed August 2007.

PRZEWORSKI, ADAM and TEUNE, HENRY (1970) *The Logic of Comparative Social Inquiry*, Malabar, FL: Krieger.

QUANDT, THORSTEN (2005) *Journalisten im Netz. Eine Untersuchung journalistischen Handelns in Online-Redaktionen*, Wiesbaden: Verlag für Sozialwissenschaften.

QUANDT, THORSTEN, LÖFFELHOLZ, MARTIN, WEAVER, DAVID H., HANITZSCH, THOMAS and ALTMEPPEN, KLAUS-DIETER (2006) "American and German Online Journalists at the Beginning of the 21st Century: a bi-national survey", *Journalism Studies* 7(2), pp. 171–86.

QUITTNER, JOSHUA (1995) "The Birth of Way New Journalism", *HotWired*, http://hotwired.lycos.com/i-agent/95/29/waynew/waynew.html, accessed February 2003.

REESE, STEPHEN D. (2001) "Understanding the Global Journalist: a hierarchy-of-influences approach", *Journalism Studies* 2(2), pp. 173–87.

REICH, ZVI (2007) "What's in the Name? A proposed framework for understanding the bylines and authorship of news reporters", paper presented to the 50th IAMCR Conference, Paris, July.

ROSEN, JAY (2006) "The People Formerly Known as the Audience", *PressThink*, 27 June, http://journalism.nyu.edu/pubzone/weblogs/pressthink/2006/06/27/ppl_frmr.html, accessed May 2007.

ROSENBERRY, JACK (2005) "Few Papers Use Online Techniques to Improve Public Communication", *Newspaper Research Journal* 26(4), pp. 61–73.

SCHULTZ, TANJEV (1999) "Interactive Options in Online Journalism: a content analysis of 100 U.S. newspapers", *Journal of Computer-mediated Communication* 5(1), http://jcmc.indiana.edu/vol5/issue1/schultz.html, accessed August 2007.

SHOEMAKER, PAMELA J. and COHEN, AKIBA A. (2006) *News Around the World: content, practitioners and the public*, New York: Routledge.

SINGER, JANE B. (2003) "Who Are These Guys? The online challenge to the notion of journalistic professionalism", *Journalism* 4, pp. 139–63.

STEPHENS, MITCHELL (1998) "Which Communication Revolution Is It, Anyway?", *Journalism & Mass Communication Quarterly* 75, pp. 9–13.

TANKARD, JAMES and BAN, HYUN (1998) "Online Newspapers: living up to their potential?", paper presented to the Annual AEJMC Convention, Baltimore, MD, August.

VAN DER WURFF, RICHARD and LAUF, E. (Eds) (2005) *Print and Online Newspapers in Europe: a comparative analysis in 16 countries*, Amsterdam: Het Spinhuis.

WEAVER, DAVID H. (Ed.) (1998) *The Global Journalist: news people around the world*, Cresskill, NJ: Hampton Press.

Chapter 8

HOW CITIZENS CREATE NEWS STORIES
The "news access" problem reversed

Zvi Reich

Introduction

Citizen journalism is a promising new breed of news-making that has been championed by various scholars as "a kind of antidote to the 'bowling alone' effect" (Schaffer, 2007, p. 6) and for its potential to empower the "former audience" (Gillmor, 2006, p. XXV; Rosen, 2005) by granting ordinary citizens a novel, hands-on role.

According to The State of the News Media report (2007), "Citizen journalism ... is becoming less something that is dismissed as the amateur hour before the professionals take the stage and more [as] something that enriches the conversation." Another study contends that the "Citizen media is emerging as a form of bridge media, linking traditional media with forms of civic participation" (Schaffer, 2007, p. 7). As a result of citizens' involvement in news production, The Economist correspondent believes that the field of journalism is undergoing no less than a "reformational moment": "[J]ust as the printing press affected the Church—people are bypassing the sacrosanct authority of the journalist in the same way as Luther asserted that individuals could have a direct relationship with God without the intermediary of the priest" (Cukier, 2006).

However, the extent to which citizen reporters are actually living up to these ambitious expectations has yet to merit attention. Notwithstanding the hundreds of citizen sites operating just in the United States (The State of the News Media, 2007), the very question of whether ordinary citizens are at all capable of producing news is the subject of an on-going dispute, which can be divided into three schools of thought: the naysayers, the well-wishers, and the mixed school.

The naysayers claim that untrained citizens can only produce commentary, analysis and opinion and can occasionally report on breaking stories when they happen to be "in the wrong place at the right time" (Allan, 2006, p. 152), such as the London bombings or Hurricane Katrina. However, as far as the naysayers are concerned, citizens are simply unqualified to produce original news content (Lemann, 2006; Lenhart and Fox, 2006; Lowery, 2006; Reese et al., 2007; Wall, 2005). Nick Lemann (2006), the Dean of Columbia Graduate School of Journalism, did not mince words in stating that "it sounds obvious, but reporting requires reporters."

The well-wishers claim that ordinary citizens can and should produce news (Allan, 2006; Gillmor, 2006; Kim and Hamilton, 2006, Platon and Deuze, 2003). Dan Gillmor, the most prominent proponent of "user-generated content," claims that "the audience is learning how to get a better, timelier news report. It's also learning how to join the process of journalism . . ., [and] in some cases, [is] doing a better job than the professionals" (2006, p. XXV).

Members of the mixed school have, *inter alia*, surveyed hyper-local citizen news outlets in the United States. In their estimation, these sites are "forming as fusions of news and schmooze" (Schaffer, 2007, p. 8); their citizen contributors tend to be "prose-shy" (Schaffer, 2007, p. 6), often supplying fragments of stories instead of full-fledged news items (Schaffer, 2007, p. 10). The mixed camp is indirectly supported by the most celebrated citizen site in the world, South Korea's *OhmyNews*. Besides its phalanx of volunteer contributors, the site has hired a team of staff reporters (Allan, 2006, p. 129; Kim and Hamilton, 2006, p. 545). As such, the *OhmyNews'* management has indirectly acknowledged that there are at least certain journalistic tasks which require "real" reporters.

The objective of the present study is to shed light on these matters by investigating the daily conduct of ordinary citizens doubling as reporters. More specifically, the researcher has endeavored to scrutinize the ways in which citizen journalists actually obtain information and produce original stories, *vis-à-vis* their colleagues in the mainstream press. Such an undertaking will help researchers and superiors of citizen organizations discern the areas in which this up and coming genre might be improved, so that it can become, if not an alternative to mainstream news, then an edifying supplement. Furthermore, it may very well yield significant insights concerning mainstream journalism as well. For instance, the present study's findings may point to those elements of journalism that can be tackled by lay citizens, on account of their developed intuition or common sense. Conversely, the findings may shed light on those areas that are best left to the discretion of professional journalists.

The study's data stem from a comparative study of the reporting practices of citizen and mainstream reporters. The former were sampled from the contributors to Israel's only nation-wide citizen journalism website (www.scoop.co.il), while the mainstream reporters work for the country's three leading news websites (www.ynet.co.il, www.haaretz.co.il, www.nrg.co.il).

Israel constitutes an outstanding case study, for it boasts one of the highest rates of broadband connection use in the OECD,[1] and, relatively speaking, its citizens are quite interested in news and politics at least according to journalistic assessments (Tsfati and Livio, 2003).[2] Furthermore, it has advanced models of both types of news organizations.

Scoop represents an ambitious, innovative, and well-funded national citizen news website, which is inspired by *OhmyNews* and shares many of its attributes.[3] The mainstream news websites also boast sophisticated formats of online news from an editorial, technological and commercial standpoint.[4]

The research method entailed a series of reconstruction interviews with citizen and mainstream journalists from the above-mentioned organizations. This approach was developed and tested in other news production contexts (Reich, 2005, 2006, forthcoming). During the sessions, the interviewees were asked to outline how they obtained a sampling of their items. Additionally, the researcher spent seven days in *Scoop*'s newsroom observing the operations and interviewing its editorial staff.

The paper opens by suggesting the "news access" model as a theoretical framework. However, the researcher has turned this same model on its head, for the sake of adapting it to the realities of citizen journalism.

Inverted News Access

In studying the practices of citizen reporters, the researcher can lean on neither the present literature on citizen journalism, which is but a pittance and hardly discusses production practices (Beckerman, 2003; Gillmor, 2006; Kim and Hamilton, 2006, Platon and Deuze, 2003), nor on the more capacious literature about alternative journalism (Atton, 2002a,b, Atton and Wickenden, 2005; Downing, 2003; Harcup, 2003, 2005; Hindman, 1998) which is far too ideologically-driven to project onto the nature of citizen websites. Studies of citizen journalism practices are not only scarce. Many of them focus on the contribution of citizens to mainstream media organizations, which tend to minimize their participation in the news production process (Domingo et al., 2007; Hermida and Thurman, 2007; Oakham and Murrell, 2007; Örnebring, 2007; Ryfe and Mensing, 2007; Ugille and Paulussen, 2007).

Blog studies, some of which have already been mentioned, do contribute to the discussion of lay people's journalistic competence, but lack the organizational context of citizen journalism.

In light of the above, this paper suggests an adaptation of the "news access" concept, which has already proved its theoretical mettle in all that concerns mainstream news (cf. Cottle, 2000, Gitlin, 1980; Hall et al., 1978; Molotch and Lester, 1974; Schlesinger, 1990). This concept elucidates the crucial link between production and representation by explaining why certain news sources are consistently privy to extensive and favored coverage. However, in citizen journalism the focus should be shifted from the superior access of mainstream sources to the restricted access of ordinary citizens.

The researcher's interviews and observations, as well as the existing literature on citizen journalism, alternative journalism and the sociology of news, point to the fact that citizen reporters are restricted by the following characteristics of their enterprise:

- *Non-established organizations.* Since citizen news outlets are fledgling, unconventional organizations, possessing limited exposure, revenue, and public prestige, potential news sources are often unfamiliar with them and do not read their publications. Consequently, the sources are not inclined to perceive them as a forum in which they would like to appear. Practically speaking, this means that citizen reporters are usually kept out of the loop of routine source-controlled exchanges, such as press conferences, press releases, and updates.

- *A confluence of weaknesses.* Of the four power combinations of source–media encounters, the present topic pits a weak media outlet against similarly weak news sources (Reese, 1991, p. 326). Even when citizen journalists rely on human agents, the latter are more likely to be ordinary citizens and not the mainstream circles consisting of senior officials and PR practitioners.

- *Inefficient division of labor.* Similar to their alternative counterparts (Atton, 2003; Harcup, 2005; Hindman, 1998), citizen news outlets are generally unable to divide their staff into news beats (Schaffer, 2007). This has far-reaching implications on reporters' access to news sources, for citizen journalists have little opportunity to cultivate long-standing relations with them. Their constant meandering between new topics and new sources is thus most reminiscent of general beat reporters (Gans, 1979, p. 31; Marchetti, 2005), who are characterized by a superficial acquaintance with both news sources and the manifold subjects that they cover.

- *Limited journalistic know-how.* Most citizen reporters not only lack prior journalistic training, but their learning curve is slower than professionals. Firstly, as volunteers without enough time to invest in news-making, the output of citizen journalists is usually limited and this constraint slows down their socialization process. Second, as in alternative organizations (Atton, 2002a; Gibbs, 2003), citizen journalism outlets face high burnout and rapid turnover rates, so that most of the contributors are inexperienced. Process-oriented practices, like sourcing, are all the more difficul to learn, for the pages of mainstream news outlets contain very few clues as to the nature of their work methods (Manning, 2001; Zelizer, 1990).

- *Weak organizational control.* Compared to their mainstream counterparts, citizen news outlets are generally under-funded threadbare organizations (Nip, 2006; Schaffer, 2007) with loose organizational structures. Its contributors tend to be scattered, isolated, and preoccupied with making a living in other pursuits, so that it is difficult to consolidate its far-flung parts into a functioning news organization in the ordinary sense of the word. Relying on volunteer-based production by unskilled and uncompensated manpower undermines the organizational hierarchy, especially before the copy is submitted. As such, the editors' jurisdiction is limited to *post hoc* veto or redaction. In light of the above, citizen news organizations have little choice but to adopt an "inclusive" editorial policy (Allan, 2006, p. 126; Schaffer, 2007, p. 9), which basically invites anyone to write about anything at anytime.

Notwithstanding the rhetoric of "giving a voice to the voiceless" (Downing, 2003, p. 633; Gillmor, 2005, p. XXIX), citizen organizations do not necessarily suffice themselves with the niches that are ignored or under-reported by the mainstream media. Unlike alternative journalists, whose selection of sources is ideologically motivated (Atton, 2002b; Atton and Wickenden, 2005; Harcup, 2005), the sources in citizen journalism are largely defined by the serendipitous encounters and idiosyncratic choices of lay people as well as their inability to access better-positioned sources.

As their alternative counterparts, citizen organizations are basically "hybrids" of mainstream and alternative media (Atton, 2002a, p. 151; Kim and Hamilton, 2006). Consequently, their aspirations often coincide with those of mainstream news organizations: broad audiences and maximum revenues (Schaffer, 2007, p. 43). Likewise, citizen news organizations occasionally seek to cover similar stories and turn to the same sources as their mainstream counterparts. For example, during in-house meetings at *Scoop*, the editors' repeatedly expressed their desire for news that caters to wider audiences, especially in the midst of major events, when their homepage can seem to be a bit out of touch. This objective requires not only more mainstream topics, but more mainstream sources.

The fact that ordinary citizens are relatively ill-equipped to access and use news sources goes without saying. Much less obvious, though, are the methods that ordinary citizens turn to for sourcing their stories and the consequences, for better or worse, of their limited access *vis-à-vis* mainstream journalists. These issues thus stand at the heart of the research questions that follow.

Research Questions

Given the exploratory nature of the topic and the dearth of comparable research, the study employs research questions in lieu of a formal hypothesis.

RQ 1:   Do the news sources that citizen journalists avail themselves of constitute a unique compendium of sources compared to those of mainstream reporters?

In light of their limited access to news sources—especially senior sources and PR practitioners, both of which were found to be the dominant sources of mainstream journalism (Reich, forthcoming)—citizen reporters could be expected to rely on a unique mix of sources. Overall, they could be expected to bypass human interactions, while those human sources that they do use probably include a greater representation of ordinary citizens, who are rarely accessed by mainstream outlets (Gans, 1979, p. 15; Hallin, 1992, p. 12).

RQ 2:   Do citizen journalists rely on less news sources than mainstream reporters?

On account of their poor access to news sources and insufficient knowledge in all that concerns the construction of full-length stories, even when they already have a lead (Schaffer, 2007, p. 10), citizen reporters could be expected to make relatively little use of news sources in their items.

RQ 3:   Do citizen reporters initiate more contacts with their sources?

The question of who initiates the news assumes a greater importance if we assume that the initiators, be they reporters or sources, may determine the existence of the item, the timing of the story's release, its topic, content (at least to some extent), and sometimes even the manner in which the piece is framed. What is more, they may even choose the identity of the other party (the particular source or reporter).

Lacking the necessary conditions to foster an environment of regular, accountable, and committed sources with whom they manage an intricate web of relationships (Manning, 2001; Roshco, 1975), it would appear that citizen reporters cannot depend on their sources to initiate the contacts that yield new stories.

RQ 4:   Are the relations between citizen reporters and their contacts less established than mainstream reporters?

One of the expected symptoms of citizen reporters' limited news access is that their relations with their sources are less established than conventional reporters. While the latter tend to rely on a relatively steady diet of sources (Sigal, 1986; Tuchman, 1978), citizen reporters can be expected to only turn to sources on an occasional basis or were previously unacquainted with. Likewise, many of their collaborations are carried out on a one-time basis.

The answer to this question should determine not only the frequency, intensity, and openness with which citizen reporters communicate with sources, but the social nature of these contacts.

> *RQ 5: Do citizen journalists interact with their news sources less frequently than mainstream reporters?*

Even when they avail themselves of human sources, citizen reporters could be expected to minimize their interactions with them and eschew the mainstream practice of interactively negotiating their source's versions (Berkowitz and TerKeurst, 1999, Manning, 2001; Tuchman, 1978). Instead, citizens could be expected to place a greater emphasis on text-mediated and non-mediated channels (i.e. on-the-scene coverage and face-to-face interviews).

Methodology

The primary mode of research, reconstruction interviews, has proven to be an effective and reliable tool for systematically studying the actual performance of journalists, as it provides the researcher with access to even the most sensitive news processes (Reich, 2005, 2006, forthcoming). Some of these practices tend to slip under the radar screen of the more traditional methods.[5] The reconstruction interview involved asking a group of reporters to expound upon the manner in which they acquired a set of specific news items, to include the frequency with which they employed different practices. To the best of my knowledge, this marks the first time that the reconstruction interview has been implemented in either a comparative context or the field of citizen journalism.

The study entailed three distinct steps:

1. *Assembling the items.* The present researcher compiled all the news items that were published in one of *Scoop*'s news sections during the sampling month (November 15 to December 15, 2006). A time period of 30 days was chosen in order to strike a balance between the need for fresh items—so the reporters could accurately recall how they constructed each story—and the need for a sample comprised of manifold stories, dates and circumstances.

2. *Identifying and selecting the news items.* In order to filter out non-news items, which were not always readily discernible in the citizen website's own definitions of news (Kim and Hamilton, 2006), two coders classified all the items into three categories: definitely news, definitely not news, and undecided. The coders agreed on 86 percent of the items, and the rest was handed over to the website's editor-in-chief to decide, under the assumption that he was the best judge of what his own organization classifies as news. He deemed less than half of them to be news stories.

3. *Interviewing the reporters.* The reconstruction interviews were conducted over the phone, as soon as the sampling period was over. In order to minimize the gaps between the first and the last interviewee, this stage was completed within a month. *Scoop*'s editor-in-chief sent the reporters emails encouraging them to participate in the study. Most of them immediately agreed to participate. The following measures were taken to compensate for the limited number of news items that were published during the sampling month:

instead of merely constructing a sample, the entire population of news items was reconstructed; and a sample was constructed of another entire month (January 15 to February 15, 2007).

For the sake of comparison, the three leading Israeli mainstream news websites were studied at the same time as the first wave of citizen items, and every effort was made to use the same methodology. Nevertheless, there were three unavoidable differences.

First, since the mainstream websites offered a wide enough variety of reporters and items, there was no need to reconstruct every single item or take a second sample. Accordingly, 10 reporters were randomly chosen from each website. Second, the mainstream reporters were quite sensitive about the confidentiality of their sources. Consequently, we conducted face-to-face interviews with them so the researcher could take the necessary precautions. Each reporter was asked to reconstruct a sample of 10 randomly-chosen items. The seating arrangement—the reporter and the interviewer sat at the opposite sides of the table and were separated by a small screen—made it impossible for the researcher to discern which of the 10 items was being described at any given moment. Third, we avoided intrusive questions about the specific identity of the source, which in any case was not of any research value to the present study. For example, the questionnaire consisted entirely of general categories, such as "Senior Source" or "PR Practitioner."

Despite the above-mentioned differences between the citizen and mainstream samples, the data are expected to be highly representative and comparable, in light of the fact that both classes of reporters were reconstructing specific actions rather than evaluating individual behavior. In addition, both populations were meticulously repre-sented, as the sample covered almost every element of the citizen website (83 percent of all news items and 77 percent of all reporters), and provided a proportional representation of the different beats in the mainstream sites. The use of a uniform questionnaire throughout the study period and the fact that the reconstruction of the citizen items covered the same time period as the mainstream sample, at least during the first wave, further enhanced the sample's reliability. In all, 206 citizen news items by 47 reporters were reconstructed, alongside 278 mainstream items[6] by 30 reporters.

Following in the footsteps of McManus (1994), the study distinguishes between two main stages of the news-making process. During the first stage, which is referred to as the news-discovery phase, the reporter first becomes acquainted with the existence of a potential new story. In the subsequent news-gathering phase, the reporter obtains further information which constitutes the building blocks of the news item, since the data acquired during the discovery phase is often incomplete and insufficiently substantiated.

Besides for the first two stages, the study also refers to another "twilight" stage, wherein the initial source supplies a mix of data that fall under the category of both new-discovery and news-gathering information. These "bi-faceted" contacts (which were found in 84 percent of the citizen items and 86 percent of the mainstream items) were thus analyzed as both a discovery contact and as a gathering one.[7] However, this measure did not skew the overall number of contacts, which was calculated in a straightforward, singular fashion.

In order to avoid long-winded interviews, the space for detailed responses in the questionnaire was limited to a maximum of four news-gathering sources per item.

Nevertheless, the study covered nearly all the contacts: 94 percent of *Scoop*'s items and 95 percent of the mainstream items.

On account of its exploratory nature, the study used effect size measures (D-statistic),[8] rather than significance tests. As suggested, effect sizes of 0.20–0.49 were considered small, 0.50–0.79 medium, and 0.80 and greater were considered large (Cohen, 1992, p. 157). Unless otherwise indicated, the unit of analysis is a single item. Most of the tables contain mean proportions rather than percentages, for the purpose of addressing the complexities of the gathering phase, which may involve as much as four contacts per item. Therefore, percentages in the gathering phase were first calculated within each item, before being calculated across the board and presented by mean proportions.

Findings

The findings provide an unprecedented insight into the ways in which ordinary citizens make news, compared to their mainstream counterparts. The differences between the two groups point to some of the fundamental strengths and weaknesses of the burgeoning field of citizen journalism.

Let us begin by focusing on the "big picture," namely the capacity of citizens to produce original news. Out of all the items that *Scoop* published over the course of the study's two months (N = 533), over half (52 percent, N = 278) were found to be news items. These items were indeed fresh news stories thanks to the strict measures that the site maintains to ensure that the pieces it publishes are original.[9] In fact, a significant portion of these items were apparently of considerable news value,[10] as some of them subsequently found their way into the mainstream media.[11]

The next step is to analyze the results of the research questions.

The Mix of Sources

The analysis of the source types that citizen journalists avail themselves of *vis-à-vis* mainstream media revealed two striking phenomenon, which accord with the researcher's expectations: citizen reporters rely much less on human sources than their mainstream counterparts; and the human sources that they do use are unique (see Table 1).

While human agents (senior + non senior + PR and spokespersons) constituted about 90 percent of mainstream reporters' contacts in both phases, citizen reporters turned to them in only 63 percent of the discovery contacts and 53 percent of the gathering contacts. The effect size was large: −0.93 for the discovery and −0.89 for the gathering.

There was also a dramatic difference between the internal alignments of human sources. While mainstream reporters leaned on senior sources and PR practitioners in three out of every four items during both news phases, these types of sources were found in only 0.30 of the citizens' contacts during the discovery phase and 0.25 in the gathering phase. The most egregious disparity concerns the use of PR practitioners and spokes-persons, as the amount of times that citizen journalists turned to them during both phases amounted to only a quarter of the spokespersons' contacts with mainstream journalists.

In contrast, citizen reporters are most likely to avail themselves of non-senior sources. Further analysis shows that these sources are by and large ordinary citizens.[12]

TABLE 1

Reliance on different source types in mainstream versus citizen news items

Source type	Mainstream news items (N=278)	Citizen news items (N=206)	Effect size (D-statistic)
News-discovery phase			
Senior sources*	0.21	0.17	−0.10
Non-senior sources†	0.14	0.33	0.49
PR and spokespersons	0.55	0.13	−0.96
Other‡	0.11	0.37	0.66
Total	1.00	1.00	
News-gathering phase			
Senior sources*	0.30	0.14	−0.47
Non-senior sources†	0.18	0.29	0.32
PR and spokespersons	0.45	0.10	−1.05
Other‡	0.06	0.47	1.23
Total	1.00	1.00	

*Chiefs and deputy-chiefs of organizations and corporations, including the representatives of local and national governments, parliaments, and political parties, and high-ranking army (colonel and above) and police officers (deputy commissioner and above).
†Sources subordinate to senior sources, sources unaffiliated with any agency, and private individuals.
‡The Internet, firsthand encounters, information published by other media outlets, news room updates, documents, and archival material.

Number of Sources

As expected, citizen journalists tend to be less reliant on news sources. While mainstream reporters used 2.52 human sources per item, there were only 2.18 sources per item in the output of citizen reporters (D-statistic = −0.20). However, this small difference was rendered negligible in the final copy, as *Scoop*'s editors routinely added source responses at their own initiative and thereby ratcheted up the final tally to 2.34 sources per item. According to the editors, they routinely add source responses to their contributors' stories because the writers often do not realize that parties that stand to be hurt by their items have a right to respond before publication.

In addition, the researcher broke down the data into source numbers and examined one-source items. While mainstream reporters availed themselves of a single source in 29 percent of their items, this was the case in no less than 47 percent of the citizen items (D-statistic = 0.44).

News Initiative

In order to avoid overstatements, reporters' initiative was inferred from the technologies and communication channels that were used to acquire information. These have already proven to be effective indicators of which party (source or reporter) initiates each contact (Reich, 2006).[13] Table 2 outlines the percentage of contacts initiated by citizen and mainstream reporters in the different news phases.

The likelihood of mainstream reporters taking the initiative in the news-discovery phase pales in comparison to their citizen counterparts. During the gathering phase, the

TABLE 2
Contacts initiated by the reporters

News phase	Mainstream news items (N=278)	Citizen news items (N=206)	Effect size (D statistic)
News discovery phase	0.28	0.57	0.62
News gathering phase	0.59	0.68	0.21

difference is still substantial, but by that stage mainstream reporters are already aware of the potential items and are thus more capable to solicit their sources for more information.

Intensity of Contacts

Another facet of the citizen journalists' limited access emerges from an analysis of the history of reporter–source contacts. As expected, Table 3 shows that the relations between citizen reporters and their sources are far less established than those of their colleagues in the mainstream press.

While the information provided by mainstream reporters is largely predicated on a regular stable of sources, who are usually contacted on a daily or weekly basis, citizen reporters primarily rely on new sources, who are contacted for the first time in order to produce the specific item at hand.

Interaction

Both types of reporters acquired their row data with the help of 16 different channels and technologies.[14] Table 4 categorizes these means of communication into four

TABLE 3
The intensity of prior contacts with news sources

Intensity of contacts	Mainstream contacts (%)	Citizen contacts (%)	Effect size (D-statistic)
News-discovery phase	N=278	N=206	
Initial contact	6	47	1.09
Irregular source*	9	11	0.09
Monthly	17	8	−0.25
Weekly	31	20	−0.23
Daily	37	2	−0.90
Irrelevant†	1	11	0.43
Total	100	100	
News-gathering phase	N=634	N=340	
Initial contact	11	54	1.11
Irregular source*	16	11	−0.16
Monthly	16	5	−0.36
Weekly	30	13	−0.41
Daily	26	2	−0.65
Irrelevant†	0	15	0.67
Total	100	100	

The unit of analysis is a single reporter–source contact.
*Contacted several times before, but not on a regular basis.
†News-scene reporting or the Internet.

TABLE 4

Types of communication channels used to acquire information in both news phases

Channel type	Mainstream news (N=278)	Citizen news (N=206)	Effect size (D-statistic)
News-discovery phase			
Telephone-mediated*	0.45	0.19	−0.59
Text-mediated†	0.41	0.46	0.09
Non-mediated‡	0.10	0.33	0.59
Other§	0.03	0.01	−0.11
Total	1.0	0.99	
News-gathering phase			
Telephone-mediated*	0.55	0.17	−1.00
Text-mediated†	0.26	0.49	0.55
Non-mediated‡	0.18	0.31	0.35
Other§	0.01	0.02	0.07
Total	1.0	0.99	

*Land-line and cellular telephones.
†The Internet, email, fax, pager, mail, documents, and archival material.
‡Face-to-face interviews and news-scene coverage.
§Mass media and reporter's experience.

basic groups. The breakdown sheds light, for instance, on the extent to which the channel allowed for interactive reporter–source contacts—thereby enabling the reporter to negotiate the source's version—and the prevalence of firsthand witnessing *vis-à-vis* technology-mediated coverage.

As expected, citizen reporters interact less with their sources than their mainstream counterparts. While telephone-mediated channels are the most common method in mainstream reporting, especially in the news gathering phase, citizen reporters unequivocally prefer text-mediated channels in both the discovery and gathering phases. On the other hand, citizen reporters make much wider use of non-mediated contacts than mainstream reporters, in both phases.

Discussion

The limited use of human sources, who contribute virtually all the raw data in mainstream news (Maier and Kasoma, 2005; Sigal, 1973, p. 123; Strömback and Nord, 2005), constitutes firm evidence that citizen reporters have limited access to news sources. By avoiding human sources, the citizen journalists are freed of the burden of having to confront, negotiate with, and come to terms with fellow human beings. Instead, they are more inclined to show up at the news scene and use the Web as a news source.[15]

The mainstream media's most prevalent source type—PR and spokespersons—is the least accessible type with respect to the citizen news outlet. However, this is not necessarily due to the editorial vigor of the citizen reporters;[16] instead it stems from the PR industry's tendency to ignore citizen journalism. This may change if citizen outlets attract greater market share.

On the other hand, the input of senior sources is sorely lacking in the stories of citizen journalist, as their remarks tend to add a sense of legitimacy, credibility, and prestige to news items, along with the general outlook of a major stakeholder (Becker, 1970; McShane, 1995).

Citizen journalism endeavors to offer a platform for ordinary citizens, who are consistently deprived of a voice in the mainstream media (Gans, 1979, p. 15; Hallin, 1992, p. 12). However, ordinary citizens comprise only 22 percent of their total contacts, so that citizen journalism's claim to be the mouthpiece of the common people has only been partially fulfilled.

The composition of citizen reporters' source lists elucidates two of the mechanisms that they avail themselves of in an effort to compensate for their limited news access. The first mechanism is their reliance on personal contacts (family, friends, co-workers, and acquaintances). These types of sources constitute 29 and 21 percent of their contacts in the discovery and gathering phases, respectively.

The second mechanism involves using one's personal experience as a news source. This practice constituted 17 percent of the sources in the discovery phase and 19 percent in the gathering phase. While the alternative media considers underscoring one's own experience to be "native reporting" (Atton, 2002a, p. 112), the mainstream media deems it to be a controversial practice, for it blurs the line between reporter and source, and the reporter's additional roles as a citizen, consumer, professional, or activist are liable to compromise his or her journalistic impartiality. That said, one cannot deny the added value of involvement, commitment, orientation, and experience that these "natives" bring to the table, as these virtues provided the impetus for some of their finest pieces.[17]

Although one would expect limited access to result in fewer sources per item, the final gap between citizen and mainstream journalism is minimal, probably due to the fact that mainstream reporters themselves are not inclined towards diversified sourcing (Brown et al., 1987; Hansen, 1991). However, the high percentage of one-source items corresponds with the difficulties that citizen writers have developing full-fledged news items (Schaffer, 2007, p. 10; Wall, 2005, p. 162) as well as with *Scoop*'s editors who reported that their contributors' stories tend to be excessively short.

The willingness of citizen reporters to take the initiative, especially during the discovery phase, is indeed a positive development, but it would be naive to attribute this solely to their unbridled journalistic vigor, rather to their lack of a foothold in the routine loops of source-initiated information and updates, which nourish their mainstream counterparts.

According to the well-wishers, leaving the news initiative in the hands of lay citizens liberates citizen reporters from the grip of the mainstream news agenda. However, the naysayers would claim that this freedom tends to divert citizen reporters' attention away from the leading news agendas and onto idiosyncratic stories, so that they are out of touch with mainstream developments.

On the face of things, the dependence of citizen reporters on new contacts in half of their stories, during both news phases, appears to breath some fresh air into news-making circles, for it enables people to serve as news sources even if they never did so in the past (Gans, 1979, p. 129). However, the findings suggest that, compared to mainstream journalism, the stock of news sources at the disposal of citizen reporters is rather meager and recurrent use of a particular source is rare. These trends are indicative of their limited access to news sources.

The lack of previous encounters between citizen journalists and most of their news sources relegate both parties to *ad hoc* short-term exchanges, rather than role relations

(Blumler and Gurevitch, 1981; Nimmo, 1964). On account of the unfamiliarity and low level of commitment, trust and accountability, citizens' sources may very well be reluctant to entrust them with sensitive or exclusive information, which happens to be the most difficult sort of data to attain (McManus, 1994, p. 88).

The manner in which citizen reporters avail themselves of communication channels and technologies is symptomatic of their limited news access. In consequence, they cannot even consider using the more sophisticated set of confrontational interview techniques that telephone-mediated contacts allow for.

On account of their aversion of human agents, citizen journalists also prefer non-mediated contacts, especially on-the-scene reporting. However, the prevalence of non-mediated contacts may also stem from the "inefficiency" of citizen reporters. In contrast, mainstream news reporters are less inclined to show up on the news scene (Christopher, 1998; Russell, 1999; Zelizer, 1990).

Conclusion

Contrary to the criticism of the naysayers, who question the journalistic competence of ordinary individuals, the citizen reporters that took part in the study displayed the wherewithal to produce a steady flow of original news. However, they sourced and produced their material from the vantage point of outsiders—beyond the purview of the existing machinery that is geared towards providing mainstream news with a constant flow of raw data.

Whereas mainstream reporters have been described as wielding the camera while their sources hold the lighting (Sigal, 1973, p. 189), citizen reporters often assume both tasks. Similarly, the collaboration between mainstream reporters and sources has been likened to a tango in which it is usually the latter that takes the lead (Gans, 1979, p. 116). In contrast, when citizen journalists take to the dance floor, they tend to lead the sources and sometimes even go solo.

On account of the practices and tendencies of citizen reporters, there are certain types of stories that are best left to mainstream journalists. Conversely, citizen journalists are well-equipped to cover the following types of stories:

- Stories that are not overly dependent on human agents, especially the regular suppliers of mainstream content and situations in which the sources are expected to make the first move.
- Stories that can be obtained from technical or textual sources (e.g. the World Wide Web), personal experience (e.g. as citizens or activists), and personal acquaintances.
- Straightforward issues, such as stories that do not require the following activities: negotiating with and interrogating several sources; juxtaposing disparate versions and voices; or elaborate processing.
- Occurrences that can be observed on a firsthand basis, instead of relying on the testimony of others.
- Items without row information that the trustees are likely to consider too sensitive or precious to be disclosed to people they barely know, have never met before, or will never meet again.

In sum, citizen reporters are quite capable of producing news, but they are hampered by a set of undeniable weaknesses, which invite a wide array of interpretations.

Insofar as the naysayers are concerned, these weaknesses are a relief, for they bolster the argument that citizen reporters are not "real" journalists. Furthermore, the naysayers contend that the increased access of ordinary citizens to news production has resulted in reporters with less access to news sources, who constitute the main pillar of journalism. If mainstream "news is not what happens, but what someone says has happened or will happen" (Sigal, 1986, p. 15), then less access to that same key player means less news and newsworthiness.

Citizen reporting appears to challenge mainstream journalism more seriously than past contenders, such as PR practitioners (Abbott, 1988, p. 225) and bloggers (Lenhart and Fox, 2006; Lowery, 2006; Reese et al., 2007; Wall, 2005), as unlike the former citizens are not professionals and they are more effective news makers than the latter.

There have been attempts to placate mainstream outlets' fears by establishing a clear division of labor, according to which citizen journalism will stick to a well-defined, lower echelon of journalism (Lemann, 2006). However, the present study suggests that the output of citizen reporters goes well beyond the purview of the small fry. At least some of them measure up to the conventional standards and may even surpass their colleagues' efforts with respect to initiative and legwork.

Citizen journalism's well-wishers deem the limited access of citizen reporters to be a fair price to pay for their admission to news-making. They also contend that citizen reporters should not be appraised in accordance to mainstream benchmarks, for the genre has its own social objectives and criteria for success (Gillmor, 2006; Nip, 2006; Schaffer, 2007, p. 43).

However, in light of the study's findings, the well-wishers must acknowledge the citizen journalists' considerable limitations as producers of news. If further studies confirm these findings, the well-wishers should consider ratcheting down the role that they wish to confer upon citizen journalism and drawing a clear line between the roles and capacities that are attributed to citizen and mainstream reporters.

Both the naysayers and the well-wishers may perhaps agree on the points in which citizen journalism can be improved, so that this fledgling field can serve as a more efficacious compliment to mainstream outlets. If citizen journalism were to attain a critical mass of contributors and/or audiences, it would be able to take the proverbial leap forward. A critical mass of contributors would not only outnumber the limited ranks of mainstream journalism, but would benefit on the whole to more access, which would markedly improve their reporting. Alternatively, were they to attain a critical mass of readers, institutions would probably come to the conclusion that is was in their best interest to provide citizen reporters with equal access and treat them with due respect.

In the meantime, so long as the aforementioned scenario has yet to come to fruition, I would like to suggest three measures that promise to enhance citizen journalists' access to news sources and their overall performance. First, the citizen outlets should develop incentives to stabilize the workforce or, at the very least, keep the blistering burnout rate of its volunteers in check. Longer career spans would afford citizen reporters to develop better access to news sources. Second, the editors should encourage their reporters to specialize, if not in traditional beats at least in wider domains that satisfy their aspirations and background. This measure can transform the nature of their contacts with sources from *ad hoc* exchanges to full-fledged role relationship.

The third measure is the establishment of a framework for journalistic guidance that is decidedly more robust and systematic than the system currently in place (Allan, 2006;

Ryfe and Mensing, 2007; Schaffer, 2007). Sourcing practices encompass a wide range of strategies and tactics that are neither intuitive nor leave enough traces in mainstream final products for lay people to decipher and internalize their techniques. The editorial staffs, at least in those citizen forums that maintain editors, are too small and busy to offer sufficient instruction on their own. Therefore, the editors should even consider having mainstream veterans train citizen reporters.

Citizen journalism and the attendant literature are still in their infancy, but given the field's impressive scope and rapid growth, the topic merits across-the-board research. One of the most urgent research targets is the launching of a new sub-domain—the sociology of citizen journalism. Nevertheless, comparative studies should also be conducted in order to determine the added value that citizen journalism brings to the equation as a complement to mainstream news. In particular, researchers should place an emphasis on the degree to which citizen content adheres to professional journalistic standards and whether the results of this sort of research is consistent with the processes explicated in the present study.

ACKNOWLEDGEMENTS

The author is indebted to the Burda Center for Innovative Communication for its generous support. Thanks are also due to Mr. Tomer Hendl and Mr. Guy Levi, from the Department of Communication Studies at Ben Gurion University of the Negev, for helping to compile the data and Mrs. Tali Avishay-Arbel for her statistical advice.

NOTES

1. Forty-nine percent of all Israelis use broadband (Mor, 2006; OECD, 2007).
2. Tsfati and Livio studied *inter alia* the extent to which reporters believe their audiences are interested in news and politics. The interest levels reported by Israeli reporters were much higher than those of their counterparts in the United States, Germany and Mexico.
3. Similar to its South Korean role model, *Scoop* is predicated on the contributions of ordinary citizens (about 1000 registered contributors at the time of the study). The site also employs four full-time editors, who are responsible for the news selection and editing. The site is profit-oriented and its business plan includes advertising revenues and a business partnership with a cellular operator.
4. *Ynet* and *NRG* employ considerable staffs of their own reporters and thus generally avoid repurposing "shovelware" from the print edition of the same publishing groups.
5. Content analysis is limited to the news product, so that the researcher can only speculate as to the nature of the underlying process (Manning, 2001, p. 48). Interviews can be somewhat problematic when the interviewees themselves are professional interviewers. Although observations can solve some of these problems, citizen reporters are too scattered to allow for systematic observations and mainstream news organizations are inclined to refuse requests for observations (Underwood, 1996).
6. *Ynet* and *NRG* were represented by 100 news items a piece. In the case of *Haaretz Online*, which relies on the same staff for its online and print editions, reporters were asked to reconstruct eight items that only appeared on the online version, in order to keep the interviews down to size (another eight items that only appeared in the print version were

reconstructed by these reporters for another study). Two items were missing, leaving a total of 78 samples.

7. The advantage of the double analysis is that the data reflect the peculiarities of each phase. Despite the double analysis, the differences between the two stages were still remarkable.

8. D-statistic was used to gauge differences between the averages of the citizen and mainstream interval variables. They were calculated as the average of the citizens, minus the average of the mainstream reporters, divided by the pooled estimate of standard deviation.

9. Upon receiving a new submission, the first thing that *Scoop*'s editors do is Google the story's keywords in order to make sure that the item was not already published. According to the editor-in-chief, Yossi Saidov, some 10 percent of all the submissions are rejected on these very grounds.

10. In order to give the reader a taste of *Scoop*'s finest work, I asked the editor-in-chief to choose the three best pieces from the list of the sampled items. To follow are his choices (headlines are followed by a short recap):

    - Chief Doctor of the Parachuters Brigade: "We Were Forced to Leave Wounded Soldiers in the Field During the War." Elad Shalev, a soldier, reported on an internal meeting that was held by combat medical officers in the aftermath of the Second Lebanon War (published March 7, 2007).
    - The Office of the Prime Ministers' Response to Citizen's Appeals: "Olmert Is Busy with the Reform of the Vehicle Tax." This was the official response that Jacob Avid, the story's author, received to queries on different matters that he had sent to the website of the Office of the Prime Minister (published February 28, 2007).
    - Clalit Health Services Turned Down a Cancer Patient's Request for a Metastasis Test. Dany Bar broke the story of a cancer patient. The test was ultimately approved thanks in part to Bar's appeal (published February 26, 2007).

11. A few of the items were presented in a weekly segment on *Channel Two*, Israel's most popular television network, featuring the best citizen stories of the past week. According to the editor-in-chief, mainstream reporters plagiarized some of the stories.

12. While in both phases mainstream news reporters had 134 contacts with non-senior sources—20 percent of which involved private individuals—the citizen reporters had 102 contacts with non-senior sources, 72 percent of which involved private individuals.

13. All the technologies and communication channels were divided into two groups: *reporter-initiated contacts*, including outgoing land-line and cellular telephone calls, Internet searches, face-to-face interviews, on-the-scene reporting, archival research, and documents handed over at the reporter's request; and *source-initiated contacts*, which comprise incoming land-line and cellular telephone calls, faxes, pagers, e-mail and instant messages, information published by other media, and documents that sources handed over at their own initiative.

14. See Note 13.

15. The discrepancies here are striking. During the discovery phase, on-the-scene reporting comprised 0.12 of *Scoop*'s contacts versus only 0.04 of the mainstream websites' reporters (D-statistic $= -0.29$); the numbers swelled to 0.16 and 0.07 in the gathering phase (D-statistic $= -0.32$). The Internet accounted for 0.15 of the discovery information and 0.22 of the gathering data at *Scoop*, but only 0.03 of mainstream websites'

information in both phases (D-statistic = −0.44 for the discovery phase and 0.73 for the gathering phase).

16.   During internal staff meetings, several reporters reiterated their desire for more PR material.

17.   Among the top-notch stories was a paramedic who reported on his team's efforts to resuscitate a patient; a passenger who found himself on the same flight as the prime minister; a social activist reporting on the court proceedings of a salary dispute pitting an employee (who he was assisting) against an employer.

REFERENCES

ABBOTT, ANDREW (1988) *The System of Professions*, Chicago: University of Chicago Press.

ALLAN, STUART (2006) *Online News*, Maidenhead: Open University Press.

ATTON, CHRIS (2002a) *Alternative Media*, London: Sage.

ATTON, CHRIS (2002b) "News Cultures and New Social Movements: radical journalism and the mainstream media", *Journalism Studies* 3(4), pp. 491–505.

ATTON, CHRIS (2003) "What Is 'Alternative' Journalism?", *Journalism* 4(3), pp. 267–72.

ATTON, CHRIS and WICKENDEN, EMMA (2005) "Sourcing Routines and Representation in Alternative Journalism: a case study approach", *Journalism Studies* 6(3), pp. 347–59.

BECKER, HOWARD S. (1970) "Who's Side Are We On?", in: Jack D. Douglas (Ed.), *The Relevance of Sociology*, New York: Merdith, pp. 99–111.

BECKERMAN, GAL (2003) "Edging Away From Anarchy: inside the Indymedia collective, passion vs. pragmatism", *Columbia Journalism Review* 5, September/October, http://cjrarchives.org/issues/2003/5/anarchy-beckerman.asp, accessed 26 June 2008.

BERKOWITZ, DAN and TERKEURST, JAMES (1999) "Community as Interpretive Community: rethinking the journalist–source relationship", *Journal of Communication* 49(3), pp. 125–36.

BLUMLER, JAY G. and GUREVITCH, MICHAEL (1981) "Politicians and the Press: an essay on role relationship", in: Dan Nimmo and Keith R. Sanders (Eds), *Handbook of Political Communication*, Beverly Hills, CA: Sage, pp. 467–93.

BROWN, JANE DELANO, BYBEE, CARL R., WEARDEN, STANLEY T. and STRAUGHAN, DULCIE MURDOCK (1987) "Invisible Power: newspaper news sources and the limits of diversity", *Journalism Quarterly* 64(1), pp. 45–54.

CHRISTOPHER, CAROL L. (1998) "Technology & Journalism in the Electronic Newsroom", in: Diane L. Borden and Harvey Kerric (Eds), *The Electronic Grapevine – Rumor, Reputation and Reporting in the New On-Line Environment*, Mahwah, NJ: Lawrence Erlbaum, pp. 123–39.

COHEN, JACOB (1992) "A Power Primer", *Psychological Bulletin* 112(1), pp. 155–9.

COTTLE, SIMON (2000) "Rethinking News Access", *Journalism Studies* 1(3), pp. 427–48.

CUKIER, NEIL (2006) "The Future of Journalism", Open Business blog, 24 June, http://www.openbusiness.cc/2006/06/24/the-future-of-journalism/, accessed 20 September 2007.

DOMINGO, DAVID, QUANDT, THORSTEN, HEINONEN, ARI, PAULUSSESEN, STEVE, SINGER, JANE and VUJNOVIC, MARINA (2007) "Participatory Journalism Practices in the Media and Beyond: an international comparative study of initiatives in online newspapers", paper presented to the Future of Newspapers Conference, Cardiff, September.

DOWNING, JOHN D. H. (2003) "Audiences and Readers of Alternative Media", *Media, Culture & Society* 25(5), pp. 625–45.

GANS, HERBERT J. (1979) *Deciding What's News*, New York: Pantheon Books.

GIBBS, PATRICIA L. (2003) "Alternative Things Considered: a political economic analysis of labour processes and relations at a Honolulu alternative newspaper", *Media, Culture & Society* 25(5), pp. 587–605.

GILLMOR, DAN (2006) *We the Media*, Sebastopol, CA: O'Reilly.

GITLIN, TODD (1980) *The Whole World Is Watching*, Berkeley: University of California Press.

HALL, STUART, CRITCHER, CHARLES, JEFFERSON, TONY, CLARKE, JOHN and ROBERT, BRIAN (1978) *Policing the Crisis*, London: Macmillan.

HALLIN, DANIEL C. (1992) "Sound Bite News: television coverage of elections, 1968–1988", *Journal of Communication* 42(2), pp. 5–24.

HANSEN, KATHELEEN A. (1991) "Source Diversity and Newspaper Enterprise Journalism", *Journalism Quarterly* 68(3), pp. 474–82.

HARCUP, TONY (2003) "'The Unspoken—said': the journalism of alternative media", *Journalism* 4(3), pp. 356–76.

HARCUP, TONY (2005) "'I'm Doing This to Change the World': journalism in alternative and mainstream media", *Journalism Studies* 6(3), pp. 361–74.

HERMIDA, ALFRED and THURMAN, NEIL (2007) "A Clash of Cultures: the integration of user-generated content within professional journalistic frameworks at British newspaper websites", paper presented to the Future of Newspapers Conference, Cardiff, September.

HINDMAN, ELIZABETH BLANKS (1998) "'Spectacles of the Poor': conventions of alternative news", *Journalism & Mass Communication Quarterly* 75(1), pp. 177–93.

KIM, EUN GYOO and HAMILTON, JAMES W. (2006) "Capitulation to Capital? OhmyNews as alternative media", *Media, Culture & Society* 28(4), pp. 541–60.

LEMANN, NICHOLAS (2006) "Amateur Hour: journalism without journalists", *The New Yorker*, 7 August, http://www.newyorker.com/fact/content/articles/060807fa_fact1, accessed 30 August 2007.

LENHART, AMANDA and FOX, SUSANNAH (2006) "Bloggers", Pew Internet & American Life Project, 19 July, http://www.pewinternet.org/pdfs/PIP%20Bloggers%20Report%20July%2019%20 2006.pdf, accessed 30 August 2007.

LOWERY, WILSON (2006) "Mapping the Journalism–Blogging Relationship", *Journalism* 7(4), pp. 477–500.

MAIER, SCOTT and KASOMA TWANGE (2005) "Information as Good as its Source: an examination of source diversity and accuracy at nine daily U.S. newspapers", paper presented to the Journalism Studies Division at the International Communication Association, New York, May.

MANNING, PAUL (2001) *News and News Sources: a critical introduction*, London: Sage.

MARCHETTI, DOMINIQUE (2005) "Sub-fields of Specialized Journalism", in: Rodney Benson and Erik Neveu (Eds), *Bourdieu and the Journalistic Field*, Cambridge: Polity Press, pp. 64–82.

MCMANUS, JOHN H. (1994) *Market Driven Journalism: let citizen beware?*, Thousand Oaks, CA: Sage.

MCSHANE, STEVEN L. (1995) "Occupational, Gender, and Geographic Representation of Information Sources in US and Canadian Business Magazines", *Journalism & Mass Communication Quarterly* 72(1), pp. 190–204.

MOLOTCH, HARVEY and LESTER, MARILYN (1974) "News as Purposive Behavior: on the strategic use of routine events, accidents, and scandals", *American Sociological Review* 39, pp. 101–12.

MOR, GAL (2006) "2.7 Million Israelis are Browsing Daily", *YNET*, 31 July, http://www.ynet.co.il/ articles/0,7340,L-3284199,00.html (in Hebrew), accessed 30 August 2007.

NIMMO, DAN (1964) *News Gathering in Washington*, New York: Atherton Press.

NIP, JOYCE (2006) "Exploring the Second Phase of Public Journalism", *Journalism Studies* 7(2), pp. 212–36.

OAKHAM, KATRINA MANDY and MURRELL, COLLEEN (2007) "Citizens at the Gate, But Whose News Are They Peddling?", paper presented to the Future of Newspapers Conference, Cardiff, September.

OECD (2007) "Broadband Statistics, Information and Communication Technologies", December, http://www.oecd.org/document/7/0,3343,en_2649_37441_38446855_1_1_1_37441,00.html, accessed 30 August 2007.

ÖRNEBRING, HENRIK (2007) "The Consumer as a Producer—of what? User-generated tabloid content in *The Sun* (UK) and *Aftonbladet* (Sweden)", paper presented to the Future of Newspapers Conference, Cardiff, September.

PLATON, SARA and DEUZE, MARK (2003) "Indymedia Journalism: a radical way of making, selecting and sharing news?", *Journalism* 4(3), pp. 336–55.

REESE, STEPHEN D. (1991) "Setting the Media's Agenda: a power balance perspective" in: James A. Anderson (Ed.), *Communication Yearbook 14*, pp. 309–40.

REESE, STEPHEN D., RUTIGLIANO, LOU, HYUN, KIDEUK and JEONG, JAEKWAN (2007) "Mapping the Blogosphere Professional and Citizen-based Media in the Global News Arena", *Journalism* 8(3), pp. 235–61.

REICH, ZVI (2005) "New Technologies, Old Practices: the conservative revolution in communication between reporters and news sources in the Israeli press", *Journalism & Mass Communication Quarterly* 82(3), pp. 552–70.

REICH, ZVI (2006) "The Process Model of News Initiative: sources lead first, reporters thereafter", *Journalism Studies* 7(4), pp. 497–514.

REICH, ZVI (forthcoming) *Sourcing the News*, Cresskill, NJ: Hampton Press.

ROSEN, JAY (2005) "Bloggers Versus Journalists Is Over", Pressthink, 21 January, http://journalism.nyu.edu/pubzone/weblogs/pressthink/2005/01/21/berk_essy.html, accessed 30 August 2007.

ROSHCO, BERNARD (1975) *Newsmaking*, Chicago: University of Chicago Press.

RYFE, DAVID and MENSING, DONICA (2007) "Doing Journalism Together: experiments in collaborative newsgathering", paper presented to the Future of Newspapers Conference, Cardiff, September.

SCHAFFER, JAN (2007) "Citizen Media: fad or the future of news?", Knight Citizen News Network, http://www.kcnn.org/research/citizen_media_report, accessed 30 August 2007.

SCHLESINGER, PHILIP (1990) "Rethinking the Sociology of Journalism", in: Marjorie Ferguson (Ed.), *Public Communication: the new imperatives*, London: Sage, pp. 61–83.

SIGAL, LEON V. (1973) *Reporters and Officials*, Lexington, MA: D. C. Heath.

SIGAL, LEON V. (1986) "Sources Make the News", in: Robert K. Manoff and Michael Schudson (Eds), *Reading the News*, New York: Pantheon, pp. 9–37.

STRÖMBÄCK, JESPER J. and NORD, LARS W. (2005) "Who Leads the Tango? A study of the relationship between Swedish journalists and their political sources", paper presented to the Political Communication Division International Communication Association, New York, May.

THE STATE OF THE NEWS MEDIA (2007) "Citizen Media", Project for Excellence in Journalism, http://www.stateofthemedia.org/2007/narrative_online_citizen_media.asp?cat=8&media=4, accessed 30 August 2007.

TSFATI, YARIV and LIVIO, OREN (2003) "Israeli Journalists Flunk the Israeli Media", *The Seventh Eye* 43, pp. 4–9 (in Hebrew), March, http://www.idi.org.il/english/download.asp?id=65, accessed 26 June 2008.

TUCHMAN, GAYE (1978) *Making News*, New York: Free Press.

UGILLE, PIETER and PAULUSSEN, STEVE (2007) "Moderation, Conversation and Collaboration? Organisational implications of citizen journalism projects in professional newsrooms", paper presented to the Future of Newspapers Conference, Cardiff, September.

UNDERWOOD, DOUG (1993) *When MBA's Rule the Newsroom*, New York: Columbia University Press.

WALL, MELISSA (2005) "'Blogs of War': weblogs as news", *Journalism* 6(2), pp. 153–72.

ZELIZER, BARBIE (1990) "Where Is the Author in American TV News?", *Semiotica* 80, pp. 37–48.

Chapter 9

DELIBERATIVENESS OF ONLINE POLITICAL DISCUSSION
A content analysis of the *Guangzhou Daily* website

Xiang Zhou, Yuen-Ying Chan, and **Zhen-Mei Peng**

Introduction

The expressive potential of citizens has been transformed with the development and spread of the Internet. Although citizen participation in online political discussion has become an important research field with regard to how the Internet affects Chinese society, much less is known about its communicative processes and implications in China, which now boasts 16.2 million Internet users as of June 2007 (CNNIC, 2007). Few studies have specifically examined the utilization of interactive functions, such as online discussion forums, by traditional media to facilitate online discussion of civil issues in terms of the quality of public deliberation.

The current study aims to fill that gap by analyzing the content of posts in interactive public affairs forums on Dayoo.com, a website affiliated with the *Guangzhou Daily*,[1] utilizing the theoretical framework of the public sphere. This study has significance for the debate about the potential of information and communication technologies (ICT) for democracy as well as the social conditions surrounding ICT use. In the battle between technological liberation and censorship, other social changes in China such as the incipient yet dynamic trends of civil society raise hopes for a more democratic society (He, 1997; Yang, 2003).

Newspaper-affiliated websites are commonly established for online news reporting. Yet they can be also used as a sphere for citizens to discuss public affairs, in that they provide users with interactive services such as chat rooms, online forums, and blogs to exchange information or express opinions, which can encourage interaction among citizens (Cao, 2005; Yan, 2000; Yu and Wu, 2007). The study of Zhan and Zhu (2005) found that about 61 percent of 45 websites associated with newspapers in China have online forums or chat rooms.

The website Dayoo.com was co-founded by the *Guangzhou Daily* and Guangzhou Press Publishing Company in December 1999. It has developed as a portal site mixed with features such as news reporting, e-commerce, fashion and entertainment, and virtual communities. Virtual communities on the website include various interactive functions such as online forums, chat rooms, newsgroups, digital magazines and blogs, in which people can freely communicate with each other.

The online forum on the website, Dayoo Forum, includes 23 sections, covering public affairs, health care, feelings and emotions, traveling, and so on. In addition to citizen-based sections for civic participation, the forum also hosts polls and public debates to catch public opinions on controversial issues. According to the instructions provided on the website, Web users are not required to register first before taking part in the forum. Users with no accounts can write follow-up posts as guests. Yet they cannot originate a post.

Despite the importance of interactive functions for civic engagement, Chinese scholars interested in Chinese newspaper websites are overwhelmingly concerned with the development and current status of these websites in terms of business operations or journalistic practices (e.g. Yu and Wu, 2007). Though some of them touch upon the issues of interactive functions (e.g. Cao, 2004; Yan, 2000; Yu and Wu, 2007; Zhan and Zhu, 2005), no systematic studies have been found to examine how these websites facilitate interaction among citizens in terms of political discussion. Therefore, the current study particularly examined three citizen-based sections of the Dayoo Forum regarding issues of public affairs to explore the potential and limitations of the Internet in fostering civic engagement.

Political Discussion and Civic Participation

The widespread adoption of the Internet has triggered utopian predictions about its democratic potential in terms of creating unprecedented opportunities for public discourse and political engagement. Optimists believe that the Internet provides a sphere for political expression, and that political discussion raises awareness about collective problems, highlights opportunities for involvement, and thereby promotes civic participation (Dahlberg, 2001; Kwak et al., 2005), and thus new forms of "teledemocracy" (Arterton, 1987; Becker and Slaton, 2000).

However, views about future prospects and more particularly the capacities of Internet-based communication to foster political discussion and heighten engagement vary widely. Dahlberg (2001), for instance, identifies three camps: the communitarian camp, which promotes the potential of the Internet to promote shared values and community spirit; the liberal individualist camp, which makes much of the role of the Internet in facilitating the expression of individual interests; and the deliberative camp, which holds that the Internet is an expansion of the public sphere based on rational-critical discourse.

Regardless of their relative optimism or pessimism, most theorists and researchers share the fundamental notion that discussion among citizens is the foundation of sound public life, contributing to better-informed opinions and fostering civic engagement. Some scholars assume that individuals who discuss politics frequently are exposed to a wider range of political perspectives, and this exposure increases their interest in politics, the quality of their opinions, and their social tolerance (Mutz, 2002).

Brezovšek (1995) identifies four basic criteria for participation: (1) individuals are included; (2) it is voluntary; (3) it refers to a specific activity, which is (4) directed towards influencing the government or authorities in general. Therefore, participation essentially is the process through which private citizens communicate their political interest and willingness to be engaged in political information, thus affecting decision making within various spheres of social life (Oblak, 2003). Citizen participation is seen not only as the most fundamental building block of democracy (Barber, 1984; Habermas, 1989) but also as a vital process to make a better citizenry (Gastil, 2000).

Regarding the prospect and reality of online political participation, enthusiasts, who eagerly promote the societal benefits of computer networking often point to the unique features of new ICTs: affordability, easy access to information, interactivity, and decentralization (Negroponte, 1998). The potential of ICTs to enable the formation of a virtual meeting place and enhance citizen networking and participation in political affairs is seen as a catalyst of a more direct "electronic democracy" (Barber, 1984). Given the growing prevalence of virtual association, deliberative democracy based on notions of the public sphere (Dahlberg, 2001; Habermas, 1989; Papacharissi, 2002) and deliberation (Chambers, 2003; Coleman and Gøtze, 2001) have gained considerable prominence.

The Public Sphere and Deliberative Democracy

Developing as a space between the private sphere and the state sphere, the public sphere, as described by Habermas (1989), is "a realm of our social life," in which individuals come together as a "public" to discuss and comment on political issues and something approaching public opinion can be formed. The concept of the public sphere remains today as a useful analytical tool to explore civil society and democracy. With the development and penetration of the Internet, a network characterized by equality and openness, observers have seen new potential to revive the public sphere (Chen, 1999), for its ability to provide an interactive function to foster true dialogue and deliberation, which are the cornerstones of a well-functioning public sphere (Brants, 2005).

To become a public sphere, a space should be a private realm, in which equal and unfettered participation, the quality of discourse and the quantity of participants are prerequisites (Grbeša, 2003). The former dimension represents the central norm of public deliberation, determining what kinds of public opinions will be formed and how well the public is informed. Deliberativeness, to a great degree reflected in reasoned argument, "involves recognizing, incorporating, and rebutting the arguments of others—dialogue and mutual respect—as well as justifying one's own" (Ferree et al., 2002, p. 222). Meanwhile, the number of participants is equally important, in that "the more people participate as citizens in politics, the closer one comes to the ideal of a public sphere" (Schudson, 1992, p. 147, as cited in Grbeša, 2003).

The concept of public sphere always goes with the idea of deliberative democracy. Theories of deliberative democracy emphasize differences of opinions and participants:

"Dialogue and difference are central to the deliberative model" (Dahlberg, 2001, p. 616). A process of rational-critical discourse is also needed to transform privately oriented individuals to publicly-oriented citizens. Additionally, participants in discussion are addressed as equal, so that they can build mutual respect and concern by debate (Christiano, 1997, as cited in Grbeša, 2003). In a successful deliberative model, arguments can be expounded so as to help other citizens to understand them, accept them and respond to them freely with their own words (Bohman, 1996, as cited in Grbeša, 2003).

The rapid development of the Internet has generated concerns about the online public sphere and e-democracy among scholars. Two major camps—optimists and skeptics—debate whether the Internet would revive or expand the public sphere. Optimists believe that the Internet provides a perfect place to encourage different points of view and disagreements that are critical to public deliberation (Weber and Murray, 2004). The Internet helps to build a new kind of distributive rather than unified public sphere. On the other hand, skeptics are cautious about equating the virtual sphere to a public sphere. Oblak (2003) warns that informed, interested, and technically literate citizens as well as accessible, simple, and interactive technologies are more assumptions than realities.

Scholars in China hold an optimistic view about the Internet, hoping that an online public sphere could emerge from the open access to the Internet. Analyzing the *Shen Hongjia* event[2] as an example suggesting an emerging online public sphere in China, Xu (2002) expects a great opportunity for the development of democracy facilitated by the Internet.

Partly due to the lack of empirical evidence, the potential of the Internet to promote an online public sphere remains unknown in China. Scholars in China's political communication must pay close attention to particular patterns of Internet use, especially those encouraging political dialogue, to understand how new technologies exist alongside traditional modes of gaining information and expressing opinions. For instance, Leib is particularly concerned with the quality of political participation in China by differentiating mass participation from deliberative participation and the necessity of identifying "what sorts of participation could truly be held to be or designed to be deliberative" (2005, p. 6). This is particularly meaningful considering most scholarly discussions focus on the participatory and democratic potential of the Internet instead of whether political participation online qualifies as deliberative in any real or useful way.

Research Queries

With these concerns in mind, the researchers conducted a content analysis of the discussion forum on the *Guangzhou Daily* website, to examine the quantity and quality of online discussion, as well as the existence of criticism of government officials and policies, if any, to learn whether group discussion indeed improves the quality of public opinion, and to explore to what extent a public sphere might be expected to emerge on the Internet in China in terms of the deliberativeness of online discussion. This study addresses the following queries to clarify the degree to which political discussion migrating to new communication networks in China displays or approximates any of the characteristics of deliberation.

The first concern is the issue of the quantity of posts and participants. The second query is related to topicality, the content of the dialogue or the topics that are discussed, which is one of the key characteristics of the political public sphere. The researchers argue that the notion of diversity of ideas is critical to an understanding of deliberation, because varying and conflicting views ought to be made available for public consideration. Therefore, the researchers look at how the topics discussed in the forum, especially those with meaningful political importance, would be distributed, whether the patterns of topic distributions would change over time, and to what extent participants would criticize government policies or government officials.

The third query is related to the critical-rational dimension of posts, that is, the rationality of argument and/or discussion. Rationality is a key measure of deliberativeness, which is assessed in light of Habermas' (1984) distinction among the semantic content of these expressions, their conditions of validity and the reasons for the truth of statements. In this study, rationality is defined in terms of three elements, justification, complexity, and civility. Justification, a most basic element of deliberativeness, is operationalized as the supply of reasons in defense of a certain proposition, that is, whether arguments supportive of posters' ideas or opinions would be provided. In the absence of reasons, it is unlikely that claims will be adjudicated. Complexity is defined in this study as the presence of an idea that incorporates different or opposing ideas. The challenge in public deliberation consists precisely in converting conflict into debate, into argumentatively processed dissent. The element in this study is taken as a measure of the co-presence of different or opposite ideas in a given post and different ways to express a given idea. The conversion of conflict into argumentative debate is dependent upon a degree of civility in the dispute, which is coupled with the central norm of deliberativeness. Civility is thus operationalized, following the definition of Ferree et al. (2002, p. 239), as the absence of "hot button" language, words that are likely to outrage opponents, or the avoidance of inflammatory speech and personal attacks.

The last research interest of this study is the interaction between participants, responsiveness (or mutual responsiveness) and/or reciprocal acts occurring in discussion in which participants articulate their interests through "talking," sharing ideas and negotiating differences. As suggested in the literature review, political messages of substance should be processed interactively, with opinions being tested against disagreement, which is one of the conditions that make deliberation possible (Ferree et al., 2002; Fiskin, 1992). Participants in democratic deliberation validate their ideas against those of their peers in the public sphere (Elshtain, 1982). This can be measured by looking at rebuttals, defined as ideas that "refer to and argue against ideas that they oppose" (Ferree et al., 2002, p. 241) and the degree of consensus in discussion. Concerning the outcome of public deliberation, the discursive tradition favors the closure of public deliberation only after a consensus has been achieved—or at least "a working consensus—enough of an agreement on the general direction of public policy" (Ferree et al., 2002, p. 221).

Methodology

This study used the quantitative content analysis method to analyze posts on the Dayoo Forum of the *Guangzhou Daily* website, Dayoo.com. The forum includes five sections related to public affairs, *Minsheng Huati* [Topics on People's Livelihood], *Yueyu Qunluo* [Cantonese Communities], *Dushi Zaixian* [Online Cities], *Zhujiang Liaowang* [Overlooking Pearl River], and *Xinwen Shequ* [News Community]. The first three were all established in late 2001, and the other two were launched in 2006. Only the first three sections were examined in this study with a time frame from January 2002 to December 2006.

During the five-year period, 79,492 sets of entries with follow-up posts, if any, were found in the three sections. A sample of 380 sets of posts was drawn from the total sets using the method of systematic sampling stratified by sections with 95 percent confidence level and ±5 percent confidence interval.

The unit of analysis was a set of posts with an initial entry and its follow-up postings, if any, sharing the same topic on one single Web page. Initial entries and their first and second follow-up posts were separately coded for categorical variables. The number of total follow-up posts was counted. The subtotal numbers of follow-up posts with certain attributes in each unit of analysis, such as the number of follow-up posts with supportive arguments, the number of follow-up posts with opinions unfavorable to the government or criticism of officials, and so on, were also separately counted.

A coding frame was developed with a focus on the deliberativeness of online discussion. Subject matters of discussion were divided into eight groups, such as policies and institutions, public figures, China's diplomacy and international affairs, economic development, administrative districts, culture and life (including education and sports), social and environmental problems, and others.

A series of questions were developed to examine how deliberative discussions were in the three sections of the Dayoo Forum. (1) Did a given participant pose any argument(s) to support his/her viewpoints? (2) Did a given participant mention or propose any different or opposite idea(s) in one single post? (3) Did a given post include any opinion(s) unfavorable to government policies or any criticism of officials? (4) Did a given participant use any "hot button" words in posts? (5) Did he/she explain his/her viewpoints with different expressions? These questions were addressed for each entry and its first two follow-up posts, if any. If there were more than two follow-up posts, the numbers of posts with certain attributes addressed in the questions above were separately counted.

For follow-up posts, the researchers additionally examined the issues of responsiveness and consensus by asking questions from a variety of aspects, such as the attitudes expressed in follow-up posts towards the views or opinions proposed in a given entry, whether the views or opinions proposed in the follow-up posts were consistent with those in the entry, and whether the information provided in the follow-up posts were consistent with those in the entry.

In order to establish intercoder reliability figures, two coders were trained to code 26 percent of postings randomly drawn from the posts other than the sample. The Scott's *pi* coefficients for the main variables mentioned above ranged from 0.70 to 1.00, beyond the generally accepted level.

Findings

The Quantity of Posts and Participants

Descriptive statistics suggested that the distribution of the quantity of posts was heavily skewed with a median, 2, and an average number of follow-up posts, 6.08 (SD = 14.396) in each single unit of analysis. About 11 percent of sample entries (42 of 380) had an extremely large number of follow-up posts ranging from 14 to 159. Nearly 31 percent (116 of 380) had no responses, together with 35.5 percent of entries with one to three follow-up posts, and 15 percent with four to seven follow-up posts, accounting for the majority of entries. A chi-square test suggested that the distribution patterns of follow-up posts changed over the years, with a trend that the number of follow-up posts increased with time ($\chi^2 = 49.078$, df $= 16$, $p < 0.0001$). The majority of samples from 2002 had no follow-up posts (47.8 percent, 44 of 92), or only one to three follow-up posts (40.2 percent, 37 of 92). The percentage of entries with no follow-up posts decreased to 16 percent (13 of 81) in 2005 and 20.3 percent (15 of 74) in 2006. In contrast, the percentage of entries with an extremely large number of follow-up posts increased from 1.1 percent (1 of 92) in 2002 to 18.5 percent (15 of 81) in 2005 and 18.9 percent (14 of 74) in 2006.

On average, there were about five participants (SD $= 8.822$) in each single unit of analysis. The majority of post sets (43.2 percent, 164 of 380) had two to five different writers. Nearly 11 percent (41 of 380) had an extremely large number of participants ranging from 11 to 85.

Topicality and Criticism of Government and Officials

Overall, topics discussed in the forum on the website Dayoo.com were quite unevenly distributed. The most frequently discussed topic was culture and life (including education and sports), which accounted for 34.2 percent in total (130 of 380 entries), followed by social and environmental problems, 15 percent (57 of 380), and economic development, 11.1 percent (42 of 380). These three assumed prominence over the other specified topics, such as policies and institutions, China's diplomacy and international affairs, public figures, and administrative districts, respectively accounting for 8.9 percent (34 of 380), 8.7 percent (33), 5.5 percent (21), and 0.5 percent (2).[3] A chi-square test confirmed that these topics with meaningful political nature were discussed less often than culture and life issues, but more often than economic development and social and environmental problems ($\chi^2 = 63.868$, df $= 4$, $p < 0.0001$).

The extent to which participants presented unfavorable opinions about government policies or criticism of officials was limited. Posts without such critical opinions dominated discussions and accounted for 88.9 percent of all sets of entries with follow-up posts (338 of 380). There was only an average 4.77 percent of posts in one single unit of analysis presenting such opinions or criticism. Only 7.6 percent of the total sample entries (29 of 380) presented opinions unfavorable to government policies or criticism of officials. The percentage of posts with such opinions or criticism was 0.8 percent (2 of 264) for the first follow-up posts and 0.5 percent (1 of 202) for the second follow-up posts.

Rationality of Argument and Discussion

In this study, rationality was measured in terms of justification, complexity and civility. Justification was examined by looking at whether participants presented their viewpoints with supportive arguments. In one single unit of analysis including an entry and follow-up posts, if any, there were about three posts on average (mean $= 2.923$, SD $= 6.451$) presenting viewpoints with supportive arguments. The percentage of entries with supportive arguments was 70.3 percent (267 of 380).

To address the issue of complexity, the researchers specifically looked at the extent to which participants incorporated different or opposing ideas into a given post, and whether they used different ways to express a given idea. Entries without any different or opposing ideas accounted for 68.7 percent (261 of 380); 22.6 percent (86 of 380) of entries mentioned opposing ideas with arguments, and 8.7 percent (33 of 380) mentioned opposing ideas without any arguments. In terms of expression forms, entries expressing a given idea in different ways, accounting for 53.4 percent (203 of 380), were slightly more commonplace than those which did not use any different expressions in one single post (46.6 percent, 177 of 380). In addition, complexity was significantly associated with justification. Compared to those not providing supportive arguments, participants who provided supportive arguments in their entries were more likely to incorporate different or opposing ideas into discussion ($\chi^2 = 54.069$, df $= 1$, $p < 0.0001$; 4.4 percent versus 42.7 percent), and more likely to express their ideas in different ways ($\chi^2 = 155.158$, df $= 1$, $p < 0.0001$; 4.4 percent versus 74.2 percent).

To assess the civility of discussion, another element to measure the rationality of argument and/or discussion, researchers looked to establish whether any "hot button" words were used; 85 percent (323 of 380) of all units of analysis did not mention these kinds of words. In each unit of analysis, 4.12 percent of posts on average used "hot button" language. By using bad personal remarks, some participants poured scorn on other discussants or certain social phenomena. For instance, they used words such as bitch (*biaozi*), booby (*shazi*), "*zougou*" (referring to people who help powerful figures to do something bad) etc., to humiliate other participants who they thought to be mindless or unable to make sense of their opinions, or those who disagreed with them.

Responsiveness and Homogeneity of Discussion

Scholars promoting deliberative democracy believe that one does not have true public opinion without the back-and-forth of disagreement and discussion (Fiskin, 1991, 1995). Furthermore, the concept of public sphere presumes the homogeneity of participants and a potential to reach consensus (Grbeša, 2003), with the main purpose of reaching a common understanding among citizens, so that it can serve as a guideline for political decisions (Ferree et al., 2002). Therefore, this study paid attention to interaction between participants, particularly how posters incorporated others' ideas or responded to other participants, how follow-up posts responded to a given entry and whether a certain degree of in-group homogeneity was reached in terms of generalizing social phenomena and the degree of agreement on discussed issues among participants.

It was found that 64.7 percent of the 380 examined units of posts did not have one single post directly addressing or discussing other participants or posts. In each set of posts, 13.5 percent of posts on average included such information. The average number of this type of post in each unit of analysis was less than two posts (mean $= 1.871$, SD $= 7.18$), which was a little more than posts with references to the words, perspectives and/or viewpoints of participants (mean $= 1.179$, SD $= 4.532$), accounting for 8.27 percent of posts on average in each unit of analysis. Most sets of posts (73.9 percent, 281 of 380) did not have one single post referring to the words, perspectives and/or viewpoints of other participants. In addition, an overwhelming majority of post sets (97.6 percent, 371 of 380) did not mention other participants' emotions or describe others' emotional expressions. All these suggested that participants tended not to incorporate or relate themselves to others' viewpoints and/or emotions in general.

As to how posters looked upon social phenomena, more than half (55.3 percent, 210 of 380) of all sample units contained posters' commentary on social phenomena, with a percentage of 32.53 on average. Specifically, 14.75 percent of these posts emphasized the homogeneity of society only, followed by those addressing both the homogeneity and diversity of social phenomena, and those stressing the diversity side only, respectively accounting for 12.13 and 3.22 percent on average.

Among the 264 units of analysis with at least one follow-up post, 71.2 percent (188 units) did not present one single post against the viewpoints or ideas of a given entry. The average number of follow-up posts in opposition to a given entry in one single set of posts was about one post (mean $= 0.939$, SD $= 3.215$), and the average percentage was 12.54. Follow-up posts tended to be consensus with a given entry; 49.2 percent of all sets with follow-up posts (130 of 264) had at least one post presenting agreement to a given entry. The average number of these kinds of follow-up posts with an average percentage of 17.66 in one unit of analysis was about two posts (mean $= 1.705$, SD $= 5.939$).

Discussion and Conclusion

The current study was conducted with a particular interest in examining and analysing the extent to which newspaper-affiliated websites might help foster an online public sphere. Our content analysis of the discussion forum on the *Guangzhou Daily* website offers a mixed and richly layered picture concerning the deliberativeness of online discussion in China.

Citizens seemed to become more and more active in online discussion in terms of the increasing quantity of posts and participants over the five-year period, although the average number of follow-up posts and participants generated by an entry was not large enough to claim that there was a large-scale group participating given the rapidly growing number of Internet users in China's major cities. Evidence of the diversity of topics discussed in the Dayoo Forum was established to some degree, although the topic of culture and life dominated online discussion. However, considering that topics with a meaningful political nature accounted for only a small percentage, the researchers are not able to argue that the online space on the *Guangzhou Daily* website is mature enough to be a public platform for discussing political issues and public affairs.

Rationality of argument, justification and civility were evidenced by the fact that a large percentage of participants could provide supportive arguments for their opinions and/or views. "Hot button" language was rare in discussion. However, the level of complexity, another element to evaluate the quality of dialogue, was relatively low, since most posters did not incorporate opposing ideas or others' views in their ongoing quest for information and conversation. A majority of posters did not directly respond to others' viewpoints. Furthermore, participants' exposure to disagreement in discussion was limited in the sense that writers of follow-up posts tended to be more likely to present agreement with a given entry instead of proposing opposing ideas or viewpoints.

According to the theory of deliberative democracy, a critical dimension of opinion quality is the understanding of arguments on various sides of issues. Exposure to disagreement in particular has many of the putative benefits. Arguments for and against force people to consider and defend their views and foster understanding of multiple points of view—namely the "consideredness" of one's opinion, not only in the sense of having developed a viewpoint anchored in argument, but also in the sense of having seriously considered other opposing views (Gutmann and Thompson, 1996). In this sense, discussions in the Dayoo Forum are not very deliberative. At the very least, there is insufficient evidence to support the view that a representative picture of the political public sphere is shown in the forum. Instead, we might be more comfortable in taking the sphere as an incipient one.

Considering the strong correlations between socio-economic status and ownership rates of basic and advanced telecommunications services, including computers (see the semiannual reports released by CNNIC), we may hold that inequalities from outside online discourse—by formal or informal restriction to access—can seriously influence the diversity of groups participating in political forums and the content of their messages. A survey would be helpful to identify people who are unable or unwilling to engage in these sorts of discursive practices.

In summary, the public sphere will not be extended merely through the diffusion and application of new technologies. As Barber notes, there must be "a will toward a more participatory and robust civic society" (1998, p. 263). The beginning of such a will may be seen in Chinese online discussion forums. Yet, more effort is needed from both inside and outside forums. From inside, discussion participants must be drawn into a higher level of rational-critical discourse. From outside, it is necessary to promote universal use of new technologies and push for protection and finance of online discursive spaces.

NOTES

1. The *Guangzhou Daily* is a paper organ of the Municipal Communist Party of Guangzhou, the capital city of Guangdong province. It is also the best-seller among all the organs of the Chinese Communist Party. In 1996, the Guangzhou Daily Group was established as the first press group in China. Guangdong, a province in Southern China, has consistently stood in the forefront in most indicators of modern telecommunications and Internet development in China.

2. In March 1998, Shen Hongjia, a college faculty member, wrote a letter to the *Southern Weekend* to complain about the services of the Shangdong Administration of Post and Telecommunication and the Jinan Telecommunication Bureau. The publication of the letter led to a large-scale public debate on China Telecom. However, soon after the intervention from the top administration, newspapers had to stop the debate, and the debate moved to online discussion forums in China. The heated online discussion turned out to be a focal point of coverage on the CCTV, which had pushed forward the reforms of China Telecom.

3. There were 61 entries, 16.1 percent of the total, with a topic other than the ones above.

REFERENCES

ARTERTON, CHRISTOPHER (1987) *Teledemocracy: can technology protect democracy?*, Newbury Park, CA: Sage.

BARBER, BENJAMIN (1984) *Strong Democracy: participatory politics for a new age*, Berkeley: University of California Press.

BARBER, B. (1998) *Strong Democracy: participatory politics for a new age*, Berkeley: University of California Press.

BECKER, TED and SLATON, CHRISTA DARYL (2000) *The Future of Teledemocracy*, Westport, CT: Praeger.

BOHMAN, JAMES (1996) *Public Deliberation: pluralism, complexity and democracy*, Cambridge, MA: MIT Press.

BRANTS, KEES (2005) "Guest Editor's Introduction: the Internet and the public sphere", *Political Communication* 22, pp. 143–6.

BREZOVŠEK, MARJAN (1995) "Political Participation", *Teorija in Praksa* 17(3/4), pp. 199–211.

CAO, XIAO-YING (2005) "Woguo Chuantong Meiti Wangzhan de Shengcun Fazhan Zhuankuang Jiqi Duice [The Existence and Development Strategies of Traditional Media Websites in China]", *Science Mosaic* 7, pp. 109–11.

CHAMBERS, SIMONE (2003) "Deliberative Democratic Theory", *Annual Review of Political Science* 6, pp. 307–26.

CHEN, JIE (1999) "BBS: Zhongguo Gonggong Lingyu de Shuguang [BBS: The Dawn of China's Public Sphere]", *China Youth Study* 5, pp. 52–4.

CHRISTIANO, THOMAS (1997) "The Significance of Public Deliberation", in: James Bohman and William Rehg (Eds), *Deliberative Democracy: essays on reason and politics*, Cambridge, MA: MIT Press, pp. 213–77.

CNNIC (2007) "Semiannual Survey Report on the Development of China's Internet", http://www.cnnic.net.cn/, accessed 23 July 2007.

COLEMAN, STEPHEN and GØTZE, JOHN (2001) *Bowling Together: online public engagement in policy deliberation*, London: Hansard Society.

DAHLBERG, LINCOLN (2001) "Democracy via Cyberspace: mapping the rhetorics and practices of three prominent camps", *New Media and Society* 3(2), pp. 157–77.

ELSHTAIN, JEANBETHKE (1982) "Democracy and the QUBE Tube", *The Nation* 234, pp. 108–10.

FERREE, MYRA MARX, GAMSON, WILLIAM ANTHONY, GERHARDS, JURGEN and RUCHT, DIETER (2002) *Shaping Abortion Discourse: democracy and the public sphere in Germany and the United States*, Cambridge: Cambridge University Press.

FISKIN, JAMES (1991) *Democracy and Deliberation: new directions for democratic reform*, New Haven, CT: Yale University Press.

FISKIN, JAMES (1992) "Beyond Teledemocracy: America on the line", *The Responsive Community* 2, pp. 13–19.

FISKIN, JAMES (1995) *The Voice of the People: public opinion and democracy*, New Haven, CT: Yale University Press.

GASTIL, JOHN (2000) *By Popular Demand: revitalizing representative democracy through deliberative elections*, Berkeley: University of California Press.

GRBEŠA, MARUANA (2003) "Why If at All Is the Public Sphere a Useful Concept?", *Politicka Misao* 6(5), pp. 110–21.

GUTMANN, AMY and THOMPSON, DENNIS (1996) *Democracy and Disagreement*, Cambridge, MA: Belknap Press.

HABERMAS, JÜRGEN (1984 [1981]) *The Theory of Communicative Action, Vol. 1, Reason and the rationalization of society*, Thomas McCarthy (Trans.), Boston, MA: Beacon Press.

HABERMAS, JÜRGEN (1989) *The Structural Transformation of the Public Sphere: an inquiry into a category of bourgeois society*, Thomas Burger (Trans.), Cambridge, MA: MIT Press.

HE, BAO-GANG (1997) *The Democratic Implications of Civil Society in China*, London: Macmillan Press.

KWAK, NOJIN, WILLIAMS, ANN, WANG, XIAO-RU and LEE, HOON (2005) "Talking Politics and Engaging Politics: an examination of the interactive relationships between structural features of political talk and discussion engagement", *Communication Research* 32, pp. 87–111.

LEIB, ETHAN (2005) "The Chinese Communist Party and Deliberative Democracy", *Journal of Public Deliberation* 1, pp. 1–7.

MUTZ, DIANA (2002) "Cross-cutting Social Networks: testing democratic theory in practice", *American Political Science Review* 96(1), pp. 111–26.

NEGROPONTE, NICHOLAS (1998) "Beyond Digital', *Wired* 6, pp. 288.

OBLAK, TANJA (2003) "Boundaries of Interactive Public Engagement: political institutions and citizens in new political platforms", *Journal of Computer-mediated Communication* 8(3), http://jcmc.indiana.edu/vol8/issue3/oblak.html, accessed 16 March 2007.

PAPACHARISSI, ZIZI (2002) "The Virtual Sphere: the Internet as a public sphere", *New Media & Society* 4, pp. 9–27.

SCHUDSON, MICHAEL (1992) Was There Ever a Public Sphere? If so, when? Reflections on the American case, in: Calhoun Craig (Ed.), *Habermas and the Public Sphere*, Cambridge, MA: MIT Press, pp. 143–63.

WEBER, LORI and MURRAY, SEAN (2004) "Interactivity, Equality, and the Prospects for Electronic Democracy: a review", in: Peter M. Shane (Ed.), *Introduction: The prospects for electronic democracy*, New York: Routledge.

XU, YING (2002) "Hulianwang, Gonggong Lingyu yu Shenghuo Zhengzhi" ("The Internet, the Public Sphere and Living Politics"), *Humanities Magazine* 2, pp. 141–46.

YAN, SAN-JIU (2000) "Dangqian Woguo Shangwang Baozhi Wenti Tanxi [An Exploratory Analysis of the Problems of Current Chinese Online Newspapers]", *Editor's Friends* 6, pp. 2–4.

YANG, GUO-BIN (2003) "The Internet and the Rise of a Transnational Chinese Cultural Sphere", Media, *Culture & Society* 25, pp. 469–90.

YU, GOU-MING and WU, WEN-XI (2007) "Shuzi Baoye: Cong Wangluoban de Jingying Zuoqi [Digital Press: start with the management of electronic editions]", *News and Writing* 2, pp. 11–13.

ZHAN, ZHENG-MAO and ZHU, FU-RONG (2005) "Woguo Baoye Jituan Wangzhan Neirong he Gongneng Sheji de Xiangzhuang yu Wenti [The Status Quo and Problems of Newspaper Websites in the Design of Content and Functions in China]", *News and Writing* 10, pp. 12–13, 29.

Chapter 10

THE CONSUMER AS PRODUCER—OF WHAT?
User-generated tabloid content in *The Sun* (UK) and *Aftonbladet* (Sweden)

Henrik Örnebring

Introduction

The rise of user-generated content (UGC) sites online (e.g. *YouTube, Flickr, Wikipedia*) provides a striking illustration of the oft-suggested blurring of the distinction between (media) producer and (media) consumer. *YouTube, Flickr* and *Wikipedia* are all dedicated UGC sites. However, a significant portion of UGC creation online is "channelled" through traditional media organizations: users are invited to create their own movie trailer, their own blog, their own comedy video, submit their own news etc. under the auspices of an established media organization, most often via the website of that organization. Many newspapers have developed extensive UGC sections on their Web pages. But there is still relatively little discussion of the exact relationship between producing and consuming in these sections. What types of content are being produced? Does the blurring of the producer–consumer represent a real shift in power away from traditional media/news organizations, or is the rise of UGC just a way for newspapers to get content produced "for free"?

This study attempts to provide a tentative answer to these questions by comparing the UGC provision of two online tabloid newspapers, *The Sun* (UK) and *Aftonbladet* (Sweden).

UGC and Online Newspapers

While there have not been any previous studies of UGC in online newspapers, there have been plenty of studies on the wider subject of user influence and interactivity in online newspapers. *Interactivity* in particular has been a major area of study (Boczkowski, 2004a,b; Chung, 2007; Dibean and Garrison, 2001; Massey and Levy, 1999; Schultz, 1999; Singer, 2006). Interactivity is a fragmented and contested concept (Downes and McMillan, 2000; Schultz, 2000). Of particular usefulness to this study are the definitions of Steuer (1992) and Massey and Levy (1999), since their definitions encompass the UGC phenomenon. Steuer's definition focuses on the user's ability to "participate in modifying the form and content of a mediated environment in real time" (Steuer, 1991, p. 84). Specifically relating the concept to news and journalism, Massey and Levy introduce the term *content interactivity* and define it as "the degree to which journalists technologically empower consumers over content" (Massey and Levy, 1999, p. 140).

Massey and Levy's definition places issues of *power* and *control* at the centre of the research agenda. Some observers have pointed out that traditional news organizations have been quite resistant to the idea of ceding powers of selection and accreditation to consumers (for an overview of this argument, see Lasica, 2002; a related argument can be found in Stromer-Galley, 2000), whereas others have found that while some journalists are very resistant to user/customer involvement in the news process, others are keen to embrace methods for further audience involvement and wholly or partly cede their gatekeeping power (Singer, 2006). This study follows this research agenda and asks to what extent users have control over the UGC provision in the studied newspapers, and what types of content it is that they are given the opportunity to create.

Tabloids Online: The Sun and Aftonbladet

The two tabloids studied, *The Sun* (UK) and *Aftonbladet* (Sweden), occupy similar positions in their respective markets: they are both the best selling (i.e. highest circulation) daily newspaper in their region (Hadenius and Weibull, 2003, pp. 73, 86). Both tabloids are also widely considered to be very successful online—*Aftonbladet* is the biggest online newspaper in Sweden in terms of unique visitors (Hadenius and Weibull, 2003, p. 116), and by the same measure *The Sun Online* was the second biggest online newspaper in the United Kingdom at the time of the study, trailing the *Guardian Unlimited* (Stabe, 2007a). The online media landscape changes very rapidly, however, and since this study was conducted, *The Sun Online* has gone through yet another relaunch of their website (the main characteristics and content categories remain very similar to before, however), and their position as "online market leader" among UK tabloids has been overtaken by the *Daily Mail*, whose successful *Mail Online* now has a competing claim to be the second-most read UK newspaper site (Stabe, 2007b).

However, both *The Sun* and *Aftonbladet* are still noted for their online presence and innovation in terms of online content—*The Sun* redesigned its website in 2006 specifically to include more UGC and community features (Leggatt, 2007), and *Aftonbladet* has a long-standing online presence (since 1994) and has continuously developed more features to make it a popular portal site (Bergström, 2005; Hadenius and Weibull, 2003, p. 434). The two tabloids chosen for this comparison thus are both "market leaders" among online newspapers, and are likely to have a number of different UGC features on their Web pages.

There are also important differences between the two tabloids, the most obvious one of course being that they are active in different countries. However, the main reason for comparing these two tabloids is not to highlight *national* difference, but rather differences between *types within the tabloid newspaper category*. As S. Elizabeth Bird has noted, "tabloid" does not mean the same thing in different cultural contexts: in the United States, a "tabloid" is generally a weekly magazine focusing not on news but on bizarre and often blatantly untrue stories about celebrities, UFOs, conspiracies etc. (Bird, 1992). In Europe, "tabloid" generally refers to both a particular newspaper format and a particular type of journalism (described in the opening paragraph of this section)—populist and entertainment oriented, but still mainly focused on news. But even within this category there are differences: *The Sun* represents a more "extreme" type of tabloid, with much more explicitly populist rhetoric and strong entertainment orientation—outside the UK tabloids of this type are prevalent in many Eastern European nations (see the various chapters in Spassov, 2004). Comparatively, *Aftonbladet's* populist rhetoric is more toned down (though still undeniably present), and in some aspects is more similar to "quality newspapers" (for example, *Aftonbladet* carries literary criticism, essays etc., something not present in *The Sun*). These differences between the two tabloids is clearly visible in their general Web page design (see www.aftonbladet.se and www.thesun.co.uk): *Aftonbladet.se* frequently leads with a story that could equally well be the lead story in a quality daily, whereas *The Sun Online* most often leads with stories from the world of entertainment and celebrity culture. It should be noted that both newspapers are unmistakeably tabloid in character, but they are sufficiently different to illustrate the breadth within the overall category of "tabloid newspaper'—and therefore interesting subjects for comparison.

UCG in Online Newspapers: An Analytical Framework

The main research questions of this study are: what kinds of content are users generating, and in what contexts is content generated? I attempt to answer these questions by analysing three aspects of UGC provision in the two chosen online newspapers: the *level of involvement* expected from users, the *types of content* produced, and the overall *mode of production*.

Level of Involvement: Customization Versus Production

Different types of UGC require different levels of involvement from users. Producing your own video and posting it online requires more work than customizing existing content, for example. Alvin Toffler's concepts of *prosumer* and *prosumerism*, and his related distinction between *customization* and *production*, provide a useful theoretical basis for analysing levels of involvement.

In his book *The Third Wave* (1980), Toffler identifies prosumerism as the increased involvement of customers in the production process, typified by the use of customer feedback and direct design request in high-tech industries like computer-aided manufacturing systems (Toffler, 1980, p. 285), and the rise of customization in both goods and services markets. Thus, Toffler's concepts of prosumerism and prosumer have two aspects. The first, "production for use", where consumers produce goods and services for their own personal use; the second, customization and customer involvement in a production process still on the whole controlled and managed by someone else. Customization requires lower levels of involvement than production.

Incidentally, there is a concept closely related to prosumerism that is specific to newspapers: the notion of the "Daily Me", a virtual daily newspaper customized for the individual user, as introduced by Nicholas Negroponte (1995). In the early days of the Internet, the "Daily Me" idea failed to take off, but some news organizations have gradually added various personalization tools to their online sites—and with the arrival of RSS (Really Simple Syndication) and other feed systems, personalization is readily available for the user without having to go through established news organizations.

Customization features would then include the possibility to get news through an *RSS feed* or other type of feed, the opportunity to *grade/mark* various types of content, the opportunity to *directly comment* on different types of content (for example, a comment function in conjunction with an article, or via an email to the article writer), and the opportunity to customize the online interface through some type of *"Daily Me"*-function (e.g. the opportunity to choose what types of news items will be displayed when you log into the Web page). In all these cases, the user is either (1) not generating actual content, but rather commenting on existing content (an action that might then influence the content structure and/or design, which is why I still classify it as a form of UGC), or (2) generating relatively small amounts of content (i.e. brief comments and reviews to go with a mark or grade). This form of UGC creation can therefore be said to be characterized by a lower level of user involvement than the second type, production.

Production refers to the other side of prosumerism: actual production of content which is then consumed by the users. On an online newspaper, this would include different forms of *textual production* (the major possible types being user *blogs* and blog posts, user comments and posts on *forums*, and user-produced *news items and/or features*), *video production* (most commonly in the form of digitally produced short video clips) and *audio production* (like user-generated podcasts).

Types of Content: Information and Entertainment, Public and Private

There are many ways to classify content—for this study, I have chosen some very simple (some would probably say simplistic) distinctions, the first one being the oft-recurring one between information and entertainment, or more specifically, between a *news/information-oriented* context of consumption and production, and a *popular culture-oriented* context of production and consumption. I am of course aware of all the problems inherent in such a distinction, but I would argue that it still serves as a good, if broad, indicator of what kind of content audiences are invited to produce.

That this distinction may still be important is hinted at by Henry Jenkins in his 2006 book *Convergence Culture*:

> Right now, we are learning how to apply these new participatory skills through our relation to commercial entertainment—or, more precisely, right now some groups of early adopters are testing the waters and mapping out directions where many of us are apt to follow. These skills are being applied to popular culture first for two reasons: on the one hand, because the stakes are so low; and on the other, because playing with popular culture is a lot more fun than playing with more serious matters. (Jenkins, 2006, p. 264)

Jenkins rightly points out that most of the phenomena analysed in his book (a lot of them having UGC production as a central feature) are in the sphere of popular culture and oriented towards commercial entertainment. This can be contrasted with the UGC phenomena Benkler (2006) describes, which are all more oriented towards information production and is more related to what we might call traditional, "Habermasian" public sphere-type activities (debate, discussion, information provision, political action etc.). The difference is one of degree rather than absolutes, however: different types of UGC can be more or less popular culture-oriented or news/information-oriented than other types, and some types can incorporate both popular culture and news/informational elements, but for the most part, one context of consumption and production will dominate.

Also note that I am not in this study trying to suggest that news/informational content is intrinsically more "valuable" or "better" than popular culture-oriented content—but I do suggest that it may be of interest to know whether online newspaper UGC provision is mainly oriented towards one or the other. This in particular because of the rhetoric that often surrounds UGC and interactive features in online news, i.e. that they "empower" users, "allow users more control over the news", and such (see for example Chung, 2007, p. 52f). This "empowerment" is frequently implicitly linked to news/informational content, so it would be of interest to find out to what extent online newspaper UGC features give users direct influence over the newsgathering, news selection and news presentation process. Are online newspaper users invited to generate their own, traditional "hard news", or are they primarily engaged in generating other types of content?

I also propose a further simple distinction. News/informational content and popular culture content have one thing in common—both content types are based on events and persons in the *public* domain. But many forms of UGC production are not concerned with documenting or commenting on the public domain, but rather on the personal or *private* domain (videos and pictures of family members, blogs used as diaries documenting everyday life etc.). Needless to say, this distinction is also problematic, but for the purposes of this study I have considered UGC that primarily deals with the private and everyday lives of users as distinct from content based on public persons, events and phenomena. Private citizens commenting on public phenomena (be they celebrities or political initiatives) have been considered to be essentially public and either informational or entertainment-oriented, whereas private citizens commenting on their own private lives without much attempt to connect it to a wider public sphere (broadly defined) has been considered to be exactly that: part of a *personal and everyday life-oriented* context of production and consumption.

Mode of Production: Centralized or Decentralized

Benkler (2006) points to the success of the technology news site *slashdot.org* as a prime example of how work previously done almost solely in centralized news organizations can be done just as well or even better using decentralized, collaborative models of peer-production. A similar site, also focusing on science and technology news, is *digg.com*, according to some a serious competitor to *slashdot* (Andrews, 2005; the following presentation is based on Benkler, 2006, p. 76ff; Leonard, 1998; Poor, 2005).

Slashdot and *Digg* assign *relevance* (i.e. a judgement about whether a particular item of information is of relevance to its audience or not) and *accreditation* (i.e. producing news according to a set of practices that make the news trustworthy) to news items in a decentralized fashion: a user submits a news item that is then graded (both in terms of relevance and trustworthiness) by other users. There are also various systems in place to avoid abuse: for example, you need to be registered for a certain time before you can grade or comment. The system is designed for distributed, decentralized peer-production: rather than giving a few people a lot of power to assign relevance and accreditation to an item (like editors on a newspaper), it gives many users a little power to assign relevance and accreditation.

While we might not reasonably respect to find any large-scale participation of audiences in the newsgathering process on *The Sun Online* or *Aftonbladet.se*, systems where users collaboratively grade, rank and/or comment on online content, either through simple voting or through technologies like "tagging" (as used by *Slashdot*, *Digg*, and blog portal *Technorati.com*, for example), could conceivably exist on the websites of traditional news organizations like *Aftonbladet* and *The Sun*. And it is itself interesting if extensive recommendation/ranking systems do *not* appear on these websites, as that shows that the newspapers are not at present prepared to divest power over the news selection and production process to any radical extent. Some suggest that news organizations would be very resistant to this type of decentralization of their authority (e.g. Lasica, 2002), whereas others suggest that traditional news organizations will have to incorporate more distributed, user-led content generation in the future (Quinn, 2005; Singer, 2006).

Possible examples of distributed UGC production on online newspaper sites similar to those analysed by Benkler could be user-created *wikis*, a *distributed system for assigning accreditation and relevance* to news items in the way of *Slashdot* and *Digg*, or *collaborative newsgathering and production* done by users.

Centralized UGC production would then be all kinds of UGC production that are actively solicited and managed by the news organization itself, e.g. asking users to contribute material on particular subjects or in response to particular questions. That is, the production is not user-led, nor does it involve large-scale collaboration between users: a typical example of centralized UGC production would be if the news organizations invited users to submit their "best holiday video"—these videos would then likely be produced and submitted by individual users, rather than as a result of a massively collaborative effort by many different users. As a further example of centralization, the editors of the newspaper rather than the readers would then decide the "best" video.

Empirical Data

I observed the dedicated UGC/reader's material sections (see next section) of *The Sun Online* and *Aftonbladet.se* daily for six weeks (June to mid-July 2007). In the course of this observation, I also surveyed the websites as a whole looking for UGC outside the dedicated UGC sections—however, I did not perform this overall survey daily but weekly, or when UGC material appeared elsewhere on the site. This might seem unsystematic, but my six weeks of observation indicated that use of UGC outside the dedicated UGC sections was generally very clearly indicated and an important part of the presentation of those particular news items (i.e. the phrase "Reader's own pictures of the event" or something similar would appear quite prominently in the coverage).

It is outside the scope of this small pilot study to do a complete quantitative analysis of forum posts, blogs etc. hosted on the studied Web pages. Instead, I have confined myself to briefer overviews of only those forum threads, blogs and video clips that appear on ranking lists on the site. An overview of the orientation of the most popular user-submitted items should suffice to give at least some indication of the types of content that users are mainly invited to submit (and presumably interested in submitting).

Since websites are dynamic as well as ephemeral, it can be difficult to track changes and patterns: to that end, I used image capture software (called *Paparazzi!*) to save screenshots of relevant UGC sections on a weekly basis, or when some important change occurred (it soon emerged that doing the screenshots on a weekly basis seemed sufficient, as section design, top-ten lists and the like actually did not change that quickly). Thus, most comparisons and analysis of popular content is based on week-by-week tracking rather than day-by-day tracking.

Analysis: UGC Provision on *The Sun Online* and *Aftonbladet.se*

Both *The Sun Online* and *Aftonbladet.se* have designated sections where UGC is concentrated and collected. On *The Sun Online*, this is called *MySun.com* and requires free registration to access, whereas access to *Läsarbladet* [Reader's Paper] on *Aftonbladet.se* is open to all Web visitors without cost (free and separate registration is required to get access to some UGC provisions, e.g. starting your own blog and submitting your own video clips, however). There are also various forms of UGC provision outside these designated sections, which I will comment on as they appear in the following sections.

Level of Involvement

First, we will look at customization features on the two websites: i.e. elements that are UGC in the sense that they allow users to manipulate existing content thereby (potentially) changing the nature and character of the content they are accessing. Customization features I have looked for are *RSS feed*, *grading/marking* features, the opportunity to *directly comment* on content, and the opportunity to choose the content displayed through some kind of *"Daily Me"* feature.

Table 1 presents an overview of the customization features on the two sites. Both sites make use of *RSS feeds* to allow users to customize their own content, and both sites make it easy for users by publishing extensive and easy-to-use instructions for how to install a feed reader, how to link to the feeds etc. The feed categories are fairly similar (more on this in the following section), though they have been chosen to emphasize different types of content: *The Sun Online* has many feeds dedicated to its podcasts, whereas *Aftonbladet.se* has a feed for each individual regularly contributing columnist. Indeed, the majority of feed categories of *Aftonbladet.se* are feeds from individual columnists, creating a strong focus on individual "star" journalists. However, some of *The Sun Online*'s podcast links also have similar characteristics, as some are advertised using the participating journalist's name, such as "Victoria Newton's Bizarre Podcast" or "Bell and Mitchelson's Laughable World of Football", for example.

Grading and marking features are fairly limited. *The Sun Online* only uses "indirect" marking, i.e. blog posts, videos etc. with many page views move up in the rankings, and users cannot actively recommend individual blogs, blog posts, videos, forum posts etc. On *Aftonbladet.se*, users have two grading opportunities: they can grade video clips on the video clip home page *Mitt Klipp* [*My Clip*]; and they can recommend (but not *grade*) blog

TABLE 1
Customization features on *The Sun Online* and *Aftonbladet.se*

Customization features	The Sun Online	Aftonbladet.se
RSS feeds?	Yes—Several linked to podcast feature	Yes—Several linked to individual columnists
Grading/marking?	No—Indirect marking only (i.e. popular blogs, blog posts, virals etc. move up the rankings)	Yes—(1) Marking of video clips in *Mitt Klipp* [*My Clip*] section; (2) recommendation of individual blog posts
Commenting?	Yes—(1) Direct comments on possible (though moderated); (2) links to relevant forum discussions	Yes—But direct comments only possible in response to columnists, not to news articles (except when solicited)
Other "Daily Me" features?	Yes—Users can choose preferred categories of news to be updated/ displayed on *MySun* when signing up	No—No features besides the RSS feeds

posts of other user bloggers. Highly recommended posts/clips will move up in the rankings and be displayed more prominently.

The Sun Online consistently gives users the opportunity to *directly comment* on articles: almost every single news item in every news category is accompanied by two buttons: "Add comment" and "Join discussion". All comments are moderated before they are published and not all comments may be published. If a comment is added, it will be displayed below the article in question. Clicking the "Join discussion" button takes the user to the Forum section. However, articles do not get a corresponding Forum thread created automatically, so unless a Forum thread has already been created by someone, the link will just lead to the general Forum area. In other words, there are a number of steps users must go through to be allowed to create their own comments. *Aftonbladet.se* does not generally allow users to directly comment on articles, though in some cases comments will be solicited from users (often under the banner "What do YOU think?"). *Aftonbladet.se* reserves opportunities to comment to its columnists' pages: all columnists have their email displayed online (*Sun* journalists' emails are not posted online), and all columns have a "Join the discussion" link that takes users to the Forum section. All columnists have their dedicated "area" of the Forum where their columns can be discussed.

Besides the RSS feeds, *Aftonbladet.se* does not have any other "*Daily Me*"-style features. *The Sun Online*, on the other hand, allows users who sign up for *MySun* to tick boxes corresponding to the areas that they would like to receive news on—this is linked to the feed feature, though the feeds users can choose between when on *MySun* are not quite the same as the ones listed in the general feed list (see Table 2).

TABLE 2
Customization features on *The Sun Online* and *Aftonbladet.se*

Production features	The Sun Online	Aftonbladet.se
Textual production	Yes—Forums, blogs	Yes—Forums, blogs (*Reader's Articles* section part of Forums)
Image production	Yes—User-submitted photos and virals	Yes—User-submitted photos
Video production	No	Yes—on *Mitt Klipp* [*My Clip*] section
Audio production	No	No

Both sites thus offer a number of customization features which could be described as "low involvement" UGC: users either do not create their own content but manipulate or comment on existing content, or only create very brief snippets of content, like comments to an article. Both sites use feeds to allow users to customize their content (*The Sun Online* emphasizing podcast content, *Aftonbladet.se* emphasizing individual columnists), the sites use grading/marking features sparingly or not at all (and never in conjunction with news content or articles), and opportunities to directly comment are more extensive on *The Sun Online* (where users theoretically can comment on any article) than on *Aftonbladet.se* (where users can only comment on columns, or when comments are solicited).

Shifting from customization to production, an overview shows that both sites have extensive provisions for *textual production* (focused on blogs and forums), but not for other types of content (none of the sites provide opportunities for audio UGC, for example).

On both sites, forums and blogs form a key part of the designated UGC area (*MySun* and *Läsarbladet*, respectively). Both sites invite users to start their own blogs, and both sites provide extensive forums for user discussions. On both sites, the forum section is divided into subject areas that follow the subject area divisions in the online newspaper (i.e. there are forum sections for news discussions, sports discussion etc.).

The main difference between the forum sections is that *Aftonbladet.se* uses a much more detailed forum subject categorization: *Aftonbladet.se* has a total 259 forum sections, spread across 34 categories, whereas *The Sun Online* has a more modest 36 sections with no subsections except for the Football forum, which has 20 subsections (one for each Premiership team), and the Sport section, which has five subsections. Overall, the forums on *Aftonbladet.se* are more extensive and forums generally have more posts than on *The Sun Online*—however, this is likely to be due to the fact that the *Aftonbladet.se* forum pages have been online for much longer (*The Sun Online*'s forum pages were part of the redesign and relaunch in 2006 and thus have not had the time to accumulate more archived forum posts). Also, the total number of forums might not be wholly relevant to the overall scope of the forum provision, as many of the discussion areas on *Aftonbladet.se* contain no discussions at all (29 areas contain no discussions, and a further 48 areas contain only one to three discussion threads, as of 15 July 2007).

It is a bit more difficult to get a general sense of the blog provision, as both newspapers make it rather difficult to track individual blogs: the main navigation page lists "Latest posts" and "Latest comments", and then you have to click on the name of the poster or on a link "Go to full blog" (*MySun*) to reach the individual blog home page. *MySun* lists a "Top blog" and three other "Popular blogs" every day, and *Aftonbladet.se* lists the three blogs "Most recommended in the last 2 hours" on their blog section main page, but other than that it is not made obvious which blogs are consistently popular. Considering that blogs are a very individual medium, the blog sections on *MySun* and *Aftonbladet.se* are curiously "de-individualized"—the main navigation is done through the *individual posts*, rather than the *people* who post.

Both online newspapers invite readers to submit (still) images: both have a "tipster" hotline/email users are invited to use if they have images of some breaking news event or something else that might be of interest to the newspaper (like celebrity pictures, for example). Both newspapers make it clear that users may be paid if their images are used. *The Sun* further invites users to submit their favourite viral email image to the *Virals* section of *The Sun* online. In the latter case, however, the "invitation" to submit is (1) not displayed very prominently, and (2) it is never made clear whether the pictures submitted are actually produced by the readers that submit them.

Aftonbladet.se has a designated area for video production. This section, *Mitt Klipp* [*My Clip*], is separate from the general UGC section, *Läsarbladet*. In order to submit a video, users have to register (currently free). Not all video clips on *Mitt Klipp* are produced by users; *Aftonbladet*'s own journalists produce some. It is generally made clear when a video clip is produced by *Aftonbladet* and when it is produced by users.

Types of Content

What types of UGC are users creating on *The Sun Online* and *Aftonbladet.se*? What kinds of content do users have the power to customize and create? First, let us look at the *RSS feed* categories available (Table 3)

It is not very surprising that the categories overall are focused on popular culture-oriented content, as this is consistent with tabloid content in general (note, for example, the relatively detailed sub-categorization of sports in both online newspapers, compared with only one general category for "News"). However, through its columnists, *Aftonbladet.se* seems to present more news/information-oriented content for customization (most of the blogs are about current affairs).

What are the most popular *forums* (as measured by the total number of threads in each forum) on the two tabloid websites? On *Aftonbladet.se*, *Politics & Society* is the most popular forum section (with 2844 discussion threads as of 15 July 2007) followed by *News* (i.e. where users discuss news items from the online and paper version of the newspaper; with 1542 discussion threads). The next most popular forum is a distant third, *TV*, with 312 threads (excepting the archived *Election 2006* forum with 602 threads). By contrast, the three most popular forums on *The Sun Online* by the same measure are *News*, with 1433 threads, followed by *Big Brother*, 693 threads, and *The Pub* (186 threads). So for both sites, while the general forum provision is popular culture-oriented, the most popular discussion forums are the news/information-oriented ones—but TV/Entertainment forums also feature among the more popular ones.

On *MySun* the *blogs* are categorized (*Entertainment*, *General*, *News*, *Personal*, *Sport* and *Paranormal*), with Personal blogs being most popular. *Aftonbladet.se*'s categorization of their blogs is based on the "tags" that individual users add to their posts (this tagging then appears on the main blog page as a navigation tool). Category tags that remain popular throughout the studied period are *Love*, *Sex*, *Blog*, *Children*, *Work*, *Life* and *Thoughts*. An overview of the "Latest update"/"Latest post" lists in the period studied, as well as overviews of the "Top blog" and "Most recommended"-lists indicate that blog content on both *Aftonbladet.se* and *The Sun Online* is overwhelmingly *personal* in character, i.e. blogs mostly function as an online diary where the most popular topics are everyday-life things such as love, work, children etc. A minor note is that the category tag "Blog" is popular on *Aftonbladet.se* throughout the studied period, which seems to indicate that it is popular to blog about other blogs, about the activity of blogging and/or about the blogosphere in general (again, the overview of recent updates and most recommended posts give some support to this impression). A general observation is that the content generated on blogs and that generated on forums seem to be of different character: textual production on forums has a closer relationship to other content on the site (i.e. people use forums to discuss the news), whereas textual production on blogs is

TABLE 3

RSS feed categories on *The Sun Online* and *Aftonbladet.se*

RSS feeds on *The Sun Online*		RSS feeds on *Aftonbladet.se*	
Big Brother	Podcasts feeds:	News	Columnists (*main* theme/
News	Victoria Newton's	Reader's Paper	subject area of columnist in
Sport	Bizarre	Entertainment	parenthesis):
Supergoals	The Sun's Ashes	Sports	Robert Aschberg (current
Bizarre	Highlights	Football	affairs)
Sun Woman	The Sun's Comedy	Ice Hockey	Nima Daryamadj (current
Viral Vault	Podcast	*Aftonbladet* Woman	affairs)
Motors	Bell and Mitchelson's	Plus (premium service	Jan Guillou (current affairs)
TV	Laughable World of	of paid subscribed	Monica Gunne (lifestyle)
Gizmo	Football	content)	Johan Hakelius (current affairs/
Podcasts (this is a	Joel and Simon's	IT	culture)
general feed that	Wrestlecast	Love & Sex	Carl Hamilton (political
collects the up-	The Sun's Motoring	Travel	analysis)
dates for all the	Podcast	Users can also	Staffan Heimersson (foreign
other podcasts)	The Sun's TV and Film	subscribe via RSS feed	affairs)
	Podcast	to individual threads	Johanne Hildebrand (foreign/
	Arhur Edward's Royal	on the various forums	current affairs)
	Pictures		Elin Lindqvist (current affairs)
	The Sun's Political		Herman Lindqvist (popular
	Podcast		history)
			Belinda Olsson
			(entertainment/lifestyle)
			Yrsa Stenius (political analysis)
			Lena Sundström (current
			affairs)
			Kerstin Thorvall (culture/
			lifestyle)
			Anders Westgårdh (lifestyle)

Feed categories available when
registering on *MySun* are: News, Bizarre,
Sport, Features*, Sun Woman, Fun*,
Competitions*, Gizmo, Gizmo Gaming*,
Wrestling*, Football (general)*, England
(football)*, Championship*, Champions
League*, Tennis*, Golf*, Ashes, FA Cup*

*Feeds not available in the regular feed list.

more "disconnected" from the rest of the content available online and more personal in nature.

When it comes to the video clips on *Mitt Klipp*, popular culture-oriented material (along with everyday life-oriented material) dominates over news/information-oriented material. Interestingly, the clips that are by far the most popular in the period studied are an ongoing series of comedy/celebrity clips featuring *Aftonbladet* entertainment journalist Alex Schulman—i.e. they are not user-generated at all. However, personal/everyday life-oriented clips in turn dominate over popular culture-oriented material: the most popular clips besides the Alex Schulman series of clips are of children, pets and sometimes adults doing amusing things. Only one clip categorized as *News/politics* makes the top 100 (most views) in the studied period; this is a clip from 2004 of an *Aftonbladet* journalist interviewing then-Prime minister Göran Persson about why he likes reading *Aftonbladet.se* (the journalist also gives the Prime minister a cake). Again, this clip is not user-generated.

In the period studied, UGC images used in conjunction with traditional, hard news only appear twice, both times in *Aftonbladet*. On 16 June, *Aftonbladet.se* reports that Swedish pop star Leila K has been hit by a car, and on 21 June, *Aftonbladet.se* reports on the arrest of a suspected cop killer. In both cases, the articles are accompanied by images submitted by a reader present at the scene of the event.

In summary, we can note that user-produced news texts, interviews and other types of news material is virtually non-existent except for the articles on *Läsarbladet*'s *Reader's Articles* forum—this section contains a total of 19 reader articles, most of them between 200 and 500 words long. News/informational content is generated mostly on the forums, when users discuss news items from the newspaper or other current events. Blogs are mostly focused on personal/everyday life content, as are the video clips on *Aftonbladet.se*. A very small proportion of UGC is "hard news".

Mode of Production

As predicted, this categorization turned out not to be that relevant to the UGC provision in the two analysed online newspapers. Neither newspaper use wikis. Neither newspaper uses a distributed system for assigning accreditation and relevance. Neither of the two newspapers provides opportunities for collaborative newsgathering and production. Both newspapers solicit readers' images of breaking news events, as detailed in the previous section, but the readers are addressed and interacted with on an individual basis rather than collectively. On *Läsarbladet*, readers are invited to produce their own articles (again, as individuals), but these articles are not assigned the same status as articles authored by the newspaper's own journalists: the *Reader's Articles* section is in fact a section of the Forum area and articles are displayed as forum posts rather than as articles proper. In the period studied, only 19 readers have taken the opportunity to write their own article, and the most popular thread (in terms of total number of posts) on the *Reader's articles* forum is the *How to write an article* thread started by an *Aftonbladet.se* staff member.

In terms of their production, online newspapers thus still resolutely follow an "old media" model—while a lot of content on the website is no longer centrally produced (i.e. produced by users in the form of blogs, forum posts and videos), the majority of news/ information gathering, selection and presentation (a core activity of any newspaper, tabloid or not) still takes place in a centralized system where users have little or no direct input, and where users do not participate. The model for most content production is still of the "we write, you read" variety—innovations like the ones presented by *Slashdot* (accreditation and relevance), *Congoo* (user-recommended news) and *Assignment Zero* (crowdsourcing) have not spread to the two studied tabloids.

Concluding Remarks: UGC in Two Online Tabloids

This is a limited study and thus only limited conclusions can be drawn—however, some tentative observations about general patterns of UGC provision can be made. The answers to the main research questions, i.e. the level of *control* the users have over the UGC production, and what *types* of content they produce, are clear.

While both the analysed online newspapers have quite extensive systems for customization and production of content, the overall impression is that users are mostly empowered to create popular culture-oriented content and personal/everyday life-oriented content rather than news/informational content. Direct user involvement in newsgathering, news selection and news production is minimal, and when it is (as in *Läsarbladet*'s *Reader's Articles* section), it is not displayed in the same way as articles produced by the regular journalists of the paper. The only reader material that is given similar status to material produced by the news organization is reader photos of breaking news events. News/informational UGC (mainly forum posts) is produced mainly in response to or in relation to material produced by the news organization (i.e. users commenting on and discussing published news items). The structures for UGC provision are provided by the newspapers rather than being "self-organizing" and produced by the users themselves. Production is still centralized rather than distributed.

The focus on both sites is on *textual* UGC production (forum posts and blogs), with the popular forums being more oriented in the first instance towards news/information and in the second instance towards popular culture, and the blogs being overwhelmingly oriented towards personal/everyday life-type content. The most popular video content on *Aftonbladet.se*'s *Mitt Klipp* section is not user-generated at all, and the material that is user-generated is popular culture-oriented and personal/everyday life-oriented.

In terms of comparing tabloid types, the expected differences between *Aftonbla-det.se* and *The Sun Online* failed to emerge—while the overall websites are clearly different, with *Aftonbladet.se* presenting "hard news" content much more prominently than *The Sun Online*, they are not very different in how they present UGC. *Aftonbladet.se*'s comment and RSS functions are primarily linked to their columnists and *The Sun Online* focuses on its podcasts, but other than that both sites offer very similar contexts for producing UGC: popular culture/entertainment-oriented and personal/everyday life-oriented.

The results of this study thus seem to support the argument of Lasica (2002), i.e. that traditional news organizations are unwilling to add features that give users more control and influence over the content. The policies behind the UGC provisions in *Aftonbladet.se* and *The Sun Online* fit with Singer's finding that while journalists may be willing to let audiences respond to and interact with already-produced material, they are less willing to give audiences any real influence over the news process (Singer, 2006, p. 275f), for example, by marking news items, ranking their relevance, or engaging in collaborative newsgathering. Looking at what kind of content users are invited to produce, and the conditions under which they produce them, both online tabloids seem to fit more within the categories of media producers that Chung term "purists" or "cautious traditionalists" rather than "innovators" (as innovators are the most willing to cede journalistic decisions to users) (Chung, 2007): UGC is used to create more popular culture-oriented or everyday life-oriented content (both very traditional tabloid categories), not news/information-oriented content.

REFERENCES

ANDREWS, ROBERT (2005) "Digg Just Might Bury Slashdot", *Wired*, http://www.wired.com/science/discoveries/news/2005/11/69568, accessed 12 July 2007.

BENKLER, YOCHAI (2006) *The Wealth of Networks: how social production transforms markets and freedom*, New Haven, CT: Yale University Press.

BERGSTRÖM, ANNIKA (2005) *nyhetsvanor.nu—Nyhetsanvänding på Internet 1998–2003 [news-habits.nu—News readership on the Internet 1998–2003]*, Göteborg: Department of Journalism and Mass Communication, Göteborg University.

BIRD, S. ELIZABETH (1992) *For Enquiring Minds: a cultural study of supermarket tabloids*, Knoxville: University of Tennessee Press.

BOCZKOWSKI, PABLO J. (2004a) *Digitizing the News: innovation in online newspapers*, Cambridge, MA: The MIT Press.

BOCZKOWSKI, PABLO J. (2004b) "The Process of Adopting Multimedia and Interactivity in Three Online Newsrooms", *Journal of Communication* 54(June), pp. 197–213.

CHUNG, DEBORAH SOUN (2007) "Profits and Perils: online news producers' perceptions of interactivity and use of interactive features", *Convergence* 13(1), pp. 43–61.

DIBEAN, WENDY and GARRISON, BRUCE (2001) "How Six Online Newspapers Use Web Technologies", *Newspaper Research Journal* 22(2), pp. 79–93.

DOWNES, EDWARD J. and MCMILLAN, SALLY J. (2000) "Defining Interactivity: a qualitative identification of key dimensions", *New Media and Society* 2(June), pp. 157–79.

HADENIUS, STIG and WEIBULL, LENNART (2003) *Massmedier: En bok om press, radio & TV [Mass Media: a book on press, radio & TV]*, Stockholm: Albert Bonniers Förlag.

JENKINS, HENRY (2006) *Convergence Culture: where old and new media collide*, New York: New York University Press.

LASICA, JOSEPH D. (2002) "The Promise of the Daily Me", *Online Journalism Review*, http://www.ojr.org/ojr/lasica/1017779142.php, accessed 12 July 2007.

LEGGATT, HELEN (2007) "Online Visitors Drawn to The Sun", *BizReport*, http://www.bizreport.com/2007/01/online_visitors_drawn_to_the_sun.html, accessed 14 July 2007.

LEONARD, ANDREW (1998) "Geek Central: at a site called Slashdot, 'news for nerds' draws a passionate crowd", *Salon*, http://archive.salon.com/21st/feature/1998/06/15feature.html, accessed 12 July 2007.

MASSEY, BRIAN L. and LEVY, MARK (1999) "Interactivity, Online Journalism, and English-language Web Newspapers in Asia", *Journalism & Mass Communication Quarterly* 76(1), pp. 138–51.

NEGROPONTE, NICHOLAS (1995) *Being Digital*, New York: Vintage Books.

POOR, NATHANIEL (2005) "Mechanisms of an Online Public Sphere: the website Slashdot", *Journal of Computer-mediated Communication* 10(2), http://jcmc.indiana.edu/vol10/issue2/poor.html.

QUINN, STEPHEN (2005) "Convergence's Fundamental Question", *Journalism Studies* 6(1), pp. 29–38.

SCHULTZ, TANJEV (1999) "Interactive Options in Online Journalism: a content analysis of 100 U.S. newspapers", *Journal of Computer-mediated Communication* 5(1), http://jcmc.indiana.edu/vol5/issue1/schultz.html.

SCHULTZ, TANJEV (2000) "Mass Media and the Concept of Interactivity: an exploratory study of online forums and reader email", *Media, Culture and Society* 22, pp. 205–21.

SINGER, JANE B. (2006) "Stepping Back from the Gate: online newspaper editors and the co-production of content in campaign 2004", *Journalism & Mass Communication Quarterly* 83(2), pp. 265–80.

SPASSOV, ORLIN (Ed.) (2004) *Quality Press in Southeast Europe*, Sofia: SOEMZ.

STABE, MARTIN (2007a) "ABCe: Sun overtakes Times as second-largest newspaper website" *Press Gazette*, http://www.pressgazette.co.uk/story.asp?sectioncode=1&storycode=38131, accessed 14 July 2007.

STABE, MARTIN (2007b) "ABCe: three newspaper sites post record traffic in October", *Press Gazette*, http://www.pressgazette.co.uk/story.asp?sectioncode = 1&storycode = 39531, accessed 23 November 2007.

STEUER, JONATHAN (1992) "Defining Virtual Reality: dimensions determining telepresence", *Journal of Communication* 42(Autumn), pp. 73–93.

STROMER-GALLEY, JENNIFER (2000) "On-line Interaction and Why Candidates Avoid It", *Journal of Communication* 50(Autumn), pp. 111–32.

TOFFLER, ALVIN (1980) *The Third Wave*, New York: Bantam Books.

Chapter 11

ATTACK OF THE KILLER NEWSPAPERS!
The "tabloid revolution" in South Africa and the future of newspapers

Herman Wasserman

Introduction

In an era when newspapers in many regions of the world seem to expect their imminent death (Philip Meyer, 2004 famously predicted that the last newspaper will be read and recycled in April 2040), a newspaper revolution has taken place in South Africa. Elsewhere the consensus in industry (Ahrens, 2005; Kinsley, 2006; Plunkett, 2005) and in the academy (Deuze, 2004; Kopper et al., 2000; Meyer, 2004; Quinn, 2005; Singer, 1997), seems to be that newspapers will have to radically adapt to new technologies and convergence culture unless they want to become redundant (even if, historically, technological transformation of the newspaper industry in itself has not proven to be a guarantee of a broadening of the range of perspectives found in the press; Curran, 2003, p. 101). The interactivity made possible by new media technologies means that professional journalists no longer determine what the public "see, hear and read about the world around us" (Deuze, 2004, p. 146). These technological, professional and cultural shifts have been termed "networked journalism" (Bardoel and Deuze, 2001). According to Beckett and Kyrke-Smith (2007, p. 56) the shift from conventional journalism to "networked journalism"—the former being "hierarchical, professionalized, and formulaic: it has deadlines, packages, and messages for its mainly passive consumers" and the latter displaying a "linear process to networked interactivity, where there is constant communication and exchange of information between journalists and society"—can also be noted in African media. The difference is that in African media, digital technologies are often used in combination with other ways of interactivity, for instance radio phone-ins and SMS.

In recent years the South African media market has been taken by storm by newspapers that seem to follow a much older tradition (according to Elizabeth Bird, 1992, going back to at least the penny press in the United States but tracing its ancestry to the 17th-century ballads in Europe and America[1]). Broadsheets in South Africa have been playing catch-up with international trends in newspaper convergence (including j-blogs, video clips on websites and cellphone news services) and interactivity (including readers' blogs, online citizen journalism etc.) in an attempt to halt declining circulation figures (apart from the tabloids, South African newspapers showed a general but moderate decline in circulation over the past couple of years, with only a few seeing a moderate increase (Grobler, 2007; Taylor and Milne, 2006).

But the newspaper market was conquered convincingly by the entry of the new tabloid newspapers—with hardly any recourse to new technologies.[2] They have turned the local media landscape upside down, and created heated controversy in South African journalism circles (Wasserman, 2006)—to such an extent that the tabloid "revolution" has attracted international attention (e.g. Beresford, 2004; Townsend, 2006). While this is in line with the fact that old media (mostly radio, due to high illiteracy rates and low circulation and advertising revenues) still dominate on the African continent (Beckett and Kyrke-Smith, 2007, pp. 24, 45), and tabloids have also gained in popularity elsewhere on the continent, e.g. Nigeria and Zimbabwe (Beckett and Kyrke-Smith, 2007, p. 55; Mabweazara, 2006), the popularity of these tabloids is without precedent[3] in the South African context, even considering its relatively strong and sophisticated print media industry. The *Daily Sun*, launched in 2002, is now the biggest newspaper in the country, with just below 500,000 copies sold and 3.8 million regular readers (according to the Audit Bureau of Circulation and All Media Products Survey released in February 2007). The publisher, Deon du Plessis, reportedly claims that there is even a second-hand market for copies—such is the demand for the paper among those that can barely afford it (Tooth, 2006).

The *Daily Sun* is aimed at the black working class, or the "man in the blue overall" as Du Plessis somewhat patronisingly describes their typical reader (personal communication, 2007)—the newspaper's Johannesburg offices are also adorned by two shop-window dolls dressed in blue overalls to symbolize this aim. It has created a mass readership out of the poor and working class (although upwardly mobile) black majority of the country that had hitherto been largely out of the focus of the post-apartheid mainstream[4] press, apart from township freesheets distributed by big conglomerates.

The tabloids have not only succeeded in creating a mass new readership among the black working class, but have also impacted on the circulation of other papers, notably the *Sowetan*[5] whose circulation figures took a nose-dive after the introduction in 2001 of the first tabloid in the country, the *Sunday Sun*, but especially the *Daily Sun* in 2002 (Taylor and Milne, 2006). Within its first year, the *Daily Sun* grew its circulation by 228 per cent (Bloom, 2003). The phenomenal commercial success of this tabloid was partly blamed for the huge circulation losses at *Sowetan* and seen as a reason for the appointment of a new editor to restructure *Sowetan* and *Sunday World* (by also incorporating tabloid elements) and reverse their circulation losses (*The Media* Online, 2004).

In the wake of its success other tabloid newspapers followed. An Afrikaans-language weekly tabloid was launched in the Western Cape province in 2003, titled *Kaapse Son*, published by the same media house, Naspers. Aimed at a "coloured" and white Afrikaans working class (Andrew Koopman, personal communication, 2005), its popularity soon became evident and it changed from a weekly to a daily in 2005. From 2006 to 2007 it launched a series of regional editions outside the Western Cape, published weekly and titled simply *Son* (Bizcommunity, 2007). Naspers' rival company, Independent, replied by launching an English-language tabloid in the same region in 2005: the *Daily Voice*. Providing much the same fare (its tagline is "Sex, Scandal, Skinner [gossip], Sport"), it challenged the *Son* head-on, inter alia by using colloquial language (Penstone, 2005) and publishing one of its three editions in a hybrid between Afrikaans and English (Karl Brophy, personal communication, 2007). Naspers again fired back by launching an English-language version of *Son* in 2006.

One could safely say that the arrival of the new tabloid newspapers has changed the media landscape in post-apartheid South Africa irrevocably. In a new democracy, they have given voice to the majority of the population who have hitherto remained on the margins of the post-apartheid mediated public sphere. Their emergence should be understood against the changing socio-political context in the country since the demise of apartheid in the 1990s. Democratization changed the regulatory as well as professional normative regime under which media operated, weakened the old ideological positions to which media houses were tied, and also opened new markets for big media conglomerates.

South Africa re-entered the globalized media sphere, which meant that influences from abroad were more easily incorporated into local media, and that global media conglomerates such as Independent made their presence felt in the South African media industry (inter alia by establishing a tabloid, the *Daily Voice*). Other salient factors underlying the rise of tabloids can be summarized as follows:

1. A vacuum had been created by the demise of anti-apartheid alternative media, which used to cater for the concerns and interests of the black majority in their struggle against apartheid. This is not to say that the tabloid media could be considered "alternative" media, nor that they fulfil similar functions than did the anti-apartheid press, but that a significant part of the potential market for print media was left untapped by the mainstream broadsheets.
2. The continued commercial logic of mainstream broadsheet newspapers, even as their editors and staff changed to reflect more racial diversity, continued to marginalize the black majority in the construction of social reality through news. News values and business models employed by the mainstream broadsheets favoured the white and increasingly black middle class and elite. To the extent that issues like poverty, social delivery, HIV/Aids and crime formed part of the news agenda of the broadsheets, more often than not it was in the form of abstract political or economic problems discussed from an elite perspective. The tabloids instead provided personalized (and often sensationalized) accounts of the effects of these social ills from the perspective of those having to live them.
3. Growing frustration at the lack of social delivery, continued poverty and unemployment, crime and other socio-economic problems (including drug abuse, HIV/Aids etc.). This frustration boiled over in street protests around the country, and was also seen as a large part of the reason for the defeat of the current president, Thabo Mbeki, at the ruling party's (the African National Congress) annual national conference in 2007 by Jacob Zuma, seen as a candidate with more grassroots appeal among the working class. In terms of the media, a platform was needed where these concerns could be voiced. In the light of the increasing perception that the public broadcaster, the South African Broadcasting Corporation (SABC) was used as a government mouthpiece, and given the dominance of commercial media (even while attempts have been made to increase the reach of

community media through licensing community radio stations and the establishment of a Media Diversity and Development Agency to fund community media), a print media outlet that could articulate these frustrations would find itself in a popular position. The tabloids, especially the *Daily Sun*, seized the opportunity. It conducted a campaign highlighting the failings of local government, and reported on the eruption of community protests against lack of social delivery (Deon Du Plessis, personal communication, 2007). In the run-up to the election of Jacob Zuma as ANC president, the *Daily Sun* ran commentary on its front page explaining how Zuma's popularity related to Thabo Mbeki's lack of leadership on social issues such as HIV/Aids, public service inefficiency, crime, and reconstruction and development (*Daily Sun* 2007e).

4.   The social changes occurring in South Africa after apartheid resulted in a process of social mobility for a young black working class, who needed information to navigate their social progress. News consumption also formed a part of their aspirations to a middle-class lifestyle. Through pages and supplements on "lifestyle", home ownership and financial matters, the tabloids engaged with this young, upwardly mobile audience and created a new advertising market in the process.

The tabloids have, however, not been welcomed by the journalistic establishment, who perceived them as flaunting conventional norms like objectivity, neutrality and truthtelling through their sensationalist, opinionated and seemingly far-fetched stories as well as objectifying women by publishing pictures of scantily clad or topless women and fascination with sex. In a process that can only be described as "paradigm repair" (Wasserman, 2006), the country's professional journalist organization (Sanef), media monitoring groups (like the Media Monitoring Project and Genderlinks) and media academics have on various occasions lashed out at them for bringing the profession of journalism into disrepute and undermining the human rights culture of the new democracy, without interrogating the existing journalistic orthodoxy.

These tabloids raise interesting questions for scholars trying to understand the role of media in the (incomplete) transition from apartheid to democracy in South Africa. They should also remind journalism studies scholars that the question regarding the future of newspapers should remain cognizant of different contexts. Too often these debates are predicated on media-saturated societies with broad access to new media technologies that have extended the range of media options available to consumers, or on the news habits of audiences whose lived experience differs vastly from those in other parts of the world.

This is not to argue for a type of cultural relativism that would make any conversation about shared challenges of journalism in diverse contexts impossible, nor is it to enter into special pleading for contexts in Africa or elsewhere in the global South because journalism there has just fallen behind on a trajectory that will in the end lead to the same place where journalism in the global North has already arrived.

Academic and journalistic attention to South African tabloids should avoid the pitfall of creating an exotic Other of Northern journalism studies. Rather, it should stimulate a rethink of the relationship between newspapers and publics in ways that pay close attention to contexts and local specificities in such a way that new lines of comparison with journalism in the dominant North can be opened.

At the heart of this exploration is a central question for this discussion of the future of newspapers in the era of convergence and interactivity: how do these tabloids manage to create a reciprocal, interactive relationship with their readers?

"People That Are Still Not in Count": South African Tabloids and Society

Can we understand the popularity of the South African tabloids as something more than just the result of a "race to the bottom" or a pandering to the lowest common denominator? If so, could the reason for their success also tell us something about the future of newspapers in a more general sense?

A common reaction to the high circulation figures of tabloids is to dismiss them as vulgar and sensational and therefore popular—"popular" here used not only to denote their mass appeal, but also marking a class distinction between "popular" and "quality" journalism which conventionally has been at the basis of normative criteria for the media's role in the public sphere (Meijer, 2001). Such a view would associate tabloids with the homogenization of the public sphere rather than the diversification thereof—as Louw (2001, p. 48) points out with reference to the emergence of "sensationalism" as a means to attract mass audiences. Tabloids are associated with an appetite for scandal, celebrity, superficiality, lack of seriousness and entertainment/"infotainment" rather than serious news (Gripsrud, 2000; Hinerman, 1997; Sparks, 2000). In sum, they are seen as contributing to the depoliticization of publics and the "lowering of journalistic standards" (Curran, 2003, p. 93). The spread of these characteristics to broadsheet papers or other media platforms like television or magazines is often referred to as "tabloidization" or "dumbing down", and takes place around the world (Bek, 2004; Conboy, 2005; Glynn, 2000; Grabe et al., 1999; Hallin, 2000; Jones, 2002; Ursell, 2001).

Counter-perspectives from cultural studies scholars like John Fiske (1989, 1992) and Elizabeth Bird (1992) have included arguments that tabloids undermine the high culture–low culture hierarchy, provide a voice to marginalized publics and serve as a site for resistance against cultural hegemony. Some are of the opinion that tabloids maintain a society's dominant values and norms by showing up spectacular instances where these norms are transgressed (Grabe et al., 1999, p. 636), while others (e.g. Conboy, 2005) point out that tabloids have throughout their history contested bourgeois societal values.

Which of these two views hold true for South African tabloids? Probably both.

Looking at their content,[6] these tabloids, on the one hand, eschew formal political coverage, sensationalize news and publish excessively lurid or graphic pictures (including portrayals of violence). There is a strong focus on sports and entertainment and through the avoidance of controversial political or ethnic positioning they ensure that as large an audience as possible is delivered to advertisers.

But the picture is contradictory and complex. These tabloids also provide a voice to the working-class majority in the country whose perspectives remain marginalized in the mainstream print media of the post-apartheid era. Stories about crime, drugs and social problems that beset their communities are covered in-depth, extensively and from a personalized perspective rather than as merely social pathologies marked by race and class or formal economic and political issues; allegations of racism in the workplace or in the social sphere are treated seriously, and the daily struggles brought about by the confluence of historical inequalities and post-apartheid neoliberal economic policies are viewed from the perspective of those that have to deal with them. For instance, the evicted illegal occupants of council houses are represented as "defenceless women and children" that "had to look on yesterday as the contents of their houses were carried away under the surveillance of heavily- armed cops" (*Son*, 2007a) rather than lawbreakers as they might have been in the mainstream press—if their plight even made the pages of the mainstream newspapers (which in this case it did not). The unequal access to health care (with the poor reliant on under-resourced state hospitals and the elite having access to well-equipped private care) is foregrounded through individual accounts (e.g. *Daily Sun*, 2007a), as is the powerlessness of individuals against systemic incompetency that robs them of chances to better themselves (like the inability to get the correct identity document needed to apply for study or work or even to retire (*Daily Sun*, 2007b, 2007c).

While recounting individual experiences could be seen to neglect larger structural issues or formal politics, conventional reporting with its preference for "hard facts" like statistics or policy documents would in all probability only serve to remove formal politics even further from the daily experience of tabloid readers. The same approach goes for reports that hold government or officialdom to account. First-person accounts of police violence (*Daily Voice*, 2007a, 2007b) and incidents of racism (e.g. Cruywagen, 2007) are splashed on the front page and often continued across several inside pages. These individual accounts of system failure and personally experienced prejudice are what constitute tabloid politics in the post-apartheid democracy. This is why, in contrast to the mainstream stalwart of black journalism, the *Sowetan*'s announcement of the death in February 2007 of Adelaide Tambo (the wife of former ANC president) on its front page with the headings "Mama Tambo dies" and "A nation mourns", the tabloid *Daily Sun* on the same day ran with a front-page headline, "No Mercy!", on a hospital that barred patients from parking their cars, resulting in a car jacking (*Daily Sun*, 2007d). In an interview the publisher[7] of the *Daily Sun*, Deon du Plessis, ridiculed the *Sowetan*'s choice of leading with the Tambo story, saying that the "collective is dead" (personal communication, 2007).

The shift from the collective to the individual can also be seen in the presence of articles, supplements and columns that interpolate tabloid readers as consumers and facilitate their entry into the middle class. For the owners and publishers of these tabloids this social mobility is what makes their readers attractive to advertisers. Economic news is provided in practical terms, e.g. "Budget and You" (*Daily Sun*, 22 February 2007), the *Daily Sun* gives new homeowners advice in a supplement "Sun Houses" (with the tagline "Getting a place of your own") and the *Daily Voice* has a section called "Kwaai (cool-HW) Cabbies" that "keeps you up to date on motoring news" (*Daily Voice*, 2007c). The *Son* regularly publishes advice and tips on health, household and safety matters, and has even published a self-help medical booklet for separate sale.

These consumer-oriented features remain in tension with the reports of the despair and precariousness of township life. Such are the contradictions of a society in rapid and unequal transition, and the tabloid media as commercial entities reliant on a public caught between history and progress, reflect this.

But it is by providing validation to the daily lived experience of a public who otherwise mostly enters mainstream print media discourse as statistics or objects rather than the subjects of news, that the tabloids maintain close involvement with their public through "stories of working class life that manage to be both humdrum and dramatic" (Kruger, 2006). One could point to cynical commercial motives of the owners and publishers of these tabloids, yet their readers see tabloids as their advocates, often their only hope of being heard or taken seriously. In the post-apartheid society, the tabloids provide a space where dominant post-apartheid narratives of democratic progress and the "better life for all" promised by the ANC when it came to power, can be contested.

The extent of this reciprocal relationship between tabloids and their publics far exceeds that of the mainstream press, if it is to be measured in the number of letters received—figures run into several hundreds per day (Beresford, 2004)—or the trust readers bestow on these publications. The *Daily Sun* ran a campaign about social delivery, for instance, and received an overwhelming response:

> We invited people to write to us, daily, and tell us about the failings of local government in their area, ranging from no ambulance to no streetlight to shit in the streets to crime. We got—I never counted exactly—ten thousand letters a month. We ran ten a day for a year about these crises. (Deon Du Plessis, personal communication, 2007)

The editor of *Son* testifies to a similar relationship between this tabloid and its readers:

> People call us often. "Come and look, the city council is evicting us (from our homes)" or "the police are beating us" and then we go out. It's actually tragic how much pain the people we work with have to go through. And they are people that are still not in count. And they see *Son* as a way of bringing out their voice, of being heard. Often people phone us and say "we went to the police but the police didn't help us". The police are now also anti-*Son* because people come to us, we are their watchdog. Everywhere I go, I hear that people aren't saying "we are going to take you to the police" anymore, but instead "we are going to take you to *Son*". So *Son* is used as a threat. (Andrew Koopman, personal communication, 2007)

The three tabloids also each have their own regular features (Captain Voice Power, Sun Power, Mr Fixit, Son gee om) where help is provided in practical ways from fixing leaking toilets, reuniting loved ones or handing out Easter eggs to township children. This is another way in which interactivity between the newspapers and readers is maintained in a visible and tangible way.

Preliminary Concluding Remarks

What does the case study of South African tabloids tell us about the future of newspapers, and perhaps journalism studies more generally? I will only venture some preliminary remarks:

- The debate about the future of newspapers—in fact the question that led to the debate in the first place—has been dominated by dilemmas and crises experienced in the media-saturated global North, where audiences are deserting newspapers because of a proliferating range of media consumption choices linked to social and lifestyle changes. The ways in which newspapers are countering this trend—e.g. through convergence and interactivity—are mostly predicated on the access their readers have to new media technologies. The case of South African tabloids (and tabloids elsewhere in Africa) indicates that this situation is not universal. Newspapers are still important in these contexts, and where they are overtaken by other media it is because of other reasons related to the socio-economic context (e.g. radio being preferred because of low literacy rates and affordability). Acknowledging this is not the same as viewing African

newspapers as lagging behind on a universal evolutionary trajectory towards technological innovation. Change and evolution in newspaper journalism is a heterogeneous
and contextually dependent process. A multi-linear, multi-perspectival view on journalism studies should be followed, with more perspectives from the global South entering
the debate.

- The success of South African tabloids is linked to the social and political changes taking
place in the country after democratization. Their emergence and popularity cannot be
reduced only to the format, style or genre taken over from similar newspapers elsewhere,
but should be considered against the political economy of the South African media
landscape as well as the social and material conditions shaping the lived experience of
their readers. This underscores the importance of viewing newspapers within their
historical, social and material contexts, which are constantly changing and shifting. Such
a contextual approach would prevent a discussion about the future of newspapers and
journalism from extrapolating the status quo in certain parts of the world as if this could
unproblematically apply universally.

- Even while the South African tabloids present us with an argument for the importance of
particularities and specificities of local contexts, this on the other hand does not mean
they can be seen in isolation from larger global processes. South African tabloids, even in
their specificity, are manifestations of a very old genre, and reflect tabloidization trends
occurring across media platforms internationally. Yet they are not mere copies of pre-
existing blueprints. The future of newspapers in the era of globalization lies in a space
between the local and the global. In considering these trends we should remain mindful
of these flows, contraflows and interconnections.

- Evaluating the South African tabloids against the emerging literature on convergent and
networked journalism, they would seem to follow a conventional journalism model,
where information is gathered by journalists (albeit with the help of correspondents and
informants in the field), packaged according to conventional journalistic routines in the
newsroom, and then disseminated to a mass audience. However, considered against
the broader picture of the structural exclusions still experienced by a large section of the
South African public with regards to mainstream print media, these tabloids manage to
elicit from their readers a significant amount of trust and reciprocity. There is an element
of interactivity between the tabloid editorial staff and their readership that extends
beyond the conventional one-dimensional model of news dissemination and consumption, even if this interactivity is not mediated extensively through new media
technologies. In fact, if new media technologies were to be introduced into this
relationship it would perhaps even broaden the divide between elite, urban-based
journalists and the working-class and largely rural constituencies these tabloids serve.
Bardoel and Deuze (2001) suggest that "networked journalism" results from technological, professional and cultural changes that re-invigorate the values of civic journalism in
the new media age. The South African tabloids may well fulfil some of the ideals of
orientation towards the audience that civic journalism holds dear. One should, however,
not push this analogy too far. Just as the interactivity created by new media technologies
can seduce one to view the reader-as-consumer relationship through rose-tinted glasses
without recognizing persistent inequalities and power differentials, one could romanti-
cize the South African tabloids as well. The fact remains that they are big business
ventures with an eye on profits, and that they still operate very much according to

commercial logics and hierarchies. The opportunities for feedback and user-created content remain limited.

Perhaps the most important point that the South African tabloids illustrate is that, whether a newspaper has all the technological bells and whistles, or whether it is printed on paper and passed on from hand-to-hand at taxi ranks and on the factory floor, interactivity takes many forms. What form it takes will depend on material conditions, historical context and social formations. And these conditions will keep changing constantly, now and in the future.

NOTES

1. If her assertion is correct that tabloid narratives are based on oral culture, it could be argued that the South African tabloids tap into an ancient tradition of African storytelling (this already forms the topic of a postgraduate dissertation at the Tshwane University of Technology) (Machelene Joubert, personal communication, 2007). The oral tradition in other forms of media in sub-Saharan Africa, for instance television, has also been noted by Bourgault (1995, p. 140)

2. The *Daily Sun* at the time of writing had only a masthead on its website with the message "under construction" (www.dailysun.co.za); the *Kaapse Son*'s website (www.dieson.co.za) contains mostly an archive of its page three girls, with a random selection of recent sports stories and video clips; and typing in the URL for the *Daily Voice* redirects the browser to Independent Newspapers' general news site, Independent Online (www.iol. co.za). Articles that have appeared in *Son* can be found in the online archives of *Die Burger*, its sister newspaper in the Naspers stable, but only via the search engine on *Die Burger*'s website.

3. There have been earlier manifestations of tabloid-type newspapers, like the Afrikaans *Dagbreek en Landstem* in the 1960s (De Villiers, 1992), and *Bantu World*, founded in 1932 (see Switzer, 1988), to which the veteran black editor and since 2007 Press Ombudsman Joe Thloloe has compared the *Daily Sun* for what he saw as its stereotypical portrayal of black people by a paper "owned by white editorial directors who 'knew' the Bantu". He described the *Daily Sun* as a "patronizing throwback to the *Bantu World* of the 1950s" (Thloloe, 2004). Although the context in which these tabloids operated was very different from that of the post-apartheid tabloids, the latter example is noteworthy. The relationship between white owners/publishers and black audiences against the background of a big commercial enterprise, as in the case of *Bantu World*, as well as the articulation of working-class aspirations in terms of the accoutrements of the petty-bourgeoisie (Switzer, 1988, p. 352) is relevant (although not entirely similar) to the current tabloids.

4. The editor of the Cape Town daily tabloid *Daily Voice*, Karl Brophy, sees the term "mainstream media" apply to tabloids rather than broadsheets: "Given that the *Daily Sun* is, quite clearly, the biggest selling newspaper in the country and accepting that the *Daily Voice* is, by far, the biggest selling newspaper in Cape Town how do we (i.e. us and the *Daily Sun*) not qualify as the 'mainstream media'? Surely we are the mainstream media and the *Cape Times* et al. are 'niche media'" (personal communication, 31 January 2007). In this article I nevertheless prefer to use the term "mainstream press" to refer to broadsheet newspapers, since these media preceded the entry of the tabloids on the

market and still dominate the discourse about professional journalism, as was evident from the clash between tabloid editors and other members of the South African National Editors' Forum, notably at the 2005 Sanef Annual General Meeting in Cape Town (Barrett, 2006). Although the tone of debate at the latter was "exclusionary" (Ferial Haffajee, personal communication, 2007), Sanef issued a statement in which the tabloids were welcomed as a "vibrant part of the changing landscape" (Barrett, 2006, p. 57). My choice to refer to broadsheets as "mainstream" is therefore informed not by circulation figures but the balance of power in journalistic discourse in the country, which might well change over time.

5. The *Sowetan* has a history of being a well-established paper aimed at "urban-based, relatively affluent African readers" and under apartheid challenged the ruling order (Tomaselli, 2000, p. 378). Other notable mainstream newspapers (albeit sometimes also showing a tabloid influence) aimed at a urban black readership are the Zulu-language papers *Isolezwe*, *Ilanga* and *UmAfrika*. The latter three have shown growth in circulation and revenue over the last few years (Bloom, 2005).

6. The themes outlined here are not exhaustive and are based on an exploratory reading rather than a quantitative content analysis. My reading of the tabloids is also informed by interviews with journalists and focus group interviews with readers of different tabloids in various parts of the country.

7. The *Daily Sun*'s editor is Themba Khumalo, but Du Plessis fulfils most of the executive editorial functions, like convening the daily news conference and deciding on the lead stories, which he often rewrites himself.

REFERENCES

AHRENS, FRANK (2005) "Hard News: daily papers face unprecedented competition", *Washington Post*, 20 February.

BARDOEL, JO and DEUZE, MARK (2001) "'Network Journalism': converging competences of old and new media professionals", *Australian Journalism Review* 23(2), pp. 91–103.

BARRETT, ELIZABETH (2006) *Part of the Story—10 years of the South African National Editors' Forum*, Rosebank: South African National Editors' Forum.

BECKETT, CHARLIE and KYRKE-SMITH, LAURA (2007) *Development, Governance and the Media: the role of the media in building African society*, London: Polis.

BEK, MINE GENCEL (2004) "Tabloidization of News Media: an analysis of television news in Turkey", *European Journal of Communication* 19(3), pp. 371–86.

BERESFORD, DAVID (2004) "South Africa Gets the Newspapers It Deserves", *The Observer*, 14 November.

BIRD, ELIZABETH (1992) *For Enquiring Minds—a cultural study of supermarket tabloids*, Knoxville: University of Tenessee Press.

BIZCOMMUNITY (2007) *Kaapse Son* profile, http://www.biz-community.com/PressOffice/AboutUs. aspx?i=115059, accessed 20 August 2007.

BLOOM, KEVIN (2003) "Daily Sun Outshines All", *The Media Online*, 3 March.

BLOOM, KEVIN (2005) "Untapped Markets", *Mail & Guardian Online*, http://www.mg.co.za/ articlePage.aspx?articleid=200953&area=/media_insightfeatures, accessed 16 August 2007.

BOURGAULT, LOUISE (1995) *Mass Media in Sub-Saharan Africa*, Bloomington: Indiana University Press.

CONBOY, MARTIN (2005) *Tabloid Britain*, London: Routledge.

CRUYWAGEN, VINCENT (2007) "Wit rassis het my sus net so laat verdrink [White racist left my sister to drown]", *Daily Voice*, 11 April.

CURRAN, JAMES (2003) "The Press in the Age of Globalization", in: James Curran and Jean Seaton (Eds), *Power without Responsibility*, Abingdon: Routledge, pp. 67–105.

DAILY SUN (2007a) "The Hospital of Horrors!", 1 January.

DAILY SUN (2007b) "I Am Not a Woman!", 22 February.

DAILY SUN (2007c) "She Can't Retire!", 24 May, p. 12.

DAILY SUN (2007d) "No Mercy! Hospital bars family—then they're hijacked!", 1 February.

DAILY SUN (2007e) "Where Mbeki Went Wrong!", 28 November.

DAILY VOICE (2007a) "Koeëlbloedig [In Cold Blood]", 12 April, p. 1.

DAILY VOICE (2007b) "Cop Skoot [Head Shot]", 11 April.

DAILY VOICE (2007c) "Kwaai Cabbies", 13 April, p. 29.

DE VILLIERS, DIRK (1992) "Die Beeld (Sondagblad)", in: W. Beukes (Ed.), *Oor Grense Heen: Op pad na 'n nasionale pers 1948–1990*, Cape Town: Nasionale Boekhandel, pp. 220–53.

DEUZE, MARK (2004) "What Is Multimedia Journalism?", *Journalism Studies* 5(2), pp. 139–52.

FISKE, JOHN (1989) *Understanding Popular Culture*, Boston: Unwin Hyman.

FISKE, JOHN (1992) "Popularity and the Politics of Information", in: P. Dahlgren and C. Sparks (Eds) *Journalism and Popular Culture*, London: Sage, pp. 45–63.

GLYNN, KEVIN (2000) *Tabloid Culture—trash taste, popular power and the transformation of American television*, Durham, NC: Duke University Press.

GRABE, MARIA, ZHOU, SHUHUA and BARNETT, BROOKE (1999) "Sourcing and Reporting in News Magazine Programs: *60 Minutes* versus *Hard Copy*", *Journalism & Mass Communication Quarterly* 76(2), pp. 293–311.

GRIPSRUD, JOSTEIN (2000) "Tabloidization, Popular Journalism and Democracy", in: C. Sparks and J. Tulloch (Eds), *Tabloid Tales: global debates over media standards*, Lanham, MD: Rowman and Littlefield, pp. 285–300.

GROBLER, FIENIE (2007) "Latest Circulation Numbers Show Decline in Consumer Titles" [electronic version], *E-Media*, 16 August.

HALLIN, DANIEL (2000) "La Nota Roja: popular journalism and the transition to democracy in Mexico", in: C. Sparks and J. Tulloch (Eds), *Tabloid Tales: global debates over media standards*, Lanham, MD: Rowman and Littlefield, pp. 267–284.

HINERMAN, STEPHEN (1997) "(Don't) Leave Me Alone: tabloid narrative and the Michael Jackson child-abuse scandal", in: J. Lull and S. Hinerman (Eds), *Media Scandals*, Cambridge: Polity Press.

JONES, ADAM (2002) "From Vanguard to Vanquished? The tabloid press in Jordan", *Political Communication* 19, pp. 171–87.

KINSLEY, MICHAEL (2006) "Do Newspapers have a Future?", *Time*, 25 September.

KOPPER, GERD, KOLTHOFF, ALBRECHT and CZEPEK, ANDREA (2000) "Research Review: Online Journalism—a report on current and continuing research and major questions in the international discussion", *Journalism Studies* 1(3), pp. 499–512.

KRUGER, FRANZ (2006) "It's Only News if It's True", http://www.journalism.co.za, accessed 14 August 2007.

LOUW, P. ERIC (2001) *The Media and Cultural Production*, London: Sage.

MABWEAZARA, HAYES (2006) *An investigation into the Popularity of the Zimbabwean Tabloid Newspaper, uMthunywa: a reception study of Bulawayo readers*, Grahamstown, South Africa: Rhodes University.

MEIJER, IRENE (2001) "The Public Quality of Popular Journalism: developing a normative framework", *Journalism Studies* 2(2), pp. 189–205.

MEYER, PHILIP (2004) *The Vanishing Newspaper: saving journalism in the Information Age*, Columbia: University of Missouri Press.

PENSTONE, KIM (2005) "Sex Sells, Says Independent Newspapers", *Marketingweb*, 17 March.

PLUNKETT, JOHN (2005) "Murdoch Predicts Gloomy Future for Press", *The Guardian*, 24 November.

QUINN, STEPHEN (2005) *Convergent Journalism—the fundamentals of multimedia reporting*, New York: Peter Lang.

SINGER, JANE (1997) "Changes and Consistencies: newspaper journalists contemplate online future", *Newspaper Research Journal* 18 (1–2), pp. 2–18.

SON (2007a) "Sent Packing by the Sheriff", 13 April, p. 2.

SPARKS, COLIN (2000) "Introduction: the panic over tabloid news", in: C. Sparks and J. Tulloch (Eds), *Tabloid Tales: global debates over media standards*, Lanham, MD: Rowman and Littlefield, pp. 1–40.

SWITZER, LES (1988) "Bantu World and the Origins of a Captive African Commercial Press in South Africa", *Journal of Southern African Studies* 14(3), pp. 351–70.

TAYLOR, ANNE and MILNE, CLAIRE (2006) *South Africa AMDI Research Report: newspapers*, London: BBC World Service Trust.

THE MEDIA ONLINE (2004) "Johncom Restructures Sowetan, Sunday World", *The Media Online*, 19 August.

THLOLOE, JOE (2004) "Desperately Searching for Staff", paper presented to the colloquium "Taking Stock of 10 Years of Media Training and Education at Tertiary Institutions—addressing an agenda for the next decade", http://journ.ru.ac.za/colloquium/papers/ETV.pdf, accessed 14 August 2007.

TOMASELLI, KEYAN (2000) "Ambiguities in Alternative Discourse—*New Nation* and the *Sowetan* in the 1980s", in: L. Switzer and M. Adhikari (Eds), *South Africa's Resistance Press—alternative voices in the last generation under apartheid*, Athens: Ohio University Press, pp. 378–403.

TOOTH, GERALD (2006) "Totally Tabloid", http://www.abc.net.au/rn/talks/8.30/mediarpt/stories/s1560445.htm, accessed 15 August 2007.

TOWNSEND, KATE (2006) "Tabloid Grabs South African Market", *BBC Two This World*, http://news.bbc.co.uk/nolpda/ifs_news/hi/newsid_6045000/6045650.stm, accessed 16 August 2007.

URSELL, GILLIAN (2001) "Dumbing Down or Shaping Up? New technologies, new media, new journalism", *Journalism & Mass Communication Quarterly* 2(2), pp. 175–96.

WASSERMAN, HERMAN (2006) "Tackles and Sidesteps: normative maintenance and paradigm repair in mainstream media reactions to tabloid journalism", *Communicare* 25(1), pp. 59–80.

Chapter 12

THE HISTORY OF A SURVIVING SPECIES
Defining eras in the evolution of foreign correspondence

Jaci Cole and **John Maxwell Hamilton**

Introduction

Foreign correspondence has a natural history.[1] Like a living creature, it has adapted over time to a changing environment in order to survive. This concept was originally propounded in a classic 1925 essay by sociologist Robert Park to describe newspapers generally. The history of the newspaper, he wrote, "is the history of the surviving species. It is an account of the conditions under which the existing newspaper has grown up and taken form" (Park, 1960 [1925], pp. 8–9).

In a previous study (Cole and Hamilton, 2007), we showed how this approach could be used to understand the evolution of the first great American newspaper foreign service, that of the *Chicago Daily News*, and by extension the evolution of modern American foreign newsgathering. But more can be done to realize the full value of Park's observation as it applies to foreign news.

The history of foreign newsgathering is typically approached by analyzing coverage of individual events rather than by tracing systemic change over time. We seek to advance the latter, largely overlooked avenue of research by proposing a historical framework for the study of foreign newsgathering by US media. This essay outlines distinct, if overlapping, stages in its evolution. It carries this history up to the present, a nascent stage that contains elements from the evolutionary past. As Park wrote, the press is "all that it was and something more. To understand it we must see it in its historic perspective" (Park, 1960 [1925], p. 11).

Literature Review

No scholar has attempted to give foreign news a coherent historical framework. Even book-length histories of foreign news have tended to be, like news itself, episodic. They deal with individual wars or other events, chronicle the lives of outstanding correspondents, or look at one aspect of coverage. In this latter category, one exemplar is Phillip Knightley's *The First Casualty: the war correspondent as hero and myth-maker from the Crimea to Kosovo* (2004). Only one broad historical survey is in print: John Hohenberg's *Foreign Correspondence: the great reporters and their times* (1964). It is an encyclopedic name–date–place history of great value to scholars but makes no attempt to delineate changing approaches to newsgathering. Written in the same spirit but limited to a handful of 20th-century events is Michael Emery's brief *On the Front Lines* (1995). Also of value for basic facts, but dated and out of print, are Robert W. Desmond's five descriptive histories, beginning with *The Press and World Affairs*, published in 1937, and ending with *The Tides of War: world news reporting: 1931–1945*, published in 1984 (Desmond, 1937, 1978, 1980, 1982, 1984).

Journal articles on the history of foreign news also tend to look at episodes,[2] with the exception of articles that measure changes in the amount and focus of international news in newspapers and on television.[3] Such longitudinal studies tend to track changes against normative assumptions about what the news ought to be. They generally are not designed to understand the broad evolution of foreign newsgathering.

A historical framework will, we hope, facilitate a better understanding of why journalists do what they do in any given period and help scholars see that a dynamic process shapes and reshapes the news. This would benefit not only historians but also social scientists, who are prone to look at individual events as "the way foreign news is" rather than as the way it is at a given point in time.

The Approach

Our focus is the basic act of newsgathering. In identifying individual periods, we give special weight to changes in four factors that in turn combine to produce major shifts in foreign newsgathering from one time to another. These are: ownership, technology, America's place in the world, and correspondents' roles and routines.[4] In some periods, change in one or the other of these is far more important than in others.

We give approximate but not exact dates for these eras—journalistic periods of change are not landmarked like innings in a baseball game. In foreign correspondence, the second inning is played even as the fourth begins. For example, it is not that special correspondents no longer exist at the end of the era of The Specials, but they exist in a brand new context. They no longer are the defining element of that era.

Because of the limitations of space, we briefly sketch these eras. We intend for this framework to serve as a starting point for other scholars' work.

Eras in the Evolution of Foreign Correspondence

The Casual Correspondents, 1700–1840

America's first newspapers did not have reporters or, really, editors at home let alone abroad. The first foreign correspondents were friendly souls in London or Paris who wrote letters home as well as passengers and crew who hove into port with newspapers from abroad and their own stories to tell. Acknowledging the importance of free help in supplying his *Pennsylvania Gazette* with material, Benjamin Franklin once wrote in its pages, "There are many who have long desired to see a good News-Paper in Pennsylvania; and we hope those Gentlemen who are able, will contribute towards the making this such."[5]

European newspapers and journals brought by ship were the equivalent of today's overseas wire services. Colonial newspapers freely reprinted official government pronouncements and other news found in those journals. Franklin's *Gazette* piped more than four-fifths of its news about the British Isles directly from other newspapers. When harsh winter weather disrupted shipping or someone lost precious printed cargo, news dried up.

Ownership.   Early American newspapers were by-products of the colonial printer's trade and, as merely another part of the business, largely passive and opportunistic in terms of newsgathering. Three-fourths of colonial printers between 1700 and 1765 published newspapers (Botein, 1975, p. 147). The highly entrepreneurial Franklin printed almanacs and other books, Pennsylvania's currency, *and* his *Gazette.* Franklin's appointment as royal postmaster was an important part of his business operation. Newspaper publishers cum postmasters sat comfortably at the center of the information flow into and out of their communities. This allowed them to collect information simply by sitting in their offices or strolling down to the port to greet incoming ships.

Ownership evolved as political parties came to dominate American political life around the turn of the 18th century. The founding fathers divided over policies of the new republic and financially supported the newspapers that sided with them. Franklin's grandson, Benjamin Franklin Bache, created one of the most well-known of these party papers, the *General Advertiser*, later called the *Aurora.* Thomas Jefferson supported the *General Advertiser* by helping Bache acquire copies of foreign newspapers and urging party leaders to pen articles for his paper. Alexander Hamilton also authored pieces for his party's prize journal, the *Gazette of the United States*, and once saved that paper from financial ruin.[6]

Although partisan involvement in ownership did not change the basic newsgathering model, it could affect content. In coverage of the French Revolution, for example, the leading Federalist paper was more negative than Bache's Republican paper (see Cole and Hamilton, 2008).

Technology.   Technology in this stage would have been familiar to Johannes Gutenberg. The news arrived no faster than a horse or ship could carry it. For foreign news, this meant well over a month could pass before a story reached the United States from Europe. A news item about Italy could be two or three months old because the British paper from which it was taken had to wait weeks to get the original report. Speed was not possible even if it was desired, and it was not desired because no one could realistically think in those terms.

America's place in the world.   The high-water point of foreign news—measured by the amount of space given to it—was in the 18th century. Common explanations for the emphasis on foreign news are that most people knew what was going on anyway in their small communities and that foreign news was less likely to impinge on local sensitivities.[7]

Printers all over the colonies took pains to remind their readers that they strove, as one New York publisher vowed, *"not to be any Ways concerned in Disputes"* (Botein, 1975, p. 190). Powerful positive reasons argued for foreign news as well. Foreign affairs had considerable interest for the colonists, who had strong ties to the Old World, especially to England, which dominated the foreign news. Those ties were practical as well as emotional. Businessmen needed to know the "Price Currant" of imported and exported goods. Economic and political policy made in London, Paris, Vienna, and Madrid materialized in the Americas. The Seven Years War in Europe spilled over to the colonies in the form of the French and Indian War; a central issue in that conflict was which European nation would control North America. Americans celebrated the English victory, signed at the 1763 Treaty of Paris, and rued news about the resulting English taxation policy implemented to defray war debts. British newspapers themselves provided extensive coverage of foreign affairs for much the same reason American newspapers did: readers saw foreign news as relevant (see Bailyn, 1990, p. 190; Copeland, 1997; Hester et al., 1980, p. 22; Merritt, 1963, pp. 368–9).

Correspondents roles and routines.   Newspaper editors thought of themselves as printers. Although they saw themselves performing a public service, the limitations under which they worked made original foreign newsgathering virtually impossible. Instructively, when Franklin wrote letters back from England in the mid-1700s, he no longer had day-to-day responsibility for his newspaper. In fact, he went there not to provide news, but as a diplomat. He was a casual correspondent instead of a casual editor.

The Specials, 1840–1900

With the advent of the penny press in the early 1800s, American newspapers began to have specialized reporters and editors who sought to fill the news pages with information that would attract a large audience.[8] In the case of foreign news, this led to the development of special correspondents who filed from abroad. In the beginning, when the role of the reporter, domestic or foreign, was still ill-defined, foreign correspondents were often part-timers with other jobs. Many were still volunteers. James Gordon Bennett, the most successful of the early penny press editors, had specials in Glasgow, Berlin, Brussels, London, Paris, Rome, Jamaica, Liverpool, LeHavre, and elsewhere for his *New York Herald* (see Bjork, 1992, pp. 10–13; Desmond, 1978, pp. 92, 93; Hudson, 1873, p. 482). In time, these specials became more entrepreneurial in their newsgathering. One example is Henry Morton Stanley, who famously set out to find David Livingstone in Africa for the *Herald*, then run by Bennett's son.

Ownership.   Journalism became a business, not a side trade or a politically subsidized enterprise. The editors who dominated this period were entrepreneurs who focused on making a profit. Their business model worked basically like this: run reports of lively local news, attract the great mass of readers local advertisers want to reach, and make a handsome profit.

Although this model introduced the idea of original reporting abroad, it led to a decrease in the amount of foreign news. This occurred because the new model emphasized local news and because newsgathering abroad was expensive. From this point forward, foreign news would be a small part of the average newspaper except during wars and other crises. The newspapers that did emphasize foreign news were likely to be members of the prestige press,[9] which sought to extend its readership to elites, as Bennett aspired to.

Technology.   Editors in this era enthusiastically talked about "the annihilation" of time and space. During urgent events, editors became particularly creative. When the Mexican War broke out, the New Orleans *Daily Picayune* created a relay system to get news from the battlefields. "Mr. Kendall's Express," named after the paper's editor, began with riders carrying dispatches to the Mexican coast. Regular mail boats carried the news onward to New Orleans. When it was especially eager to get a jump on competitors, the *Picayune* sent a small, fast steamer fitted out with typesetting equipment to meet the mail boat.

The prospect of getting news even faster came with the completion in 1858 of a transatlantic cable. Although the cable line soon went permanently dead, eight years later a new "ocean greyhound" hummed with foreign news, which flew across the country. Cables were strung between Java and Port Darwin in Australia in 1873, and between Europe and Brazil the following year. To help reduce the costs of foreign newsgathering, newspapers pooled resources to gather routine distant news. This became the basis for the Associated Press.

America's place in the world.   Free of its colonial master and largely self-sufficient in resources, America was a relatively insulated country. This, too, worked against more aggressive foreign news coverage.[10] Even though the Associated Press was created during this period to cut down on the costs individual newspapers had to shoulder, the Associated Press had few foreign bureaus. The association instead carried the news of services from other countries.

Correspondents' roles and routines.   Although ethical codes were non-existent in the era of The Specials, a professional ideal began to take shape. Quasi-correspondents early in this era distinguished themselves journalistically by taking a break from fighting to report what they saw. By the end of this era, such half measures had become passé. Correspondents were expected to be dedicated to newsgathering. And given their small numbers and the importance of their job, they began to be seen as professional elites. "The special correspondent must be 'to the manor born,'" observed a *Scribner's* author in 1893. "He must be as sanguine as a songbird, and as strong and willing as a race horse" (Ralph, 1893, p. 154).[11]

The Foreign Service, 1900–1930

In the era of The Specials, there was a strong emphasis on the sensational and the episodic, the culmination of which was seen in coverage of the Spanish–American War. This new era of the Foreign Service saw a more systematic approach to the news, in which individual correspondents became part of a larger network of newsgatherers.

A glimmer of this was George Washburn Smalley, correspondent for the New York *Tribune*. From his base in London, he was a genius at organizing the flow of European news around special events, whether the Franco-Prussian War of 1870–1 or the Oxford–Harvard boat race of 1869 (Smalley, 1984, 1911). But the epitome of organization in newsgathering, arguably the inventor of it, was Victor Lawson, owner and editor of the *Chicago Daily News*. The *Chicago Daily News* foreign service was the first thoroughly professional corps of American correspondents abroad. Their reporting was eventually syndicated widely (see Cole and Hamilton, 2007; Dennis, 1935).

Ownership.   Although less flamboyant than the Pulitzers and Hearsts of the era of The Specials, owners were still an important factor in this period. These were still businessmen who cared about the bottom line, especially since the cost of publishing had increased. But profit motives were also mixed with a sense of public spiritedness.

Lawson was one of the first to display this mix of business sense and responsibility, but he was soon followed by Adolph Ochs of the *New York Times*. The *Christian Science Monitor*, which began in 1908 as a Christian Science counterweight to yellow journalism, was to have one of the strongest foreign services in the 20th century. The *Philadelphia Public Ledger*, New York *Evening Post*, the *New York Herald Tribune*, the *New York World*, and the *Chicago Tribune* all started foreign services in due course. In addition, there were specialized syndicates, one example being the Consolidated Press.

Technology.   The Era of the Foreign Service saw the advent of greater speed over cable and telegraph lines. This enabled journalists to file important news quickly, which the wire services specialized in. Newspapers tried different approaches, but one that was especially effective was to focus on less time-sensitive, in-depth reporting that could be sent through the mail, which was less costly (see Cole and Hamilton, 2007, p. 159). Improved communication allowed coordination among the home office, foreign bureaus, and correspondents. But because of the irregularities and high cost of transmission, correspondents still enjoyed a high degree of independence.

America's place in the world.   This is perhaps the most important factor of change during this period. With the Spanish–American War in 1898, the United States had become a world power. "It is no longer desirable, or even safe," Lawson told one of his editors at the end of the war, "for public opinion in this country to rely, as it now does, almost exclusively on foreign agencies, most of them subsidized by foreign governments, for their news of foreign countries" (Dennis, 1935, p. 264). Recognition of this change did not bring an upsurge in the amount of foreign reporting by the average newspaper. But it did bring a much higher quality of reporting by the best newspapers.

Correspondents' roles and routines.   Lawson's vision created a template for other prestige papers like the *New York Times*. He favored American reporters reporting for Americans, and he believed these journalists needed to go beyond the common practice of combing foreign publications for the news and gather it themselves. He also left them in the field for years. In a 1920 internal *Daily News* memo, Lawson's Paris bureau chief, Paul Scott Mowrer, wrote, "If public opinion is to conduct our foreign affairs wisely, it must be rightly informed, by expert observers."[12]

The Compleat Correspondents, 1930–1970

The years between the two world wars were the beginning of a golden age for foreign correspondence, a high point in terms of professionalism and competence and clearly defined ideas of what quality foreign news was.[13] Outlets for foreign reporting proliferated, most dramatically in the new medium of broadcast. News magazines like *Time*, *Newsweek*, *Life*, and *Look* began. General interest magazines with a broad readership, such as the *Saturday Evening Post* and the *New Yorker*, showed a strong interest in foreign affairs and also gave reporters scope to write longer pieces.[14] Beginning in the mid-1930s, scores of books and memoirs by foreign correspondents began to appear. Other forces, too, combined in this period to optimize the work of foreign correspondents.

Ownership.   Individuals continued to dominate newspapers as well as other media, either owning individual news properties or presiding over media empires, some of which sold shares to the public. A relatively large number took Lawson's point of view on social responsibility and subsidized foreign news coverage. When one correspondent told CBS board chair William Paley his plans for foreign correspondence were going to "cost you a lot of money," Paley famously replied, "You guys cover the news. I have Jack Benny to make money for me."[15]

Technology.   An enormous audience for foreign news emerged with the advent of an entirely new medium, radio, which took root and then burst into flower when overseas crises erupted and the public wanted up-to-the-minute reports. By the end of the 1930s, millions of Americans had their ears turned toward their radio sets. Some correspondents became fulltime broadcasters. But in its early stages radio also made use of experienced print journalists for on-air reporting and observations.

America's place in the world.   In this era, news took on grand, urgent proportions for Americans. Fascism rose in Germany, Italy, Spain, and Japan; after the war, communism emerged in Russia and China; the seeds of independence germinated in India and other colonized lands. The issues were sweeping, the consequences for people everywhere staggering. "The phenomenon of contemporaneity is one that has never been experienced by the world as a whole until now," wrote correspondent Vincent Sheean (1939, p. 343).

The United States' direct involvement in the world grew dramatically after World War II, but even in the isolationist 1920s, when the American government tried to avoid entanglements, individual citizens were deeply involved overseas. As Paul Scott Mowrer, correspondent for the *Chicago Daily News* observed, Americans were "traveling or trading, for business, science, art, education, or pleasure, in every corner of the six continents and all the islands of the oceans" (1924, p. 308).

In line with the old adage about coups and earthquakes commanding the most attention, foreign news fluctuated, especially among medium and smaller news outlets that could not afford their own foreign correspondents. Coverage reached greater intensity during outright wars, such as World War II and Vietnam.

Correspondents' roles and routines.   With their names on books, greater use of bylines in newspapers, and on-air reporting—all against the backdrop of roiling international issues—correspondents reached a high point in terms of celebrity. This contributed to their autonomy and, because many were still allowed to stay abroad for long periods, their expertise. As a relatively small group with direct links to the American public, correspondents were treated with difference by the foreigners they covered as well.

The Corporate Correspondent, 1970–2000

In this period, foreign correspondence tended to move away from the paths trod during the era of the Compleat Correspondents. Correspondents were far less free-wheeling and flamboyant, less likely to spend decades overseas. Even their numbers seemed to go down.

Ownership. A key factor in this change was the nature of ownership. More corporate ownership and a greater concern for profit combined with concerns about a dwindling audience for news. Foreign news, the most expensive kind of news, was not the best way to attract viewers, listeners, and readers. As more media companies went public, grew larger, more diversified, and more corporate, in some cases becoming part of non-media companies (e.g., NBC owned by General Electric), their executives sought bragging rights on Wall Street. On that boulevard, few were impressed that an editor spent more of their money on foreign news coverage.

Technology. Technology was an equally important factor in these changes. Reporters traveled farther and faster to get to stories. They reported live from anywhere. But the ability to file instantly also became a requirement, not just a luxury, and it had costs. Speed tended to trump depth. There had always been a concern on the part of correspondents that technology makes it difficult to have thoughtful journalism. But correspondence in this era reached the ultimate in terms of immediacy. The time between witnessing a story and writing about it was reduced to basically no time at all (see Foote, 1998).

Also, instant communication made it possible for the home office to closely coordinate the work of correspondents. This allowed the creation of packages but also made correspondents less free to look for news on their own. No matter how insistent foreign editors were about wanting to give correspondents plenty of latitude, large organizations run by executives with MBAs, boards of directors, and mission statements inevitably placed a high value on controls. Worldwide communications that facilitate instant daily communication with correspondents gave added muscle to this managerial discipline. With modern travel, journalists with media that were strictly local could go abroad to do a story. While this added to foreign reporting, major media that had correspondents abroad permanently used parachute journalism as a way to cut corners.

America's place in the world. The global responsibilities and ties of the United States are enormous. Coverage, however, did not keep up with this. Up to the fall of the Berlin Wall and the end of the Cold War, there was quite a lot of foreign news. But afterward, when communism was no longer a world threat, the amount fell off considerably. In the words of Herbert Swope, who made notable scoops for the New York *World* during World War I, foreign news was normally to be given to the reader "in spoonfuls and damned small ones at that" (van Paassen, 1939, p. 109).

Correspondents' roles and routines. Correspondents tended to be company men. It was much harder to be an independent freelance correspondent for traditional media. Living abroad was no longer cheap, and the attraction of a fulltime job was much more powerful because of the need for benefits (Jurden, 1993, p. 115; Scofea, 1994, p. 6). Earlier correspondents did not concern themselves with health insurance. (In 1940, less than

10 percent of Americans were covered by some sort of health plan. Fifty years later, with the costs of health care escalating, only 14 percent of Americans did *not* have health coverage—and 71 percent of those who did acquired their insurance through an employer.) Said one freelance correspondent covering the Middle East, "There's probably a limit to how long I'll be interested in coming to places like Iraq. There's also a part of me that wants to have a normal life; an apartment in a cool American city, a job with health benefits, and the rest of it" (Gallagher, 2004). The modern foreign correspondent, concluded the author of a 1967 study of correspondents' work habits, was unlike his dashing predecessors "in at least one significant respect: he is not a loner but an organization man" (Bogart, 1968, p. 305).

In this environment, correspondents were far less often eccentric or flamboyant. "It's a corporation, and it's a business; it's a brand," said *USA Today World* Editor Elisa Tinsley, "and there is less tolerance for the kind of eccentricities that you used to always see in our profession."[16] Her newspaper has a written "USA Today Overseas Journalist Safety Policy." "You must obtain permission from your editors before entering a hostile environment," it states. "You must routinely advise your editors of your movements."

Today's Surviving Species: Our Current Era in the Natural History of Foreign Correspondence

A Confederacy of Correspondences

Foreign correspondence enters a new era: newsgathering abroad appears to be moving toward a system of multiple models co-existing and collectively providing information. In this Confederacy of Correspondences, serious foreign newsgathering by the *New York Times* and other prestige media continues, although with continual experimentation, such a greater use of nationals in the countries covered. Other species of foreign newsgathering and distribution have emerged that, while new, carry the DNA of much earlier forms thought to be extinct. These new forms include:

- *Premium service foreign correspondents* report from bureaus overseas for "gated," high-cost news services. Bloomberg News and the Dow Jones News Wire are examples of this. The services for which these correspondents report have a global audience. A Bloomberg correspondent in Singapore is a foreign correspondent as far as a client in Minneapolis is concerned, but local for a Singapore subscriber.
- *In-house foreign correspondents* are employees of a non-news organization whose exclusive job is to provide updated and high-quality news and information related to the organization's mission. Sometimes they do original reporting; more often they aggregate news that appears in traditional and non-traditional media and distribute it over their own networks.
- *Citizen foreign correspondents* are individuals without journalistic training or affiliation who become *de facto* journalists when they report on foreign events and issues, often by posting the information directly on the Internet. They also can be their own foreign editor by accessing information without relying on the editorial function of a newspaper, magazine, or broadcast entity.
- *Foreign local correspondents* are non-Americans who work and report for a foreign news organization whose news is available worldwide on the Internet. An example is an Indian journalist reporting for a New Delhi newspaper or broadcast station whose work is

accessed via the Internet or satellite from Indianapolis. One of the chief audiences for such news is an Indian emigrant.

The overall result is a broader, more variegated class of foreign correspondents that, if still imperfect, ensures continued foreign news flow and forms a basis for improvement.[17]

Ownership.   Ownership is in flux. First, traditional media companies are changing hands, in some cases going from being a publicly owned company to being privately held. Paralleling this change in ownership is mounting concern over the viability of traditional media. Hence, a return to private ownership does not guarantee strong foreign reporting. Bloomberg, however, began as a private company and remains that way—and has a strong commitment to foreign news. In addition, the liberating quality of new technology allows individuals to become virtual owners of their own news networks.

Technology.   Behind all of the new types of correspondence is technology, chiefly the Internet. "Technology," said Frank Governale, CBS vice president for operations, "has advanced to the point where the only limitation is in the imagination of the correspondent."[18]

America's place in the world.   The United States is back to a point where foreign affairs are again urgent. The traditional media have given considerable attention to the war in Iraq. But traditional media foreign affairs coverage still is strikingly limited because of the constraints the media faces. New alternative media have helped supplement this coverage. For all the talk about declining numbers of foreign correspondents, no census takes into account the fact that in 2007 Bloomberg had 1,000 radio and television journalists inside the United States in some 50 bureaus and 1,250 outside in about 80 bureaus.

A constraint that has been building for some time has now acquired considerable force, anti-Americanism. This has had an impact on correspondents' work, making it more dangerous and limiting their access. "Anti-Americanism is on the rise throughout the world," the Council on Foreign Relations noted in 2003 (Peterson et al., 2003, p. 5). Foreign peoples, as polls show, have "a mostly negative picture of . . . America, its people and policies" (Jurgen, 2003, p. 1; see also DeFleur and DeFleur, 2003, p. 57). Correspondents no longer go abroad, as Vincent Sheean did, believing their citizenship "was a kind of insurance against misfortune" (1939, p. 345).

Correspondents' roles and routines.   There are different ways to be a foreign correspondent, as we described above. Also, we see a return to some earlier forms of reporting: the casual correspondent, who is not even a journalist, filing by himself on the Web, or a special correspondent, like Kevin Sites who is a sort of one-man foreign service for Yahoo! We also have highly-sophisticated experts filing over the Web, for example, Dow Jones News Service reporters and those for Bloomberg.

Conclusion

The ambition for this paper has been to begin to build a historical framework for foreign news. Considerable meaning and richness is lost when more than two centuries are lumped into an undifferentiated mass, just as would be the case if one did not distinguish between the Renaissance and the Enlightenment.

Our model is not perfect. It is a first attempt at the challenging task of creating a historical framework for delineating changes in American foreign newsgathering and understanding the broad forces that work on foreign news, for better or worse. Developing a coherent, complete model will require considerable give and take among scholars.

One way to build on this model is to look at the evolution of foreign correspondence in other countries. Another is to look at newsgathering in the context of thousands of years of history as opposed to two hundred or so.

In any event, such a model is of value not only to historians. Social scientists also can make good use of it to place their in-depth case studies in perspective. Perspective is especially important today when the model for foreign newsgathering is becoming far more complicated. With so much Darwinian conjecture about the extinction of foreign news, we need history to help us think creatively about how to make new models function optimally.

NOTES

1. We have argued this point, building off the insights of sociologist Robert Park, in Cole and Hamilton (2007). For Park's essay, see Park (1960 [1925]).
2. See, for example, Hutchenson et al. (2004), Bennett (1990) and Althaus et al. (1996).
3. Examples of these longitudinal studies include: Hachten and Beil (1985), Potter (1987), Ogan et al. (1975), Emery (1989), Riffe (1994), and Riffe and Budianto (2001).
4. These factors are different from those we outlined in "A Natural History of Foreign Correspondence" (Cole and Hamilton, 2007), which were ownership, product differentiation, cost, the urgency of world events, and correspondents' self-perceptions. There is good reason for this. That study was generally narrower than this essay. It focused on a span of 20 years in the evolution of one newspaper and asked what forces affected change during that period. This study looks at the three-century-history of American foreign newsgathering and asks what factors shaped broad changes in newsgathering within an entire press system.
5. See Clark and Wetherell (1989)—for piping foreign news, see p. 295. Also see Copeland (1997).
6. For this period, see Knudson (2006) and Stewart (1969).
7. Discussions from this point of view can be found in Leonard (1986, p. 18) and Botein (1980, p. 22). In *The Good Citizen*, Michael Schudson says foreign news appeared in colonial newspapers "primarily . . . because it afforded local readers and local authorities no grounds for grumbling" (1998, p. 36).
8. For this period, see Crouthamel (1964) and Mott (1947, pp. 216, 222). For an important discussion of the economic success of penny papers such as the *New York Sun* and the *New York Herald*, see Hamilton (2004, chap. 20).
9. Figures on the decrease of foreign news can be found in Wilke (1987, p. 1570). Other studies show a similar pattern, for instance, Shaw (1981, pp. 38–50). Donald R. Avery (1984, 1986) has noted a decline in foreign news in the years before the War of 1812.
10. See Avery (1982), who argues foreign news declined because editors and readers began to think of themselves as American and thus were more oriented toward domestic affairs.

11.   The term *special correspondent*, as Ralph used it, applied to any reporter outside of the newspaper's hometown, be it Washington, DC, or Vienna; the foreign application became more firmly rooted in the argot of journalism.

12.   Paul Scott Mowrer, "Suggestions for Reorganizing the Foreign Service," May 6, 1920, Edward Price Bell Papers, Midwestern Manuscripts Collection, Newberry Library, Chicago.

13.   The term "Golden Age" is thrown around a good deal. Phillip Knightly has dated the age for war correspondence as running from 1865 to 1914 "because of the rise of the popular press, the increasing use of the telegraph, and the tardy introduction of organized censorship" (2004, p. 43). Among those who consider the interwar years the Golden Age is Morrell Heald (1988, p. xi).

14.   On the proliferation of outlets for foreign news, see Desmond (1982, chaps 12, 14, 16), Goulden (1965, p. 29), Lynd and Lynd (1965, p. 386), Ryant (1971, p. 680), and Peterson (1964, pp. 57–64).

15.   Interview with Marvin Kalb, who was CBS correspondent in Moscow when the Paris meeting took place, January 8, 2004. As yet another example of this attitude, a CBS executive is credited with saying, "The entertainment end of the network business did its worst so that CBS News could do its best" (Salant, 1999, p. 147).

16.   Interview with Elisa Tinsley, February 2, 2005. Safety policy supplied by Elisa Tinsley (email March 27, 2005) is dated September 16, 2002.

17.   This discussion is drawn from Hamilton and Jenner (2003, 2004).

18.   *New York Times*, March 24, 2003.

REFERENCES

ALTHAUS, SCOTT L., EDY, JILL A., ENTMAN, ROBERT M. and PHALEN, PATRICIA (1996) "Revising the Indexing Hypothesis: officials, media, and the Libya crisis", *Political Communication* 13, pp. 407–21.

AVERY, DONALD R. (1982) "The Newspaper on the Eve of the War of 1812: changes in content", PhD thesis, Southern Illinois University.

AVERY, DONALD R. (1984) "The Emerging American Newspaper: discovering the home front", *American Journalism* 1, pp. 51–6.

AVERY, DONALD R. (1986) "American Over European Community? Newspaper content changes, 1808–1812", *Journalism Quarterly* 63, pp. 311–4.

BAILYN, BERNARD (1990) *Faces of Revolution: personalities and themes in the struggle for American independence*, New York: Knopf.

BENNETT, W. LANCE (1990) "Toward a Theory of Press–State Relations in the United States", *Journal of Communication* 40, pp. 103–25.

BJORK, ULF JONAS (1992) "The Commercial Roots of Foreign Correspondence: the *New York Herald* and foreign news, 1835–1839", paper presented to the annual convention of the Association for Education in Journalism and Mass Communication, Quebec.

BOGART, LEO (1968) "The Overseas Newsman: a 1967 profit study", *Journalism Quarterly* 45, pp. 298–306.

BOTEIN, STEPHEN (1975) "Meer Mechanics and an Open Press: the business and political strategies of colonial American printers", *Perspectives in American History* 9, pp. 127–225.

BOTEIN, STEPHEN (1980) "Printers and the American Revolution", in: Bernard Bailyn and John B. Hench (Eds), *The Press in the American Revolution*, Worcestor, MA: American Antiquarian Society.

CLARK, CHARLES E. and WETHERELL, CHARLES (1989) "The Measure of Maturity: The Pennsylvania Gazette, 1728–1765", *William and Mary Quarterly* 46, pp. 279–303.

COLE, JACI and HAMILTON, JOHN MAXWELL (2007) "A Natural History of Foreign Correspondence: a study of the *Chicago Daily News*, 1900–1921", *Journalism & Mass Communication Quarterly* 84, pp. 151–66.

COLE, JACI and HAMILTON, JOHN MAXWELL (2008) "Another Test of the News", *Journalism History* 33, pp. 34–41.

COPELAND, DAVID A. (1997) *Colonial American Newspapers: character and content*, Newark: University of Delaware Press.

CROUTHAMEL, JAMES L. (1964) "The Newspaper Revolution in New York: 1839–1860", *New York History* 45, pp. 91–113.

DEFLEUR, MELVIN L. and DEFLEUR, MARGARET H. (2003) *Learning to Hate Americans*, Spokane, WA: Marquette Books.

DENNIS, CHARLES (1935) *Victor Lawson: his time and his work*, Chicago: University of Chicago Press.

DESMOND, ROBERT W. (1937) *The Press and World Affairs*, New York: D. Appleton-Century.

DESMOND, ROBERT W. (1978) *The Information Process: world news reporting to the twentieth century*, Iowa City: University of Iowa Press.

DESMOND, ROBERT W. (1980) *Windows on the World: world news reporting 1900–1920*, Iowa City: University of Iowa Press.

DESMOND, ROBERT W. (1982) *Crisis and Conflict: world news reporting between two wars 1920–1940*, Iowa City: University of Iowa Press.

DESMOND, ROBERT W. (1984) *Tides of War: world news reporting 1940–1945*, Iowa City: Iowa University Press.

EMERY, MICHAEL (1989) "An Endangered Species: the international newshole", *Gannett Center Journal* 3, pp. 151–64.

EMERY, MICHAEL (1995) *On the Front Lines: following America's foreign correspondents across the twentieth century*, Washington, DC: American University Press.

FOOTE, JOE S. (1998) *Live from the Trenches: the changing role of the television news correspondent*, Carbondale: Southern Illinois University Press.

GALLAGHER, AILEEN (2004) "Dateline Baghdad, Capital of Chaos", 14 July, www.blacktable.com/gallagher040714.htm.

GOULDEN, JOSEPH C. (1965) *The Curtis Caper*, New York: G.P. Putnam's Sons.

HACHTEN, WILLIAM A. and BEIL, BRYAN (1985) "Bad News or No News? Covering Africa, 1965–1982", *Journalism Quarterly* 62, pp. 626–30.

HAMILTON, JAMES T. (2004) *All the News That's Fit to Sell: how the market transforms information into news*, Princeton, NJ: Princeton University.

HAMILTON, JOHN MAXWELL and JENNER, ERIC (2003) "The New Foreign Correspondence", *Foreign Affairs* 82, pp. 131–8.

HAMILTON, JOHN MAXWELL and JENNER, ERIC (2004) "Redefining Foreign Correspondence", *Journalism* 5, pp. 301–21.

HEALD, MORRELL (1988) *Transatlantic Vistas: American journalists in Europe, 1900–1940*, Kent, Ohio: Kent State University Press.

HESTER, AL, HUMES, SUSAN PARKER and BICKERS, CHRISTOPHER (1980) "Foreign News in Colonial North American Newspaper, 1764–1775", *Journalism Quarterly* 57, pp. 18–22.

HOHENBERG, JOHN (1964) *Foreign Correspondence: the great reporters and their times*, New York: Columbia University Press.

HUDSON, FREDERIC (1873) *Journalism in the United States from 1690 to 1872*, New York: Harper & Brothers.

HUTCHENSON, JOHN, DOMKE, DAVID, BILLEAUDEAUX, ANDRE and GARLAND, PHILIP (2004) "U.S. National Identity, Political Elites, and a Patriotic Press Following September 11", *Political Communication* 21, pp. 27–50.

KNIGHTLY, PHILLIP (2004) *The First Casualty: the war correspondent as hero and myth-maker from the Crimea to Kosovo*, Baltimore, MD: Johns Hopkins.

KNUDSON, JERRY W. (2006) *Jefferson and the Press: crucible of liberty*, Columbia: University of South Carolina Press.

LEONARD, THOMAS C. (1986) *The Power of the Press: the birth of American political reporting*, New York: Oxford University Press.

LYND, ROBERT S. and LYND, HELEN MERRELL (1965) *Middletown in Transition: a study in cultural conflicts*, New York: Harcourt Brace Jovanovich.

MERRITT, RICHARD L. (1963) "Public Opinion in Colonial America: content-analyzing the colonial press", *Public Opinion Quarterly* 27, pp. 356–71.

MOTT, FRANK LUTHER (1947) *American Journalism: a history of newspapers in the United States through 250 years, 1690 to 1940*, New York: Macmillan.

MOWRER, PAUL SCOTT (1924) *Our Foreign Affairs: a study in national interest and the new diplomacy*, New York: E.P. Dutton.

OGAN, CHRISTINE, PLYMAKE, IDA, SMITH, D. LYNN, TURPIN, WILLIAM H. and SHAW, DONALD LEWIS (1975) "The Changing Front Page of the New York Times, 1900–1970", *Journalism Quarterly* 52, pp. 340–4.

PARK, ROBERT (1960) "The Natural History of the Newspaper", in: Wilbur Schramm (Ed.), *Mass Communications*, Urbana: University of Illinois Press, pp. 8–25.

PETERSON, PETER G., BLOOMGARDEN, KATHY, BRUNWALD, HENRY, MOREY, DAVID E., TELHAMI, SHIBLEY, SIEG, JENNIFER and HERBSTMAN, SHARON (2003) *Finding America's Voice: a strategy for reinvigorating U.S. public diplomacy*, Washington, DC: Council on Foreign Relations.

PETERSON, THEODORE (1964) *Magazines in the Twentieth Century*, Urbana: University of Illinois Press.

POTTER, W. JAMES (1987) "News from Three Worlds in Prestige U.S. Newspapers", *Journalism Quarterly* 64, pp. 73–9.

RALPH, JULIAN (1893) "The Newspaper Correspondent", *Scribner's*, August, p. 154.

RIFFE, DANIEL, AUST, CHARLES F., JONES, TED C., SHOEMAKE, BARBARA and SUNDAR, SHYAM (1994) "The Shrinking Foreign Newshole of the New York *Times*", *Newspaper Research Journal* 15, pp. 74–88.

RIFFE, DANIEL and BUDIANTO, ARIANNE (2001) "The Shrinking World of Network News", *International Communication Bulletin* 36, pp. 18–35.

RYANT, CARL G. (1971) "From Isolation to Intervention: The Saturday Evening Post, 1939–42", *Journalism Quarterly* 48, pp. 679–87.

SALANT, RICHARD S. (1999) *Salant, CBS, and the Battle for the Soul of Broadcast Journalism*, Boulder, CO: Westview Press.

SCHUDSON, MICHAEL (1998) *The Good Citizen: a history of American civic life*, New York: Free Press.

SCOFEA, LAURA A. (1994) "The Development and Growth of Employer-provided Health Insurance", *Monthly Labor Review* 117, pp. 3–10.

SHAW, DONALD LEWIS (1981) "At the Crossroads: change and continuity in American press news 1820–1860", *Journalism History* 8, pp. 38–50.

SHEEAN, VINCENT (1939) *Not Peace But a Sword*, New York: Doubleday Doran.

SMALLEY, GEORGE W. (1894) "Chapters in Journalism", *Harper's New Monthly Magazine*, August.

SMALLEY, GEORGE W. (1911) *Anglo-American Memories*, New York: G.P. Putnam's Sons.

STEWART, DONALD H. (1969) *The Opposition Press of the Federalist Period*, Albany: State University of New York Press.

VAN PAASSEN, PIERRE (1939) *Days of Our Years*, New York: Hillman-Curl.

WILKE, JURGEN (1987) "Foreign News Coverage and International Flow of News Over Three Centuries", *Gazette* 39, pp. 147–80.

WILKE, JURGEN (1993) *Statistical Abstract of the United States*, Washington, DC: Department of Commerce.

WILKE, JURGEN (2003) *Views of a Changing World*, Washington, DC: Pew Research Center for the People and the Press.

Chapter 13

INTERNATIONAL NEWS FROM PARIS- AND LONDON-BASED NEWSROOMS

Michael Palmer

First a Language Point

The word "news" refers both to "new things" and to reports of those things. In French, "*nouvelles*" has a similar meaning, but it also has literary connotations. Some dictionaries—both English and French—hint at the French provenance of the word "news"; many also go back to the Latin, indeed to the Greek. Here, I would simply note that *nouvelle* has kept its literary connotations; a little like the word "novel" in English, even if the *nouvelle*, as a literary form is more akin to what in English is called a "novella".

I begin thus for two reasons. One is relatively straightforward: many 19th- and early 20th-century books in English about the French press, or in French about the English (rarely "British") press made the point that the French press was more "opinionated" and "literary", the English press more "fact-centred" and attentive to the divorce between fact and comment—the famous C.P. Scott formula: "comment is free, but facts are sacred" (1921) (*Guardian*, 2002).

In 2008, such distinctions appear out-of-date in many regards. In January 1995, the relaunch of the *Le Monde*, a leading quality daily, referred once again to the Anglo-American tradition of separating news from comment. In Agence France Presse (AFP), the leading French international news agency, the centre-piece of every news-file is called: "*un factuel*". Such a text, like millions produced daily worldwide, addresses the famous W Questions—who, which, what, when, where, why, how; to which AFP, like RTR, adds another question: "so what/*et alors*": why should the reader care, be bothered? To work on both AFP and RTR copy is to note that "fact-centric" news-reporting is the common parlance of news editors worldwide. This is hardly a revelation. But is perhaps worth recalling at the outset.

The second reason is more "cultural". Some French journalists—newspersons included—still see themselves as "men of letters", *hommes de lettres*. There is a long tradition of journalists, *"grands reporters"*—Hemingway-like figures in a way—who are also *"grandes signatures"*; they combine journalism and a literary career. I think here of French reporters turned novelists and authors investigating what one might term the extremes of the human condition: one such is Jean Hatzfeld. He was maimed when covering the wars in ex-Yugoslavia for the left-of-centre daily *Libération*; he subsequently wrote a poignant book on war-reporting as a result (Hatzfeld, 1994). Hatzfeld then "experienced"—I use the word intentionally—the horrors of the massacres between Hutu and Tutsis in Rwanda. He has since produced three books on this, including the prize-winning *La stratégie des antelopes* (Hatzfeld, 2007). And a novel, *La ligne de flottaison* (Hatzfeld,), where his enthusiasm as a sports-reporter also comes across. To be haunted and write movingly about a traumatic blood-letting experience that one covers as a bystander and lives and relives time on end is obviously not just peculiar to the French; among journalist-writers publishing in English, one might mention Martin Bell, Janine di Giovanni (2004) of *The Times* or the Australian-born John Pilger. Yet Francophone war reporters are a distinctive breed; many of them see themselves in the reflective mode of the Polish correspondent and literary figure Ryszard Kapuscinski, whose *Travels with Herodotus* were translated into French (2006) from the Polish original (2004) before their appearance in English (2007)—always a sign, I would suggest, that the reporter turned explorer of the human predicament is more common in the French tradition than the affected cynicism or world-wise (and amusing) approach of US and UK journalists in the vein of Edward Behr (1926–2007). His best-selling, trenchant memoire contains the following passage on his experience as a young journalist, around 1950, first in London, then in Paris:

> I sat at the end of a table in the Reuters News agency newsroom … Gradually the dismal craft of rewriting agency copy came to me … Originality was not encouraged. Speed was. Every day supervisors … noted the hour, the minute and probably the second that Reuters had annouced a major news break, comparing it with monitored reports on the same story from Associated Press and the old United Press … Then I was sent to Paris … At first the same agency routine applied as in London, but with the additional barrier of the French language. Who really makes the news? I began asking myself. In London Agence France-Presse (AFP) correpondents rewrote Reuters' copy, as fast as they could, and the finished product ended up as part of the AFP news service. In Paris, we shamelessly rewrote Agence France Presse copy, serving it up as Reuters' fare. All over the world lesser news agencies were writing up *their* versions of Reuters' stories and serving them up as authentic Indian, Spanish, or Brazilian news agency stories. Somewhere, at the bottom of this inverted pyramid, someone was getting a story at first hand. But who was he …? (Behr, 1981, p. 181)

What Relevance to the Future of News, You May Wonder?

I shall reply obliquely, in crab-like style: forward one, sideways one. Nearly all my points are going to come from international news agency copy and in-house comment: mostly RTR and the Paris headquartered AFP—their Internets and intranets.

Five examples will serve. The media in France have long debated what is known by the *"pipolisation"* ("people"). The election of a new President, in May 2007—Nicholas

Sarkozy—occasioned renewed debate on a phenomenon that in spring/summer encompassed Sarkozy and his wife and, among others, the complex domestic arrangements of the couple heading the socialist party—François Hollande and his "companion"—until the end of the Presidential and parliamentary elections (May/June 2007)—Ségolène Royal, the socialist party candidate who came second to Sarkozy in the Presidential campaign. Some argue that the French media still lag behind the London-based media in the cult of "celebs" and the *pipolisation* of politics. France does not have, unlike Britain "a brutal tabloid culture that regards elected officials mostly as scoundrels, liars or fools" (James P. Rubin).[1] Not quite.

The result of a presidential election campaign is a top story in (most) democracies. Here, I would merely highlight how the Reuters news agency congratulated its Paris bureau for their coverage of the campaign, and of the final election round in particular. A RTR photographer on a motorbike caught the moment when Sarkozy gave the thumbs-up sign as his motorcade sped to celebrations in the place de la Concorde; this made the splash in British nationals like *The Times*.

For many years, media academics and journalists have recognised the importance of "INAs" as "TNCCs"—international news agencies as transnational communication corporations and purveyors of news worldwide.[2] INAs, it is argued, have the staff out in the field when so many other TNCCs and national media cut back their resources "overseas", "abroad", in "foreign postings". In many respects this is still true and likely to remain so. But three factors—and it is these that I would argue bode large for the future of international news—are ever-more present. Or, I should say, as a qualifier, seem to grow in importance when one looks at matters from the viewpoint of one who researches Reuters and AFP.

The first is possibly the least well discussed. A shorthand term helps describe the formatting of international news, information and data streams. Since the mid-1990s, a professional body of news-purveyors/providers (the IPTC: international press telecommunications council), headquartered in Britain, works on the compatibility of news formats in the era of Internet and hypertext mark-up languages. A News Industry Text Format (NITF) is one of the results. In recent years, journalists—following on from computer engineers—are having to work with the "slugging" and related technical key-words, when they file their copy, in line with NITF requirements. The NITF, on the one hand, allows for exchange of material (whether from audiovisual or print outlets), and on the other, classifies all matter into 17 categories—some of which, such as sports, have as many as 117 sub-categories.

There were sometimes heated debates as to how to classify such material: representatives whose cultural background was British wanted bull fighting classified under sports (bloodsports) whereas Romance language cultures (the Spanish, the French) wanted it under "arts, culture and entertainment". The latter lobby won. Another debate concerned classifying material related to wars and all non-domestic violence. Photographers and video-news personnel were active in establishing the appropriate nomenclature for acts of non-domestic violence: wars, massacres, conflicts etc. (Palmer, 2007).

This classification of material for transfer and compatibility between news-purveyors and end-users has existed since at least the 1880s, and the development of exchange of material between international news agencies like Reuters and Havas, the predecessor of AFP. Such collaboration has increased over the past 150 years and is likely to further increase. It has partly to do with computer-to-computer data transfer compatibility. In some texts "humans" are referred to as "the child element".

Point two has to to do with a more commonly known but vexed issue when one studies the role of international news organisations channelling the interational news flow: the relationship between the news products and news markets. To put it crudely: who is willing to fund the cost of collecting, editing and delivering "general news" worldwide? Here again, old arguments are repeated. Customers from niche-markets are more willing to pay than "the general public". Traders, bankers, managers of hedge funds, and other members of the financial community worldwide pay for customised access via Bloomberg or Reuters terminals to data-streams that, to use a euphemism, are a necessary professional tool. Many traders do not (have time to) read news stories; the headline or slug (40/50 characters) has to suffice. Breaking news, analytics, or/and the information–decision–action process is the name of the game; whether to buy, sell or not to move: *that* is the question. On the other hand, as Reuters and other news executives have long argued, economic news and "general" news often go hand-in-hand, impinge on one another within a very short time-span. In June 2006 when the news of the death of the al-Qaida leader in Iraq, killed in a US air attack, was released, oil prices fluctuated: Iraq was the world's third largest producer of petrol. "Market-moving news" is the name of the game, in RTR parlance, for over 30 years or so. The interdependence of so-called general news and niche news for professional markets is likely to intensify, not decrease, for two reasons, perhaps. The more news outlets there are—podcasts, websites, SMS among them—the more both professionals and what for lack of a better shorthand term I will call the international middle class or bourgeoisie, want access to material—to a range of material and to the computer programs that help "customise" it or to tailor it to their purposes, to what a few years ago was called the electronic "Daily Me". Put another way, the young executive on the London tube travelling to Canary Wharf, podcast in ear, *Financial Times* in hand, cell phone at the ready, a discarded freesheet nearby, wants to check sports results and his/her horoscope as well as company market prices; behind the outspread, hand-held copy of the *Financial Times* may indeed lurk *The Sun* or the *Daily Mail*. Sarkozy's France like Thatcher's (and post-Thatcher) Britain champions the advent of stockholder, shareholder, house-owning democratic societies. In both countries, there are more and more (relatively small) stockholders who follow market prices; their pension may depend on market-movements.

Third factor, after the technical and economic points, the shifting sands of the international news scene. This applies to both the news industry and to the role and strategies of major news-vendors, a term that gains increasing currency, as opposed to "news agencies". To simplify: in the past, some RTR executives stressed that AFP only kept going because of an indirect state subsidy, and their AFP counterparts returned the compliment noting that over 90 per cent of RTR revenue came from its non-media clients.[3] Reuters and AFP executives alike agreed that the biggest single external factor explaing the growth of Reuters' revenues in the 1980s was that of the global foreign exchange market.

Today, some of us struggle with how to find the appropriate terminology: "news, information, data-streams", on the one hand; vendors and outlets, on the other, seem more apposite than "international news agencies". The point is that many actors play or fulfil several roles; and they may be partners in some ventures, competitors in others. For instance, until recently, the Factiva database (culling material from some 10,000 sites) was a joint operation, launched in 1999, by Dow Jones and Reuters, otherwise competitors. Reuters had CNN as a subscriber until CNN terminated the contract in August 2007, shortly before—it so happened—RTR got a world scoop with an extract of a Bin Laden video. RTR is accessed—in the United States at least—via Yahoo! Yet end-users, Internet users, sometimes critique how, say, CNN or Yahoo have presented RTR material in ways different from that in which the feed was supplied. And, of course, if many established actors play several roles, so do many Internet users. I shall not repeat well-known arguments about the material provided by people via hand-held videophones of the London July 2005 bombings to broadcasters like the BBC. More and more end-users may also be provers of material via what in English are called "social media"—*YouTube, My Space, Facebook.* Is there any reason why this will not end?[4] Or will perhaps the all-importance of *branding*, of the value (in terms of credibility, but also of market capitalisation) of an established reputable professional new-organisation, win out? I suspect that the ability of established players—including the very recently established: think of Google, created in 1998—to take on board "social" media, will win out. The pressure to be *"numero uno"*—to figure in the top five or ten, or whatever, market leaders—irrespective of the market—appears to grow. In a globalised financial data-led economy many fall by the wayside, in the news business as elswhere. The blurring of news, data, and information industries, while anathema to many journalists, is accentuated by—say—the number of online media groups chasing what is not a bottomless pit of advertising revenue.

A further point concerns the future of "international news". Many observers have long commented on the decline of resources alloted to international news-gathering by major national media; how, for example, the traditional leading US broadcasting "majors" (ABC NBC, CBS) cut back on staff and bureau abroad. Or else, how a form of *pipolisation* affects such coverage; at times when Iraq was a top story, immediately after the US–UK invasion of Saddam Hussein's Iraq, Dan Rather, a household name of US TV news, was sent to front umpteen programmes. Thus, the "familiar" messenger fronts stories from physically unfamiliar places where "our boys" are present. Such presentational tactics are hardly novel. Will they increase, notably on what remains of "mainstream media" targetted at broad public audiences?

The (World) Regionalisation and the Language Zoning of output does not necessarily reduce the prospects of established INAs. Reuters during the US–UK 2003 "move on" Saddam Hussein's Iraq provided video-"footage" with "Q and A" sessions with its Lebanese Palestinian-born Bagdad bureau chief correspondent, Sadmia Lakhoul; she was injured (8 April) and other RTR staff were killed; page visits reportedly peaked at 5 million per day, up 500 per cent on pre-invasion figures. "Western" international news organisations develop Arabic-language video feeds and Arab-based news organisations develop English-language services: based in Doha (Qatar), al-Jazeera had a centralised news-editorial operation covering the 2003 invasion (cf. Ziani, 2007); did the RTR team of proven professionals, operating in Bagdad, have greater latitude? RTR and AFP have long produced Arab-language services; the al-Jazeera English-language service, the CNN Spanish-language service are of more recent vintage; "professionalism" is a common goal, the increasingly diverse ethnic mix of INA staff likewise; the reference to BBC, RTR or AFP proven tracken-records is a frequent *leitmotif*.

The growth of diasporic communications introduces variations on the theme. The Chinese community in Toronto, Vancouver and London follow news of floods and other nature (and human)-induced disasters affecting family members "back in China". The Kobe earthquake in Japan in January 1995 and the tsunami of December 2004 symbolise worldwide stories impacting on Internet traffic, between "kith and kin" worldwide as well as on what is perceived as the general world market for human-interest news.

Yet there lies the rub. We may have more and more customised news, and news that is sanitised—for a three-minute (or 5–45-second) mainstream soundbite culture. But it is no less unlikely that the "news-on-demand" culture leads to diasporas worldwide—say the Chinese in Toronto, London and China itself—accessing more and more news of primary interest to that diaspora. The decline of mainstream news programmes is accompanied by more and more "glocalised" news: the more the channels, the more the sites, the less the "national" frame? And perhaps, the greater the difficulty of detecting what is happening when trained in a metropolitan, capital city (London, Paris, etc.)-based media culture.

The term "international" does not figure in the above-mentioned IPTC categories. Faced by the streams of material (data, news, information) in circulation, it is for each media outlet to fashion the news agenda and re-impose, as appropriate "national", "international", "local" etc. prisms or *topoi*. When working from Britain, or within what used to be call—*à la* Winston Churchill—the English-speaking world, it is sometimes difficult to realise the importance of another prism: the English *language*. International news depends primarily on English as the *lingua franca* of world communications— whether it be British-English, American-English, international English or indeed, "globish", that user-friendly pidgin or creole which some French detractors call *Anglo-ricain*. Will this change, with the growth of the Spanish (and Spang-*lish*), of Mandarin Chinese usage worldwide, etc? I suspect not. Mainstream news outlets will be served by a template of English-language material and by English-language professionals; their output, expressed in a global American-English, with regional variants, will remain the main language vehicle. However, much diasporic communication will be nurtured—in Chinese, in Spanish, even in French, by "susbstantive minority media". Before recent cost-cutting measures Reuters had services (mostly for financial, non-media subscribers) in up to 23 languages; this figure is now below 20.[5]

Yet a final point, before closing, returns to the issue of the number of reputable, reliable, established organisations—considered to be so by their fellow-profesionals, as much as among a broader public. A few months after the "move on/invasion of Iraq", an American journalist working in Washington for AFP reviewed his agency's experience compared to that of Reuters (among other competitors). He provided examples of where London-based RTR and New York-based Associated Press (AP) had enjoyed advantages, including facilities afforded to embedded correspondents that were denied to journalists from AFP and other international news organisations that were not headquartered in one of the "belligerent" countries. Journalists press for a level playing field yet know this rarely exists. Reviewing its own performance during the same period, Reuters pointed out that a US-based American news agency, a major competitor in financial news, did not have correspondents in the field, in Bagdad, etc., and was presenting as its own ... material collected and transmitted at cost (personal safety as well as monetary) by correspondents from the BBC, Reuters, AFP etc. Two reports on this: "being there is better; being there is still better", circulated within RTR and were picked up by the US trade magazine and website, *Editor and Publisher* (Palmer, 2006).

There are no level playing fields in international news. In Iraq today, in ex-Yugoslavia in the past, reporters and news personnel—both "locals" and "foreign nationals"—die on assignment. Few major media organisations stay the course in long-running news venues, which sometimes go "off-screen" from the international news agenda only to return centre-stage at some undetermined date (a process the French call "news-latency"). Will leading news organisations like RTR and AFP maintain bureaux in proven news centres? Probably yes; this is possibly more likely the case than, say, for some prominent international braodcasting corporations. This is partly because of journalistic commitment, partly because of the multi-media and multi-platform nature of the diverse feeds news agencies supply; their track-record is proven, and despite hiccups, is sufficiently reliable and relatively low-cost that many many others rely on them. But not only on them. There is always the possibility that the seeming availability (via blogs, etc.) of material on the Net may grow as a substitute for having staff in the field, on the hotspot. Fears about the reliabilty and accuracy of the Net in the mid-1990s led several top AFP and RTR executives to be wary indeed. Such qualms persist even if company strategies more than take Internet and video feeds on board. Blogs—to judge from the impact of the "Salam pax" blog produced out of Baghdad, prior to the invasion of Iraq, when so few on-the-ground sources seemed available—may serve as a complement to professional news organisa-tions: can they be a substitute? [6] The tension between, on the one hand, media managers and accountants eyeing news-editorial budgets and the bottom-line, and, on the other, those wanting journalists in the field "on the spot", "where it's at" . . ., will not decrease—even if accountants appreciate that the company brand depends in part on "beats and exclusives" due to cultivating contacts and having people in the field. Soft news and social media are not enough. But the constant repackaging, recycling, re-translating and re-formatting of "news material" will increase, as will the rhetoric of "one-stop shopping" and "customised, tailored to measure" services. Some agency executives issue wake-up calls: the AP's Tom Curley (2007) warns: "the portals are running off with our best stuff" (as) "more people are accessing news more frequently than ever before the world over".

Ryszard Kapuscinski (1932–2007) was both the Polish news agency, PAP's, first foreign correspondent and the author of the heartfelt lines : "we know how language fails us, how often we feel helpless, how the experience is, finally, incommunicable".[7] He noted also how his situation differed from that of Reuters, AFP or AP correspondents: these agencies "have a correspondent in nearly every African country; working for Poland, I was asked to be the correspondent for the entire continent".

The seasoned agency "pro" produces copy tailored to story length guidelines—"newsbreaks": no more than two paragraphs if the news is unexpected. Write three paragraphs only if the material is so complex that it requires additional background and context or a crucial quote (up to 10 lines/100 words).[8]

And s/he exercises news judgement: following the controversy about the footage shown worldwide of the execution of Saddam Hussein (end of December 2006), a RTR video editor noted: "every day we cover hundreds of subjects—from war to showbiz, from the unexpected to life-style pieces—as a result we acquire a form of institutionalised understanding" of what, when and how to produce and distribute what meets the norms of mainstream news values.

ACKNOWLEDGEMENTS

My thanks to Reuters and AFP for granting access to in-house material.

NOTES

1. Assistant secretary of state for public affairs during the Clinton administration; a "world affairs" commentator for Sky News in Britain—the companion of CNN's Christiane Amanpour (of Iranian and English parentage) (book review of *Alistair Campbell's Diaries, The Blair Years, I.H.T.*, 1–2 September 2007).
2. House-histories of news agencies provide the data to support the remark of E. Herman and R. McChesney's, *The Global Media*: 'the wire-based international news agencies were the first significant form of global media' (1987, p. 12); and less directly, the assertion of D. L. Winseck and R. M. Pike: 'the advent of the global media system ... was driven mainly by the logic of imperialism and rivalry among the imperial superpowers' (2007, p. xv).
3. A Reuters memo, "Review of French Operations, 10.2.1976", asked rhetorically: for how much of the 20 per cent of Reuters revenue coming from the media does the AFP compete? (Reuters' Archive, London).
4. At a world editors forum in Cape Town, in May 2007, a Reuters editor noted how the director, news and information, of France's leading circulation daily (the Rennes-based *Ouest-France*, 800,000 copies), claimed that local bloggers provided about half of its material; R. Mackinnon, a co-founder of Global Voices, an aggregator of blogs worldwide, co-sponsored by RTR, stressed that blogs show journalists what people care about. The CEO of Pluck, in which RTR has a stake, showed how US newspaper sites began to cover subject areas without using journalists by syndicating material from bloggers.
5. Between 1985 and 1988, Reuters launched services in Japanese, Dutch, Italian, Swedish and Norwegian.
6. This is the argument that underlies promotional rhetoric about some blogs. Riverbend's news has nothing to do with troop movements, casuality figures, or the latest from the Green Zone—the subjects of mainstream news reports (Riverbend, 2005, p. v).
7. "Words Without Borders", an interview with Ryszard Kapuscinksi, *Granta* magazine, 1989, reprinted in *Adbusters*, 1 May 2007.
8. Reuters eBriefs, 30 May 2007.

REFERENCES

BEHR, EDWARD (1981) *Anyone Here Been Raped and Speaks English?*, London: Hamish Hamilton.

CURLEY, TOM (2007) "We Have Come to a 'Fork in the Road'", *Editor and Publisher*, 1 November.

DI GIOVANNI, JANINE (2004) *Madness Invisible*, London: Bloomsbury.

GUARDIAN (2002) *History of the Guardian*, http://www.guardian.co.uk/information/theguardian/story/0,,1038110,00.html, accessed 25 July 2008.

HATZFELD, JEAN (1994) *L'air de la guerre*, Paris: Éditions de l'Olivier.

HATZFELD, JEAN (2007) *La stratégie des antelopes*, Paris: Le Seuil.

HATZFELD, JEAN (2005), *La ligne de flottaison*, Paris: Le Seuil.

HERMAN, E. and MCCHESNEY, R. (1987) *The Global Media*, London and Washington, DC: Cassell.

KAPUSCINSKI, RYSZARD (2007 [2004]) *Travels with Herodotus*, New York: Knopf.

PALMER, M. (2006) *Dernières nouvelles d'@mérique*, Paris: éditions de l'Amandier.

PALMER, M. (2007) *Nommer les nouvelles du monde*, No. 46, Hermès: CNRS.

RIVERBEND (2005) *Baghdad Burning*, London and New York: Marion Boyars.

WINSECK, D. L. and PIKE, R. M. (2007) *Communications and Empire*, Durham, NC: Duke University Press.

ZIANI, ABDULKRIM (2007) "La chaine Al-Jazira et la guerre contre l'Iraq; couverture médiatique et traitement de l'information", PhD thesis, University of Grenoble 3.

Chapter 14

WHAT FUTURE FOR LOCAL NEWS?
The crisis of the French regional daily press

Aude Rouger

Introduction

The circulation of French daily newspapers has been decreasing for several decades, which has caused much debate about a "press crisis", both in academic and professional circles. Compared to the national press, the position of the regional dailies seemed relatively safe until the 1980s and 1990s. However, since then, despite a much higher circulation than that of the national dailies, the regional dailies have been experiencing a continuous loss of readership. Local news, their main strength, has been insufficient to counter this decline.

This paper aims to examine the crisis of the French regional daily press, drawing on PhD research that focuses on the changes in the relations between these newspapers and territories, as well as in their treatment of local news. It is based on a comparative survey of three French regional newspapers: *Ouest-France* (Rennes, the largest French daily newspaper in terms of circulation), *Le Parisien* (Paris) and *Le Progrès* (Lyon). Several corpora are analysed: 50 interviews with editorial staff and people in charge of other departments in the newspaper companies; ethnographic observations within national and local newsrooms; a more heterogeneous corpus of in-house documents; and newspaper files, of which content analysis is still to be completed.

First, some general elements about the press crisis in France are discussed. Then the paper deals with the possible reasons for this crisis. While some factors are economic and common to the daily press as a whole (problems of distribution, high sale prices, decrease of advertising, and the competition of various other media, the most recent ones being the free daily press and the Internet), others are sociological and more specific to the regional press: changes in lifestyles, especially in big cities with the increased importance of transport and mobility; generational problems; changes in identities and processes of individualisation, resulting in a lack of interest in certain types of local news.

How do the newspapers react to the crisis? In addition to efforts to get to know their readers better (through marketing as well as research and development, which are relatively new to this kind of press in France) and the policy of the press companies to increase their presence in the "new media" (especially the Internet and the free press), new formulae are regularly tested. However, going beyond mere changes of format and design can prove difficult, as the newspapers are reluctant to risk losing their traditional readership. Changes in the content of the newspaper, especially in the treatment of local news, are crucial to the survival of the regional dailies, but encounter many obstacles.

General Facts About the Press and Press Crisis in France

The Relations Between the "National" and the "Regional" Daily Press

Before addressing the question of the crisis of the daily press in France, it is necessary to clarify the general organisation of this press, which is based on the traditional centralised organisation that still prevails in this country. French daily newspapers are divided into two categories: the "national" newspapers (10 titles), based in Paris and circulating in the whole country, and the "regional" newspapers (65 titles), which are distributed in various parts of France.

The catchment areas of regional newspapers spread out from their main town and vary in size. Most of these newspapers are based in towns other than the capital, the only exception being *Le Parisien*, which defines itself as the only regional newspaper in the Paris region.[1] Apart from their geographical locations, the key characteristic of the French regional newspapers is that they publish regional and local news concerning their catchment areas, whereas the national newspapers only deal with "national" news.

Since the end of the Second World War, the circulation of the French regional daily press has largely exceeded that of the national dailies.[2] The highest circulation in the French daily press is that of *Ouest-France*, with 783,000 copies per day in 2004—far above that of the national daily *Le Monde* (second daily newspaper in terms of circulation with 380,500 copies per day), and that of *Le Parisien* (352,500 copies) (OJD, 2004). However, even though the regional newspapers' circulation has been higher for more than 60 years, the national newspapers are still considered as lodestones. They benefit from a much heavier symbolic weight than their regional counterparts. This is largely specific to France. Some countries, such as Great Britain and Japan, have national newspapers that are economically stronger than their regional dailies. Others, such as Germany, Italy, Belgium, Switzerland and the United States, have a more decentralised system; in those countries, daily newspapers are based in various towns throughout the country (Charon, 1991, p. 137).

The Crisis of the Daily Press in France

While the national daily press is symbolically dominant in France, it is economically weaker than the regional press. The crisis of the French daily press became clear in the 1970s, the national newspapers being the first and most badly hit by the loss of readership. From the end of the 1960s, the circulation of the national newspapers started decreasing: in 1969, the circulation of the national dailies was 4.5 million per day, whereas in 1980, it was only 2.9 million, and in 2002 it had fallen to 2.2 million. In contrast, the regional dailies' circulation remained relatively stable until the 1980s, with 7.5 million copies per day in 1980 as well as in 1969. However, from the 1980s onwards, it started decreasing steadily—if not as fast as that of the national daily press. In 1990, it was 7 million copies, and in 2002, it had fallen to 6.7 million (Direction du développement des médias, 2005, p. 116).[3]

The regional dailies thus seem relatively safe compared to their national counterparts. Marc Martin, a historian, author of a reference book about the regional daily press in France, writes about "a slow, continuous dwindling, ... a moderate decrease that seems to go on and on inexorably" (Martin, 2002b, 238)[4]. However, the regional dailies' situation still concerns the professionals as well as the researchers, especially since the ratio of the circulation to the population is decreasing fast: in 1968, almost one in two households bought a regional daily; in 2003, only one in four households bought one (*Ouest-France, 2005*). In addition, the newspapers' readership is growing older and older,[5] and the regional dailies face more difficulties in urban areas (while a growing proportion of the population is urban). Finally, occasional reading has increased, while the proportion of regular readers has decreased. According to Olivier Donnat's study on cultural practices in France, in 1989, 43 per cent of people above 15 years old read a daily newspaper every day or almost every day. They were only 36 per cent in 1997. In the meantime, the proportion of non-readers has increased less rapidly (Donnat, 1998, p. 169).

How can such a crisis be explained? This paper first mentions the economic factors that affect both the national and regional newspapers. Then, the sociological causes of the crisis of the regional press are pointed out. Until the end of the 1960s, local news constituted a crucial means of development of the regional daily press. This kind of news is the main specificity of the regional dailies in France, which publish pages of local news from towns and districts (they are called "micro-local" in France). Local pages appeared in the regional dailies by the end of the 19th century, and they played a great part in these newspapers' development at least until the Second World War (Martin, 2002a). The hypothesis raised in this paper is that economic factors are crucial, but do not constitute a sufficient explanation for the regional dailies' crisis. Certain sociological factors can partly explain why interest in local news is no longer enough to ensure the expansion of the regional daily press in France.

Looking for an Explanation to the Regional Press Crisis

Economic Factors

Authors trying to elucidate the reasons behind the crisis of the French daily press point out economic factors that can explain both the regional and the national dailies' decline. Researchers and professionals generally agree that the price of newspapers is an obstacle to their development. Laurent Martin stresses that the daily newspapers' price index grows faster than the cost of living index (2005, p. 194). French newspapers are sold at a higher price than German and British ones. Even though the French regional dailies are cheaper than the national ones, they remain more expensive than those of other European countries (Martin, 2002b, p. 247).

Problems of distribution are also highlighted. In France, the newspaper companies can choose between two systems of distribution. They can either be distributed by their own means—which is more flexible, but also more costly—or depend on a collective system: either the Nouvelles Messageries de la Presse Parisienne (NMPP) or the Messageries Lyonnaises de Presse (MLP). In effect, only the regional dailies are distributed by their own means (Dupuy-Busson and Sonnac, 2002, p. 394). In addition, subscribers can receive their newspapers by post or through distribution rounds organised by the newspaper companies themselves. The latter are more efficient, but also more costly. With sales decreasing since the 1970s, retail outlets are closing without always being replaced, creating a vicious circle, their disappearance causing in turn a decrease in circulation.

Advertising also tends to decline with the loss of readership, the advertisers turning to other media (such as radio or television), other types of print media (magazines in particular) or to billboard advertising. In 1970, 71.3 per cent of advertising revenues in the media was present in the written press. This media represented only 37.1 per cent of advertising revenues in 2002. On the other hand, television represented 10.3 per cent of advertising revenues in 1970, and 34.8 per cent in 2002 (Charon, 2005, pp. 62–3).[6]

Finally, French daily newspapers experience the consequences of increased competition with other types of press or with other media. Radio and television come to mind, as well as magazines. The situation of the latter is specific to the French press: while daily newspapers are declining, magazines benefit from a much better outlook. As far as local news is concerned, new types of competition have emerged in the last 30 years. Local weeklies have been established in some areas, especially the most rural ones. Local TV channels and radios are also beginning to appear, although not everywhere in the country. Local authorities tend to develop their own free sheets, which publish local news. Besides those media, new competitors have appeared more recently, on the Internet and with the free daily press. They compete with regional dailies in terms of advertising, but also in terms of content, with an increasing focus on local news.

Sociological Causes of the Regional Press Crisis

In addition to the economic causes of the press crisis, which are common to the whole French daily press, sociological factors also need highlighting. They are specific to the regional dailies and they are strongly linked to the publication of local news by these newspapers. As is explained earlier in this paper, this type of news used to be a major element of development for the French regional dailies until the end of the 1960s. Through local news, the French regional daily press maintains links between its readers and their territories and reflects territorial identities (Pailliart, 1993). Why is local news no longer sufficient to ensure the development of the regional daily press in France? What does the decline of local news mean in terms of geographical identities?

The relations between the individual and society are at the very core of the notion of identity. According to Renaud Dulong and Louis Quéré, the main function of the regional press is to forge links between individuals and society within the territories that are covered by the regional newspapers:

> The function of the press is not to tell events, but to daily reinforce the ideological or territorial reference points through which the individuals define themselves as members of a society ... These reference points are primarily ideological in the case of the national press, mainly territorial in the case of the local press. (Dulong and Quéré, 1978, pp. 23–4)

Aside from the economic factors that have been addressed earlier in this paper, it can be hypothesised that the difficulties of the French regional press are due to changes in the links between the individual and society that affect the readers' (or potential readers') relation to the area where they live.

The issue of the link between the individual and society is a major sociological question. Several sociologists have looked into the changes affecting this link during the "second modernity" (that is, since the 1960s). The second modernity is a concept first introduced by Anthony Giddens (1994) and Ulrich Beck (2001). It opposed the notion of "post-modernity", which implies a break with the period of modernity. The sociologist François de Singly distinguishes three periods: that of "the pre-modern society"; that of the first period of modernity, from the end of the 19th century to the 1960s, which is a transitional period; and finally the "second modernity", from the 1960s to nowadays (De Singly, 2003, p. 234). According to these authors, changes affecting the link between the individual and society during the second modernity include greater individualisation, autonomy of the individual towards institutions, and the development of multiple and temporary forms of commitment and identification.

Claude Dubar analyses the changes in what he calls "forms of identities". He identified a series of changes within French society during the 1960s which challenged the traditional social cohesion. These changes weakened the legitimacy of the "forms of identities" that characterised the previous period. Drawing on Max Weber's writings, he talks about a shift from "communautary" to "societal" forms of identities. In the "societal" forms, each individual belongs to "multiple, variable and temporary groups, to which they subscribe for limited periods of time and that provide them with resources of identification they deal with in diverse and temporary ways" (Dubar, 2003, p. 5).

Changes in the relation between the individual and society alter territorial identities, as well as lifestyles—especially in the urban areas, with the increased importance of transport and mobility. Jean-Marie Charon writes:

> Within two decades, the phenomenon of big urban areas and vast suburbs has triggered profound modifications of time management, of the organisation of work and leisure. A significant part of the population experience a break with their district, town or region of origin, because an important part of the population moves several times in a lifetime. (1991, p. 334)

Jean-Marie Launay points out the "development of transports and big cities", which changes the themes of "daily conversation"—more oriented towards "individual concerns" and less towards "neighbourhood relations" and local life. He considers that these changes can explain why local news is no longer sufficient to attract new readers to the regional dailies: he states that "society and local news have not evolved in the same way" (1980, pp. 216–7). For Marc Martin, the crisis of local news "reflects the decline of a form of social cohesion based on proximity, in a society in which the groups tend to multiply" (Martin, 2002b, p. 248).

The audience of the regional dailies is lower in urban areas than in rural ones. While in 2005, it reached more than 40 per cent of the population in rural habitat and in towns between 2000 and 100,000 inhabitants, it was only 36.9 per cent in towns over 100,000 inhabitants, and 18.2 per cent in the urban area of Paris (TNS Sofres, 2006). Even though the French regional press first developed in big cities at the end of the 19th century, it was designed for a society that was still, at the time, mostly rural, with multiple local editions publishing "micro-local" news. Today, this model has difficulties adapting to the big regional metropolis, where there is not necessarily a significant interest in local news. This has to do with several factors: an important proportion of young people, particularly students, who do not read the press as much as older people;[7] the presence of a lot of "newcomers", from other regions or countries, for whom reading the regional newspaper has not yet become a habit; the importance of lifestyles influenced by mobility (be it for work, consumption or leisure).

During the second modernity, the development of multiple and temporary forms of commitment has changed individuals' relations to institutions. These changes affect all kinds of institutions: family, church, political parties, etc. As local institutions, the French regional daily newspapers went through the same changes.[8]

All these sociological changes led some researchers and professionals of the regional press to question the content of the regional dailies, especially of their local pages. According to Jean-Marie Launay, local news, as covered by French regional newspapers, "has become obsolete": "a study made by SOFRES in 1968 reveals that the readers' stronger motives of attachment to their regional newspaper are all related to habits and tradition" (1980, p. 223).

However, the French regional daily press can hardly count on tradition nowadays, when occasional reading is progressing and new forms of press, such as the free daily press, are creating new habits among readers, especially the younger ones. How do the newspapers adapt to the changes highlighted in this paper in order to stop the fall of their circulation? How are they trying to attract new readers? Have the sociological causes of the press crisis had an impact over the content of the newspapers?

The Newspapers' Reactions to the Crisis

Getting to Know the Readers

In order to deal with the decline of their circulation, the French daily newspapers have highlighted their efforts to better know their readers. The word "marketing" has for long been taboo in the French daily press, as Jean-Marie Charon notes:

> For a very long time, daily newspapers have remained convinced that their circulation was automatically linked to the quality of their editorial content and to the cultural, political, social, ideological tendencies that were expressed in it. Using commercial notions of promotion and "marketing", reserved to regular consumer goods, was a matter of obvious perversion. (1991, p. 270)

However, some regional dailies created research departments earlier than others. *Ouest-France* was a precursor (Charon, 1991, p. 275) in 1965. Jean-Pierre François, one of the assistant managers of the research and development department of *Ouest-France*, discussed the beginnings:

> The specificity of this department was that it was unique in the regional daily press, and even in the daily press. That people, in a newspaper company, got paid to think about the content of the newspaper, and above all about what the readers thought about it, was quite new.[9]

Other regional dailies, such as *Sud-Ouest*, followed *Ouest-France* in creating marketing or research departments. *Le Parisien* developed its marketing department in the 1980s. Research departments in the newspaper companies conduct or order both quantitative and qualitative studies about the readership, as well as various themes concerning the content, forms and editorial strategies of the newspaper and other media owned by the company (Internet websites, radio or TV channels, weekly or free daily newspapers, etc.). They also advise the editorial board and journalists about the transformations undergone by the newspaper.

Even in titles that had long been reluctant to conduct readership studies, initiatives have been taken in this field over the last 10 years. For instance, in *Le Progrès*, an "editorial development manager" was hired in 2003, prior to a major change of formula, to conduct a series of studies from 2003 to 2006. However, newspapers vary in their attempts to get to know their readers: *Le Progrès* does not have a permanent research department, but instead relies on temporary work groups surrounding changes of formulae.

Traditional Press and the "New Media"

The question of the complementarity between traditional press and the "new media" is of concern for all French daily newspapers. Today, the titles which do not have a website giving access to at least part of their content are quite rare.[10] Regional titles often choose to give free access to part of their content, mostly national news, while most of local news remains paid-for. This can be explained by the fact that this type of news is often exclusive to these newspapers, while national news is carried by other types of newspapers and media. Some regional newspapers have invested more than others in developing their website. In addition to a general website that publishes national and regional news, *Ouest-France* has created a network of websites especially dedicated to local news, called maville.com ("mytown.com"). A small proportion of this news is free, most of it is paid-for.

Aside from the Internet, some newspaper companies also invest in local radio or television stations. They are also more and more present in the free daily press. After the launch of the *Metro* and *20 minutes* newspapers in France in 2002, several regional newspapers decided to create their own free dailies, in order to counter these two titles in their main towns. Free newspapers owned by regional dailies are now distributed in Lille, Lyon, Bordeaux, Marseille and Montpellier. A network, called Ville Plus, has been created to federate these publications. Each newspaper is in charge of its own local news, while national news is produced in Paris by the free newspaper *Matin Plus*, owned by *Le Monde* group.

New Formulae and Changes in the Treatment of Local News

The initiatives of the regional dailies on the Internet, in audiovisual media or in the free press are relatively recent and still generate much debate within newspaper companies. However, the most crucial question probably remains that of the content of the newspaper itself. Over the last 15 years, regional dailies in France have made considerable efforts to rethink their formulae. But, while the forms of the newspapers have changed dramatically, the question of their content remains more problematic.

As was explained earlier, local news in particular appears to be inadequate for the kinds of relations to territories that have developed since the end of the 1960s. Nevertheless, the interviews conducted in the three newspapers show that editorial managers are not unanimously in favour of a radical change in the way their newspapers treat local news. To which kind of public should the regional dailies give priority?

Conquering a younger, fickler audience would require modifying the treatment of local news: such a decision seems risky to many newspapers' managers, as it might alienate older, more faithful readers.

However, a few ideas about changes to be made in the treatment of local news can be pointed out in the interviews that have been conducted during this research. The necessity to publish less "institutional", more "personalised" news, in the form of interviews and portraits, is often stressed. Certain topics, such as education, environment, accommodation, employment, health, are also seen by editorial managers as subjects of particular interest in urban areas. The need to promote "interactivity", through the publication of readers' mails and "forum" pages, is also addressed, as well as the importance of writing shorter papers, with more entries in one page, and several entries per story (i.e. several small papers instead of one single big paper). To see whether these ideas are put into practice in the newspapers, the interviews will have to be conducted in conjunction with content analysis of newspaper files, which is still in progress.

Conclusion

This paper has tried to address the question of the future of one specific type of news (local news) in one specific country (France) and in one medium: the regional daily newspapers. The daily press is suffering from a decline of its readership in many countries around the world. However, in France, this recession has been particularly severe since the 1970s. Even though the regional dailies are in better condition than the national dailies, there is a growing concern about their situation, especially since local news has stopped ensuring their development.

This situation can partly be explained by economic factors, such as problems of distribution, high sale prices, decrease of advertising and the competition of other media. But these causes are not enough to explain the crisis of the regional dailies. Sociological factors must be highlighted.

In order to reinforce an interest in local news, especially from younger people, the regional dailies will have to face the challenge and treat local news according to the changes that have affected people's relations to their localities over the last 30–40 years. But any change in the content of the newspapers is risky, as it exposes the titles to the possibility of losing more readers than they gain.

NOTES

1. Until the 1960s, *Le Parisien* used to be a national newspaper. In the 1960s, it started publishing local editions containing local news of the Paris region. During the following decades, its catchment area was gradually restricted to this region. This "regionalisation" was motivated by the success of the regional press compared to that of the national press at the time, as well as the important proportion of this newspaper's readers who lived in the Paris region and the lack of a regional newspaper in this region.

2. For the first time, the circulations of the national and regional dailies were equal in 1939. After the Second World War, the regional dailies' circulation exceeded the national dailies', with 9.1 million copies per day in 1946 for the regional dailies and 5.9 million for the national dailies. In 2002, the gap between these two types of press was even more

important, with a circulation of 2.2 million for the national press and 6.7 million for the regional press (Direction du développement des médias, 2005, p. 116).

3.   The fall of circulation has not been as bad for every regional daily. However, almost all of them have lost readers since the 1980s, and even more since the 1990s. The situation of the newspapers that are studied in this paper is contrasted: while *Ouest-France* has lost 1.3 per cent of its circulation since 1990, *Le Parisien* has lost 4.4 per cent, and *Le Progrès* has lost 25 per cent (Balle, 2003, p. 91). However, all of the interviewees expressed concern about the press crisis and the possible ways to overcome it.

4.   All quotes extracted from references in French have been translated by the author.

5.   A study, published in 2003 and based on the audience figures of the regional daily press from 1957 to 2001, concluded that there was a "generational effect" on the regional dailies' audience: the more recent a generation is, the less its members are likely to read a regional newspaper regularly (BIPE, 2003).

6.   Jean-Marie Charon quotes the Institut de recherches et d'études publicitaires (IREP).

7.   While 48.5 per cent of French people over 60 years old and 37.4 per cent of people between 35 and 59 read a regional daily in 2005, only 26.8 per cent of people between 15 and 34 did so (TNS Sofres 2006).

8.   Although not central to this paper, sociological causes of the national press crisis could also be stressed. For instance, it could be hypothesised that the changes in the relations to political institutions have played a part in a decrease of interest in politics in general—a topic that is abundantly covered by the national dailies.

9.   Interview with the author, Rennes, April 2006. Translation by the author.

10. In November 2007, among 65 regional daily newspapers, only 11 had no website listed by the French association of regional daily newspapers (SPQR, Syndicat de la presse quotidienne régionale, http://www.pqr.org).

REFERENCES

BALLE, FRANCIS (2003) *Médias et sociétés*, Paris: Montchrestien.

BECK, ULRICH (2001) *La société du risque, sur la voie d'une autre modernité*, Paris: Flammarion.

BIPE (BUREAU D'INFORMATIONS ET DE PRÉVISIONS ÉCONOMIQUES) (2003) *Les générations de lecteurs face à la PQR. Rapport final*, Paris: BIPE.

CHARON, JEAN-MARIE (1991) *La presse en France de 1945 à nos jours*, Paris: Seuil.

CHARON, JEAN-MARIE (2005) *La presse quotidienne*, Paris: La Découverte.

DE SINGLY, FRANÇOIS (2003) *Les uns avec les autres: quand l'individualisme crée du lien*, Paris: Armand Colin.

DIRECTION DU DÉVELOPPEMENT DES MÉDIAS (2005) *Tableaux statistiques de la presse, édition 2004*, Paris: Documentation française.

DONNAT, OLIVIER (1998) *Les pratiques culturelles des Français: enquête 1997*, Paris: Documentation française.

DUBAR, CLAUDE (2003) *La crise des identités: l'interprétation d'une mutation*, Paris: PUF.

DULONG, RENAUD and QUÉRÉ, LOUIS (1978) *Le journal et son territoire, presse régionale et conflits sociaux, Rapport final de recherche*, Tours: CNRS-EHESS-Université de Tours.

DUPUY-BUSSON, SEVERINE and SONNAC, NATHALIE (2002) "Les relations entre éditeurs et marchands de journaux: les dérives d'un système", in: Gilles Feyel (Ed.), *La distribution et la diffusion de la presse, du 18ᵉ siècle au 3ᵉ millénaire*, Paris: Panthéon-Assas, pp. 391–408.

GIDDENS, ANTHONY (1994) *Les conséquences de la modernité*, Paris: L'Harmattan.

LAUNAY, JEAN-MARIE (1980) "L'information locale et les quotidiens régionaux", in: Albert Mabileau and André-Jean Tudesq (Eds), *L'information locale*, Bordeaux: Pedone, pp. 213–23.

MARTIN, LAURENT (2005) *La presse écrite en France au 20e siècle*, Paris: Le Livre de Poche.

MARTIN, MARC (2002a) *La presse régionale: des Affiches aux grands quotidiens*, Paris: Fayard.

MARTIN, MARC (2002b) "Information locale et diffusion de la presse quotidienne régionale (fin du 19e siècle et 20e siècle)", in: Gilles Feyel (ed) *La distribution et la diffusion de la presse, du 18e siècle au 3e millénaire*, Paris: Panthéon-Assas, pp. 217–50.

OJD (OFFICE DE JUSTIFICATION DE LA DIFFUSION) (2004) *Procès-verbaux 2004, diffusion totale en nombre d'exemplaires*, Paris: OJD.

OUEST-FRANCE (2005) *Evolution de la presse quotidienne régionale par départements, 1968–2003, diffusion par foyers*, Rennes: *Ouest-France* Research and Development Department.

PAILLIART, ISABELLE (1993) *Les territoires de la communication*, Grenoble: PUG.

TNS SOFRES (2006) *EPIQ—Etude de la presse d'information quotidienne, Audience 2005* [CD-Rom], Paris: TNS Sofres.

Chapter 15

PARTICIPATORY JOURNALISM PRACTICES IN THE MEDIA AND BEYOND
An international comparative study of initiatives in online newspapers

David Domingo, Thorsten Quandt, Ari Heinonen, Steve Paulussen, Jane B. Singer, and **Marina Vujnovic**

Introduction

Now that newspapers are exploring newsroom convergence and eroding the boundaries between print, broadcast and online media, participatory journalism seems to add another dimension that questions previous boundaries—and definitions—of professional journalism. The borderline that separates professional journalists and their audience seems to be blurring (Bruns, 2005; Jenkins, 2006).

Until recently, the working routines and values of journalistic culture had remained highly stable for almost a century (Schudson, 2003; Tuchman, 2002), even after being declared in crisis (Blumler and Gurevitch, 1996; Dahlgren, 1996). Traditionally, journalism has been attached to the institution of the media, based on the production of news by dedicated paid labour, the journalists. The term "gatekeeper", used to describe a main task of journalists, indicates their claim to be the ones who decide what the public needs to know, as well as when and how such information should be provided. The gatekeeper role is maintained and enforced by professional routines and conventions that are said to guarantee the quality and neutrality of institutional journalism (Reese and Ballinger, 2001; Shoemaker, 1991).

But contemporary critics have proposed alternative models such as public journalism (Massey and Haas, 2002; Rosen, 1999) that asked for a more reciprocal relationship between reporters and their audience, suggesting news should be a conversation rather than a lecture (Gillmor, 2004; Kunelius, 2001). In the past decade, new communication technologies, particularly network communication, have made it possible for others also to publish content for a potentially global audience. Of course, the arenas of public communication and especially news production still are dominated by the media, but in certain spheres, alternative agenda-setting actors do exist, and they are producing news themselves. Thus, institutional journalism has encountered—for the first time—a serious challenge to its social function, an activity parallel to its own.

A new and relevant object of study is how journalists in the established, institutionalised media react in this situation (Chung, 2007; Hermida and Thurman, 2008; Lowrey, 2006). This article is an initial effort to explore the extent to which the current development of audience participation opportunities in online newspapers is redefining journalistic culture, values and practices. We want to examine online media to see when and how institutional journalism accommodates the public's capacity to participate in news communication as more than mere receivers. This is not a normative statement implying that media institutions and journalists in fact should abandon traditional core tasks in favour of participatory journalism, but scholarly curiosity about whether institutional journalism empowers and engages citizens in public communication with newly available means.

We have two main objectives in contributing to this inquiry: (1) making conceptual sense of the phenomenon of participatory journalism in the framework of journalism research, and (2) determining the forms that it is taking in different European countries and the United States. In the following pages, we develop a theoretical and methodological model to analyse audience participation opportunities in journalism. The model is tested with a preliminary overview of participatory options in 16 leading online newspapers from eight European countries (Belgium, Croatia, Finland, France, Germany, Spain, Slovenia, United Kingdom) and the United States. The international sample enables a comparative perspective that aims to overcome the deterministic idea that participatory journalism is a must for professional media and to start a more fruitful and contextualised discussion on the benefits, risks and possibilities of this trend (Paulussen et al., 2007).

The groundwork provided by this article places participatory journalism in the historical context of the evolution of journalism and public communication. We propose operational concepts for a systematic analysis of user participation in news websites, understanding it as a very flexible process defined by different roles of content contributors and managers in different stages of the news production process. We end by suggesting further research that could be developed with the analytical model presented here.

Participatory Journalism: A Theoretical Model and Analytical Proposal

In early societies, with small and densely knit social networks, communication on matters of public interest took place through direct interaction among community members. Events that mattered could be communicated by word of mouth, without the necessity of media to transport or convey ideas. Some member of the community would observe an event and tell others, who might then pass the information on. Access to and observation of events, as well as the filtering of relevant information, were contingent on individual and situational factors. The same was true for the processing and editing of information; some community members might be excluded from news or get an altered version of the story.

Both distribution and interpretation of news stories in personal networks were thus highly dynamic and dependent on individuals, personal relationships and various external factors. Only rarely did members of different social networks engage in informational interaction, typically through some connecting node such as a messenger or a traveller who spread the news from one village to the other. However, most of the necessary information for the functioning and survival of each social network was contained in the network itself. These same communication principles of "unmediated" public communication are with us today, not only within small communities but also in many everyday contexts that do not primarily rely on mass media as a means of transporting information.

Why is this relevant for the study of journalism? While this ideal model of unmediated public communication (see Figure 1) oversimplifies the community structures at play here, it helps us identify the basic communication principles that constitute *all* types of public communication. Common components of communication processes include access to and observation of something that can be communicated; selection and filtering of information; processing and editing that information; distribution; and interpretation.

This process is certainly more complicated than just "transporting" information from point A to point B, as is sometimes still implicitly assumed in communication models and public discussion alike, and it depends on mutually accepted rules and roles for all the individuals involved in the process. Furthermore, such processes do not necessarily or

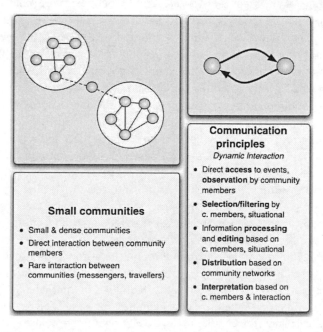

FIGURE 1

Public communication principles in small communities

directly lead to a final element of the chain in each case. Communication processes can stop, for example, if the selection does not lead to a positive result. There are "loop points", where the process might go into a repetition circle; for example, edited information can be further selected and filtered by individuals. And each chain might lead into another chain; for instance, the last steps of the original observation chain could be the first steps of a second-order chain that relies on already-communicated information.

In complex societies, we find the same communication principles (see Figure 2). However, as the size and level of complexity in societies rise, it becomes more and more difficult for individual community members to perform the necessary functions in the process. The social networks in complex societies contain both stable groups and quickly changing ones. There are dense, clustered network structures and loosely knit ones, as well as central and peripheral nodes. Depending on where something happens or is observed in the network, and where the relevant interest groups for news are, the information still might reach its goal by direct interaction. But the farther the source is away from the "goal" person, the more likely it will get lost somewhere in the structure of the networks.

Therefore, institutions developed in order to solve the problem of limited individual reach and communication-processing capability; some sociologists see this institutionalisation of communication as a process of societal evolution (e.g. Luhmann, 1975; Parsons, 1964; compare also Görke and Scholl, 2006). Institutionalised communication, supported and enabled by media that help bridge space and time differences between members of large and complex communities (Carey, 1998), can be seen as a part of a more general social development toward "modernity" (Haferkamp and Smelser, 1992), with new divisions of labour, the birth of modern social institutions, and so on.

As a result of this socio-historical development, professional observers and communicators (agencies and journalistic media) work full-time to access, select and filter, produce and edit news, which is then distributed via the media to network members. The interpretation of information is also partially journalism driven, as the media imply interpretation patterns by providing comments and opinions. The institutionalisation process is connected to technological advances and to the development of working rules, professional roles and organisational structures. As a result, discussions of journalism today incorporate consideration of distribution technologies; the industrial formations organising the production processes; a complex system of social rules and roles connected with production, distribution and reception processes; and a large number of cultural myths connected with all these aspects. However, the processes described above are by no means linear, and institutionalised media did not replace the "earlier" type of communication. From early two- and multi-step flow approaches up to recent network-based analyses, communication research has shown that mediated and interpersonal communication work together to disseminate news in a society.

The fact that journalism has emerged through the historical and social development process roughly sketched above makes some of its constitutive features more obvious: while journalism is a social phenomenon with a high level of internal differentiation, it still follows the basic communicative principles identified for early societies. Furthermore, its development is certainly not "finished"; as a solution to the challenges of organising communication processes in complex societies, it will be altered and modified, depending on new challenges and options that emerge. Journalism studies scholars currently discuss

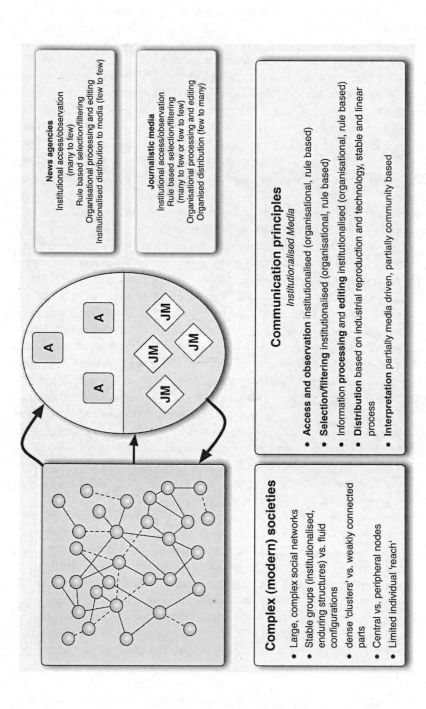

News agencies
Institutional access/observation
(many to few)
Rule based selection/filtering
Organisational processing and editing
Institutionalised distribution to media (few to few)

Journalistic media
Institutional access/observation
Rule based selection/filtering
(many to few or few to few)
Organisational processing and editing
Organised distribution (few to many)

Communication principles
Institutionalised Media

- **Access and observation** institutionalised (organisational, rule based)
- **Selection/filtering** institutionalised (organisational, rule based)
- **Information processing and editing** institutionalised (organisational, rule based)
- **Distribution** based on industrial reproduction and technology, stable and linear process
- **Interpretation** partially media driven, partially community based

Complex (modern) societies

- Large, complex social networks
- Stable groups (institutionalised, enduring structures) vs. fluid configurations
- dense 'clusters' vs. weakly connected parts
- Central vs. peripheral nodes
- Limited individual 'reach'

FIGURE 2
Institutionalisation of public communication

some of these possible modifications, which are triggered partly by technological advances but also by societal challenges and deficits in the current state of institutionalised journalism. These modifications *might* lead to a new model of journalism, labelled "participatory journalism" (see Figure 3).

This model implies that some of the institutionalised communication functions of agencies and journalistic media can be performed by individual society members and organisations, while others still lie in the hands of the communication institutions. The re-inclusion of the social networks and the resulting de-institutionalisation are closely connected to the emergence of new communication technologies, which expand the reach of the individual network nodes again. Computer technology and the Internet allow users, as individuals or pools, to produce and distribute news items on the basis of their observations or opinions, and computer-based selection and management systems support collective work processes to gather the information bits that are spread across the whole network.

Within some sociologically oriented approaches, this development is seen as a reaction to the growing complexity in society, with solutions developed in response to the challenges of organising public communication in an ever-expanding social network. These scholars see signs of a paradigmatic shift to a new form of societal order beyond "modern" institutionalised societies (sometimes called postmodernity, second modernity or liquid modernity, to name but a few; Carey, 1998; Deuze, 2007; Wimmer and Quandt, 2006). Others stress an economic logic behind the developments, seeing user participation as a form of (re)engaging their audiences and cutting costs by "crowdsourcing" (Howe, 2006) tasks that were formerly performed by paid professionals.

There are no easy answers to the questions of which factor or combination of factors is driving the process, or of whether a new participatory model will succeed. But it is obvious that its development does not depend solely on an internal differentiation of journalism: the emergence of participatory forms is influenced by various external factors such as technology, economy, and the larger cultural and societal framework. Out of these internal and external factors, various development logics might emerge. In this article, we analyse the status quo, as of 2007, among leading news organisations in various Western countries. We do so using an analytical grid (see Figure 4) that follows the logic of news production stages, as described in the three models above.

The grid serves as an orientation for our empirical approach to participatory journalism. Looking at each stage of the process, we separately evaluate the current state of development regarding participatory and institutionalised elements in a way that strives to be both systematic and flexible. The analytical grid suggests that audience participation in the media can take many different forms, depending on the openness of each of the news production stages. In which part of the production process audiences can participate, and to what extent, is in fact a decision of institutional media. The work of Bruns (2005) on participatory sites outside the institutional media field, from Indymedia to Slashdot, has inspired our analytical grid, but we felt that his proposal of *input*, *output* and *response* gates was not thorough enough for the analysis of professional news production stages.

In order to operationalise the analysis of the online newspaper websites, we tried to identify in each stage who were the content *contributors* and who were *managers* of the process, the ones with decision-making power. In Bruns' cases, illustrating some of the most open models of participatory journalism, citizens were in charge both of

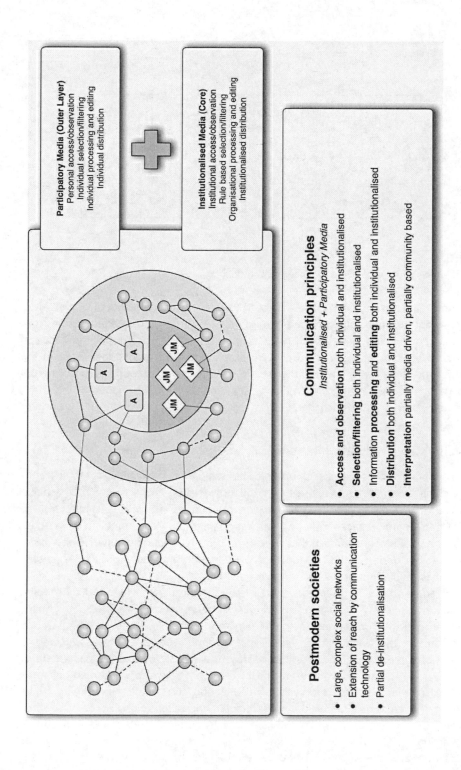

Participatory Media (Outer Layer)
Personal access/observation
Individual selection/filtering
Individual processing and editing
Individual distribution

Institutionalised Media (Core)
Institutional access/observation
Rule based selection/filtering
Organisational processing and editing
Institutionalised distribution

Communication principles
Institutionalised + Participatory Media

- **Access and observation** both individual and institutionalised
- **Selection/filtering** both individual and institutionalised
- **Information processing and editing** both individual and institutionalised
- **Distribution** both individual and institutionalised
- **Interpretation** partially media driven, partially community based

Postmodern societies

- Large, complex social networks
- Extension of reach by communication technology
- Partial de-institutionalisation

FIGURE 3
Re-inclusion of social networks in public communication

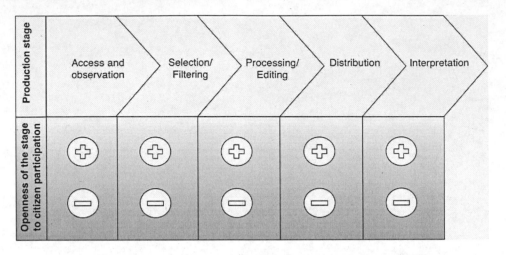

FIGURE 4
Analytical grid derived from the theoretical model

contributions and management. We expected that in institutional media news sites, journalists would have a significant degree of control in most of the stages. Besides this, we also wanted to identify the explicit *rules* and *incentives* for audience participation and the explicit *criteria* for user-generated content management in each stage. To build the checklist for the qualitative analysis of the websites, we took into account the participatory features detected by other researchers in professional and citizen media (Bruns, 2005; Hermida and Thurman, 2007; Schaffer, 2007).

Preliminary Study: An International Comparative Sample

This empirical study seeks to outline the structural characteristics of audience participation in 16 online newspapers. We did not analyse the actual content (news, photos, comments) being produced by citizens, nor did we interview the journalists in charge of participatory spaces to know their rationale when developing these features. The study is a preliminary approach that intends to identify, through qualitative analysis of the websites, the opportunities for audience participation and the explicit rules, criteria and incentives regulating them.

After agreeing on the theoretical and methodological framework and developing the analytical checklist, the team of six researchers selected two leading online newspapers in six EU countries (Belgium, Finland, France, Germany, Spain, United Kingdom) and in the United States (see Table 1). One website also was selected in Croatia and one in Slovenia. The countries represent a sample of Western parliamentary democracies, both old and new, and include EU newcomer Slovenia and member-to-be Croatia. Each researcher was responsible for selecting the online newspapers to be analysed in the countries he or she was familiar with. Sensationalist or specialised newspapers were not considered for the sample selection, nor were papers with a free printed version.

Structural analyses of the websites were initially conducted during June and July 2007 and recoded in December 2007, looking for participatory features in the websites

TABLE 1
Online newspapers included in the study

Country	Newspaper	Online Web address
Belgium	*De Standaard*	standaard.be
	Gazet van Antwerpen	gva.be
Croatia	*Jutarnji List*	jutarnji.hr
Slovenia	*Dnevnik*	dnevnik.si
Finland	*Iltalehti*	iltalehti.fi
	Helsingin Sanomat	Hs.fi
France	*Le Monde*	lemonde.fr
	Le Figaro	lefigaro.fr
Germany	*Spiegel* (weekly in print)	spiegel.de
	Frankfurter Allgemeine	Faz.net
Spain	*El Mundo*	elmundo.es
	El País	elpais.com
United Kingdom	*Guardian*	guardian.co.uk
	The Times	timesonline.co.uk
United States	*The New York Times*	nytimes.com
	USA Today	usatoday.com

and any explicit definitions or other information offered by the online newspaper, including the FAQ and Help pages. An analytical checklist was used to set a common data-gathering procedure, and each website was coded by two different members of the research team.[1] Differences were discussed and resolved to ensure interpretative homogeneity. More formal intercoder reliability tests were planned for a potential follow-up study including a broader sample.

Results: Professional Media Exploring Participation

A first overview of participatory features in the analysed websites indicates that most of the options explored by citizen media sites had not been widely adopted by these online newspapers at the time of the study (see Table 2). The most common features offered by the studied cases enabled users to act upon journalistic content, such as by ranking or commenting on it. Features that let citizens produce content themselves were developed in relatively few websites; most popular were invitations to submit audio-visual materials (mainly photos) and story ideas, links to social networking sites and space for citizen blogs. Few online newspapers used tools that are regarded as efficient for community-building, something that citizen media initiatives have found to be a key aspect to engage participants and make them feel responsible for the quality of their contributions (Schaffer, 2007). *USA Today* had explored these options more thoroughly than the other cases in this study, creating user profile pages as well as a system to recommend other users and their contributions and to report abuse. However, this user-centric management of comments was still minimal compared to all the other decision-making processes that remained under the sole authority of journalists.

A closer look, separating the news production process into the five stages previously discussed, confirmed that only the interpretation stage was significantly open to some sort of citizen participation for all the newspapers studied (see Table 3). The audience did not take part at all in selection and filtering; while there was considerable variation in the other three stages, most of the sampled sites exhibited little openness. This suggests that the

TABLE 2
Participatory features in the analysed online newspapers

	Yes	No	NA
News production-related spaces			
Invitation to submit photos, video, audio	10	6	
Invitation to submit story ideas	6	10	
Collective open interviews with newsmakers	3	13	
Space to publish citizen blogs	6	10	
Space to publish citizen stories	5	11	
Audience-driven citizen content selection/hierarchy	1	6	9
Audience-driven journalistic content hierarchy	11	5	
Commentary and debate spaces			
Comments embedded in journalist stories/blogs	11	5	
Comments embedded in citizen stories/blogs	6	1	9
Trackback of comments by external weblogs	6	10	
Audience-driven forums, open to any topic	5	11	
Journalist-driven forums, referred to in stories	9	7	
Polls	13	3	
Social networking features			
Public user profile page	4	12	
Karma system (user points based on activity)	1	15	
User tagging of content, serendipity tools	2	14	
Links to promote content on social sites	7	9	

institutional media had largely kept the journalistic culture unchanged even when exploring participation opportunities for the audience. The core journalistic role of the "gatekeeper" who decides what makes news remained the monopoly of professionals even in the online newspapers that had taken openness to other stages beyond interpretation. Furthermore, no single stage in any of the cases allowed for complete involvement of the citizens as managers, either on their own or in collaboration with journalists. Professionals reserved the last word in management of each stage of the production process; citizens generally were limited to a role as contributors, if they were given a role at all.

An exception to this rule confirms that institutional media are not fully releasing their power over the production process to the citizen. In some online newspapers, users can vote for the stories they like, generating a ranking of "most recommended" stories at the distribution stage. The list is usually available in a specific page of the website, one click away from the homepage in some cases. But it is rarely shown side by side with the hierarchy of stories decided by the journalists.

A comparison of the levels of openness by country did not reveal clear national idiosyncrasies. There were both differences and similarities between the two online newspapers of every country in the sample. Low levels of openness in any stage but interpretation were widespread in all the countries. In some cases (Spain, United States), the market leader showed far less openness to participation than the second pick, but in other countries (United Kingdom, Finland), it is the other way around. The relative diversity of approaches (only two online newspapers share the same openness profile) suggests that attitudes toward audience participation in online newsrooms are locally constructed not only in every country but also in every case, apparently shaped by specific contextual factors. These data suggest that beyond the common core of journalistic culture that may

TABLE 3
Openness of the news production stages in the analysed online newspapers

		Access/observation	Selection/filtering	Processing/editing	Distribution	Interpretation
Belgium	standaard.be	Closed	Closed	Closed	Slightly open	Slightly open
	gva.be	Slightly open	Closed	Closed	Closed	Slightly open
Croatia	jutarnji.hr	Slightly open	Closed	Slightly open	Closed	Moderately open
Slovenia	dnevnik.si	Slightly open	Closed	Moderately open	Closed	Moderately open
Finland	hs.fi	Slightly open	Closed	Slightly open	Slightly open	Slightly open
	iltalehti.fi	Slightly open	Closed	Slightly open	Slightly open	Very open
France	lefigaro.fr	Closed	Closed	Slightly open	Closed	Moderately open
	lemonde.fr	Closed	Closed	Slightly open	Closed	Moderately open
Germany	faz.net	Closed	Closed	Closed	Slightly open	Moderately open
	spiegel.de	Closed	Closed	Closed	Slightly open	Slightly open
Spain	elmundo.es	Closed	Closed	Slightly open	Slightly open	Slightly open
	elpais.com	Moderately open	Closed	Moderately open	Slightly open	Moderately open
United Kingdom	guardian.co.uk	Slightly open	Closed	Moderately open	Slightly open	Very open
	timesonline.co.uk	Closed	Closed	Slightly open	Slightly open	Moderately open
United States	usatoday.com	Closed	Closed	Closed	Moderately open	Very open
	nytimes.com	Closed	Closed	Slightly open	Moderately open	Slightly open

Very open to participation: citizens can both participate as contributors *and* managers in that stage. Moderately open to participation: citizens can only participate as contributors or managers in the stage, with loose criteria. Slightly open to participation: citizens can only participate as contributors, with very strict rules and filters. Closed to participation: citizens cannot contribute to this stage of the production process.

be relatively homogenous across countries, professional singularities, market characteristics, social particularities and regulatory differences may explain the diverse understandings and developments of participatory journalism in each online newspaper.

In the following paragraphs, we summarise the participation opportunities offered in 2007 by the online newspapers in each stage.

Access/Observation

Few websites explicitly invite their users to participate in the access and observation stage. In most of the cases there is some way to contact the newsroom or specific journalists, but relatively few websites explicitly invite the audience to submit story ideas. The Finnish and Croatian online newspapers do, as well as *GVA.be* and *USA Today*, which has a blurb at the bottom of the homepage asking for "tips about government corruption, business ripoffs, safety violations or other serious problems". A journalist might decide to work on the story if it is deemed newsworthy; citizens are not involved in subsequent stages of the production process. *El País*, which started its citizen journalism section in 2007, has a different strategy: the newspaper suggests topics to be covered by the amateurs, who can also decide what they want to report about. The range of topics is wide, including mostly cultural chronicles and lifestyle issues, but also hard news witnessed by contributors. Although separated from actual newsroom-produced content, it can be considered a form of crowdsourcing, where the journalists try to loosely guide the priorities of citizen journalists.

Selection/Filtering

As mentioned above, no participation opportunities are offered in this stage. Even in *El País'* "Yo, periodista" section (mimicking CNN's "I-reporter"), the newsroom is the sole entity responsible for choosing what stories will be published. *The Times* experimented with a Reader Panel, which responded to regular online surveys, with a £1,000 monthly prize as an incentive. However, this did not empower the citizens as managers or collaborators of selection and filtering.

Processing/Editing

Few online newspapers in the sample allow citizens to submit news stories. Audience blogs and audio-visual material are more common but are always clearly separated from professional content, with specific sections and labels. Blogs tend to be the most open form of participation, when they are available, as there typically is no moderation prior to publication. *Le Monde* has one of the most extensive collections of audience blogs, but authoring one is only available to paying subscribers. *Iltalehti* has an entertainment-oriented special section called "One's own" where readers can publish their own blogs. Besides this, news texts, photos and other materials are carefully selected by journalists. Furthermore, in most of the websites that enable citizen participation in producing news content, this option is limited to specific topics such as entertainment and travel, leaving hard news as a journalist-only venture. That is the case in the British websites, as well as *El Mundo*, which just lets users submit local news or TV programme reviews, and *The New York Times*, which allows registered users to rate and review movies, books, theatre plays and travel destinations.

El País and *Dnevnik* are the only cases with a user-generated content section explicitly devoted to news of all sorts. The motto presented by the Spanish online newspaper is clearly inspired by the citizen journalism movement: "If you have witnessed a newsworthy event, send it and we will publish it. Now readers become journalists". Only registered users can submit content, be it text, photos or audiovisual material. The user must agree to detailed terms of contract when registering: his or her personal data are genuine, the submitted content is original, the people shown in photos or videos agree to be in the story, and the stories do not affect the rights or dignity of other people. Selection and distribution stages related to the citizen news are controlled by journalists. One story is chosen each day by the newsroom to be shown on the main homepage, in a box that clearly states that it is a "reader" story. To further motivate audience participation, *El País* explored for six months giving out a money prize for the best story selected by the newsroom weekly (€500) and monthly (€1,500), but they have discontinued the prizes.

Some online newspapers explicitly ask the readers to submit immediate feedback if they detect a factual error on a story. This suggests a responsive attitude from the journalists, but it is hard to consider this as a real opening of the news-editing process.

Distribution

As mentioned before, the participation options at the distribution stage are very restricted. Most of the websites create user-driven story rankings based on automatic counts of most-read or -emailed stories. Some websites let users vote on the news they like, but users cannot change journalistic decisions directly. *The Times* is the newspaper that most prominently shows user news rankings, in a box at the right of the homepage. *USA Today* has a tab on the main page of every section, and *NYTimes.com* and *El País* show user rankings at the right column of each story page. Tools to ease the redistribution of news are not widely used in the sites analysed. The most popular are Digg.com, del.icio.us and Technorati. German and Spanish websites additionally provide links to social networking and bookmarking sites in their own languages.

Interpretation

Most of the online newspapers see audience participation as an opportunity for their readers to debate current events. There are two main strategies for user participation in the interpretation stage. Some websites allow user comments below each news story. Others prefer to keep participation separated from news and have forums or debate spaces, usually referenced from selected stories or other items that the newsroom feels suitable for discussion. For example, the *Guardian* has both talk boards and an extensive but distinct section of its site called "Comment Is Free," where user input is encouraged. Comment management strategies range from open options (post-publication moderation, just an email as author identification) to strict and filtered systems (supervision of posts before they are published and registration required). Guidelines are sometimes very brief (*New York Times*: "Comments will be posted if they are on-topic and not abusive. They may be edited for length and clarity"), but a full page of rules is usually provided.

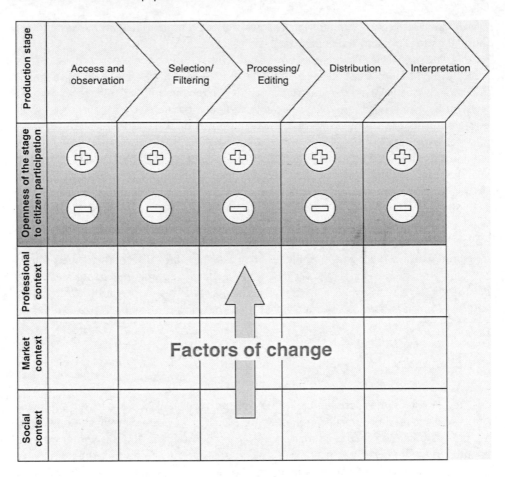

FIGURE 5
Extended analytical grid to include factors of change

The websites that opt for post-publication supervision tend to make users co-responsible for policing the submissions, offering a "report abuse" link besides every comment; some, including the *Guardian*, *FAZ.net* and *USA Today*, also enable users to recommend comments they find interesting. Some sites, such as *De Standaard*, only allow comments on blogs, op-ed columns and forums, not on news stories. *Le Monde* and *The Times* have a variable comment moderation strategy, based on the sensitivity of the news topic.

Conclusions and Further Research

This preliminary study of audience participation opportunities in online newspapers reveals useful data about media industry trends in Europe and the United States. The proposed analytical model is successful in describing the diversity of strategies and the general reluctance to open up most of the news production process to the active involvement of citizens. These results suggest that, as of the study period in 2007, core journalistic culture had remained largely unchanged in the 16 online newspapers analysed, as professionals kept the decision-making power at each stage. Journalists are retaining the traditional gatekeeping role in adopting user content on their websites (Hermida and Thurman, 2008).

It should be emphasized that much has changed since these data were collected in 2007, underlining the need for research in this rapidly developing area to be ongoing. In particular, further research should explore the motivations and context factors constraining or fostering openness at each production stage. Interviews with journalists are needed to understand the rationales for the approaches being taken, and a round of those have since been conducted. In addition, an extended version of the proposed analytical grid could incorporate such influences and help explain the different approaches to audience participation (see Figure 5). The analysis should pay attention to factors such as:

- *Professional context*: existing routines, newsroom organisation, journalistic culture, ethical guidelines, media tradition (press, broadcast, online).
- *Market context*: size of the company, ownership, competitors' strategies (both professional and citizen media).
- *Social context*: public sphere history, information society policies, media laws.

In addition, the actual quality of citizen participation also deserves research attention. From a normative point of view, researchers should question whether user-generated content improves the overall quality of news products, journalistic work and the public sphere. While interviews with online editors and journalists will be crucial to address the study of factors and motivations, content analysis is needed to assess the quality of user contributions. A bigger and more representative sample may enable researchers to draw clearer profiles of the actual development of citizen participation in the news production process.

NOTE

1. Pauliina Lehtonen was the second coder for the Finnish sample, and Nina Brnic assisted in the second coding of the Slovenian and Croatian news sites.

REFERENCES

BLUMLER, J. and GUREVITCH, M. (1996) "Media Change and Social Change: linkages and junctures", in: J. Curran and M. Gurevitch (Eds), *Mass Media and Society*, London: Edward Arnold.

BRUNS, A. (2005) *Gatewatching: collaborative online news production*, New York: Peter Lang.

CAREY, J. W. (1998) "The Internet and the End of the National Communication System: uncertain predictions of an uncertain future", *Journalism & Mass Communication Quarterly* 75, pp. 28–34.

CHUNG, D. (2007) "Profits and Perils: online news producers' perceptions of interactivity and uses of interactive features", *Convergence* 13(1), pp. 43–61.

DAHLGREN, P. (1996) "Media Logic in Cyberspace: repositioning journalism and its publics", *Javnost: the Public* 3(3), pp. 59–72.

DEUZE, M. (2007) "Journalism in Liquid Modern Times. An interview with Zygmunt Bauman", *Journalism Studies* 8, pp. 671–9.

GILLMOR, D. (2004) *We the Media. Grassroots journalism by the people, for the people*, Sebastopol, CA: O'Reilly.

GÖRKE, A. and SCHOLL, A. (2006) "Niklas Luhmann's Theory of Social Systems and Journalism Research", *Journalism Studies* 7, pp. 645–56.

HAFERKAMP, H. and SMELSER, N. J. (Eds) (1992) *Social Change and Modernity*, Berkeley: University of California Press.

HERMIDA, A. and THURMAN, N. (2008) "A Clash of Cultures: the integration of user-generated content within professional journalistic frameworks at British newspaper websites", *Journalism Practice* 2, pp. 343–56.

HOWE, J. (2006) "The Rise of Crowdsourcing", *Wired*, http://www.wired.com/wired/archive/14.06/crowds.html.

JENKINS, H. (2006) *Convergence Culture: where old and new media collide*, New York: New York University Press.

KUNELIUS, R. (2001) "Conversation: a metaphor and a method for better journalism?", *Journalism Studies* 2(1), pp. 31–54.

LOWREY, W. (2006) "Mapping the Journalism–Blogging Relationship", *Journalism: Theory, Practice and Criticism* 7, pp. 477–500.

LUHMANN, N. (1975) *Soziologische Aufklärung [Sociological Enlightenment]*, Vol. 2, Opladen: Westdeutscher Verlag.

MASSEY, B. L. and HAAS, T. (2002) "Does Making Journalism More Public Make a Difference? A critical review of evaluative research on public journalism", *Journalism & Mass Communication Quarterly* 79, pp. 559–86.

PARSONS, T. (1964) "Evolutionary Universals", *American Sociological Review* 29, pp. 339–57.

PAULUSSEN, S., HEINONEN, A., DOMINGO, D. and QUANDT, T. (2007) "Doing It Together: citizen participation in the professional news making process", *Observatorio (OBS*) Journal* 1(3), pp. 131–54, http://obs.obercom.pt/index.php/obs/article/view/148/107.

REESE, S. D. and BALLINGER, J. (2001) "Roots of a Sociology of News: remembering Mr. Gates and social control in the newsroom", *Journalism & Mass Communication Quarterly* 78, pp. 641–58.

ROSEN, J. (1999) *What Are Journalists For?*, New Haven, CT: Yale University Press.

SCHAFFER, J. (2007) *Citizen Media: fad or the future of news?*, College Park, MD: J-Lab, http://www.j-lab.org/citizen_media.pdf.

SCHUDSON, M. (2003) *Sociology of News*, New York: Norton.

SHOEMAKER, P. J. (1991) *Gatekeeping*, Thousand Oaks, CA: Sage.

TUCHMAN, G. (2002) "The Production of News", in: K. B. Jensen (Ed.), *A Handbook of Media and Communication Research: qualitative and quantitative methodologies*, London and New York: Routledge.

WIMMER, J. and QUANDT, T. (2006) Living in the Risk Society. An interview with Ulrich Beck", *Journalism Studies* 7, pp. 336–47.

Chapter 16

A CLASH OF CULTURES
The integration of user-generated content within professional journalistic frameworks at British newspaper websites

Alfred Hermida and **Neil Thurman**

Introduction

The Internet is increasingly being defined by new digital technologies that empower users to develop, create, rate, and distribute Internet content and applications (O'Reilly, 2005). Websites such as YouTube, MySpace, and Wikipedia provide platforms for so-called user-generated content (UGC), where citizens can publish their own comments, photos, videos, and more online. According to Paul Saffo (quoted in the *Economist*, 2006), in this new media culture the public is no longer a passive consumer of media, but an active participant in the creation of the media landscape.

2006 saw the purchase of MySpace by Rupert Murdoch's News Corporation for US$580 million and Google's acquisition of YouTube for US$1.65 billion, leading some commentators to state that UGC was the "paramount cultural buzz phrase of 2006" (Pareles, 2006). Indeed, such quantitative evidence as exists does seem to show that websites based on user participation generate significantly more usage than sites not based on this concept.[1]

The response of the British public to the 7 July 2005 underground and bus bombings in London showed how visitors to online news sites were ready and willing to contribute content. The BBC received 22,000 e-mails and text messages, 300 photos, and several video sequences on the day of the attacks.[2] The dramatic stills and video led BBC TV newscasts—the first time, according to Torin Douglas (2006), that such material had been considered more newsworthy than professional content.

The emergence of online tools that allow for broad participation in the creation and dissemination of content has repercussions for the role of journalists as conveyors of news and information. Gillmor (quoted by Lasica, 2003) argues that "people at the edges of the network have the ability to create their own news entries". UGC may be instigating a fundamental shift in established modes of journalism, undermining the "we write, you read" dogma of modern journalism (Deuze, 2003).

This study seeks to understand how established news organisations in the United Kingdom are responding to the emergence of UGC. We examine UGC as a process whereby ordinary people have an opportunity to participate with or contribute to professionally edited publications. It builds on research by Neil Thurman (2008) in 2004–5 that quantified and analysed the distribution of user-generated content initiatives (UGCIs) at 10 leading UK news websites and examined editors' attitudes to citizen journalism and participatory journalism.

In the first section of this study we examine the range of formats used to solicit material from readers, and the progressive adoption of UGC by UK newspaper websites. The second section explores senior news executives' attitudes towards UGC within professional news organisations. We analyse: (1) the reasons behind the adoption of UGC initiatives; (2) its editorial and financial value; and (3) editors' concerns about brand identity and reputation. More widely, our study examines the relationship between professional journalism and amateur content, and how UGC challenges the traditional gate-keeping role of journalists. The study comes as news organisations across the world are experimenting with ways of integrating UGC into professional journalistic models.[3]

Methodology

A combination of an online survey and in-depth interviews were used to examine the adoption of UGC by UK news organisations and to investigate the internal debates taking place in newsrooms over the publication of user media. The study focuses on the online experiences of the leading national newspapers in the United Kingdom, and, therefore, does not include the BBC, which is a publicly funded national broadcaster.

A survey was undertaken in November 2006 to measure the adoption of UGCIs by 12 UK newspaper websites. The websites were studied over a period of 48 hours and visited a number of times at random during the day. For the assessment of the UGC functionality of each site, the unit of analysis was a web page. All sections of the websites studied were examined to see if they contained any UGCIs.

The interviews were semi-structured and did not set out to test any specific propositions. Instead the authors set out to investigate attitudes to user media, with use of prompts and follow-up questions (McCracken, 1988). The following news executives were interviewed in August 2006:

- Richard Avery—Internet Development Controller, Northern and Shell.
- Peter Bale—Editorial Director, *Times Online*.
- Alistair Brown—General Manager, *Scotsman.com*.
- Richard Burton—Editor, *Telegraph.co.uk*.

- James Montgomery—Editor, *FT.com*.
- Pete Picton—Editor, *TheSun.co.uk*.
- Steve Purcell—Editor, *Mirror.co.uk*.
- Alan Revell—COO, Associated Northcliffe Digital.
- Annelies Van den Belt—New Media Director, Telegraph Group.
- Simon Waldman—Director, Digital Publishing, *Guardian.co.uk*.
- Richard Withey—New Media Strategies, Independent Digital.

The participants were selected as representatives of a particular position in the social system in question (Lindlof, 1995): in this case as very senior editors and managers at the most popular newspaper websites in the United Kingdom. As such the findings have relevance to other established news organisations seeking to integrate UGC into their products and services, because journalism professionals tend to have a common set of norms and values (Weaver, 1998). While the number of participants in a typical qualitative research study is too small to be representative of the general population, the number of interviewees in this study exceeds the quantity that McCracken (1988) believes is sufficient for qualitative research based on in-depth interviews. A modified version of the issue-focused method recommended by Weiss (1994) was used to analyse verbatim transcripts of the interviews.

Findings

New Formats Introduced

The website analysis identified nine generic formats used to encourage contributions from the public: "Polls", "Messageboards", "Have your says", "Comments on stories", "Q&As", "Blogs", "Reader blogs", "Your media", and "Your story" (see Thurman, 2008).

"Polls" are defined as topical questions where readers are asked to make a multiple choice or binary response. They provide instant and quantifiable feedback to readers and are easy to set up and run automatically, being inexpensive and risk-free. But they offer very limited interaction: restricted to "yes" or "no" answers, or a multiple-choice response.

"Messageboards" are areas that allow readers to engage in threaded online conversations or debates on topics often initiated by readers. They are usually reactively moderated.[4] They are structured so that users can reply to any of the posts rather than just the original one. The discussions remain open for weeks or months.

"Have your says" resemble "Messageboards" but with significant differences. These are areas where journalists post topical questions to which readers send written replies. A selection is made, edited, and published by journalists, with the submissions either fully or reactively moderated. "Have your says" usually remain open for a limited number of days. This format has proved popular with readers.[5]

The "Comments on stories" format allows readers to submit their views on a story. These comments are usually submitted using a form at the bottom of an article. This format may or may not require a reader to register with a news site.

"Q&As" are interviews with journalists and/or invited guests, with questions submitted by readers. By their very nature, "Q&As" are moderated. But since they are usually webcast in audio or video, or transcribed, as live, they offer a sense of interactivity and immediacy.

"Blogs" are a relatively new addition to news websites in the United Kingdom. These have posts laid out in reverse chronological order and most allow readers to comment on the entries. Blogs are explicitly authored by one or more individuals, often associated with a set of interests or opinions, and can include links to external websites.

"Reader blogs" are a new format launched in 2006 by the website of the United Kingdom's best-selling daily newspaper, *The Sun. TheSun.co.uk* allows readers to create a blog and have it hosted on the news organisation's web servers.

"Your media" are galleries of photographs, video and other media submitted by readers and vetted by journalists. "Your stories" are sections where readers are asked to send in stories that matter to them. These then are edited by journalists for publication on the website.

Opportunities for Reader Participation

The survey of 12 UK newspaper websites conducted in November 2006 revealed that only one, *Independent.co.uk*, was not providing any tools for reader participation. The results showed wide variation in the opportunities users have to contribute to the professionally edited publications studied. Three sites, *Guardian.co.uk*, *TheSun.co.uk*, and *Scotsman.co.uk* required users to register in order to participate. There were also variations in the use of moderation, with most of the sites (eight) exercising a high degree of control on contributions by fully moderating content.

Our study revealed substantial growth in the opportunities for readers to contribute compared to the analysis by Thurman (2008) in April 2005 (see Table 1). In particular, we identified significant growth in three formats: "Blogs", "Comments on stories", and "Have your says". The number of blogs jumped from seven to 118 in the 18 months from April 2005 to November 2006 (see Table 2), although there were wide variations in the nature of

TABLE 1

User-generated content initiatives at a selection of British newspaper websites, November 2006

News sites	Polls	Message boards	Have your says	Comments on stories	Q&As	Blogs	Reader blogs	Your media	Your story
DailyExpress.co.uk			X			X			
DailyMail.co.uk	X	X		X*	X	X*			
DailyStar.co.uk			X			X			
FT.com	X	X			X				
Guardian.co.uk		X		X*	X	X*			
Independent.co.uk									
Mirror.co.uk	X	X				X			
Telegraph.co.uk	X	X	X*	X*		X*		X	
TheSun.co.uk		X*	X*		X	X*	X*	X	
TheTimes.co.uk	X*		X	X	X	X*			X†
ThisisLondon.co.uk		X		X*		X*			
Scotsman.com				X*		X*		X	X*

*New since April 2005. Three websites, *DailyExpress.co.uk*, *DailyStar.co.uk*, and *Mirror.co.uk* were not included in the previous survey by Thurman (2008).
†Platform to showcase readers' travel stories.

TABLE 2
Progressive adoption of blogs at a selection of British newspaper websites

News site	April 2005			November 2006		
	Blogs	Comment moderation		Blogs	Comment moderation	
		Full	Reactive		Full	Reactive
DailyExpress.co.uk				1	X	
DailyMail.co.uk				7	X	
DailyStar.co.uk				2	X	
FT.com						
Guardian.co.uk	6		X	12		X
Independent.co.uk						
Mirror.co.uk				2*		
Telegraph.co.uk				37	X	
TheSun.co.uk				12*		
TheTimes.co.uk				39	X	
ThisisLondon.co.uk				5	X	
Scotsman.com	1	X		1	X	
Total	7			118		

*Comments not allowed.

the blogs and how often they were updated. The largest increase was seen at *Telegraph.co.uk*, which introduced 37 blogs; and at *Times.co.uk*, which created 39 blogs. *TheSun.co.uk* also introduced blogs for readers, with comments enabled.

Most of the newspaper blogs allowed comments, though they were almost all vetted by journalists before publication. Only one site, *Guardian.co.uk*, allowed users to post comments directly to a blog, but readers had to register and confirm their e-mail address first.

The "Comment on stories" format also saw rapid expansion in the 18-month period between surveys (see Table 3). The number of UK publications adopting this feature rose from one to six. Two-thirds of the sites were moderating comments, while those that did not required registration.

"Have your say" sections grew more slowly than "Comments on stories" (see Table 3). The number of UK newspaper websites using this format rose from three to five. Four of these were fully moderated, with only *TheSun.co.uk* adopting the use of registration and reactive moderation.

Attitudes to User-generated Content

The Fear of Marginalisation

The interviews with senior news executives revealed some of the factors that influence editorial attitudes towards audience participation. Our findings suggest that the growth identified in the survey is partly the result of editors' and executives' fear of being marginalised by user media. Richard Burton, editor of *Telegraph.co.uk*, suggested that "the idea of becoming a forum for debate was an area that newspapers had to get into, otherwise they'd get left behind". Richard Withey of *Independent.co.uk* suggested user media is a "phenomenon you can't ignore", even though the newspaper group he represented did not provide platforms for participation:

TABLE 3
Progressive adoption of "Have your says" and "Comment on stories" at a selection of British newspaper websites

News site	April 2005				November 2006			
	Have your says		Comment on stories		Have your says		Comment on stories	
	Full	Reactive	Full	Reactive	Full	Reactive	Full	Reactive
Dailyexpress.co.uk					X			
Dailymail.co.uk							X	
Dailystar.co.uk					X			
FT.com								
Guardian.co.uk								X*
Independent.co.uk								
Mirror.co.uk								
Telegraph.co.uk	X				X		X	
TheSun.co.uk	X					X*		
TheTimes.co.uk	X		X		X			
ThisisLondon.co.uk							X	
Scotsman.co.uk								X*

Note: "Full" and "Reactive" refers to the type of moderation employed.
*Registration required.

The whole idea of the newspaper proprietor and his editors telling people what was going on in the world and the world neatly reading that ... that self-perpetuating oligarchy has been broken down very rapidly, and user-generated content now forms quite a big part of national newspaper websites. (Withey)

As editors jumped on board because of the perceived need to offer greater levels of interactivity with readers, they acknowledged that they were "latecomers to the party" (Burton) and that newspapers need to be in the business of interactivity. Alan Revell of Associated Newspapers said:

We firmly believe in the great conversation. These businesses are about interactivity and it's about it being a two-way street and people joining the conversation rather than being lectured to or talked to. They do want to respond, not all of them, but people do want the ability to respond instantly and contribute and add.

Retaining Staff

The widespread adoption of blogs—a common vehicle for initiating the conversation with readers—at mainstream newspaper sites cannot be attributed solely to editors' fear of marginalisation. Interviews showed that news executives were also motivated by a desire to retain control of journalists who may have otherwise created their own blogs. At *TimesOnline.co.uk*, leading *Times'* and *Sunday Times'* correspondents were offered blogs as an attempt to "give them a piece of property on the internet themselves, within our site" (Bale). At *Telegraph.co.uk*, blogs were first offered to foreign correspondents, as these were the journalists "most frustrated about not having their articles published in the paper" (Van den Belt). Blogs also allow journalists to target a different audience, perhaps one they are more comfortable with, as this quote from the editor of *Mirror.co.uk* shows: "Our science editor is keen to take a blog because he can address an audience in a way which he feels more comfortable with rather than having to dress everything up as a tabloid idea" (Purcell).[6]

Evolving Attitudes

While UK news sites have added UGCI features, there remained some concern (see Thurman, 2008) that the trend has been over-hyped (Purcell). Editors tended to view these initiatives as complementary to professional journalism, rather than replacing it. There was a common view that "a good story will beat anything", as Pete Picton of *TheSun.co.uk* put it, implying the superiority of professionally produced content to that from readers. Steve Purcell also argued that "there's no substitute for a good story" and estimated that a story would receive "ten times" the amount of hits "than the comments attached to it". Nevertheless he did agree that it was "still valid to give that feedback area".

There has, however, been a shift in attitudes to UGC since Thurman's study. In 2004 some editors described blogs as "extremely dull", "mediocre" or of "very marginal interest" (Thurman, 2008). Our research showed a recognition by editors that they may have been too dismissive of blogging and that journalists appreciated the "extra flexibility that the dialogue with readers have given them" (Bale). There was an acknowledgement that a newspaper's audience can be "very knowledgeable about certain areas", as the editor of *FT.com* described his readers, adding that he was "very interested in unlocking that information". The *FT.com* was debating how best to tap into the knowledge of its readers. Montgomery suggested the newspaper was considering creating "niches" online to provide space for like-minded readers to discuss a topic, rather than "talking across a broad canvas".

Questions remained, however, over the role of blogs within established news organisations. While endorsing blogs, Burton expressed reservations about the long-term value of blogs to *Telegraph.co.uk*, reflecting general concerns about how blogging fits within a traditional journalistic framework. Burton described blogs as "massively overrated" and as "a bit of fun".

Shift to Gate-keeping

Protecting the Brand

Our study found that news professionals were still working out whether and how to integrate user participation within existing norms and practices. The potential that UGC has to damage a newspaper's brand remained a prevailing concern among some editors. The idea of publishing a comment without checking it first was described as "very dangerous" (Avery), while Bale said that not to moderate content would be an inappropriate brand risk.

The Scotsman was among the few UK newspapers that allowed readers to post comments to its website without moderation. The general manager described this as a "work in progress", deciding at an article level whether comments should be pre- or post-moderated. The site attempted to mitigate risk by requiring all users to register and by avoiding allowing unmoderated posts on contentious subject matters. Brown said *Scotsman.com* was "from an editorial perspective, quite careful about where we enable post-moderation".

One approach adopted by *The Sun* newspaper has been to create different areas online for professionally produced content and for user media. In October 2006, *TheSun.co.uk* launched a second site—*MySun.co.uk*—that allowed readers to start a blog and contribute stories, pictures, and comments on breaking news. This site is editorially separate from the news site, making a distinction between professional and amateur content. Picton said *TheSun.co.uk* wanted to "encompass both spectrums" by "providing people with the ability to put their own personal journal out there". *The Sun*'s main competitor in the tabloid marketplace, *The Mirror*, was adopting a different approach, and questioned the value of allowing every reader to have a platform. Instead Purcell suggested the newspaper may run a competition offering readers the chance to be a *Mirror* blogger, "and out of that, we'll select those who actually can write and have something to say".

Controlling the Conversation

Our research found widespread moderation of UGC by UK newspaper websites. Bale stressed that, as an organisation, *The Times* wanted to use a lot of UGC but "it's got to be the right user-generated content and it's got to fit with our brands". Editors tended to want UGC that provided content that met their understanding of their readers' expectations, both online and potentially offline:

In this world where many people feel that they've got something to say, to comment and be heard, we still want to give our *Telegraph* audience the best and therefore we need moderation ... What's the percentage of our readers who have time to read through 15,000 comments on any particular article? It's our job to display the most interesting ones. What we see more and more happening now on a particular topic is that we take the best and publish it in the newspaper the next day. (Van den Belt)

Editors tended to view moderation in terms of the traditional gate-keeping role of journalists. This was considered to be one way of offering value to the audience:

We are an organisation that filters all the news and then compresses it. We do that partly because we serve a busy audience who don't have much time to read the paper, who don't have that much time to read the website, and they look to us to have done the filtering and the compression for them. (Montgomery)

The notion of moderating UGC so that it fitted in with the identity of a newspaper came across in many of the interviews. Editors expressed apprehension at the "grey area" of the law as it relates to online content (Purcell), with newspaper lawyers themselves unsure on certain areas of the law:

The law's so unclear about who's published what, because there isn't really any case law yet. In my role as new media director both here and in my previous organisation, I've taken advice from very senior law groups who've not been clear about who publishes what and what your culpability is. Therefore moderation has to be the way forward for a group that has anything to protect. (Withey)

The Cost of Control and the Role of Technology

The gate-keeping model has cost and resource implications that have impacted on UGCIs. Moderation is "a real pain, it's a real chore", Steve Purcell, editor of *Mirror.co.uk*, told us. He described a messageboard about Princess Diana they had hosted as "hugely successful", but explained how it was "invaded with abusers, and just ploughing through the number of messages every day became more effort than it was worth".

Newspapers are caught in a bind: the burden increases as the participation of users rises. Waldman said moderation becomes more difficult as blogs and other areas encouraging interactivity with the audience become more popular. He said that *Guardian.co.uk* had received so many comments on its World Cup blog that "it was almost too much". The experience has led Waldman to start looking at traffic-calming techniques.

Technology is seen as one way of alleviating a laborious and time-consuming process. The volume of comments received by the *BBC News* website has resulted in the investment in software to process and publish content, enabling journalists to scan e-mails and publish them with a click of a button.[8] This technology still requires a team of journalists to moderate comments, which may be why *The Guardian* talked about potentially outsourcing the management of its comment areas (Waldman).

Defining the Value of User Participation

The Cost–Benefit Analysis

Our research found that news organisations were struggling to balance the resources needed to control—editorially—UGCIs with the commercial potential of user media. The cost of these operations is one of the reasons smaller news organisations like *Independent.co.uk* had no mechanisms for audience participation. Richard Withey of *Independent.co.uk* expressed concern that the need for moderation would drain resources away from what he called the good side of the newspaper model, meaning journalists researching and validating stories.

There remained a concern over the lack of a model to monetise these initiatives (see Thurman, 2008). The editorial director of *TheTimes.co.uk* saw commercial potential in delivering niche audiences to advertisers. Peter Bale gave the example of a travel section, rich with UGC from a "good and interesting demographic", which could offer a "very compelling proposition" for advertisers. But this was counterbalanced by a fear among editors that UGCIs were or could become what Waldman called "self-contained playgrounds", catering to a niche audience of limited value to an advertiser. Purcell mentioned this as a concern he had about the forums of *Mirrror.co.uk*, which "attract the same people all the time".

UGC offers some value to professional journalists as a source for stories. *TheSun.co.uk* was getting three or four stories each week from readers (Picton). In this case, editors value UGC as a digital form of newsgathering, rather than as a way of allowing readers to express themselves:

> With user-generated content, people see it often in terms of what users write but quite often for us, it's in terms of the stories they bring. And users were doing this prior to the web. They were ringing newsdesks with stories. It's just a lot easier to do it online now. (Picton)

Although reader contributions can lead to stories, there was some doubt about whether this justified the cost of UGCIs. Burton acknowledged that at times a reader's comment might be passed on to the newsdesk, but disputed it justified the expenditure on UGCIs. He said this was "just a complete and utter journalistic by-product".

Levels of Participation

Our interviews revealed that editors doubted whether a large proportion of readers wanted to contribute. Withey argued "most people like to consume media as opposed to take part in it". Quantitative data supports these views. Earlier research showed that although the *BBC News* website receives thousands of user comments on many "Have your says", these contributions often come from just 0.05 per cent of the site's daily unique audience (Thurman, 2008).

For some editors, the number of people who contribute does not necessarily matter as a small number can still make a UGC forum "worthwhile" (Revell). *The Guardian* estimated that only 1–5 per cent of readers contribute. But Waldman argued they had created a "vibrant community" at the heart of the site, which is of value to advertisers and other users:

As you look at strategies around user-generated content, you need to realise that only a small number are really going to communicate, engage at that level. But that small number make it much more interesting for everyone else. (Waldman)

Several editors mentioned that the perceived quality of comments rather than the absolute number received was a factor in judging the value of UGC. Brown related an occasion at *Scotsman.com* when a story on a proposed tram system in Edinburgh generated a level of debate that was "quite remarkable", including a discussion about the geography of the city by geologists worldwide.

Discussion

Our study showed a dramatic increase in the opportunities for audience participation across all but one of the 12 national newspaper websites in the United Kingdom, building on Thurman's 2005 survey of the adoption of UGCIs by British newspaper websites (see Thurman, 2008). Four of the nine formats for UGC—"Comments on stories", "Reader blogs", "Your media", and "Your story"—were not sufficiently established to be classified by Thurman in 2005. The last three of these formats can be seen as the most radical departure from the traditional publishing model, as they seek to present "news", and comment on current events from the point of view of the audience. However, the "Your media" and "Your story" formats are still edited by journalists. By contrast, "Reader blogs", offered by *TheSun.co.uk*, are not vetted before publication. But this area of the site is clearly segregated from the professional content, creating what Bowman and Willis (2003) argue is a "closed-off annex where readers can talk and discuss, as long as the media companies don't have to be involved".

In the rapid adoption of blogging editors seem to have accepted that blogging can play a role in journalism, although they see blogs less as a platform for a conversation with the audience (Gillmor, 2004) and more as a way of taking advantage of the "limitless newshole" of the Internet (Paul, 2005) to give staff an outlet for copy.

The expansion of UGCIs is taking place despite editors' residual doubts about the contribution UGC can make to professionally edited publications. Editors primarily judged the notion of value by balancing the resource needs of UGCIs against their commercial potential. While there was a recognition that contributions from readers could help journalists identify and report on stories, the lack of a model to monetise these initiatives remained a pressing concern. Some editors talked about the potential of UGC to increase brand loyalty and some of the literature backs up this assumption. Bowman and Willis (2003) talk of the "inherent psychological value of the creative process to the individual", while Saffo (1992) argues that what he calls "participtainment" is the "most powerful hybrid of communications and entertainment".

While news organisations are opening their doors to the public, they are also retaining the traditional gate-keeping role of journalists, as witnessed by the shift towards moderation shown in our study. Only 12 out of the 118 blogs we identified allowed readers to post directly without a comment being vetted by journalists, and even then, comments were reactively moderated. Our findings are in line with other research that shows that news organisations tend to expand their operations to the Internet based on their existing journalistic culture, including the way they relate to the public (Deuze, 2003).

The integration of amateur content presents challenges to news organisations' professional identities. Established media have an identity that is defined by professional content, while websites driven by audience participation serve as publishing platforms whose brand identity is defined by the nature of the user media. Editors are putting out a call for user content to be published under the masthead of a newspaper but perceive a need for it to fit the identity and values represented by the brand. Our study suggests that, in the longer term, established news organisations are shifting towards the retention of a traditional gate-keeping role towards UGC. This fits in with the risk-averse nature of newspapers[9] and reflects editors' continuing (see Thurman, 2008) concerns about reputation, trust and legal issues.

Our findings show that news organisations are facilitating user participation, by filtering and aggregating UGC in ways they believe to be useful and valuable to their audience. This response reflects a worry also shared by some US publications that offering tools for participation could become a "free-for-all that annoys readers instead of generating useful conversations" (Williams, nd). A gate-keeping approach may offer a model for the integration of UGC, with professional news organisations providing editorial structures to bring different voices into their news reporting. Postman (quoted in Fulton, 1996) said the problem facing journalism in the 20th century was an informational glut, whereas in the 19th century the problem was a scarcity of information. Postman argued the issue for journalism is how to decide what is significant, relevant information. As some editors said, the value in user participation becomes not just the content itself, but how it is sifted, organised and presented by professional journalists.

As this study shows, mainstream journalism's approach to UGC is largely framed by its shared norms and values. While this research looked at user-generated content initiatives in the context of the UK newspaper industry, it has broad relevance, as professional journalists tend to share a similar set of norms. The British experience offers valuable lessons for news executives making their first forays into this area and for academics studying the field of participatory journalism.

ACKNOWLEDGEMENTS

Earlier versions of this paper were presented at the 8th International Symposium on Online Journalism, University of Texas, Austin, USA, 31 March 2007; and at the Future of Newspapers Conference, Cardiff University, UK, 12–13 September 2007.

NOTES

1. "The five UGC sites that ranked in the top 50 in the United Kingdom (measured by total visitors that month)—Wikipedia, MySpace, Piczo, YouTube and Bebo—generated an average of 4.2 usage days and 79.9 minutes per visitor, according to comScore. By comparison, sites in the top 50 that were not based on UGC saw far less usage" (quoted by Wunsch-Vincent and Vickery, 2007).

2. Douglas (2006) described 7 July 2005 as a turning point for the media. He wrote that it was the day user-generated content came into its own in Britain and that when there were four more attempted bombings in London two weeks later, the public knew what was expected of them and photos and videos flooded into the BBC.

3. For example, on 5 March 2007, *USAToday* unveiled a redesign of its web presence. In an editorial note published on the website, editor Ken Paulson and executive editors Kinsey Wilson and John Hillkirk (Paulson et al., 2007) said the newspaper's journalistic mission

was to "help readers quickly and easily make sense of the world around them by giving them a wider view of the news of the day and connecting them with other readers who can contribute to their understanding of events".

4.   "Messageboards" are one of the oldest forms of participation, dating back to 1999 at *Guardian.co.uk* and 2002 at *Dailymail.co.uk* (Thurman, 2008).

5.   On the day the popular British radio presenter John Peel died, in October 2004, the *BBC News* website received 35,000 e-mail submissions—rising to a total of 100,000—to the "Have your say" that had been established in commemoration (Thurman, 2008).

6.   Not all publications, however, had a rationale for selecting staff bloggers. At *DailyMail.co.uk* "the disarmingly honest answer is that it's those who stuck their hands up basically", said Alan Revell. For Revell, the COO of Associated Northcliffe Digital, it was important to have journalists who were willing to commit the time, rather than force people into it.

7.   In 2003, the former British Member of Parliament and Secretary General of NATO Lord Robertson sued *The Sunday Herald* over a posting on a messageboard hosted by the newspaper that he alleged was defamatory. The case was settled out of court (see Thurman, 2008).

8.   Based on Alfred Hermida's personal experience as a senior member of the *BBC News* website editorial team from 1997 to 2006.

9.   A study by the Readership Institute (2000) found that US newspapers fell into the following culture types: Constructive, 17 newspapers; Aggressive-Defensive, 27 newspapers; Passive-Defensive, 21 newspapers; Mixed Passive-Aggressive, 25 newspapers.

REFERENCES

BOWMAN, SHAYNE and WILLIS, CHRIS (2003) "We Media: how audiences are shaping the future of news and information", *The Media Center*, 21 September, http://www.hypergene.net/wemedia/weblog.php, accessed November 2006.

DEUZE, MARK (2003) "The Web and Its Journalisms: considering the consequences of different types of news media online", *New Media & Society* 5(2), pp. 203–30.

DOUGLAS, TORIN (2006) "How 7/7 'Democratised' the Media", *BBC News*, 4 July, http://news.bbc.co.uk/2/hi/uk_news/5142702.stm, accessed March 2007.

ECONOMIST (2006) "Survey: new media, among the audience", 20 April, http://www.economist.com/surveys/displaystory.cfm?story_id=6794156, accessed November 2007.

FULTON, KATHERINE (1996) "A Tour of Our Uncertain Future", *Columbia Journalism Review*, March/April, http://backissues.cjrarchives.org/year/96/2/tour.asp, accessed December 2007.

GILLMOR, DAN (2004) *We the Media*, Sebastopol, CA: O'Reilly Media.

LASICA, J. D. (2003) "What Is Participatory Journalism", *Online Journalism Review*, 7 August, http://www.ojr.org/ojr/workplace/1060217106.php, accessed March 2007.

LINDLOF, THOMAS R. (1995) *Qualitative Research Methods*, Thousand Oaks, CA: Sage.

MCCRACKEN, GRANT (1998) *The Long Interview*, Thousand Oaks, CA: Sage.

O'REILLY, TIM (2005) "What Is Web 2.0", *O'Reillynet.com*, 30 September, http://www.oreillynet.com/pub/a/oreilly/tim/news/2005/09/30/what-is-web-20.html, accessed July 2007.

PARELES, JON (2006) "2006, Brought to You by You", *New York Times*, 10 December, http://www.nytimes.com/2006/12/10/arts/music/10pare.html, accessed December 2006.

PAUL, NORA (2005) "'New News' Retrospective: is online news reaching its potential?", *Online Journalism Review*, 24 March, http://www.ojr.org/ojr/stories/050324paul/, accessed July 2007.

PAULSON, KEN, WILSON, KINSEY and HILLKIRK, JOHN (2007) "To Our Readers", http://www.usatoday.com/news/2007-03-02-editors-note_N.htm, accessed 7 March 2007.

READERSHIP INSTITUTE (2000) "Culture Report: a profile of the impact newspapers and their departments", July, http://www.readership.org/culture_management/culture/data/final_culture_report.pdf, accessed March 2007.

SAFFO, PAUL (1992) "Consumers and Interactive New Media: a hierarchy of desires", *Saffo.com*, http://www.saffo.com/essays/consumers.php, accessed November 2006.

THURMAN, NEIL (2008) "Forums for Citizen Journalists?: adoption of user generated content initiatives by online news media", *New Media & Society* 10(1), pp. 139–57.

WEAVER, DAVID H. (Ed.) (1998) *The Global Journalist: news people around the world*, Cresskill, NJ: Hampton Press.

WEISS, ROBERT (1994) *Learning from Strangers*, New York: The Free Press.

WILLIAMS, LISA (nd) "Frontiers of Innovation in Community Engagement: new organisations forge new relationships with communities", *Center for Citizen Media*, http://citmedia.org/reports/newscommunities.pdf, accessed March 2007.

WUNSCH-VINCENT, SACHA and VICKERY, GRAHAM (2007) "Participative Web: user-created content", *OECD's Directorate for Science, Technology and Industry*, 12 April, http://www.oecd.org/dataoecd/57/14/38393115.pdf, accessed July 2007.

Chapter 17

OLD VALUES, NEW MEDIA
Journalism role perceptions in a changing world

John O'Sullivan and **Ari Heinonen**

Introduction

Journalists are one among many vocational groups which have needed to meet the challenge of adapting to changing premises in recent years. Many professionals have experienced increased difficulty in doing good work, in the midst of growing pressures emanating from market forces, technology and the public, all of which have been in a state of flux. Lately, it has been argued that a peculiarly narrow Anglo-American understanding of professions relating to a strictly limited set of occupational groups is no longer useful, and that the appeal and application of professionalism as a means of exerting control in the face of uncertainty and change has extended to include a wide variety of knowledge workers (Evetts, 2003).

Professionals, and journalists among them, are torn between old virtues representing apparent certainties and a rapidly shifting working environment (Gardner et al., 2001). In journalism, increased pressures for profitability, changes in media consumer behaviour and changing technology have transformed both practices and values of working life—or at least created expectations towards transformation.

To examine these changes from the perspective of journalists, it is possible to conceive of a common international understanding of journalism, based on the culture and values of modern Anglophone journalism, as practices and norms are to a large extent modelled from it in an increasing number of countries (Splichal and Sparks, 1994; Weaver, 1998). It is not within our ambit here to explore how this particular understanding has developed (for that see e.g. Chalaby, 1998; Schudson, 1978), but we can say with some confidence that journalism has some defining characteristics that would be recognised in most parts of late 20th- and early 21st-century Europe, partly as a result of the spread of Western values generally, but also of the permeating presence and global predominance of Western news media (Boyd-Barrett and Rantanen, 1998; Reese, 2001, Shoemaker and Cohen, 2006, pp. 349–52). In addition, we can observe the presence of common values and concerns by reference to professional codes (Wilkins and Brennen, 2004).

Now, new media offer a prism that is useful in exploring such values, and how the ideologies and norms of the profession play out in a changing communication ecology. It is our goal here to contribute to the discussion about how journalism as an institution and as a profession responds to its encounter with the Net.

Journalists and the Internet

The volume of exploration of the profession of journalism, both generally (Zelizer, 2004, pp. 13–44) and with a particular focus on the Internet and online news, has grown apace in the past decade or so. Following Weaver and Wilhoit's (1986) seminal study of US journalists, many researchers have sought to adopt a social survey or ethnographic approach, with an increasing trend of looking into how practices and values are affected by or interact with the social and technical dimensions of the Internet (Boczkowski, 2004; Deuze and Paulussen, 2002; Heinonen, 1999; Paulussen, 2004; Quinn and Trench, 2002; Weaver, 1998). A large proportion of the questions thrown up interrogate the civic role of journalism, and whether new media either empower or compromise journalism in its self-declared mission to maintain an informed public (Coleman, 1999; Winston, 2005). Such questions can relate to the specific, for example, message boards or chat rooms (Beyers, 2004; Goss, 2007), or, sometimes, through the vehicle of such phenomena, can operate at a definitional level (Singer, 2003). Similarly, some questions focus on the routine tasks that are important in shaping journalism and news; others relate to asserted values, such as objectivity. The European-wide COST A20 content analysis of print and online newspapers which preceded this study elaborated a similar range of issues (van der Wurff and Lauf, 2005). Finally, authors such as John Pavlik (2001) and Barrie Gunter (2003) have made wide-perspective observational studies of the meeting of new media and journalism that address similar topics.

While quite probably it is futile ever to attempt to define every potential way in which the Net impinges on journalism, at this still early point in the development of online news principal areas of discussion have centred on multimedia, format and convergence; newsgathering and relations with sources and readers; news political economy and institutions; and definitions of journalism, with associated questions around values, ethics and professional identity.

The potential for news in video or audio is often emphasised promotionally and in how-to and practice-oriented texts (Foust, 2005; Kawamoto, 2003; Ward, 2002) but thus far, at least in Europe, it is arguable to what extent traditional news publishers have progressed in their online offerings beyond what is by now familiarly disparaged as "shovelware" (Boczkowski, 2004; Harper, 1996; van der Wurff and Lauf, 2005). Other format possibilities, such as longer-form, hyperlinked texts, to which there are no technical barriers, such as slow broadband adoption, on the whole have not been realised either (Jankowski and van Selm, 2000). Convergence, and in particular converged newsrooms, mostly in US organisations characterised by cross-media ownership, has also figured significantly (Huang et al., 2006; Quinn, 2005; Quinn and Filak, 2005). Much of the discussion here relates to working pressures and quality, as well as the fusing of media cultures (Singer, 2004), and the phenomenon of breaking news and the accelerated news cycle (Hall, 2001).

From an early position of exotic exclusivity in newsrooms, the Net has now become embedded in newsgathering and news-processing routines, and has altered relationships with sources. At an apparently prosaic level, email has supplanted the fax as the vehicle for the press release, but the Net also has provided journalists with an array of story research tools (Callahan, 2003; Paul, 1999; Reddick and King, 1995). The newsroom has become a hub in a digital communication arena that bestows speed and efficiency advantages but with potential consequent implications for quality and independence. Meanwhile, alongside privileged sources, reporters now also share an unmediated information space, especially in relation to government and other official publications which are likely to be published online, but potentially also may find themselves researching and gathering news on the wider Net (Berkman and Shumway, 2004; Garrison, 2000a, 2000b).

The technical potential for interactivity raises fundamental questions around the role of the journalist, and it is the locus of much of the most contested and controversial discussion related to news and the Net. One of the foremost themes that emerges from studies of online news is the absence of message boards, chat rooms, editorial contacts and the rest of the gamut of facilities that would enable a dialogue between the otherwise isolated news producer and his or her audience (Deuze, 2003; O'Sullivan, 2005; Rosenberry, 2005; Zeng and Li, 2006). Newspapers have been quick to embrace the Net and to publish and develop Web editions, but within this movement online there clearly are tensions, as illustrated in no small way by the provision of free content, or by the internal political economies of news organisations that see online journalism and journalists as marginal or of lower status (Domingo, 2006; Kiss, 2002).

Personal journalism, citizen media, and open source journalism, in the shape of weblogs and networked sites such as Indymedia and Slashdot, are posited as competitors to and potential critics of mainstream media, in a new, intertextual communication ecology in which news workers, as dedicated paid labour, form but one, albeit important, constituent (Allan, 2006; Bruns, 2005; Gillmor, 2004) and in which the distinction between news producer and "consumer" becomes blurred (Haas, 2005). The perhaps inevitable professional response has been that the practice of journalism, with its declared emphasis on objectivity and facts, is even more vital than heretofore, such is the alleged poor quality and unreliable nature of much of the "amateur" blogosphere (Carlson, 2007).

Method and Sample

The findings to be discussed are based on a survey, interviews for which were conducted in 2005–6 in 11 European countries: Cyprus, Estonia, Finland, Greece, Ireland, Italy, Lithuania, Slovenia, Spain, Sweden and the United Kingdom. In all countries, the target groups of respondents were selected by local researchers acquainted with the national media environment and journalistic culture. A total of 239 journalists in 40 news outlets were interviewed. Most of the outlets had been represented in a previous European-wide comparative study, in which the contents of print newspapers and their websites were analysed (van der Wurff and Lauf, 2005).

The respondents were seasoned professionals, since they had been working as journalists for a mean of about 14 years (see Table 1 for a general description of the respondents). For analytical purposes, respondents were split between those who had been in the profession 10 years or less, and those who had longer experience. The crucial year was thus 1995, which can be considered as a turning point in the history of journalistic use of the Internet. "The newcomers" (of 10 years or less professional age) comprised 45 per cent of the sample, "old hands" 55 per cent.

In the newcomers' group, a fifth (20 per cent) identified themselves as online journalists, and a third (30 per cent) said that they worked both as print and online journalists. The more experienced journalists were overwhelmingly print journalists (76 per cent), and only 5 per cent of them were online journalism workers. Although the majority of respondents were male, the majority (54 per cent) of online journalists were female. However, women did not seem to be more frequent Net users than men.

We consider that our approach in sketching a "portrait of a European journalist" is a valid one for the purposes of the study. Much of the European role model of the professional journalist has its shared origin in a globalised Anglo-American professional culture that has spread via education, business practices and, latterly, new media practices. Secondly, the scope and spectrum of our sample is illustrative, although not representative, in that the respondents come from many corners of Europe, and as a whole contribute to a sound enough body of data for us to draw tentative deductions of the attitudes existing among journalism professionals on our continent.

Observations

Using the Net

It appears that our European journalist has made a smooth transition to the Age of the Internet. Our respondents were asked about difficulties which they had encountered associated with the introduction of the Net into newsrooms, and the overwhelming majority said that there were hardly any problematic issues. Neither the costs associated with the Net nor the availability or otherwise of technical support staff or training were seen by most journalists as significant obstacles, although there was some minority sentiment indicating problems with attitudes of both journalists and management.

The Net, it seems, has become an indispensable part of journalists' everyday toolbox. On a scale of 1 to 5, it is considered very useful, with a median of 5 in replies, in searching for what can be called utility information, such as phone numbers, addresses and other service details (see Figure 1). As a tool for accessing national and local government

TABLE 1
Respondents' background information

Total N	239
Age	Mean 38 years
Gender	61% male, 39% female
Work profile	64% print, 12% online, 24% both print and online
Professional age (worked as journalist)	Mean 14 years
Internet age (used the Internet)	Mean 8 years
Internet use	75% access the Net >10 times a day

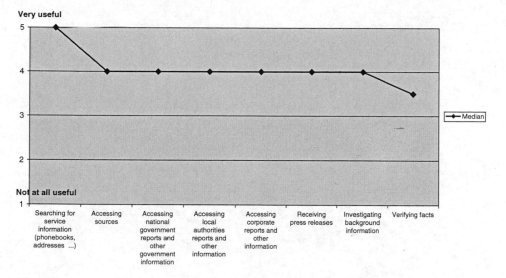

Very useful

Not at all useful

Legend: ◆ Median

X-axis categories: Searching for service information (phonebooks, addresses ...) | Accessing sources | Accessing national government reports and other government information | Accessing local authorities reports and other information | Accessing corporate reports and other information | Receiving press releases | Investigating background information | Verifying facts

FIGURE 1
Usefulness of the Internet

information, the Net was considered slightly less useful, with a median of 4; usefulness in accessing corporate information, receiving press releases and investigating background information received a similar rating.

Perhaps it reflects widespread suspicion of the Net (not solely among journalists) that it is not considered quite as useful in verifying facts, with a median of 3.5. However, of all respondents, 50 per cent considered that the Net is useful in this regard. The Net is more valued in accessing sources, with a median of 4, and almost three-quarters of respondents (72 per cent) endorsing this view. This opinion was held equally strongly regardless of length of experience, but online journalists and those of mixed profile were more enthusiastic (86 per cent) than their print colleagues (64 per cent). This may indicate that print journalists are not that familiar with finding and accessing sources online; that they are able to use more "live" sources; or that they are less willing to rely on online sources. However, the generally positive stance on the Net is further reinforced by 75 per cent agreement that the Net allows journalists to get more information into their stories, with little to separate journalists by work profile or length of service.

To reveal further the relative significance of the Internet in journalistic work, respondents were asked to assess the importance of Net-based methods in news-gathering, alongside more traditional means (see Figure 2). Respondents assessed the relative importance of methods, online and other, on a scale from 1 (not at all important) to 5 (very important), and the three most valued, each with a median outcome of 5 are, on the one hand, face-to-face conversation and telephone conversation, and, on the other hand, Web search engines. The next most valued group (median value 4) of news-gathering methods also comprises a mixture of traditional and the Internet Age: personal emails, Web news sites, newsroom colleagues, and personal archives, to name a few examples.

Looking more closely, for illustrative purposes, at two journalistic research methods, we find that face-to-face conversation, perhaps the most traditional mode of news-gathering, is the most widely valued. Of print journalists, 93 per cent said that face-to-face

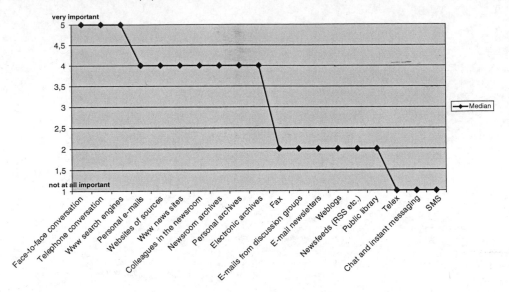

FIGURE 2
Importance of information-gathering methods

conversation is important, whereas this view was held by much fewer online journalists, at 63 per cent. Mixed-profile journalists fall in the middle, with 75 per cent saying that such conversation is important.

Clearer differences are observed in attitudes towards weblogs as research tools, on the basis of work profile. Print journalists said quite widely (84 per cent) that weblogs are not important: this opinion was expressed by substantially fewer online journalists (59 per cent), whereas mixed-profile journalists held the middle ground (67 per cent).

Given that, as shown above, it seems that European journalists indeed have taken the Net quite unproblematically into their everyday professional life, it might be interesting to know, as a measure of their perception of its centrality to their work, how they would feel the effects of ceasing to use it. We tested opinions on taking away the Internet with respect to various aspects of journalistic work (see Figure 3).

In general, respondents seem to consider the effects of ceasing to use the Net as negative or, at best, neutral. When looking at the medians of the responses, there is not a single aspect of journalistic work mentioned which it is considered would benefit in such circumstances. Medians vary from 1 (very negative effect) to 3, which can be regarded as not having much effect in either direction. No values were recorded at 4 or, the extreme, 5 (very positive effect).

It appears that the Net would be missed most by journalists in relation to news currency. Firstly, they felt that, without the Internet, it would be difficult to keep up to date with news, and there would be negative effects on the speed of information gathering as well as on access to digital archives. In addition, journalists indicated that there would be negative effects on real-time publishing of breaking news. All of these aspects of journalistic work scored a median of 1, i.e. a very negative effect would be felt.

Slightly less severe but still negative effects register in relation to some other routine chores. Tracking story topics, finding sources, data checking and simply keeping in touch with the newsroom from the field would be somewhat hampered by the removal of the

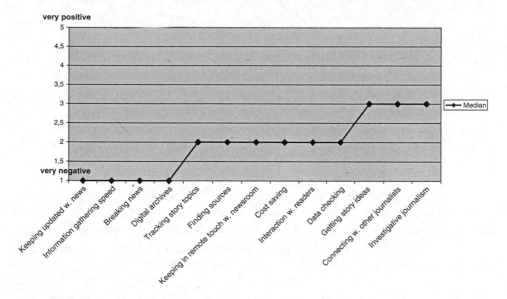

FIGURE 3
Effects of ceasing to use the Internet

Net. Medians here were 2. It is interesting that interaction with readers falls also into this slightly less negatively affected category. It may be tenuous to conclude that journalists generally consider the Net more important for keeping up to date than interacting with the audience, but we can say that, of the two, they present more anxiety in relation to news currency.

Ceasing to use the Net would seem to have the least negative effect (median 3) on getting story ideas and keeping in touch with other journalists—and, perhaps somewhat surprisingly, on investigative journalism. It would appear that the Net is not considered critical in working imaginatively or in digging up difficult material. In relation to interaction with readers, respondents in general felt that there would be some loss in the absence of the Internet, with a median of 2 on the scale of 5.

Some variation appears between respondents on the basis of whether they consider themselves creatures of print, online media, or both. For instance, while a clear majority of print journalists (74 per cent) consider that ceasing to use the Net would have negative effect on breaking news, this opinion was even more emphatically held by online journalists (97 per cent). Those with a mixed profile, i.e. identifying themselves as "both print and online journalists", took the middle ground, at 79 per cent. Similar differences between print and online journalist were found relating to interaction with readers. Although more than half (54 per cent) of print journalists said that interaction would be negatively affected by ceasing to use the Net, this stance was taken much more widely among online journalists, at 82 per cent. Again, those describing themselves as both print and online journalists were in the middle: 63 per cent said the effects would be negative.

Journalism and the Public

In theory, and technically, the Internet can bring journalists into closer contact with those outside the confines of the news organisation, whether the audience, the public at large, or the emerging and perhaps critical or competing practitioners of citizen journalism. With a series of questions, it was hoped to elicit some insight into how journalists actually see such relationships in the contexts of traditional and new media.

Given that the Web affords an opportunity for virtually perfect knowledge of which editorial output is read, it is interesting to note that only a quarter (26 per cent) of all journalists said they receive detailed information on reader behaviour, while a larger share (38 per cent) said they are confined to receiving outline information and more than a third (36 per cent) reported having no access to such information. Strikingly, no online journalist reported ignorance of such information, while almost half (48 per cent) of print journalists did.

Working journalists are relatively sanguine about the perceived challenge to the role of newspapers of DIY journalism (citizen journalism, blogs etc.). Over 64 per cent rejected the notion that there is such a threat, with a median outcome of 2 on the scale of 5 (1= strongly disagree). There was little variation according to the work profile or professional age of respondents, apart from the tendency of newer journalists to hold this view more widely.

If we are tempted to interpret this low level of misgiving as meaning that journalists take an apparently progressive or inclusive view of developments, their attitude towards the value of citizen journalism and blogs complicates matters. An overall median of 4 represents a relatively strong endorsement of the rather provocative statement that these forms of activity do not comprise real journalism. Over half (51 per cent) of respondents held this view, and less than a quarter (23 per cent) actively disputed it. One might anticipate some strong argument against this sentiment, which could be interpreted as dismissive. Print journalists displayed strongest hostility; online and mixed-profile combined tended more towards a neutral position, as did the newer professional group.

Traditional values seem to win out when respondents considered the relative advantages of print and online mediums (see Figure 4). For example, there was overall active disagreement (56 per cent) with the statement that online journalists are closer to

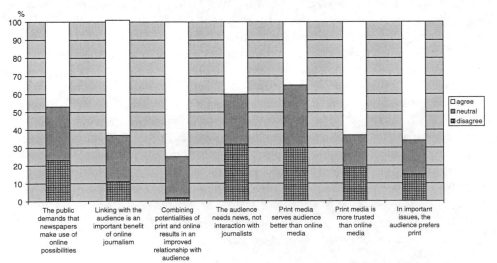

FIGURE 4
The Internet, journalism and the public

their audience, with a median of 2. The sentiment is most marked, at 63 per cent, among print journalists. Mixed-profile journalists score 46 per cent agreement with the statement, compared with only 16 per cent for their newsprint counterparts. Almost 30 per cent of all respondents preferred to take no view, or expressed ambivalence or lack of knowledge in relation to the assertion that there is a public demand that their publications exploit online possibilities. But almost half (47 per cent) agreed to some extent, with less than half that proportion disagreeing. Online (67 per cent) and mixed-profile journalists (49 per cent) show much more enthusiasm here than print journalists. Although they voiced little active opposition to exploring new possibilities, well over half of print journalists, at 58 per cent, were little exercised about them. Those fresher to the job were only slightly more likely to agree with the statement.

More than two-thirds (64 per cent) of respondents expressed an appreciation of connecting with the audience as an important benefit of online journalism. A significant proportion (26 per cent) preferred to inhabit the neutral zone here, but relatively few (11 per cent) expressed active disagreement. In spite of the median outcome of 4 (qualified agreement) a tiny 2 per cent registered opposition to the notion that combining potentialities of print and online would result in an improved audience relationship, with 75 per cent in support. Perhaps support for complementarity is the sort of apparently progressive position with which it is relatively easy to agree, without invoking difficult questions for rooted professional norms. But the seemingly pointed statement that the audience needs news, and not dialogue with news producers, evinces a muted response, with a median value of 3. This outcome reflects a relatively substantial (28 per cent) group of neutrals, but also a balancing of opinions on either side of that option, with 40 per cent agreeing, and 32 per cent disagreeing. Print newspaper journalists were most likely to agree strongly (23 per cent) with the statement, with online and mixed-profile journalists registering significantly lower enthusiasm. Nevertheless, a strong contingent, at 33 per cent, of online journalists agreed somewhat with the statement, recording opinions at 4 in the scale. Longer-serving journalists are more sceptical about audience interactivity, with around 25 per cent agreeing fully with the statement, compared with just 12 per cent of those whose careers have begun within the Internet era.

As we have seen, asking simply whether print media serve the audience better than online media draws a non-committal response from the group as a whole, with a median of 3, with this outcome strongly determined by the fact that 35 per cent of respondents have plumped for this option. However, looking more closely at responses from within particular work profiles, the assertion gets an emphatic rejection from online journalists at 68 per cent, while only 13 per cent of print journalists disagreed, with 38 per cent of them preferring to stay diplomatically neutral, and 48 per cent agreeing. Of mixed-profile journalists, 56 per cent disagreed with the statement. So, in spite of a hesitant overall response, there are some very firm views held on this admittedly bluntly put question, with a clear split between print and online or mixed-profile factions. There is little to separate journalists on the basis of professional age: both groups gravitate towards the median on this question, although the "old hands" show a little more print chauvinism.

There is less balance, or ambiguity, when it comes to trust, with a median of 4 and relatively few (18 per cent) occupying the middle ground. Overall, 63 per cent of respondents agree that print media are more trusted than online, compared with only 19 per cent who demur. All three work groups show substantial agreement with the statement, but to varying extents—print, 73 per cent (though with 42 per cent agreeing fully); mixed profile 47 per cent; and online 46 per cent. Among print journalists, only 10 per cent disagreed, compared with 35 per cent among their online counterparts. Of course, these data need to be interpreted carefully, especially as it is not clear if respondents answered the question on audience preference in literal terms, as to whether print actually is trusted or preferred more, or interpreted it to mean that print is more trustworthy. But we can see that, overall, there is a movement towards the older media form when it comes to an essential value.

Ethics and the Net

It seems that the European journalist is quite confident concerning the Internet's consequences for quality. For example, an overwhelming majority (79 per cent) agreed that the Net prompts journalists' wider use of sources (see Figure 5). And, although most (56 per cent) agreed that journalists must deal with unreliable information more often online, and a majority disagreed with the statement that separating fact from falsehood would be as easy on the Net as elsewhere, most of the respondents (58 per cent) suggested that it is easier to double-check information thanks to the Net.

A slightly larger share of journalists agreed with the statement that online journalism has sacrificed accuracy for speed than disagreed with it (41 and 35 per cent, respectively). Among those with more professional experience there was a clearer tendency to agree with this statement than among post-1995 entrants (47 and 35 per cent, respectively). It may not be surprising that almost every other print journalist (49 per cent) agreed with the statement, whereas only a third of online journalist (32 per cent) did so. But it is interesting that those working both as print and online journalists were least worried about sacrificing accuracy in the rush to publish; only a fraction of them (16 per cent) agreed with the statement.

The question of accountability has always been a crucial issue in the debate about journalistic quality and ethics, and in this regard the respondents do not seem to think

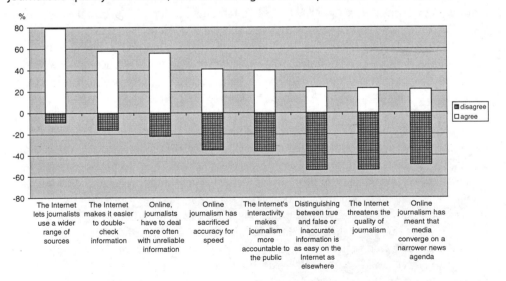

FIGURE 5
The Internet, ethics and quality

that Net-based interactivity would bring about much change. While many respondents (40 per cent) agreed with the statement that the Net's interactivity makes journalism more accountable to the public, more than a third (36 per cent) disagreed. Again, those with a longer career were more sceptical than relative late-comers (45 and 35 per cent, respectively). About a third of print journalists agreed (35 per cent) with the statement, while among online and mixed-medium journalists almost half supported the statement (46 and 49 per cent).

All in all, respondents seem to think that there is not a threat, or at least not an imminent one, to the quality of journalism. Over half (54 per cent) disputed this assertion. However, it is worth noting here that almost a quarter (23 per cent) agreed. Between older and younger professionals, the former were more worried, with more than a quarter (26 per cent) in accord with the statement, while among younger professionals less than a fifth (19 per cent) agreed. In addition, almost a third of more experienced journalists (28 per cent) were unable to comment either way. About a third of print journalists agreed with the statement (28 per cent) while only 7 per cent of online journalists did so. Male journalists were more sceptical; over a quarter of them (27 per cent) agreed with the statement, considerably more than females, at 16 per cent.

Discussion

As we progress into the second decade of news' encounter with the Net, publishers, journalists and observers are still grappling with ideas of change, and the role of journalism as a profession is central to the discussion. As print circulations continue to fall in most markets, and Net adoption strengthens, there is a degree of inevitability in the belief that, at some point, newspapers will need to unshackle themselves from their print origins and redefine themselves as online entities, potentially with attendant fundamental changes in practice, culture and content.

We have seen in this study that journalists as a group are not only more than comfortable with the Internet, having adopted it with relatively little difficulty, but now view it as essential. There is little technophobia in evidence. Far from being intimidated by the Net, they rank Net-related story research techniques as being among some of the most important in their toolbox. Overall, they do not perceive a threat from the Internet to the quality of journalism. Within that assessment, they apparently are also unperturbed at the arrival on the scene of new cohorts of online content producers. And they express warm feelings towards using the Net to connect to audiences and towards new possibilities in multimedia.

On this level, at least, it seems that journalists are happy to place themselves among Net-progressives. However, this apparent optimism comes with certain caveats that emerge when we probe a little more deeply and, perhaps, sensitively, or otherwise is tempered by remaining preferences for "old" ways. It is a trivial assertion that the Net is immensely useful to journalists: what may be more telling is that face-to-face and telephone conversation still are most highly prized as reporting methods. And, where the Net is rated as very useful, it is frequently in the pursuit of distinctly traditional news values, such as currency, where its absence would be most lamented, and less so in relation to interactivity. The significance of more inclusive online media, such as weblogs or discussion boards, as research sources in the new news ecology is given short shrift. Overall, personal, or DIY, journalism is rather strongly rejected as a form of "real" journalism. Scepticism about convergence emerges when the issue of recycling, or "shovelware" is raised, and the survey registers a note of caution when it comes to the demands of working with multimedia. Journalists also raise fears concerning the quality of information available online, and many dispute the contention that online interactivity engenders more accountability. Trust is seen to reside more in print media than online.

Two other features are salient. Firstly, it is striking that many of the questions put to our respondents, selected as expert informants, elicited neutral responses. It is difficult to interpret whether this reflects ambivalence or ignorance or confusion, but we can say that a large proportion of news workers opt for safer ground. Against that, the frequent polarisation of responses fits our expectations that print journalists would endorse more traditional values, while online and mixed-profile journalists would offer a more Net-friendly perspective.

This survey confirms that the social institution called journalism is hesitant in abandoning its conventions, both at organisational and professional levels, even in the "Age of the Net", when overall communication patterns in society are being re-shaped. There seems to be a prevailing "principle of continuity" in journalism. The profession has striven for its status among other professions in society since the 1800s. Even now, there seems to be an internal need to adhere to practices which ensure that status, and to maintain the particular values that both generate and legitimise those practices. Newspaper journalists appear to want to stay newspaper journalists. This is not to say that they are recalcitrant technophobes, but they welcome the Net when it suits their existing professional ends, and are much less enthusiastic about, and unlikely to promote, radical change in news work.

Journalists mostly continue to behave like journalists in the conventional sense, with conventional ethics and values at least evident in their professional rhetoric (Evans, 1999) and in the various texts and classrooms of journalism educators. At this point, it remains far from clear whether the profession can maintain its status quo, move towards normalisation of new potentialities (Matheson, 2004, Robinson, 2006, Singer, 2005), or is willing or able to adapt radically to new conditions (Bromley and Purdey, 1998) and to shift from its traditional role towards a more democratic community and public debate-oriented ideal heralded since the earliest days of Internet news (Bardoel, 1996).

ACKNOWLEDGEMENTS

We want to thank Aukse Balcytiene, Dimitra Dimitrakopoulou, Leopoldina Fortunati, Micke Gulliksson, Phil McGregor, Vallo Nuust, Tanja Oblak, Nayia Roussou and Ramón Salaverría for contributing to the design and data gathering for this study. Special thanks to Mauro Sarrica for help in data processing.

REFERENCES

ALLAN, STUART (2006) *Online News: journalism and the Internet*, Maidenhead: Open University Press.

BARDOEL, J.O. (1996) "Beyond Journalism: a profession between information society and civil society", *European Journal of Communication* 11, pp. 283–302.

BERKMAN, ROBERT I. and SHUMWAY, CHRISTOPHER A. (2004) "Is It Appropriate for Reporters to 'Lurk' in Online Chat Rooms?", http://www.ojr.org/ojr/ethics/1065048923.php (accessed 2 July 2007).

BEYERS, HANS (2004) "Interactivity and Online Newspapers: a case study on discussion boards", *Convergence* 10(4), pp. 11–20.

BOCZKOWSKI, PABLO J. (2004) *Digitizing the News: innovation in online newspapers*, Cambridge, MA: MIT Press.

BOYD-BARRETT, OLIVER and RANTANEN, TERHI (1998) *The Globalization of News*, London: Sage.

BROMLEY, MICHAEL and PURDEY, HEATHER (2001) "Chilling Out—But Not Yet 'Cool': new media training in a UK journalism school: a further report on 'journomorphosis'", *Convergence* 7(3), pp. 104–15.

BRUNS, AXEL (2005) *Gatewatching: collaborative online news production (digital formations)*, New York: Peter Lang.

CALLAHAN, CHRISTOPHER (2003) *A Journalist's Guide to the Internet: the Net as a reporting tool*, 2nd edn, Boston: Allyn and Bacon.

CARLSON, MATT (2007) "Blogs and Journalistic Authority", *Journalism Studies* 8, pp. 264–79.

CHALABY, JEAN K. (1998) *The Invention of Journalism*, Houndmills: Macmillan.

COLEMAN, STEPHEN (1999) "The New Media and Democratic Politics", *New Media and Society* 1(1), pp. 58–64.

DEUZE, MARK (2003) "The Web and Its Journalisms: considering the consequences of different types of newsmedia online", *New Media and Society* 5, pp. 203–30.

DEUZE, MARK and PAULUSSEN, STEVE (2002) "Online Journalism in the Low Countries: basic, occupational and professional characteristics of online journalists in Flanders and the Netherlands", *European Journal of Communication* 17, pp. 237–46.

DOMINGO, DAVID (2006) "Inventing Online Journalism. Development of the Internet as a news medium in four Catalan online newsrooms", PhD thesis, Universitat Autònoma de Barcelona.

EVANS, HAROLD (1999) "What a Century!", *Columbia Journalism Review* 37(5), pp. 27–37.

EVETTS, JULIA (2003) "The Sociological Analysis of Professionalism: occupational change in the modern world", *International Sociology* 18, pp. 395–415.

FOUST, JAMES C. (2005) *Online Journalism: principles and practices of news for the Web*, Scottsdale: Holcomb Hathaway Publishing.

GARDNER, HOWARD, CSIKSZENTMIHALYI, MIHALY and DAMON, WILLIAM (2001) *Good Work. When excellence and ethics meet*, New York: Basic Books.

GARRISON, BRUCE (2000a) "Journalists' Perception of Online Information-gathering Problems", *Journalism & Mass Communication Quarterly* 77, pp. 500–14.

GARRISON, BRUCE (2000b) "Diffusion of a New Technology: on-line research in newspaper newsrooms", *Convergence* 6(1), pp. 84–105.

GILLMOR, DAN (2004) "We the Media", O'Reilly, http://www.oreilly.com/catalog/wemedia/book/index.csp (accessed 2 July 2007).

GOSS, BRIAN MICHAEL (2007) "Online 'Looney Tunes'", *Journalism Studies* 8, pp. 365–81.

GUNTER, BARRIE (2003) *News and the Net*, Mahwah, NJ: Lawrence Erlbaum.

HAAS, TANNI (2005) "From 'Public Journalism' to the 'Public's Journalism'? Rhetoric and reality in the discourse on weblogs", *Journalism Studies* 6, pp. 387–96.

HALL, JIM (2001) *Online Journalism: a critical primer*, London: Pluto Press.

HARPER, CHRISTOPHER (1996) "Doing It All", *American Journalism Review* 18, pp. 24–29.

HEINONEN, ARI (1999) "Journalism in the Age of the Net: changing society, changing profession", University of Tampere, http://acta.uta.fi/pdf/951-44-5349-2.pdf (accessed 3 July 2007).

HUANG, EDGAR, DAVISON, KAREN, SHREVE, STEPHANIE, DAVIS, TWILA, BETTENDORF, ELIZABETH and NAIR, ANITA (2006) "Facing the Challenges of Convergence: media professionals' concerns of working across media platforms", *Convergence* 12(1), pp. 83–98.

JANKOWSKI, NICHOLAS and VAN SELM, MARTINE (2000) "Traditional News Media Online: an examination of added-value", *Communications* 25(1), pp. 85–102.

KAWAMOTO, KEVIN (2003) *Digital Journalism: emerging media and the changing horizons of journalism*, Lanham, MD: Rowman & Littlefield.

KISS, JEMIMA (2002) "UK Journalists' Union Organises Online", http://www.journalism.co.uk/news/story710.shtml, accessed 2 July 2007.

MATHESON, DONALD (2004) "Weblogs and the Epistemology of the News: some trends in online journalism", *New Media and Society* 6, pp. 443–69.

O'SULLIVAN, JOHN (2005) "Delivering Ireland: journalism's search for a role online", *Gazette* 67(1), pp. 45–68.

PAUL, NORA (1999) *Computer-assisted Research: a guide to tapping online information for journalists*, Chicago and St. Petersburg, FL: Bonus Books and Poynter Institute for Media Studies.

PAULUSSEN, STEVE (2004) "Online News Production in Flanders: how Flemish online journalists perceive and explore the Internet's potential", *Journal of Computer-mediated Communication* 9(4), http://jcmc.indiana.edu/vol9/issue4/paulussen.html (accessed 20 August 2008).

PAVLIK, JOHN V. (2001) *Journalism and New Media*, New York: Columbia University Press.

QUINN, GARY and TRENCH, BRIAN (2002) *Online News Media and Their Audiences*, Heerlen, The Netherlands: Mudia, International Institute of Infonomics.

QUINN, STEPHEN (2005) "Convergence's Fundamental Question", *Journalism Studies* 6, pp. 29–38.

QUINN, STEPHEN and FILAK, VINCENT (Eds) (2005) *Convergent Journalism, an Introduction: writing and producing across media*, Oxford: Focal Press.

REDDICK, RANDY and KING, ELLIOTT (1995) *The Online Journalist: using the Internet and other electronic resources*, Fort Worth, TX: Harcourt Brace College.

REESE, STEPHEN (2001) "Understanding the Global Journalist: a hierarchy-of-influences approach", *Journalism Studies* 2, pp. 173–88.

ROBINSON, SUSAN (2006) "The Mission of the J-blog: recapturing journalistic authority online", *Journalism* 7(1), pp. 65–83.

ROSENBERRY, JACK (2005) "Few Papers Use Online Techniques to Improve Public Communication", *Newspaper Research Journal* 26(4), pp. 61–73.

SCHUDSON, MICHAEL (1978) *Discovering the News. A social history of American newspapers*, New York: Basic Books.

SHOEMAKER, PAMELA J. and COHEN, AKIBA A. (2006) *News Around the World: content, practitioners, and the public*, New York: Routledge.

SINGER, JANE B. (2003) "Who Are These Guys?: the online challenge to the notion of journalistic professionalism", *Journalism* 4(2), pp. 139–63.

SINGER, JANE B. (2004) "Strange Bedfellows? The diffusion of convergence in four news organizations", *Journalism Studies* 5, pp. 3–18.

SINGER, JANE B. (2005) "The Political J-blogger: 'normalizing' a new media form to fit old norms and practices", *Journalism* 6(2), pp. 173–98.

SPLICHAL, SLAVKO and SPARKS, COLIN (1994) *Journalists for the 21st Century. Tendencies of professionalisation among first-year students in 22 countries*, Norwood, NJ: Ablex.

VAN DER WURFF, RICHARD and LAUF, EDMUND (Eds) (2005) *Print and Online Newspapers in Europe: a comparative analysis in 16 countries*, Amsterdam: Het Spinhuis.

WARD, MIKE (2002) *Journalism Online*, Oxford: Focal Press.

WEAVER, DAVID H. (Ed.) (1998) *The Global Journalist. News people around the world*, Cresskill, NJ: Hampton Press.

WEAVER, DAVID H. and WILHOIT, G. CLEVELAND (1986) *The American Journalist: a portrait of U.S. news people and their work*, Bloomington: Indiana University Press.

WILKINS, LEE and BRENNEN, BONNIE (2004) "Conflicted Interests, Contested Terrain: journalism ethics codes then and now", *Journalism Studies* 5, pp. 297–310.

WINSTON, BRIAN (2005) "Emancipation, the Media and Modernity: some reflections on Garnham's Kantian turn", *Media, Culture and Society* 27, pp. 495–509.

ZELIZER, BARBIE (2004) *Taking Journalism Seriously: news and the academy*, Thousand Oaks, CA: Sage.

ZENG, QIAN and LI, XIGEN (2006) "Factors Influencing Interactivity of Internet Newspapers: a content analysis of 106 U.S. newspapers' web sites", in: X. Li (Ed.), *Internet Newspapers: the making of a mainstream medium*, Mahwah, NJ: Lawrence Erlbaum, pp. 139–58.

Chapter 18

THE FUTURE OF "RESPONSIBLE JOURNALISM"
Defamation law, public debate and news production

Andrew T. Kenyon and **Tim Marjoribanks**

Introduction

Debates about newspapers have long raised questions around journalistic practice. The concept of "responsible journalism" has had no stable or assured status, within journalistic, social and academic realms. Claims by media organizations that they act to promote accountability from powerful actors rest centrally on promoting journalists and editors as professionals working to high standards (Schultz, 1998). Within the law and legal systems of commonwealth countries, however, a different view has often been taken—the fourth estate has traditionally received little praise from the judicial branch of government, and there have been limited opportunities to present evidence about news production practices in court. The juridical inquiry has focused more often on the truth or falsity of a critical publication than the process by which it came to be published.

Contemporary US instances in which journalistic standards have been questioned—involving journalists including Jayson Blair, Stephen Glass and Rick Bragg—have returned questions of responsible journalism to prominence in public debate (Bandler, 2004). Similarly, in both Britain and Australia, journalistic practices at numerous media companies have given rise to significant debate around what constitutes responsible journalism. Claims over cheque book journalism, concerns about blurring factual reporting and opinion, and low public opinion of journalists make it a pertinent issue, outside and within the media. For the newspaper industry itself, questions of responsible journalism are of critical significance. In the Australian context, for example, the code of ethics of the Media

Entertainment and Arts Alliance states that journalists "scrutinise power, but also exercise it, and should be responsible and accountable" (Media and Entertainment Arts Alliance, nd). Media organizations in the United States and the UK have similar statements related to responsible journalism.

Defamation law is one area in which this tension over journalistic standards can be seen. The traditional law in common law countries left little room for arguments that journalists had acted "responsibly". The law often demanded that publishers establish the truth, with evidence admissible in court, of defamatory allegations that were the subject of suit. Arguments of public interest or responsible news production practices received little sympathy. This has changed in important ways during the last decade in many commonwealth countries. While defamation law—particularly under the common-wealth approach, less so in the United States—has long been criticized for overly restricting journalism and public debate and lowering the quality of media speech, in recent years UK law has changed to protect "responsible journalism" (see, e.g., Robertson and Nicol, 2007). Many other commonwealth countries have seen similar developments. These changes offer real potential to support wider public debate, and to protect the place of newspapers in furthering such debate, but they also increase the importance for law of understanding news production and evaluating journalistic practices.

The change in law—which is ongoing, especially in the United Kingdom—is of particular interest for the future of news because of digital communications and the transnational circulation of content, *and* because of the history in which US journalism has faced defamation actions in the United Kingdom or Australia among other jurisdictions (see, e.g., *Berezovsky, 2001*; *Gutnick, 2002*). Debates about responsible news production sit uneasily between the local or national contexts in which many producers practice, and the transnational syndicated or online audiences that receive their content. This is evident especially to the degree that reception is moving away from the historical situation in which international news was heavily mediated through domestic outlets of translation and local diffusion. With greater international dispersal of content there is increased potential for different understandings of what constitutes good journalism to be applied to the same content. This raises challenges for journalists, editors and other organizational actors in news production as they operate in a context where their readership is more internationalized. It also highlights questions about what standards journalism might be held accountable to, whether formally or informally.

The changes in law mean that similar aspects of news production have gained *legal* relevance in the United Kingdom and some other commonwealth countries to those aspects that are influential within US law. This is true even though the overall balance of the laws—between protecting reputation, or at least the reputation of those with financial or cultural resources sufficient to sue, and protecting public speech—remains quite distinct within and outside the United States. In this paper, we analyse changes in defamation law concerning "responsible journalism" in the United Kingdom, "reason-able publication" in Australia, and the long-established strong protection in the United States for speech about public figures. In addition to outlining the law, we draw on interviews conducted with journalists and editors in all three countries. The purpose of these interviews was to explore how key informants in newspaper and other media organizations interact with defamation law in their everyday work. Through our analysis of this material—and the brief snapshot of it provided here—we argue that while recent legal developments suggest the media will be protected from defamation liability where its publications are deemed to be responsible and in the public interest, significant challenges remain for the law in understanding everyday newspaper production and content.

Journalism Standards and Responsible Journalism

Existing analyses of journalistic standards in news production reveal a highly contested terrain. Sociological and legal research suggests that practices of competent journalism can be well understood as social processes, influenced by the interaction of organizational and cultural contexts as well as the broader political economy (Cottle, 2003; Marjoribanks and Kenyon, 2003; Schudson, 2000; Ursell, 2001). In his work on objectivity in US journalism, for example, Schudson has shown "the objectivity norm guides journalists to separate facts from values" (2001, p. 150), but the norm's content varies according to the interaction of specific social, cultural and organizational circumstances. This literature raises questions for analysing journalism's self-proclaimed ideals—such as responsible journalism including fairness, lack of bias, accuracy and objectivity—all of which are central to claims of high standards in professional practice. In particular, research into what constitutes "responsible journalism" should engage with news production's societal and organizational contexts.

The media-focused literature can be related to broader sociological literature on professions, which also considers debates around standards and competence. Two issues are most relevant here in relation to responsible journalism. First, it is necessary to acknowledge the ways in which boundaries between various professional groups are the outcomes of political, social and organizational struggles, in which claims to expertise and competence over areas of practice are made, contested and transformed (Good, 1998). Second, Aldridge and Evetts have argued for the need to analyse discourses of professionalism. For journalism, professionalism is "a discourse of self-control, even self-belief, an occupational badge or marker which gives meaning to the work and enables workers to justify and emphasize the importance of their work to themselves" (Aldridge and Evetts, 2003, p. 555). They continue:

> Employers, managers and supervisors are also mobilizing the discourse of profession-alism unilaterally and instrumentally. High professional standards are required, but need to be achieved in others by a combination of individualized forms of self-control and organisational, hierarchical supervision, checking and correction. (2003, p. 556)

Such literature suggests that analyses of news production should engage with boundary contests, for example between journalists, editors and legal advisors, around what constitutes appropriate standards of journalistic practice, and the ways in which that practice can promote broader public debate.

In exploring these issues, we draw on Simon Cottle's suggestion that, to understand news production, there is a need to explore the interaction of micro-level workplace practices, meso-level organizational cultures, and macro-contexts of regulatory, techno-logical and competitive environments (Cottle, 2003). Of significance here, the macro-context of news reporting includes both legal regulation and technological change, so that any analysis of responsible journalism must engage with such factors. Particularly interesting here is the relationship between defamation law and newspaper production. In common law countries, defamation law is said to be aimed at regulating the publication of material thought likely to harm reputation. Underlying defamation law is the idea of "balancing" the protection of free speech and the protection of reputation. However, the risk of liability under traditional defamation law is thought to deter media publication and limit public debate, resulting in a "chilling effect"—an effect which has been seen in varied legal and media research (from law see, e.g., Barendt et al., 1997; Dent and Kenyon, 2004; and from media studies see the lesser "chill" for letters to the editor in a US newspaper: Wahl-Jorgensen, 2007).

Analysing the embeddedness of newspaper organizations in their institutional contexts provides important material for strategies of comparative analysis of the interaction of defamation law and news production. Notably, it suggests that while the legal context of defamation may impact on news practices, so those production practices may resonate within law. This points to the value of empirically based qualitative fieldwork concerned with uncovering and analysing the ways in which defamation law is perceived and strategically accommodated by journalists, editors, and legal advisors. Before turning to our fieldwork, however, we outline defamation law as it has sought to regulate news production historically and in more recent years, in particular focusing on the emergence of the concept of "responsible journalism" and its links with "public interest" as constituting a defence in defamation cases.

Changing Defamation Law and Responsible Journalism

While defamation law can be said to regulate the publication of material harmful to reputation through balancing interests in reputation and speech, quite different balances are struck in the United Kingdom or Australia and in the United States.

A traditional common law approach to defamation requires the claimant to prove only three things: the defendant published material, which identified the claimant, and which would harm the claimant's reputation. Once these elements are established, the material must be defended by proving it to be true, to be a matter of honest opinion or comment that is based on true facts, to be published on an occasion of qualified privilege—such as a fair report of what was said in parliament or in court—or by some other defences with less application to media publications. The defendant need not have intended any harm, nor need the defendant have been at fault in publishing. In addition, damages are presumed to flow from defamatory publications and need not be proven by claimants. Publishers' liability is strict.

It is not a defence under traditional defamation law for the publisher to show that it was not careless, or that publishing the material served some wider public interest. This approach to defamation law makes it easy for critical publications to convey defamatory meanings and for publishers to face liability. The media must carefully consider how it would defend any material criticizing individuals or companies. The common law approach calls for publishers to research before publication and err on the side of caution. Traditional defamation law is often seen to protect reputation at the expense of open debate about matters of public interest. It does not sit comfortably with idealized concepts of the media's role as a fourth estate and liberal approaches to speech (see, e.g., Peters, 2005). Nor does it fit well with ideas about the value of divergent and contradictory viewpoints—and modes of speaking—being represented in public debate, of speech being performative in the creation of publics (see, e.g., Fraser, 1992; Nolan, 2006; Warner, 2002).

The defamation law of England and Wales, and the rest of the United Kingdom, broadly follows the above outline. During the last decade, however, it has developed a wider form of privilege defence, in recognition that the traditional law was too restrictive of speech. The defence can apply to material that cannot be proven true where it was published as a result of "responsible journalism" about a matter of public interest. It is commonly known as the *Reynolds* privilege or *Reynolds* defence, after the first House of Lords case in which the defence was set out (*Reynolds,* 2001; and see, e.g., Kenyon, 2006, pp. 202–11). Later court judgments have emphasized the breadth and strength of the defence (in particular, *Jameel*, 2007) and the way in which it can apply to some "reportage" of serious allegations, even where no attempt has been made to verify those allegations. In such situations, the public interest lies in the fact that the allegations were made, rather than whether they were true. The publication merely reports the fact that that allegations exist, it does not adopt the allegations as true (see, in particular, *Roberts,* 2007). In most situations, however, the "responsible journalism" protected by *Reynolds* requires news producers to investigate material—and do so more carefully if the material contains seriously defamatory charges—to have appropriate sources, and to attempt to contact the subject of the planned publication and include their position on the situation. Overall, *Reynolds* privilege appears to offer important advances on traditional qualified privilege for media publications and perhaps also for wider public debate, although courts may envisage a limited form of investigative journalism as being the only media content worthy of the defence. For example, in the *Jameel* decision, which is discussed further below, Baroness Hale in the House of Lords noted that the defensible *Wall Street Journal* reporting could be described as both "seriously dull" and as the sort of journalism that "our defamation law should encourage" (*Jameel*, 2007, [150]).

Australian defamation law has also developed a broader privilege defence for "reasonable" publication in recent years. During the 1990s, that defence developed in relation to "political" speech (see, e.g., *Lange,* 1997), a category which appeared limited to publications about politicians, candidates and some related matters that a court would think should properly influence voters. This was a narrow, institutional vision of the political; the reformulation of the concept of politics in the latter 20th century was not drawn on in *Lange*. An effect of the *Lange* defence's narrowness was that few publications subject to suit could even be argued to come within the defence. Therefore few Australian cases exist about the *Lange* defence. Since the start of 2006, however, all Australian jurisdictions have introduced largely uniform defamation statutes, which provide a defence for reasonable publication on any matter of public interest (see, e.g., *Defamation Act 2005* (Vic) s. 30) in addition to the *Lange* defence. The new statutory defence has the potential to be interpreted in a similar manner to the *Reynolds* defence in the United Kingdom, although the history of an earlier statutory defence in the state of New South Wales suggests the Australian law may remain more restrictive (Kenyon, 2006, pp. 217–20, 374–79). Thus, Australia has developed a constitutional protection for "reasonable" political speech and its statutory defence may be interpreted as closer to the UK position.

The US approach to defamation offers a strong contrast to the traditional law and the more recent UK and Australian developments. In the United States, the "*Sullivan* rules" (Chesterman, 2000, p. 155) have developed in a long series of cases since the classic 1964 *Sullivan* decision. Before *Sullivan*, the US position was broadly similar to the traditional common law approach outlined above. Defamation was seen to lie outside the US constitutional protection for free speech until *Sullivan*, which aimed to create more room for public debate. The *Sullivan* rules require plaintiffs to prove the three elements mentioned above: publication, identification and defamatory meaning. However, plaintiffs must also prove that the publication conveys material of a factual quality—rather than being a matter of opinion—that is actually false. This limits defamation to harmful factual allegations that are proven to be false. In US law, matters of opinion that do not imply the existence of a false fact cannot form the basis for defamation claims (Murchison, 2008). In addition, plaintiffs who are public officials or public figures must also prove the defendant published with what is called "actual malice". The plaintiff must prove that the publisher actually believed the material was false at the time of publication, or at least that the publisher had a "high degree of awareness" of the publication's "probable falsity" and recklessly disregarded that danger (*St Amant*, 1968, p. 731). As well, the *Sullivan* rules require the plaintiff to establish actual malice with "convincing clarity", which is a standard of proof substantially higher than the usual standard in civil litigation. The *Sullivan* rules can be seen as the way that US defamation law supports the country's "profound national commitment to the principle that debate on public issues should be uninhibited, robust and wide-open" (*Sullivan*, 1964, p. 270).

The US requirement for the plaintiff to show actual malice applies to people or entities who are public officials or public figures. Its rationale is that public interest speech will tend to concern these figures, and so it is only appropriate to make it harder for them to sue. The law presumes that, instead of suing, they can respond to attacks in the media with their own speech in reply and their public profile will increase their media access. The law means the media can criticize public officials and public figures without facing liability for defamation, so long as the media does not knowingly publish falsehoods. That is a very different position than faces the media in other common law countries.

Given the transnational concerns of this paper, it is worth noting a little more about the most recent House of Lords decision about the *Reynolds* defence in the case of *Jameel v. Wall Street Journal Europe Sprl* (*Jameel*, 2007). *Jameel* involved a European publication from a major US-based media company being sued in London—no doubt in part because of the more favourable position for claimants there than under US law—which in itself suggests the importance of the new defences in the United Kingdom, Australia and some similar jurisdictions. In *Jameel*, the *Reynolds* defence protected a newspaper report that alleged the Saudi Arabian central bank was monitoring various accounts, at the request of US authorities, because of concerns that funds were being used for attacks on US and allied interests. Before publication, the newspaper had made inquiries and received off-the-record confirmation of the monitoring from staff at the US treasury department. It is notable that this confirmation—and evidence given by news producers that relying on such confirmation was commonplace for journalists working in Washington—was not treated as significant in lower courts. Initially, then, this style of confirmation was not recognized as part of responsible journalism, but in the House of Lords news production practices received a fuller and more sympathetic analysis. There, the details of the newsroom were appreciated and they mattered legally.

It is also notable that the *Jameel* decision provided room for editorial choices about how a particular allegation is presented, something which UK and Australian defamation law has often failed to do. As part of the *Reynolds* defence, the law asks whether an article which does deal with a matter of public interest appropriately includes the *particular* material at issue. In the *Jameel* case, for example, did bank account holders such as the claimant need to be named in the story? It would have been possible to write a story without that detail. However, the House of Lords emphasized the importance of deferring to editorial decisions about the best way in which to convey a story. It cautioned against easy recourse to evaluating editorial judgements with forensic hindsight (*Jameel*, 2007, [33]–[34], [51]) and recognized the need for media publications to be newsworthy. For example, Lord Hoffman, with whom Baroness Hale agreed, said:

> [W]hereas the question of whether the story as a whole was a matter of public interest must be decided by the judge without regard to what the editor's view may have been, the question of whether the defamatory statement should have been included is often a matter of how the story should have been presented. And on that question, allowance must be made for editorial judgment ... The fact that the judge, with the advantage of leisure and hindsight, might have made a different editorial decision should not destroy the defence. That would make the publication of articles which are ... in the public interest, too risky and would discourage investigative reporting. (*Jameel*, 2007, [51])

Interviews: "Responsible Journalism" as Contested Organizational Practice

With legal developments in the United Kingdom and some other common law countries, illustrated by the above cases, a key challenge for law remains how to understand and evaluate practices of journalism. This in turn raises the ways in which journalists, editors, and legal advisors perceive relationships among themselves, and between the law and news production practices. Our fieldwork reveals several themes about how media professionals understand their work and the operation of the law.

The larger research project from which we draw here involved more than 170 semi-structured interviews conducted between 2002 and 2005 with journalists, editors and managers within the newspaper and wider media industry and with lawyers working in media companies or private practice in the United States, United Kingdom and Australia. The interviews focused on participants' perceptions and experiences of news production generally, of defamation litigation, and of the relationship between news production and defamation law more specifically. Interviews also focused on the interactions between journalists, editors and lawyers—both in-house and external lawyers, depending on which the media outlet used—and how the different professionals perceived these interactions and their influence on news production practices. The interviews were conducted face to face by one or both of the authors. All but a handful were audio-taped and transcribed, with handwritten notes taken of the remainder. The resulting transcripts and notes were coded thematically. Here, only brief illustrations can be given of the extensive material generated. The illustrations are drawn from the 95 interviewees who were news production, editorial or managerial staff in the United States, United Kingdom and Australia.

Three key themes relevant to the concept of responsible journalism emerged from these interviews; namely the perceived effects of defamation law; standards and quality of journalistic practice; and organizational negotiations. Considered together, they raise many issues around the relationship between defamation law, public debate and journalism, in particular underlining how understandings of responsible or reasonable journalism are contested at the organizational level of everyday news production practice.

Theme 1: Perceived Effects of Defamation Law

From our research, it is evident that people working in the media across all three countries are aware of defamation law, and believe it has an effect on their work. In particular, there is a clear sense that defamation law can have a "chilling effect" on journalism, in that journalists and editors will either not pursue stories, or will pursue stories in a modified fashion, in certain circumstances for fear of being liable under defamation law. This is consistent with earlier UK studies (Barendt et al., 1997) as well as multi-country comparative research (Weaver et al., 2006). In our research perception of a "chilling effect" was particularly notable in the Australian context, but also existed in the United Kingdom and to a lesser extent the United States. In a few instances, this appeared to operate at a direct and open level, but in most cases it operated in a more indirect fashion, echoing the structural chilling effect discussed by Eric Barendt and his colleagues. Journalists and editors in all three countries acknowledged that there were certain individuals or organizations which had a reputation for being ready to sue if they were written about in the media, particularly in newspapers. (Research has long suggested that newspaper publications prompt a higher rate of defamation suits than other media forms.) When such people or organizations were known, media workers would take extra precautions. These not only included further fact checking, but also weighing up the benefits of publishing a newspaper story in a single issue compared with the potential legal and personal costs of being involved in lengthy legal proceedings over subsequent years. One respondent noted that:

> One thing we're aware of—and this is just a reality—some people are going to be more inclined to sue than somebody else. We looked at a story last year about a person of fairly high prominence and there were sensitive things and the reporter was on the phone with him a lot, and he kept saying "well, you can print that, I'll see you in court" and we had no reason to doubt that he wouldn't sue us if we didn't get it right. But we spent a lot of time talking to our lawyer about that and made sure we had all those things nailed down because we knew that if we didn't get it right, he would sue and that doesn't mean we don't try to get it right with everything else but we know that some people are more prone to do that than others. (United States, editor)

In a similar manner, an editor at another US newspaper reflected:

> When we want to press for more complex stories and get more stories with depth in them that sometimes involves law suits or going after very powerful people. I think my experience, when you go after somebody who has very powerful standing in the community and there's something in the story that they don't like, sometimes they'll get the gist of what you're going to do before you print it, and they have a relationship with maybe the publisher or the advertisers, and they'll bring some pressure and all that means as an editor here, you want to make sure all your T's are crossed and your I's are dotted, and you're not going to get your paper into trouble. (United States, editor)

Many other respondents had similar perceptions and experiences, reflecting the situation that defamation law is part of the everyday experience of media workers, even in the US context where defamation law is seen to be more accepting of media speech than the traditional law. While there was a strong recognition among newspaper journalists and editors that they have a responsibility to protect the reputations of people they write about, outside the United States in particular there was also a concern that defamation law operated too strongly to protect reputation at the expense of the media's ability to report and to promote wider public debate.

Even with major cases during the last decade that appear to hold great promise for the media—such as *Reynolds* and later UK decisions and *Lange* and subsequent statutory reform in Australia—concerns still existed that defamation law negatively affected journalistic practice. In particular, there was a common set of concerns across all three countries related to the costs of legal advice and litigation, both in terms of financial costs and time. Reflecting on the costs of defamation, a UK editor noted:

> Well the big evil of defamation here, in the past, hasn't been that you got sued for damages, it's been the lawyers' costs, which dwarf the damages, and just make it completely unprofitable for a media company to do dangerous things. (United Kingdom, editor)

While many of those that we interviewed discussed the financial dimensions of defamation damages and legal costs, and the clear potential for "chilling" speech given a need for media to operate profitably or use public funding carefully, their concerns notably included the time costs associated with defamation litigation and the potential costs to the reputation of media workers.

The concern expressed by journalists and others working in media is that defamation law can impact negatively on the practice of journalism in the ways it restricts the range of people or organizations about which journalists are able to write, or how they can be written about. Even with what appear to be stronger defences for the media created in cases such as *Reynolds*, many of our interviewees still had concerns about the impacts of defamation law. Issues related to financial and personal cost were crucial here, and were interpreted as an important part of the potential and actual chilling effect of defamation law. This concern is exacerbated when we turn to the concerns of media workers with standards and quality.

Theme 2: Journalistic and Legal Standards and Quality

A second set of issues arose around the relationship between standards and quality of journalistic practice and defamation law. In almost all instances, those we interviewed were keen to argue that while they were aware of the standards required by defamation law, in everyday practice the self-proclaimed journalistic standards of responsible journalism were in fact dominant and directed them to high standard practice. This was particularly evident in the United States, which was unsurprising given the different legal tests for defamation liability that exist under US law. As outlined above, to face liability over publications about public figures US journalists must publish something that has the character of fact, not opinion, which is actually proven to be false *and* which they knew to be false or entertained serious doubts about its falsity and published despite those doubts. One would expect that, if they follow commonly articulated journalistic standards, journalists would not publish factual material they believe to be false. The interviews supported this position:

> I honestly don't think we think about it [the role of the law] much until we have to. I think it's viewed by journalists as running on a parallel track. We're aware of it, I mean, obviously the principles of what we do—fairness, dictate, but how the law will intersect

with us isn't on our minds until it does ... Their journalistic principles are driving them, not legal principles. (United States, journalist/editor)

I think the values in the law and the values in journalism come from the same place. And that's ethics ... Journalism should be conducted responsibly and thoroughly and professionally. (United States, journalist)

The reality is that American mainstream journalistic standards are very high. And to give people the impression that all they need to do is hit the legal hurdle would really do damage to the quality of the publication. (United States, journalist)

Even if you decide you're OK to do with something legally, you've really got to think about the ethics and there's a much tougher test there. You don't feel like, "well if I can pass the *Sullivan* test, I can print." You've got to think, "do I really have enough information to print?" (United States, journalist)

However, it is important to note that such views were also evident among participants working in the United Kingdom and Australian contexts. It is salutary—for lawyers, courts and legal academics—to remember that, even where the legal burdens are far less supportive of media speech, media workers look to professional standards. As other newsroom research suggests, "those who choose news as a profession see it as a calling in the service of democracy, free speech and the public" (Wahl-Jorgensen, 2007, p. 154). In our research, this can be related to boundary contests over who is competent to regulate news standards, for example, journalists, editors, lawyers, ombudsmen or other external influences, including courts. Through such discourses, journalists and editors are making a claim that they are the people best positioned to decide the appropriate standards of responsible journalism. From such a viewpoint, attempts to regulate journalism through legal means are considered as an infringement on the autonomy of journalistic practice. In relation to such attempts by law it is worth noting that, while the US law places lesser burdens on the media than the law in England and Wales, *similar* aspects of journalistic practice can be relevant for courts determining whether actual malice or responsible journalism is established (for the US situation see, e.g., Murchison et al., 1994).

Even though journalists looked to professional standards, it was evident that lawyers had much more frequent involvement in pre-publication negotiations under the more restrictive UK and Australian defamation laws than under US law. At the same time, there was an important recognition through the interviews of the social responsibility held by journalists, given their position as members of the "fourth estate". According to an editor in Australia:

Journalists have an enormous privilege, you know, to do what they do, because they are set up as sort of critics and judges and all sorts of things. It's a process of making ... choices, and those choices are in their copy, often. So in return for that privilege, there has to be a certain amount of obligation, and the obligation, I think, is to get things right and to be fair. (Australia, editor)

That illustrative comment suggests an approach which sits uneasily with traditional commonwealth defamation law. In many situations, the law required journalists "to get things right"—that is, publish material that could be proven true in court—and it offered little room for arguments that a journalist had been "fair" or that the publication amounted to responsible journalism about something of public interest. The newer defences, in particular *Reynolds* in the United Kingdom and the statutory defence for reasonable publication in Australia, offer real scope for such journalistic standards to have greater traction within defamation law.

Theme 3: Organizational Negotiations

A third theme seen in the interviews is that law is negotiated and contested within organizational contexts. As would be expected by socio-legal researchers, defamation law is not something that exists independently of, and is not imposed on, newspaper organizations with direct effects on journalistic practice. Rather, the operation of defamation law is influenced at the level of the newspaper organization by the manner in which lawyers, editors and journalists strategize around ways in which to negotiate the influence of defamation law.

Through these organizational responses, a number of tensions emerge for journalists in their everyday practice. For example, many of our respondents were concerned about whether their legal advisors considered their role to be to protect journalistic practice or to protect the newspaper. For many of the interviewees who worked at well-resourced media organizations, their experiences with their legal advisors had been positive. This was well captured in the following comment:

> I did a piece that had to be intensely lawyered ... and I'd be backing off of something, "maybe we don't need to go with that". "No, no, no", [the newspaper's lawyer] said, "this is really important, you really need to get this in the paper. How can we get this in the paper?" And it's the antithesis of most journalists' experience of lawyers. (United States, journalist)

Discussing the same relationships, a senior Australian journalist noted:

> There are defamation lawyers who truly love the media ... and they see their job as saying, "OK, you have got the story, let's work out how we can get it in the paper." Now we might have to change this or we might have to put in a paragraph in here which just looks bizarre saying that "The [newspaper title] is in no way suggesting that the man we called a fiend is a fiend." It's a paragraph which is just a bumper paragraph [aimed at lessening the danger of conveying a defamatory allegation]. Whereas there are other defamation lawyers who see their job as protecting the corporation so they create an outer crust. They are out around Pluto and they don't want the invaders to get past there to get to Earth. So if you keep them out there in Pluto, we are OK. (Australia, journalist)

As suggested by this last comment, these organizational relations can be a source of tension. Similarly, a journalist in the United Kingdom, commenting on the challenges that confronted editors in managing defamation, noted that in his experience:

> It's the editor's decision in the end, whether [the editor's] going to take advice from lawyers or not. The thing that worried me quite a lot when I was in the first two or three years of this was the business of asking the lawyer what the probability is of someone suing ... to form part of the criteria that you're going to base your editorial judgment on, whether to run it or not, I'm still not quite sure about that as a legitimate consideration because it's another way of saying "can we get away with this?" (United Kingdom, journalist)

The close connections between journalism and pre-publication legal advice in the United Kingdom and Australia were also evident with the emergence of *Reynolds*-style defences, with a UK editor commenting that:

> [Lawyers have] an intimate involvement [in my stories], and since *Reynolds*, a more intimate one because the lawyer comes into the editorial process more. Because the lawyer is checking out, not just the words on the page, but checking out the process I'd gone through to acquire the story. She's sitting there grilling me on what I've done, you know, and I'm compiling a record of the things I've done and the letters I've sent and all that. And it does take a lot of time. (United Kingdom, editor)

Again, while many of our journalistic and editorial participants were quick to acknowledge that they valued highly the contribution of lawyers to their work, a tension could be seen around who was ultimately controlling the journalistic process and in that regard influencing what constitutes responsible journalism. This was seen particularly in the UK and Australian contexts, where lawyers were more frequently involved at the production stage. For many of our participants, there was a fine line between constructive input through legal avenues and inappropriate attempts by the law to define the boundaries of journalistic practice.

Such concerns were greatly heightened when media workers reflected on situations which reached court, with such reflections suggesting these were searing experiences. As a journalist commented:

> I sat at the defence table in a libel trial ... once, and never, ever want to have to do that again. I thought we were solid on the facts ... and they reached a settlement after, you know, half way through, and I was really pissed off. How could you do that? You know, our reputation is at stake, you take a settlement? (United States, journalist)

Conclusions

Relationships between defamation law and journalism can be illuminated by exploring how organizations are embedded in institutional contexts. As Cottle's model suggests, everyday micro-level workplace practices and meso-level organizational cultures interact with the macro-level institutional environment, including legal regulation, to produce particular forms of news production. As this paper reveals, defamation law is a significant feature of the institutional context for newspapers and other media outlets, and influences the development and practice of journalism. While recent cases such as *Reynolds*, *Jameel* and *Roberts* indicate an increasing awareness within law about the significance of socially valuable journalism, and about the need for the law to provide a context in which such journalism might prosper, it is also evident that at the organizational level of journalism these legal developments are not experienced uniformly. Indeed, a key site of tension within news organizations relates to the ways in which defamation law is experienced and negotiated in everyday practice. Under US, UK and Australian law, boundary contests continue within media organizations around who is competent to decide about journalistic standards, with journalists and editors particularly concerned when their legal advisors and the courts are perceived to be inappropriately defining the boundaries of what constitutes appropriate journalism. At the same time, the recent changes in defamation law in the United Kingdom and Australia call for a greater legal capacity to comprehend and evaluate journalistic practices, a need which has been implicit in the United States since major reforms to its defamation law began more than 40 years ago.

ACKNOWLEDGEMENTS

We acknowledge the research support of the Australian Research Council (Discovery Project DP0343258) and thank interview participants for willingly giving of their time, ideas and insights. Many thanks for research assistance to Chris Dent (CMCL, University of Melbourne)—who also conducted three out of the larger set of interviews—and Jason Bosland (CMCL, University of Melbourne). We also thank the editors and reviewers of *Journalism Practice*. Earlier versions of this paper were presented at The Future of Newspapers Conference, School of Journalism, Media and Cultural Studies, University of Cardiff, 12–13 September 2007, The Australian Sociological Association Conference, University of Auckland, 4–7 December 2007 and The Australian Sociological Association Conference, La Trobe University, 8–11 December 2004. Thanks to conference participants for their feedback.

REFERENCES

ALDRIDGE, MERYL and EVETTS, JULIA (2003) "Rethinking the Concept of Professionalism: the case of journalism", *British Journal of Sociology* 54, pp. 547–64.

BANDLER, JAY (2004) "Public Editor Daniel Okrent, Recruited After Scandal, Draws Ire of Reporters", *Wall Street Journal*, 12 July, www.newsombudsmen.org/bandler.html.

BARENDT, ERIC, LUSTGARTEN, LAURENCE, NORRIE, KENNETH and STEPHENSON, HUGH (1997) *Libel and the Media: the chilling effect*, Oxford: Clarendon Press.

BEREZOVSKY (2001) *Berezovsky v. Forbes* [2001] EMLR 45.

CHESTERMAN, MICHAEL (2000) *Freedom of Speech in Australian Law: a delicate plant*, Aldershot: Ashgate.

COTTLE, SIMON (Ed.) (2003) *Media Organisation and Production*, London: Sage.

DENT, CHRIS and KENYON, ANDREW T. (2004) "Defamation Law's Chilling Effect: a comparative content analysis of Australian and US newspapers", *Media & Arts Law Review* 9, pp. 89–111, http://papers.ssrn.com/sol3/papers.cfm?abstract_id = 586684.

FRASER, NANCY (1992) Rethinking the Public Sphere: a contribution to the critique of actually existing democracy, in: Craig Calhoun (Ed.), *Habermas and the Public Sphere*, Cambridge, MA: MIT Press.

GOOD, MARY-JO DELVECCHIO (1998) *American Medicine: the quest for competence*, Berkeley: University of California Press.

GUTNICK (2002) *Dow Jones v. Gutnick* (2002) 210 CLR 575.

JAMEEL (2007) *Jameel v. Wall Street Journal Europe Sprl* [2007] 1 AC 359 (decision handed down in 2006).

LANGE (1997) *Lange v. Australian Broadcasting Corporation* (1997) 189 CLR 520.

KENYON, ANDREW T. (2006) *Defamation: comparative law and practice*, Abingdon: University College London Press.

MARJORIBANKS, TIMOTHY and KENYON, ANDREW T. (2003) "Journalistic Practice and Defamation Law in Australia and the US", *Australian Journalism Review* 25(2), pp. 31–49.

MEDIA AND ENTERTAINMENT ARTS ALLIANCE (nd) "Media Alliance Code of Ethics", http://www.alliance.org.au/code-of-ethics.html.

MURCHISON, BRIAN C. (2008) "The Fact-conjecture Framework in US Libel Law: four problems", *Media & Arts Law Review* 13(2), forthcoming.

MURCHISON, BRIAN C., SOLOSKI, JOHN, BEZANSON, RANDALL P., CRANBERG, GILBERT and WISSLER, ROSELLE L. (1994) "*Sullivan*'s Paradox: the emergence of judicial standards of journalism", *North Carolina Law Review* 73, pp. 7–113.

NOLAN, DAVID (2006) "Media, Citizenship and Governmentality: defining 'the public' of public service broadcasting", *Social Semiotics* 16(2), pp. 225–42.

PETERS, JOHN DURHAM (2005) *Courting the Abyss: free speech and the liberal tradition*, Chicago: University of Chicago Press.

REYNOLDS (2001) *Reynolds v. Times Newspapers* [2001] 2 AC 127 (decision handed down in 1999).

ROBERTS (2007) *Roberts v. Gable* [2007] EWCA Civ 721 (21 July 2007); [2007] EMLR 11.

ROBERTSON, GEOFFREY and NICOL, ANDREW (2007) *Robertson and Nicol on Media Law*, 5th edn, London: Sweet & Maxwell.

SCHUDSON, MICHAEL (2000) The Sociology of News Production Revisited (Again), in: James Curran and Michael Gurevitch (Eds), *Mass Media and Society*, 3rd edn, London: Arnold, pp. 175–200.

SCHUDSON, MICHAEL (2001) "The Objectivity Norm in American Journalism", *Journalism* 2(2), pp. 149–70.

SCHULTZ, JULIANNE (1998) *Reviving the Fourth Estate: democracy, accountability and the media*, Cambridge: Cambridge University Press.

ST AMANT (1968) *St Amant v. Thompson*, 390 US 727.

SULLIVAN (1964) *New York Times v. Sullivan*, 376 US 254.

URSELL, GILLIAN D. M. (2001) "Dumbing Down or Shaping Up? New technologies, new media, new journalism", *Journalism* 2(2), pp. 175–96.

WAHL-JORGENSEN, KARIN (2007) *Journalists and the Public: newsroom culture, letters to the editor, and democracy*, Cresskill, NJ: Hampton Press.

WARNER, MICHAEL (2002) *Publics and Counterpublics*, New York: Zone.

WEAVER, RUSSELL L., KENYON, ANDREW T., PARTLETT, DAVID F. and WALKER, CLIVE P. (2006) *The Right to Speak Ill: defamation, reputation and free speech*, Durham, NC: Carolina Academic Press.

Chapter 19

TABLOID *NOUVEAU GENRE*
Format change and news content in Quebec City's *Le Soleil*

Colette Brin and **Geneviève Drolet**

Introduction—A Newspaper's Response to Changing Times: Format Change in Historical Perspective

After more than a century of publication as a broadsheet, the Quebec City daily newspaper *Le Soleil* changed to a smaller compact format in April 2006. The term "compact" is commonly used in the newspaper industry to designate "a broadsheet-quality newspaper printed in a tabloid format".[1] Because of the negative connotations associated with the term "tabloid", this somewhat euphemistic term is also suggestive of the difficulty for broadsheets in adopting a more popular guise without giving the impression of reducing content quality.

This article examines the newspaper's coverage of itself during the months preceding and following the format change. Articles having the "new" *Le Soleil* as their main focus, or just mentioning it, are considered here as a form of meta-discourse, revealing tensions between old and new, sometimes conflicting, ways of doing journalism, during a period of adjustment to a very visible change.

Our analysis is inspired by a general model of transformation in journalism practice developed by Jean Charron and Jean de Bonville (1996, 2004a, 2004b, 2004c, 2004d). Only a few key notions which are particularly relevant to our case study will be discussed here.

Following the model, journalism practice since the 18th century can be divided in four periods, each associated with a dominant type or paradigm with its own characteristics. This complex theory of "paradigm shifts" in journalism offers historical and theoretical perspective to explain recent and apparently disparate changes. It rests on the postulate that over several centuries, there has existed and continues to exist something called journalism, but that sweeping changes at specific junctures have led to the appearance of new sets of rules and practices. Thus, the changing nature of journalism reflects and follows changes in social structure, but also contributes to larger social change by its function of public discourse.

Although conceived in North America and based on the specific experience of journalism in Quebec, the model is designed to be acultural. Indeed, it has been used to analyze changes in journalism practice in Germany and South America (Charron and de Bonville, 1996, p. 52). The model is useful specifically in addressing recent changes also because it is not guided by normative or prescriptive purposes. It is purely analytical, and so does not concern itself to declare whether journalism is, or ever has been, in "decline" or in its golden age (Schudson, 1997). This allows us to avoid taking sides in the classic debate of quality versus popular press (Esser, 1999, p. 293; Franklin, 1997; Örnebring and Jönsson, 2004; Pradiness Stein, 2005, p. 23). Indeed, this debate can be examined, within the explanatory model, as a discursive manifestation of "crisis" within an established paradigm, a period of uncertainty where old and new sets of journalistic rules coexist. The term "crisis" is defined here as a period of intense change and questioning of established practices and norms, and carries no negative connotation. In the present context, the model offers a larger theoretical framework and historical perpective to changes often described as "tabloidization", "popularization", and "marketization" (Barnett, 1998; Conboy, 2007; Dahlgren, 1995; Esser, 1999; Fairclough, 1995).

The first paradigm, called "transmission journalism", dating back to the 18th century, implies a practice apparently existing without journalists; news circulates through the intervention of social actors (Charron and de Bonville, 2004a, p. 142). At the beginning of the 19th century, this type is progressively replaced by "opinion journalism", due among other reasons to the control of newspapers by institutions, i.e., political parties, labour movements, and the clergy. Newspaper content takes on a strongly expressive form and serves to propagate political or religious viewpoints held by the owner.

Just before World War I, the "information journalism" paradigm emerges notably because of increasing industrialization and intensification of commerce. The newspaper becomes a vehicle for transmitting primarily a new form of report, the news story (*nouvelle*), designed to be universal and objective. The norm of journalistic objectivity, although not entirely determined by economic imperatives, fits nevertheless with the industrial and commercial development of the press during this period (Charron and de Bonville, 1996, p. 73).

The exacerbation of commercial competition, technological innovation and consumer culture led to a situation of media "hypercompetition",[2] provoking, around the 1970s, another fundamental shift in journalism practice. The crisis accompanying the emergence of the "communication journalism" paradigm is characterized by the explosion (*éclatement*) of the notion of journalistic news (*information*), progressively replaced by the notion of communication, focusing on news as interaction, as mode of contact with the public. Central to the crisis is the critique and erosion of journalistic objectivity, the guiding principle of "information journalism", as well as of journalistic authority and professional specificity. Citizen journalism and user-generated content, and the hybridization of journalism and public relations, advertising, or entertainment, are manifestations of this erosion of journalistic authority.

As well, the choice of topics for journalistic coverage, and the manner in which they should be covered, become more and more diverse and largely exceed the conventional conception of news as recent events of general social and political importance (*actualité*). The figure of news user as citizen is replaced by a consumer figure (Charron and de Bonville, 1996, p. 77). Topics traditionally considered part of the private sphere and relegated to specialized sections or media appear in the front pages and headlines, leaving proportionally less space to political news (Sparks and Tulloch, 1999). The context of hypercompetition in the current paradigm also translates, from the public's perspective, into an overwhelming abundance of content and sources to sift through, requiring a different set of skills to "read the news" (Barnett, 1998; Bird, 1992; Pradiness Stein, 2005). Consumption patterns appear more and more volatile, a source of concern particularly for the newspaper industry (Charron and de Bonville, 1996).

This model of successive periods of transformation in journalism practice can be applied to specific studies of change using a series of parameters ranging from the macroscopic to the microscopic, the most general being the social, political-legal and economic-technological contexts. The most specific is the journalistic text itself (see Figure 1). These parameters are to be considered as an interweaving series of factors influencing journalism practice—though not in strictly hierarchical order—which guide the formulation of hypotheses for specific studies by analyzing the relationship between a few distinct parameters.

In this article, we will examine the relationship between change particularly as manifested in *journalistic texts within the newspaper* (parameter 1) and at the level of the *newspaper as organization* (parameter 5). There is obviously some overlap between parameters, and all levels of the schema are involved to some point to this study. The model suggests, however, that empirical research should take journalistic texts as a starting point and work outwards to more general (macroscopic) considerations.

The present study is one of short-term adjustment within a period of long-term change, spanning several decades. Attempted reforms within media organizations, whether successful or not, provide clearly circumscribed case studies of normative conflict, typical of paradigmatic crisis (Brin, 2003). During these periods of professional experimentation, tensions can be high between journalists and managers or, more specifically, between proponents and opponents of the project. What is at stake is rarely the project itself, but rather competing views of journalistic norms as well as conventional sources of organizational conflict (labour relations, rivalries, occasional coalitions, personality conflicts, etc.). In the process, journalists, editors, and managers eventually negotiate a consensus on the proposed reform, somewhat different from the initial project, but nevertheless indicative of evolution fitting into the new paradigm. The format change at *Le Soleil* was particularly visible to the public eye, as well as the internal tensions which permeated journalistic production before and during this period of adjustment.

From Competition to Hypercompetition

Competition is a major component of journalism and an important factor of paradigmatic transformation. The technical and economic conditions prevailing since the late 1970s and 1980s have created a context of competition of such intensity that it

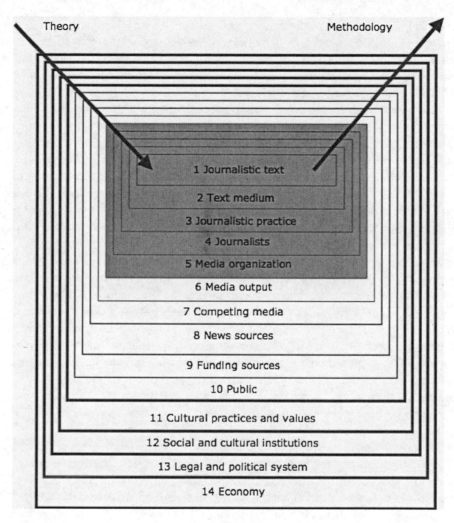

FIGURE 1
Parameters of a journalistic paradigm

approaches the theoretical model of hypercompetition (Charron and de Bonville, 2004c, p. 290). Hypercompetition, a term developed to describe the new economy, is "characterized by intense and rapid competitive moves, in which competitors must move quickly to build [new] advantages and erode the advantages of their rivals" (D'Aveni, 1994, pp. 217–8).[3]

In this context of exacerbated rivalry, conventional forms of professional and commercial competition become secondary as another competitive aspect emerges: the frantic race for the public's attention. As media consumption habits evolve, news consumption becomes more rapid and segmented. This has become a primary concern for media owners and managers, but is also now shared by journalists whose professional interests have come to converge with those of their employers during this period (Demers, 1989; McManus, 1994). The commercial imperative of retaining the public's attention has become a professional imperative and is now integrated to journalists' discursive consciousness.[4] For example, the assumption that conventional news media must adopt convergence practices for economic reasons is rarely challenged within the journalistic community. When criticism of commercial strategies is expressed by a journalist, it is usually preceded by a confession of being rather "old school" or "a dinosaur", thus defining oneself as a journalistic anachronism.

Journalists progressively adjust their practices to that of their competitors and their perception of the public's expectations. The current technological context of online news and 24-hour television news allows for increased reflexivity in that journalists can more readily and continuously observe their competitors' work and compare this work to their own, evaluating their performance based on audience expectations and making adjustments as required. In this hypercompetitive context, it becomes crucial to personalize and particularize media messages in order to make one's voice heard in the cacophony of media sources available. The cycle of production and shelf life of news are also shorter and more fragile than ever.

Charron and de Bonville assert that media firms in the communication paradigm operate simultaneously in five different markets: the advertising market, the consumer market, the source market, the financial market and the professional market. As competition levels increase, so does interdependence between agents in the media system.[5] Solutions adopted by one media firm will tend to be copied, at least in part, by its competitor or competitors. The firm's position on one specific market will influence choices and strategies used on the other markets. This interdependence of markets translates, within organizations, into contradictory and conflicting imperatives. For example, production of "attractive" content to retain the public's attention may be contradictory with a journalist's professional criteria for quality news. These conflicts can only be resolved by constant negotiation and, eventually, compromise.

The recent direct involvement of journalists in commercial competition, as it relates to intensification of competition, leads to new forms of media discourse. Themes and objects of news content are segmented and specialized, a trend that can be perceived as a threat to the universality of journalistic norms (Charron and de Bonville, 2004c, p. 309). However, the mimetic behaviour caused by surveillance of competing media of all forms leads to both homogenization and hybridization. To make their content more intelligible and more visible to the public, journalists borrow from other media genres and from rival sources. The struggle to gain the public's attention is such that journalists use discursive processes incompatible with the paradigm of "information journalism", such as humor, dramatization, familiar or colloquial expressions, etc. Hypercompetition requires news to be a spectacle, bringing to the fore processes of enunciation (form and communicative "power" of news) rather than the statements themselves (the "content" of news) (Charron and de Bonville, 2004c, pp. 310–2).

Changing consumption patterns require the media to develop a more dynamic and interactive relationship with the public. Newspaper layout in 2007 is adapted to a browsing or grazing reader, who can scan the page as quickly as a television or computer screen. This search for new strategies and innovation, specific to a context of hypercompetition, is favourable to questioning conventional assumptions and to self-criticism by journalists, raising the level of media and journalistic reflexivity. The media have never been as prompt to discuss their own practices; they are becoming more and more self-referential. This self-criticism indicates in itself the normative crisis, revealing that rules of journalism practice are no longer evident. This process of self-examination also opens the door to increased criticism from the public. Progressively, the weight of norms defining journalism as a distinct form of public discourse diminishes in favour of norms and dispositions focusing on the relationship between a medium and its public (Charron and de Bonville, 2004c, p. 315). Journalistic discourse, in its semantic and morphological aspects, is progressively characterized by the struggle for the public's attention and advertising revenue. The tabloid front page, with its glaring headlines and high-contrast visuals, although it existed prior to the communication paradigm, can be considered as somewhat of a general reference point or model, in the sense that broadsheets now need to use more aggressive visual and rhetorical strategies to call attention to themselves.

The Quebec Newspaper System

Concentration of media ownership first raised concerns in Quebec in 1967, when Paul Desmarais added the Montreal daily newspaper *La Presse* to the Power Corporation conglomerate.[6] Since then, government task forces, committees and commissions, both at the federal and provincial levels, have suggested limits or controls with varying levels of success. Ownership in broadcasting, cross-ownership and foreign ownership remain regulated in Canada, although there is continuing and intensifying debate about these measures in the present context of globalization, convergence and abundance of media sources.

The media in Quebec has developed somewhat independently from the Canadian system, insulated by a language barrier, public policy, and other historical and cultural factors relating to the classic "two solitudes" metaphor. For example, the term "national media" is commonly used to designate a broadcast network or newspaper distributed exclusively in the province of Quebec, which also points to unresolved constitutional issues.

However, the small size of the market and restrictions on foreign ownership translate into a very limited group of owners controlling the Quebec media. Since 2000, several major transactions have notably served to create new chains, consolidate existing groups, and develop convergence strategies. They have also fuelled concerns regarding the future of local news in smaller markets.[7]

Daily print newspapers show among the highest, if not the highest level of media concentration in Quebec. As shown in Table 1, multimedia empire Quebecor's two tabloids, *Journal de Montréal* and *Journal de Québec*, account for nearly half of French-language newspaper circulation in the province. Both dominate their local markets. The Gesca chain (Power Corporation), which includes the Montreal daily *La Presse*, *Le Soleil* and five regional newspapers, controls just over half of the same market, leaving just 3 per cent for the independent "quality" newspaper, *Le Devoir*.[8]

A distinctive trait of the Quebec media, as of Quebec society as a whole, is the significant role played by labour unions. About 40 per cent of the workforce is unionized, and labour federations (*centrales syndicales*) play a key role in Quebec politics. A sizable majority of full-time working journalists in the major media belong to a union (Pritchard and Sauvageau, 1999), although the industry is evolving toward a higher proportion of freelancers and short-term contracts. Through negotiation of collective agreements in individual media outlets, over several decades, unions have contributed significantly to the professionalization of journalism in Quebec (Demers and Le Cam, 2006). They also provide

TABLE 1
Weekly circulation of paid daily newspapers in Quebec, by ownership (2006)

Groups and titles	Total copies	Circulation Market share (%)	
		Total	French only
Gesca (Power)			
La Presse	1,485,088		
La Tribune	195,908		
La Voix de l'Est	95,395		
Le Nouvelliste	258,774		
Le Soleil	583,855		
Le Quotidien	164,997		
Le Droit	216,970		
Total	3,000,987	44.0	51.6
Quebecor			
Le Journal de Montréal	1,925,384		
Le Journal de Québec	714,836		
Total	2,640,220	38.7	45.4
CanWest Global			
The Gazette	984,358	14.4	
Le Devoir			
Le Devoir	177,816	2.6	3.0
Glacier Ventures International			
The Record	24,460	0.4	
Total			
12 titles	6,827,841	100.0	100.0

Source: Centre d'études sur les médias (2008).

substantial financial support to the Fédération professionnelle des journalistes du Québec (FPJQ), a voluntary association of about 2000 members.[9]

Le Soleil: 20 Years of Turbulence

The 2006 format change follows 20 years of organizational turbulence at Le Soleil, including two controversial ownership changes, management and newsroom restructuring, layoffs, a journalists' strike and ongoing labour tensions, as well as technological changes. The newspaper's offices were also moved twice during this period.

The Hollinger era (1987–2000) saw investment in a new press and technological infrastructure but also labour strife and political controversy, perhaps due in part to Conrad Black's unique personality. Undoubtedly a passionate newspaperman with a strong attachment to his home province, he is also known for his fierce attacks on journalists, unions, and separatists.

Under Black's leadership, Le Soleil was to become "the Washington Post of Quebec". Some critics have observed that this promise was never quite realized (Lesage, 1997). During a journalists' strike which lasted two months in 1992–3, the union's president raised the spectre of tabloidization: "Space reserved for real news [in Le Soleil] has rapidly diminished in favour of soft news. In-depth analysis has disappeared, while fashion, pet care, gossip and 'trendy' columns have proliferated" (Pelchat, 1992).[10] In 1994, 20 journalists and 75 other employees of the newspaper were laid off. Hollinger sold Le

Soleil's downtown building and the newsroom and offices moved to rented space in a quieter, more residential area. Some speculated this move was actually devised to leverage capital for Black's expensive pet project, the *National Post* (Lemieux, 2006).

In 2001, Hollinger sold *Le Soleil*, *Le Droit* and *Le Quotidien* and 15 weekly newspapers to Gesca. Power Corporation's previous attempts to buy *Le Soleil* in 1973 and 1987 had been blocked by Quebec premier Robert Bourassa. This time, the provincial government did not intervene directly, but rather appointed a special commission on ownership concentration. The commission's report (Commission permanente de la culture, 2001) recommended the creation of an ownership surveillance mechanism. This was further specified in a subsequent report authored by a group of experts, led by former journalist and media scholar Armande Saint-Jean (Saint-Jean and Saint-Jean 2003). The recommendation was not implemented by the provincial government.

During the commission's hearings, *Le Soleil*'s journalists' union expressed concerns over anticipated content-sharing and "montrealization" of the newspaper (Leduc, 2001). The new publisher, Alain Dubuc, freshly arrived from Montreal, assured that *Le Soleil* would keep its local identity, although some "less important" regional news could be sacrificed (Dubuc, 2001). *Le Soleil*, he insisted, would remain a "national" newspaper, featuring political journalism and international reporting, enlightened commentary, and lofty editorials.[11] Finally, the conclusion of the transaction was received with some relief by the journalists' unions, in part out of hope that their fortunes would improve under *Québécois* ownership, compared to the Hollinger era (Cauchon, 2000).

However, the tensions soon resurfaced. In 2004, Alain Dubuc, who had by then resigned as publisher of *Le Soleil*, was immediately hired as a freelance columnist for all seven Gesca newspapers (Giguère, 2004). The journalists' union denounced this as an affront to the diversity of opinion and to the autonomy of local newsrooms (Cauchon, 2004a). Among other measures of protest, reporters refused to add bylines to their articles on the days when Dubuc's column was published (Cauchon, 2004b).

During these 20 years of turbulence, *Le Soleil* has seen its circulation dwindle, then stagnate (see Figure 2), while its competitor, conventional tabloid *Journal de Québec* (Quebecor), founded in 1967, has consolidated its lead since the mid-1990s.[12] *Le Soleil* reached its peak average weekday circulation of 150,000 copies in 1965 and has been declining since the 1970s (Centre d'études sur les médias, unpublished data).

Efforts to rejuvenate content—and the newspaper's aging readership—including redesigned and expanded consumer sections, a tabloid sports section, free distribution on the university campus, a free monthly magazine distributed on city buses, and hiring younger journalists, have not succeeded in reversing the trend. It is possible, however, that these efforts have slowed the decline in readership.

A recent study of news content in three local dailies, including *Le Soleil*, between 1992 and 2007 suggests that although the news hole has shrunk with the format change, the proportion of local news has remained the same (Centre d'études sur les médias, 2007). The study found that in *Le Soleil*, the proportion of articles dealing with conventional political, social and economic affairs ("heavy" news) has diminished in favour of "lighter" content (sports, entertainment, crime, consumer news).

This apparent move toward a more popular form of journalism, aside from economic considerations, occurred in a period of labour tensions and affirmation of parochial sentiment. The recent popularity of local talk radio, exploiting the resentment of the capital toward Montreal, among other populist themes, and the rise of the political right in

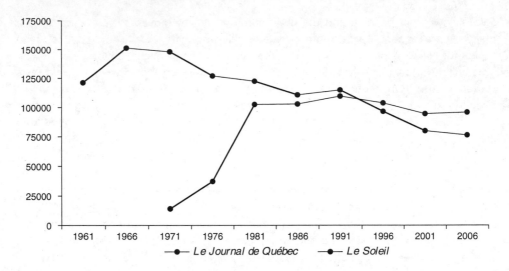

FIGURE 2

Average weekday circulation of Quebec City daily newspapers, 1961–2006. Sources: *Gale Directory of Publications* (1961–1986); *Gale Directory of Publications and Broadcast Media* (1991–2006) Detroit: Gale Research

both federal and provincial elections have been associated to what has been called, somewhat simplistically, the Quebec City "mystery" or "enigma" (Robitaille, 2006).

The Format Change Strategy

Over a period of six months, Gesca's regional broadsheets[13] all changed to a smaller format: *Le Nouvelliste* in October 2005, *La Tribune* in January 2006, *La Voix de l'Est* in February 2006, and *Le Soleil* in April 2006. As far as we know, there are no official plans for a format change at the Montreal flagship, *La Presse*, although its layout was redesigned in 2003.

This change was motivated by the popularity of the tabloid format among readers, but also, presumably, the rising cost of newsprint.[14] *Le Soleil*'s foreign models for "quality" compacts included British newspapers like *The Guardian*, but also *Zero Hora* in Brazil. The launch of the new format and design was also timed to coincide with the newspaper's 110th anniversary. The journalists' collective agreement was signed a few days before the new format's first edition (Cauchon, 2006a).

In terms of content, the new *Le Soleil* features new columns on provincial politics and municipal affairs, but also child-rearing advice (from "D^re Nadia", a psychologist and host of a popular reality show), and an expanded Arts and Entertainment section with a locally-written gossip column on Hollywood celebrities. The revamped design includes a new logo and detachable middle sections colour-coded by topic area ("arts and life" daily, "travel" and "home" on Saturdays). There are no more articles on the front page, only headlines and photos as on conventional tabloids (Figure 3).

To sell the change to its readers, and perhaps more importantly, to attract new ones, especially among young people, *Le Soleil* launched a massive advertising campaign featuring elements of the new design and focusing on the "compact" theme, associating the revamped newspaper with trendy consumer items. Subscribers could win a Smart car, an iPod, or all their living expenses paid for a year. Readers were invited to submit entries to a recipe contest and to buy encyclopaedia volumes through the newspaper. There were also several articles, mostly celebrating the new look, but also some "straight" news coverage.

A few months after the change, the change seemed to have had little impact on circulation—a 1 per cent rise on weekdays, 2.9 per cent on Sundays—while *Le Journal de Québec*'s circulation rose by 6.6 and 4.8 per cent for its weekday and weekend editions, respectively (Cauchon, 2006b). Reactions were mixed: many new readers were pleased with the smaller size, but some long-time subscribers had complaints, notably that sports and business news were not removable sections.

Journalistic Meta-discourse

In the months before and after the format change, *Le Soleil*'s publisher, managing editor, columnists and reporters wrote articles on the theme of the "new" paper. Newsroom supervisors, such as managing editor Yves Bellefleur (2006), particularly insist on the newness of the paper rather than just the format change. In total, we found 19 articles mainly about the new format and 10 with passing mentions, all published between September 2005 and June 2007. In these articles, the medium is its own discursive object, and the way in which the story is reported closely compares to the paradigm of communication journalism. These texts inform us on the discursive and semantic characteristics of journalism production in a period of change, but also on the reflexive consciousness and self-justification within the news organization, as it is shared with its public through the newspaper. The journalistic texts appear as a meta-discourse on journalism practice and newspaper management. Not only do they announce change, they contribute to justify it and invite readers to comment and react to it.

Journalistic meta-discourse is used here as an umbrella concept, covering meta-journalism, which has been defined as "journalism about journalism", specifically in the context of emerging online practices (Deuze, 2003, p. 210), and "meta-coverage", described as "the increased fascination of media actors with news management as a news topic" (Esser and Spanier, 2005, p. 29). In the case of *Le Soleil*'s format change and 110th anniversary, journalistic meta-discourse takes on the form of self-celebration and commemoration. To this effect, Tulloch (2007, p. 43) notes that "Like nations, newspapers celebrate key anniversaries and rites of passage. They lend themselves to systematic personification, and aspire to have voices, personalities, character, identities". Although it is not entirely new for newspapers to discuss their own doings, especially at the launch of a new publication or other event it considers newsworthy, this practice appears to be more frequent and perhaps more systematic in the current paradigm.

In true communication journalism form, the motivation behind the format change is clearly stated in the articles as a willingness to "adapt to readers' lifestyles" (Bellefleur, 2006, p. 4). It is also described as a necessary adaptation to general social change (N. Provencher, 2006, p. 7). Terms such as "pleasing", "easy to read" and "simple" are used to assure the reader of immediate gratification when consuming the new product. The insistence on the format's practicality points to the fact that reading a newspaper is no longer assumed to be part of a daily routine, but rather that it competes with other media-

FIGURE 3
Le Soleil's front page, broadsheet and compact. Note: the broadsheet is the March 29, 2006 edition; the compact is July 20, 2007. The two images are not on the same scale

related activities (Charron and de Bonville, 1996, p. 77). *Le Soleil* is no longer competing only with *Le Journal de Québec* and other newspapers distributed locally, but also with "new media created … to inform and entertain" (A. Provencher, 2006b, p. 32).

Consistent with the hypercompetition thesis, there is an implicit commitment to responsiveness to complaints and willingness to adjust the newspaper to readers' preferences following the launch of the new format. Thus, *Le Soleil* is described as being on "constant watch" (A. Provencher, 2006b, p. 32), always ready to show "audacity and innovation" (A. Provencher, 2006a, p. A1) to conquer its readership. In a context of source abundance, acceleration of news consumption and reader volatility, media firms find themselves in a state of almost permanent change (Picard, 2005). This state of change is accompanied by a no less constant state of interactivity with the public, a situation unique to the current paradigm (Charron and de Bonville, 2004a, p. 195). The media firm tries to establish a relation of complicity with the reader, by announcing its wish to "develop the concepts of user-friendliness and clarity … by continually adjusting and by being attentive to readers' observations" (Tanguay, 2007, p. 4).

This desire to be clear, an easy read, and especially in touch with the public's needs impels journalists to initiate a "conversation" with the public. This calls into question the conventional rule of objectivity and draws journalism practice toward other forms of public communication (Charron and de Bonville, 2004a, p. 163). This appears quite clearly in columnists' texts: "so, how d'ya like the new paper?"[15] (N. Provencher, 2006, p. 7). The columnist speaks directly to the reader, in colloquial form typically used in casual conversation, implying familiarity, informality: "once you get used to it, bunch of rascals, you won't be able to live without it" (N. Provencher, 2006a , p. 7).[16] This form of address, mimicking interpersonal exchange between close acquaintances, appears somewhat removed from the public sphere model traditionally associated with journalistic discourse (Charron and de Bonville, 1996, p. 78).

Journalistic meta-discourse also reveals tensions and contradictions specific to a context of change and hypercompetition (Hamilton, 2005). Even though managing editor Yves Bellefleur insists on substantial improvements in content, he also maintains the importance of "historic continuity at *Le Soleil*. None of the quality, the rigor, the distinction and the diversity which are our trademark have been sacrificed" (Bellefleur, 2006, p. 4). Publisher André Provencher also notes this double requirement of being both innovative and respectful of tradition (2006a, p. A1). The adoption of a smaller format, and even the term "compact" itself, implies a debate regarding what constitutes "good" and "bad" journalism, revealing tensions between constancy and change (Langer, 1998, p. 144).

Articles briefly mentioning the format change, especially columns and features, are also interesting in that they show appropriation of the new format by journalists, as well as inherent tensions within the newsroom and among readers. The format is used as a metaphor for the passing of time and resistance to change, particularly by older people, which also happen to be the newspaper's most faithful readers. Although such mentions are relatively rare, they also seem to evolve toward a gradual acceptance by journalists.

A retired journalist, profiled in a weekly feature honouring a worthy citizen, admits she is "distressed" by the change but that "things change and you have to keep up with the times" (Méthé Myrand, 2006, p. 16). A Quebec City-based biologist is apparently surprised to discover the new look of the newspaper on her return from an expedition in Antarctica. In the context of the news story, the anecdote serves to illustrate the shock of returning home after spending months in such a foreign environment, her experience compared to that of an astronaut in space (Drolet, 2006, p. 9).

In his 300th bird-watching column, a journalist draws parallels between commemorating this "anniversary" and the format change. In this case, the passage of time is cause for celebration: "what gives me the greatest satisfaction is interactivity with readers" (Samson, 2006, p. M21). A year after the format change, to describe well-off retired professionals living in a residential complex, a columnist imagines them as "nostalgic for *Le Soleil*'s stock-market pages back when it was still a broadsheet" (Bourque, 2007, p. 6).

Conclusion

Although situated in a specific local and national context, the case of *Le Soleil*'s format change undoubtedly echoes similar experiences elsewhere in the world. By analyzing a short-term case study within a larger historical model of changes in journalism, we hope to contribute to a better understanding of the forces behind these changes in order to see more clearly into the future of newspapers.

The analysis of journalistic meta-discourse shows an interesting paradox of hypercompetition which would require further study. The collective identity of the newspaper appears to be negotiated through the official voice of management (publisher and managing editor), but also the individual, more expressive voices of columnists and feature writers, whose personal style is especially valued in communication journalism. In this sense, *Le Soleil*'s coverage of its own format change is more than simple self-promotion; despite a clear positive bias, traces of reflexivity and of negotiation of the newspaper's collective identity appear in the texts.

ACKNOWLEDGEMENTS

The authors wish to thank Daniel Giroux, Jean Charron, Jean de Bonville, Ulric Deschênes, and Philippe Marcotte for their assistance and helpful comments on an earlier version of this article.

NOTES

1. See http://en.wikipedia.org/wiki/Compact_newspaper.
2. This key concept for the present study is defined in the next section of the article.
3. For a cogent analysis of the concept's application to news media production, see Hollifield (2006).
4. This notion, borrowed from Giddens (1984), designates the ability of social agents to verbalize the reasons for their actions, as opposed to "practical consciousness", i.e., knowing how to act in social situations.
5. Charron and de Bonville define the newspaper system as a population of newspapers and journalists circumscribed in time and space (2004d, p. 224), characterized by relationships of interdependence and competition between agents within the system's boundaries. For the purposes of the present study, in the current context of convergence, we have opted for a more extensive term including broadcast as well as print media.
6. See http://www.powercorporation.com/index.php.
7. The Montreal metropolitan area is the only large urban market in Quebec, with six dailies and the headquarters of all national French-language media groups. The population of Montreal area (3.6 million) is about half the population of the province of Quebec (7.6 million), while Quebec City has a population of about 540,000 (Institut de la statistique du Québec, 2008; Statistics Canada, 2008).
8. These figures do not include two free dailies distributed in Montreal, *Métro Montréal* (owned by Transcontinental, 60 per cent; Metro International, 25 per cent; Gesca, 15 per cent) and *24 heures* (Quebecor), as circulation numbers do not represent readership in the same proportions (Centre d'études sur les médias, 2008).
9. See http://www.fpjq.org.
10. All quotes from *Le Soleil* have been translated by the authors of this article.
11. This editorial was written two weeks after the attacks of September 11, 2001, which may explain in part the insistence on international news. Still, Dubuc explains the changes were made during the summer months of 2001.
12. *Le Soleil*'s circulation appears to have benefited, perhaps temporarily, from a labour conflict at *Le Journal de Québec* from April 2007 to August 2008. During this period, locked-out journalists also published their own free daily, *MédiaMatinQuébec*, with funding from various labour organizations.
13. *Le Quotidien* and *Le Droit* were already tabloids before the transaction.

14. A slight reduction of the broadsheet format design was done for this reason a decade earlier (Corbeil, 1996).

15. "[P]is, vous le trouvez comment votre nouveau *Soleil*?"

16. "[E]t une fois l'habitude prise, ma bande de snoros, vous allez être les premiers à ne plus pouvoir vous en passer, vous m'en donnerez des nouvelles."

REFERENCES

BARNETT, STEVEN (1998) "Dumbing Down or Reaching Out: is it tabloidisation wot done it", *The Political Quarterly* (b) 69, pp. 75–90.

BELLEFLEUR, YVES (2006) "Découvrez votre nouveau *Soleil*", *Le Soleil*, 24 April, p. 4.

BIRD, S. ELISABETH (1992) *For Enquiring Minds: a cultural study of supermarket tabloids*, Knoxville: University of Tennessee Press.

BOURQUE, FRANÇOIS (2007) "Le meilleur des mondes", *Le Soleil*, 5 May, p. 6.

BRIN, COLETTE (2003) "L'organisation médiatique et le changement des pratiques journalistiques: adaptation, innovation et réforme", in: Jean Crête (Eds), *La science politique au Québec: le dernier des maîtres fondateurs*, Québec: Presses de l'Université Laval, pp. 417–31.

CAUCHON, PAUL (2000) "Plus de prudence que d'inquiétude. Les syndicats et les organismes représentent les médias réagissent sans état d'âme à l'acquisition d'Unimédia par Power Corporation", *Le Devoir*, 11 November, p. B1.

CAUCHON, PAUL (2004a) "Concentration de la presse. Les pratiques journalistiques de Gesca sont remises en cause", *Le Devoir*, 7 May, p. B2.

CAUCHON, PAUL (2004b) "Les journalistes du *Soleil* protestent contre la 'montréalisation' du quotidien de Québec", *Le Soleil*, 17 June, p. B7.

CAUCHON, PAUL (2006a) " Le passage du quotidien *Le Soleil* au format tabloïd va de l'avant", *Le Devoir*, 20 April, p. B8.

CAUCHON, PAUL (2006b) "*Le Soleil* en format tabloïd maintient son tirage", *Le Devoir*, 17 November, p. B4.

CENTRE D'ÉTUDES SUR LES MÉDIAS (2008) "Portrait de la propriété dans le secteur des quotidiens au Québec et au Canada", http://www.cem.ulaval.ca/concentration.html, accessed 12 August 2008.

CENTRE D'ÉTUDES SUR LES MÉDIAS (2007) "Les quotidiens régionaux de Gesca toujours aussi fidèles à leur milieu", http://www.cem.ulaval.ca/portraits_sectoriels/, accessed 12 August 2008.

CHARRON, JEAN and DE BONVILLE, JEAN (1996) "Le paradigme du journalisme de communication: essai de définition", *Communication* 17(2), pp. 51–97.

CHARRON, JEAN and DE BONVILLE, JEAN (2004a) "Typologie historique des pratiques journalistiques", in: Colette Brin, Jean Charron and Jean de Bonville (Eds), *Nature et transformation du journalisme. Théorie et recherches empiriques*, Québec: Les Presses de l'Université Laval, pp. 141–219.

CHARRON, JEAN and DE BONVILLE, JEAN (2004b) "Les mutations du journalisme: modèle explicatif et orientations méthodologiques", in: Colette Brin, Jean Charron and Jean de Bonville (Eds), *Nature et transformation du journalisme. Théorie et recherches empiriques*, Québec: Les Presses de l'Université Laval, pp. 87–120.

CHARRON, JEAN and DE BONVILLE, JEAN (2004c) "Le journalisme et le marché: de la concurrence à l'hyperconcurrence", in: Colette Brin, Jean Charron and Jean de Bonville (Eds), *Nature et transformation du journalisme. Théorie et recherches empiriques*, Québec: Les Presses de l'Université Laval, pp. 273–316.

CHARRON, JEAN and DE BONVILLE, JEAN (2004d) "Le système de journaux: définition et modélisation du concept", in: Colette Brin, Jean Charron and Jean de Bonville (Eds), *Nature et transformation du journalisme. Théorie et recherches empiriques*, Québec: Les Presses de l'Université Laval, pp. 219–42.

COMMISSION PERMANENTE DE LA CULTURE (2001) *Mandat d'initiative portant sur la concentration de la presse*, Québec: Assemblée nationale, Secrétariat des commissions.

CONBOY, MARTIN (2007) *Tabloid Britain*, London: Routledge.

CORBEIL, MICHEL (1996) "Les quotidiens se font petits!", *Le Soleil*, 14 February, p. A9.

DAHLGREN, PETER (1995) *Television and the Public Sphere: Citizenship, Democracy, and the Media*, London and Thousand Oaks, CA: Sage.

D'AVENI, RICHARD A. (1994) *Hypercompetition*, New York: The Free Press.

DEMERS, FRANÇOIS (1989) "Journalistic Ethics: the rise of the 'Good Employee's Model': a threat for professionalism?", *Canadian Journal of Communication* 14(2), pp. 15–27.

DEMERS, FRANÇOIS and LE CAM, FLORENCE (2006) "The Fundamental Role Played by Unionism in the Self-structuring of Professional Journalists from Québec", *Canadian Journal of Communication* 31, pp. 659–74.

DEUZE, MARK (2003) "The Web and Its Journalisms: considering the consequences of different types of newsmedia online", *New Media & Society* 5(2), pp. 203–30.

DROLET, ANNE (2006) "Retour sur terre", *Le Soleil*, 27 November, p. 9.

DUBUC, ALAIN (2001) "Le Soleil en changement", *Le Soleil*, 29 September, p. A1.

ESSER, FRANK (1999) "Tabloidization News: a comparative analysis of Anglo-American and German press journalism", *European Journal of Communication* 14, pp. 291–324.

ESSER, FRANK and SPANIER, BERND (2005) "News Management as News: how media politics leads to metacoverage", *Journal of Political Marketing* 4(4), pp. 27–57.

FAIRCLOUGH, NORMAN (1995) *Media Discourse*, London and New York: Arnold.

FRANKLIN, BOB (1997) *Newszak and News Media*, London: Arnold.

GIDDENS, ANTHONY (1984) *The Constitution of Society. Outline of the theory of structuration*, Berkeley: University of California Press.

GIGUÈRE, MONIQUE (2004) "André Provencher succède à Alain Dubuc", *Le Soleil*, 25 March, p. A1.

HAMILTON, T. JAMES (2005) "The Market and the Media", in: Geneva Overholser and Kathleen Hall Jamieson (Eds), *The Press*, New York: Oxford University Press, pp. 351–71.

HOLLIFIELD, C. ANN (2006) "News Media Performance in Hypercompetitive Markets: an extended model of effects", *International Journal on Media Management* 8(2), pp. 60–9.

INSTITUT DE LA STATISTIQUE DU QUÉBEC (2008) "La Capitale-Nationale ainsi que ses municipalités régionales de comté (MRC) et territoire équivalent (TE)", http://www.stat.gouv.qc.ca/regions/profils/region_03/region_03_00.htm, accessed 12 August 2008.

LANGER, JOHN (1998) *Tabloid Television. Popular journalism and the 'other news'*, New York: Routledge.

LEDUC, GILBERT (2001) "Concentration de la presse: non à la 'montréalisation'", *Le Soleil*, 12 February, p. A10.

LEMIEUX, LOUIS-GUY (2006) "Les années Black", *Le Soleil*, 28 December, p. B8.

LESAGE, GILLES (1997) "Magie des mots, des ondes, de Québec", *Le Devoir*, 14 June, p. A10.

MCMANUS, JOHN (1994) *Market-driven Journalism. Let the citizen beware?*, Thousand Oaks, CA: Sage Publications.

MÉTHÉ MYRAND, LÉA (2006) "Monique Duval: pionnière et passionnée d'histoire", *Le Soleil*, 4 June, p. 16

ÖRNEBRING, HENRIK and JÖNSSON, ANNA MARIA (2004) "Tabloid Journalism and the Public Sphere: a historical perspective on tabloid journalism", *Journalism Studies* 5, pp. 283–95.

PELCHAT, PIERRE (1992) "*Le Soleil* en lambeaux", *Le Devoir*, 17 December, p. B8.

PICARD, G. ROBERT (2005) "Money, Media, and the Public Interest", in: Geneva Overholser and Kathleen Hall Jamieson (Eds), *The Press*, New York: Oxford University Press, pp. 337–50.

PRADINESS STEIN, AMBER NICOLE (2005) "Politics, Citizenry and Tabloid Style of Journalism: the case of Clinton/Lewinsky scandal", MA dissertation, Florida Atlantic University.

PRITCHARD, DAVID and SAUVAGEAU, FLORIAN (1999) "English and French and Generation X: the professional values of Canadian journalists", in: Harvey Lazar and Tom McIntosh (Eds), *Canada: the state of the federation 1998/1999. How Canadians connect*, Montreal and Kingston: McGill-Queen's University Press.

PROVENCHER, ANDRÉ (2006a) "*Le Soleil* publié en format compact le 24 avril", *Le Soleil*, 24 March, p. A1.

PROVENCHER, ANDRÉ (2006b) "Aujourd'hui pour demain", *Le Soleil*, 24 April, p. 32.

PROVENCHER, NORMAND (2006) "La constance du changement", *Le Soleil*, 26 April, p. 7.

ROBITAILLE, ANTOINE (2006) "Le 'mystère de Québec' expliqué", *Le Devoir*, 25 January, p. A1.

SAINT-JEAN, ARMANDE and SAINT-JEAN, CHARLES-OLIVIER (2003) *Rapport sur les effets de la concentration des médias au Québec: problématique, recherche et consultations*, Comité conseil sur la qualité et la diversité de l'information, Québec: Ministère de la culture et des communications.

SAMSON, JACQUES (2006) "C'est la 300e", *Le Soleil*, 15 July, p. M21.

SCHUDSON, MICHAEL (1997) "Toward a Troubleshooting Manual for Journalism History", *Journalism & Mass Communication Quarterly* 74, pp. 463–76.

SPARKS, COLIN and TULLOCH, JOHN (1999) *Tabloid Tales: global debates over media studies*, Lanham, MD: Rowman & Littlefield.

STATISTICS CANADA (2008) "Portrait of the Canadian Population in 2006: findings", http://www12.statcan.ca/english/census06/analysis/popdwell/index.cfm, accessed 12 August 2008.

TANGUAY, LOUIS (2007) "Le Soleil mise sur la qualité et la proximité", *Le Soleil*, 1 February, p. 4.

TULLOCH, JOHN (2007) "Tabloid Citizenship. The Daily Mirror and the invasions of Egypt (1956) and Iraq (2003)", *Journalism Studies* 8, pp. 42–60.

Chapter 20

GOSSIP, SPORT AND PRETTY GIRLS
What does "trivial" journalism mean to tabloid newspaper readers?

Sofia Johansson

Introduction

As worries about the "dumbing down" of the media abound, the British tabloids are often placed at its centre. With a typically sensationalist news style, a celebrity-oriented and sexualized news agenda, and the use of aggressive journalistic methods such as paparazzi coverage and chequebook journalism, tabloids continue to stir emotions. One reason for the controversy they have raised throughout their colourful history is the sheer numbers of readers these newspapers often attract. Competing for the largest group of British newspaper readers, with the lowest incomes and educational levels, tabloids have been criticized for trivializing journalism, to the detriment of the general media climate.

But despite an ongoing debate about tabloid journalism, little academic research has focused on what readers appreciate and get out of these papers. Why are they popular? In discussions about tabloid news, readers are routinely reported as stereotypes—assumed to be uninterested in life beyond their private worlds, and certainly not interested in politics or in public life. Elsewhere (Johansson, 2007a, 2007b), I have argued against such simplification on the grounds that the way that readers use tabloid news—both political and entertainment-oriented news—in relation to public sphere discourse is more complex than previously assumed. In this article, I concentrate instead on readers' views of what is often considered the "soft" side of journalism, such as celebrity gossip, humorous stories and sports coverage. Drawing on interviews and focus groups with 55 male and female regular readers of the *Sun* and the *Daily Mirror*, the two best-selling popular tabloids in the United Kingdom, the article seeks to open up an analysis of the cultural and even political roles of a type of newspaper journalism often considered to be "trivia".

Approaches to Tabloid Journalism

Tabloid newspapers and their historical predecessors, such as the "penny dreadfuls", have long raised controversy among critics concerned with the influence of sensationalist and populist journalistic traditions on society (see Conboy, 2002, pp. 30–1). But, as the characteristic features of the tabloid newspaper are thought to have spread to other media formats, a main framework for the analysis of tabloids today is the much-debated "tabloidization". Against the backdrop of economic, technological and social trends, tabloidization is an umbrella-term for a variety of claims about shifts in the production and content of contemporary media (see Sparks, 2000, for a full discussion), which, as Steven Barnett noted, often are placed in the context of "a pervasive sense of declining cultural, educational and political standards" (1998, p. 75). The news media, traditionally regarded as safeguarding democratic practices by providing information on matters of public interest, are perceived as increasingly turning to entertainment and the realm of private affairs. Here, media audiences are thought to be diverted away from issues of political relevance, from "hard" news on to "soft" tabloid focuses such as human interest, sport, scandal, celebrity and entertainment, or simply not provided with enough wide-ranging analyses and debates about current affairs to function as citizens (e.g. Franklin, 1997).

However, while arguments about tabloidization give an account of economic and social constraints affecting the media, they do not explain the popularity of tabloid journalism. In trying to understand the attractions of this type of journalism, it is important to acknowledge its social uses and interpretive cultural frameworks. Such an approach is outlined by John Langer in relation to "tabloid" TV news. Langer emphasizes that "viewer linkages to the news ... may be more ritualistic, symbolic and possibly mythic than informational, and ... news might better be conceptualized as a 'form of cultural discourse'" (1998, p. 5). While not disregarding news as a source of information, this line of enquiry recognizes that news also serves purposes beyond simply conveying politically relevant information. Indeed, this may be an especially important approach in terms of tabloid news, where some of the main attractions could be found precisely in the way that it fits in with routines and social contexts of everyday life.

Crucially, when thinking about the appeal of tabloid journalism, audiences need to be recognized as active producers of meaning. Reception research during the past couple of decades has insisted that knowledge of how people relate to media cannot be drawn solely from studies of media texts (see Alasuutari, 1999, for an overview). Yet, there is a scarcity of qualitative reception studies on news in general, and of printed news in particular. We therefore know relatively little about the actual contexts and experiences of tabloid reading.[1]

Research Methods

To find out more about readers' experiences of tabloids, I interviewed 55 London-based, regular readers of the *Sun* or the *Daily Mirror* either individually or in small focus groups between May and January 2004–5. The sample is not drawn from affluent, well-educated sections of readers, but readers drawn from the social segments constituting the majority of the readerships. Participants were aged 18–35,[2] a crucial age group for the competition between the two papers, and in the C1C2DE social categories—such as clerical workers and skilled and unskilled manual labourers—which represented over three-quarters of both papers' readerships at the time of the research.[3] Access to "naturally" occurring groups, such as groups of friends or colleagues, was achieved by the use of contacts and "snowball" sampling (see May, 2001, p. 132): eventually 35 male and 20 female readers participated. Most were white and British, with six participants of colour, two non-Western immigrant readers (from Jamaica and Nigeria) and four immigrant readers from countries in the West (Portugal, Greece, Poland, Australia). In total, 11 groups of three to six readers were interviewed, with at least two groups of male/female for each paper and one group each of mixed gender. These were semi-structured and taped, taking place where participants were thought to feel comfortable, such as quiet pubs and cafés, and in several cases at workplaces. The individual interviews were arranged similarly to the focus groups, but provided more personal data.[4]

Tabloid Reading as "Fun"—Gossip, Sport and Pretty Girls

When talking to readers about what they liked about either newspaper, a recurring description was of reading as "fun". Exemplified in explanatory statements such as "It makes me laugh" or "it's a fun newspaper to read" this was deemed a primary reason for buying the papers, with central experiences of amusement. The examination of these responses is therefore important to gain an understanding of the attractions of the popular tabloids, which, as I will attempt to show in the following, are connected to a number of deep-seated social and cultural structures.

Part of this enjoyment was centred on humorous headlines, jokes used in stories and pictures, and a clever deployment of word-games and puns. Readers would, for example, commend the journalists on their skill with headlines with admiring acknowledgments such as "I don't know how they do it, but they crack me up". But the "fun" of reading was also derived from joking about scandalous or strange stories. An example can be given from an interview with a secretary (aged 33) who recounted how a bizarre news story in the *Mirror* provided an opportunity to share an amusing moment with colleagues:

> Interviewer: Do you talk about what you read in the *Mirror* with other people?
> Victoria: Some of the articles, yeah. If I find a good article in there. I found one in the paper not too long ago, and I cut it out and photocopied it and sent it round the office!
> Interviewer: Oh, ok. What was that about then?
> Victoria: It was about the . . . the man that kept spiders and they broke free of their glass . . . and they actually bit him and he died.
> Interviewer: Oh . . .
> Victoria: And . . . he had snakes, he had spiders, he had . . . And they had actually started eating his body. And cockroaches all over . . . [Laughs] It's true! I put it on my wall upstairs [in the office]!
> Interviewer: How funny. Oh well, I mean . . .
> Victoria: Yep. Then I photocopied it. I gave a copy to Alex [a colleague], to all the girls in the office.

As evident in Victoria's jovial fascination for this story, it is notable that readers might use "sombre" content to fit into a general frame of humour—again demonstrating how entertainment and amusement were over-riding aspects of the reading.

While pleasure was connected to lively tabloid narratives and humour, some genres appeared more closely connected to the prevalent idea of the newspapers as "fun". These included bizarre human-interest stories such as the one detailed above, as well as agony aunts and horoscopes. However, not surprisingly given the tabloid focus on these areas, "sport" and celebrity "gossip" dominated discussions of particularly well-liked reading material. These content types were subjects of much amusement in the groups, and appeared relatively easy to talk about—at least within gender confinements. For example, although celebrity gossip was described as a "guilty pleasure" by some female readers, it was still often given as a reason for reading either paper. Male readers, on the other hand, showed reluctance to admitting liking "gossip", with initial reactions either distancing, such as "Who cares?" or derogatory, such as "I think it's rubbish". But, as shown in this extract from a group of *Mirror*-readers in their late twenties, negative perceptions of "gossipy" coverage did not rule out enjoyment:

> Andrew: And it's like, "who's been seen messing about in Hampstead Heath with his boyfriend?" You know? What's the point?
> Mike: Yeah, why have it?
> Douglas: Having said that I do . . . when I buy the *Mirror*, I do read all this . . .
> Andrew: Oh, absolutely! . . . So, everyone says that, like, they hate gossip, but when it comes down to it, everyone reads it.

Responses to celebrity coverage will be considered in the next part of this paper, but it is worth noting that taking an interest in "gossip" is contradictory to traditional masculine areas of interest (see Jones, 1990 [1980]), and such contradictions can signify a struggle between competing notions of masculinity amongst readers.

Conversely, while female readers were largely negative about the sport coverage, for example describing it as "a waste of the back of a newspaper", male readers praised the *Sun* or the *Mirror* for their extensive football coverage and breaking sports news. An appreciated feature was of the sports writers' ability to come across as "ordinary" football fans, and the enjoyment taken from the football coverage was significantly interlinked with televised coverage. Probing further into experiences of tabloid sports coverage, however, it became clear the newspapers' opinions were valued not just for the game commentary, but, interestingly, for "transfer gossip" and features that would go beyond the sport itself. As one construction worker explained his penchant for the *Sun*'s football coverage:

> I just think that they [other papers] tend to pick the mundane sort of thing, which . . . No one really wants to know if . . . sacked their manager. But everyone wants to know what Ferguson's done, or what Chelsea are doing. Or someone putting coke up their nose. These . . . That's the sort of thing you wanna know what's going on in football. (Daniel, 35)

While sport has historically been one of the key signifiers of masculinity in many Western societies (Wheaton, 2003, p. 193), such responses serve as reminders of how, on a reception level, it can mask pleasure gained from its co-existence with the more feminized pursuit of insights into human relations—a pursuit clearly pleasurable to both male and female readers.

Not surprisingly, for the male readers a content type equally regarded as part of the "fun" was the tabloid presence of topless or scantily clad women. "Pretty girls", as one *Sun*-reader described them, would sometimes be held up as a main attraction of both newspapers. Yet, there was generally a deep sense of embarrassment in talking about this for both male and female readers, particularly when it came to the *Sun*'s infamous, bare-breasted, Page Three pin-up. Due to the sensitivity of the subject, likely to have been heightened by my presence as a young female, male readers would come up with a number of "defences" for looking at "boob pictures", as another *Sun*-reader described them. These included emphasizing that pictures of girls were not essential to the reading, as in "it's not that important, but it does brighten up your day", as well as assertions such as "it's a paper everyone can read, my wife reads it" in connection with discussion about Page Three.

Yet, while the enjoyment gained from Page Three was difficult to pin down, the conversations at times offered vital glimpses into how it was experienced by male readers. As shown in the following example, a main pleasure appeared related to taking part in a typically "masculine" activity:

> I mean, women, they probably look at Page 3 and then move on but a man would look at the page a bit longer [laughs] and then flick through ... Women, they're not interested in that but a man would stop and just read the caption at the bottom. And that caption, ... it's written in a masculine way so a man would appreciate it. It's a bit, it would be a bit smutty, and so, a man could have a little giggle about this girl in a skirt and blah blah. It's a masculine paper. (Kiani, 28, cinema worker)

The references to "a man" and "masculine" in this extract highlight the strong links being made between identification with the male gaze (Mulvey, 1992 [1975]) in the consumption of Page Three and *being* a man. Aside from the sexual allure, tabloid pin-ups appeared to provide opportunities to strengthen a masculine identity. Such an interpretation is supported by the fact that this was an area that seemed to allow male bonding across cultural boundaries. For example, a Nigerian, Muslim, *Sun*-reader explained that at the building site where he worked "we talk a lot about ladies". For him, the interest in Page Three had become a way to identify with and be accepted by his mainly British colleagues.[5]

Female *Sun*-readers, conversely, unilaterally expressed aversion for Page Three. They often displayed very fierce reactions, shown in the use of emotive language such as "disgusting" and "hate". One reader demonstrated how she would cover Page Three with her hand while reading, whereas another explained how the feature made her feel low in self-esteem:

> Maria (age 20): I don't like her. I don't like any of them! I don't think ... I prefer ... not to open the paper and see them in there. I mean, I don't think, you know, if you're gonna have a newspaper, I don't think you should have some ... whoever it is ... Some girl in there taking her clothes off and having pictures of them. I don't like it.
> Interviewer: Why don't you like it, then?
> Maria: I just don't think that ... To me, I don't think it's right and ... especially if I have a partner and he's sitting there and opens the paper and he sits there staring at them. I mean you'd get jealous if it was your, your man was walking down the road with you and

he was looking at somebody else, and it's the same thing ... I mean it's not just that ... They put in someone skinny, with a nice body or whatever. Never do you see a woman with a fuller figure ... Why does it have to be skinny, white ladies with blonde or brown hair?

Such obvious tension between experiences of disempowerment by Page Three, and the women as regular readers, was dealt with through what, paraphrasing French sociologist Michel De Certeau (1984), could be seen as "strategies of resistance", whereby the female readers had developed ways of thwarting their dissatisfaction. Toying with demands of a "Page Three man" to counteract the impact of the Page Three girl can be seen in this light. Ridiculing the glamour models likewise appeared to offer another strategy of resistance and a way to gain superiority over the image:

> Tina (age 25): I just think it's like, embarrassing. It's, like, I don't know ... People call them models. Like, people that ... Like, the Page Three girl, is like, "oh, the model ..." She's not a model!
> Interviewer: What is she, then?
> Tina: She's just ... just a girl, ain't she?
> [Laughter]
> Tina: She's just a tart ...

There is moreover a tension here since this contempt could exist alongside what seemed a fascination for the model's perceived lucrative, perhaps glamorous, career, with frequent references made to the models as being financially successful. Hence, as with the male readers' responses to tabloid pin-up images, those of female readers are far from straightforward.

While what can loosely be defined as "entertaining" content, then, is important to tabloid reading, it is worthwhile going beyond ideas of this as simple and self-explanatory. The centrality of fun in these discourses, moreover, requires further analysis in relation to everyday life. Here, having "fun" while reading the newspaper gave a welcome break from mundane habits and routines, such as commuting or repetitive job tasks:

> Like on the bus to work, you're tired, and you just wanna be entertained. You know, get the latest on the sports, get a peep into the glamour world [laughs]. So the *Sun* is good for that. (Adam, 28, shop-fitter)

For some, the idea of "fun" appeared a way to cope with experiences of events and circumstances of the surrounding world as threatening or depressing, where the newspapers would have a "cheering-up" function:

> I don't wanna wake up in the morning and read about a rail crash that's happened in Iraq, or Taiwan, or Australia. I don't wanna be depressed when I read the news. I wanna be cheered up. (Daniel, 35, construction worker)

Thus, although these newspapers can be enjoyed in a number of ways, the emphasis on fun overall might be understood as a response to day-to-day routines, where, in some cases, the newspaper reading can work both as a way to release unwanted emotions and as dealing with general anxieties. The next part of the article looks at how, in the area of tabloid celebrity, content included in the framework of "fun" can also be used to cope with and criticize wider social structures.

Tabloid "Celebrity-bashing" as an Attack on Social Privilege

As mentioned, celebrity stories were part of the especially popular reading material in the *Sun* and the *Mirror*. Celebrity stories were the cause of much amusement and animated conversation, and, as with the Page Three feature for male readers, it appeared to bridge cultural divisions. Tabloid celebrity stories seemed to share functions with other celebrity media in these respects (see e.g. Holmes and Redmond, 2006; Johansson, 2005; Turner, 2004; for overviews), but the conversations pointed to a more genre-specific role—bringing up questions of social class in relation to the reception of tabloid journalism.

Readers, on the one hand, understood celebrities as inhabiting a distinct, glamorous existence, while on the other, they emphasized basic human connections. Some conversations showed an occasional ironic remoteness from the "fantasy" of the celebrity, with readers stressing the discrepancy between a routine existence and the glamour of celebrity life, whereas others pointed to the balancing act between a distancing from celebrities and recognizing aspects of their lives. The following example from a group of retail trainees (aged 18–21), shows how notions of individual vulnerabilities appeared to be the main area of affinity—but also how reading about celebrities could serve as a harsh reminder of their different circumstances.

> Interviewer: Do you think that celebrity stories somehow relate to your lives, or . . .
> Helena: No.
> Marissa: No.
> Helena: I like, I like hearing about how they started, like, before they became famous, yeah. I like to know them things. But when they . . . [become successful] they don't interest me. I don't think their lives are like ours at all.
> Joanne: Some of them are though, like Britney Spears. Yeah, she's got her millions and they don't have nothing to do with me, but she's got boyfriends and arguments and . . .
> Helena: But they have arguments with their boyfriends and they go on TV and they can get their boyfriends back by . . . making a song or something, do you know what I mean? And they flippin' got money. They split up with their boyfriends, they can go out and spend, cause they've got loads of money. When we split up with our boyfriends, I ain't got loads of money to go out and spend nothing.

I have in a more detailed analysis of tabloid celebrity consumption (Johansson, 2006) argued that this "painful" aspect of celebrity coverage is related to how contemporary celebrity discourse embraces a notion of social mobility, where the enjoyment of tabloid celebrity stories can be seen as connected to a hope of self-transformation. As shown, such a notion often appeared contradicted by the lived experiences of these readers and not surprisingly, therefore, an important tenet to the talk about celebrity in this study was that it was marked by frustration, enmity and anger.

Readers were certainly clear that for the tabloids celebrities were "fair game", with the newspapers felt to be "picking on" celebrities or displaying them "making a fool of themselves". Here, some readers expressed concern for how individual people were treated in the tabloids, feeling "sorry" for someone like David Beckham. But a common (and sometimes simultaneous) response was to take pleasure in this treatment, well illustrated in following quote from a 35-year-old construction worker, whose main enjoyment from celebrity stories related to seeing unflattering depictions of "top celebs":

Daniel: They, cover, yeah, they seem to pick on the top celebs. Catherine Zeta Jones can't move without the *Sun* doing it. Jordan can't change her underwear without the *Sun* knowing about it [laughs] . . . They must hang around night clubs 24/7 waiting for a celebrity to fall out the door.
Interviewer: Yeah . . . Is it something you like to read about, or . . .?
Daniel: Oh, I'd gloss over it. Unless, there's . . . it's an amusing picture of Naomi Campbell or someone, falling over with her legs in a twist [laughs].

This type of response must be placed in connection to the everyday life of readers, where the perceived glamour of the celebrity's life brought attention to experiences of social inequality. Indeed, readers would sometimes connect their resentment of celebrities to dissatisfaction with their own circumstances. Ronnie, a 35-year-old bus-driver, put it like this:

I couldn't care less about them lot [the celebrities]. It just makes me jealous. Especially when I'm out there driving a bus picking up all them people all day.

Here, the newspapers' exposes of celebrity misdeeds provide a temporary vindication of injustices, as it allows what Catherine, a 21-year-old shop assistant, described as a "hate" for celebrities:

Sometimes you just wanna hate celebrities, you know? They've got money, and the life . . .

As the newspapers invite a temporary reversal of experiences of disempowerment, hating celebrities through these stories can be a way to cope with their own situation. There is thus some empirical support for Ian Connell's (1992) hypothesis that claims that the significance of tabloid celebrity stories is that privilege is presented and understood as *attackable*. The interviews with readers showed that celebrities were understood to represent privilege and these stories did appear to nourish an irreverent attitude to this. While not necessarily leading to actual socio-economic change, the interest in tabloid celebrity stories can certainly be seen as a commentary on some very real social tensions and power-struggles in the society in which they operate.

Tabloid Reading as Sociability, Community and Certainty

The attractions of reading as discussed so far in this article—the way these papers provide an entertaining break from day-to-day struggles and the way they can simultaneously be experienced as a momentary attack on privilege and power—are bridged by a third, fundamental aspect of their enjoyment. For, connected to the idea of the *Sun* and the *Mirror* as vents for dissatisfaction with social subordination, are those which inspire a sense of affinity among readers, for ordinary people and against elitist structures in society. As demonstrated by Conboy (2002, 2006), popular newspapers generally draw on sentiments of collectivism and a dialogic approach to conjure up an image of the reader–paper relationship as based on shared values and interests.

On a reception level, perhaps the most obvious way in which the idea of "community" is useful is when thinking about the importance of these to the sociability of readers. Tabloid reading was without exception described as a social activity, exemplified in how some of the participants would read the papers together, in the focus on "gossip" and evident in the often lively focus group discussions. Likewise, comments on the newspapers' inclusiveness and popularity, such as "It's an everybody's paper" or on social interaction on a wider level, such as "I can talk about what I read in this paper with anybody" reflect the way sociability as part of tabloid reading is not only a question of day-to-day interaction, but also of experiencing oneself as part of a more widespread collective of readers. Although one should be cautious about asserting the media's impact on collective identities (see Schlesinger, 1991), there is some room for thinking about tabloid reading in terms of *belonging*. These newspapers were generally seen to aim for "ordinary people", and there was evidence of how, particularly the blue-collar workers, would identify themselves with the papers in this respect, evident for example in how the newspapers were regarded to voice the concerns of relevance to a majority, in a language close to the everyday—"like we talk" or "like something I'd say myself". This experience of being part of a large collective of "ordinary people", further, in some instances appeared related to identification with the nation at large. Whether in talks about particular content types such as sports or about general impressions of the journalism, both newspapers were commonly referred to as especially "British" papers, and reading them corresponded with an experience of "Britishness":

> Kiani: I think the *Sun*, it is a paper that I think to really understand you have to have been born in this country. I think that there are a lot of people from overseas especially that . . . It is a bit of a jokey newspaper, but they can't quite grasp that the paper is the best-selling newspaper. It's not really an in-depth read, it's not really a . . . that's why I think it's a very British paper that people from overseas don't really understand.
> Interviewer: So, if you're British, how would you get it more?
> Kiani: I think cause of the humour of the paper as well. Cause the humour is a very British humour. English humour. Like Page Three for example, ever since I've grown up, whenever the *Sun*'s there, Page Three has always been there. But in all the foreign papers, Page Three is never ever there. And then people come over and go "what!". So it is in a way like a British institution where, me personally, I think that you can only really understand the paper if you were born here. Cause then you understand the *Sun*'s mentality and the whole thing the *Sun* does.[6]

The papers' invitation to identification with a collective was thus interpreted through the very experience of being part of something popular, ordinary, anti-establishment and "British".

In other ways too, these newspapers were perceived as bringing an element of stability. For example, both papers were linked to *certainty* in the way they were perceived as "opinionated" and "black-and-white", transparent in ideas and with writers firm on their views. "You know their angle", as one reader described her appreciation for the *Sun*, whereas another felt it "spells it all out", enabling the forming of own opinions in relation to the view of the newspaper. Such qualities provided a frame of reference in which the readers would develop their own standpoints, but, paradoxically, could also be linked to the pleasure taken from knowledge free from contradiction. The enjoyment that male readers in particular derived from the stress on traditional attributes linked to gender could possibly, too, be placed in this context.

The observations made in this last part of this paper point to tabloid reading as connotative of the warmth of human interaction, of belongingness and security. These are precisely the features that sociologist Zygmunt Bauman, in his *Community: Seeking Safety in an Insecure World* (2001), suggests are most sorely missing from modern life, which he sees as increasingly marked by flexible social relations, competition and indifference. Perhaps here, there is a final clue as to how the popularity of tabloid journalism can be explained within the fabric of society at large. Certainly, it is interesting to juxtapose the emphasis on "black-and-white-ness", graspable morals and community against the context of an increasingly complex society, where forces of globalization and commercialization have been seen to contribute to eroding traditional values and working-class forums, such as trade unions and the security of a lifetime workplace. The search for community, real or imagined, appears crucial to understanding the reception of tabloid journalism.

Conclusion

In this article, I have, through a small-scale empirical study with readers, provided an analysis of the appeal of the *Sun* and the *Daily Mirror*, two of the most well-read British newspapers. I have focused on readers' responses to content perceived as typically "soft" tabloid focuses, such as human interest, sport and celebrity stories—a kind of journalism often considered to trivialize the media but which appears to be pleasurable to many readers. The aim has thus been to provide a better understanding of the popularity of this kind of journalism, rather than to discuss its role within political communication and public life. However, an analysis of this side to tabloid reading reveals much about the complex ways in which tabloid newspapers link in with readers' everyday lives, contributing to knowledge of how tabloid journalism is to be explained within the fabric of society at large.

The analysis has emphasized three important aspects to the appeal of the two newspapers studied. On one level, the enjoyment of reading can be understood as a way to deal with day-to-day struggles, which, particularly through the deployment of humour, provides an opportunity for relaxation and the release of general everyday anxieties. Demonstrated here through responses to celebrity stories, these newspapers on another level act as a vent for frustration rooted in experiences of social inequality, which means that an equally significant attraction is being able to criticize social privilege within the reading experience. Finally, over-lapping both of these tangents is what, drawing on Bauman's analysis of modern Western culture, I have called the "search for community", which helps explain the appeal of the sociability, collective identity and clarity as experienced through the *Sun* and the *Mirror*.

Taken together, these three ways of explaining responses to the newspapers show how tabloid material often considered trivial is made meaningful in the linkages between the papers, readers and the social structures surrounding readers' everyday lives. Thus, what this discussion has attempted is to shed light on how main attractions of the newspapers relate to human desires, life experiences and uncertainties, as well as how these are shaped by a social context.

NOTES

1. Two previous qualitative, English-language studies of the context and experience of tabloid reading—Elisabeth Bird's (1992) study of US supermarket tabloids, and Mark Pursehouse's (1992) article on a small number of *Sun*-readers—have provided insights, with both for instance finding that tabloid reading was related to an alienation from, as

Bird puts it, "dominant narrative forms and frames of reference" (1992, p. 109). Ongoing doctoral research by Mascha Brichta on tabloid reading in the United Kingdom and Germany will shed light on cross-cultural comparisons. See also Brichta (2002) on the reception of the German *BILD-Zeitung*.

2.   The initially selected age category following industry quotas was 18–34, but two group members were aged 35.

3.   Figures from the National Readership Survey 2004.

4.   All names are pseudonymous to protect respondents' privacy.

5.   While this reader liked talking about these "ladies", he also stated that as a muslim, he ought to think pin-ups should not be in a newspaper. His resolve for this obvious contradiction was that although "muslims are religious people", "when they come to the Western [*sic*] it's okay". This response to Western media exposure of nudity illustrates how identity positions shift over different sets of values, and how the reading is one area where different aspects of these are emphasized and juggled with.

6.   As a second-generation immigrant from Pakistan, the daily connection with the *Sun* for Kiani appeared to strengthen his own identification with "Britain". It highlights how perceived stable identities, such as the security that comes with belonging to a nation, may be especially appreciated in the context of volatile identificatory relations in other areas.

REFERENCES

ALASUUTARI, PERTTI (1999) "Introduction: Three Phases of Reception Studies", in: Pertti Alasuutari (Ed.), *Rethinking the Media Audience*, London: Sage, pp. 1–21.

BARNETT, STEVEN (1998) "Dumbing Down or Reaching Out", in: Jean Seaton (Ed.), *Politics and the Media*, London: Blackwell, pp. 75–90.

BAUMAN, ZYGMUNT (2001) *Community: Seeking Safety in an Insecure World*, Cambridge: Polity Press.

BIRD, S. ELIZABETH (1992) *For Enquiring Minds: A Cultural Study of Supermarket Tabloids*, Knoxville: University of Tennessee Press.

BRICHTA, MASCHA (2002) "Die BILD-Zeitung aus der Sicht ihrer Leserinnen und Leser: Eine qualitative Rezeptionsstudie", MA thesis, University of Hamburg.

CONBOY, MARTIN (2002) *The Press and Popular Culture*, London: Sage.

CONBOY, MARTIN (2006) *Tabloid Britain: constructing a community through language*, Abingdon: Routledge.

CONNELL, IAN (1992) "Personalities in the Popular Media", in: Peter Dahlgren and Colin Sparks (Eds), *Journalism and Popular Culture*, London: Sage, pp. 64–83.

FRANKLIN, BOB (1997) *Newszak and News Media*, London: Arnold.

HOLMES, SU and SEAN REDMOND (2006) "Introduction: understanding celebrity culture", in: Su Holmes and Sean Redmond (Eds), *Framing Celebrity: new directions in celebrity culture*, London: Routledge.

JOHANSSON, SOFIA (2005) "Editorial", *Westminster Papers in Communication and Culture*, 2(2), pp. 1–5.

JOHANSSON, SOFIA (2006) "'Sometimes You Wanna Hate Celebrities': tabloid readers and celebrity coverage", in: Su Holmes and Sean Redmond (Eds), *Framing Celebrity: new directions in celebrity culture*, London: Routledge.

JOHANSSON, SOFIA (2007a) "'They Just Make Sense': tabloid newspapers as an alternative public sphere", in: Richard Butsch (Ed.), *Media and Public Spheres*, Basingstoke: Palgrave Macmillan.

JOHANSSON, SOFIA (2007b) *Reading Tabloids: tabloid newspapers and their readers*, Huddinge: Södertörn Academic Studies.

JONES, DEBORAH (1980) "Gossip: notes on women's oral culture", in: Deborah Cameron (Ed.), *The Feminist Critique of Language: a reader*, London: Routledge.

LANGER, JOHN (1998) *Tabloid Television: popular journalism and the "other news"*, London: Routledge.

MAY, TIM (2001) *Social Research: issues, methods and process*, 3rd edn, Buckingham: Open University Press.

MULVEY, LAURA (1992 [1975]) "Visual Pleasure and Narrative Cinema", in: Gerald Mast, Marshall Cohen and Leo Braudy (Eds), *Film Theory and Criticism: introductory readings*, Oxford: Oxford University Press, pp. 746–57.

PURSEHOUSE, MARK (1992) "Looking at the Sun: into the 90s with a tabloid and its readers", in: *Cultural Studies from Birmingham Number 1 1991*, Nottingham: Russell Press, pp. 88–133.

SCHLESINGER, PHILIP (1991) "Media, the Political Order and National Identity", *Media, Culture and Society* 13, pp. 297–308.

SPARKS, COLIN (2000) "Introduction: the panic over tabloid news", in: Colin Sparks and John Tulloch (Eds), *Tabloid Tales: global debates over media standards*, Oxford: Rowman & Littlefield Publishers, pp. 1–40.

TURNER, GRAEME (2004) *Understanding Celebrity*, London: Sage.

WHEATON, BELINDA (2003) "Lifestyle Sport Magazines and the Discourses of Sporting Masculinity", in: Bethan Benwell (Ed.), *Masculinity and Men's Lifestyle Magazines*, Oxford: Blackwell Publishing, pp. 193–221.

Chapter 21

NEWSPAPERS IN EDUCATION IN FLANDERS
A press policy to support the future readership market for newspapers

Karin Raeymaeckers, Tim Hoebeke, and **Laurence Hauttekeete**

Introduction

The present-day decline of the circulation and reach figures suffered by traditional newspaper publishers is a phenomenon that is encountered in practically all countries throughout the Western world. In an already difficult market newspaper publishers are increasingly faced with competition from other media as well as with the abundant offers of free news and entertainment. All the figures show that the time spent on reading newspapers has also been falling sharply. They also indicate that in every age cohort the more highly educated spend relatively more time reading newspapers. However, this correction for education should be interpreted with some caution, as some reduction of reading time is found to be common to all age groups. This leaves little room for optimism about the future of newspaper reading (Knulst and Kraaykamp, 1996; Raeymaeckers, 2002).

A further general observation that can be derived from the successive research studies of the time spent reading is that young people always spend less time reading newspapers than their elders (Lauf, 2001). This makes them the Achilles heel in the development of the readership market as it has been projected in the traditional newspaper publishers' plans (Bogart, 1991; Buckingham, 1997; Chisholm, 2005). Publishers of free papers are apparently better armed against the substantial loss of young readers, as their appeal clearly lies in offering fast news, although the price element also plays a major role in the development of a youth readership for newspapers (Buckingham, 2000; Raeymaeckers, 2004).

Socialising factors traditionally appear to be the strongest engine for establishing a steady reading habit (Bonfadelli, 1993; Chaffee and Choe, 1981; Cobb-Walgren, 1990). In this respect an environment that may or may not provide young people with access to newspapers is of cardinal importance to the subsequent development of an independent reading behaviour and for buying newspapers for themselves. Segmentation of the survey of newspaper buyers reveals that in an increasingly high number of families with young children, parents no longer buy a newspaper daily. This clearly impedes the future preservation of newspaper readership (Bogart, 1989; Gustafsson and Weibull, 1997).

This paper describes a strategy that combines the efforts of newspaper publishers, participants from the educational sector, and politicians who design the government's media policy in Flanders. It presents the results of the study that was conducted into the effects of the reading promotion project Newspapers in Education (NIE) in Flanders. Specifically, NIE has been receiving ample financial backing from the Flemish media Minister, Geert Bourgeois, and from the Innovation and Media Department of the Ministry of the Flemish Community, which regards the project as an opportunity to develop initiatives directed at the qualitative support of the future readership market.

In point 3.2 of its Report on Media Policy, the Flemish Government (2005–6) explicitly states that it wants to create the context and conditions in which each individual can be a full participant in the information society. The document further states that to this end it is necessary to remove any impediments to access to both the new and the traditional media.

After a period in which the Flemish newspaper publishers had set up and financed small-scale reading promotion projects, the Newspapers in Education Project was re-launched in 2004. Its broad target group was all 16–18-year-olds from the most various sections of secondary education. In that first year the Flemish Government backed the project with 500,000 euros for purchasing newspapers at a reduced rate and distributing them among schools. At the same time it also invested in starting up academic research that, over the successive years, was to highlight certain separate constituent aspects of the project and develop a tool for a longitudinal monitoring of the project's results in various social segments and in different educational settings.

The project's notable success with participating teachers and pupils convinced the political authorities of its value and it has been continued year after year, with increasing financial support. Moreover, the initial results of the academic research study (Raeymaeckers et al., 2007) demonstrated that the project had positively acted as a substitute socialising factor within the school environment, and that its socialising potential was increasing as the home environment was failing in its socialising role.

As from 2006 the Flemish Government steeply increased its contribution to 1.2 million euros, i.e. half of the total cost, it has been possible to expand the original target group (pupils aged 16–18) considerably by adding other age groups and other social groups such as certain "groups at risk". The latter are defined as newcomers to a society whose native language is different from the dominant language, as well as adults in special education programmes. At the same time the project was also introduced to teacher training curricula and models were developed for special targets, such as hospital schools.

In the same year about 1,800,000 free newspapers were distributed to a large number of participating schools, reaching at least 150,000 children and young people. In that year the project was made available to primary school pupils. Primary school teachers were so eager to accept the invitation that they subscribed to the project in such large numbers that eventually one of out three children in the project belonged to the 10–12-year-old group. The action, which is launched at the start of each new school year, has been such a success that the available means have been insufficient to meet all applications. The fact that the application period had to be closed before all potential subscribers had been satisfied created such hype that it had to be closed earlier each successive year, even after an increase of the financial input. An unprecedented flood of applications for the 2007–8 action exhausted all subscriptions in a matter of days. Indeed, in less than a week's time the maximum number possible of subscriptions had been reached.

The results we present in this paper refer to the action during the 2006–7 school year, and focus on the shifts in the participants' attitudes towards newspapers and reading newspapers from before to after the action. We also examine whether over the years the action has succeeded in producing some sort of cumulative effect. The results have been obtained from the average school population in the 10–18-year age range.

Innovative Opportunities for a Media Policy

Any government-financed action that aims to support and shape the future readership of traditional print media might be regarded as an alternative form of press subsidy. The reference work by Hallin and Mancini (2004), which attempts to classify media systems, also pays much attention to various forms of media subsidies as they are found in Western countries. In what they define as the North/Central European or Democratic Corporatist Model, the authors include the following countries: Germany, the Scandinavian countries, the Netherlands, Switzerland, Austria and Belgium, all of which have certain parameters for press subsidies. Several other authors who have outlined the different systems of press support have emphasized the various individual national differences, but have always pointed out the common factor that all policy measures are aimed at effecting an active press policy. In each case they mention the possibilities for press support to those commercial enterprises that are faced with a readership market that is too limited and/or generates insufficient advertising revenue (Charon, 1994; Grisold, 1996; Holtz-Bacha, 1993; Kopper, 2004, Meier and Trappel, 2007). Also in each case we find arguments that are based on the presumption that press support, in particular of the selective kind, can underpin media diversity and take the rough edges off media concentration. However, study of the eventual effectiveness of a range of such measures shows that their outcome is diffuse and equivocal (Charon, 1994; Picard, 2003).

Apart from direct and general as well as selective press support, we also find forms of government intervention that are less economic interventions than an ensemble of measures aimed at providing qualitative support for the media. These are mainly to be found in the countries with the North/Central European or Democratic Corporate Model (Hallin and Mancini, 2004). Hallin and Mancini (2004), Heinrich (2001) and Holtz-Bacha (1993) itemize different examples of selective support to investigative journalism, journalist training, professional journalist associations, etc. Also projects that are specifically developed to promote reading in general and newspapers in particular may be regarded as examples of this kind of implementation of qualitative support measures that aim at a mainly long-term effect.

Newspapers in Education (NIE): A Newspaper Publishers' Project that Functions as an Instrument for Qualitative Press Support Aimed at Underpinning the Future Readership Market

NIE's long tradition started in the 1930s as an educational project that was coordinated by the Newspaper Association of America and established as a collaboration between schools and partners from the newspaper industry. It has been funded by contributions from the educational sector and from the publishers, who have acknowledged it as a marketing tool for giving their titles a privileged status in a specific school or a comprehensive school. Today NIE has developed into a project that has been implemented worldwide in various forms. Its financial backing comes from different sources, including UNESCO, various national newspaper publishing associations, and the paper giant Norske Skog. And today there are countries where the project is supported by the government as part of a qualitative press support policy. While small-scale instances of the project that are financed by local publishers or publishing syndicates often also comprise a commercial component, the governments which officially invest in the project are likely to ensure that it is carried out without any manifest commercial aim, that the project involves all publishers, and that the newspaper package that is distributed in the schools conveys a representative sample of the entire press landscape.

In the NIE project in Flanders, participating teachers receive a daily newspaper package for a fortnight containing enough copies of each title for pupils to be able to perform class and individual tasks. All participating pupils receive a one-off workbook, matching their various ages, with assignments that may guide the teachers in their approach to the theme of newspapers and newspaper reading. These tasks are quite diverse and range from playful search tasks to critical reflection, confronting the young readers with assignments that sharpen their critical skills concerning news content by having them compare various sources of information in terms of news value, journalistic approach and critical commentary of the news that is presented.

For children aged between 10 and 12 the workbook assignments are oriented to developing reading skills, to learning to search for information, and to the critical reflection on information. For this group a quiz has been designed in which participating classes compete against each other, culminating in a final round in a spectacular mass event that the participating children attend with an enthusiasm that is truly touching.

By positioning schools and teachers as additional socialising actors and as facilitators for learning to handle newspapers and to reflect critically on the information that is on offer, the widest possible range of children and young people are reached. The interest shown by the Flemish government has added extra spearheads to extend the project to specific target groups. These include adult education courses or special programmes for the integration of newcomers to Flemish society. In these cases the emphasis of the various application modalities will be on literacy in general or on Dutch language fluency in particular.

Aim of the Study

Central Question

The central question of this study remains the same as in previous research into reading promotion campaigns such as NIE: to what extent can these campaigns promote young people's interest in reading newspapers? These campaigns are not created to effect directly demonstrable behavioural changes, such as adequate purchasing behaviour or media use. However, what these reading promotion projects can promote is a change in attitude in the short term, as well as, and especially, in the long term. Therefore, it is this attitudinal change that occupies a central position in this study, which seeks to answer the question whether NIE can affect young people's attitudes in the short and in the long term, and if so, whether this effect may be cumulative?

Methodology

A random sample was taken from a list of participating units. As all age categories and all types of education were represented in this list, our sample reflected the real NIE landscape. We opted for a written questionnaire to be completed anonymously, so as to avoid a social desirability bias in the replies. The questionnaire design was an iterative process: different test stages made the questions sufficiently clear and one-dimensional as well as adjusted to the different age groups of participating pupils. The pre-test/post-test design we opted for allowed us to analyse the short-term effect of NIE. The pupils were required to complete the first questionnaire before the start of the project and the second after the end of the two-week project.

The results presented in this paper refer to the 2007 NIE campaign and are based on 2470 questionnaires completed by pupils aged between 10 and 18. On a total sample of 4960 units, this represents a response of nearly 50 per cent. The non-response rate is partly explained by our decision to process only those questionnaires that covered both the pre-test and the post-test scores.

Socio-demographic Profile

Slightly more boys (56.6 per cent) than girls (43.4 per cent) took part in the survey. Divided according to age, the 14–16-year-olds (54.8 per cent) form the largest group, followed by the 16–18-year-olds (23.7 per cent). While the Flemish publishers' own survey figures indicate that the group of the 10–12-year-olds covers about 33 per cent of the participating pupils, they make up only 15.2 per cent in our study. This is because it was decided to keep the youngest age group deliberately small in the sampling process. The 12–14 age group (4.3 per cent) is by far the smallest both in our study and in the data provided by the Flemish publishers. Research in previous years has shown that teachers in the first two years of secondary education argue that the curricula of this age group notably leave little room for alternative activities during lessons.

Media Use Profile

Our survey first inquired into a number of variables that chart media use. Reading newspapers is not self-evidently an activity that fascinates young people. Indeed, about one-third (33.1 per cent) declare they never read a newspaper. And those who do read a newspaper occasionally, present a rather fragmentary reading behaviour and spend little time on it. Fewer than 17.4 per cent report spending less than five minutes, which probably allows them to scan the front page, have a quick glance through the paper, or look for the evening's television programme listings. Just over 50 per cent of young people hardly have any newspaper contact to speak of. The low rate of newspaper use is not so much a matter of availability of newspapers. Indeed, we find that nearly 80 per cent of our respondents' homes have a newspaper, and about 40 per cent even have a newspaper daily. The overall time spent on newspapers is extremely short in all age groups in our study, with the exception of the 16–18 age group which shows a clear positive shift in the pattern of use. Irrespective of their age the number of non-readers fluctuates round 30 per cent, but the number of young people who declare to spend 10–30 minutes a day on reading newspapers changes strongly. As the ages advance, this percentage mounts from 15 per cent of the 10–12-year-olds to 32 per cent in the 16–18 age group.

What Are Young People's Attitudes to Newspapers?

Let us first consider the results of those study variables that gauged the pupils' attitudes towards newspapers and newspaper reading. The pre-test contained 15 statements for the pupils to either agree or disagree with on a five-point scale. Table 1 shows the average scores for the various statements.

Although some statements elicit replies in the safely neutral central range, the majority of statements are given a distinctive score. Young people agree most strongly with the statement that everything that is in the papers can also be found on the Internet and on television. Yet, they agree least with the statement that reading newspapers is a waste of time. It thus appears that young people believe that the information in newspapers can equally be found in other media, but also that spending time on newspapers is not necessarily useless. In other words, they continue to regard newspapers as a useful source of information.

The pre-test results show that young people in Flanders have a predominantly positive attitude towards newspapers. They deny that they dislike reading newspapers, they do not regard newspapers as an old-fashioned medium and they even find it necessary to read newspapers. They admit that it is a way to remain well informed and to understand current affairs more deeply. They concede that the information offered by a newspaper is also useful to them in their daily life. While the pupils find that newspapers contain a lot of interesting information, they are also of the opinion that they contain a lot of superfluous data and that television offers much better information.

Relating the results in the attitudes section to the access variables (availability of newspaper in the home environment) leads to a number of remarkable observations. On each of the 15 statements there is a significant difference between both groups insofar as pupils who have a newspaper at home rate newspapers more positively. And when we relate the results to the age variable, we find that the 16–18 age group rates most positively on the attitude variables. The larger the age difference, the more significant the differences on the statements. The 16–18-year-olds differ significantly from the 10–12-year-olds on eight items and with the 12–14-year-olds on three items. This no longer holds when considering the 14–16-year-olds. On no fewer than 12 statements this

TABLE 1

Changes of the average scores on the statements on the attitude towards newspapers (five-point scale)

	N	Average pre-test	Average post-test	Shift	Significance
I find reading newspapers entertaining*	2451	2.98	3.21	0.23	0.000
Newspapers are old-fashioned*	2443	2.40	2.35	−0.05	0.022
Reading newspapers is a waste of time	2415	2.15	2.16	0.01	0.666
Newspapers contain information that is useful in daily life	2448	3.63	3.63	0.00	0.875
Television news offers better information than the newspaper*	2439	3.39	3.27	−0.12	0.000
I can easily find the information I am looking for in the newspaper*	2437	2.99	3.13	0.14	0.000
The information in the newspaper is reliable*	2441	3.00	3.12	0.12	0.000
The newspaper contains a lot of information that does not interest me*	2447	3.55	3.40	−0.15	0.000
I do not feel the need to read a newspaper*	2439	2.85	2.66	−0.19	0.000
The newspaper contains interesting information	2427	3.67	3.69	0.02	0.169
Everything that's in the newspaper, I can also find on TV/the Internet*	2430	3.94	3.81	−0.13	0.000
I only look at the pictures in the newspaper*	2419	2.37	2.45	0.08	0.000
Newspapers help me better understand current events*	2425	3.34	3.44	0.10	0.000
Readers of newspapers have more to talk about*	2426	3.53	3.62	0.09	0.000
I do not like reading the newspaper*	2448	2.77	2.54	−0.23	0.000

*$p < 0.05$.

group diverges from the 16–18 age group. The 14–16 age group adopts the least positive and the least interested attitude towards newspapers. Puberty appears to have a major impact on the formation of attitude.

As the Department of Communication Sciences at Ghent University, commissioned by the Innovation and Media Department of the Ministry of the Flemish Community, has been carrying out research into the impact of the NIE project for some years, we also wanted to find out whether the successive project years have had a cumulative effect on the formation of attitude. Among pupils who have participated in the project before we have found six statistically significant differences from those who have not participated before (Table 2). Those who have participated in NIE previously experience newspaper reading as more entertaining and tend to agree less with the statement that newspapers are old-fashioned. They make a stronger distinction between newspapers and television and they have more appreciation for the informative function of a newspaper, as they understand that someone who reads a newspaper is better and more widely informed.

TABLE 2
Average scores of the statements on the attitude towards newspapers (totally disagree → totally agree), divided according to previous participation

	Have you participated in "Newspapers in Education" before?	N	Average	SD
I find reading newspapers entertaining*	No	1914	2.96	1.065
	Yes	522	3.07	1.094
Newspapers are old-fashioned*	No	1911	2.43	1.142
	Yes	521	2.29	1.142
Reading newspapers is a waste of time	No	1907	2.16	1.127
	Yes	518	2.10	1.090
Newspapers contain information that is useful in daily life	No	1915	3.60	0.954
	Yes	520	3.69	0.961
Television news offers better information than the newspaper*	No	1913	3.42	1.044
	Yes	521	3.28	1.067
I can easily find the information I am looking for in the newspaper*	No	1912	2.96	1.039
	Yes	521	3.05	1.037
The information in the newspaper is reliable*	No	1913	2.98	1.028
	Yes	519	3.06	1.006
The newspaper contains a lot of information that does not interest me*	No	1914	3.56	1.091
	Yes	521	3.53	1.106
I do not feel the need to read a newspaper*	No	1916	2.89	1.224
	Yes	521	2.73	1.234
The newspaper contains interesting information	No	1904	3.65	0.973
	Yes	518	3.73	0.912
Everything that's in the newspaper, I can also find on TV/the Internet*	No	1907	3.94	1.095
	Yes	519	3.89	1.137
I only look at the pictures in the newspaper*	No	1904	2.37	1.136
	Yes	517	2.37	1.138
Newspapers help me better understand current events*	No	1902	3.32	1.044
	Yes	519	3.42	1.000
Readers of newspapers have more to talk about*	No	1909	3.50	1.116
	Yes	519	3.61	1.097
I do not like reading the newspaper*	No	1917	2.80	1.415
	Yes	521	2.64	1.434

*$p < 0.05$.

Therefore, they feel a greater need to read newspapers and they do so with considerably more pleasure. This shows that NIE unmistakably has a longer-term effect.

Does a Campaign Such as NIE Bring About Any Shifts in Attitude? A Comparison of the Results from the Pre- and Post-test Phases

Juxtaposing the post-test results with those of the pre-test phase allows us to compare the replies immediately before the start of the project with those after the project has ended. Table 3 shows that after the project the pupils assess newspapers and reading newspapers differently. On no fewer than 12 items there are statistically significant shifts. They indicate the short-term effect that a project such as NIE can have, i.e. removing the negative prejudices towards a medium that was to a large extent unknown to many of the participants. These shifts do not quite constitute a landslide, but the differences are large enough to be significant. What is more, all shifts are changes towards a more positive rating on items concerning newspapers and reading newspapers.

Parallel with our reporting of the pre-test results, we examine whether as far as the attitudinal shifts are concerned any relevance emerges by relating the results to access variables. We can observe that young people who have a newspaper available at home, tend to further strengthen the positive attitude they already had shown in the pre-test. The observation applies to no fewer than 12 of the 15 items in the questionnaire.

Also pupils who never or very rarely have a newspaper available, positively change their attitude after the project. This applies to eight of the 15 items. It is remarkable, however, that in this group the shifts in attitude are much more pronounced. This group started with a far less positive attitude towards newspapers, which gave them a wider margin that left room for more intense changes. NIE more often has an impact on pupils who have contact with newspapers in their home environment, although those who in their home environment have the least socialising impulses more frequently display a stronger and more intense change in attitude.

When we go more deeply into the differences in changes according to the extent to which the pupils experience these socialising effects at home, we can see a clear and evident trend emerging. The less time pupils spend on newspapers at home, the more their attitudes towards the medium are influenced positively by the NIE project. Pupils who declare never to have read a newspaper change their opinion significantly on 13 of the 15 statements, in the group that spends less than five minutes on newspapers we find nine significant shifts, in the group that spends 5–10 minutes on newspapers we can see eight shifts, and in the group that is occupied with newspapers for as long as 10 minutes to half an hour, we find only six shifts. In the cohort that invests half an hour to one hour in reading newspapers there are only four significant shifts. It thus appears that NIE has the strongest impact on those young people who spend little time reading newspapers and have least access to newspapers in their home environment.

A further useful approach consists in linking the shifts in attitude in their turn to the various age groups in the project. We can notice that after participating in the NIE project, both the 10–12 age group and the 12–14 age group adjust their attitude positively on eight of the 15 statements. The 14–16-year-olds do so on 10 statements, and the 16–18-year-olds on nine statements. Especially the 14–16-year-olds, with 10 significant shifts, appear to undergo a positive impact from the project. Since this group showed, as we

TABLE 3

Changes of the average scores on the attitude statements towards newspapers (five-point scale), divided according to previous participation

	Participation	Average pre-test	Average post-test	Change
I find reading newspapers entertaining	Not the first time*	3.07	3.26	0.19
	The first time*	2.96	3.20	0.24
Newspapers are old-fashioned	Not the first time	2.29	2.30	0.01
	The first time*	2.43	2.37	−0.06
Reading newspapers is a waste of time	Not the first time	2.10	2.11	0.01
	The first time	2.16	2.17	0.01
Newspapers contain information that	Not the first time	3.69	3.63	−0.06
is useful in daily life	The first time	3.61	3.63	0.02
Television news offers better	Not the first time*	3.29	3.17	−0.12
information than the newspaper	The first time*	3.42	3.30	−0.12
I can easily find the information I am	Not the first time*	3.05	3.17	0.12
looking for in the newspaper	The first time*	2.96	3.12	0.16
The information in the newspaper	Not the first time*	3.06	3.15	0.09
is reliable	The first time*	2.98	3.12	0.14
The newspaper contains a lot of	Not the first time*	3.53	3.39	−0.14
information that does not interest me	The first time*	3.56	3.41	−0.15
I do not feel the need to read a	Not the first time*	2.73	2.56	−0.17
newspaper	The first time*	2.89	2.68	−0.21
The newspaper contains interesting	Not the first time	3.73	3.79	0.06
information	The first time	3.65	3.67	0.02
Everything that's in the newspaper,	Not the first time	3.89	3.80	−0.09
I can also find on TV/the Internet	The first time*	3.95	3.82	−0.13
I only look at the pictures in the	Not the first time	2.37	2.41	0.04
newspaper	The first time*	2.37	2.46	0.09
Newspapers help me better	Not the first time*	3.42	3.52	0.10
understand current events	The first time*	3.32	3.42	0.10
Readers of newspapers have	Not the first time	3.61	3.66	0.05
more to talk about	The first time*	3.51	3.61	0.10
I do not like reading the newspaper	Not the first time*	2.64	2.48	−0.16
	The first time*	2.80	2.55	−0.25

*$p < 0.05$.

have indicated above, also the most negative attitude before the start of the project, they obviously had more scope for positive changes.

Regarding three statements that positive shift may be called absolute, because all the responses to them constitute changes, irrespective of the age category. It is obvious that in these young people participation in NIE has increased the need to read newspapers. After participating they regard reading newspapers also as a more entertaining activity and therefore they tend to enjoy newspapers more. This change in attitude, certainly as regards these three statements in particular, provides evidence for the effectiveness of the project as an engine for raising awareness among young people of school age.

And just as we did above, we can relate the attitudinal shifts to previous participation in the project. We find that pupils who in 2007 participate for the first time in the NIE project show a positive shift on a larger number of items (12 significant shifts as opposed to eight significant shifts for pupils who have participated in previous years). One must not forget, however, that the group who had participated previously started with a more positive start score, which in principle left less scope for a further change in attitude.

The replies to four particular statements show that NIE has not only a short-term effect, but also a cumulative impact. These statements are the following: television news offers better information than the newspaper, I do not feel the need to read a newspaper, I do not like reading a newspaper, I find reading newspapers entertaining. First of all, the results show a significant shift in terms of positive adjustment and therefore a shift in the short term. In spite of their more positive start scores, the group who had participated previously also shows a further adjustment towards a more positive attitude, which indicates a cumulative effect that develops as young people participate in the project several times in the course of their school years.

Conclusion

Our research, which has been gradually creating approaches to examining the impact of reading promotion projects among a wide range of participants, has been running for several years. In this paper we comment on our latest data that, like those in previous years, demonstrate the opportunities offered by this kind of project to engage young people in what newspapers have to offer. Because the NIE project has been organised for several years on a regular basis, our research may provide some insight in its impact beyond the current year. This paper shows that the NIE action, as it is conducted in Flanders, succeeds in having a long-term impact on those who have participated more than once. The outcome is quite promising and points at an indirect kind of impact as participants positively change their attitude towards reading newspapers, towards newspapers in general and the kind of information offered by newspapers.

Because it is financed partially with government funding, the project can be carried out without direct commercial intentions. This means that publishers are prevented from having the project focus on those segments of the potential youth readership market that hold most promises for them. Indeed, NIE, as it is organised in Flanders, specifically aims at making itself accessible to the widest possible range of participants, while also emphasising arguments such as the need for equal opportunities in access to information. That is why it should be regarded as a further positive factor that the results for 2007, just like those from previous studies, show that participants change their attitudes positively and that these shifts are strongest in those groups with a lower degree of access to newspapers in their home environment.

The research results also point at an impact beyond the period immediately after participating in the project. The 2007 results show that young people who have participated before have a more positive start score when rating the statements concerning newspapers and reading newspapers. Also for these pupils this additional participation results in a further, though more limited, positive shift in attitude.

With age comes wisdom and this also goes for the young people's attitude towards newspapers. The older the pupils become, the more highly they tend to appreciate newspapers. However, there is no straight positive connection between maturity and attitude, as the replies of the second-grade secondary pupils are peculiarly distinctive. These 14–16-year-olds probably have to cope with the rebellious nature of their age.

The study also focuses on the extent to which the campaign has succeeded in changing the attitudes of those young people who were newspaper-illiterate because they had no or only very limited access to newspapers in their home environment. Our results clearly testify to the need to promote the habit of newspaper reading in the school environment. Campaigns conducted at school level will reach the broadest possible range of young people and will help redistribute access opportunities, thus benefiting the groups with the lowest access rates regardless of educational levels.

REFERENCES

BOGART, LEO (1989) *Press and Public: who reads what, when, where and why in American newspapers*, 2nd edn, Hillsdale, NJ: Erlbaum.

BOGART, LEO (1991) *Preserving the Press: how daily newspapers mobilised to keep their readers*, New York: Columbia University Press.

BONFADELLI, H. (1993) "Adolescent Media Use in a Changing Media Environment", *European Journal of Communication* 8, pp. 225–56.

BUCKINGHAM, DAVID (1997) "News Media, Political Socialization and Popular Citizenship", *Critical Studies in Mass Communication* 14, pp. 344–66.

BUCKINGHAM, DAVID (2000) *The Making of Citizens: young people, news and politics*, London: Routledge.

CHAFFEE, STEVEN H. and CHOE, S. Y. (1981) "Newspaper Reading in Longitudinal Perspective: beyond structural constraints", *Journalism Quarterly* 58, pp. 201–11.

CHARON, JEAN M. (1994) "A propos des aides à la presse", *Médiapouvoirs* 33, pp. 110–14.

CHISHOLM, J. (2005) *Shaping the Future of the Newspaper: analysing strategic developments and opportunities in the press industry*, Vol. 4, No. 2, Paris: World Association of Newspapers.

COBB-WALGREN, C. J. (1990) "Why Teenagers Do Not 'Read All About It'", *Journalism Quarterly* 67, pp. 340–7.

FLEMISH GOVERNMENT (2005–6) "Media Policy Document", www.jsp.vlaamsparlement.be/docs/stukken/2005-2006.

GRISOLD, ANDREA (1996) "Press Concentration and Media Policy in Small Countries", *European Journal of Communication* 11, pp. 485–509.

GUSTAFSSON, KARL E. and WEIBULL, LENNART (1997) "European Newspaper Readership: structure and development", *Communications* 22, pp. 249–73.

HALLIN, DANIEL and MANCINI, PAOLO (2004) *Comparing Media Systems. Three models of media and politics*, Cambridge: Cambridge University Press.

HEINRICH, JÜRGEN (2001) *Medienökonomie. Band 1: Mediensystem, Zeitung, Zeitschrift, Anzeigenblatt. Überarbeitete und aktualisierte Auflage*, Wiesbaden: Westdeutscher Verlag.

HOLTZ-BACHA, CHRISTINA (1993) "Presseförderung im westeuropäischen Vergleich", in: Peter A. Bruck (Ed.), *Medienmanager Staat. Von den Versuchen des Staates Medienvielfalt zu ermöglichen. Medienpolitik im internationalen Vergleich*, München: Verlag Reinhard Fischer, pp. 443–567.

KNULST, W. and KRAAYKAMP, G. (1996) *Leesgewoonten. Een halve eeuw onderzoek naar het lezen en zijn belagers*, Rijswijk: Sociaal en Cultureel Planbureau.

KOPPER, GERD (2004) "The German Newspaper Industry: a case study in changing media markets and strategic options for the European newspaper industry", in: Robert Picard (Ed.), *Strategic Responses to Media Market Changes*, Jonkoping: Jonkoping International Business School.

LAUF, EDMUND (2001) "Research Note: The Vanishing Young Reader. Sociodemographic determinants of newspaper use as a source of political information in Europe, 1980–1998", *European Journal of Communication* 16, pp. 233–43.

MEIER, WERNER A. and TRAPPEL, JOSEF (Eds) (2007) *Power, Performance and Politics. Media policy in Europe*, Baden-Baden: Nomos.

PICARD, ROBERT G. and GRÖNLUND, MIKKO (2003) "Development and Effects of Finnish Press Subsidies", *Journalism Studies* 4, pp. 105–19.

RAEYMAECKERS, KARIN (2002) "Trends in Reading. Young people and patterns of time consumption in relation to print", *European Journal of Communication* 17, pp. 369–83.

RAEYMAECKERS, KARIN (2004) "Newspaper Editors in Search of Young Readers: content and layout strategies to win new readers", *Journalism Studies* 5, pp. 223–44.

RAEYMAECKERS, KARIN, HAUTTEKEETE, LAURENCE and DEPREZ, A. (2007) "To Read or Not to Read: Flemish press assistance aims to support the future readers market", *European Journal of Communication* 22, pp. 89–107.

Chapter 22

THE SIMULTANEOUS RISE AND FALL OF FREE AND PAID NEWSPAPERS IN EUROPE

Piet Bakker

Introduction

Traditional paid newspapers, always a stronghold of journalism, have lost circulation and readership in almost every Western country in the last decade (*World Press Trends*, 2007). Other media like commercial television and Internet compete for the attention of the audience, but newspapers themselves have also changed. They launched online versions and spin offs, while many titles are now printed in smaller formats, particularly in the North Western part of Europe. The most recent development is the rise of free daily newspapers. All over Europe free dailies were introduced in little more than a decade, leading to a total market share of more than 25 per cent in 2007. In four countries more free than paid newspapers are distributed while in more than a dozen countries the best-read paper is a free daily.

This article focuses on the rise of free daily newspaper circulation and the possible effects on the decline in paid circulation in Europe where two-thirds of the total circulation of free dailies is distributed. If there has been substitution, it would mean that readers have moved to "lighter" products in terms of news coverage in a number of ways. Free newspapers offer less news than paid papers. Free dailies, moreover, are published as tabloids or even smaller formats; the vast majority is only published from Monday till Friday and offer lower pagination than paid papers. During the summer holiday many free dailies, particularly in Southern Europe, cease publishing altogether. Free papers also rely more on press agencies' material than paid papers who originate more of their news in house. The number of journalists employed is smaller and less experienced (younger) than that of paid newspapers. Metro International, for example, responsible for 20 per cent of the world circulation in free newspapers, reported in their 2006 annual report (2007) that there were only 500 journalists working for the 70 editions in 20 countries.

If, on the other hand, there is no relation between the rise in free and the decline in paid circulation, it would mean that free dailies find an audience that is not reached by paid papers, and although they provide these readers with less news than paid papers, without free dailies these readers would not read newspapers at all.

The aim of this article is to map the development of the European newspaper market with special emphasis on both paid and free dailies, to explain the rise of this new form of newspaper, and to assess whether there is a relation between the emerging new free daily newspapers and the declining circulation of paid newspapers.

Literature Review and Theoretical Framework

Research on free newspapers is relatively scarce, probably because of the relatively recent introduction of this medium. The studies available are often limited to the introduction period (Arnoud and Peyrègne, 2002; Bakker, 2002; Picard, 2001; Vogel, 2001) or to specific regions like Sweden (Wadbring, 2003, 2007; Wadbring and Weibull, 2000), Switzerland (Bachman et al., 2001; Haas, 2005), Spain (Sporstøl, 2003), Germany (Holznagel, 2006), Chile (Larenas Martinez et al., 2002), Italy (De Chiara, 2002), Denmark (Bakholdt Andersen and Husted Rasmussen, 2007) or France (Trouniard, 2004).

Substitution is hardly considered. Wadbring (2002), however, tracks circulation of Stockholm papers (the first free commuter daily *Metro* was published in Stockholm in 1995) back to 1990 and concludes that circulation of three leading dailies was already declining between 1990 and 1995 and did not suffer more after 1995. Focusing on Göteborg between 1996 and 2004 Wadbring (2007) again found little substitution. Picard (2001) hypothesises that free papers mainly serve readers who normally read newspapers only occasionally, thereby also suggesting modest substitution at the most. In 2004 Bakker calculated that the four national paid morning newspapers in the Netherlands lost 25 per cent of their single copy sales to free newspapers. Single copy sales, however, are only responsible for 10 per cent of the total circulation of paid papers making total substitution less than 3 per cent. The total circulation of free dailies was much higher than the total loss of paid papers, meaning that reading both free and paid newspapers or reading only free papers was much more common than substitution. Also Röper (2006) claims that substitution on the readers' market is minimal, although there might be competition and some substitution on the advertising market. The report *N2 Newspaper Next; the Transformation Project* (The American Press Institute, 2006), however, claims that substitution by free papers may be modest initially but eventually increases. This hypothesis is based on theories of disruptive innovation by Christensen (1997). There is, however, evidence that free newspapers compete mostly among themselves; readership of existing titles seems to decline as new titles are introduced, as was reported by Callius and Lithner (2007) for Sweden and by Bakker (2007) for Denmark. In general, substitution is not overwhelmingly supported by research although data on some markets show some substitution while longer-term developments are not yet studied.

Also for other media, substitution is not often found. Dutta-Berman (2004) concludes on the basis of research conducted on traditional broadcast media and new electronic media that complementarily is more likely than substitution. A somewhat similar conclusion was reached by Wolfgang Riepl (1913). He stated after studying 2000 years of media history that media don't disappear although they tend to change in function and use.

From the perspective of paid newspaper publishers, free papers are a threat. A spokesman for Alex Springer, publisher of the European paper with the highest circulation, *Bild Zeitung* in Germany, stated "Jeder Tag ohne Gratis-Zeitung ist ein guter Tag" ("Any day without a free paper is a good day") (*Die Welt, 2005*). Rupert Murdoch, owner of the second biggest European newspaper *The Sun*, estimated that his flagship lost 30,000–40,000 copies because of competition from free daily *Metro* (Cozens, 2005). For these statements there is little empirical evidence, a day without a free paper might be a good day for Springer but *Bild Zeitung* went down in circulation from 4.5 million in 1995 to 3.7 million in 2006—without competition from free dailies. *The Sun* lost half a million copies in circulation before the introduction of free dailies in the United Kingdom (from 4.1 million in 1995 to 3.6 million in 1999) and another half million in the next seven years.

On a theoretical level a direct relation between the rise of free newspapers and the problems of the paid ones is not obvious. It might very well be that free newspapers attract readers that did not read a newspaper before (Bakker, 2007; Wadbring, 2007) and that the decline in circulation of paid newspapers is the result of other forces. In Europe and the United States readership is also declining because young readers do not tend to read newspapers to the same degree as older groups (Lauf, 2001; Meyer, 2004). The percentage of readers below the age of 35 is declining in almost every Western country (*World Press Trends, 1996*–2007). The reasons why young people do not read newspapers could be various, but the growing importance of other media and entertainment sources, like television, computer games, cell phones and the Internet, seem to play a significant role (Dimmick et al., 2004).

There might be other explanatory factors for the success (in terms of circulation) of free dailies as well. Price could play a role as the high cost of paid newspapers might drive substitution. Also the share of single copy sales could be important, as it is easier to stop buying a single copy than to end a yearly subscription. Another aspect could be the mode of delivery, as home delivery of free papers also makes substitution easier. Also, if the content of a free daily is more or less similar to a paid paper, substitution might be more likely. Other aspects, like the nature of the media system (Hallin and Mancini, 2004) do not seem to play an important role as free dailies have gained substantial market shares in almost every European country.

Definition, Method and Data Collection

A free daily newspaper is published at least from Monday till Friday (some titles in Sweden, Denmark, Italy, Iceland and the Netherlands have or had a weekend edition). Tabloid is the most common format, although some smaller formats exist. In the first years, free papers were mainly distributed through public transport systems: subway, trains, buses, airports, and ferries. When competition between free titles increased, alternative ways of distribution are used increasingly: racks in shopping malls, universities, post offices, parking lots, hospitals, filling stations, restaurants and other places where commuters pass like shopping areas. Home delivery is used in some markets in Denmark, the Netherlands, Switzerland and Iceland.

Free commuter dailies were introduced in 1995 in Sweden[1] and were launched in the Czech Republic and Finland in 1997, Hungary and Germany followed in 1998 while in 1999 there were papers in 10 countries. We focus in this research on the period 1995–2006 which means that for every country (except Sweden) we include years with and without free dailies. Wadbring (2003) covered the earlier Swedish years. We limit our research to countries where free papers were introduced before 2005 and have gained a substantial market share—10 per cent or more of total circulation in 2006.

Some countries were excluded from the analysis because of insufficient data. Circulation data for paid newspapers is taken from *World Press Trends* (1996–2007), a yearly publication by the World Association of Newspapers. For all Western European countries, Poland, Hungary and the Czech Republic data are complete. To assess whether free papers have an impact on paid circulation we also use data, if available, from comparable countries without free dailies.

Circulation data of free papers is obtained from various sources. In a growing number of countries, circulation is officially audited by national organisations. When official audited data are absent, data from research reports, the publishers themselves or press releases are used. Publishers of papers with missing data were contacted via e-mail. In a few cases missing circulation data were estimated on the basis of available data from other years.

Table 1 lists the markets studied with market share and the number of titles available. Free newspaper circulation exploded in 2006—Europe saw a rise in circulation of 68 per cent compared to 2005. Growth in 2007, however, is moderate with only 13 per cent.

In Europe four groups of countries are distinguished: Nordic countries, Central Europe (United Kingdom, German-speaking countries, the Netherlands, Belgium), Eastern Europe and Southern Europe. In two groups there is at least one country (almost) without free newspapers. In Germany there were only free papers in the period 1998–2001 in four markets (500,000 copies, market share 2 per cent) and some very small papers in 2006

TABLE 1
Free dailies in 17 markets

Country	Introduction of free dailies	Market share in 2006 (%)	No. of titles in 2006
Sweden	February 1995	28	4
Finland	April 1997	10	2
Czech Republic	July 1997	38	4
Hungary	September 1998	19	1
United Kingdom	March 1999	12	9
Netherlands	June 1999	19	4
Switzerland	December 1999*	34	6
Spain	February 2000*	55	32
Italy	July 2000	46	9
Belgium	October 2000	14	1
Greece	November 2000	27	4
Poland	November 2000	14	2
Austria	March 2001	26	5
Iceland	April 2001	81	2
Denmark	September 2001	62	11
France	February 2002	24	8
Portugal	November 2004	36	3

*In Switzerland a local door-to-door free paper with a modest circulation was published in Zurich from 1995 to 1999; free commuter dailies were introduced in 1999. In Spain a small free local daily was launched in 1992 in Valencia. Free commuter dailies were introduced in 2000.
Sources: *World Press Trends* (2007) (total market), own research for free titles.

(120,000 copies, market share less than 1 per cent), while Luxembourg (until 2007) and Norway have no free dailies. In the southern group, Portugal saw free papers only at the very end of 2004. In the Eastern Europe group we have no country without free newspapers with full data available.

The differences between these groups are not only based on geographic considerations. Newspaper reading differs in these groups from very high in the Nordic countries to low in the southern part of Europe. In Eastern Europe, however, reading habits differ, with Poland and Hungary having low readership figures compared to the Czech Republic (Table 2). We use readership data from 2001 and 2002 because after these years sometimes readership data for all newspapers (including free ones) were used.

Paid Circulation

In Europe,[2] circulation of paid dailies has decreased by an average 14 per cent between 1995 and 2006. In the two largest markets, Germany and the United Kingdom, the drop in circulation has been even more dramatic: 17 per cent in Germany and 19 per cent in the United Kingdom. The rest of the top five markets performed somewhat better. In France circulation was down by 12 per cent, in Italy by 7 per cent while Spain saw a small decline (−3 per cent). Along with the United Kingdom and Germany, the Netherlands, Denmark, Greece and Luxemburg also lost considerably more than average, while Austria, Ireland and Portugal saw circulation increase. In Austria, however, a large part of the circulation was not officially audited for some years while the increase in 2006 can be attributed to the introduction of a new title—the nine leading titles in Austria have lost 12 per cent of their circulation since 1995. In Ireland UK-papers have launched Irish

TABLE 2
Daily reach of newspapers, 2001–2 (%)

Nordic countries		Middle Europe		Eastern Europe		Southern Europe	
Sweden	88.0						
Finland	86.0						
Norway	86.0						
Iceland	80.5						
		Germany	77.3				
Denmark	74.5						
		Switzerland	73.1				
		Netherlands	66.1				
		Luxembourg	63.5				
		UK national*	50.4				
		Belgium	50.0	Czech Republic	50.3		
						Italy	40.1
						Spain	37.4
						Portugal	37.0
				Poland	31.7	France	31.4
				Hungary	30.1		
						Greece	18.2

*For the UK regional readership is 31.1 per cent. Because of people possibly reading both regional and national papers total readership is higher.
Sources: *World Press Trends* (2002, 2003).

editions while also most other titles have gained circulation in the last years. Poland, the Czech Republic and Hungary saw huge drops in paid circulation. For other Eastern European countries circulation data are missing for several years. For the 21 European countries with complete data there is a clear trend: a 1–2 per cent decline in almost every year with particularly big losses in Central Europe (German-, Dutch- and English-speaking countries) and Eastern Europe (Figure 1).

The Rise of Free Daily Newspapers

Circulation of free daily newspapers in Europe rose from 231,000 in 1995 to 5.5 million in 2000 and 26 million in 2006; at the end of 2007 circulation was 28 million with 130 titles with 350 editions published in 31 countries (Table 3).

In Europe free dailies almost cover the whole continent. The only market gaps in 2007 are Norway, and some Eastern European countries. In Germany free dailies are almost invisible, only distributed on a very small scale in first-class trains and to business-class airline travellers.

After a slow start-up period until 1998, growth in Europe started in 1999 and lasted until 2001. After the recession, circulation remained stable until 2003 after which it increased at a rapid pace (Figure 2). The amount of titles published grew much faster than the number of countries with free dailies, indicating that within these countries competition between free dailies increased. In fact, a free newspaper monopoly in Europe is rare, only found in Belgium, Hungary, the Baltic States and Serbia in 2006.

The total market share of free papers in Europe in 2006 was 24 per cent. The share differs between less than 1 per cent in Germany to more than 80 per cent in Iceland. In three countries more free than paid papers were published on an average weekday in 2006; Portugal joined that group in 2007. In those markets, but also in Greece, Croatia, Hungary, Italy, Latvia, Portugal, France, Switzerland, Slovenia and Sweden, the paper with

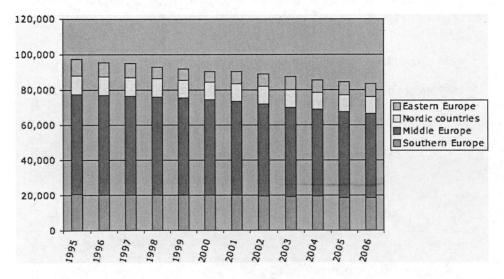

FIGURE 1
Paid circulation in 21 European countries, 1995–2006

TABLE 3
Free daily newspapers (millions) in Europe, 1995–2007

	1995	1996	1997	1998	1999	2000	2001	2002	2003	2004	2005	2006	2007
Circulation	231	249	558	918	2.711	5.542	8.071	8.851	8.768	11.109	15.400	26.280	28.862
Countries	2	2	4	6	10	14	17	16	16	19	24	29	31
Titles	2	2	4	6	16	29	35	35	40	63	81	129	133
Editions	4	3	5	8	25	46	61	70	83	128	200	313	338

the highest circulation is a free title. For Serbia and Russia no market share can be calculated because there is no information on paid circulation.

Substitution

In the Nordic countries (Table 4), free dailies were introduced in Sweden in 1995. As noted above, Wadbring (2003) found that in Stockholm circulation was already dropping before 1995, this trend accelerated in 1996 but although circulation and market share of free papers increased, circulation of paid papers kept reducing at a moderate level of 1–2 per cent and it stabilised between 2001 and 2004. In the last two years a small decrease is evident. In Finland the same pattern emerges: a modest decline in the year before the introduction with no additional decline subsequently.

In Denmark, a country with a high market share for free papers, the picture seems somewhat different because the decline is higher than in the two other countries, but it should be noted that in the years before the introduction of free papers, circulation also declined. Consequently, if there is an effect, it is only modest. Iceland, however, shows a different pattern. From the beginning a high market share of free papers and a steady and substantial circulation decline of the paid press. It is likely that substitution is evident here. Also in Norway, a country without free papers, circulation went down mostly in the last four years, the period when other countries in the same group also lost more than before.

In Eastern Europe the picture is slightly blurred by sudden shifts in paid circulation in the Czech Republic and Poland. There is, however, no clear indication of dropping circulation because of free papers. In all three countries paid circulation took substantial hits before the introduction of free papers (Table 5).

In Central Europe the picture is more consistent. In the Netherlands and Switzerland there is almost no decline in the first three years after the introduction of free papers, but a more substantial decline in the last years. In Belgium there seems to be an impact in the second and third year but less after that. In the United Kingdom, effects—if any—seem to show pretty late: in the fifth and sixth year only. Austrian data are hard to interpret

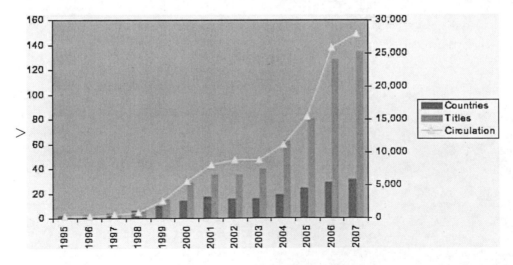

FIGURE 2
Free dailies in Europe, 1995–2006: countries and titles (left axis) and circulation (right axis)

TABLE 4

Free daily newspaper circulation (thousands) in the Nordic countries, 1995–2006

	1995	1996	1997	1998	1999	2000	2001	2002	2003	2004	2005	2006
Sweden												
Paid (%)	4.041	3.874	3.871	3.807	3.721	3.700	3.685	3.671	3.668	3.652	3.603	3.526
−/+		−4	0	−2	−2	−1	0	0	0	0	−1	−2
Free	211	229	228	298	360	772	604	621	628	824	912	1.376
Share free (%)	5	6	6	7	9	17	14	14	15	20	20	28
Finland												
Paid (%)	2.368	2.335	2.324	2.343	2.331	2.304	2.309	2.268	2.243	2.255	2.240	2.224
−/+		−1	0	1	−1	−1	0	−2	−1	1	−1	−1
Free			110	110	242	227	215	209	194	194	260	260
Share free (%)			5	4	9	9	9	8	8	8	10	10
Denmark												
Paid (%)	1.613	1.631	1.617	1.583	1.528	1.481	1.456	1.433	1.381	1.325	1.290	1.268
−/+		1	−1	−2	−3	−3	−2	−2	−4	−4	−3	−2
Free							248	405	422	604	658	2.086
Share free (%)							15	22	23	31	34	62
Iceland												
Paid (%)	98	93	92	94	91	91	79	76	71	63	62	48
−/+		−5	−1	2	−3	0	−13	−4	−7	−11	−2	−23
Free							70	76	86	101	183	202
Share free (%)							47	50	55	62	75	81
Norway												
Paid (%)	2.582	2.578	2.603	2.600	2.591	2.578	2.527	2.524	2.450	2.405	2.338	2.270
−/+		0	1	0	0	−1	−2	0	−3	−2	−3	−3

TABLE 5
Free daily newspaper circulation (thousands) in Eastern Europe, 1995–2006

	1995	1996	1997	1998	1999	2000	2001	2002	2003	2004	2005	2006
Czech Republic												
Paid (%)	2.542	2.224	2.082	1.802	1.764	1.704	1.727	1.690	1.467	1.661	1.742	1.711
−/+		−13	−6	−13	−2	−3	1	−2	−13	13	5	−2
Free			200	200	200	200	174	173	173	173	420	1.028
Share free (%)			9	10	10	11	9	9	11	9	19	38
Hungary												
Paid (%)	1.980	1.646	1.742	1.700	1.659	1.624	1.665	1.595	1.540	1.470	1.460	1.451
−/+		−17	6	2	−2	−2	3	−4	−3	−5	−1	−1
Free				190	207	239	302	322	320	320	341	341
Share free (%)				10	11	13	15	17	17	18	21	19
Poland												
Paid (%)	4.846	4.352	4.194	3.011	2.958	2.820	3.592	3.571	4.077	3.979	4.369	4.462
−/+		−10	−4	−28	−2	−5	27	−1	14	−2	10	2
Free						198	485	412	295	526	526	756
Share free (%)						7	12	10	7	12	11	14

because of the inconsistent behaviour of paid circulation. It is hard to imagine that the drop of more than 700,000 copies within two years can be attributed to the 150,000 (not audited) copies of free daily *U-Express*. Data from Germany and Luxemburg indicate that countries without free newspapers also witness declines in paid circulation (Table 6).

Southern Europe seems hardly affected. In Spain, a country with a high market share of free papers, there seems to be no impact at all while in Greece paid papers seem to perform even better after the introduction of free papers. In Italy there also seems to be no discernible connection between the fortunes of free and paid newspapers while in France there is a decline in 2002: the drop in circulation seems to be accelerating modestly in the last two years. It is hard to make sense of the Portuguese data because of sudden movements in paid circulation, but there is no persuasive evidence of substitution (Table 7).

All European markets taken together show a consistent picture: a steady drop of 1 or 2 per cent in circulation for every year except in 2001 when circulation was stable—a decline which seems not to be affected by the growth in free circulation that differs very much over the years (Figure 3).

Limitations of the Study

Although substitution on a national level in most European countries is not likely, it could still be that individual titles are affected by free competitors, especially in markets with a high penetration of free newspapers, like most European capitals and other major metropolitan areas. Further research should focus on these markets and also distinguish between morning and afternoon markets. This is complex since such research involves more than a dozen markets within one country (like in the United Kingdom, France, Italy and Spain) while detailed information on these local markets is not available in many cases.

In this study free and paid circulations were compared, but circulation of paid papers does not equal *paid circulation*. The circulation reported in *World Press Trends* includes in almost every case also *unpaid* circulation of paid papers. To measure market shares this total circulation is a reliable indicator. To assess substitution it would be better to measure only paid circulation, but these data are not available for the vast majority of the markets.

In this study, moreover, we focused on circulation substitution. Further research would benefit if also readership substitution would be analysed.

Conclusion and Discussion

Free papers are attracting substantial audiences while paid papers in almost every market face a decline in circulation. Free newspapers are apparently successful where traditional paid newspapers have been struggling to sustain circulation. In particular, it seems that traditional papers have problems attracting the younger audience (Lauf, 2001). Free newspapers, however, seem to be quite successful in reaching this age group (Bakker, 2007; *Pressevielfalt Schweiz*, 2007).

In the results there is actually only one clear example of substitution: Iceland. In some markets like Denmark, the Netherlands and Switzerland, and maybe in Belgium and France, there are indications that free papers had some (minimal) impact. The results from

TABLE 6

Free daily newspaper circulation (thousands) in Middle Europe, 1995–2006

	1995	1996	1997	1998	1999	2000	2001	2002	2003	2004	2005	2006
Netherlands												
Paid (%)	4.658	4.658	4.652	4.421	4.374	4.323	4.375	4.311	4.204	4.061	3.912	3.831
−/+		0	0	−5	−1	−1	1	−1	−2	−3	−4	−2
Free					515	694	795	670	655	698	870	881
Share free (%)					11	14	15	13	13	15	18	19
Switzerland												
Paid (%)	2.721	2.715	2.711	2.676	2.679	2.666	2.634	2.594	2.539	2.486	2.405	2.344
−/+		0	0	−1	0	0	−1	−2	−2	−2	−3	−3
Free					346	787	728	663	563	564	784	1.232
Share free (%)					11	23	22	20	18	18	25	34
United Kingdom												
Paid (%)	19.742	19.226	18.994	18.666	18.839	18.609	18.297	18.349	17.250	16.485	16.494	16.056
−/+		−3	−1	−2		−1	−2	0	−6	−4	0	−3
Free					321	820	837	832	827	1052	1167	2144
Share free (%)					2	4	4	4	5	6	7	12
Belgium												
Paid (%)	1.628	1.621	1.602	1.588	1.564	1.568	1.531	1.475	1.478	1.486	1.466	1.424
−/+		0	−1	−1	−2	0	−2	−4	0	1	−1	−3
Free						160	159	196	203	220	227	227
Share free (%)						9	9	12	12	13	13	14
Austria												
Paid (%)	2088	2382	2500	2669	2896	2503	2151	2137	2126	2144	2153	2356
−/+		14	5	7	9	−14	−14	−1	−1	1	0	9
Free							150	150	150	150	200	815
Share free (%)							7	7	7	7	8	26
Germany												
Paid (%)	25.557	25.456	25.260	25.016	24.565	23.946	23.838	23.267	22.571	22.095	21.543	21.091
−/+		0	−1	−1	−2	−3	0	−2	−3	−2	−2	−2
Luxemburg												
Paid (%)	135	135	121	124	124	120	120	118	115	115	115	114
−/+		0	−10	2	0	−3	0	−2	−3	0	0	−1

TABLE 7

Free daily newspaper circulation (thousands) in Southern Europe, 1995–2006

	1995	1996	1997	1998	1999	2000	2001	2002	2003	2004	2005	2006
Spain												
Paid (%)	4.237	4.180	4.265	4.300	4.173	4.261	4.274	4.157	4.185	4.240	4.200	4.110
−/+		−1	2	1	−3	2	0	−3	1	1	−1	−2
Free						270	1.026	1.071	1.541	1.878	3.499	5.078
Share free (%)						6	19	20	27	31	45	55
Greece												
Paid (%)	728	758	719	672	637	681	671	628	622	618	593	593
−/+		4	−5	−7	−5	7	−1	−6	−1	−1	−4	0
Free						125	101	88	215	217	217	227
Share free (%)						16	13	12	26	26	27	28
Italy												
Paid (%)	5.977	5.890	5.894	5.889	5.914	6.073	6.057	5.806	5.726	5.737	5.739	5.569
−/+		−1	0	0	0	3	0	−4	−1	0	0	−3
Free						400	1.729	2.025	1.507	1.805	2.493	4.696
Share free (%)						6	22	26	21	24	30	46
France												
Paid (%)	8.770	8.656	8.498	8.593	8.447	8.423	8.429	8.151	8.037	7.934	7.807	7.686
−/+		−1	−2	1	−2	0	0	−3	−1	−1	−2	−2
Free								938	989	1.363	1.485	2.491
Share free (%)								10	11	15	16	24
Portugal												
Paid (%)	610	697	634	673	686	556	614	551	571	593	570	621
−/+		14	−9	6	2	−19	10	−10	4	4	−4	9
Free										200	251	347
Share free (%)										25	31	36

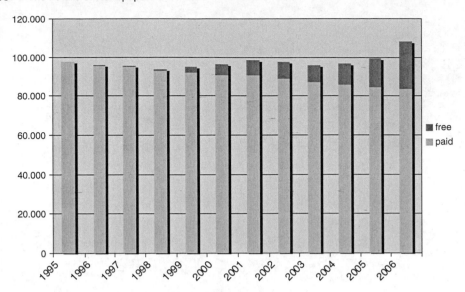

FIGURE 3
Paid and free circulation in 21 European countries

Eastern Europe are inconclusive. Substitution seems even more unlikely when we look to countries without free papers, also in those markets paid circulation declines.

Free newspapers depend only on advertising revenues. There is ample evidence that the state of the economy (recessions, upheavals—measured as changes in Gross Domestic Product) and advertising expenditures are related (Jones, 1985; Swerdlow and Blessios, 1993; Van der Wurff et al., 2008). The state of the economy could therefore be a predictor for the number of launches in a given period. Almost every country saw GDP decline in 2001–3 compared to the years before (OECD, 2005, p. 30). These same years show the slowest growth in free newspaper circulation as well (see Figure 2).

Pricing, distribution and quality of content may play a role in Denmark and Iceland. Denmark has the highest (absolute) newspaper prices in the world (*World Press Trends*, 2007) while free dailies in Iceland are both home delivered and offer a quality that could be compared to some paid dailies: *Frettabladid* is delivered to most homes in the capital and the surrounding area seven days a week and often counts more than 80 pages.

The fact that younger readers in particular do not turn to paid newspapers because there are so many other alternatives is probably a better explanation for the decline in paid circulation than the advance of free papers. For the markets studied there are more newspapers distributed in 2006 than in 1995. There is also evidence that these papers are actually read—both by readers that read paid papers as well as by new readers. In Belgium 7 per cent of the newspaper readers (370,000) only read a free daily, in the Netherlands more than a million readers (8 per cent of the population) only read free newspapers (Bakker, 2007).

Two problems emerge for researchers. The first is that we do not know much about the content of free papers. They lack weekend editions, their format is different while the page count is lower than that of paid newspapers—but is there also less diversity, less coverage of politics or foreign affairs. These questions are mostly unanswered until recently.

The second problem is that we do not know how readers appreciate free dailies, or whether they trust them and whether they serve social and political functions for readers. Newspapers were always considered to be a medium that provided society with a wide choice of news, information and opinions, and served as a platform for different groups. Their importance was also related to their availability to many, to a wide choice of different titles, and the space they devoted to political issues and other content important for modern societies (McQuail, 2005). A decline in circulation of paid papers could be interpreted as a decline of their societal influence. It is not clear, however, whether free newspapers can play the same role.

NOTES

1. Some free dailies were introduced before 1995; in Australia (1906), the United States (1971), Brazil (1974), Spain (1992) and Russia (1992). These, however, did not have the features of the Stockholm *Metro* and their introduction did not lead to the epidemic spread of free dailies like *Metro* did.
2. For 21 European countries with (almost) complete data for the whole period. For Luxembourg one missing year was estimated, for Greece the 2005 data were also used for 2006 because of inconsistent measurements. Not included are the former Yugoslavian and Russian Federation countries, Albania, Turkey and Slovakia.

REFERENCES

ARNOUD, VALÉRIE and PEYRÈGNE, VINCENT (2002) *Free Newspapers—an international market survey*, Ifra Special Report 6.25, http://www.ifra.com, accessed 20 May 2002.

BACHMAN, A., BRANDER, CHANTAL and LENZ, SARAH (2001) *Gratiszeitungen im Raum Zürich; Eine Befragung der Leserinnen und Leser*, Zurich: Universität Zurich, IPMZ.

BAKHOLDT ANDERSEN, MARIE and HUSTED RASMUSSEN, CHRISTOFFER (2007) "Det Danske Marked For Gratisaviser" ["The Danish Market for Free Newspapers"], Thesis, Copenhagen Business School.

BAKKER, PIET (2002) "Free Daily Newspapers; Business Models and Strategies", *Journal of Media Management* 4, pp. 180–7.

BAKKER, PIET (2007) "Free Newspaper Readership", in: *Worldwide Readership Research Symposia Vienna 2007*, Harrow, UK: Worldwide Readership Research Symposium/Ipsos, pp. 63–74.

CALLIUS, PETER and LITHNER, ANDERS (2007) "Daily Reach and Beyond", in: *Worldwide Readership Research Symposia Vienna 2007*, Harrow, UK: Worldwide Readership Research Symposium/Ipsos, pp. 357–72.

CHRISTENSEN, CLAYTON (1997) *The Innovator's Dilemma: when new technologies cause great firms to fail*, Boston: Harvard Business School Press.

COZENS, CLAIRE (2005) "Young People Shunning Papers, Warns News Corp Boss", *The Guardian*, 7 June, www.guardian.co.uk/media/2005/jun/07/newscorporation.pressandpublishing, accessed 20 November 2007.

DE CHIARA, ARIANNA FABIANA (2002) "Leggo City in Metro: viaggio nel fenomeno della free press" ["Leggo City in Metro; a travel through the phenomenon of free dailies"], Thesis, Rome.

DIE WELT (2005) "Alex Springer plant 'Gratissimo' als Abwehrmaßnahme" ["Alex Springer plans 'Gratissimo' as defense"], 12 September, http://www.welt.de/data/2005/09/12/773738. html, accessed 13 September 2005.

DIMMICK, JOHN, CHEN, YAN and LI, ZHAN (2004) "Competition Between the Internet and Traditional Media: the gratification-opportunities niche dimension", *The Journal of Media Economics* 17(1), pp. 19–33.

DUTTA-BERMAN, MOHAN J. (2004) "Complementarity in Consumption of News Types Across Traditional and New Media", *Journal of Broadcasting & Electronic Media* 48(1), pp. 41–60.

HAAS, MARCUS (2005) *Die geschenkte Zeitung: Bestandsaufnahme und Studien zu einem neuen Pressetyp in Europa* [*The Free Paper: description and studies on a new press type*], Münster: Lit. Verlag.

HALLIN, DANIEL C. and MANCINI, PAOLO (2004) *Comparing Media System: three models of media and politics*, Cambridge: Cambridge University Press.

HOLZNAGEL, BERND (2006) "Gratiszeitungen—ein Verstoß gegen die Pressefreiheit? Befunde eines Rechtsgutachtens" [Free Dailies a Threath to the Freedom of the Press? Analysis of a law case], *Media Perspektiven* 10, pp. 529–37.

JONES, JOHN PHILIP (1985) "Is Total Advertising Going Up or Down?", *International Journal of Advertising* 4, pp. 47–64.

LARENAS MARTINEZ, MARICELA RAMOZ FLORES, CLAUDIA and SIEGEL SILVA, MARIÁ PIÁ (2002) "El Fenomeno de los Diarios Gratuitos" ["The Phenomenon of the Free Daily Newspapers"], Thesis, Santiago, http://www.udp.cl/comunicacion/publicaciones/periodismo/t2002/Larenas_Ramos_y_Siegel.pdf, accessed 20 September 2004.

LAUF, EDMUND (2001) "The Vanishing Young Reader: sociodemographic determinants of newspapers use as a source of political information in Europe 1980–98", *European Journal of Communication* 16, pp. 233–43.

MCQUAIL, DENIS (2005) *McQuail's Mass Communication Theory*, 5th edn, London: Sage.

METRO INTERNATIONAL (2007) *Annual Report 2006*, Luxembourg: Metro International S.A.

MEYER, PHILIP (2004) *The Vanishing Newspaper: saving journalism in the information age*, Minnesota: University of Missouri Press.

OECD (2005) *OECD Factbook 2005*, Paris: OECD.

PICARD, ROBERT G. (2001) "Strategic Responses to Free Distribution Daily Newspapers", *International Journal on Media Management* 2(III), pp. 167–72.

PRESSEVIELFALT SCHWEIZ, EIN ÜBERBLICK (2007) Schweizerische Eidgenossenschaft: Neuchâtel.

RIEPL, WOLFGANG (1913) *Das Nachrichtenwesen des Altertums mit besonderer Rücksicht auf die Römer* [*News in Early Times, with Special Focus on the Romans*], Leipzig: Teubner.

RÖPER, HORST (2006) "Gratiszeitungen und etablierte Zeitungsverlage: (Mögliche) Effekte eines neuen Pressetyps" ["Free Dailies and Incumbent Publishers: (possible) effects of a new press format"], *Media Perspektiven* 10, pp. 521–8.

SPORSTØL, ELLEN (2003) "Free Papers in Spain: 20 minutes of fame or here to stay?", Thesis, Norwegian School of Management.

SWERDLOW, ROBERT A. and BLESSIOS, V. I. (1993) "A Model for Predicting Advertising Expenditures: an inter-industry comparison", *International Journal of Advertising* 12, pp. 143–53.

THE AMERICAN PRESS INSTITUTE (2006) *N2 Newspaper Next; the Transformation Project*, Reston (USA): The American Press Institute.

TROUNIARD, AMELIE (2004) "Les bouleversements des champs organisationnels: quelles leçons tirer de la Presse Quotidienne Parisienne?", paper presented to the XIIIème Conférence de l'Association Internationale de Management Stratégique Normandie, Vallée de Seine, 2–4 June 2004.

VAN DER WURFF, RICHARD, BAKKER, PIET and PICARD, ROBERT (2008) "Economic Growth and Advertising Expenditures in Different Media in Different Countries", *Journal of Media Economies* 21(1), pp. 28–52.

VOGEL, ANDREAS (2001) "Die tägliche Gratispresse: Ein neues Geschäftsmodell für Zeitungen in Europa" ("Daily Free Newspapers: a new business model for newspapers in Europe"), *Media Perspektiven* 11, pp. 576–84.

WADBRING, INGELA (2003) *En tidning i tiden; Metro och den svenska dagstidningsmarknaden [A Paper for This Time: Metro on the Swedish newspaper market]*, Göteborg: Institutionen för Journalistik och Masskommunikation.

WADBRING, INGELA (2007) "The Role of Free Dailies in a Segregated Society", *Nordicom Review* Jubilee Issue, pp. 135–47.

WADBRING, INGELA and WEIBULL, LENNART (2000) "Metro on the Swedish Newspaper Market", *Mediatique* 20, http://www.comu.ucl.ac.be/ORM/Mediatique/metro.htm, accessed 13 December 2001.

WORLD PRESS TRENDS (1996–2007) Paris: World Association of Newspapers.

Chapter 23

OBITUARIES FOR SALE
Wellspring of cash and unreliable testimony

Nigel Starck

Life Stories at a Price

The mortuary hostess of Evelyn Waugh's *The Loved One*, a satire on the more extreme aspects of America's funeral industry, offers these services to the clients of the mythical *Whispering Glades*:

> Our crematory is on scientific principles, the heat is so intense that all inessentials are volatilized ... Normal disposal is by inhumement, entombment, inurnment, or immurement, but many people lately just prefer insarcophagusment. That is *very* individual. (Waugh, 1966, p. 37)

The paid obituaries of today's American and Canadian press furnish a reprise of that extravagant language and a mix of threat and nourishment for the obituary art. They are in essence extended death notices published within classified advertising sections, generally celebratory in tone, sometimes endearing in spirit, wonderfully remunerative to the host newspaper, and yet grossly unreliable as capsules of history. When the "Reverend Doctor" Gregory Wayne Spencer died, in June 2003, *The Fort Worth Star-Telegram* carried a lavish paid obituary, describing him as

> pastor and founder of The Church at Philadelphia ... founder of R.O.C.K. House (Residents of Christ Kingdom—a chemical dependency renewal center), member of the Progressive Gents Social Club and executive producer of *By His Grace* television

ministry on Daystar Television Network . . . a psalmist and composer of 220 religious songs. (*Legacy*, 2003)

Mourners were asked to assemble on the lawns of a Baptist church "as the Spencer white glass horse-drawn chariot, led by the Spencer Celebration Band, arrives with the golden solid bronze couch of Dr Spencer". The good pastor, readers were assured, had on the 24th of June, "surrendered his life into the arms of Jesus" (*Legacy*, 2003). A more clinical, and more reliable, rendition of his life and death included these factors: his honorary doctorate was awarded by a college subsequently forced to close for lack of competence; he was an undertaker suspected of leaking damaging information concerning rival operators to a state investigation agency; he had dominated the Fort Worth market and was trying to break into the Dallas market; he was hog-tied, strangled, gagged and shot in the back of the head in a motel room a few blocks from his fundamentalist church (Carolyn Gilbert, personal communication, 7 July 2003). The paid obituary, predictably, had provided a bowdlerised version for posterity. This obliquity in obituary worries Tom Hobbs (2001), research librarian at the University of South Carolina who serves as archivist for the International Association of Obituarists. Writing in *Grassroots Editor*, an American newspaper industry journal, he has registered his concern at the potential for inaccuracy, exaggeration and deliberate distortion of fact, and the consequent disservice to history in print.

There is some considerable disservice, too, to the cause of vigorous English expression. Paid obituaries frequently engage in the language of *The Loved One*, actually using "inurnment" (the act of placing an urn, containing the ashes, into a columbarium) and "inhumation" (an inventive, and euphemistic, opposite of "exhumation"). The reader is often told also that the subject was "preceded in death" by a life partner and (not surprisingly) by parents. Yet they are popular, and they are significant suppliers of classified advertising revenue. Consider these purchases, all of recent vintage:

- An indication of the typical cost structure, and of customer expenditure, is found at the *Plain Dealer*, Cleveland's morning newspaper. It charges $44.99 for the first 10 lines, and then $5.86 for each additional line. American society is known for its gregarious and loquacious qualities—so paid obituaries of 50 or so lines (at a total cost of $275) are commonplace. According to the editor of "legitimate" journalism obituaries at the *Plain Dealer*, Alana Baranick, there have been instances of $2000 purchases (personal communication, 21 June 2007).

- The family of Sara Adelaide Hallack bought two full columns of *Dallas Morning News* classified advertising space to relate the life story of her 93 years. It appeared twice, on successive days in June 2002, at a total cost of $2700. Such munificence is not unusual in the Bible Belt (Starck, 2004).

- Some papers are able to fill two or three pages, every day, with paid obituaries. In Utah, the *Salt Lake Tribune* is a notably enthusiastic practitioner of the art. Note (in Figure 1) the high incidence of paired photographs, depicting the "decedent" (as they are known) in youth and in old age. Men, as in the case here of Calvin Ray Hatch (a World War Two B-17 bomber tail-gunner), are often depicted in military uniform. The language tends to the discursive, thereby adding to the expenditure, as demonstrated by this *Salt Lake Tribune* (2002) vignette of Clare F. Jones (who, on the evidence of the text, was surely not a practising Mormon):

FIGURE 1

Tribune tributes. Pages of paid obituaries, such as these in the *Salt Lake Tribune*, have revived the advertising revenue of newspapers across the United States.

She married her military sweetheart, T. Sgt Cyril Jones, and they became the parents of two children ... and they in turn had children ... making six grandchildren and nine great-grandchildren in all. Clare lived a life full of spunk and was feisty to the end. She was a Utah Jazz and Atlanta Braves fan through and through. She never missed an opportunity to play the slots in Wendover [gambling, over the border in Nevada] with her family or friends ... She loved talking on the phone to her two sisters Dozie and Berta.

- In an instance of posthumous vanity publishing, the bereaved family of Charles Henry Lundquist, an entrepreneur and University of Oregon benefactor, bought an entire page in Portland's *Sunday Oregonian* (2006b) for $4700. He is pictured (see Figure 2) three times: in what appears to be a corporate setting, in his World War Two Quartermaster's Corps uniform, and on a visit to Disneyland.
- The family of Carl Millard, a Canadian aviation pioneer, also purchased a whole-page obituary. His appeared in the *Globe and Mail*, a newspaper of some greater influence than the *Sunday Oregonian*; it cost them, in the edition of Saturday 25 November 2006, $30,000 (*Globe and Mail*, 2006b).

Editorial Rewards, Costs to Reputation

Clearly, then, the paid obituary is a lucrative instrument. In discussing the prospects for survival and revival within the context of the future of newspapers, it emerges as a mechanism demanding reflection. The revenue potential is phenomenal, offering a refreshing wellspring of cash when classified advertising is constantly challenged by online competition. As the American journal *U.S. News & World Report* has found: "For many newspapers, charging for obituaries may be the only way to avoid following their readers to the grave" (Noah, 1997).

These pages can also serve as a source for obituaries of the unpaid kind. Indeed, American and Canadian editors draw, cautiously, on such notices for the conventional practice of obituary in the newspaper. When paid obituaries are free of artifice, those editors welcome the flow of information and endorse the means for bereaved families to have a voice. The obituaries editor at Cleveland's *Plain Dealer*, Alana Baranick (personal communication, 21 June 2007), supports their existence because they "are a great source of revenue, relieve the reporting staff of extra responsibilities, and appease the family who want the obit to run exactly as they wrote it". Colin Haskin, who edits a page of considerable editorial presence at Toronto's *Globe and Mail*, has welcomed their emergence in Canada: "I'm a great supporter of the paid obituary. It's human nature ... readers should be allowed to say what they want to say. They get to mention all the grandchildren and all the nurses involved" (Starck, 2006, p. 154). At Dallas's *Morning News*, Joe Simnacher agrees, pointing to the opportunity afforded for reader satisfaction and appeasement: "No problem. It gives them the freedom to say things that can't be said in the news formula" (Starck, 2006, p. 154).

However, the paid variety can create a dilemma for obituary editors in search of material for their columns: to what extent should they believe, and capitalise upon, published sources of information appearing in their own newspapers? There is evidence that the paid obituary can be manipulated for a variety of purposes, as in the divisive

Charles Henry Lundquist

August 1920–November 2006

Charles H. Lundquist dies at 86;

Fostered an entrepreneurial zeal and impetus for mutually beneficial business growth in the San Francisco and Los Angeles County South Bay regions

TRADITIONAL VALUES WITH AN ENTREPRENEURIAL SPIRIT

**Founder and Chairman of the Board – Continental Development Corporation
Naming Benefactor – Charles H. Lundquist College of Business,
University of Oregon, Eugene**

**HIS WORLD WAR II
AND HARVARD
UNIVERSITY YEARS**

HIS EARLY YEARS

**HIS ENTREPRENEURIAL
YEARS**

**HIS CONTINENTAL
DEVELOPMENT
CORPORATION YEARS**

**HIS PHILANTHROPIC
YEARS**

HIS MANY PASSIONS

FIGURE 2

Life story. Charles H. Lundquist's lavish instant biography, in the *Sunday Oregonian*, cost $4700. But did the "typo" in the final headline deck qualify for a subsequent discount?

intent apparent from a series of notices placed in the *Hartford Courant*, Connecticut. It began with a paid obituary for a Palestinian woman, with no connection to Hartford, who had been killed by an Israeli soldier. Gale Courey Toensing, a local newspaper correspondent of Palestinian-Lebanese descent living in Connecticut, admitted that she had placed it "as a political statement" (Weiss, 2002). The Jewish community responded with paid obituaries for two Israeli women killed by a suicide bomber. While the affair appeared to be over by November 2002, Toensing told the *Courant* that she would repeat her actions if she "was moved in the same way again".

A less serious political statement, though expressed in a terribly lame gag, was composed for North Carolina's *Winston-Salem Journal* by John Payne. He wrote (and possibly paid for) his own obituary, declaring: "If you're reading this right now, I guess I'm dead ... I've got some bad news for you ... just as I had always suspected, God is a Republican" (Starck, 2004).

Then there were the conflicting statements made by two paid obituaries in the same edition of the *Dallas Morning News*. Steve Blow, a staff writer, based his entire column one Wednesday morning on the posthumous recognition given in his paper's classified columns to Melodi Dawn Knapp. Melodi, a 27-year-old nurse, had made the news pages in a spectacular way too, when she "died and killed three others while going the wrong way" along a freeway (Blow, 2002). Steve Blow's interest was stimulated by the appearance of two separate obituaries, with references to two funerals and displaying markedly different photographs, which appeared on the same day. The paid notice lodged by her father, a Dallas police officer, carried a glamour image of Melodi when she was 16. In listing the bereaved, it referred only to relatives. It stated that the funeral would be held at a Baptist church the following day.

Hard alongside that notice was a second paid obituary, placed by her mother, depicting Melodi in a scrubbed, wholesome, yet less glamorous fashion. The text had a markedly different emphasis too. There were specific references to "her very best friend", Elizabeth Hudson, and to "her life partner", Tina Merritt. It invited acquaintances to attend a funeral two days later, at Dallas's Cathedral of Good Hope, a church described by *Morning News* columnist Blow as "predominantly gay". His report told of a family divided: parents long divorced; a father who refused to acknowledge his daughter's homosexuality; a mother who accepted it.

Reader confusion of a deliberate kind was generated by a paid obituary, of farcical content and laborious delivery, appearing in three successive editions of California's *Sacramento Bee*. It said that Paul Jackson, a shipping pilot, had collapsed and died while guiding a container vessel along Oregon's Columbia River. According to the text, he had fallen on the controls, causing the ship to plough into "the combination Sardine Canning & Dynamite Factory on the wharf, resulting in a huge explosion and raining sardines all over the town" (Marcano, 2003). An investigation by the *Sacramento Bee* staff ombudsman found that, although the death was real, the sardine storm was a hoax. The pilot's son confessed to inventing it because, he said, other obituaries in the paper had looked "boring".

Questions arise, accordingly, about the reputation of newspapers which publish these life stories without verifying the content. The paid obituary cannot entirely be trusted. It is in essence a personal and untested statement about a life lived; as such, it is not subject to the regulations that govern the advertising of products and services. Editors drawing on this soft underbelly of the obituary art as a resource, therefore, must beware elision and fabrication. Failed marriages (and the children of those unions) are inevitably overlooked, non-existent degrees are claimed, military service is exaggerated, career achievement is overcooked. By way of contrast, the professional obituarist will always seek independent testimony. Jim Sheeler, whose work for the *Denver Post* and the *Rocky Mountain News* has been recognised with a Pulitzer Prize, epitomises a more pronounced commitment to historicity: "I seek out the evidence of awards. I check with the military on Purple Hearts and I check with universities on degrees" (Starck, 2006, p. 153).

To help writers in this regard, information is shared among members of the International Association of Obituarists and through an online exchange entitled Obituary Forum. In a recent instance of co-operative effort, Trudi Hahn, formerly the principal obituary writer at the *Star Tribune* in Minneapolis, posted advice on the exchange about fake claims of prisoner-of-war status. It followed the publication by a Texas newspaper of an apparently gallant, but thoroughly invented, army career. Hahn's subsequent message contained precise contact details for the Department of Defense Prisoner of War/Missing Personnel Office in Washington, so that any future claims of this type could more readily be subjected to verification (*Obituary Forum*, 2007). The obituarists had been told enough lies.

Words and Dollars

Although the paid obituary has not yet established its presence outside North America, it is apparent that classified advertising in general is extending its range elsewhere. In the British and Australian press, generous declarations of affection are now encountered on Valentine's Day. Announcements of birth and death are frequently illustrated by photographs and by clip art, and quests for romance and dalliance are proposed in print. With such readiness to change and relax the medium, it would seem that obituaries—as a source of revenue—might be ripe for exploitation at large.

Putting aside for the moment those concerns about textual mendacity, one encounters a compelling truth in terms of cash flow. In Portland, the *Sunday Oregonian* (2006b)—as we have seen—pocketed $4700 for the instant biography of Charles H. Lundquist (Figure 2). An outmoded series of headline decks told readers that Mr Lundquist had "fostered an entrepreneurial zeal and impetus for mutually beneficial business growth in the San Francisco and Los Angeles County South Bay regions"; that, through the profits of this entrepreneuring, he was naming benefactor of the Charles H. Lundquist College of Business, University of Oregon, Eugene; and that he espoused "traditional values with an entrepreneurial spirit". Unfortunately, the fifth of those decks contained a "typo": he was described as "chariman [*sic*] of the board".

While its expression is not as exaggerated as that employed in *The Loved One*, there are recurring strains of hyperbole and breathless narrative on the Lundquist page. A legitimate obituary would surely have excised such terms as "very distinguished and uniquely efficient", "bravely and confidently investing in a new greater vision", and "fruitful, giving and inspirational". Every detail of an 86-year life was recounted in the prolix. He was a clerical officer in the Q stores of Chicago during World War Two, but the readers were still assured that "Chuck" was awarded the American Theatre of Operations Ribbon and the Victory Medal. "Chuck" liked luxury cruising, deep-sea fishing, and spaghetti westerns. He had been, inevitably, a "tender husband", possessed of a "loving" wife and "beautiful grandchildren", and a "compassionate and caring friend to many". He also gave $11 million to his alma mater: or, as the obituary could not resist putting it, his "beloved" alma mater.

So what else confronted obituary readers of the *Sunday Oregonian* in that edition of 19 November 2006? The section entitled "Obituaries" ran to five pages:

- The first of them contained a legitimate obituary, of about 1000 words with five photographs (Martinez Starke 2006). The text, in this instance telling the life story of an ambulance paramedic, offered some moments of candour: it said that he contracted his fatal dose of hepatitis C from a needlestick accident, and that he had a "brusque demeanour" which led to confrontations with doctors.
- Towards the bottom of that first page, and continuing on the fourth, were 23 short obituaries written in a formulaic style. Their main purpose, apart from conveying a brief biography, was to provide funeral service information and tell mourners where to send their donations (or "remembrances", as they are called in this newspaper). This is a free service offered by the *Oregonian*.
- Then there are the paid obituaries, stretching on that day of Charles Lundquist's generous notice, to three full pages. Those for Polly Ann Cohan and Zean Raymond Moore (*Sunday Oregonian*, 2006a) offered typical examples. Each ran to about six inches over two columns, and was illustrated with a pair of photographs (the Moore obituary used the favoured male combination of wartime uniformed youth and peacetime old-age). The cost of each: approximately $450. Mr Moore, incidentally, had a rather more adventurous war than Mr Lundquist the quartermaster's clerk; he flew, and somehow survived, 92 bombing missions.

Just as the *Oregonian* enjoyed a financially rewarding Sunday, over the border in Canada the *Globe and Mail* recorded an even more profitable experience the following Saturday. The Carl Millard full-page account, for which the paper charged $30,000, was an odd affair. There were five photographs, but no captions, so the reader had to assume— for example—that a woman so depicted was the subject's wife, Della; the relentless biographical detail made reading difficult; and right at the end there was the banal assertion that, in death, Carl Millard had been reunited with his wife: "The Dynamic Duo are back together to start the next leg of the Great Journey. They'll probably change a few things along the way" (*Globe and Mail* 2006b). In short, it is not journalism. But it is, undeniably, remunerative.

It is also indicative, though decidedly at the top end, of an advertising feature which is as common in Canada as it is in the United States. On that same day, the *Globe and Mail* (2006a) filled a dozen columns with more modest life histories. They included those of Mildred Isabel Hall, a nursing sister "famous for her duck dinners and lemon pies", and Kimberley Ann Hiltz, who worked in marketing and was devoted to "her precious Golden Retriever". For notices such as these, the *Globe and Mail* charged: $9.21 per line for a single appearance; $8.70 per line for two appearances; and $7.74 per line for three. In addition, inclusion of a photograph cost $175 and a 6% tax was applied, producing a standard charge of about $575. Such posthumous vignettes are found every day, in virtually every paper, across North America.

Conclusion

The paid obituary has established itself as a source of advertising revenue in the United States and Canada. Doubts persist, however, concerning its lack of regulatory control and its capacity for deliberate misrepresentation. Although this phenomenon has so far not surfaced within other newspaper markets, it is apparent that classified columns at large are extending their scope. British and Australian newspapers experience an annual explosion of love-in-print on Valentine's Day; in recent years, too, illustrated birth and death announcements have become commonplace, along with a vigorous quest (in type) for partnership and personal encounter. It would take some loss-leading, and some courage, to extend such developments to include the paid obituary. Nevertheless, in the realm of unexplored opportunity for increasing classified revenue, it surely warrants consideration. That process of reflection might yet generate the earning power achieved on the other side of the Atlantic.

REFERENCES

BLOW, STEVE (2002) "Dueling Obituaries Reveal Depths of Tragedy", *Dallas Morning News*, 5 June, p. 19.

GLOBE AND MAIL (2006a) "Mildred Isabel Hall", "Kimberley Ann Hiltz", 25 November, p. S8.

GLOBE AND MAIL (2006b) "Carl Millard", 25 November, p. S9.

HOBBS, THOMAS C. (2001) "A Librarian Looks at Obituaries", *Grassroots Editor* 42(3), pp. 1, 5.

LEGACY (2003) "Gregory Wayne Spencer", http://www.legacy.com, accessed 11 July 2007.

MARCANO, TONY (2003) "The Ombudsman: when sardines fall from heavens, do ad guidelines too?", *Sacramento Bee*, http:www.sacbee.com, accessed 26 April 2007.

MARTINEZ STARKE, AMY (2006) "Sirens in the Night Called to Paramedic", *Sunday Oregonian*, 19 November, p. E1.

NOAH, TIMOTHY (1997) "For Newspapers, the Obit Pages Aren't Sad; the nation's dailies turn bad demographics into a good business opportunity", *U.S. News & World Report* 122(13), p. 58.

OBITUARY FORUM (2007) "Trudi Hahn", http://www.obituaryforum.blogspot.com, accessed 11 May 2007.

SALT LAKE TRIBUNE (2002) "Obituaries", 22 December, p. B8.

STARCK, NIGEL (2004) "Writes of Passage: a comparative study of newspaper obituary practice in Australia, Britain, and the United States", PhD thesis, Flinders University.

STARCK, NIGEL (2006) *Life After Death*, Melbourne: Melbourne University Press.

SUNDAY OREGONIAN (2006a) "Polly Ann Cohan", "Zean Raymond Moore", 19 November, p. E2.

SUNDAY OREGONIAN (2006b) "Charles Henry Lundquist", 19 November, p. E3.

WAUGH, EVELYN (1966) *The Loved One*, Harmondsworth: Penguin.

WEISS, TARA (2002) "Death Notices, Politics Mixed", *Hartford Courant*, http://www.ctnow.com, accessed 22 April 2007.

Chapter 24

FROM NEWSPAPERS TO MULTIMEDIA GROUPS
Business growth strategies of the regional press in Spain

Miguel Carvajal and **José A. García Avilés**

Introduction

The Spanish regional newspaper industry enjoyed a long period of economic boom up to 2004. Signs of advertising slowdown and readership loss have become evident since then. The rise of free newspapers, the Internet and the new audiovisual platforms are undermining the news and advertising hegemony of regional media. Publishers have attempted to defend their market positions, among other responses, with a corporate diversification strategy in the audiovisual industry and the development of online editions. However, companies with a multimedia business portfolio face important challenges in order to be more efficient in their new businesses, such as finding possible synergies as a result of newsroom convergence or selling common advertising packages. And their regional audiovisual businesses do not yet operate as efficiently as national commercial television channels.

The purpose of this article is to explore Spanish regional publishing companies' strategic responses to the above threats. Multimedia diversification strategy, platform convergence and online development are among the most significant responses adopted by publishers. To a large extent, their reaction has been triggered by technological convergence and the absence of legal obstacles. This trend is examined with a comparative analysis of two large Spanish regional media groups, Vocento and Prensa Ibérica. We look at the different steps they have taken in order to become strong multimedia groups in their markets. Both companies own radio and television stations which intend to broaden the audience of their newspapers. They have used their horizontally integrated corporate structures, so as to diminish the effects of weak performance in the local television market, through economies and synergies.

Theoretical Background

Multimedia diversification is one of most frequent growth strategies of media companies. This strategy has been widely studied in the field of media economics. In this paper, we focus on the managerial side, as a strategic response to market competition. Both audiovisual diversification and cross-media strategies have been examined from the market structure and company performance viewpoints.

Albarran and Dimmick (1999) analysed the levels of "within and across industry-concentration" in the communication industry. Diversification strategy has been adopted by media companies but with regard to cross-media ownership of television *and* newspapers there is no compelling evidence that diagonal integration brings about inherent synergies, economies of scale or other economic benefits (Doyle, 2000). An analysis of the performance of diversification might require further study with a longer time period (Kolo and Vogt, 2003). In fact, both authors argue that the next generation, the so-called "convergence generation" will probably obtain better results from those strategic options.

Deregulation and the convergence of different media, information and communications markets have led the corporate diversification strategy (Van Kranenburg, 2004; Wirth and Bloch, 1995). Technological convergence facilitates the creation of new operational synergies between newspapers and broadcasting (Doyle, 2000). Companies with a multimedia business portfolio are able to implement convergence processes (Dennis, 2006; Gordon, 2003), so as to integrate the various media platforms.

According to Dennis, media executives who have developed convergence strategies consider three options: "(1) operational convergence wherein internal infrastructures conform to digital standards; (2) cross-platform marketing in which companies leverage their platforms and repurpose old content; and (3) delivering on-demand content in addressable form for viewers and users" (Dennis, 2006). Cross-promotion and content sharing among platforms were the main goals of media diversification. Synergy was the key issue to media conglomerates. However, many of those promises are still questioned and there are no empiric evidences to support this theory (Doyle, 2000).

The cross-media strategy is based on external growth processes, such as acquisition, mergers or joint ventures. The benefits of growth are well known: it provides stability, it reduces competitors' market share, it allows new business opportunities, and it generates internal company promotion. According to Sánchez-Tabernero and Carvajal (2002), diversified companies enjoy three types of advantages: (1) they are able to diversify risks; (2) they enter sectors with potential growth in the advertising and information markets; (3) synergies might be found in several areas, such as content sharing, cross-promotion, advertising commercialization; marketing coordination to share information about readers and integration of production structures.

Technical innovations and the increase of format standardization allow, for example, production of a newspaper and its online edition simultaneously, using a content management system. Intangible resources, such as brands and corporate reputation, could additionally offer scope for economies because of the prospect of transferring them from one business area to another at low marginal costs (Kolo and Vogt, 2003). However, it has not yet been demonstrated that cross-media strategies between print and television are profitable both for the business area and the company (Doyle, 2000). Besides, the coordination of both platforms usually involves high management costs because it is difficult to integrate different journalistic cultures which cater for distinct audiences. In regional markets, it might be possible to mitigate those adverse effects because broadcasting and newspapers are primarily domestic products.

Newspaper companies have historically been the first to initiate diversification because they considered that television and radio were their natural growth markets (Gordon, 2003). In the Spanish regional market, there is a growing trend for newspapers to evolve into multimedia groups. Company managers adopted a corporate focus that has now broadened to embrace business, tactical and operational aspects. In smaller, more versatile companies with a regional multimedia structure, it might be the key to obtain a better performance.

Strategic Responses of Spanish Regional Media

The Spanish regional media market is stronger than the national market. The number of regional newspapers and their circulation figures show its dominance over the national press (Table 1). Besides, regional publishers enjoy greater percentages of advertising incomes, from local and national advertisers interested in their proximity value. Thus, leading media in most cities tend to be local newspapers, which are mostly owned by large companies.

The Spanish regional newspaper market has developed within a mature market dominated by a small number of newspapers chains. Leading newspapers enjoy an excellent economic performance, while their competitors face greater difficulties to achieve economies of scale and other performances. The local media market is very competitive, reflected in the increasing number of mergers and acquisitions in recent years, as newspaper chains vie fiercely to become market leaders.

The traditional publishing landscape has changed significantly during the past decade. The Spanish regional newspaper industry has been the last sector to feel the slowdown of the newspaper readership crisis. In Spain, as in other countries, newspaper market penetration began to decline in the mid-1990s and they have consistently decreased with each subsequent year. The loss of advertising income worsened with the arrival and the consolidation of new platforms, specially the Internet. Advertising

TABLE 1

Spanish newspaper market, 2007

Daily paid newspapers	Number of dailies	Circulation (%)
Regional	84	64.8
National	6	35.2

Source: OJD audit bureau.

migration to the Web is already hitting both smaller advertisers and large global trademarks. It has been predicted that Internet ad spend will grow dramatically in the next years, overtaking radio or outdoor (Zenith Optimedia, 2006).

The wide popularity of the Internet, the booming of the free newspapers distribution and the multiplication of audiovisual media outlets are severely damaging newspapers circulation figures. Daily paid newspapers have lost market leadership, exclusivity as a public service news outlet, immediacy and brand values. In Spain, publishers have regarded free newspapers as a common enemy since 2001. At first, they underestimated their impact; they later attempted to slow down their growth but have finally been obliged to compete with them (Bakker, 2002; Picard, 2001).

Spanish regional newspaper companies face up to the crisis with an unprecedented business activity in several areas. First, publishing companies have followed a corporate diversification strategy increasing their business portfolio in order to become local multimedia groups. They have organized mergers, acquisitions and joint ventures with local television stations in order to compete in the audiovisual market. Secondly, companies with a multimedia business portfolio have invested in their online editions so as to consolidate them as multimedia platforms and users' participation channels. Thirdly, they have set up advertising sales offices to harmonize the commercialization strategy of their media outlets. Fourthly, they have initiated processes of newsroom integration in order to consolidate their weaker platforms, to support the Web as a distribution structure and to reduce costs both in news production and gathering. Finally, the previously competing publishing companies are now cooperating with joint ventures in printing or distribution businesses.

The Cases of Vocento and Prensa Iberica

Two case studies of large-scale publishing companies Vocento and Prensa Iberica (measured in terms of their newspaper portfolios in Spain) have been selected for particular consideration in this paper. According to OJD (circulation audit bureau), they enjoy the highest circulation in the Spanish regional publishing sector. Both companies are highly competitive and are involved in diversification activities.

Editorial Prensa Iberica, one of the largest regional media groups in Spain, was created in 1984, with the acquisition of three large newspapers in Alicante, Valencia and Asturias. Today, the group operates in nine autonomous communities and it owns 15 newspapers, four television stations and three radio stations, together with other publishing ventures and online companies (Table 2). Their regional newspapers achieved a circulation of 319,186 in 2006 (Table 3).

TABLE 2
Regional multimedia portfolio of Vocento and Prensa Ibérica, 2007

	Newspapers	Television	Radio local stations	Online editions
Vocento	12	46	24*	12
Prensa Ibérica	15	4	5	15

*Plus 43 stations with a minority participation.
Source: Companies' annual reports.

TABLE 3

Media audience of Vocento and Prensa Ibérica, 2006

	Circulation	Daily TV audience	Daily radio audience	Online users (Nielsen)
Vocento	751,102	2.7 million	451,000	4.1 million*
Prensa Ibérica	319,186	700,000	–	1 million*

*Monthly unique users estimated (OJD).
Source: OJD, EGM and Sofres audience research.

Vocento is one of the biggest media holdings in Spain, reflecting the merger of two multimedia groups in 2001. Their historical strengths were regional newspapers, but they have pursued an aggressive strategy of diversification towards audiovisual and online media. Vocento currently owns 12 large regional multimedia groups that comprise a newspaper, its online edition, a local radio station, a local television network and an advertising sales company (Table 2). It also owns both local television (*Punto TV*) and radio (*Punto Radio*) networks, also embedded in the Vocento Media Group. Vocento enjoys the largest combined circulation of the Spanish newspaper market (Table 3).

Both companies are family owned and they have been growing with a corporate specialization strategy in the regional newspaper market over the last 20 years. However, they have developed different levels of audiovisual diversification. Vocento's regional newspapers represent the best business area, with a contribution to total EBITDA (Earnings Before Interest, Taxes, Depreciation and Amortization) of 87.6 per cent. The audiovisual business area is less important than print media for Vocento's EBITDA and local television stations still face a negative performance (− 11.7 per cent). Advertising income for regional newspapers is distributed into local advertising expenditure (72 per cent) and national advertising expenditure (28 per cent). Display advertising (48 per cent) and classified ads (19 per cent) support their economic performance.

From Newspapers to Multimedia Groups

The micro study of both companies shows five main tendencies in the Spanish regional newspaper market.

Cross-media Strategy

Vocento was the first Spanish media group that implemented a regional multimedia strategy as its core business in 2001. Publishers developed a multimedia strategy to gain several competitive advantages in their local markets. To achieve these goals, Vocento followed two main tactics: to generate synergies on advertising through coordination and the unification of spaces in all its media outlets, and to consolidate its bargain power in the advertising market as an institution in its local area.

As Figure 1 shows, the number of Vocento's local television stations has increased significantly over the last four years. Punto TV is the brand under which all Vocento's local televisions operate and it comprises 46 local stations that reach about 12 million people throughout Spain, which means they are the leading local television network. Moreover, Vocento launched a national radio network in 2002, which links all its local radio stations and supports them with content and advertising. These media outlets are integrated in

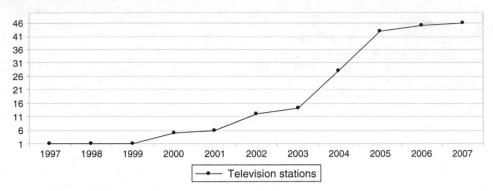

FIGURE 1
Evolution of the number of Vocento's local television stations integrated in the Punto TV network

what management calls "multimedia groups" that comprise a newspaper, its online edition, a local radio station, a local television station and an advertising sales company.

Prensa Iberica has also developed a cross-media strategy although to date it is at an incipient stage. The audiovisual market position of Prensa Iberica is based on production and broadcasting businesses. Until 2007, Prensa Iberica owned just four local television stations but it is expecting to receive several administrative broadcasting licences in the next few months. In 2007, Prensa Iberica launched a brand new company, Prensa Iberica Media, to produce and manage all its local stations. Similar to Vocento, the company aims to develop a radio network in its local newspaper markets. Both Vocento and Prensa Iberica have integrated the newspaper online editions of all their local dailies into their own service provider that syndicates content for their respective newspapers. Management in both companies is investing a great deal of economic resources to improve its technological applications. They have recently signed an agreement with Nielsen Net Ratings to test its monthly average of Web pages and to research their new digital audiences.

Besides cross-promotion and advertising aggregation, local newspapers' online editions are multimedia platforms which generate, distribute and promote audiovisual content. Radio and television newsrooms are often supplying some features and news to improve the online editions. The sites also provide links to Vocento's and Prensa Iberica's other media.

Internet as a Multimedia Platform

Vocento's and Prensa Ibérica's strategy in the Internet market is geared to turning their local online editions into multimedia portals which integrate a wide variety of information and entertainment services. Newspapers' online editions are suitable platforms to distribute multimedia content and the best area to generate content, advertising and marketing synergies. At an early stage, news and editorial content generated by its regional newspapers was useful to build up all its Internet editions. Up to 2005, publishers limited themselves to just publishing the contents of their print editions on their websites and they were hardly innovative. Currently, their cross-media strategy provides their online editions with multimedia packages, online chats, blogs, exclusive online content, video reports and other resources.

Vocento was the first Spanish company to syndicate all its regional newspapers' online editions. It created an in-house service provider, Sarenet, which is also responsible for the design and hosting of all its webs. Vocento's management decided to split off its online editions in order to look for new companies, aiming to consolidate its performance through generating scope economics and several technical synergies. The main operation was carried out in 2007 when Vocento's Internet subsidiary company acquired a classified advertising company which operates in the Internet market, which is increasingly migrating online.

Prensa Iberica also launched its own company, "Recursos en la red" in 2000 to develop products and supply services to its local newspapers' online editions. This company offers a multi-edition system to package and distribute content for all newspaper online editions, as well as to syndicate news and resources for newsrooms.

Through these subsidiary companies, the two main newspaper groups have positioned their local newspapers' online editions as the best multimedia platform to distribute content, which has resulted in improved economic performance in their own businesses. In the case of Vocento, online income represented a 5.8 per cent contribution to Vocento's EBITDA in 2006.

Moreover, they are implementing new applications for Web 2.0, integrating a variety of services devoted to promote readers' participation. Early in 2007, Vocento carried out a redesign of its local newspapers' online editions. Main changes included the enlargement of page width, implementing a horizontal navigator menu as well as new full sections devoted to readers and new tools to enable users' participation and collaboration.

Prensa Iberica also unleashed a redesign of its online editions in July 2007. Prensa Iberica websites offer options for users to get involved in news production at some level (stories, photos, videos). Comment opportunities for the audience are more typical, especially in journalists' blogs. This leadership of newspapers is also found in Web 2.0 services, those that let users connect news stories to websites for the collective sharing of relevant materials (such as Technorati). Actually both Prensa Iberica and Vocento's online newspapers offer these options.

Advertising Packaging and Cross-promotion

Advertising migration to the Web, the popularization of free newspapers and the increasingly audiovisual availability, has fragmented local advertising markets. The marketing of brands combines local and global strategies, which implies important diversification of advertising expenditure. Regional dailies have attempted to defend their market positions as advertising outlets by improving space commercialization with pricing strategies. Therefore multimedia groups are seeking to increase their advertising market share in all their different platforms.

Vocento has used a subsidiary company, CM Vocento, to commercialize its multiple advertising spaces. This company was born with the aim of promoting the commercial area of the parent company's regional newspapers. These aggregated spaces are more competitive in the national market through high bargain power and unified rates. Managers decided to split off their commercialization units into new companies in 2000. These businesses integrate newspapers' marketing offices to promote huge market shares to its dailies. Local television and radio networks, as well as online newspaper editions, share company's services and thus are able to generate synergies both in advertising and marketing areas. The company's economic performance has been excellent and it has increasingly grown since 2000. This company is the result of a defensive strategy to protect its newspaper market and consolidate leadership in advertising and circulation.

Newsroom Convergence and Content Sharing

Newsroom convergence is an emerging issue in Spanish regional media. Partnerships and collaboration among the various newsrooms have developed as digital technology allowing journalists to produce news across several multimedia platforms at increasing speed. The relationships became more attractive as declining or flat circulation numbers forced newspapers to look for new ways to market their product to younger audiences.

Vocento is starting to share journalists, news and production stages between its print and online newsrooms. Sharing content of text-based products is easier than generating combinations between text and audiovisual-based news stories. At Vocento, they have created the role of "multimedia coordinator" in each of the regions, in order to foster content sharing and common strategies among the different newsrooms. This strategy is technologically backed by a content management system shared by all the newsrooms nationally. Since 2006, this system has allowed different media in the same region, but also media from different regions, to use stories produced by other newsrooms. This coordination never crosses the point of having journalists of one medium working for another one; the newsrooms stay completely independent.

Vocentos's multimedia strategy allows for each media outlet to share information gathered by its cross-media partner and to publish it after it has been repackaged by journalists. Partners might also share news budgets or attend the other partner's planning sessions. News directors from the various outlets meet regularly to exchange ideas, provide feedback to each other, share some material from the stories they have covered, plan longer investigative pieces together and share the cost for special projects.

Multimedia convergence at Prensa Iberica has contributed to generate synergies between paper and online editions since 2005. The company "Recursos en la red" provides a central newsroom which is devoted to updating news content in the 15 newspaper online sites and to sending headlines through e-mail and PDA alerts. A content management digital system allows for automatic downloading of all print material into the online edition. "Recursos en la red" also employs some Web staff in three regional newspapers but, by and large, the online newsroom works independently. Collaboration between print newsrooms and the central online newsroom is scarce.

Managers of both companies ask themselves to what extent they should integrate the different newsrooms, which kind of skills are now required by journalists and how they should cover information together and if they could combine different edition systems to syndicate content efficiently.

"Coopetition" in Printing and Delivering

Collaboration and competition are no longer opposite concepts. So-called "coopetition" is increasingly developing in the Spanish regional newspaper industry. After a period of fierce competition, both Prensa Iberica and Vocento are involved in several joint ventures in non-strategic areas. Printing and delivering are expensive economic activities that have become a matter of negotiation. Although distribution was never the core business of this industry, some publishers have been operating together in this sector, in order to save costs and to develop a deep sales marketing strategy.

In 2006, Vocento and Prensa Ibérica agreed on a joint venture to launch Localprint, the biggest printing plant in Spain, located in Elche (Alicante). The plant uses the latest technology available to publish five different newspapers from both groups, as well as magazines, books and other publications. It is a pioneering agreement between two very competitive newspaper chains in the Spanish publishing industry to share a printing plant which covers a large geographic area and will serve other national and international publishers.

As an innovation in the distribution business, Prensa Iberica is planning to implement a new smart card that allows users to buy a newspaper at newsstands. Using a chip, the card will gather information about newspaper circulation and the data will be automatically transferred to the publisher by an electronic system. Moreover, this card will offer several promotions and discounts in the purchase of newspapers, and it will also operate as a credit card for small purchases.

Conclusions

The study of operations, structures and strategies of Vocento and Prensa Iberica suggests that the main strategic response to the crisis of newspapers in the Spanish regional publishing industry is a corporate cross-media strategy. Newspapers' audiovisual diversification seeks to protect its core business by promoting new media outlets to deter new entrants and to improve its economic performance. Consolidation of market leadership, both into the advertising and information markets, has triggered this corporate diversification strategy.

Most regional publishing companies operate in more than a single media market. Both Vocento and Prensa Iberica are trying to improve operational and corporate performance through a multimedia portfolio to protect their advertising and circulation markets. The new business portfolio has not yet achieved a positive economic outcome, so publishers are trying to reduce operational costs. Managers do consider the new multimedia business as new areas of growth and profitability within the next few years.

Regional newspapers have moved markedly in the direction of becoming multimedia platforms. Major advantages performed by local multimedia groups include joint advertising bargaining and cross-promotion. Both in traditional outlets, as in digital ones, cross-branding and advertising space aggregation increase performance and give higher negotiation power to media companies. Convergence or collaboration between print and online newsrooms is also increasing. Besides, competitive regional publishers such as Vocento and Prensa Iberica have started collaboration in printing and delivering to save cost in non-strategic areas.

Diversifying on to new platforms has enabled the newspapers of Vocento and Prensa Iberica to reach new markets such as younger people and readers outside the print distribution area, more efficiently. Consumption of news stories has increased and this benefits news publishers who can leverage new technologies. Cross-platform advertising packages mean that newspapers recoup substantially more marketing income than those traditionally limited to display and classifieds. Convergence will strengthen the core business if its values are successfully migrated to new platforms.

It is too early to tell whether these online newspapers will generate competitive advantages to their parent companies. Spanish regional publishers do consider the Internet as a strategic option and the best way to face newspapers' economic crisis. The editors of Vocento and Prensa Iberica believe that news related to society, events that are covered from readers' perspective and their newspaper brand values, are their best resources to win success in the digital age.

REFERENCES

ALBARRAN ALAN B. and DIMMICK, JOHN (1999) "Concentration and Economies of Multiformity in the Communication Industries", *The Journal of Media Economics* 9(4), pp. 41–50.

BAKKER, PIET (2002) "Free Daily Newspapers: business models and strategies", *Journal of Media Management* 4, pp. 180–7.

DENNIS, EVERETTE E. (2006) "Television's Convergence Conundrum", *Television Quarterly* 37(1), pp. 22–7.

DOYLE, GILLIAN (2000) "The Economics of Monomedia and Cross-media Expansion: a study of the case favouring deregulation of TV and newspaper ownership in the UK", *Journal of Cultural Economics* 24, pp. 1–26.

GORDON, RICH (2003) "The Meanings and Implications of Convergence", in: Kevin Kawamoto (Ed.), *Digital Journalism: emerging media and the changing horizons of journalism*, Lanham, MD: Rowman & Littlefield Publishers, pp. 57–73.

KOLO, CASTULUS and VOGT, PATRICK (2003) "Strategies for Growth in the Media and Communications Industry: does size really matter?", *The International Journal on Media Management* 5, pp. 251–61.

PICARD, ROBERT G. (2001) "Strategic Responses to Free Distribution Daily Newspapers", *The International Journal of Media Management* 2, pp. 167–72.

SÁNCHEZ-TABERNERO, ALFONSO and CARVAJAL, MIGUEL (2002) *Media Concentration in the European Market*, Media Markets Monograph, Pamplona: Servicio de Publicaciones de la Universidad de Navarra.

VAN KRANENBURG, HANS L. (2004) "Diversification Strategy, Diversity and Performance Among Publishing Companies", paper presented to the 6th World Media Economics Conference, Montréal, Canada, 12–15 May.

WIRTH, MICHAEL and BLOCH, HARRY (1995) "Industrial Organization: theory and media industry analysis", *The Journal of Media Economics* 8(2), pp. 15–26.

ZENITH OPTIMEDIA (2006) "Online Advertising to Grow Seven Times Faster Than Offline Advertising in 2007", *Advertising Expenditure Forecasts*, Press release, December.

Chapter 25

"IF YOU CAN'T EARN ENOUGH—TEACH"
Newspaper journalists as journalism lecturers in Israel

Hagar Lahav

Introduction

Journalism in Israel is currently undergoing extensive changes reflecting develop-ments in new media technologies, as well as economic and social changes (Limor, 2003; Peri and Tsfati, 2007). No matter how journalism is conceptualized—as profession, craft, an industry, a market, an institutional practice of representation, a literary genre, an ideology or a culture—it is changing (see, for example, Altheide and Snow, 1991; Anderson, 2007; Benson, 2005; Bloebaum, 2007; Deuze, 2005; Frith and Meech, 2007; Hamilton, 2004; Schudson, 2003; Zelizer, 2004).

This article explores two particular changes within this broad alteration, using them to provide a context to illuminate a particular outcome. Specifically, it focuses on the present situation of newspapers and journalism education in Israel and considers the recent tendency of newspaper journalists to take a second job as journalism teachers. Although the changes in the newspaper industry, as well as in journalism education have been studied and well documented internationally, their specific influence on the phenomena of newspaper journalists-as-teachers has not yet been explored. Nationally, the current situation of both the newspaper industry (Limor, 2006; Limor and Mann, 1997) and journalism education (Adoni and First, 2006) in Israel remain less than fully researched and consequently the data presented here will also contribute to those two branches of the journalism field in Israel.

There is a common agreement that the newspaper industry is facing difficult times. The general decline in news reading (Patterson, 2007), the establishment of on-line news organizations and blogs, and the rapid growth of convergence journalism (*Nieman Reports, 2005*) have each impacted on newspaper circulations, revenues and readerships. Even if Meyer's (2004) prophecy of "the vanishing of newspaper" is precociously gloomy, there is a broad consensus that newspapers in the United States and northern Europe are suffering sustained circulation decline (NRG, 2006). According to a report published by the Center on the Press, Politics and Public Policy at Harvard University (July 2007), only 16 percent of Americans between the ages of 18 and 30 read a newspaper every day, compared to 35 percent of older adults (Patterson, 2007). Data by the world association for newspaper and media publishing, IFRA, reveal that in 1995 newspapers held 36 percent of global advertising budgets which dipped to 30 percent in 2005. Estimates signal that newspapers will lose another 5 percent sales per annum until 2015, and that across the coming decade, a quarter of the classified ads will migrate online (NRG, 2006).

Newspapers' requirement for substantial investment exacerbates the financial consequences of their loss of sales revenues. To sustain, much less increase, circulation, newspapers need to modernize their styles of writing, design and page layout to meet the shifting needs of readers in a changing media market. Newspapers must also carry the costs of establishing and operating online editions and sites. One evident victim of this "pincer movement" in which income declines while costs expand is the journalistic staff. In recent years newspapers in a number of national settings have reduced the number of journalists employed to cut labor costs and have even reduced salaries, etc. (NRG, 2006).

Paralleling these industry changes are developments in journalism education. Journalism studies has become an academic field, embracing both an intellectual subject area of study as well as a vocational training track; there is a steady increase in journalism education globally. Universities, schools and colleges dedicate departments and programs to journalism teaching and research (Deuze, 2006, 2005; Frith and Meech, 2007; Hanna and Sanders, 2007; Kraeplin and Criado, 2005; Lowrey et al., 2005; Skinner et al., 2001).

The interrelations between the journalism industry at large (and newspapers in particular), and journalism education are not simple (Frith and Meech, 2007; Limor, 2006; Skinner et al., 2001). At the ideological level both sides reflect a mutual antipathy. Journalists tend to disregard journalism education and its connection to "real life." The *Guardian Media Guide*, for example, cited by Frith and Meech (2007, p. 149) claimed: "media studies course content is sub-Marxist gobbledygook and courses are taught by talentless individuals who can't get jobs in the media, so they teach instead." Similarly, journalism educators and researchers tend to be broadly critical of the journalism industry and its products. They tend to conclude that currently journalism is "bad", and to see the majority of journalists as either too naïve, too cynical, too badly trained, too limited by the organizational and economic constraints within which they are obliged to work, or too weak, lazy, disreputable and dishonest to produce "good" journalism (see, for example, Bennett, 1996; Gitlin, 1980; Herman and Chomsky, 1988; Schudson, 2003). Although this mutual disregard is occasionally accompanied by mutual jealousy, there is little doubt that a deep suspicion exists between the practitioner and educational groups. Even in North America, where journalism education is well established, there is a constant tension between practical journalism teaching and more academic-based approaches to journalism (Skinner et al., 2001).

On the practical level, however, these two branches of journalism are inextricably interwoven and mutually feed each other. Researchers study journalism, journalists report academic findings and use academic professionals as sources. The journalism industry, moreover, recruits more and more young journalists, who were trained in academic journalism programs, making journalism a graduate occupation (Frith and Meech, 2007). In turn, education institutions offer more and more teaching positions to journalists in their vocational programs (Frith and Meech, 2007). Changes in the journalism industry bring changes in the educational curriculum (Deuze, 2006; Lowrey et al., 2005; Kraeplin and Criado, 2005).

Although the existence of mutual relations is well established in previous studies, the particular connection between the developments in journalism education and the developments in newspapers, as well as their impact on the journalism field more generally, are yet to be studied. What, for example, is the place of newspaper journalists in journalism educational programs? What are the reasons for the growing trend for newspaper journalists to lecture on graduate journalism programs? What is journalists' motivation? And why do the heads of programs hire them? And maybe the most important question—if and how this situation influences the field of journalism? By posing these questions to the situation in Israel, this study suggests that two processes— declining journalism jobs and newspaper revenues in tandem with increasing provision of journalism education—occur in Israel. It suggests that one outcome of the interaction between these two processes is the tendency for newspaper journalists to "moonlight" as teachers in academic journalism programs.

Methodology

In-depth interviews were conducted to provide the qualitative data informing this study. Twenty interviewees belonging to three different groups—(1) newspaper journalists teaching in journalism programs in academic institutes (10), (2) heads and senior staff in academic schools, departments or programs of journalism, media and communication (five), and (3) newspaper executives (five)—were interviewed with interviews conducted as free conversations.

The journalists were asked about the academic program in which they participated, their position in the program, their attitudes towards the program and its modules/ distinctive course components, their motivation in taking the position and their (journalism) professional background and history. The program's executives were asked, among other questions, about the programs of study/training in journalism, the policy and practice of recruiting journalists, the range and levels of seniority of posts filled by newspaper journalists, the motivation to hire journalists, and the advantage and disadvantage of their work, along with the history of the program. Newspaper executives were asked to address questions concerning their newspaper's economic situation, the paper's employment policy concerning journalism staffs, organizational changes at the newspapers and their triggers, the news organization's history, and the difference between conditions of employment in newspapers and for other sectors of the journalism field.

Additional quantitative data on newspaper organizations and on higher education organizations and journalism programs was also gathered from public surveys on communication consumption and from official information about journalism or practical media work studies programs in colleges and universities.

Newspapers and Journalism Education in Israel

With a population of almost seven million, of which 70 percent are Hebrew-readers, three national Hebrew daily newspapers are published in Israel. The two popular (*Yediot Achronot* and *Ma'ariv*) newspapers along with the quality paper *Ha'aretz* constitute the core of mainstream daily newspapers. Each of them is the main component of a larger private business group, which also publishes regional weeklies, magazines and books.

Recent Developments in Newspaper Journalism

The last two decades have been problematic for the mainstream Israeli press, which has been obliged to confront and address problems arising from the growing popularity of on-line journalism, as well as the establishment of commercial broadcasting and the emergence of free newspaper competitors.

Until the early 1990s, broadcast journalism in Israel was uniquely public sector with a single TV channel (without commercials) and two radio stations (only one station includes commercial advertising). In 1993 the first national commercial TV channel (channel 2) was opened, followed by a second (channel 10) a few years later; the establishment of cable and satellite TV as well as regional commercial radio stations followed promptly (Limor and Mann, 1997). Newspaper executives claimed in interview that these changes presented difficulties for newspapers in two ways. First, the arrival of competitors prompted a fall in the price of advertisements and hence advertising revenue. Second, newspapers lost their exclusiveness as primary and major sources of information. Consequently, newspapers had to invest heavily to change page layout and design and writing style to accommodate to the changed media market, while also losing readers.

Problems were enhanced by the subsequent challenge of on-line journalism. To resolve this latter difficulty requires Israeli newspapers to invest significant parts of their budget in developing online editions and websites. Although very popular, newspaper executives estimate that they are responsible for less than 10 percent of the newspaper's revenues and are not yet covering set up costs.

A final difficulty for newspapers was offered by the emergence of a few freely-distributed daily newspapers ("Metro" in style but national in distribution) which were launched from 2006. The establishment at one of them, which by 2008 became the second most circulated newspaper in Israel (Zoref, 2008), was accompanied by vast investments, including the recruitment of some high-profile journalists from the larger mainstream newspapers. This new paper is financed by the American multi-billionaire Sheldon Adelson, listed in fourth place in *Fortune Magazine*'s "list of the wealthiest." His investment is not prompted by financial motivation so much as ideological-political reasons. "We are surely nervous", said one executive in a large newspaper, "we prepare ourselves, but there is no doubt that we are facing a tough battle. The market is too crowded. Not every one will survive."

The impact of these combined pressures on mainstream newspapers has been considerable. According to communication consumption surveys, the number of news-paper readers in Israel has declined by more than 10 percent in the last 10 years (TGI, 2006), while newspaper executives interviewed estimate that newspapers' current share of advertising revenues today is 30 percent lower then 15 years ago.

Asked about the influence of this situation on journalistic staff in the newspapers, one executive said: "To be sure, this has an enormous effect. We fired quite a lot of 'expensive' journalists with high salaries, and hired new young 'cheap' journalists that earn less money. We froze the salaries of other senior journalists and we refuse salary rises." Other newspaper executives estimate that the journalist's average salary in newspapers today is approximately 30 percent lower than it was a decade ago when allowances for inflation are taken into account.

Drawing on executives' descriptions of the organizational position of journalists in the Israeli media market, a schematic description of journalists' employment (data are not published and considered to be a business secret) is summarized in Table 1.

When asked to explain these varying circumstances and conditions of employment, newspaper executives mentioned a range of factors including: medium-specific character-istics (for example, the importance and value of well-known faces and names on TV, compared to online journalism); the medium/organization's history (for example, the fact that commercial TV and online journalism are relativity new, while printed newspapers are relatively old was offered as an explanation for the age differences between journalists in different media); and the past or present existence of a journalists' union in the medium/organization.

All interviewees acknowledged that present employment conditions in newspapers obliged many newspaper journalists to take a second job. "Our salary is just not enough", said one journalist, "so we have to 'moonlight.'" Newspaper executives estimated that about 40 percent of newspaper journalists in Israel are holding a second part-time job. "Dozens" of them are "moonlighting" as teachers in vocational journalism programs.

Developments in Israeli Journalism Education and Training

The employment conditions for journalists in newspapers undoubtedly have relevance and consequence for media education in Israel; in recent years this field has developed rapidly and continues to do so. The development reflects both changes in the conceptualization of the field and in its boundaries. As Adoni and First (2006) point out, influenced by the historical development of communication teaching and research in the United States, the academic progress of the field in Israel has been shaped by a tension between "communication" and "journalism". "Communication" was understood as a scientific research discipline, while "journalism" was largely perceived to be a vocational field. But these definitions, or perhaps widespread understandings, are somewhat misleading. The vocational field of mass media, for example, includes not only journalism but other professions such as advertising, PR and television production. Similarly, "communication" is not only the study of news reporting and its social effects. It is probably wiser to follow the distinction offered by Skinner et al. (2001) between theoretical research and vocational training (what they call "the theory/practice gap"), while bearing in mind that "communication" and "journalism" are still serving as code words for many Israeli scholars.

Unlike the United States, academic developments in the field initially favored the development of a scientific discipline in universities ("communication departments"). Those departments gave only a modest space, if any, to vocational training and concentrated on theoretical teaching (Adoni and First, 2006). In the 1990s the Council for Higher Education (CHE) encouraged the establishment of public and private academic

TABLE 1
Journalists' employment conditions in Israel

Medium or organization	Estimated number of employed journalists	Salary policy	Additional information offered by the executives
Mainstream newspapers (national)	About 1000	Average salary declining. Moderate (but growing) income differentiation between high- and low-profile journalists. Until 20 years ago, most journalists were employed on unionized contracts. Today, the vast majority have individual contracts of working conditions	"They don't work too hard"; "They are relatively old"
Free distributed newspapers (national) (Metro-like)	About 100	A few well-known talents, many low wages	"Low on journalistic staff and expenses"
Magazines and sectarial newspapers (national)	Not estimated	Mainly freelancers	
Commercial TV (national)	About 100	Strong differentiation between highly paid and well-known "talents" and "regular" journalists that earn more modest salaries	"The 'regular' journalists earn more or less the same as national newspaper journalists, but work harder"; "The 'regular' journalists are relatively young. The 'talents' are older"; "many of the ' talents' used to work in national newspapers or radio stations before moving to TV"
Public TV and radio stations (national)	About 100	Primary unionized public salaries	"The stations and their journalistic staff are in deep stagnation"; "old and outdated"; "no one knows what is going on there, and no body cares"; "irrelevant"; "practically non existing"; "cor-rupted", "pathetic"
Military radio station (national)	Less than 50	Two kinds of employment: most of the journalists are very young men and women conducting their obligatory military service in the station and receive only pocket money. A few older journalists are defined as civilians who work for the army, gaining unionized public salaries	"Those are young people who receive a very good professional training in the army, and then join the civic media"; "A primary journalism school for the civic media". "They work hard and gain nothing now, but they will cash-in later, when they leave the army"

TABLE 1 (*Continued*)

Medium or organization	Estimated number of employed journalists	Salary policy	Additional information offered by the executives
On-line news sites (national)	Less than 200	Low salaries	"The 'slaves' of news media markets"; "Very young and badly paid"; "On the net the journalist's name doesn't count. Any one can be replaced at any time. So there is no justification for high salaries"; "Not as prestigious as TV, newspapers and radio"
Local newspapers (regional)	A few dozen	Low salaries. Mainly freelancers	"More or less the same as on-line journalism: young and cheap manpower"; "It is not prestigious. Every local journalist dreams on becoming national"
Cable and satellite TV and local radio stations (regional)	A few dozen	Differentiation between well-known and highly paid "talents" and "regular" journalists	"In any station there is a 'talent' or two, who is being paid fairly enough, and a small staff of 'regular' journalists"; "mostly salaries are not very high"

colleges. According to the CHE policy, universities should focus on research while colleges place their emphasis on teaching (Committee for an Examination of High Education in Israel, 2007). It was only with the opening of these colleges that the training in practical media work began to develop as part of an academic curriculum. According to CHE sources (CHE, 2006) there are 10 non-university academic institutes that include communication departments or schools (i.e. departments that offer theoretical education). Two other programs are waiting for the approval of the CHE. In all of those institutes theoretical teaching is accompanied by (at least some) practical media training. The curricula in four institutions includes formal vocational programs in journalism, while the others offered courses in journalism as part of a more general media-work practice training. At the same time, the traditional communication departments in universities increased the number of practical workshop they offer to their students.

Consequently, within 15 years, Israel moved from having no vocational journalism higher educational, to the present situation, in which the scope of vocational journalism academic education is constantly growing. This vocational training enjoys very high student demand. More and more graduates of those programs are joining the media market. So the way of becoming a journalist in Israel is currently in a state of change. In the past journalists' professionalism was acquired by practical work in the media industries: today, increasing numbers of young journalists are trained on courses offered by journalism education institutes. These growing numbers of students increased the demands for vocational journalistic teaching staff. This demand is being met by employing experienced journalists to deliver courses and workshops on the various and specialist practical aspects of journalism. Here lies the connection between the employment conditions in newspapers described earlier and journalism education. I turn now to consider this connection.

Newspaper Journalists in Journalism Education in Israel

Although journalism programs and courses do not offer print journalism exclusively, examination of the vocational programs' components—in university, college and journalism school brochures—reveals a strong emphasis on traditional print/newspaper journalism. The head of one program explained that this emphasis has three intersecting dimensions. First, the curricula contain many courses that deal directly with newspaper journalism with module titles such as "News Writing", "Newspaper Editing" and "Newspaper Design"). Second, some courses deal with journalism in general, without specifying a particular medium and titles such as "The Reporter's Work", "News Gathering" signal an emphasis on newspaper work. Third, most of the journalists who offer professional workshops do work for their main job on newspapers.

About 80 reporters and editors, who work at the three main newspapers in Israel, are currently giving courses on different aspects of journalism in high education institutions. They constitute the vast majority of the vocational (non-academicals) staff in academic journalism education. Usually they are employed as adjunct lecturers, holding a part-time job. All the newspaper journalists, who teach in those vocational programs and that were interviewed to this study, emphasize the financial factor as their main reason for teaching. As one of them expressed it: "Sure, I enjoy teaching, I love to share my knowledge with young people, and it's a nice way to break the working routine. But if it wasn't for the fact that I have a family to support and that my salary in the newspaper is a disgrace, I wouldn't have done it."

Heads of journalism and practical media work programs also emphasize financial motives. One of them said: "I have a very long list of newspaper journalists who called me, asking for a job. I have no problem to fill all my teaching positions, and I have to reject many of the appeals. They need a second income, because they don't earn enough in the newspapers." When asked to describe the socio-professional profile of newspaper journalists that teach on his program, another director said: "they belong to the middle ranks in the newspaper hierarchy. Their name is known enough to attract students, but their income as journalists is not high enough to satisfy their standard of living."

The tendency of academic institutes to hire newspaper journalists as teachers and lectures is, then, good news for newspaper reporters and editors struggling to earn a living. From the journalism education angle, however, it might very well be a problematic trend. If press journalism is indeed decreasing, then a strong emphasis on newspaper journalism skills means that the vocational programs train their students in the journalism of the past rather than focus on tomorrow's journalism. It means that the programs supply their students with outdated professional knowledge. As Frith and Meech (2007, p. 143) explained:

> Journalist educators must realize that their graduates will be working not just in newspapers but on all kinds of corporate, consumer and trade magazines, for radio and television outlets of various sorts, with new web-based publications, in media serving all

kinds of reader and audience from the most geographically local to the most loosely global.

An obvious question arises here: Why are the heads of vocational programs so willing to hire mainstream newspaper professionals, leaving only a marginal teaching space for programs focused on online, radio, television and local media journalists? Interviews with directors and executives of vocational programs indicate a number of possible reasons for this preference for newspaper journalists.

Some of the interviewers attributed this tendency to the heads of the programs' own ideological, social or professional backgrounds. One interviewee, for example, referred to himself and his colleges by saying:

We are all between the ages of 45 to 65. As such we believe in "serious", "quality" journalism, as well as automatically associate this kind of journalism with mainstream newspapers. Being relatively old, we are less engaged in non-traditional media and journalism, and tend to be much more critical towards them.

Another said:

Some of the heads of programs are either retired journalists, or academics who used to be journalists before they joined the academic world. As such, they tend to choose teachers from the people they knew when they were journalists. Those, of course, are not young journalists, but middle age or even retired reporters and editors. And the old journalists in Israel work in newspapers.

Another interviewee added:

Communication departments and schools tend to duplicate each others' curricula, but more importantly—to duplicate each others' teaching staff. Each one of us sees what courses the others offer, and who gives them. If you are an academic scholar, who never had any direct personal contacts with journalists, the only way you would know whom to approach is by seeing someone's name in the curricula of other programs.

The interviewee gave a list of names of journalists, all of them from mainstream newspapers, who each constitute "a one-man-conglomerate" in journalism teaching. "The same people teach everywhere. You look at the teaching plan of different programs, and see the same names again and again. And those are newspaper journalists."

Other interviewees referred to the employment conditions in the media field as a whole to explain their tendency to hire newspaper journalists. One of them said:

It's not that I prefer newspaper journalists, it's just the easiest way to go. Talents don't need the extra income and it is very hard to convince them to come and teach. Young television reporters are just too busy. Public media journalists need a special approval to have an extra job, and this is a bureaucratic hassle. On line and local media journalists are just not known enough to attract students. So I'm left with mainstream newspapers journalists. There are many of them, they are well trained, they are more or less known, and they are handy.

A complementary explanation focused on the working routine in different media. "Radio, television or on-line reporters," an interviewee explained, can't just disconnect themselves from everything for two or three hours during daytime and give a class. They cannot commit themselves to a fixed day and hour to come and teach. Something always happens: an event to cover, a story to work on or a place to be in. The newsroom's editors always need the report now—immediately, fast, urgently. Also, the reporter has to be in the arena to report from. It is much easier with newspaper reporters. They have a fixed deadline—late at night. Even if they missed an event, they can always gather the information later. They don't have to be present in the arena to report, they can just pick up a phone, call their sources whenever they want to and update. So I can count on a newspaper reporter to appear to class in time, to finish it in time and to give his whole attention to the students.

One interviewee claimed the predominance of print journalists was irrelevant given the generic character of journalism across platforms. "Journalism is journalism is journalism," this person argued;

> Recognizing a good story, gathering information, handling relations with sources, checking facts, evaluating news worthiness, telling a story, choosing an angle, formulating a lead—that's what journalism is about. It is the same in all journalism outlets. So it doesn't matter which medium the journalist is coming from, as long as he or she is a good teacher and an experienced journalist.

The other interviewees, however, acknowledged this over-reliance on newspaper journalists might be problematic. Some of them said that they are making an effort to vary their teaching staff as well as their curricula to give more weight to electronic media. However, all of them estimated that the situation will not change dramatically in the coming years, and change will occur slowly and gradually.

Possible Effects

It seems then that the present conditions of employment in Israel's journalism industry combined with the deterioration of newspaper journalists' salaries and with the growth in journalism education, to make newspaper journalists the main vocational educators of the next generation of journalists. It is a deeply ironic circumstance: as newspaper journalism is declining, its professionals might become more and more important in the formulation of future journalism, by educating the next generation. What effects, if any, will this situation have on the future of journalism in Israel?

The answers to this question, offered by both journalists and academic interviewees, divided concerning the estimated strength of the effect. Some interviewees denied any consequence. "It doesn't matter what we teach and who teaches it," one of them said. "Courses can never substitute practical training. When the students get a real journalistic job, they learn everything from the beginning. In two days they forget everything they learned in school." By contrast, another newspaper journalist that works in higher education claimed, "our ethic, our do's and don'ts and our knowledge are planted in the students' heads and will accompany them forever in their media work and media consumption. There is no doubt that what they learned here will affect the journalism that they produce." Straddling these two extremes is the position offered by a third interviewer who suggested, "Organizational socialization is very strong. As new journalists the students will have to adopt the professional values and practices of the news organization.

But I believe that something stays. As they will climb in the organizational hierarchy they will find more and more spaces to express what they picked up at school."

But even if we assume that vocational teaching has a significant influence on students' future work as journalists, two other questions arise. The first is whether the content of journalism practical education is different in any way from the actual reality of journalism practice in Israel? The second concerns whether this difference, if any exists, has something to do with the fact that many journalism vocational educators are newspaper journalists?

Here too the answers vary greatly. Offering positive answers to both questions, a retired newspaper journalist who teaches on a number of vocational programs argued,

> It is not a secret that journalism today is poor. It is a shallow, a sensational, and an irresponsible journalism. It is less the case in mainstream newspapers, as well as with older journalists. Even the popular mainstream press is still conserving an ethos of deeper investigative reporting than TV, on-line and local journalism. In the quality newspapers this ethos is even stronger. So when we, as old newspaper journalists, teach students, we teach them better journalism. When they are integrated into a television, on-line or local journalism organization, their knowledge and understandings will diffuse into the organization and hopefully improve journalism. I sincerely believe that we are training better journalists than the ones who are currently working, and better than we were as young journalists. They are better trained, more critical and less ignorant. They, the next generation, are our hope.

A different view was offered by many interviewees who dismissed the very idea that journalism education had anything but the slightest consequence for practice. "I teach what I do, and I do journalistic work. I am no different from any other journalist," an interviewee claimed. "In the media there are good journalists, who do the work as it should be done as best they can, and bad journalists—lazy, fool, talentless. It has nothing to do with medium, training, education or age. The same goes for the students. What is, and what will be, have different reasons, but journalism education is not one of them," said the interviewee.

Again, adopting the middle ground, some interviewees tended to agree that there are differences between the contents of journalism education and journalism practice, and that those differences might reflect the fact that many practitioner educators are newspaper journalists. However, they were uncertain in their assessments of the effects, or possible future effects, on Israeli journalism. "There are too many factors that can interfere, too many things that might happen. We just have to wait and see, and even then I'm not sure we will ever know," one interviewee concluded.

Summary

This article has mapped the employment conditions in Israeli journalism organizations and the institutions of academic journalism education in Israel, to illuminate the tendency for print journalists in Israel to "moonlight" as teachers and lecturers on vocational journalism programs. Two opposite tendencies are combining to create a new professional trend. On the one hand, mainstream newspapers are persistently declining in terms of circulation and revenues. On the other, journalism studies in Israel are booming.

This two-fold trend encourages more and more newspaper journalists to take up a second job as a lecturer.

This development invokes a very interesting effect. At the same time that newspaper circulation—and probably also press influence on public discourse—is declining, the influence of their workers on the formulation of the next generation of journalists is increasing. By analyzing understandings of this phenomenon offered by journalists and journalism educators, it seems it is too early to say if tendency will influence journalism practices and texts in the coming years, but it seems likely that the newspaper journalists' heritage will prove influential. Print journalism, allegedly dying, may not yet have spoken its last word, and may find new ways to be a relevant agent in the future of journalism.

REFERENCES

ADONI, HANNAH and FIRST, ANAT (2006) *Communication Research and Teaching: structural dilemmas and changing solutions*, Jerusalem: The Hebrew University Magnes Press (Hebrew).

ALTHEIDE, L. DAVID and SNOW, P. ROBERT (1991) *Media Worlds in the Post-journalism Era*, New York: De Gruyter.

ANDERSON, CHRIS (2007) "Journalistic Professionalism, Knowledge, and Cultural Authority: towards a theoretical framework", paper presented to the International Communication Association, San Francisco, May.

BENNETT, W. LANCE (1996) *News—the politics of illusion*, 3rd edn, New York: Longman.

BENSON, RODNEY (2005) "American Journalism and the Politics of Diversity Media Culture Society", *Media, Culture & Society* 1, pp. 5–20.

BLOEBAUM, BREND (2007) "Journalism and Change: theoretical framework and empirical research", paper presented to the International Communication Association, San Francisco, May.

COMMITTEE FOR AN EXAMINATION OF HIGH EDUCATION IN ISRAEL (SHOCHT COMMITTEE) (2007) "The Final Report of the Committee for Examination of High Education in Israel", http://www.che.org.il/download/files/shohat-report_e.pdf (Hebrew).

COUNCIL FOR HIGHER EDUCATION (2006) "Reports from the Planning and Budgeting Committee", http://www.che.org.il/template/default.asp?maincat = 2 (Hebrew).

DEUZE, MARK (2005) "What Is Journalism? Professional identity and ideology of journalists reconsidered", *Journalism* 6, pp. 442–64.

DEUZE, MARK (2006) "Global Journalism Education: a conceptual approach", *Journalism Studies* 1, pp. 19–34.

FRITH, SAIMON and MEECH, PETER (2007) "Becoming a Journalist: journalism education and journalism culture", *Journalism* 8, pp. 137–64.

GITLIN, TODD (1980) *The Whole World Is Watching*, Berkeley: University of California.

HAMILTON, T. JAMES (2004) *All The News That's Fit to Sell: how the market transforms information into news*, Princeton, NJ: Princeton University Press.

HANNA, MARK and SANDERS, KAREN (2007) "Did the Educators Make a Difference? Journalism students and news media roles and ethics", paper presented to the International Communication Association, San Francisco, May.

HERMAN, S. EDWARD and CHOMSKY, NOAM (1988) *Manufacturing Consent: the political economy of the mass media*, New York: Pantheon Books.

KRAEPLIN, CAMILLE and CRIADO, CARRIE ANNA (2005) "Building a Case for Convergence Journalism Curriculum", *Journalism and Mass Communication Educator* 60(1), pp. 47–56.

LIMOR, YEHIEL (2003) "Mass Communication in Israel", in: Ephraom Yaar and Zeev Shavit (Eds) *Trends in Israeli Society Vol. 2*, Tel Aviv: The Open University Press, pp. 1030–95 (Hebrew).

LIMOR, YEHIEL (2006) "A Response to Theodore L. Glasser", paper presented to the Communication Research and Teaching Conference, The Hebrew University, Jerusalem, 24 December.

LIMOR, YEHIEL and MANN, RAFI (1997) *Journalism*, Tel Aviv: Open University Press (Hebrew).

LOWREY, WILSON, DANIELS, L. GEORGE and BECKER, B. LEE (2005) "Predictors of Convergence Curricula in Journalism and Mass Communication Programs", *Journalism and Mass Communication Educator* 60(1), pp. 32–46.

MEYERS, PHILIP (2004) *The Vanishing Newspaper: Saving Journalism in the Information Age*, Columbia: University of Missouri Press.

NIEMAN REPORTS: THE NIEMAN FOUNDATION FOR JOURNALISM AT HARVARD UNIVERSITY (2005) "Citizen Journalism", *Meinan Report* 59(4), http://www.nieman.harvard.edu/reports/05-4NRwinter/05-4NFwinter.pdf

NRG (2006) "The Newspapers Declaiming", *NRG-Ma'ariv*, 29 December, http://www.nrg.co.il/online/4/ART1/522/582.html (Hebrew).

PATTERSON, E. THOMAS (2007) "Young People and News", *A Report from the Joan Shorenstein Center on the Press, Politics and Public Policy*, http://www.ksg.harvard.edu/presspol/carnegie_knight/young_news_web.pdf.

PERI, YORAM and TSFATI, YARIV (2007), "To See is To Believe? Lack of Confidence in Mainstream Media", in: Dan Caspi (Ed.) *Political Communicatiom in Israel*, Jerusalem: The Van Leer Institute/ Hakibbutz Hameuchad Publishing House, pp. 162–84 (Hebrew).

SCHUDSON, MICHAEL (2003) *The Sociology of News*, New York: Norton.

SKINNER, DAVID, GASHER, J. MIKE and COMPTON, JAMES (2001) "Putting Theory to Practice: a critical approach to journalism studies", *Journalism* 2, pp. 341–60.

TGI (2006) "Israel Media Surveys", http://www.tgi.co.il/tgi/www/html/tgi_heb.html.

ZELIZER, BARBIE (2004) *Taking Journalism Seriously: news and the academy*, Thousand Oaks, CA: Sage.

ZOREF, AYALA (2008) "'Israel Today' overtakes 'Maariv'", *The Marker Business News*, 29 July, p. 24.

Chapter 26

NEWSPAPER NEGOTIATIONS
The crossroads of community newspaper journalists' values and labor

Wendy M. Weinhold

Introduction

The canons of American newspaper journalism—among which are an obligation to truth, dedication to the creation of a high-quality product, objectivity and responsibility to readers—are the foundation of journalists' work ethic. Journalists' activities inside and outside newsrooms, as well as their self-understanding, are guided by these principles (see Kovach and Rosenstiel, 2001). But American newspapers are also profit-driven businesses that operate in the free-enterprise economy, and journalists' credo lacks an acknowledgement of how or whether their work should answer their employers' capital demands (Udell, 1978). When research does address this topic, it addresses it only tangentially.

Drawing from existing research, my five years work experience as a professional newspaper journalist, and study of journalists at *The Southern Illinoisan* (*The Southern*), a community newspaper in Carbondale, Illinois, I use ethnographic methods to examine how journalists negotiate the tension between their commitment to serve the public and professional obligation to a business. I conducted fieldwork in *The Southern's* newsroom during spring 2006 to expand my knowledge of the decision-making process journalists use when confronted by business pressures during their routine workdays. My analysis of *The Southern* suggests the newspaper's finances and concern with circulation are outside journalists' control; obligations to the commercial imperatives of newsroom decision-making are the necessary evils of doing business.

Political economy serves broadly as my theoretical lens for this examination of why and how American community newspaper journalists' labor has the potential to bring about structural changes that influence shifts in journalists' work and values as they negotiate the juxtaposition of their public service mission against their employers' profit motives. Mosco defines political economy as "the study of the social relations, particularly the power relations, that mutually constitute the production, distribution, and consumption of resources" (1996, p. 25).

The political economy approach to media studies has been used to examine the historical roots of professional journalism in offering a critique of contemporary journalism's problems. McChesney (2003b) highlights the rise of professional journalism in the 20th century in his critique of the "commercial attack" on journalism (p. 308). He explains that pressures on journalists to shape stories that meet advertisers' and owners' desires are nothing new, and journalists' professional code of autonomy and objectivity was designed to prevent "or at least minimize" these pressures (2003b, p. 310). But market influences continue to seep into journalists' work at a rapid pace, and McChesney suggests that "in an increasingly commercialized journalism 'market,' where profit maximization is the firm's explicit defining objective, journalists figure they might as well get their's [sic] too" (2003b, p. 311).

As media conglomeration and economic constraints force the continued decline of community newspapers, this ethnography offers a rare approach to the study of journalists and seeks to fill a gap in existing journalism research dominated by scholarly studies of large newspapers. My research question attempts to address an issue unexplored by current scholarship on journalists: Do the products of community newspaper journalists' labor reflect their ability to follow the principles of journalism? In order to answer this question, first, I review literature that provides a background on professional print journalists' current labor conditions and identifies the roots of their professional principles. Second, I establish critical theory as my framework for examining how journalists' work experiences and resulting products have the potential to bring about structural changes that influence shifts in journalists' work and values. Third, I use a methodology that juxtaposes the principles of journalism with an ethnographic case study of journalists at a community newspaper to see if the journalists' work experiences uphold or counter the principles. Finally, I draw conclusions about the need for a new articulation of journalists' principles that accommodates increased transparency in the connection between journalists and their labor.

Literature Review

Cutting the Cord: The Rise of Professional Journalism

Kovach and Rosenstiel (2001) outline nine principles of journalism that serve as the foundations of journalists' work ethic in their book, *The Elements of Journalism*. The principles emerged from a three-year study by practicing journalists concerned about business's growing hold on the press. Kovach and Rosenstiel's theories are repeatedly offered as evidence of a clear dictum for journalists, and their book is a standard textbook in journalism schools across America. In fact, a journalism degree is generally recognized as a prerequisite to obtaining an American newspaper job, and journalists are indoctrinated as part of their professional education with the belief they should to march to the tune of these principles. According to McChesney (2003b), nearly 90 percent of American newspaper journalists had college degrees by 2002.

According to Kovach and Rosenstiel, the nine principles of journalism are:

1. Its first obligation is to truth,
2. Its first loyalty is to citizens,
3. Its essence is a discipline of verification,
4. Its practitioners must maintain independence from those they cover,
5. It must serve as an independent monitor of power,
6. It must provide a forum for public criticism and compromise,
7. It must strive to make the significant interesting and relevant,
8. Its practitioners must keep the news comprehensive and proportional, and
9. Its practitioners must be allowed to exercise their personal conscience. (2001, p. 13)

Taken at face value, these are worthy principles. But they are not without limitations. The full text of Kovach and Rosenstiel's text, which several colleagues I met at The Future of Newspapers Conference (Cardiff, 2007) jokingly called the "book of lists," does address the need to hire managers with editorial experience and not just business savvy. Kovach and Rosenstiel (2001) reason editorial-minded editors will put the news before their companies' profit-making priorities. This approach is a start, but it is not a fail-safe remedy. By placing responsibility for guarding the news and protecting against business pressures on editors, the text leaves reporters without solutions of their own. Beyond asking journalists to espouse the problematic notions of objective truth, the principles fail to recognize the underlying reason the principles were created in the first place—journalists' growing desire to stave off and separate from the demands of business. Furthermore, the credo lacks an acknowledgement of how or whether journalists' work should answer their employers' capital demands. In turn, the principles encourage journalists to sublimate their values and accept their roles as commercial newspaper employees.

Economic and institutional pressures led to the divorce of journalists' public service mission from recognition of the profit motive of the businesses they serve. Journalists' work is in many ways the "product of a social institution . . . [and] professionalism" that transforms information, observation or event into a "shared phenomenon" for public consumption (Tuchman, 1978, pp. 5–6). Udell explains the "dual role" of journalists' reliance on newspapers to inform the public while turning a profit through use of the words of media critic Ben Bagdikian:

> On the one hand, the daily paper in the United States is a product of professionals whose reporting is supposed to be the result of disciplined intelligence gathering and analysis in order to present an honest and understandable picture of the social and political world. If this reportage is in any way influenced by concern for money-making it is regarded as corrupt journalism. On the other hand, the American daily newspaper . . . has to remain solvent and has to make a profit or else it will not survive. If it doesn't make money there will be no reporting of any kind. (Udell, 1978, p. 65)

As advertising revenue became an increasingly important source of newspaper revenue and newspapers became increasingly commercial enterprises, editorializing on the front page became bad for business because it threatened to turn away some readers and in turn led advertisers elsewhere in search of an audience. The professional code of journalism emerged when newspapers "put profit-making in the driver's seat" (McChesney, 2003a, p. 2). According to McChesney, partisan journalism was routine before 1900, and the political leanings of a newspaper owner were overtly expressed throughout the paper's news content. McChesney explains: "Professional journalism was born from the revolutionary idea that the link between owner and editor could be broken ... Journalists would be given considerable autonomy to control the news using their professional judgment" (2003a, p. 2).

Research that examines the intersection of journalistic values and market-driven demands that shape routine workdays of full-time American journalists is dominated by random surveys and case studies of large newspapers (e.g. Gaziano and Coulson, 1988; Konner, 1996; Johnstone et al., 1976; Lacy and Fico, 1991; Landon, 2004; Pease, 1991; Tuchman, 1978; Udell, 1978; Weaver and Wilhoit, 1996). Large, metropolitan newspapers, such as *The New York Times* and *Washington Post*, are the most universally recognized icons of American newspapers, but most journalists do not work for one of these giants. According to the most recent statistics available from the Newspaper Association of America (2006), of the 1437 daily newspapers operating in the United States, only 104 had circulations above 100,001. Circulation is understood to mean the number of audited copies sold daily. Daily community newspapers, which Landon (2004), p. 14) defines as papers with circulations of less than 100,000, employ a majority of American journalists and serve as professional training grounds for young journalists. According to the American Society of Newspaper Editors (2007), of the 56,982 full-time journalists working for daily American newspapers, 30,125 are employed by daily community newspapers. The society reports 56 percent, or 27,563, white journalists and 33 percent, or 2562, of minority journalists work for newspapers with circulations under 100,000 (American Society of Newspaper Editors, 2007).

Studies of the field of journalism tend to focus on the effects of competition and economic constraints on the quality of journalism or on the ethical constraints influencing journalists. For example, Weaver and Wilhoit's (1996) *The American Journalist in the 1990s* finds journalists at odds with their editors over issues of newspapers' quality and profitability. Journalists who participated in Weaver and Wilhoit's study "sometimes portrayed their differences with management in terms of the pressures of 'reader-driven' news values" and cite a younger journalist at a medium-sized paper who says, "I find that the newspaper and news room management here is insensitive and mean-spirited and confused by conflicting corporate goals" (1996, p. 106). But beyond noting journalists growing awareness of "the corrosive effects of a concern for profit over quality," the researchers bypass examination of the interrelationship and effects between newspaper journalists and employers' profit motives (1996, p. 65).

American newspapers provide information and entertainment to their readers, but profit is king in determining how they meet this mission. Newspapers use circulation rates to recruit advertisers and set advertising rates, which serve as their major revenue source (Meyer, 2004b). Schudson claims "the profit motive is a major factor in shaping the lion's share of news in the United States" (2003, p. 32). But he views economics as a potentially crushing force on "the spirit of journalists who come to their work with much more than profit in mind" (2003, p. 123).

Because circulation is more volatile at community newspapers, it is possible the journalists they employ experience greater fluctuations in day-to-day business pressures. Meyer (2004b) reports his empirical analysis of circulation in 24 US newspaper markets found that circulation is much more volatile at smaller papers than at large ones. He observes small papers operate in "environments so different (from large papers) that they probably need to follow different rules" (2004b, p. 79). Many small papers are victims of the rapid pace of media concentration and have been gobbled up by giant corporations, placing control of editorial and business power in the hands of a few companies and threatening the operations of the free press.

More than any other journalists, reporters serve as newspapers' representatives to the public by attending community events and reporting on the scene of breaking news, but research suggests they have limited input into decisions about newspaper content and direction. Pease (1991) illustrates the tension between journalism and business through a national job satisfaction survey of reporters at newspapers with circulations of more than 50,000. He cites a white male Californian reporter in his early 30s, who says, "I'd just like to do more satisfying reporting that addresses the needs of my community instead of my paper's marketing goals" (1991, p. 7).

Reporters' expectations of their work and work products are reflected in their self-definitions. Konner offers insight into how young journalists perceive their work when she includes Columbia Graduate School of Journalism students' responses to the blank line, "A journalist is . . ." (1996, p. 4). Although the question uses the broad term, "journalist," most of the responses refer to writing, data collection and interpretation, which are among reporters' primary tasks. An unidentified student offers this definition: "Journalists are people entrusted with defining reality" (1996, p. 4).

Critical Theory 1.0[1]

Developments in media technology have historically been lauded and lamented as potential tools for challenging the traditional principles and practices of journalism. Critical theorists, particularly Walter Benjamin, held that new media have emancipatory potential. Benjamin's theories lay the groundwork for understanding the complexities of technological change. In his classic text, "The Work of Art in the Age of Mechanical Reproduction," Benjamin (1969) explores technological and cultural shifts as harbingers of promise rather than doom. He examines the repercussions of rapid technological change and argues techniques used to reproduce artworks, such as photography and film, have significantly influenced human perception and interaction with their world and their conceptualization of the relationship between art and society at large (Franklin, 2002). Benjamin probes the increased interconnectivity between journalists and the press and notes how the "increasing extension of the press" led a growing number of readers to become writers (1969, p. 232). At that time, the content readers could contribute was largely limited to letters to the editor, but Benjamin suggests little remains to separate author from reader when the "difference becomes merely functional" (1969, p. 232).

While the audience in Benjamin's work may be liberated by new technologies, I contend journalists are less able to seize this opportunity under the rules of their existing systems. The conflict between journalism's guiding principles and newspapers' profit motives functions to isolate print journalists from the business of their business. Benjamin warns that humans' gradual and habitual mastery of tasks helps routinize their behavior as they operate in a constant state of distraction. He explains:

> The distracted person, too, can form habits. More, the ability to master certain tasks in a
> state of distraction proves that their solution has become a matter of habit. Distraction as

provided by art presents a covert control of the extent to which new tasks have become soluble by apperception. (1969, p. 240)

Benjamin's caution is significant in that it reveals how the misappropriation of mass production holds potentially corrosive effects on human autonomy.

Journalists' high-pressured work and limited control over their product can be a source of conflict. Ajrouch's (1998) ethnographic study identifies the front page as the newsroom staff's central focus each day. Reporters' workdays are organized around the problematic process of "landing a story on the front page," but their editors have the final say in where and when stories are published (1998, p. 348). The study found reporters were more focused on coverage of government and business news while editors wanted stories of personal drama. Emotionally evocative stories were most likely to find their way to the front page at the major newspaper in metropolitan Detroit that was the focus of Arjouch's study. She concludes the human element in editors' judgments of news value separates reporters from their canons of autonomous and objective creation and places them in an "awkward paradox" (1998, p. 349). Gaziano and Coulson's (1988) empirical analysis of reporters finds their news judgment rarely is controlled through direct instructions from management. They explain, "The process is far more subtle. Through newsroom socialization, journalists learn the established routines and paths to advancement" (1988, p. 870).

Methodology

Research for this paper relies on participant-observation and in-depth interviews conducted during a three-month-long period of ethnographic study at *The Southern*. More than 100 hours of on-site research, in addition to my daily reading of the newspaper between February 1 and April 30, inform my analysis. I was a participant-observer in the work of two reporters, the education reporter and the county government reporter; conducted three hour-long, in-depth interviews with the city editor; and sat in on five management meetings where stories for the next day's newspapers were selected.

In the following analysis, I juxtapose the principles of journalism with a case study of the reporters, editor and managers to understand when journalists' online work upholds or counters Kovach and Rosenstiel's (2001) principles. I organize the principles into three groups. The first group encompasses principles that describe journalists' behaviors: independence from those they cover, loyalty to citizens, and use of their personal conscience. I apply these principles to my observations of the county government reporter's expectation of the publication and treatment of her coverage of a politician's visit to the area. The second group encompasses principles that describe how journalists should structure their content: provide a forum for public criticism and compromise, make the significant interesting and relevant, and keep the news comprehensive and proportional. I juxtapose these principles with statements *The Southern*'s city editor made during our conversations. The third group encompasses principles that endorse journalists' roles as watchdogs: obligation to the truth, reliance on disciplined verification, and independent monitoring of power. I apply these principles to analysis of the management meetings I attended.

Analysis and Findings

The Daily Grind

The research I have conducted thus far identifies how reporters use similar definitions to describe their work, indicating their desire to fulfill idealized roles while recognizing when their work is directed toward answering the demands of their business. During participant-observation at *The Southern*, I listened as the county government reporter joked with another that she views stories reserved for the newspaper's free weekly publication delivered to non-subscribers to sell ads and solicit subscriptions as "news that didn't make the news section."

On the day in the first week of March 2006 I shadowed the county government reporter to cover a speech by a state representative to the area. Before the event, we drank coffee and chatted at her desk in the newsroom. She told me she had completed her bachelor's degree in journalism the previous year. When the city editor walked by, she called out to him, "Hey, can you carve me out some real estate on the front today?" and then mumbled under her breath, "I'm sick of the local front." The reporter explained the story she would write about the politician's visit would likely be printed in a section called "Plus," which she described as a "zoning section" that is distributed free to homes in Jackson County. She called the section the "pancake section." She said she did not care about story placement but then changed her mind and said she wanted all her stories to be published in the newspaper's online version because that was where most of her readership came from. This free distribution practice is used by many newspapers to shore up circulation numbers and bolster advertisement rates.

As we drove toward the community college where US Rep. Jerry Costello would speak, she said she admired how much attention the politician paid to southern Illinois and criticized other elected officials for not making regular stops to the region like Congressman Costello. "Southern Illinois is an easy place to forget about, and he comes down here. It's good," she said. After the speech, she joked with Costello about seeing him the previous weekend at a St. Louis' Rams football game. She did not ask any follow-up questions on issues he raised in his speech—taxes, agriculture, education costs—and she did not interview any of the audience members, who were students from the college's government classes. Once we were back in her car and headed for the newspaper, she confessed that she had considered leaving journalism and would switch careers if she could secure a job as a political spokesperson. I asked her what she would write about the event we had attended. "Congressman Costello comes to the fucking blah blah," she said. In applying the first group of principles—independence from those they cover, loyalty to citizens and use of their personal conscience—the county reporter's attitude toward the place secured for her stories in the paper seems to shuck the content of all but the newspaper's front page. She did not voice concern for informing the public about the politician's visit or the content of his speech; instead, her primary concern was where the products of her day's labor would land in the paper. In addition, her remarks that she admired the politician for his interest in the area suggest that she is concerned about the life and work conditions of the citizens she writes for but not that interested in maintaining an autonomous stance from the government officials who dominate her day-to-day work.

The Businessman's Business

Journalists perform and produce the news, but editors dictate their work, its function and use in answering the demands of the business. Editors are leaders, teachers and decision makers, and they set the tone of the newsroom by directing reporting and business strategies. Profit is a primary concern for managers, and Meyer suggests they weigh profit concerns above quality (2004a, p. 56). During the first of our three interviews, *The Southern*'s city editor said his work was focused primarily on the business side of the newspaper, and increasing circulation was a key focus of his work each day. In this capacity, his job is to create papers that will sell. He said this portion of his job "really has nothing to do with journalism or anything like that."

This editor served as the gatekeeper for my participant observation fieldwork, and reporters often peeked into his office to ask questions during our interviews. Several times during our conversation, the editor mentioned the newspaper was short staffed. He said he had fewer reporters than he would like, and he worked two jobs at *The Southern*. When he was hired, the newspaper's local editor position was open. Over the course of the three months of my ethnographic research at *The Southern*, the newspaper not only failed to hire an additional editor, the managing editor resigned. So the city editor then did the work of three people. He explained, "I told people, I'm doing my job, the person under me's job, and the person above me. I'm thinking about firing myself from one or two of those jobs." He explained that he had more than 15 years in the newspaper business and had worked a variety of reporting positions. He said he wished an editor's job was more like my job as a writing coach, but his job required him to stay focused on selling papers.

He compared this part of his job to "being like a baseball coach or a baseball manager. You're making out your lineup for the game, I mean, 'cause you got 25 players and you only got nine spots." Because *The Southern* is what he described as "a regional paper," stories that focus on events in a specific town are rare on the front page. But he said that a story about a murder in a town would go on the front page. When I asked why this kind of story has front-page appeal, the editor offered the example of a story printed the previous week. This story detailed a little girl who was attacked by a pit-bull. He said even though the story was about an event in one town, it went on the front page because "it's something that even if you don't live in the town, you'd want to read."

The editor explained his labor is focused primarily on the business side of the newspaper. He told me that "art is a big factor" in his selection of what goes on the front-page stories because photos are a "selling point" or "marketing tool." He feels "better once I get the two pieces of art because then, you know, news happens." The business side of the editor's job seemed to be a source of inner conflict for him. He explained, "I still don't really care about sales, but I know it's part of my job . . . Obviously when you're a reporter, you could care less. You have no idea. In management, on the news side, you realize that's part of your job, to make it attractive." As he spoke about this part of his job, his voice lowered in volume, and he picked at his fingernails.

When applying the editor's approach to the news he selects for publication to the second group of principles that guide how journalists should structure their stories' content—provide a forum for public criticism and compromise, make the significant interesting and relevant, and keep the news comprehensive and proportional—he seems so keen on selling papers that he is rarely able to actualize his stated interest in serving the public good. Despite his contention that he wants his staff to write interesting, community-minded stories, he recognizes that these are rarely the stories that entice readers to buy papers. The editor says one thing, but he does another. As a result, the principle is not upheld.

The Tough Decisions

The city editor presided over each of the managers' meetings I attended where stories for the next day's front page were decided. In each of the meetings, the conversation went back and forth between newsworthiness and market potential for selling papers. During one meeting in early March, the main topic of discussion was the college basketball tournament game coming up that weekend. Readers in the newspaper's circulation are adamant supporters of the hometown team, the Southern Illinois University Carbondale Salukis. When the discussion turned to the sports editor's waning interest in the Saluki basketball team, whose season had been extended into playoff games the previous week, the editor-in-chief told the group a basketball story belonged on the front. "These are the last couple of gasps for the Salukis, and we need to play them big to sell papers," he said. When a manager asked the sports editor to predict the game's outcome, he responded, "Go Evansville. I want the season to be over." Another manager replied, "Spoken like a true sports editor." The group erupted in laughter.

The conversation then turned to a story about an upcoming weekend concert by a country music star scheduled to perform in the area. The entertainment editor said she thought the concert story deserved a space on the front page because it had the potential to sell more papers. The group agreed after determining a photo of the star was available to lead the page.

When applying the newspaper managers' statements during their meetings to the third group of principles—obligation to the truth, reliance on disciplined verification, and independent monitoring of power—I contend the managers rarely placed stories' newsworthiness above their market potential. Many of their statements unabashedly lift the veil and show that their true concern is with profits. Each of these stories was selected for its ability to sell papers over its news value. None of the stories that were selected for the front page dealt with government, schools or other aspects of infrastructure in the communities *The Southern* covers.

Conclusions

This project contributes to the literature on journalism education, journalists' values and labor, and the newspaper business. My analysis of the principles of journalism and application to a single, American, daily community newspaper has limited potential to explain journalists' work across the newspaper terrain. However, I believe this examination of real-time journalism reveals the need for a new articulation of journalists' principles that accommodates increased transparency in the connection between journalists and their labor. Future studies are needed to explore how journalists at newspapers of all sizes, particularly the community newspapers that dominate the American market, adhere to or resist the principles as they produce and disseminate the news.

The journalists I worked with at *The Southern* negotiated their values and internalized business demands to answer their employers' profit motives. Whether fresh out of school or seasoned veterans of the newspaper industry, these journalists strive to do quality work. They face business pressures every day, but the principles they were trained to follow do not offer advice for resolving these frequent challenges to their work. The pressures of reporting while meeting newspapers' profit demands seem to intensify reporters' need to condense, and as a result omit, important and illuminating content, and citizens are the losers in the end.

Perhaps the most important conclusion that can be drawn is for the need to think about new values and cease our celebrations of the possibility of objectivity. American journalism is undergoing drastic changes, and this reality presents an opportunity to amend journalists' principles to accommodate a direct and material recognition of the connection between journalists, their labor, and their employers' market-driven demands. There is no better time than now to restructure journalists' training on the job and in the classroom to incorporate an understanding of the economic imperatives at work in newspaper decision making.

ACKNOWLEDGEMENTS

My thanks go to Walter Jaehnig, Cinzia Padovani and Lisa Brooten for their careful readings of earlier versions of this article. I am also grateful to the organizers of The Future of Newspapers Conference and to the colleagues I met while in Wales.

NOTE

1.   This sub-heading is inspired by John Tudor's witty one-liner, "If at first you don't succeed, call it version 1.0."

REFERENCES

AJROUCH, KRISTINE (1998) "Personalization and the Determination of News", *Qualitative Sociology* 21, pp. 341–50.

AMERICAN SOCIETY OF NEWSPAPER EDITORS (2007) "Diversity Slips in U.S. Newsrooms", *News Releases*, http://www.asne.org/index.cfm?ID =6506, accessed 1 May 2007.

BENJAMIN, WALTER (1969) "The Work of Art in the Age of Mechanical Reproduction", in: Hannah Arendt (Ed.), *Illuminations*, New York: Schocken, pp. 217–42.

FRANKLIN, M. I. (2002) "Reading Walter Benjamin and Donna Haraway in the Age of Digital Reproduction", *Information, Communication & Society* 5, pp. 591–624.

GAZIANO, CECILIE and COULSON, DAVID C. (1988) "Effect of Newsroom Management Styles on Journalists: a case study", *Journalism Quarterly* 65, pp. 869–80.

JOHNSTONE, JON W. C., SLAWSKI, EDWARD J. and BOWMAN, WILLIAM W. (1976) *The News People: a sociological portrait of American journalists and their work*, Urbana: University of Illinois Press.

KONNER, JOAN (1996) "A Journalist Is . . ." *Columbia Journalism Review* 35(4), p. 4.

KOVACH, BILL and ROSENSTIEL, TOM (2001) *The Elements of Journalism: what newspeople should know and the public should expect*, New York: Crown Publishers.

LACY, STEPHEN and FICO, FREDERICK (1991) "The Link Between Newspaper Content Quality & Circulation", *Newspaper Research Journal* 12(2), pp. 46–57.

LANDON, KIM (2004) "Editors' and Young Reporters' Differing Views on Community News", *Grassroots Editor* 45(1), pp. 14–6.

MCCHESNEY, ROBERT W. (1997) *Corporate Media and the Threat to Democracy*, New York: Seven Stories Press.

MCCHESNEY, ROBERT W. (2003a) "The '"Left-Wing' Media?", *Monthly Review: An Independent Socialist Magazine* 55(2), pp. 1–16.

MCCHESNEY, ROBERT W. (2003b) "The Problem of Journalism: a political economic contribution to an explanation of the crisis in contemporary US journalism", *Journalism Studies* 4, pp. 299–329.

MEYER, PHILIP (2004a) "Saving Journalism: how to nurse the good stuff until it pays", *Columbia Journalism Review* 43(4), pp. 55–7.

MEYER, PHILIP (2004b) "The Influence Model and Newspaper Business", *Newspaper Research Journal* 25(1), pp. 66–83.

MOSCO, VINCENT (1996) *The Political Economy of Communication*, London: Sage Publications.

NEWSPAPER ASSOCIATION OF AMERICA (2006) "U.S. Daily Newspaper Circulation", in: *The Source: newspapers by the numbers*, http://www.naa.org/thesource/the_source_newspapers_-by_the_numbers.pdf, accessed 30 April 2007.

PEASE, TED (1991) "Blaming the Boss", *Newspaper Research Journal* 12(2), pp. 2–21.

SCHUDSON, MICHAEL (2003) *The Sociology of News*, New York: W. W. Norton & Company.

TUCHMAN, GAYE (1978) *Making News: a study in the construction of reality*, New York: Free Press.

UDELL, JON G. (1978) *The Economics of the American Newspaper*, New York: Hastings House.

WEAVER, DAVID and WILHOIT, G. CLEVELAND (1996) *The American Journalist in the 1990s: U.S. news people at the end of an era*, Mahwah, NJ: Lawrence Erlbaum.

Chapter 27

THE PASSIVE JOURNALIST
How sources dominate local news

Deirdre O'Neill and **Catherine O'Connor**

Introduction

Sources, as Leon Sigal has stated (1986), make the news; moreover "who the sources are bears a close relationship to who is news" (Sigal, 1986, p. 25). Similarly, while "the effects of the way the reporter gathers information and the dynamics of the reporter–source relationship may be unintended, often unperceived, and sometimes unpredictable, nevertheless they are real and a part of the power and influence of the press" (Strentz, 1989, p. 22).

This article seeks to establish which primary sources are defining or "making" local news and to assess whether sufficient secondary sources are being used to validate a story or provide alternative views. It provides an empirical record of which sources are dominating news coverage, from which future trends in local journalism might be assessed.

Exploring Sources

Ask any journalist, and they will probably agree that sources are always at the heart of news selection and production. Harcup (2004, p. 46), for example, lists 72 common sources of news. But Bell (1991) notes that in their day-to-day practice journalists use a relatively narrow range of sources, favouring authoritative sources and marginalising alternative sources such as more socially disadvantaged people. Journalists cannot be in all places at all times and in his study of the routinisation of news, Gans (1980) recognised that, with deadlines to meet, journalists' over-riding concern is to assess the *efficiency* of news sources thereby increasing the likelihood that "journalists are repeatedly brought into contact with a limited number of the same sources" (Gans, 1980, p. 144) or "primary definers", the sources that "frame" the subsequent tone or perspective of a given news story (Hall et al., 1978, p. 58).

Newspapers have a paradoxical role in that they exist to make profit, yet the information they provide is central to most understandings of democracy. Therefore research into sources can shed light on the quality of information, the diversity of perspectives and the interpretative frameworks on offer to the news consumer. Which sources are favoured and how they are used goes to the heart of the debate about power relationships in society, since sources given news access have an opportunity to set the news agenda, define the parameters of debate, and shape ideology.

Sources and reporters share what is typically described as a symbiotic relationship. A study of local news by Walter Gieber (1964) revealed that journalists, despite believing themselves to be freely acting agents, finding and investigating their own stories, rarely behaved independently of their sources; instead they generated stories based on information from sources who stood to benefit from the transaction as much as the journalist.

The potentially mutual benefit of this journalism–source relationship is not problematic if it does not affect the journalist's ability to act in the public interest. The degree to which a journalist can discharge this duty, however, will involve going beyond initial source information—routine, official, authoritative or otherwise—to verify and check facts by using other sources. This may necessarily entail adversarial, independent and investigative journalism, which Sigal (1973) termed enterprise methods, and which require time and resources.

But when time and resources are at a premium, commonsense dictates that journalists will turn to those sources most eager to provide information and such sources will, in turn, become *regular* sources (Gans, 1980). Efficient sources can take this a step further. Studies of news values, for example, have identified the production of ready-made copy as significantly increasing the chance of a story being selected by journalists for publication (Allern, 2002; Bell, 1991). In these ways, journalism has allegedly entered into an unholy alliance with the public relations industry.

As a profession, public relations has been developing throughout the 20th century but has rapidly expanded in the last 20 years (Davis, 2003, p. 28). A flurry of scholarly books and academic studies has charted its rise in the field of political communication—in particular, how news is packaged and spun to journalists (Barnett and Gaber, 2001; Franklin, 2004; Jones, 1995). Schudson claims that "Journalists face a vast world of parajournalists—public relations firms, public information officers, political spin doctors, and the publicity staffs of a wide variety of institutions, both corporate and nonprofit" (Schudson, 2003, p. 3).

In the same way and by the same processes that national news and the national public sphere are influenced and shaped by news sources, regional and local news agendas and the local public sphere are likewise shaped by local sources. Local newspapers have traditionally played a significant role in recording local public life and promoting local democracy, using their unique local knowledge and journalistic skills to dig out genuine exclusives and quirky "people" stories from their patch, reports that have, in effect, made them a feeding ground for the nationals. As Franklin argues, "Local newspapers should offer independent and critical commentary on local issues, make local elites accountable [and] provide a forum for the expression of local views on issues of community concern" (2006a, p. xix), but to what extent are journalists discharging these duties? One approach is to examine the sources reported in local newspapers to help shed light on the diversity of voices and perspectives that are contributing to the public sphere.

But a study of news sources needs some discussion about wider trends in regional papers, particularly managerial strategies, since these have a "critical impact" on newsgathering and reporting processes (Franklin, 2006b, p. 10).

Changes in Local Journalism

In recent years, local newspapers have faced the challenges of changing patterns of newspaper consumption and changing communities whose inhabitants may be more transitory than in the past (Aldridge, 2003).Yet while the number of titles in circulation have declined, regional newspapers have maintained high levels of profitability (Franklin, 2006b, p. 3), while profit margins are higher than those achieved in national newspapers as well as other comparable industries (Williams and Franklin, 2007). Trends in ownership are towards monopoly (Murphy, 1998; Williams and Franklin, 2007), with three major media groups—Trinity Mirror, Newsquest Media Group and Johnston Press—dominating the local newspaper sector, highly responsive to the requirements of shareholders but essentially removed from the local communities of readers. Despite operating in a highly competitive marketplace driven by new technology, conglomeration, deregulation, competition from free newspapers and declining circulations, newspapers' managements have squared the circle by paying staff low salaries, shedding staff and cutting training, while simultaneously increasing output, including online content (Curran and Seaton, 1997; Davis 2003; Franklin, 1997; Murphy, 1998; Tunstall, 1996, Williams and Franklin, 2007). Time available for journalists to speak to contacts, nurture sources, become familiar with a "patch" and uncover and follow up leads has become a "luxury" (Pecke, 2004, p. 30).

It is the emphasis currently being placed on online content which has resulted in one of the most significant changes of recent years; namely many traditional, multi-edition evening newspapers in the United Kingdom have moved to print only a single early morning edition each day. The rationale offered by managements suggests that local newspapers cannot—and should not be trying to—compete by offering breaking news when TV and the Internet are able to deliver news faster, unconstrained by fixed print schedules. The argument suggests that by focusing effort into a single edition on sale for the maximum length of time, local newspapers can play to their USP—their ability to provide an in-depth local news service, to be "a local paper for local people ... a unique product in which on-the-day news is no longer the priority" (Kirby, 2006).

Despite a trend towards graduate employment, turnover of staff is high, and career prospects are poor. Questioned about falling standards, trainee journalists "pointed to the age-old problems of low pay, poor working conditions, the complete absence of training, long hours, understaffed newsrooms, and a managerial emphasis on quantity not quality" (Pecke, 2004, p. 27). Pilling (1998, p. 184) has likened local papers' newsrooms to "sweatshops". In such a pressurised and demoralised working environment it is all too easy for journalists to become dependent on the pre-fabricated, pre-packaged "news" from resource-rich public relations organisations or the familiar and easily accessed routine source or re-writes of news agency copy—what BBC journalist Waseem Zakir coined as "churnalism" (Harcup, 2004, p. 3). One local journalist based in the south of England, commented: "Every day I see absolute reliance by an under-manned newsroom on ready-made copy supplied by public sector organisations with an axe to grind: propaganda masquerading as news" (personal communication). These trends suggest that while "local newspapers are increasingly a business success" they increasingly constitute "a journalistic failure" (Franklin, 2006b, p. 4).

The Passive Journalist?

This study examines the identity and character of primary and secondary sources used in a sample of local newspapers, as well as the percentage of articles using secondary sources to provide an additional or alternative viewpoint to the reader. In other words, we wished to know the extent to which *sources* were influencing the selection and production of news and rendering the role of the local journalist essentially *passive* or reactive, with all the subsequent implications for the quality of local reporting and the public interest.

Methodology

The type and number of sources reported in 2979 news stories published in four daily West Yorkshire papers, owned by the three main proprietors of local newspapers in the United Kingdom, were examined and recorded over a period of a month (February 2007). The sample newspapers included the *Huddersfield Daily Examiner* owned by Trinity Mirror, the *Bradford Telegraph & Argus* owned by Newsquest and the *Yorkshire Evening Post* and the *Halifax Courier* both owned by Johnston Press.

In particular, we identified and recorded the primary sources from which the main substance of an article was sourced; in other words, the sources informing the newspaper reader. Thus, we were not necessarily categorising those quoted, but the main published source from which information for a story emanated, and which framed the story. While any decisions about categorisation necessitates some degree of subjectivity, this proved relatively easy to judge in most instances: for example, a story about a new service in a local hospital would be categorised as a "health" source; a story describing a bad experience in hospital by a patient would be categorised as a "reader" source; while a report on standards of care in local health services would normally be attributed to the organisation that carried out the report (this might be a government department, a charity or some other public body, and would be categorised accordingly). Any stories where the source was unclear we categorised as "other". We also recorded which stories used just a single primary source and those which used secondary sources. The aim was to establish whether readers were receiving alternative, contrasting or validating perspectives from relevant multiple sources within a single report or whether relevant voices or views were, as a matter of routine, not being consulted or recorded. This seemed to offer a useful indicator of the standard of the journalistic service being provided by these newspapers to their readers. We also talked to some local journalists and ex-editors for their views.

The news pages were the only editorial content analysed. Features, opinion pieces, News in Briefs, sports and business pages were not included in the study, nor pages devoted entirely to photographs of people involved in staged events (though these were included and analysed when they appeared among other news reports on the news pages).

Findings

Some of the frequency findings from the content analysis are presented in Tables 1–3; these findings are then discussed further below. Table 1, for example, identifies the different types of news sources used by journalists in the sampled newspapers and their prominence in news coverage, in relation to other sources (expressed as a percentage of overall source citation in the newspapers' editorial). Local journalists' reliance on police (11 per cent), court (<11 per cent), local government (>9 per cent) and (pseudo) events (<9 per cent) sources becomes evident because of their prominence in journalists' reports. By contrast the inclusion of MPs (<2 per cent) and local councillors' as sources (>2 per cent) and even the newspapers' readers (<5 per cent) is relatively sparse.

TABLE 1

Sources by type and prominence in local newspapers (as percentage of all sources)

	Halifax Courier	Huddersfield Examiner	Bradford Telegraph & Argus	Yorkshire Evening Post	Average
1. Police	12	>11	>11	>10	11
2. Court	<14	>7	<12	<11	<11
3. Local government	<10	<10	<10	<9	>9
4. Organisers of/ participants in staged events*	<3	>6	>11	<13	<9
5. Charity	>6	>5	7	<4	<7
16. Education	<13	>4	<4	<7	<6
7. Commercial	<6	10	>2	5	<6
8. Culture (arts, music, exhibitions, museums)	5	>4	<5	<7	>5
9. Public bodies	>3	<7	>5	<4	>5
10. Readers	>3	3	>6	<7	<5
11. Action groups	<4	<4	<2	<3	<3
12. Fire service	3	<4	>2	<1	>2
13. Councillors	>1	3	>2	<1	>2
14. Health service	>1	>1	>2	<2	<2
15. MPs	>1	<2	>2	>1	<2
16. National government	<1	2	>2	>1	<2
17. Other†					13

The number of coded items is 2979 (all percentages are rounded to nearest whole number).

*These are, in effect, pseudo-events. They have not occurred spontaneously, but have been "staged" in some way. Some are rather inconsequential, little more than a photo opportunity (e.g. "Keen Gardeners Learn Tricks of the Trade", *Halifax Courier*, 28 February 2007), while others may have a more serious public interest role such as an event staged to coincide with the launch of a campaign to tackle domestic violence in Bradford (*Telegraph & Argus*, 15 February 2007). The vast majority were of the former type and were sourced from one person or organisation (85 per cent, see Table 2).

†"Other" sources included unions, armed forces, religious organisations, accountancy firms (where companies had gone into receivership), public meetings (non-council), stories emanating from the newspaper itself (such as new online services or the launch of a campaign), follow-ups to national stories, professional bodies—all of which were less than 1 per cent of total sources used—and articles where the source was not apparent.

TABLE 2
Sample newspapers' uses of secondary sources by identified source category (%)

	Halifax Courier	Huddersfield Examiner	Bradford Telegraph & Argus	Yorkshire Evening Post	Average
1. Police	21	11	27	22	20
2. Court	12	15	9	14	>12
3. Local government	36	9	46	26	29
4. Organisers of/ participants in staged events	14	2	16	21	15
5. Charity	<6	>4	20	<25	13
6. Education	<12	10	55	45	<28
7. Commercial	23	8	25	21	>15
8. Culture (arts, music, exhibitions, museums)	7	<12	>12	<12	11
9. Public bodies	>29	9	<28	>17	19
10. Readers	47	54	51	70	<59
11. Action groups	30	33	50	45	>38
12. Fire service	>8	<1	14	0	>8
13. Councillors	38	25	44	17	<33
14. Health service	25	10	42	50	29
15. MPs	43	27	33	20	30
16. National government	0	19	81	50	50

Table 2 highlights the varying degrees to which particular newspapers use secondary sources; it also reveals the extent to which the four sampled newspapers use secondary sources differentially according to source identity. The *Huddersfield Examiner*, for example, uses secondary sources in 11 per cent of stories sourced by the police whereas the Bradford *Telegraph & Argus* use them in 27 per cent of stories. Similarly, while only 8 per cent (average across all sampled papers) of journalists' reports sourced from the fire service use secondary sources, 33 per cent of stories sourced from councillors cite them (see Table 2).

Table 3 identifies the sampled local newspapers' uses of single and secondary sources in news reports, revealing that a substantive majority of local news reports are reliant on only a single source.

Discussion

Local journalism is about producing newspapers of record, so one would expect routine sources such as the council or courts to have a strong presence within any local

TABLE 3
Local newspapers' uses of single and secondary sources in news reports (%)

	Halifax Courier	Huddersfield Examiner	Bradford Telegraph & Argus	Yorkshire Evening Post	Average
Use of secondary sources	21	<14	31	>27	<24
Use of one source	79	>86	69	<73	>76

paper (as Table 1 indicates that they do) despite an overall decline in such coverage in local newspapers in recent years (Glover, 1998; Pilling, 1998). Moreover a high profile for the police in local news might be anticipated given readers' interest in and concerns about local crime. Likewise, there is an expectation that a local newspaper will chart the landmarks, events and achievements that are individual to their readers.

The issue here, however, is how far the balance has tipped in favour of sources, and, given that the findings reveal a high proportion of articles (76 per cent) relying on just *one* source (see Table 3), sources appear to be in a relatively strong position to influence the subsequent framing of articles in most of the local news reported. There is little evidence of "original journalism", in Marsh's (2007) sense that journalists might ask "What if the opposite is true?"

The findings suggest that journalists' reliance on a single source for stories, possibly reflecting shortage of time and resources, combined with sources' skills in presenting positive public images, is a significant contributory factor to uncritical local press reporting. The 76 per cent of stories using single sources were rarely contentious (at least in the way they were written) or critical of the source providing the story. As Hitchens observed, "When there is only one source of information . . . that the media want, then the potential to manage that information is absolute" (1997, in Harrison, 1998, p. 166). This seriously undermines the *trust* that the public can place in information from local papers.

Of the 24 per cent of articles with a secondary source, most were still framed by a primary source, with a brief alternative quote included at the end of the report. What this means in practice is a formulaic style, superficially giving the appearance of "objective news", but which fails to get to the heart of the issue, or misses the real story. There was little evidence of the sifting of conflicting information or contextualising that assists readers' understanding and makes for good journalism (Williams, 2007). There were also examples of high-profile and significant community stories where opportunities to canvas all voices relevant to the stories were simply not taken. If an unquestioning and uncritical culture is emerging in newsrooms, this is highly damaging to journalism. As one experienced journalist put it, "I am concerned about the training given to new-entry reporters who no longer have the questioning attitude inculcated into me and my peers when training in the late 1980s. It doesn't occur to them to tone down the shameless propagandising in their source material, and the idea of looking for an alternative viewpoint, which might create a better story, seldom seems to arise" (personal communication).

In addition, "events", charity, commerce and culture sources—hardly the stuff of hard news—were in the top 10 categories (see Table 1), forming stories with the lowest rates of secondary sources (see Table 2). The remainder of this section addresses local press reporting of specific subject areas.

Local Government Reporting

This study found that almost two-thirds (61 per cent) of local government-sourced stories (one of the main routine source categories) had no discernible secondary sources and suggests a significant unquestioning reliance on council press officers or press releases (see Table 2). Compared to an earlier study of local papers where "information subsidies" from government information officers did *not* [our emphasis] constitute the main source of information in resulting coverage (Franklin and Van Slyke Turk, 1988, in

Harrison, 1998, p. 157), the situation would appear to have deteriorated, leading to a democratic deficit in local government reporting. This has a profound impact on the public interest and the fourth estate role of the regional press.

For example, the *Yorkshire Evening Post* covered a story on 22 February 2007 about local authority performance league tables ("Three-star Rating for City Council's Good Showing"), but framed it only in terms of the report and the views of the council leader and chief executive, with no alternative or dissenting views presented, despite the fact that the authority had dropped one star in the ratings.

While local government formed one of the main source categories, given the potential effects of local government on local communities, it is surprising that only 9 per cent of articles were sourced by the council (see Table 1). The decline in local government reporting has often been laid at the door of readers, who, editors argue, are not very interested in public life (Pilling, 1998). However, it could be argued that, rather than ignoring many of the stories that emanate from local government due to a perceived lack of audience interest, more investigative journalism and engagement with readers would uncover interesting and highly relevant stories relating to local political decisions and local services. The shift in power from local to central government or to unelected public bodies, such as the regional development organisation Yorkshire Forward, may play a part in this trend, but, it remains important to report about the effects of policies and plans on local communities, whoever is responsible. Indeed, with more unelected bodies assuming responsibility for such decisions, it might be argued that the need for the local media's watchdog role has never been greater. Glover has identified decreasing coverage of local issues, particularly local government, as central to accelerating sales decline. "[Local] newspapers", he claims, "seem to have forgotten what they do well and diverted limited resources into what they do less well" (1998, p. 119).

This state of affairs has been compounded by the fact that local government has become highly adept at media relations. By 1994, 90 per cent of metropolitan local authorities had established PR departments, employing 2000 full-time staff; by 2004 Unitary Authorities were employing up to 50 PR staff and spending up to £1,949,000 per annum on PR while the biggest spending London Borough enjoyed a PR budget of £3,945,000 (Franklin, 2004, pp. 104–5). By 2005, all local authorities had some professional media relations function (Harrison, 2006, p. 177). Today's journalists are far more likely to have dealings with press or communications officers than senior council staff, and hard-pressed journalists are increasingly reliant on the information the former provide. "I fear", claimed Aiken, "that increasingly council media officers are used as an extension of local newsrooms" (Aiken, cited in Harrison, 2006, p. 188). But these PR professionals are not merely benign conduits of information. They are employed to place a positive spin on the information they provide and attract publicity for those issues the council wishes to highlight, while downplaying those the council wish to "bury". Harrison (2006, p. 187) has acknowledged that the information subsidy provided by local sources to local newspapers is "great, and growing" but she does not believe that this trend has undermined the credibility of local media to be an independent commentator on the affairs of local government. However, with nearly two-thirds of articles emanating from local government having no alternative or secondary sources, our findings contest this view, confirming the earlier comments put forward by Harrison: "Local newspapers are ceasing to fulfil their former role as guardians of the truth, and keepers of the public record" (1998, p. 167).

Crime Reporting

Two of the other main sources for stories were the police (11 per cent) and courts (11 per cent), in keeping with the key role of the regional press in reporting crime. But overall this, too, has been decreasing in recent years (Glover, 1998; Pilling, 1998). Many newspapers no longer employ specialist court reporters to cover the courts directly. For example, at the time this study was conducted the *Telegraph & Argus* and *Huddersfield Examiner* employed an agency to provide this coverage, confirming Aldridge's assessment that "the financial imperatives of corporate ownership are limiting papers' capacity even to pursue reliable news sources like court proceedings" (2003, p. 499). Just 12 per cent of articles sourced from the courts cited secondary sources (see Table 2).

In line with other major institutions, the police also now have highly developed media relations. Journalists now anticipate interviewing a media relations professional when covering crime, losing out on the opportunity directly to question relevant senior investigating officers who can provide essential background details. And stories sourced by the police in the research sample used secondary sources in only 20 per cent of cases, indicating that news from this source is primarily being shaped by the source. A study which interviewed journalists extensively cited one reporter who claimed "We're not going out and challenging people like the police and local council" (Editor quoted in Williams and Franklin, 2007, p. 17). And one local journalist told us, "In my town, where public concern about crime and public disorder is growing, we produce a weekly crime page consisting entirely of blurry CCTV pictures of suspects in petty thefts and minor assaults, supplied by the police and often several months old—but it's a doddle to write" (personal communication).

Commerce

Commercial sources are also regularly used but most of the stories that appeared as a result of commercial sources referred to *no* secondary source (85 per cent, see Table 2) and were banal, non-contentious, and provided free publicity for commercial enterprises. The *Huddersfield Examiner*, for example, produced a page lead and accompanying large photograph about a hypnotherapist who, in the run-up to Valentine's Day, was handing out roses to promote his confidence-boosting services ("Help at Hand for the Town's Shy and Lonely", *Huddersfield Examiner*, 2 February 2007); the story guaranteed that he was receiving his own free helping hand from the paper. In the *Telegraph & Argus*, a page lead was devoted to the opening of a fun barn at a local farm, which runs a visitor centre ("Farm's Fun for All the Family", 13 February 2007). The information may well have been of interest to readers but the farm is a commercially run business and the equivalent space in advertising would have cost hundreds of pounds, yet the "plug" was free thanks to its inclusion as "news". It is noteworthy that the newspapers concerned do run business pages but there is relatively little evidence of reporting of the business sector making any sizeable impact on general news pages which, arguably, it should, given its importance to local communities.

Health Service

Just 49 articles out of 2979 appeared to be directly sourced from the health service itself (though the number of stories about the health service was higher, but more likely to be sourced from the public who were victims of or complainants about the standards of care and usually categorised as a "reader" source). It is worth noting that only 15 of these 49 stories had a secondary source (29 per cent) and in the *Huddersfield Examiner* only 10 per cent of health stories cited secondary sources (see Table 2).

Education

Education sources were dominated by schools, and were primarily from organisers of school "events", such as a healthy eating day, or a story-telling session, usually accompanied by appealing photos of primary school children, with the "story" constituting little more than a caption. Most articles were positive. In-depth articles about the education service were singularly lacking. Only 28 per cent of articles had secondary sources, and often these were merely another voice involved in the organisation of the event or congratulating the school. University and college stories were similar in style, usually publicising success or a new course or partnership. While these types of articles certainly have a place in the local paper, it was hard to believe that national debates and policies such as concerns about city academies, the Building Schools for the Future initiative, the controversial Private Finance Initiative, the shortage of head teachers, education standards and the testing of young children were not impacting on local communities. It is true that the press has sometimes been criticised for dwelling on the negative and amplifying fears and problems, but the other extreme presents just as false an impression and does not engage with the very real concerns of parents, young people, and those working in education.

Events and Charities

Nearly a quarter of reports (22 per cent) stem from "events" of some kind (general events, listed in Table 1, and also school events, charity events, arts events—included in education, charity and culture categories but also noted by us separately) and the vast majority of these, when recorded together (but not expressed in a table), had no secondary source (89 per cent). While we would not expect many of these types of stories to have secondary sources, the point is that these stories are helping fill up nearly a quarter of the news space at the expense of what may well be more important stories. Many of these "articles" would not have been elevated to news in the past, merely appearing in "What's On" listings. Clearly, there will be some reports which have an exceptional human-interest angle, but this was not usually the case in the articles analysed.

There are other "events" where it was questionable what benefit readers might gain from knowing about them, particularly given their prominence. For example, the *Yorkshire Evening Post* dedicated its page 9 lead on 28 February ("Powerful Draw at Celebration of Northern Art") to an exhibition celebrating northern artistic works and organised for MPs and peers at the House of Commons. It may well have been worth recording as a event which local MPs were attending but, given that it was not an event with which readers were likely to engage with, then its prominence can be questioned.

The Voice of the Local Public?

Readers were sources in just 5 per cent of the sampled articles (see Table 1). This compares unfavourably with a 2006 study (Ross) where 12 per cent of articles had readers as sources, indicating that journalists appear to be increasingly out of touch with their readers. As Ross noted, "If the local press is to continue to call itself 'local' in any meaningful way, it probably needs to work a bit harder to more genuinely reflect the views and interests of local communities back to themselves" (2006, p. 243). But when readers were used as a primary source, the subsequent articles contained the highest percentage of secondary sources (59 per cent) (see Table 2). This begs the question: What is it about other sources which means they do not warrant the same treatment by journalists? Are these dominant sources, such as the police or commerce, often with vested interests, really so credible and do they provide such a full picture that they do not require balance or verification with a secondary source?

It was notable that the *Telegraph & Argus* ran vox pops on a number of occasions, thereby canvassing the views of a number of readers on key issues. However, there were also examples of poor practice in giving readers a voice on stories which cried out for a public view. The *Yorkshire Evening Post*, for example, ran a report about the success of an action group preventing development at Yeadon Banks, Leeds ("Cause for Celebration on the Village Green", 16 February 2007). The chairman of the group is mentioned and praised and members of the group are photographed but the only quotes in the story are from local MP Paul Truswell. Mr Truswell may well have played a role in the campaign and it may be the case that the chairman of the group was not available for comment but it seems a major flaw that a local newspaper cannot express the success of the campaign directly through the voices of the ordinary people involved. The same story ran in the *Telegraph & Argus* ("Land-fight Residents Win Round One", 15 February, 2007) and again Mr Truswell is quoted, saying, "This is a victory for the little people", though once more the voices of "the little people" were absent and silent. These examples and our findings in general raise questions about what perspectives, what views, what facts, what *real* stories are being missed. This was well expressed by a local journalist who claimed that, "As the person responsible for compiling the letters page, I often find potentially good stories in letters to the editor and used to pass these on to the news desk, but I no longer bother because they almost never appear. Instead, six-paragraph press releases from the council advertising some dreary non-event or other are elevated to the status of page leads and given four-deck 70pt headlines, twice the size of the story beneath them" (personal communication).

Conclusion

Aldridge has argued that "regional newspapers should have little difficulty in addressing multiple dimensions of readers' and potential readers' lives: for most people, their home, employment, at least some of their kin network, their friendships, their consumption of essential and optional goods and services, and their leisure are largely geographically co-terminous" (2003, p. 497). With a little imagination and some curiosity, journalists should be able to mine a rich seam of stories relevant to local communities.

However, the combination of the pressures on journalists and the increased expertise in organisations' media relations which have generated the findings presented here, have a number of implications for journalists, readers and the public. First, journalists are becoming more passive, often merely passing on information to the public that they have been given. The local journalist's role as the gatekeeper in the news selection and production process (White, 1950) is diminishing and shifting towards the source, often a public relations professional, who selects and packages news within the internal confines of their organisations before external presentation to journalists.

As a passive recipient of information rather than an active investigator, the local journalist is not keeping an ear to the ground and interacting with the local community. Journalists are relying less on their readers for news (less than 5 per cent of all primary sources were readers), and are consequently less in touch with a broad cross-section of their readers on a regular basis. As an Editor in a recent study claimed, "[Journalists are] not actually out there connecting with the community" (Williams and Franklin, 2007, p. 17). This passivity also leads to an over-reliance on single sources, excluding certain views and issues relevant to the readership, and allowing routine sources to dominate the news agenda and frame subsequent stories.

While many of the news stories sourced in this study probably do have a place in a local paper, stories which have little weight are being elevated to significant positions, or are filling up news pages at the expense of more important stories that, put simply, are being missed. Too frequently the result is bland, banal copy at best; or free advertising and propaganda at worst. All these trends are a serious threat to local democracy, the public interest, public trust, the local public sphere, and the standards of journalism.

By attempting to extract every last drop of profit, the owners of regional papers are producing newspapers that reveal contempt for their readers. Crozier (quoted in Lagan, 2006) has asserted that local newspapers can only survive with investment and by becoming more local. This view was echoed by former *Western Morning News* editor Barrie Williams who "believes that costs in the regional press will continue to be 'screwed to the floor' as the big corporate owners continue their 'management of decline'" (Ponsford, 2007). Williams went on to argue that, in the past, local proprietors "wore the ownership of a newspaper like a badge of honour" and that a shift back to local ownership could reverse this decline (Ponsford, 2007). Geere (quoted in Lagan, 2006) has claimed that, "The regional press needs to wake up quickly and reinvent itself before the only readers left are those officials, PR people and pressure groups who make up the news conspiracy along with bored reporters and unimaginative editors."

While editors preach the virtues of interactivity with communities, parent companies pursue policies and profits that serve to undermine contact with the public and journalistic endeavour and enterprise. At the heart of the debate about declining sales is the realisation by readers that there is precious little in their local paper that is engaging, trustworthy, or that reflects the genuine concerns of local communities and gives local people a voice. Unless the local press improves standards of journalism, the health of local papers will continue to decline.

REFERENCES

ALDRIDGE, MERYL (2003) "The Ties That Divide: regional press campaigns, community and populism", Media, *Culture and Society* 25, pp. 491–509.

ALLERN, SIGURD (2002) "Journalistic and Commercial News Values: news organizations as patrons of an institution and market actors", *Nordcom Review* 23(1/2), pp. 137–52.

BARNETT, STEVEN and GABER, IVOR (2001) *Westminster Tales: the twenty-first-century crisis in political journalism*, London and New York: Continuum.

BELL, ALLAN (1991) *The Language of News Media*, Oxford: Blackwell.

CURRAN, JAMES and SEATON, JEAN (1997) *Power Without Responsibility*, London: Routledge.

DAVIS, AERON (2003) "Public Relations and News Sources", in: Simon Cottle (Ed.), *News, Public Relations and Power*, London: Sage.

FRANKLIN, BOB (1997) *Newszak and News Media*, London: Arnold.

FRANKLIN, BOB (2004) *Packaging Politics: political communications in Britain's media democracy*, London: Arnold, Second Edition

FRANKLIN, BOB (2006a) "Preface", in: Bob Franklin (Ed.), *Local Journalism and Local Media: making the local news*, London: Routledge.

FRANKLIN, BOB (2006b) "Attacking the Devil?", in: Bob Franklin (Ed.), *Local Journalism and Local Media: making the local news*, London: Routledge, pp. 3–15.

GANS, HERBERT J. (1980) *Deciding What's News: a study of CBS evening news, NBC nightly news, Newsweek and Time*, London: Constable.

GIEBER, WALTER (1964) "News Is What Newspaper Men Make It", in: A. Dexter Lewis and David Manning White (Eds), *People Society and Mass Communication*, London: The Free Press of Glencoe, pp. 289–97.

GLOVER, MIKE (1998) "Looking at the World Through the Eyes of . . .: reporting the 'local' in daily, weekly and Sunday local newspapers", in: Bob Franklin and David Murphy (Eds), *Making the Local News: local journalism in context*, London: Routledge, pp. 117–24.

HALL, STUART, CRITCHER, CHAS, JEFFERSON, TONY, CLARKE, JOHN and ROBERTS, BRIAN (1978) *Policing the Crisis: mugging, the state, and law and order*, London: Macmillan.

HARCUP, TONY (2004) *Journalism: principles and practice*, London: Sage.

HARRISON, SHIRLEY (1998) "The Local Government Agenda: news from the town hall", in: Bob Franklin and David Murphy (Eds), *Making the Local News: local journalism in context*, London: Routledge, pp. 157–69.

HARRISON, SHIRLEY (2006) "Local Government Public Relations and the Local Press", in: Bob Franklin (Ed.), *Local Journalism and Local Media: making the local news*, London: Routldge, pp. 175–88.

JONES, NICHOLAS (1995) *Soundbites and Spin Doctors: how politicians manipulate the media and vice versa*, London: Cassell.

KIRBY, ALAN (2006), "There's Nothing Fishy About Becoming a Morning Paper", *Press Gazette*, 11 August, www.pressgazette.co.uk/story.asp?sectioncode = 1&storycode = 36174, accessed 25 June 2007.

LAGAN, SARAH (2006) "Searching for a Cure for Local Newspaper Ills", *Press Gazette*, 27 January, www.pressgazette.co.uk/story.asp?sectioncode = 1&storycode = 33071, accessed 25 June 2007.

MARSH, KEVIN (2007) "Original Journalism Is About What You Don't Know, Not What You Do", *Press Gazette*, 18 June, www.pressgazette.co.uk/story.asp?sectioncode = 1&storycode = 37952, accessed 26 June 2007.

MURPHY, DAVID (1998) "Earthquake Undermines Structure of Local Press Ownership: many hurt", in: Bob Franklin and David Murphy (Eds), *Making the Local News*, London: Routledge, pp. 80–90.

PECKE, SAMUEL (2004) "Local Heroes", *British Journalism Review* 15(2), pp. 26–30.

PILLING, ROD (1998) "The Changing Role of the Local Journalist: from faithful chronicler of the parish pump to multiskilled compiler of an electronic database", in: Bob Franklin and

David Murphy (Eds), *Making the Local News: local journalism in context*, London: Routledge, pp. 183–96.

PONSFORD, DOMINIC (2007) "How to Save the Local Press—give it back to the locals", *Press Gazette*, 5 November, www.pressgazette.co.uk/story.asp?sectioncode = 6&storycode = 39330, accessed 14 November 2007.

ROSS, KAREN (2006) "Open Source?", in: Franklin Bob (Ed.), *Local Journalism and Local Media: making the local news*, London: Routledge, pp. 232–44.

SCHUDSON, MICHAEL (2003) *The Sociology of News*, New York: Norton.

SIGAL, LEON V. (1973) *Reporters and Officials: the organisation and politics of newsmaking*, Lexington, MA: Lexington Books.

SIGAL, LEON V. (1986) "Sources Make the News", in: Robert Karl Manoff and Michael Schudson (Eds), *Reading the News*, New York: Pantheon Books, pp. 9–37.

STRENTZ, HERBERT (1989) *News Reporters and News Sources*, Ames, IA: Iowa State University Press.

TUNSTALL, JEREMY (1996) *Newspaper Power: the national press in Britain*, Oxford: Oxford University Press.

WHITE, DAVID MANNING (1950) "The 'Gatekeeper': a case study in the selection of news", *Journalism Quarterly* 27, pp. 383–90.

WILLIAMS, ANDREW and FRANKLIN, BOB (2007) *Turning Around the Tanker: implementing Trinity Mirror's online strategy*, Cardiff: School of Journalism, Media and Cultural Studies, Cardiff University, http://www.cardiff.ac.uk/jomec/en/pubs/200/376.html, accessed 12 June 2007.

WILLIAMS, GRANVILLE (2007) "Visions of the Online Age", *Free Press* 157(March/April), pp. 4–5.

Index

Page numbers in Italics represent Tables. Page numbers in Bold represent Figures.